# A History of Prince Edward Island

JACQUES CARTIER

# A History of Prince Edward Island

FROM ITS DISCOVERY IN 1534 UNTIL THE DEPARTURE OF LIEUTENANT-GOVERNOR READY IN A.D. 1831

### A. B. Warburton, D.C.L., K.C.
*Surrogate and Judge of Probate;*
*Ex-Premier of Prince Edward Island;*
*Ex-M. P. for Queen's County*

HERITAGE BOOKS
2012

# HERITAGE BOOKS
*AN IMPRINT OF HERITAGE BOOKS, INC.*

Books, CDs, and more—Worldwide

For our listing of thousands of titles see our website
at
www.HeritageBooks.com

A Facsimile Reprint
Published 2012 by
HERITAGE BOOKS, INC.
Publishing Division
100 Railroad Ave. #104
Westminster, Maryland 21157

Copyright © 1923 A. B. Warburton, Canada

Originally published
St. John, N.B.:
Barnes & Co., Limited, Printers
84 Prince William Street
1923

— Publisher's Notice —
In reprints such as this, it is often not possible to remove blemishes from the original. We feel the contents of this book warrant its reissue despite these blemishes and hope you will agree and read it with pleasure.

International Standard Book Numbers
Paperbound: 978-0-7884-0993-6
Clothbound: 978-0-7884-3422-8

DEDICATED
TO
MY WIFE

# A History of Prince Edward Island

# Preface.

IN preparing this volume, my object has been to place before the public an authentic record of Prince Edward Island's early history. I have experienced great difficulty in procuring material, as comparatively little was to be found here where one would naturally look for it. To that mine of information, the Canadian Archives, I am indebted for a great part of the facts which I have been able to collect. I wish here to express my warm appreciation of the unfailing courtesy and assistance that I have received from Dr. Doughty, the distinguished head of the Archives, and his splendid staff of assistants. I have also derived much information from articles published in the Prince Edward Island Magazine, notably from those by the late Professor John Caven. It is to be regretted that this valuable Magazine ceased publication. Dr. Dawson's "St. Lawrence" and Mr. Bagster's "Jacques Cartier" have been most useful with regard to the "Discovery."

I have been able to consult a considerable number, though not all, of the Journals of the old Legislative Council and House of Assembly. Several are not to be found.

Newspapers were published in Charlottetown from an early date, but for the period covered by this narrative, none of these were fyled and only odd numbers of most of them are to be found.

I was able to procure portraits of four of our earliest Lieutenant-Governors, as well as of Bishop McEachern and John Stewart. I was unable to procure likenesses of Rev. Theophilus DesBrisay and of the first pioneer heads of denominations, who came to the Island in its formative period.

I am well aware that there is much that could be added to this volume, if one could find the scattered material. I can only hope that, whatever its short-comings may be, this narrative may prove informative and of use to enquirers into Prince Edward Island's past.

A. B. WARBURTON.

CHARLOTTETOWN,
   10th September, 1923.

# Contents.

## PART I.
THE DISCOVERY . . . . .     Pages 1–15

## PART II.
THE "FRENCH REGIME" . . . . .     16–83

## PART III.
THE DEPORTATION . . . . .     84–117

## PART IV.
ANNEXED TO NOVA SCOTIA . . . .     118–149

## PART V.
SEPARATE GOVERNMENT . . . .     150–494

### CHAPTER I.
PATTERSON, GOVERNOR . . . . .     150–234

### CHAPTER II.
FANNING, LIEUTENANT-GOVERNOR . . .     235–290

### CHAPTER III.
DESBARRES, LIEUTENANT-GOVERNOR . .     291–312

### Chapter IV.

Smith, Lieutenant-Governor . . . 313–361

### Chapter V.

Ready, Lieutenant-Governor . . . 362–382

## PART VI.

Miscellaneous . . . . . 385–439

## SECTION I.—THE CHURCHES.

### Chapter I.

St. Paul's Church and the Parish of Charlotte . 385–392

### Chapter II.

The Roman Catholic Church in P. E. Island . 393–398

### Chapter III.

The Presbyterian Church in P. E. Island . . 399–404

### Chapter IV.

The Methodist Church in P. E. Island . . 405–408

### Chapter V.

The Baptist Church in P. E. Island . . . 409–411

## MISCELLANEOUS.

### SECTION II.—THE EARLY CHIEF JUSTICES.

#### CHAPTER VI.

Duport, First Chief Justice . . . 415–418

#### CHAPTER VII.

Stewart, Second Chief Justice . . . . 419–423

#### CHAPTER VIII.

Cochran, Third Chief Justice . . . 424–426

#### CHAPTER IX.

Thorpe, Fourth Chief Justice . . . . 427–430

#### CHAPTER X.

Colclough, Fifth Chief Justice . . . 431–434

#### CHAPTER XI.

Tremlett, Sixth Chief Justice . . . . 435–437

#### CHAPTER XII.

Archibald, Seventh Chief Justice . . . 438–439

# APPENDICES.

## APPENDIX A.

Patterson's Commission as Governor of the Island of St. John . . . . . . . 443

## APPENDIX B.

Patterson's Instructions . . . . 450

## APPENDIX C.

Further Instructions . . . . . 465

## APPENDIX D.

Additional Instructions . . . . 466

## APPENDIX E.

Patterson's Commission as Lieutenant-Governor . 469
Bibliography . . . . . . 471
Index . . . . . . . . 475

# Illustrations.

1. Jacques Cartier......................................................Frontispiece

                                                                                                Opposite Page

2. John Cabot and Son (Imaginary) prepared for the Cabot Celebration in A. D. 1899. Modelled by John Cassidy of Manchester, England, Exhibited in London, 1897......... 2

3. Section of Champlain's Map (1634) showing the Island of St. John in its correct position and crescent shape......... 14

4. Franquet's plan of a fort to defend Port la Joye, A. D. 1751......... 42

5. Franquet's plan of a fort for the defence of St. Peters......... 44

6. Franquet's plan of a fort for the defence of Three Rivers...... 46

7. Governor Walter Patterson......... 150

8. Plan and Section No. 1 of redoubt for the defence of Charlottetown, by Captain Spry, Chief Engineer of Nova Scotia, for Phillips Callbeck, A. D. 1776......... 192

9. Plan and Section No. 2 of redoubt for the defence of Charlottetown, by Captain Spry, Chief Engineer of Nova Scotia, for Phillips Callbeck, A. D. 1776......... 193

10. Lieutenant-Governor Fanning......... 235

11. Lieutenant-Governor DesBarres......... 291

12. John Stewart of Mount Stewart......... 343

13. Lieutenant-Governor Ready......... 263

14. Bishop McEachern......... 395

(xv)

# History of Prince Edward Island

## PART I.

## THE DISCOVERY

THE noble Gulf of St. Lawrence bore an unwonted burden on its fair bosom the afternoon of 30th June, A. D. 1534, the day when Prince Edward Island smiled her welcome to Jacques Cartier, first of white men to scan her shores. This was the great Breton's earliest voyage to the New World, and until that summer day, save the bark canoes of the Indians, his two small vessels, of some sixty tons each, were the first craft to plough the waters within the bight of Prince Edward Island.

Jacques Cartier was the earliest of the great French explorers of Canada. He was the first European to ascend the St. Lawrence River. This he did on his second and third voyages; but with these expeditions we have, at present, nothing to do. He was a man of courage and resource, as well as of great force of character, qualities essential to one of his adventurous calling. With these he combined the skill of an experienced sailor and a practical knowledge of navigation, not surpassed by any of the sea-faring men of his time.

In almost every walk of life, the closing years of the fifteenth century, and the whole of the sixteenth, were rich in great and enterprising men. In the earlier part of this long period, it may almost be said that in no field of activity were there to be found more far-seeing and adventurous men than were the great navigators and explorers, whose discoveries changed the known face of the globe and resulted in an absolute revolution in the conditions of the civilized world. This extraordinary class of men was not confined to any one nationality. It almost seemed as if Nature had bidden the different European peoples, regardless of racial differences, to beget men, whom she could send forth to seek out and explore the hidden places of the earth, and make them known to civilized man. They hailed from no single country. They gave allegiance to no single rule. Portugal, Spain, the Italian coast cities, France, England -- all could boast of members of this class, whom they sent forth on their daring quests.

For several of these navigators, besides Jacques Cartier, the credit of discovering Prince Edward Island has been claimed. Such claims do not seem to rest on a substantial basis. The strongest has been made on behalf of John Cabot. In the earlier histories and by the earlier writers he is usually credited with the discovery.

## CABOT.

Mr. Stewart, who published an excellent account of Prince Edward Island in 1806, says: *"This Island was first discovered by the English navigator, Cabot, in 1497, June 24, from which circumstance it took the name of St. John. From the abstract of his voyage published in Lediard's Naval Chronicle, it appears to have been the first land he met after leaving Newfoundland. It was probably foggy weather when he entered the Gulf of St. Lawrence, or he must have seen the Island of Cape Breton, the North Cape of which is high land, and only eighteen leagues distant from Cape Ray in Newfoundland." Sailing west by the compass the variation would take him south, how far is impossible to tell. It likely took him south of Newfoundland and the Labrador.

There is nothing to show that he saw Newfoundland, even if he were far enough north to see it; it is likely that Cape Race was hidden by fog and not to be seen. Fog prevails there a great part of the time; but the same cannot, with equal truth, be said of Cape Breton. Moreover, sailing in waters never sailed over by white men before, it does not seem likely that he would have kept on through the dense fog. But he does not mention this fog, and surely he would have done so had there been one. If there was no fog he must, according to Mr. Stewart, have seen Cape Breton, and there is no reason to suppose there was a fog to prevent him from seeing it. The inference seems clear that he did see it and that it was his land-fall. Moreover, if Prince Edward Island was the land-fall, where was the second island lying opposite and close to the land-fall?

In 1903, in a paper styled "Latest Lights on the Cabot Controversy," read before the Royal Society of Canada, the Right Rev. M. F. Howley, Bishop of Newfoundland, contended that the site of Cabot's land-fall was St. John's, Newfoundland. He thinks that

*Page 147.

JOHN CABOT AND SON (Purely Imaginary) PREPARED FOR THE CABOT CELEBRATION IN A. D. 1899.

the theories as to site may be reduced to two main heads; 1st. Theory held by those who maintain that the land-fall must have been on the east coast of Labrador or Newfoundland; 2nd. Theory held by those who believe that Cabot, having passed Cape Race without seeing it or any part of the coast of Newfoundland, drifted some five or six hundred miles further and struck Cape Breton Island or land in the Gulf of St. Lawrence.

The latter he brushes aside as so utterly impossible; so utterly irreconcilable with the facts we now have about this voyage that he cannot conceive how any person could for a moment maintain it, and he, passing by without delaying to refute it, makes St. John's, Newfoundland, the land-fall. This is a very off-hand way of disposing of the second theory, but it is not a satisfactory way. It so happens that the second view is held by such men as Dawson, Bagster and others; but clear of such distinguished advocacy, how could the Bishop reconcile the appearance of the coast at St. John's or any part of the eastern coast of Newfoundland with Cabot's description of the first land seen by him. "The land is excellent and the climate temperate," he says, "suggesting that brasil and silk grow there." Dr. Dawson points out that brasil is a tropical dye wood, imported from the East, and that silk culture is an industry of warm climates. This description surely cannot be applied to Newfoundland.

Dr. Stewart, in his article in the Encyclopædia Britannica* tells us that the claim was made on behalf of Sebastian Cabot. He evidently confounds the son with the father. There are no grounds on which any claims of the former can be based, beyond the uncertain fact that he accompanied his father on his first voyage. The supposed discovery was by the father, John Cabot, a greater man than the son. In May, 1497, he sailed on his first voyage from Bristol, in the "Matthew," a small, unarmed vessel, with a crew of only eighteen men. It was really a preliminary or preparatory expedition. The objective point was Cathay, or Northern China, or the land of the Great Khan. In those days the belief prevailed that a way lay through these new regions to the East, to China, to India, to the fabled realm of the Great Khan. This belief long prevailed. Magellan found a way at the southern extremity of America, round the "Horn," dreaded by sailors. It was a terrible

---
*Ninth Edition.

route of storm, mist and fog. Yet the belief endured that another and better passage could be found through or around the northern parts of the New World. It lingered long and was the cause of many an adventurous voyage to the Arctic seas. The method of these old navigators, in making their voyages, was, after leaving their home port, to sail northwardly until they reached a latitude judged sufficiently high for their purpose, and then to steer a course due west by the compass, This is what Cabot did. He seems to have had very rough weather. He made the land on the 24th of June, old style, which would be the first week in our July, so that his voyage must have taken six or eight weeks. There has been much dispute as to what land that was, which Cabot made. Sailing to the westward it must have been the east coast of whatever land it was. It has been variously contended that it was the east coast of Newfoundland, the coast of Labrador, or the east coast of Cape Breton. But the report of the voyagers on their return to England was that the land was fertile, with a mild climate as if silk or Brazil wood (a tropical dye) might be grown there. In other words it looked like a semi-tropical land. This description effectually disposes of Newfoundland and Labrador, as by no stretch of the imagination could it be made to apply to those storm-beaten and barren coasts, to the rocky, ill-shaped and frightful land which, some decades later, Cartier rather deemed to be the land God gave to Cain. Now, in the beginning of July, part of the east coast of Cape Breton is a land very fair to the eye. At that season it might well impress one, who saw and heard of it for the first time, and whose wearied gaze had for weeks rested on nothing but a stormy waste of waters. Moreover, in A. D. 1500, LaCosa, a companion of Columbus, made a map of North America for the King of Spain, which is still extant. It was long lost, but was found in the middle of last century. It is certainly based, so far as this part of Canada is concerned, upon information furnished by Cabot or by some of his companions. It is the earliest map of North America, and on its face mentions the "sea discovered by the English." As John Cabot and his ship's company were the only Englishmen who had yet been there, this can only refer to his discoveries. On the English section, it refers to the Cape of Discovery, which coincides with Cape Breton, and which thus seems to be established as the land made by John Cabot. Further, Sebastian Cabot, in a map made by him in 1544, while giving no name to this Cape, refers to it as the "first land seen." He must have had his information from his father, or he may have known of it himself, as it is very likely that he was one of the Matthews company. On the same day an island was found close to this "first land seen," which was named "St. John," because it was seen on John the Baptist's day. Cabot did not know of the Gut of Canso, which was not discovered until 1525, and he thought that Cape Breton was part of the mainland. Even had he known of this passage, by no possibility could he, in the slow-sailing craft of his time, which could only make four or five knots an hour, have got through and seen the coast of Prince Edward Island the same day. It would be scarcely possible with our present day craft. Not knowing of the Gut of Canso's existence, he could scarcely have reached Prince Edward Island inside of a week. Moreover, he landed twice the day he made his land-fall, spent some time inspecting the land and, on the second landing, took off a supply of fresh water for his ship, so that he must have spent the greater part of the day there.

But Cabot, on this first voyage, when he had found the land, had accomplished his quest. He had found land to the west, which he thought to be, and reported to be, the land of the Great Khan, the land for which he was seeking. Then, skirting the coast of Newfoundland, he returned to Bristol, where he arrived in September, having been absent on this voyage about four months.

It seems beyond doubt that Cabot never saw Prince Edward Island. The island named by him St. John, found the same day that he made the land, was almost certainly Skatari, off the cape where he made his land-fall. There is no other island off that coast which complies with Cabot's description. By no possibility could it have been Prince Edward Island.*

---

*The late Archbishop O'Brien, in an erudite paper on Cabot's land-fall and chart published in the Transactions of the Royal Society of Canada for 1899, disputes the view adopted in the text, which is the one advanced by Dr. Samuel E. Dawson in his valuable work, "The Saint Lawrence." Some of the crew, he argues, landed at Cape North "on the very Cape," and then sailed four leagues west to St. Lawrence Bay, within the Gulf, where they again landed for water. Entertaining, as he does, a profound respect for the late prelate's erudition, the writer yet feels that his distinguished fellow Prince Edward Islander's patriotic love for the land of his birth misled him in this matter. The facts as set out in his article would seem to be fatal to his contention. Cabot made his land-fall about 5 a. m. True this was on one of the longest days of the year. He had been storm-tossed for six to eight weeks without seeing land. The crew, before landing "on the Cape," had to make some preparations, get boats ready, etc., and would spend some time going and returning from the shore, and would also spend some time on the land, when they reached it

## VERAZANNO.

Verazanno, a Florentine navigator in the employ of Francis I of France, made a voyage in 1524, and it has been alleged that the credit of discovering Prince Edward Island may belong to him, but that idea may be dismissed. He made the land to the south, near the Carolinas. He sailed along the coast of the present United States and the shores of Nova Scotia and Newfoundland. It was largely upon his discoveries that the French founded their claim to New France. He also coasted along Cape Breton, but there is nothing to show that he went further, and, as already pointed out, the Gut of Canso, through which he might have sailed, was not yet known. As he sailed thence along the coast of Newfoundland, he could not have come within sight of Prince Edward Island.

## GOMEZ.

Another noted explorer was the Portuguese, Stephen Gomez. Like so many of the sea-faring men of his country and day, he was a most skilful navigator. He had sailed with Magellan, when that great sailor discovered the strait which bears his name; but Gomez was of a jealous and treacherous nature. Taking one of the ships, he deserted his chief at the strait and returned to Spain, in the

---

Men, who had been so long at sea in bad weather, would be apt to linger on shore. Then they returned on board, got the ship under way and sailed four leagues to St. Lawrence Bay, where they again went on shore for water. The reports they make are that they saw no inhabitants, but that they saw traces of them. This shows that they took time to look around. It is almost safe to conjecture that Cabot himself landed. Besides the time taken in getting their water which they had to find, dip up and put into their casks, they remained on shore long enough to form an estimate of the quality of the soil and of the products they deemed it adapted for raising. They evidently looked about them, seemingly without hurrying. Now, if they made the North Cape of Cape Breton in the early morning, landed and spent some time there, then sailed four leagues, in a vessel whose rate of sailing would be little, if at all, over four to five knots an hour, landed again, procured water for the ship, had a look at the land, returned with their casks to the Matthew, and got them on board again the same day, that day, even though a long one, would have been pretty well spent. To the writer it seems quite impossible that, in the slow-sailing Matthew, they could have reached Prince Edward Island the same day. Moreover, if he had made Prince Edward Island, he would not have known it to be an Island or part of the mainland, as subsequent explorers believed. No doubt his Grace was right in his description of the headland of Cape Breton, as not agreeing with Cabot's description, but it was not necessary for the navigator to step on shore at the Cape itself. There are landing places near the Cape. It seems possible that the Cape made by Cabot may have been one of the headlands or points in the same neighbourhood, but, even if that were the case, it would not destroy the force of Dr. Dawson's contention, which the writer has adopted in the text, and which seems to him to be conclusive. Another point which the Archbishop does not seem to have considered, but which seems to the writer to be of weight against his contention, is the fact that when Cabot, sailing to the west, made his land-fall, he had accomplished the purpose of his expedition, and had no occasion to continue his voyage further. In fact, having, as he believed, attained his object, and being short of provisions, he did turn back.

service of which country the expeditions to the south had been made.

Under the patronage and with the support of the emperor, Charles V., Gomez, in 1525, fitted out a ship and made an exploring voyage to North America. A methodical and skilled explorer, he minutely examined the coast from somewhere near Florida to Cape Breton and Newfoundland. He discovered the Gut of Canso and that Cape Breton was an island. It had previously been thought to be part of the mainland. The name, St. John, had been given by John Cabot to the small island off the east coast of Cape Breton discovered by him. Gomez gave it to Cape Breton itself, and the Gut was called the Channel of St. John or St. Julian. But he did not go beyond that. He examined the coasts of Nova Scotia and seems to have struck Halifax as well as other harbours. The reports of his voyage, which are pretty full, give no hint of Prince Edward Island, or that he was ever in its immediate neighborhood. Had he seen an island the size of Prince Edward Island there would surely be some mention of it. He was too painstaking and methodical an investigator to omit so important a discovery. In fact, his explorations from the Gut were in a direction away from this island.

## CARTIER.

But while it may now be safely asserted that none of these great explorers ever saw the "Garden of the Gulf," there can be little doubt that Jacques Cartier did make its shores. He made three voyages, possibly four, to these regions. At present we are only concerned with the first made in 1534. Of this voyage he left a record which was long lost, but of which at least two translations, one in Italian and one in English, translated from the Italian, were known. For centuries information as to his voyage was derived from these translations. In 1867, however, there was found in the Imperial Library in Paris, what was evidently the original account or report of his voyage made by Cartier himself. It is clear and succinct, and the explorer's routes, with its aid, may fairly well be traced. From it we see that Cartier was not only a great and skilful navigator but that he was also a most observant man. Many of the localities described by him can, to this day, be recognized from his description.

The name of Jacques Cartier is so important a one in connection with the discovery of Prince Edward Island, that the writer feels justified in going into some detail with regard to his life and environment. He was a native and resident of St. Malo in France, where he first saw the light in the closing years of the fifteenth century. Little is known of his youth. He evidently became a respected and prominent citizen of his native town. The people of St. Malo were a sea-faring folk noted for skilful and daring seamen, a distinction shared with others of the coast towns of France. From the rather meagre accounts we have of his earlier days, we gather that he, like other of his townsmen, went to sea, early in life, and rapidly developed into one of the foremost sailors of a community famed for its seamen. Even at that date, the voyages of the ships of St. Malo extended to what were then the remote parts of the globe. Among the hardy voyagers it is clear that Cartier soon took a prominent place. He was acquainted with Portugese sufficiently to act as an interpreter of that tongue, and it is fairly certain that he had been in Brazil and possibly in other parts of South America. While still a young man he became a master pilot, a fact which is evidence in itself that he was a first-rate seaman. Of the excellence of his seamanship, however, his voyages of exploration in North America are in themselves sufficient proof.

Subsequently to Verazanno's voyage in 1524, war between France and Spain prevented Francis I from continuing his interest in New World exploration. At the great battle of Pavia, in February, 1525, Francis was defeated and made prisoner by the Emperor Charles V. He did not regain his freedom till the following year, when peace was made between the warring countries. In 1532-3, Francis began to again concern himself with the New World. His re-awakened interest was encouraged by Philippe de Chabot, Seigneur de Brion and Admiral of France, who recommended that the command of an expedition be given to Cartier, to whom, in consequence, a Royal Commission was issued. The fisheries of Newfoundland, already made known by the expeditions of the Cabots and other early explorers, were attracting many fishing vessels to their teeming waters. The Strait of Belle Isle was itself known, though possibly not throughout its whole length. Cartier, himself, on this voyage found a large ship of Rochelle in one of the harbours of the Strait. It is not unlikely that Portugese mariners had found their way through the Strait and into the Gulf of St. Lawrence, but, if they did, they left no record of their voyage.

The proposed expedition, under the Royal Commission, to explore the Canadian seas met with scant favour from the seafaring magnates of St. Malo, who were much more concerned about the Newfoundland fisheries than they were about the realm of the Great Khan, and looked askance at the skilled seamen of the port being taken away to man Cartier's ships, while their own vessels had difficulty in obtaining experienced crews. The hindrances to his obtaining men became so serious that he had to appeal to the authorities, when orders were issued that he would get his men, and to make sure that he got them, the merchants were prohibited from shipping their crews until Cartier's ships were manned. This drastic procedure proved effective, and in the spring of 1534 he was ready for sea. He had two vessels of about sixty tons each, together carrying a total complement of sixty-one persons, including the commander.

Leaving his home port of St. Malo on 20th April, 1534, he directed his course towards Newfoundland, even then noted for her great fisheries, to which European vessels, in increasing numbers, were resorting. He had a very good run of twenty days and made the land at Bonavista. Owing to great quantities of ice lying along the coast, he could not at once proceed on his voyage and made for the harbour of Catalina, where the ships were held for ten days, during which time the boats were fitted out. Leaving Catalina on 21st May, he reached an island, to which, owing to the enormous numbers of fowl which congregated there, he gave the name, Isle of Birds, or Bird Island. It was surrounded by ice, through which he sent his two boats to the land where, in half an hour, they were loaded with birds. Of these each ship, in addition to those they used fresh, salted four or five casks full. He gives a brief description of the different species of fowl frequenting the island.

On 27th May he reached the Strait of Belle Isle. For a month he explored the Strait and the Newfoundland coast. He reported that the harbours were good, but that this region should not be called "New Land," but instead, a rocky, ill-shaped, and frightful land which he rather deemed to be the land God gave to Cain. Having explored the coast of Labrador and the shores of Newfoundland, he reached out into the Gulf of St. Lawrence where he discovered the Magdalen Islands. Of these the first seen were the Bird Rocks, which he described as consisting of three small islands. At that time there was a third island, but it has been worn away since Cartier's time. Its position is now indicated by the waters breaking over the shoal where it once had been. The islands are readily recognized from Cartier's description. They were, he says, as "full of birds as a field of grass." The voyagers were unable to ascend the largest and landed at the base of the smaller one, where they killed more than a thousand birds. They could have loaded thirty boats had they so desired. About five leagues to the westward was another island where they procured water and firewood. Cartier praises the land as being the best he had seen, full of goodly trees, meadows, wild corn, gooseberries, strawberries, parsley and other herbs. Here also they found many great beasts, like huge oxen, with teeth (tusks) like an elephant, that go in the sea. This is the first we hear of the walrus or sea cow of which, later, we shall hear much. There were also foxes and bears. To this island Cartier gave the name of Brion Island, in honour of Philippe de Chabot, seigneur de Brion, grand admiral of France, a name it still bears. The 27th June and following day he sailed along the islands, passing several till he reached a very high pointed one which he called Allezay. There has been much dispute as to what island is here meant. Pope, Ganong, Dawson and Bagster recognize it as "Deadman's Island," and the writer accepts their finding. On the 29th of June the wind changed to the southwest, and they ran until Tuesday the 30th at sunrise. At sunset the previous day they saw land like two islands which lay to the west-south-west nine or ten leagues. Bagster assumes that he anchored on the night of 28th June near Southwest Cape. As he wished to explore the coast, which he could not well do, at night, this is a most likely assumption, and may fairly be adopted. The next morning he sailed. Mr. Bagster in his note at this point says: "Sailing westward in order to fetch clear of Amherst Island, he would have to stand out on a course east by south, a quarter south, for about ten miles. He would then tack and steer west three-quarters south, which, with moderate wind and the tide setting out of the Gulf, as it always does at that time of the year, would bring him by sunset into a position to see Campbell's Point and Cape Sylvester on the northerly shore of Prince Edward Island. He must have approached the coast, for he discovered the next day that it was the mainland, along which he sailed for forty leagues to Cap D'Orleans, doubtless the present Kildare. Mr. Bagster's argument commends itself to the writer as being sound.

There has been much difference of opinion as to Cartier's land-fall. It certainly was where he saw the two seeming islands. Some years ago, in preparing a sketch of Prince Edward Island the writer was much indebted to the excellent work of Dr. S. E. Dawson and, in deference to his authority, adopted Capes Turner and Tryon as the two seeming islands first seen by Cartier, in which case the "River of Boats," which Cartier saw the following day, would be the entrance to Richmond Bay. He also consulted Mr. Popes' "Jacques Cartier," in which the lands seen were placed further west. In that case, Kildare River would be the River of Boats. Cartier, approaching the island, saw two high lands, which looked like islands in the distance. There were formerly some high sand-hills, known as the Seven Sisters, to the eastward of Cascumpec or Holland Bay, off the shores of Township No. 11. These were swept away some time in the first half of the last century. Till then they were prominent objects, particularly when approached from the sea. These the writer suggested were the two high lands seen by Cartier. A very strong objection to this view was the distance (about forty leagues) which Cartier says he sailed to the westward after seeing the two supposed islands. If these sand-hills were the land-fall, the distance would not be more than ten leagues. If the high lands were Capes Turner and Tryon, then the distance sailed would not exceed twenty leagues. Hence Cartier's forty leagues did not apply to any of these supposed land-falls.

Since that sketch was written, new data have been obtained, which, in the writer's opinion, effectually dispose of the question and fix Campbell's Point and Cape Sylvester as being Cartier's land-fall in Prince Edward Island. Mr. W. F. Tidmarsh, of Charlottetown, who, for many years has had extensive business relations with the Magdalen Islands and who has always been deeply interested in the early history of this province, decided, if possible, to settle this vexed question of Cartier's land-fall. In the closing days of June, some years ago, he sailed on a schooner from the Magdalens for Prince Edward Island, taking as nearly as possible the courses taken by Cartier. Like Cartier he saw land in the distance, that appeared like two small islands. On nearer approach they were seen to form part of the mainland of Prince Edward Island, and were, in fact, Campbell's Point and Cape Sylvester, on the north shore of the island, some four or five miles west of East Point. In the writer's opinion this quite disposes of the question as to Cartier's land-fall. The distance westward along the coast from these two points (about forty leagues) fits in with Cartier's narrative. Mr. Bagster, in his work already referred to, adopts these two capes as the land-fall, and the writer has no hesitation in taking the same view.

Having made the land, Cartier, as already mentioned, coasted to the westward about forty leagues, landing in his boats at several places. He was greatly impressed with what he saw of the richness and fertility of the land. He described the country as a beautiful one, speaks of its low level land, "The fairest that it may be possible to see," and full of goodly trees and meadows; but he could not find a harbour, because the land is low and wholly ranged with sands. This is true of the north side. Cartier, who did not know that his discovery was an island, never saw the south side where are our splendid harbours.

The explorers landed, in their boats, at several places, among others at a river, which they named the "River of Boats," a fair stream where they saw boats of savages crossing the stream, hence the name. This may surely be identified with Richmond Bay and the entrance to the Narrows.

The wind hauling in from the sea, Cartier withdrew to his ships and made to the northeast until next day at sunrise, when as it became foggy and stormy, he struck sails until about ten o'clock, when they saw Cape Orleans, now Kildare Cape, and further to the north another cape which he named Cape Savage, clearly the North Cape. He saw more natives towards this cape, near which he again landed. He tried to communicate with the savages but without success. Rounding the Cape of Savages, he noted the long and dangerous reef. This day (1st July) he sailed for nine or ten leagues up the coast towards the West Cape, thinking to find a harbour, which he failed to do, as the land was low.

He landed at four places and found the trees wonderfully fair and that there were cedars, pines, white elms, ash, willows and many other species of trees unknown to him, all without fruit. He describes the lands where there were no woods as very fair and so full of peas, gooseberries, other small fruits and corn, that it seemed to have been sown and cultivated there. The land he described as of the best quality that can be seen, and of great warmth, and that there were many turtle-doves, wood pigeons and other birds. There was nothing lacking save harbours.

As he sailed up the coast he saw the land apparently closing in on both sides, whence he concluded he was in a large bay. On 2nd July he sighted land to the north which held with that already skirted, from which he was satisfied that it was a large bay about twenty leagues in depth and the same in width. He was at the western entrance of the Strait of Northumberland, but failed to see it. He had sailed along the whole length of the north shore of Prince Edward Island and rounding the North Cape, had sailed up some nine or ten leagues along the western shore, without knowing it to be an island, and believing it to be part of the continent. It was not known to be an island until long afterwards.

Mr. John Calder Gordon, in "Americana" for September, 1913, page 773, says that: "The first mention of the 'Isle of St. John,' as unquestionably applied to Prince Edward Island, is attributed to Champlain. He knew of it as early as 1603, but by hear-say only. In 'Des Sauvages,' published in 1604, Chapter XII, he tells us the story of Sieur Prevert's attempt to find mines on the Bay of Fundy, by crossing over-land from the Gulf, in connection with which he mentions 'The Island of St. John,' which is some thirty or thirty-five leagues long and some six leagues from the main land on the south.

"We first hear of this island of St. John (for there were others) in 1623, when the Basques, who, for a time, resisted the royal concessions to the companies trading and fishing in the Gulf, seized one of Champlain's vessels and took it to a port they had fortified on the island for their own account."*

---

*Dawson, The St. Lawrence, page 422.

St. John the Baptist seems to have been the cause of much of the confusion and doubt that exist, and have long existed, regarding the early history of Prince Edward Island. His was a favorite name with the old navigators, and we find it in many different places, hence the confusion. There were Cabot's Island of St. John, off the east coast of Cape Breton; Gomez's Island of St. John, meaning Cape Breton itself; on Sebastian Cabot's map of 1544 the Magdalens are called St. John; then there are St. John's, Newfoundland; St. John, New Brunswick, the river St. John and others. Small wonder that, at a later date, Governor Patterson complained of mails going astray and asked to have the name changed.

Nothing further is known of the Island for a century. Not even that greatest of French explorers, Champlain, seems to have set foot on its shores, although he was aware of its existence.

In his first map, made in 1610, there is nothing to show that he knew anything about the Island, as an island, In that of 1612 it appears as a sort of dot, showing that Champlain must have learned of the Island since his first map was made.\* In his last map, made in 1634, it is clearly and correctly shown. While he was never on the Island, it is evident that Champlain learned of and profited by the researches of others; or it might very possibly be from the reports of fishermen.

Cartier's discovery would certainly have conferred upon France the first claim to the ownership of the Island, but it was long overlooked, or, probably, the French were too much engrossed with affairs at home, where they had plenty of troubles to engage their attention, to give much thought to their North American possessions. The Bretons and the Basques, as well as the Portugese, the English and other nationalities, resorted more and more to the Newfoundland fisheries, which were carried on before Cartier's time, and assuredly they would not have neglected the rich fisheries of Cape Breton. It is most unlikely that these hardy fishermen did not seek their fares round the Magdalens and in the teeming waters off the shores of Prince Edward Island. In fact, as already seen,† the Basques had a fortified post there in 1623, but their business was catching and curing fish, reaping the harvest of

---

\*See section of Champlain's map of 1634, in this volume.
†Dawson, The St. Lawrence, page 422.

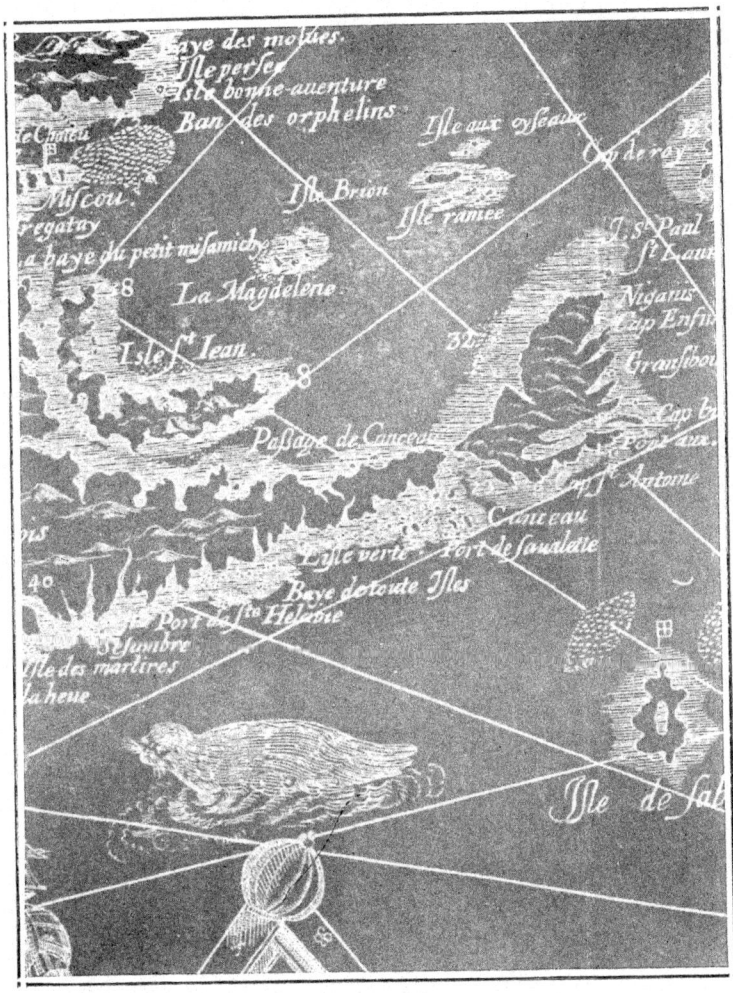

SECTION OF CHAMPLAIN'S LAST MAP (1634) SHOWING THE ISLAND OF ST. JOHN IN ITS CORRECT POSITION AND CRESCENT SHAPE.

the sea, and not settlement or exploration. It is even likely that they would land and erect their flakes and shelters on the coasts of these different lands, but there is nothing to tell us of what they saw or did, or how the Island fared, or how its swarthy inhabitants occupied themselves during the long years when, after Jacques Cartier's visit, it slumbered and slept in all the beauty of its forests and streams, its bright skies and glorious summer climate, or how the months of isolation sped away.*

*The Indian name of the island was Abegwet. It had several variations and slight differences of meaning. The following are from "Micmac Place Names," recorded by Rev. Dr. S. T. Rand, collected and arranged by Lieut.-Col. Wm. P. Anderson, C. M. G., F. R. G. S., etc., member of the Geographic Board of Canada:

(1) "Abagwit" (long soft a), meaning, "Moored in shelter," "Cradled alongside," "Sheltered by the encircling shore."

(2) "Abegwet" (long final e) meaning, "Afloat, at rest on the wave close by," "Moored in the shelter of the encircling shore."

(3) "Apagwit" (long a) meaning, "Afloat, at rest on the wave close by," "Moored in the shelter of the encircling shore."

(4) "Epagwit" (long a) meaning, "Reposing on the wave," or in simple prose, "Lying on the water"—"Afloat and lying still on the water."

Another Indian name was "Minegoo," meaning "The Island," showing Prince Edward Island to have been "The" Island, par excellence, back in pre-historic aboriginal times.

## PART II.

## THE FRENCH REGIME.

### Captain Doublet.

IN 1663 Captain Doublet of the French navy (ship's captain), obtained a concession from the Company of New France, then nearing the end of its powers, of the Island of St. John, together with the Magdalens, for the purpose of carrying on the fisheries in their waters. Associated with him were two companies of fishermen from the towns of Granville and St. Malo. They seem to have confined their operations to a few harbours, and not to have attempted any permanent settlement, beyond such as was necessary to the carrying on of their industry. The writer has been unable to ascertain how long Doublet held this concession. It recites that, wishing to help those who can work in colonizing the country, it (the Company of New France), at the request of M. Doublet, ship's captain, for the Islands Magdalens, St. John, Bird and Brion, in the Gulf of St. Lawrence, to colonize the same and to send thither the necessary ships, and to carry on all kinds of fisheries round about and on the banks of said islands, and clear and cultivate the said lands, concerning which, after due deliberation and pursuant to the power given to it (the Company) by His Majesty, has given, granted and allotted the said islands of Magdalens, St. John, Bird and Brion, with all rights, to the said M. Doublet; yielding rent to our said Company of Miscou and charged in its favour with fifty livres per annum, for all rent, which shall be paid during the first three years, without the said M. Doublet trading in skins or pelts in the said places or elsewhere. That is, Doublet was not to engage in the fur trade.

Rev. A. E. Burke* says that he had the following, concerning the concession to Doublet, from Dr. Dawson, an excellent authority, who said that he had the original concession before him. Dr.

*Prince Edward Island Magazine, Vol. II, 136.

Dawson says: "At the date of the grant to Doublet, the King was not making grants. Grants were made by the Company of New France, and it was not until February 24th, 1663, that the country was turned over to the King, and the deed was not registered until September of that year."

The concession of January 19th, 1663, was made to Le Sieur Doublet, Capitan de Navire, by La Campagnie de la Nouvelie France, and was signed at the office of the Company by A. Chiffant, the secretary. This Doublet was François Doublet. He was an apothecary at Harfleur, but when he got up a company to explore his grant, he sank the shop and, in the deed, figures as captain of the ship S. Michel, 200 tons.

The concession was of the following islands:

(a) De la Magdaline.
(b) St. Jean (Prince Edward Island).
(c) Aux Oiscaux.
(d) Brion.

A company known as the Miscou Company, united with that of New France, were parties to the concession, for they held a prior grant to all that region, and Doublet was to have held as their vassal. François Doublet formed an association to settle and work the grant, in April, 1663, with one Gaignast at Harfleur. His training as an apothecary would not seem to be one conducive to his making a success of his new venture, which seems to have been a failure.

## NICHOLAS DENYS.

The Abbe Casgrain in his work, "La Seconde Acadie," discredits the record of Doublet, and suggests that English writers have confused him with Nicholas Denys.

According to M. Casgrain, Nicholas Denys, an enterprising and industrious merchant, who came to Acadia at the same time as the Commander de Razilly in 1632, obtained from the Company of New France, in 1656, the concession of the country and islands situate in the great Bay of St. Lawrence, stretching from Cape Canso as far as Cap de Rosier. In a history of his domains which he published and dedicated to Louis XIV in 1672, Denys styled himself Governor, Lieutenant-General for the King, and proprietor of all these lands and islands.

The Island of St. John was included in his territory, and he gives an interesting description of it. At eight or ten leagues, he tells us, from Brion and the Magdalen Islands is the Island of St. John, twenty-five to thirty leagues in length and one in bread that the centre, somewhat crescent shaped. There was an abundance of game on the Island, including caribou, a species of elk. He adds that the old descriptions of the Island of St. John have an interest and a merit, which the best, that have since been made, cannot have; because the former show the gradual progress of exploration. To Jacques Cartier the island, seen from afar, seemed like a point of land. Later, Champlain determined its general form; then Denys came, who penetrated the interior, lived there, and described its vegetation, its forests, animals, etc.

The Island of St. John, as Denys said, has the form of a crescent, of which the horns point one to the northeast, the other to the northwest.

Denys had obtained great privileges, which had not the result, hoped by the Company of New France, of encouraging settlement. He concerned himself solely with trade and the fisheries. Neither in the Island of St. John nor in the other parts of his possessions did he leave any permanent establishments.

Some English writers, the same authority intimated, such as Stewart and Osgoode, have maintained that, prior to 1663, a grant of the Island of St. John for the purpose of establishing a fishery was made to a captain in the French Navy named Doublet. He thinks it probable that these authorities have confused the name of Denys with that of Doublet, because that Denys, who worked his concession before and after Doublet's time, and who had to defend it on two different occasions, the first against the attack of Le Borgue, one of the feudatories of Acadia, the second time against those of a privateer of the name of Girandiere, makes no mention of Doublet.

The Abbe Casgrain is seemingly in error in this matter. The concession of 1663, a copy of which the writer has before him, was made out in the name of Doublet and his partners, whose names appear more than once in it, while that of Denys is not even mentioned in the grant, etc., so that there can be no doubt as to the concession to Doublet. Nicholas Denys, who also had extensive concessions in Acadia, came out from France in 1632, and in 1654 was made Governor in the Gulf of St. Lawrence and the islands from Cape Canso to Cape Rosier. He was, as M. Casgrain says, a man of enterprise. Dawson described him as a man of peace, a colonizer and organizer. For some time he carried on a shore fishery at what is now Liverpool, in Nova Scotia. Owing to difficulties with his neighbours he removed to the eastern end of Nova Scotia and established posts at Chedabucto, St. Peter's and St. Anne's on Cape Breton Island, and at Miscou at the southern point of the opening of Chaleur Bay. His grant, dated in 1654, was from the King of France, and extended from Canso in Nova Scotia to Cape Rosier in Gaspe. The coal of Cape Breton was first exploited by him. There was no reason why his interests and those of Doublet should clash.

In 1682-3 the Island was granted to a company formed by one Bergier and others, whose object was to establish fisheries along the coast of Acadia and to prosecute the seal fishery. They were not successful.

Mr. Stewart, in his "account of Prince Edward Island," a valuable little work published in 1806, tells us that "From the best information, it does not appear that any settlements, with a view to cultivation, were made by the French on the Island till after the Peace of Utrecht; and it is said the Government never encouraged the settlement, and refused after Sieur Doublet's patent was vacated, to give grants in perpetuity to the people who had settled in the Island, with a view to forcing the settlement of Cape Breton, and of drawing as many people as they could round the different fortified posts they held on the continent.

### Treaty of Utrecht.

After the Treaty of Utrecht in 1713, ceding Acadia and Newfoundland to Great Britain, by the terms of which the French inhabitants were to have liberty to remove, within a year, to any other place, many Acadians settled in the Island of St. John, preferring it to Cape Breton, to which the French authorities were desirous that they should emigrate.

The French inhabitants of Acadia resorted thither, but seem to have, subsequently, abandoned it. This is to be gathered from the correspondence of Lieutenant-Governor Caulfield of Nova Scotia, with the Home Government in London, to be found in Akin's Nova Scotian Archives. Writing from Annapolis Royal, on 16th May, 1716, to the Board of Trade and Plantations, he says that "The Island of St. John's, which the French of this colony seemed to like, in case they were obliged to quit us, is entirely abandoned by these inhabitants, who went there out of this Government." From this it seems clear that there had been a considerable efflux of Acadians from Nova Scotia to the Island of St. John's. This may have taken place before the cession of Acadia by the Treaty of Utrecht in 1713, though of this we know nothing, and immediately after the treaty there probably would be a considerable though temporary exodus from Nova Scotia to the Island, which still continued to be French.

Caulfield's letter indicated that this movement, doubtless inspired by fear of their new rulers,— by panic in fact,— very soon spent itself, and the refugees shortly found their way back to Acadia, or even to Quebec and France. Certainly they seem to have made no serious attempt at permanent settlement in the Island of St. John.

As there were no English in the Island of St. John when Caulfield wrote, it is evident that, save for Indians, the Island was then uninhabited. But this abandoned condition did not long continue. The French authorities at length recognized the Island's importance to them and decided to settle it. No doubt they came to this decision because they saw how conveniently placed the Island was, as a source of supplies for their forces in Cape Breton and elsewhere in its vicinity. This view continued to prevail with regard to the Island of St. John. Nearly forty years later, after its capture by the British in 1758, Villejon, the last French commandant, writes to his Government that: "Three years ago the Island was stocked with cattle, in the hope of its being able to supply efficient and annual help to Louisbourg."

After 1716, the savage Micmac tribes who inhabited the Island of St. John remained in peaceable possession until 1719 when a new concession of the Island and of Miscou was granted to the Count de St. Pierre, with a view to establishing a permanent colony there.

## St. Pierre.

In January of the following year, St. Pierre procured new letters patent for concessions on the same terms, for the Islands of

Magdeline, Boton or Ramees, neighbouring islands and islets, as much for the cultivation of the soil as for the cod, seal and sea cow fisheries. One of the chief reasons actuating the French Government in conferring such great privileges was to favour the Acadians of Nova Scotia, who wished to locate in French territory, and who found it more profitable to settle in the Island of St. John than on the less hospitable coasts of Cape Breton. Count St. Pierre associated with him two wealthy speculators, MM. Farqes and Moras. All three shared in the expenditure, which ran up, it is said, to over twelve hundred thousand livres (about $240,000), but conflict of interests caused the enterprise to miscarry. The Count de St. Pierre, said Charlevoix, would likely have succeeded in his design, had all his associates been like himself. He soon experienced the disgust inseparable from associations, whose members are incapable of large thoughts, and who are united by self interest only.

The Island was also deemed of importance as commanding the trade of the neighbouring territories. The English in Nova Scotia were not less alive to its importance. Paul Mascerine, in a description of Nova Scotia, transmitted in 1720 by Governor Phillips to the Lords of Trade, clearly points this out. He advocated the construction of a small fort on the neck of land between Bay Verte and the Bay of Fundy, and to show its necessity says: "This is more so by reason that the French have sent four ships this summer, with two hundred families, with provisions, stores and materials for the erecting of a fort and making a settlement on the Island of St. John's, which lies in the Bay of Verte, part of the Gulf of St. Lawrence, part of which Island (which is near fifty leagues long) is but three or four leagues distant from the Main, and six in all from Chignecto. When the settlement is made by the French, they will, from thence, command all the trade, and carry a greater sway over all the Bay of Fundy than the English, who are the undoubted owners, but have only the name of possession of it, till such measures are taken as are hereby humbly proposed." He emphasized his contention by adding: "For it is to be remembered that each of these places has a French Popish missionary, who is the real Chief Commissioner of his flock and takes his commands from his superior in Cape Breton," a statement interesting in itself because of the side-light it throws upon the rancour and intolerance which prevailed in religious matters a couple of centuries ago, when the feelings of suspicion between people holding differing religious beliefs, would almost seem to be stronger than the influence of the religions they respectively professed; a feeling, which, in this twentieth century, it is difficult to appreciate.

These two hundred families must have been settled there by Count St. Pierre, to whom, in 1719, as we have seen, the French King had granted the Island for the purpose of carrying on the fisheries.

The grant to St. Pierre recites that having favourably heard the request of Count St. Pierre, first equerry to the Duchess of Orleans, for a grant of islands in the Gulf of St. Lawrence in order to settle them and to establish a permanent fishery, which would be for the benefit of our kingdom and of the commerce of our subjects and for other reasons, and by the advice of the Regent, and by our special favour, full power and royal authority, we have granted to the said Count de St. Pierre the Islands of St. John and of Miscou, with the small islands and banks adjacent, situate in the Gulf of St. Lawrence, and to his heirs in perpetuity as of a freehold title, without, however, judicial authority, which we have reserved, giving the said Count de St. Pierre power to grant leases of the lands contained in said islands, without having to pay to us or our successors any payment or indemnity, of which we have made a gift to him, subject, however, to fealty and homage to the Castle of Louisbourg, which he shall hold without any rent, to conserve oak trees of use in the building of our ships, to notify us or the Governor and Commander of Isle Royal (Cape Breton) of mines and minerals, if any be found on the lands granted by these presents, which we have reserved. He shall retain or indemnify any settler now on said lands; to convey to said islands, next year, one hundred persons to settle there, and fifty other persons a year during succeeding years, until the said islands shall be fully settled, and supplied with cattle necessary for permanent settlement. He is to clear the lands and cause them to be cleared by the settlers thereon. He is to lay out roads necessary for public use. Should we at any future time need any portion of said lands for the erection of forts, batteries, parade grounds, magazines or other public works, we reserve power to appropriate such lands as well as such trees as may be necessary for said works, and firewood for the garrisons of said forts, without being liable in damages, except to pay the cost of clearing said lands, and the buildings and fences at the valuation of an expert. St. Pierre was also permitted to construct ships and other sea-going vessels from the wood on the granted lands, as also to put up such mills as he should deem necessary for the well-being of said lands. Should he cause to be erected one or more churches of stone, he should have the patronage and should enjoy the honours due to the patron. The Count and his settlers in said islands were permitted to have negro slaves, on condition that they comply with the ordinances and rules which shall be made with respect to said negroes. On non-compliance with the conditions contained in the concession, the islands and lands granted thereby should revert to the Crown.

St. Pierre's attempt was not as useless to the Island of St. John as might be supposed; because it gave birth to several small centres of colonization, which, by virtue of the heavy expenditures that the Company had incurred in establishing their factories, were not slow to develop and prosper.

Concerning these early establishments there are few and brief accounts, but what there are, are invaluable, because official; they are the first registers of baptisms, marriages and burials, by the missionaries from the year 1721. Also there are the censuses taken on the Island in the year 1728, 1735 and 1753. The first two of these censuses are the more valuable as they give the names. By the help of these, the route of the first immigrants from their start at the points of departure can be traced, step by step, to the foundation and development of each group of colonists.

During the time the Count St. Pierre was engaged in France, gathering the elements of the colony which he purposed founding in the Island of St. John, he happened upon a Sulpician priest, the Abbe Breslay, recently come from Canada, where he had been successively cure of Montreal and missionary among the savages of Sault St. Louis. The Abbe Breslay was a man of rank, who had lived in the world before entering the Sulpician order. Count St. Pierre must have met him more than once at the Court of Versailles, where he had served as a gentleman of the royal bed-chamber. The Count, who was on the lookout for a missionary for his new colony, asked the Abbe de Breslay to undertake this work. He found no difficulty in persuading him to accept, because de Breslay was of a fervid temperament and full of zeal for the rough labours of the Canadian missions. He sought only to procure the authorization of his Superior-General, who was then M. Leschassier. He was readily induced to give his consent, because he had inherited from his predecessor, M. Trouson, the idea of founding a seminary in the regions of the Gulf of St. Lawrence. A previous attempt had even been made at Port Royal some years before, but it had miscarried. M. Leschassier deemed the occasion favourable for carrying it out in the Island of St. John.

M. de Breslay was a man eminently fitted for this undertaking. He had experience in mission work and knew the languages kindred to those of the Indians of Acadia and of the islands in the Gulf of St. Lawrence. But being about sixty years of age, his strength sapped by long labour and hardship, he hesitated about going alone and asked for a missionary assistant. A young Sulpician, Abbe de Metivier, was assigned to the work and embarked with him.

Marie-Anseleme de Metivier, a native of the Diocese of Orleans, had already spent six years in Canada. He had been stationed at Montreal and at Long Point, of which he was one of the first cures, and was now back in France on some business matters, when he received his instructions for the Island of St. John. These two had been on the Island some months when M. de Breslay made the first entry in the register of the church. It was the entry made on 10th April, 1721, of the marriage of Francis du Rocher, fisherman, a native of Brittany, with Elizabeth Bruneau. This is, presumably, the first Christian marriage in the Island of St. John.

The ministry of de Breslay was exercised over a congregation few in numbers, but scattered over the Island of St. John as well as other localities. It necessitated frequent journeys, which had to be made in Indian style in canoe, on foot through the woods, or, for the service of other islands, on boats, schooners or other craft capable of holding the sea. Twice a year, autumn and spring, he made regular visitations to the different places, principally to the harbour of St. Peters, next to Port la Joie, the most important station, as well as to Malpeque, a section of country preferred by the Micmacs, and which appealed to him more than other parts of his mission, because it recalled to his mind his old mission of St. Louis, near Montreal.

We cannot readily imagine that St. Pierre, whose interests in the Gulf were so large, and who was forming considerable establishments there involving large expenditures, did not come in person to inspect them, at least at the outset. However, no direct trace of him is to be found in the records of his adventure. It seems likely, however, that his wife passed some time at Port la Joie, where she acted as godmother to a child of one of the company's officers. Even in this it is possible that Madame St. Pierre was not personally present, and that she was represented by a proxy.

When he sent his first lot of settlers to the Island in 1720, St. Pierre was represented by a Governor, M. Gottenville de Belle-Isle, who seems to have remained in command until about 1730.

The organization of St. Pierre's company was a reproduction in miniature of the government of New France, with its good points and its bad; its machinery too complicated, its ways too European, its affable treatment of the native races, its anxiety to civilize and to christianize.

The fisheries in these parts were the most direct source of gain. That, it was, which induced the company to locate at St. Peter's Harbour, named after the Count, the neighbourhood of which also offered land suitable for tillage. In the course of the years 1720 and 1721 ten families were settled there, all of whom were engaged in the fishery. Five others settled at Port la Joie, three on the Northeast (Hillsborough) River and two at East Point.

In the Island of St. John, prior to 1720, there were only two French families, one at St. Peter's Harbour, the other at East Point, both living by fishing. By the end of 1721 the first nucleus of colonization was formed. It consisted of nineteen families, making in all one hundred souls. Then there set in two currents of immigration, one directly from France, the other from Acadia. The Acadians were the best colonists. The little colony during the following year continued to receive new settlers, some bringing with them families already formed, others marrying after their arrival.

The Rev. John C. McMillan, referring to this grant, says: "With this concession to Count St. Pierre, the history of St. John's Island properly begins. Heretofore almost entirely neglected, it now becomes the point towards which converged two streams of emigrants, the one from France, the other from Acadia or Nova Scotia."*

The settlement by Count St. Pierre was made in 1720. He procured his letters patent in January, and in April he sent out three vessels from Rochfort, carrying three hundred immigrants with their supplies, for St. John's Island by way of Louisbourg. They were under the command of Daniel de Gottenville de Belle-Isle, who was to act as governor of the new colony. In September, St. Ovide de Brouillan, Governor of Louisbourg, wrote to Vaudreuil that on 23rd August two of the vessels had arrived and gone on and that he had permitted Denys de la Ronde, an officer of experience, to accompany them. When de Gottenville arrived at Port la Joie, the landing was well advanced. Neat and solid log houses were constructed and breastworks thrown up, mounted with eight cannon and manned by thirty soldiers. A tall cross was set up. A church dedicated to St. John the Evangelist was erected and M. Breslay placed in charge.†

In August, 1723, a new missionary was installed at Port la Joie, under the roof lately occupied by M. Breslay and his assistant, M. Metivier. The new missionary was a member of the Franciscan order,— Brother Louis Barbet Dulonjin, who had landed but a few days previously at Port la Joie, with the title of chaplain of the garrison and at the same time charged with the services of the whole island. What had brought about this change?

The company of St. Pierre grew alarmed at the enormous expenditure he was incurring and which appeared to its members out of all proportion with the profits they had hoped to realize. Among the economies they saw were those which might be made in the religious services of the colony. The support of secular clergy was clearly more burdensome than that of the monk or friar satisfied with the soldier's ration. A branch of the order, the Recollets of Brittany, had founded a convent at Louisbourg.

---

*"Early History of the Catholic Church in Prince Edward Island," page 3.

†From 1721, when M. M. Breslay and Metivier founded the mission, till 1751, there was only one parish in the island, that of Port la Joie. Here the parochial records already referred to were kept. The formation of four new parishes, those of Point Prim, Louis, St. Peter's and Malpeque, did not take place prior to 1752, in consequence registers were kept there only for about the six years from 1752 to 1758. At the time of the evacuation of the Island of St. John the registers were carried to France. I have seen no record as to what became of the registers of the four new parishes, but the more ancient and the more important, those of Port la Joie, have been preserved and are to be found in the archives of the Ministry of Marine and Colonies in Paris. They form three volumes in small folio, in a good state of preservation.

Some time before a monk of the same house, Michel Brulai, who served the small groups scattered along the banks of the Bay Chaleur, and especially of the Micmac village of Rustigouche, had landed at Port la Joie. He was followed by the Abbe Ganlin from Acadia, where he represented the Bishop of Quebec as Vicar-General.

The conferences of these missionaries at Port la Joie with the two Sulpicians serving the colony had a significance explained by subsequent events. Doubtless they had discussed together and with the Governor, the company's plans, and propounded a new scheme of missions in the islands of the Gulf of St. Lawrence. M. de Breslay did not require to make a long stay in the Island to convince himself and satisfy M. Leschassier that the founding of a seminary was premature. Some months later, after the Recollets had replaced the two Sulpicians, the Abbe de Breslay left the Island in the spring of 1723, and was followed in July by M. de Metivier, who returned to France. The Recollets remained on and were in charge of the Island of St. John until 1752 when secular priests were again called in to take their place.

The year 1728, the same in which the first census of the Island was taken, was marked by an increase of immigration, such as had not been seen till then. There arrived no less than twenty-five new settlers, of whom eighteen brought with them their wives and families. That influx, together with the natural increase, brought the population, at the close of that year, to a total of three hundred and thirty-six souls, distributed among seven different settlements as follows: Fourteen families at Port la Joie; eighteen at St. Peter's Harbour; three at East Point; fifteen at Savage Harbour; four at Tracadie, and three at Malpeque and East River. The census of that year gave the names of the settlers at each place, following the date of their arrivals.

St. Pierre, as we have seen, spent a large amount of money to settle and carry on business in the Island. He claimed an exclusive monopoly of all fishing rights. This claim was disputed by the French fishermen of Isle Royale, who paid no attention to his claims and fished despite of them. He sent out an armed vessel to enforce his demands, which seized several of their vessels and cargoes in the open sea. When these doings became known, the traders and independent fishermen took measures to have his exclusive privileges revoked and complained to the home authorities of their injustice. In addition to maintaining an armed ship and seizing their vessels on the sea, they accused him of favoring the English. They set out that if his privileges were sustained, the French fisheries would suffer a great decrease. The result was that on 13th October, 1725, his letters patent were revoked, and the group of islands over which his concession extended reverted to the Crown. Previously, in November, 1724, St. Pierre having failed to render any assistance, nearly all the inhabitants retired to Cape Breton. This exodus was the real end of his colonization scheme.

In 1730 the Island of St. John had a new Governor, M. de Pensens. He had occupied an important position at Louisbourg in 1714, and was sent to Port Royal, with M. de la Ronde, to induce the Acadians to remove from the territories ceded to the British and to settle in Cape Breton.

During 1735 the second census was taken and showed a total of eighty-one families settled in the Island, of whom fifty-seven were farmers. Thirty-five of these came from Acadia; twenty-one from Normandy; seven from Saintonge; four from Brittany; two from Canada and one from Spain. All the Acadians were sprung from families originally settled in the Island of St. John, with the exception of a family named Dubois, a family named Vecco, composed of twelve persons, and two Porrier families.

This population was distributed, one hundred and fourteen souls at Port la Joie; at St. Peters, two hundred and ninety-four; at Savage Harbour, thirty-five; at Tracadie, thirty-nine; at Malpeque thirty-one; at East Point, eighteen; at Three Rivers, ten.

During the thirty-eight years, covering the French regime from the settlement by Count St. Pierre till the capture of Louisbourg in 1758, with the consequent surrender of St. John's Island to the British, we get several very full descriptions of the Island written by officials or others who travelled over a great part of the settlements and have left accounts of these journeys, of the several settlements and of the appearance and resources of the country. They were observant men and have left informative accounts of what they saw. The earliest of these was La Ronde.

## La Ronde.

The settlement at Port la Joie was not intended to be a fishing centre. It was not well situated for that purpose. Little, if any, fishing was carried on there. It was situated about half way from either end of the Strait, hence too far from the great fishing waters to be suitable for that industry. It was better adapted for agriculture and cattle raising. The settlers, whose newly built houses were scattered about the rivers and harbour, were a farming community who gave little or no attention to other employments. LaRonde seems to have devoted his first year on the Island to the establishing and fortifying of Port la Joie. But, at the same time, St. Pierre and his associates were establishing fishing stations in the harbours on the north side of the Island. There can be no doubt but that La Ronde, who took a very active part in the work of settlement, had visited and assisted in the establishment of these stations prior to his journey in 1721 when he carefully enquired into the condition of the new settlements and also into the natural resources of the Island.

De la Ronde had organized the settlement at Port la Joie. It might fairly be expected to prosper. On 6th November, 1721, he wrote the Minister of Marine and Fisheries, giving an account of the other parts of the Island. He described its harbours, rivers, timber, soil, birds and animals. The Island itself he described as crescent shaped, fifty leagues in length by eight in width. Port la Joie, he wrote, was one of the most beautiful harbours the eye could behold. Three rivers flowed into it. Timber was abundant and of excellent quality. The streams inland were suitable for mills, which could be profitably employed cutting pine and oak for ship-building. Of harbours he speaks only of the northern. St. Peter's, named after the president of the company, he says, admits vessels of sixty tons safely. Savage Harbour was fitted for boats only. Tracadie was safe for vessels of one hundred tons. The next harbour to the west he called by its Indian name, "Quiquibougat." Professor Caven thought that Rustico Harbour was meant. It was suitable for boats. Then came Malpeque, into which vessels of two hundred tons could safely enter. The last was Cascumpec, six leagues farther west, safe for vessels of three hundred tons. In all these harbours fish abounded, and there was every facility for curing them. Many of the animals and birds mentioned by La Ronde have long since disappeared. There were stags in the woods, he wrote, but the Indians had destroyed the elk and moose. The country was infested with wolves. A skin of one of these was sent, in the ship that carried the despatch, as a present to the wife of the French admiral. Marten, otter, squirrels and foxes of various colours also abounded. He says there were no beaver, but to this statement Professor Caven and Sir Andrew McPhail take exception. Both point out that La Ronde was incorrect, as remains of old beaver dams are still to be found on some of the streams. Of birds he mentions geese, duck in many varieties, plover, partridge, turtle-doves and others.

Of the harbours mentioned by La Ronde, three, Franche Montagne (identified by Professor Caven with South Lake), St. Peter's and Tracadie were settled the first year. Of settlers twenty families, sixteen from France and four from Acadia, aggregating, probably, one hundred souls, were located at Port la Joie, while a couple of hundred more might be estimated as settled at the other three harbours.

Returning to the business of the expedition, he becomes optimistic, and estimates St. Pierre's annual net profits at one hundred thousand livres.

The company lost no time in getting to work. A ship of one hundred tons was built to carry codfish to Europe. Another of twenty-five tons was intended for the sea cow and seal fisheries. Still another of sixty-five tons was built for the West Indian trade. Sixteen families from France and four from Acadia had settled at Port la Joie. The remainder of the immigrants from France had settled at Three Rivers (now Georgetown), St. Peter's and Tracadie.

The expedition seemed to be an assured success. The prospects were of the brightest. The nucleii of several settlements had been formed. Shipping, quite sufficient for present needs, had been provided. The trouble arose over the fishing privileges, between St. Pierre, the people of Cape Breton and the merchants of St. Malo. An investigation having been held, it was reported that these exclusive privileges were contrary to good of trade and to public policy. The letters patent were cancelled, and the Island reverted to the Crown. The buildings of the company were occupied by the Government's servants and were utilized until 1749, when they were replaced by others built then. The colony was ruined, and, in the autumn of 1724, nearly all the inhabitants had left and the director had returned to France.

For several years after the cancellation of St. Pierre's letters patent and his return to France, little or nothing seems to have been done to promote settlement in the Island. The immigrants, whom St. Pierre had brought there, had largely gone from the Island, particularly from Port la Joie, and made their homes in Cape Breton. Some, doubtless, returned to France.

## DE ROMA.

In 1731 a new company was formed having its headquarters at Three Rivers. Its concession was issued on 17th July, 1731. It recites the royal approval of the scheme for a grant which Messrs. Claud Catterel, merchant at Rouen; Joseph du Boccage de Blansville, merchant at Havre; Joseph Phillip Narcis and John Peter Roma, merchants at Paris; had applied for. They had resolved to enter into a partnership in the Island of St. John situate in the Gulf and Stream of St. Lawrence, and His Majesty, being informed of their experience and ability to trade with the colonies, had favoured their request for a concession in that Island for the formation of establishments to carry on farming and fishing, that the King had given them the space of three thousand five hundred acres frontage by forty acres in depth, in the locality called the Three Rivers, situate near the East Point of the Island of St. John, on both sides of the rivers and in the parts formed by them, thence running towards the seashore and the north shore, to include three thousand five hundred acres frontage and forty acres in depth, and of which none of the land had been granted to settlers or cleared by them. They were to hold the said lands to them and their heirs forever as a freehold estate. They were not to have the right to administer justice, which His Majesty reserved to himself. They were empowered to grant leases of the said lands, but they would not, by reason of such grant, have to pay to His Majesty, or to his successors, any quit rent or fine, notwithstanding any increase in the rents. His Majesty was making them a gift, subject to fealty and homage to the palace at Louisbourg in Isle Royale, without rent. They were to conserve, and cause to be conserved by their tenants, oak timber useful in the construction of His Majesty's ships. They were also to notify His Majesty's commissioners of minerals, if any, found on the said lands, they being reserved to the Crown.

Should default be made in performing the conditions set out in the grant, which is to be recorded in the Superior Council at Louisbourg, the lands so granted should revert to His Majesty's domain. His Majesty desiring to deal generously (favourably) with Messrs. Catterel, du Boccage, Narcis and Roma, and to facilitate the erection of private establishments in the ports, harbours, roads or rivers of the Island of St. John, which their business might or could require, gave them permission to erect stages on the north shore, and shops in the said ports, harbours, roads or rivers as they may see fit. His Majesty also ordered that there be allotted to them lands in the same manner as to the other settlers in proportion to the number of boats employed by them.

It will be observed that the privileges granted in this concession were much more limited than those formerly conferred upon St. Pierre, and they covered a comparatively small territory. Of this new company it is evident that De Roma was the leading spirit. He seems to have been the managing director of the company's affairs in the Island of St. John.

The company received grants of land for agricultural purposes and for sites of buildings to be erected to carry on fishing operations along the eastern shores of the Island. Three ships bearing liberal supplies, and having on board skilled artizans and Breton fishermen to inaugurate the colony, had arrived from France, and were lying in the splendid harbour of Three Rivers. The company's shareholders hailed from Bordeaux and St. Malo.

At Brudenell Point, in what is now Georgetown Harbour, de Roma established his company's headquarters. By the late autumn a considerable tract of land had been cleared. Nine solidly constructed log buildings were erected, two being each eighty feet in length. One of these was for the residence of de Roma and the other for the fishermen. Of the other seven, three were for the labourers, ships' crews and for overseers and tradesmen. Another was for stores and a bakehouse. There were, also, a forge and a stable. Each house had its own garden. A stone jetty suitable for small vessels was built at Brudenell Point. The site of what is now Georgetown furnished the heavy timber. The brick required was made on the ground from clay found nearby. A road was cut through the woods to Sturgeon Bay, to get grass for the live stock. Roads were also constructed to connect with

Cardigan, St. Pierre and Port la Joie. There were five sea-going craft capable of long voyages. Yearly two voyages were made to Quebec and two to the West Indies, while smaller craft were employed to bring in the fish from the different stations. Forty acres of woodland were cleared, the stumps removed and the surface levelled for the growth of grain and vegetables, of which splendid crops were raised. Truly elaborate preparations were made for the launching and prosecution of the enterprise. Were they too elaborate?

Surely an undertaking so well started and established must succeed. Prospects could not be brighter or more promising. De Roma was charged by his shareholders with extravagance and divers offences. Certainly the initial preparations and settlement were on a very elaborate if not extravagant scale, but he continued to carry on and to manage the company's affairs in the Island of St. John. Finally, a few days before the first capture of Louisbourg by the British in 1745, a hostile warship, one of a small squadron of New England origin, appeared in the harbour, plundered and utterly destroyed the whole settlement. They looted the place, carried off what, to them, seemed of most value, and burned with the buildings what they could not carry away. The destruction was complete. When the fires died down, nothing but the blackened sites remained to show where a promising establishment had been. De Roma, his family and servants, escaped into the woods, and made their way to St. Pierre, thence to Quebec. From Quebec they went to the West Indies and eventually returned to France. Thus ended in disaster and ruin an enterprise which had promised so well. Three Rivers as a settlement had ceased to exist.

De Roma had been one of the principal personages of the Island of St. John. He was a man of ability but Utopian in his disposition and caustic in his manner, which rendered it difficult to get on with him. After the destruction of his properties, and some time spent in Quebec, he went to the Antilles to seek fortune there, but ever with the hope of returning. From Martinique, where he was in March, 1750, he wrote the Minister of Marine propounding a scheme for colonizing the Island of St. John, the success of which, according to his view, would make an Eldorado of the Island. Abbe Casgrain refers to him at some length in "Une seconde Acadie."

Some days before the first siege and capture of Louisbourg by Pepperell in 1745, he had detached a body of four hundred men to take possession of the establishments of Isle Royale and the Island of St. John. They were ordered to destroy everything and remove the inhabitants. The first landing made in the Island was at Three Rivers. The story of this devastation is very fully told by the French Commissary General Prevost in a despatch to the Minister of Marine in November, 1752, in which he proposed sending some settlers to the abandoned establishment. It is quoted at length by M. Casgrain. He says that the English entered the harbour on 20th June, 1745, when a privateer landed some men on the point where de Roma's buildings were situated. De Roma, his son, daughter, two domestics and three servant men, had scarcely time to gain and hide themselves in the woods. De Roma, he says, suffered by this the loss of a large wooden house divided into four parts, besides warehouses and other buildings. He goes on to give in detail a large list of the live stock, wheat and other grains destroyed.

The site, he adds, which de Roma occupied is unquestionably beautiful, having a delightful outlook on a very fine harbour. The land seems good and well adapted for all sorts of crops. It would be a mistake if settlers were not placed there. They would find farming facilities at once, because of clearings made either by the company or by de Roma.

After the privateer had made a wilderness of the Port of Three Rivers, the expedition continued its cruise and made a descent on Port la Joie. There remained there, after the recall of the garrison to Isle Royale, only fifteen soldiers and a sergeant under the orders of an ensign of infantry, M. Duport Duvivier, probably the son of a commander of that name, noted in connection with the siege of Port Royal. That similar ravages were committed here as at Three Rivers seems to be indicated by the engineer Franquet, who says that "before the last war, all the part cleared (to the left of the entry of Port la Joie) was under cultivation, but today,— it is not cultivated."

A party of the British advancing incautiously into the interior of the country was ambushed by a band of Indians supported by Duvivier's little force and by a good number of the settlers, who killed or made prisoners of twenty-eight men. The remainder turned back in haste and made the best of their way towards the river. Duvivier pursued the fugitives with his soldiers and some settlers, attacked them on a vessel where several had taken refuge, and took possession of it after having killed or wounded one man.

Some weeks later, having spent all his ammunition, Duvivier embarked with his little garrison for Quebec. There he presented to the Governor a petition from the inhabitants of the Island in which they made known their evil plight. Shut off from all help they had been obliged to send a deputation to the British authorities at Louisbourg, offering their submission, conditionally on their not being disturbed on their lands. At the close of the year 1745 they had not yet received a reply, but they had not again been subjected to attack. The garrison of Louisbourg was in a feeble condition. The weather, which had been very fine during the siege, had later changed to storms and torrential rains. The troops were badly housed in the half-demolished buildings of the town. They had suffered much and a contagious disease had broken out among the soldiers, of whom nearly one thousand had been buried in the cemetery of Rochfort before the end of the following winter. Such, doubtless, was the cause of the immunity from attack which the Island of St. John enjoyed during this period.

In the spring of 1746 a flotilla of seven sail was prepared at Quebec, intended to carry to Bay Verte an expeditionary force of seven hundred Canadian officers and men under command of M. de Ramezay. It sailed on 5th June and reached Gaspe on the 16th without incident other than a heavy squall which surprised it below Mont Lewis. Here important news was received. Two frigates, L'Auron and Le Castor, commanded by Captains duVignan and de Saillies were arrived at Chebuctou. On the other hand a launch from the Island of St. John brought word of the presence at Port la Joie of two English men-of-war of forty guns each, which threatened to close the entrance of Bay Verte.

MM. de Saint Ours and de Montesson, with a party of two hundred Micmacs, set out in boats on 21st July, 1746, from Bay Verte for Port la Joie on a scouting expedition. They learned that there had been there not more than two English vessels, one a frigate of twenty-four guns, engaged in taking in provisions. Their crews were not suspicious of attack and often went ashore.

De Montesson was ordered to set out immediately with a detachment of Canadians and Micmacs to attack them. He fell unexpectedly upon the English spread out along the bank, and killed, wounded or captured forty of them and put the others to flight. A few escaped by swimming, but most of them were taken prisoners, and sent afterwards to Quebec. A schooner taking in freight at some distance up the river might have been captured had the Indians acted upon the orders of the commander, but they had killed a quantity of oxen and other cattle kept on shore by the British, for provisions, which they were looting, and were beyond his control. This enabled the few English, who escaped, to rejoin their vessels.

Among the prisoners were found two hostages belonging to the Island. It will be remembered that the French inhabitants, when the English captured Port la Joie, were unable to make a resistance and had sent a deputation to the British, who had agreed not to disturb the islanders, who on their part agreed to give six hostages and supply the English with provisions.

In this attack on the English the settlers took no part. It seems clear from this and from the presence of the two hostages that the offer of submission must have been accepted after the close of 1745 and before Montesson's attack.

Under the terms of the submission of the settlers after the British invasion of Port la Joie, that they should observe neutrality and supply provisions, their condition was apparently pretty much on a par with that of the Acadians on the peninsula. They lived in this way until the Treaty of Aix-La-Chapelle when Cape Breton and the Island of St. John were restored to France.

It is impossible to arrive at any reliable estimate of the losses occasioned to the inhabitants by the Anglo-American descent and occupation. The repulse sustained by the invading force on their first descent on Port la Joie seems to have checked their depredations, which were limited to the razing of de Roma's establishment at Three Rivers and to some destruction wrought at Port la Joie. At the outbreak of the war the Island contained a population of seven to eight hundred souls whose lands, increasing in value every year, yielded bountiful harvests and supported a large number of cattle.

# HISTORY OF PRINCE EDWARD ISLAND.

The war, which continued for four years, kept the inhabitants in a constant state of alarm, but it was far from being as destructive as they had feared.

The twenty years which preceded this war may almost be regarded as the golden age of the colony. It had not known the hardships which are the usual accompaniment of new settlements in regions where the colonist must attack the forest, cut it down and clear the land before he can crop it.

It covered the time when the company of Count St. Pierre were disbursing great sums in the creation of factories and fishing establishments. Energy, trade, industry, were the rule there, creating a general well-being among all classes. Composed, as we have seen, of Acadian farmers, fishermen and labourers from France, their habits were frugal and their manners simple. Such enjoyments or amusements as they desired, they found by their firesides or among their neighbours.

## ISLAND'S IMPORTANCE RECOGNIZED.

From the coming of St. Pierre, the importance of the Island of St. John rapidly increased. Its owners, the French, at length recognized the great advantages its possession offered them, and, though late in doing so, now began to make the most of these advantages.

The British, in Nova Scotia, were not slow to grasp the significance of this new departure on the part of their opponents. They saw the effect this settlement would have upon the trend of affairs and upon the business interests of the province of Nova Scotia. This is evidenced by an undated despatch of about this time, to Mr. Popple, secretary to the Board of Trade in London, in which Governor Phillips, the writer, complains that "There is continual intercourse between Minas, Chignecto and the Island of St. John, the traffic of those parts is wholly turned that way, the inhabitants go and come daily, and all this is not in my power to prevent, with the garrison at the distance of thirty leagues."

Evidently the aspect of affairs grew rapidly more alarming, and the government of Nova Scotia became more anxious. On 27th September, 1720, the Governor-in-Council memorialized His Majesty, the King, urging the strengthening of Chignecto, because "it requires the more to have a considerable strength in regard that the trade is clandestinely carried to Cape Breton, by means of the trafitt (portage) from the Bay of Fundy into the Gulf of St. Lawrence, and that the French have sent, this summer, four ships, two of which, we hear, are actually arrived at the Island of St. John, not above six leagues distant from Chignecto, where they intend to have a considerable fort and settlement and by means of it will be able to command the trade, as well as the French inhabitants in these parts."

That the Island of St. John was a cause of much anxiety to the Government of the British Province, and that it was looked upon by the French authorities in Cape Breton as of much importance, is shown by the despatches of Governor Armstrong, who, writing on 27th July, 1726, from Canso to the Secretary of State, says: "I understand that Governor St. Ovide, with some troops and his Council, are gone to the Island of St. John, in the Bay of Verte, in order to mark out the lands of that Island for such people and inhabitants as will quit the province and retire under the Government of France; this has been managed under the missionary priests among the Indians and French inhabitants in the province."

Again, writing on 9th July, 1728, to the Duke of Newcastle, with regard to the refusal of the French on the mainland to take the oath of allegiance, he informs his Grace, that "they want neither invitations nor promises from the Islands of Cape Breton and St. John for that purpose." The purpose was to quit their plantations and improvements in Nova Scotia and to make new settlements in the territories belonging to France.

In 1728, the population had increased, new settlers had been coming in from France, while the local policy of inducing residents of Nova Scotia to join their compatriots in the Island of St. John had borne fruit. Seven considerable settlements had been formed, namely, Port la Joie, situate between Rocky Point and the West River and the south shore, where strong evidence of their settlement is still to be seen; St. Peter's, considered then and till the close of the French regime, the commercial capital; Savage Harbour; East Point; Tracadie; Malpeque and East River.

About Port la Joie there were now scattered the log houses of one hundred and fifteen settlers. Guarding the settlement was a breastwork, overlooking the harbour, mounting eight cannon, and usually manned by thirty to fifty men from the Louisbourg forces. Government buildings consisted of a dwelling and offices for the commandant, quarters for the soldiers and junior officers, a bakehouse, a forge, and three storehouses. These were the buildings erected by St. Pierre's company and were now falling into decay. De Pensons, writing to the Minister in 1728, says it would be impossible to live there longer unless new buildings were constructed. Those left by St. Pierre were so rotten as to be unsafe to live in. No new buildings, however, were erected and none were constructed until 1749, twenty years later. Port la Joie was the settlement, or the centre of the settlements, which appealed to those who wished to go in for agriculture and to found homes for themselves on the fertile soil. The woods there and up the rivers had been largely cleared away and rich grain fields were now showing in the openings where the forest had been. Fishermen did not settle there. It was a community of farmers and soldiers. The log houses of the farmers, built by themselves, were sufficiently roomy and were solid and comfortable. The crops were abundant, giving a rich return to the farmer for his labour. Eye witnesses declared they equaled any in France or in other parts of Europe. In 1730, the crop of grain at Port la Joie and its neighbourhood, according to the Government's reports, amounted to two thousand bushels. This was ample for all their needs. It consisted of wheat, barley, oats, peas, and rye. The settlers were principally Acadians with a few emigrants from France. These had chosen to leave their homes in Acadia, after it passed under British rule, and to live under their country's flag in the Island of St. John, which was still French, rather than to own allegiance to their former foes and continue in their old homes. It was the same spirit that, in later years, sent the United Empire Loyalists, in thousands, from the United States to settle in Canada rather than live with people who had severed their allegiance to their mother land. The Acadians were well adapted for pioneer settlement in the forest. They could turn their hands to almost everything. They not only cleared the land and raised the crops. They also manufactured the clothes they wore, putting the wool through all the stages of manufacture from the sheep's back to their own. They sheared the sheep, they spun the fleece, they wove, shaped and sewed it into the garments they wore. They grew flax, which they manufactured in their homes into coarse linen for domestic purposes. They also raised their own tobacco. When they made their little clearings, the fertility of the soil was such that merely scratching the ground, planting and sowing the seed, produced fine crops of potatoes, barley, wheat, Indian corn and all kinds of garden vegetables.

Among the settlers at Port la Joie lived Rene Rassicot, who, with his family of ten children, came from Normandy in 1724. Some of his family seem to have moved to the north shore, perhaps attracted by the fisheries there. There they gave the family name to Rustico. An anonymous writer in the Prince Edward Island Magazine, vol. V., p. 369, treating of the settlement of Rustico, says, as already stated, that "The name of the district is derived from a Frenchman named Racicat. He came from Port la Joie and settled at the head of the creek where Stevenson's mill now stands."

Communication with the various settlements was mainly kept up by water or over the ice. From Port la Joie there were the three rivers over which the settlers, in the summer, travelled by boat or canoe and on the ice in winter. A short portage at the head of the East River enabled them to reach the north side of the Island and to communicate with the settlements along that shore.

In 1728, the inhabitants of Savage Harbour, according to a census (the first) taken about that year, numbered fifty-eight, all farmers. They included individuals from Acadia, from Canada, from Normandy, from Bayonne and St. Malo. A Canadian came in 1725, all the others settled here in 1728. From the first this settlement grew and prospered. Visitors spoke with admiring surprise of the excellence of the crops. The people were well off in flocks and herds. They had erected both saw and grist mills. The census of 1752 showed the farms to be well stocked and the harvest abundant. It was a farming community.

A road started from or near French Fort on the East River and ran in a straight line to the southern waters of Tracadie Harbour, thence to Savage Harbour and St. Peters'. A flourishing settlement had been formed at Tracadie. There were few settlers on the Harbour in 1728. Four Acadian families, twenty souls in all, were the first to arrive. The country hereabouts, however, gradually grew in population and in time became well settled.

HISTORY OF PRINCE EDWARD ISLAND.                    41

At South Lake, which Professor Caven identified as the Franche Montagne of the French, three French fishermen settled, one (Matthew Turin) in 1719, the other two in 1720. They were among the earliest settlers on the Island of St. John. In 1728, only eight years after their arrival, they each owned three shallops. Turin had in his employ seven men and two hired servants. One of the others employed four sailors and one servant. The several families, together, numbered twenty souls. They caught and cured thirteen hundred quintals of codfish.

Malpeque was the principal Indian village. Three Acadian farmers, with their families, seventeen in all, settled there in 1728 and were the first white settlers. This was the beginning of settlement in Malpeque.

Considering that the settlements were, as already indicated, formed so systematically in so many differing localities and lying, as the Island of St. John did, so close to the British possessions on the main land, it is not surprising that the authorities there should regard it with suspicion and alarm. The Indian inhabitants are said to have been a warlike race, although we of the present time long found it difficult to imagine anything of the kind. The splendid response of the descendants of these Indians to the call for men in the Great War, however, has most effectually demonstrated that the red blood of their forefathers still coursed through their veins and that the warlike spirit of their race was not dead; it merely slumbered.

The French inhabitants themselves were a hardy people, inured to privation. They had suffered much, both real and fancied wrongs, and both the Indians and they were largely under the influence of unscrupulous leaders, of whom Le Loutre was, perhaps, the most notorious, as well as the most to be feared. For years, this man kept the colonies, both French and British, in a ferment. Possessing great influence over the Indians and the French inhabitants, he was a veritable thorn in the side of the Governor of Nova Scotia. The English authorities were kept in a continual state of alarm and unrest and the Island of St. John was a centre from which danger was always to be apprehended. Writing from Chebucto to the Duke of Bedford, on 11th September, 1749, Governor Cornwallis says: "I have intelligence from all parts of the province and from Cape Breton, that the Indians of

Acadia and St. John's Island, headed by Loutre, design to molest us this winter. The French do everything in their power to excite them to it. The settlers don't seem at all alarmed. All precautions that can be thought of are taken for their security."

Writing from Halifax to the Lords of Trade and Plantations, on the 17th October of the same year, Cornwallis returns to the subject as follows: "I acquainted you in my last, I was apprehensive that the Indians called 'Micmacks,' in this peninsula, encouraged and set on by the French, would give us trouble, as all my accounts from Cape Breton denoted it, and more, that they would attack the settlement. These Micmacks include the Cape Sable, St. John's Island, Cape Breton and all inhabiting the peninsula. La Loutre, a priest sent out from France as a missionary to the Micmacks, is with them, as good-for-nothing a scoundrel as ever lived."

"The St. John's Indians I made peace with, and am glad to find by your Lordship's letter of the 1st August, it is agreeable to your way of thinking, their making submission to the King before I would treat with them. . . . I intend, if possible, to keep up a good correspondence with the St. John's Indians, a warlike people, though treaties with Indians are nothing. Nothing but force will prevail."

Even as late as 1756, only two years before the fall of Louisbourg and the British occupation of St. John's Island, it was a subject of anxious thought, not only by the Government of Nova Scotia, but also by the New England Colonies, who recognized the importance to themselves of British rule being maintained in what are now the Maritime Provinces of Canada. Being much better informed as to existing conditions, they were much more alive to the danger than were the Lords of Trade in London. Writing to Governor Lawrence on 13th March of that year, Shirley, the famous governor of Massachusetts, urged the fortifying of the neck of land between the Bay of Fundy and Bay Verte to secure the province (of Nova Scotia) against sudden attacks of the French from Quebec, . . . "not to mention St. John's Island which is so very near a neighbour to the Peninsula, and from whence danger may arise to it, when the Island shall be settled by the French."

It would likewise prevent the French from making any considerable settlements upon St. John's Island, from whence further

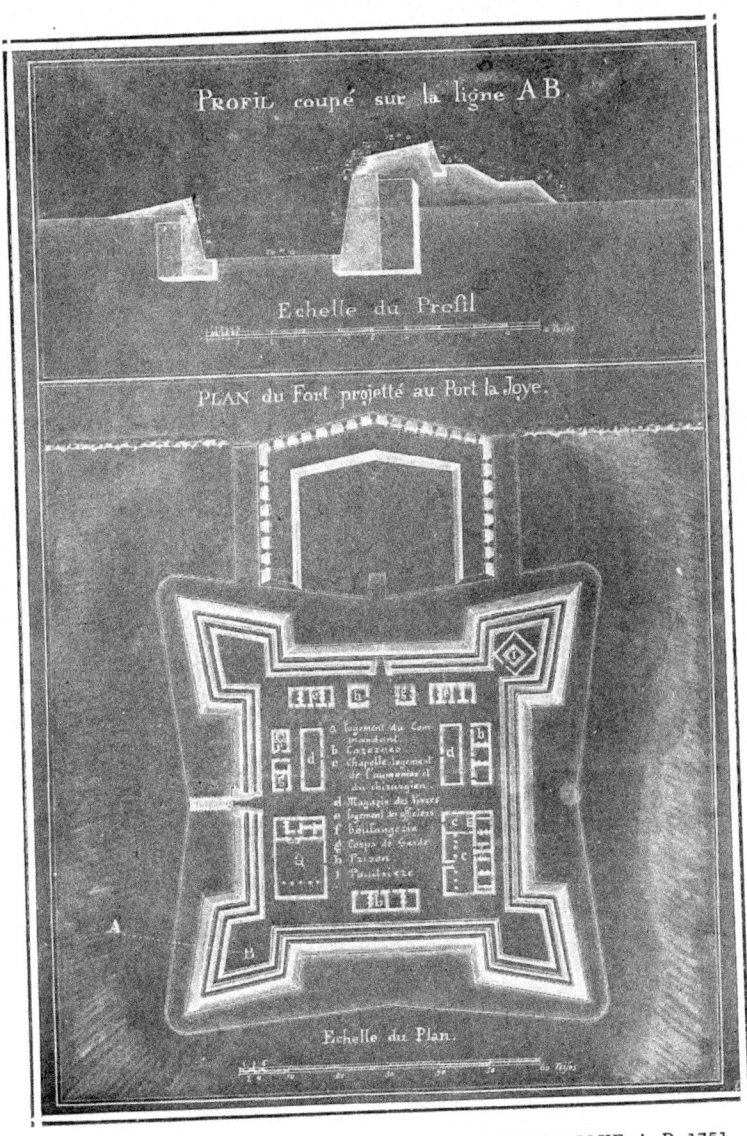

FRANQUET'S PLAN FOR A FORT TO DEFEND PORT LA JOYE, A. D. 1751

danger might arise, in time, to the Peninsula, and from carrying on any fishery there.

## TREATY OF AIX-LA-CHAPELLE.

After the first capture of Louisbourg in 1745 by the New Englanders, it was restored to the French by the Treaty of Aix-la-Chapelle in 1749. Soon after M. de Bonaventure, with one hundred men, sailed for the Island of St. John. The old buildings were in ruins, the fields were becoming a wilderness again. A few of St. Pierre's settlers were still there. They and the newcomers had to be provided for. This de Bonaventure did. The buildings were to be used as temporary shelters. Later Colonel Franquet prepared plans for fortifications, but they never materialized.

## FRANQUET'S VISIT.

In 1751, Colonel Franquet visited St. John's Island for military purposes, and while there made an extensive tour of the settled parts of the Island. The following year Pichon spent part of the summer there and also travelled over the country. Each of these men left a lengthy report of his visit, which is of interest.

Colonel Franquet was an officer of Engineers, sent out by the French Government to superintend the new fortifications of Louisbourg. He was also to work out a system of defence for the French possessions in the Gulf of St. Lawrence. In the performance of his duties he visited the Island of St. John in the summer of 1751. He prepared and submitted to his Government a report with plans of the military works necessary for the defence of the French colonies. He prepared plans, along modern lines, of fortifications to be erected at Port la Joie. They were to be built for a garrison of four hundred men, with stores for two years. The bastions, of which there were to be four, and the curtains were to be of solid brick and stone. To further protect the harbour, a redoubt for a permanent garrison was to be erected on the east side of the entrance to the harbour, while a station at the western side was to be strengthened. But like the "best formed schemes of mice and men," neither fort nor redoubt ever got beyond the plans. Outside his military duties, Franquet carefully noted and reported on the appearance of the country, its products and capabilities, the condition of the settlers and their prospects.

On 3rd August, 1751, Franquet entered the harbour of Port la Joie and anchored off what is now called Warren Farm. He was delighted with the magnificent natural harbour with its three wide rivers emptying into it.

On 9th August he set out to visit St. Peter's and other settlements on the north side. To do so he took a barge with six rowers up the East River. Settlers were already establishing themselves along both sides of the river. The crops, seen from the stream, were flourishing in the new soil. Opposite what is now Scotchfort, the tide falling, he landed and was welcomed at the home of an Acadian, the Sieur Gauthier. He and another Acadian, the Sieur Bugeau, each occupied a farm of one hundred and sixty acres. They had been settled there for eighteen months. Franquet walked around Gauthier's cleared lands and new fields bearing wheat, peas, oats and many kinds of vegetables, such as he had not seen surpassed in the most fertile parts of France.

The following morning, a number of settlers from both sides of the river waited on him to consult as to the site for a church, the question being as to which side of the river it should be built on. Franquet agreed to act as umpire, but asked all interested to meet him at Gauthier's on his return journey when he would hear the different views and decide. He then embarked and, ascending the stream, saw a brook on which one of the pioneers had erected a saw-mill. Further on he came to the Pisquid River with settlers on either bank. The settlement, he was informed, was an old one. Every farmer had ample livestock and they raised all that their needs required. Admiringly Franquet says that "life in such a spot could not be otherwise than agreeable."

About a league above what is now Mount Stewart, he put up at an inn kept by a widow named Gentil, where he admired the fine fields of grain about her residence. From there a road six or seven feet wide had been cut through the woods to St. Peter's. It was without bridges, though it crossed swamps and streams. The construction of the road merely meant cutting down the trees and removing the stumps. A species of cart, drawn by oxen, was the only vehicle that could be put through it.

The journey to Three Rivers was more easily made than that to St. Peter's. Franquet was impressed by the splendid harbour and by its great potential importance as a seaport. He viewed it

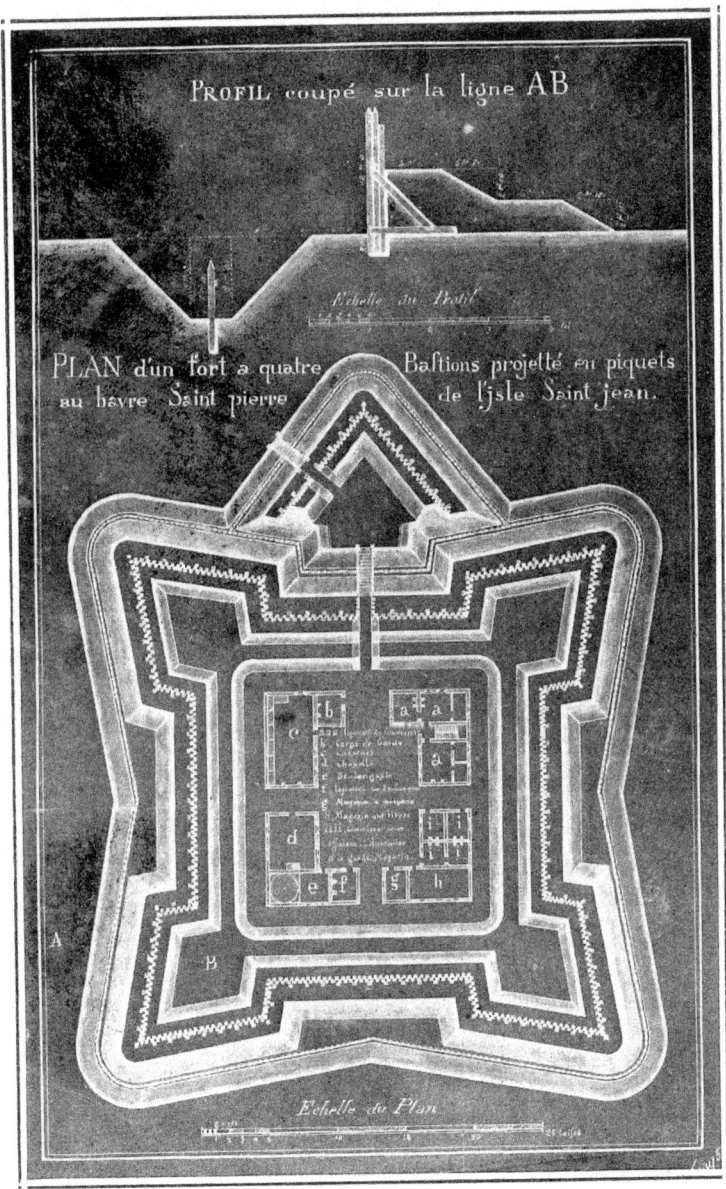

FRANQUET'S PLAN OF A FORT FOR THE DEFENCE
OF ST. PETERS

with a soldier's eye. A fleet, with headquarters here, could guard the Strait of Canso, the Gulf, the communication with Canada and with Cape Breton. Nature had done her utmost, but there was no sign of population. The land was a wilderness. Brudenell Point itself, from which the woods had been cleared, had not a building standing. The New England cruiser had destroyed everything, only the lands were left, and they were unoccupied. The reason for there being no settlers at Three Rivers was that the rights conferred by its charter on de Roma's company were still in force. Three thousand five hundred acres of water front, besides areas inland, had been granted to it by the Crown, and its charter was still outstanding, hence the immigrant avoided Three Rivers, preferring the Crown lands where their titles would be good. Franquet urged upon the Government to remedy this and open up to settlement the magnificent harbour with its surrounding fertile lands. To protect it he planned a redoubt of stone and brick to be erected on Brudenell Point. He eulogized the fertile soil, the rich pastures, the natural harbours and the navigable character of the rivers, really arms of the sea, but to no effect.

Communication between the settlements was chiefly by canoe, a slow, laborious and time-killing means, but, practically, it was the only means, as there were no roads. Count de Raymond ordered a road five feet wide to be opened between St. Marguerit's and Three Rivers. It was intended to build another from Three Rivers to St. Peter's. Franquet advised a change and that a road be carried as straight as possible between Brudenell Point and the Northeast River opposite the Grand Source, and a third to St. Peter's Harbour. They seem to have been partly made. The settlers of the Island of St. John did not excel as road-builders.

The road to St. Peter's lead through from Brudenell Point to Savage Harbour and round the coast to the homes of the settlers and thence to the entrance of St. Peter's Harbour. The settlement was entirely composed of old settlers. The Acadian immigration had not reached it. The farms were large and bore crops that Franquet had never seen surpassed. Fishermen's houses were scattered along the sloping lands, where also were stores and warehouses. On the higher ground was a large church dedicated to St. Peter. A grist mill was badly needed and Franquet strongly urged the Government to build one. For defence Franquet designed a fort of four bastions to be built on the high ground close to the church. St. Peter's was looked upon as the commercial capital of the island. It was really of more importance than Port la Joie, the political or civil capital.

Having finished what he had to do at St. Peter's, Franquet set out on his return journey, and arrived at Madame Gentil's house. The road was even worse than when he had travelled it on his outward journey. He decided to plan a better route. Tracing a stream near Madame Gentil's abode he found, in less than a mile, a spring with a great volume of clear water forming a brook which ran to the river. The French called it "La Grande Source." He decided that, with little labour, a good road could be made on almost a straight line from "La Grande Source" to the church at St. Peter's. He made plans of it, which he sent to the Government and strongly urged its construction.

Continuing his journey down stream, he reached Sieur Gauthier's house and spent the night there. In the morning the people gathered to get his decision as to the site of the proposed church. He decided in favour of the north side of the river, as people from Tracadie, two leagues distant, could come there rather than to St. Peter's. Moreover, Sieur Bugeau had made a free gift of land for a site, his orchard for a priest's residence, and his garden for a cemetery. This decision was accepted without demur and the people agreed to build the church on the northern site. It was also agreed that a ferry should be kept up at the expense of both sides. Franquet promised to ask the Government to give a bell for the church. Eight months after Franquet's visit, Gauthier died and was probably the first to be buried in the new cemetery. He was no common man. He came from Rochelle to Port Royal when a young man, twenty-three years of age. He resided there forty years. In Cornwallis' time he left Port Royal for the Island of St. John to be under the French flag. It is said that he left seventy thousand livres worth of property behind him at Port Royal. Through his influence some two hundred or three hundred families came to the Island and settled there.

## GAUTHIER.

Nicholas Gauthier was an outstanding figure in Acadia. Besides large business transactions carried on by him and his family, they played a prominent part, on the French side, in the

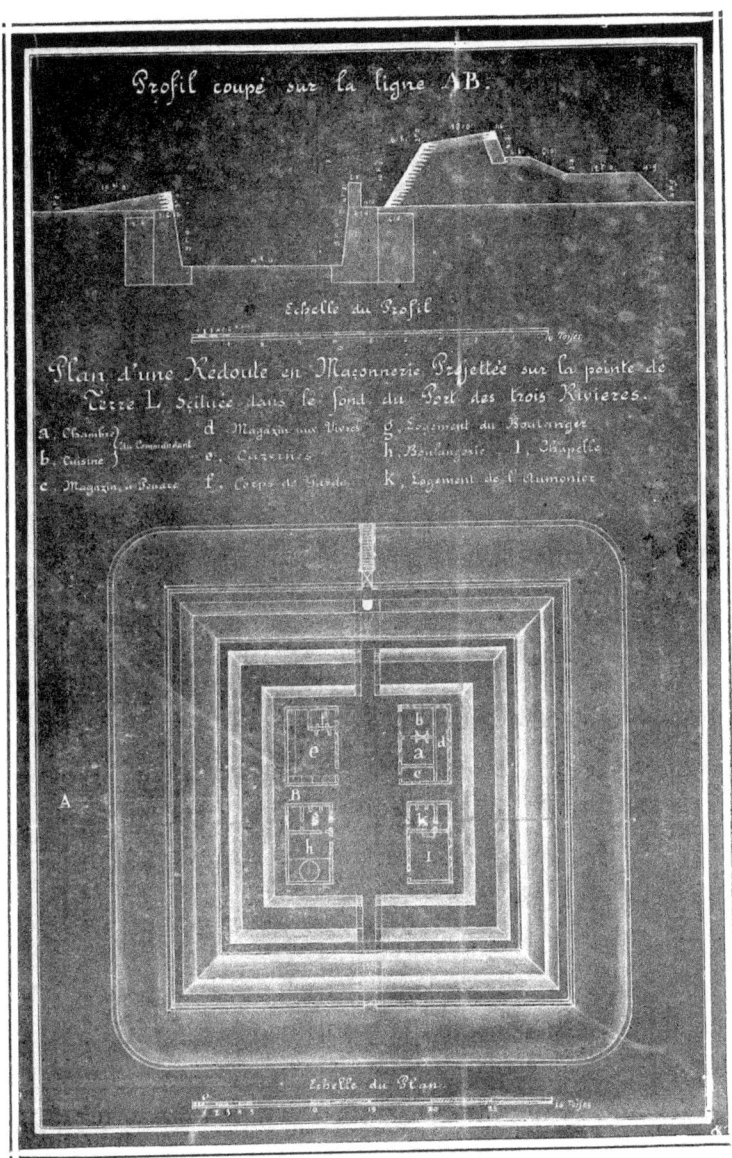

FRANQUET'S PLAN FOR A REDOUBT TO DEFEND
THREE RIVERS (Georgtown)

years from 1744 to 1749. On the return of peace he became one of the leading personages of the Island of St. John. He was animated by a spirit of patriotism akin to that which, at a later period, actuated the United Empire Loyalists when, abandoning comfort and wealth, they sought new homes in the Canadian wilds, rather than own allegiance to any flag but their own. One cannot but admire this man.

His business headquarters were situated a short distance from Port Royal on the Dauphin River. It was well chosen, picturesque and beautiful, if it be judged by the name he gave it, of Bel Air or Belair. Besides a good residence and immense outbuildings he owned two flour mills and one saw-mill. He employed two vessels of his own in his trading ventures.

Business did not prevent him from successfully managing a large farm, part of Belair, as well as a property situate at Pree-Ronde in the upper part of the river, on which he had erected a house valued at ten thousand francs. His father, a native of Aix-in-Province, had been a captain in the forces at Port Royal. He was now long dead.

It is likely that he had been engaged in two sieges of Port Royal, or had formed part of the privateers' crews which assisted in its defence. There is nothing definite known. He had married, in 1715, Marie Alain, daughter of Louis Alain, who had been concerned with numerous maritime and colonial enterprises. He was associated with a man named Naquin, who resided at Belair. It was from him that the Alain's held this property, and Nicholas Gauthier derived it from his father-in-law. When he assumed control he extended his business activities. He had a capital of twenty to thirty thousand francs (from $5,000.00 to $6,000.00) which he had so skillfully managed, that in 1744 he had become one of the richest inhabitants of Acadia. His fortune amounted to at least one hundred thousand francs (about $20,000.00) a large sum for the time and for the place. Belair, with its outbuildings, its warehouses, its mills, was valued at forty-one thousand francs, without mentioning his residence of the Pree-Ronde, reckoned at ten thousand francs.

His dealings in the products of the soil and sea necessitated large premises. His vessels carried flour, lumber, cattle, fish and other articles to Boston, Louisbourg and even to the Antilles. He brought back such merchandise as his people needed, sugar, molasses, etc., which he warehoused, not at Port Royal, but at his own properties, whence it was distributed throughout the neighbouring settlements and at Mines, where his vessels could enter directly, and on the east side as far as Beaubassin. The detailed story of his life and doings is set out at great length in a petition forwarded by him to M. de Maurepas, Minister of Marine, praying to be indemnified for his losses during the war of 1744-1749.

He was worthily supported in his affairs by his wife, a strong and courageous Acadian woman, and by his large family. In 1744, his two eldest sons, Joseph and Pierre, were over twenty-five years of age. They were brave, sprightly fellows, who sailed in their father's vessels, transporting their merchandise, and already able to take his place, if need be, at home or at sea.

The Gauthiers lived quietly at Belair from 1715 to 1744, engaged in their varied occupations. In 1730 they had reached the height of their fortune. The father was chosen by the Acadians of the Port Royal district, deputy to the Council of Annapolis; but it is probable that his zeal for the French cause was already noted, as his nomination was not assented to by Governor Armstrong of Nova Scotia.

In 1735 he visited Duvivier at Louisbourg. It had become known to him, that one of his wife's relatives had died leaving property, and that the Governor had seized the heritage for the Crown. This visit and the relations which resulted with Duvivier, were possibly among the main reasons for the activity displayed by Gauthier in the events of 1744. When Duvivier entered Acadia and came to besiege Port Royal, it was at Belair he established his headquarters. The owner of Belair became the principal purveyor for the little French army.

It is not known what were the immediate consequences to himself of the position thus taken by Gauthier. It seems, however, that he was not, at once, disturbed. It may be that Mascerine, a brave and tactful man, hoped that Gauthier would remain where his home was, and where his wealth had accumulated, or that he feared to irritate the Acadians, among whom Gauthier reckoned many relatives and friends. However that may be, Gauthier and his sons, during the following campaigns, more than ever threw their lot in with the French.

When Franquet visited Gauthier and Bugeau in their new homes at the Northeast River in the Island of St. John, they had been there long enough to have become settled in their new surroundings. They might be described as proscribed Acadians who had been in Nova Scotia, on the side of France, in the late war. They were still in comfortable circumstances, but Gauthier no longer possessed the wealth that had been his in Acadia, the remembrance of which he fondly sought to perpetuate by giving the name of his old home, Belair, to a clear and fresh spring of crystal water, which gushed out over his new lands. The chief support of his advancing years was still his eldest son, that Pierre Gauthier, who served as pilot to M. de la Jonquierre, when that commander sailed, from Chebuctou Harbour, with the remains of the Duke d'Anvilles fleet, to lay seige to Port Royal. On the return of peace, when Shirley, Governor of Massachusetts, offered a general amnesty to the Acadians, he refused, it is said, to include in it Nicholas Gauthier and his two sons, Pierre and Joseph, or Amand Bugeau who, like them, had warmly supported the cause of France. Their names figured at the head of the list of the proscribed. All their property, that they were unable to remove, was confiscated, their dwellings razed, and themselves condemned to prison. They found safety in flight.

In Canada they found friends among those in authority, who knew their devotion to the Court of Versailles, and who procured for them, in part reparation for their losses, a money gratuity and grants of land in the Island of St. John.

In 1750, they, with their vessel, were engaged in transporting Acadians, who were fleeing from the English, from Tatamagouche and from Bay Verte to the Island. It will be seen from this that the Gauthier family were resuming in the Island, though in a small way, the kind of life they had led at Port Royal, creating means of subsistence from the land and from the sea.

Nicholas Gauthier and Amand Bugeau, united by common misfortunes, were neighbours settled near to each other, and, as could be readily seen, were at the head of a group of colonists, mostly newcomers like themselves, numerous enough and sufficiently supplied with means to provide a church for themselves. Prompted by good dispositions, they set an example of generosity.

Nicholas Gauthier, writing to the Minister shortly after Franquet's departure, says: "I take the liberty of representing to you the situation of the Island of St. John, where I am actually settled with all my family, and where a great number of the Acadians, upon my example and urging, are settled on this Island to the number of two hundred or three hundred families, with their live stock. This is what makes the place today appear so different from what it was before, owing to the work done by all the inhabitants, which they are every day doing, clearing the lands with which they are well satisfied."

The day when Amand Bugeau had made a gift of a site for the church and parish house, Gauthier supplied a great part of what was required for the buildings. Thanks to these two men, harmony reigned among the settlers, and together they assembled the materials necessary for the construction.

Shortly after Franquet's visit, Gauthier went to Louisbourg. The career of the brave old Acadian was nearing its close. The strenuous life he had led, the loss of his wealth, continual fatigues had sapped his powers. He died at Louisbourg in April, 1752, happy to have escaped misfortunes even greater than those which he had seen and which were to mark the coming years,— proscription of all his compatriots, the second capture and destruction of Louisbourg, followed by that of his last establishment, finally the occupation of Canada by the people whose uncompromising foe he was.*

The restoration, under the provisions of the Treaty of Aix-la-Chapelle, in 1749, of Louisbourg to France, more than ever drew the attention of the French Court to the Island of St. John, because it was hoped that from that Island, before many years, might be drawn the supplies necessary for the great Cape Breton fortress.

An officer of distinction, who had figured at the siege of Louisbourg, M. Denis de Bonaventure, was appointed Governor of the Island. He had under his orders at Port la Joie a garrison of one hundred men (A. D. 1749). He constructed, on the old sites, the principal buildings necessary for a small garrison — a barrack, quarters for the commandant, the officers, the surgeon,

---
*Of Bugeau, Provost,— on 28th November, 1751,— writing to the Minister says, that the Sieur Amand Bugeau, Acadian settler and navigator, who erected a permanent establishment on the North East River (The Hillsborough), is a very honest hard-working man, and has rendered services to the King in Acadia.

the chaplain, as well as large depots for provisions and merchandise. With the exception of the powder magazine, which was built of stone and was the only one of the old buildings still standing from the last war, all these structures were of wood.

On his return to Port la Joie, Franquet found the frigate, Gracienne, anchored a league out from the harbour's mouth. The commander, Lieutenant de Tourin, thought it risky to come closer in. Franquet got a young lieutenant from the ship to make soundings, from which he prepared a chart into the Three Tides. This was likely the first chart of Charlottetown Harbour.

Referring to the arrival of M. Bonaventure in 1749, to his buildings and to Franquet's plans for fortifying Port la Joie, Professor Caven summarizes the condition of affairs, closing with a fine bit or irony. He says: "A few weeks after Isle Royale had been given back to the representatives of France, M. Bonaventure, an officer who had distinguished himself in the defence of Louisbourg, sailed with his company of one hundred men and established himself at the heights of Port la Joie. It was the month of August, 1749. The pursuits of peaceful industry had either been abandoned or were carried on fitfully and in fear. Some of the less resolute settlers fled to Quebec or elsewhere, and left their homesteads to whatever fate the fortunes of war might bring. Others hovered between their hiding places in the thick woods and their dwellings, watching the approach of danger. The buildings he erected were built in haste to meet a pressing need and to serve as temporary shelters until works constructed on the most advanced principles of military engineering should take place. Such plans were drawn with minute details by Colonel Franquet, but they never rose in stone or mortar on the heights of La Joie; they found a more peaceful resting place in the archives of the Marine and Colonies in Paris."*

We have seen that the great majority of the missionaries in the different centres of population were of the Recollet Order, who received their appointments from the Superior of the Order residing in Louisbourg. About this period the Indians of the Island were visited once or twice a year by the missionaries who had spiritual charge of the Micmacs of Acadia and Isle Royale. In October, 1749, the Abbe Mallard, writing from Louisbourg to the Abbe du

*Prince Edward Island Magazine, Vol. I, page 94.

Fau of the Quebec Seminary, said that he was alone for Isle Royale, Malogomiche and the Isle Saint John. The following year writing, probably, to the same correspondent of Abbe Monach, his then colleague among the Micmacs, he said that M. Monach was intended for the Island of St. John where he was to report the coming spring.

In the following of Governor Bonaventure came a new chaplain to Port la Joie, M. Patrice Lagree, whose predecessor was M. Ambrose Aubre, of whom the Abbe of the Isle Dieu said in a memorial to the King, that he was a very good monk (religious), recognized as such and a man in the confidence of the government even.

In 1748, le Sieur Benoist was charged with the duty of transferring to the Island of St. John all the Acadian families that he could get. On 6th September of the same year, M. de Galissonniere, Governor of Canada, wrote to M. de Mauripas, Minister of Marine, that he was furnishing him with a list of a detachment sent to the Island of St. John commanded by the Sieur Benoist, as much for the purpose of assisting the inhabitants, who were ready to abandon it for want of supplies as to facilitate the immigration of Acadians into that Island.

The Government at London, alarmed by the threatened exodus from their territory in Nova Scotia, sent ships of war to cruise in the strait, with instructions to seize all the Acadian craft which attempted to cross over to the Island. These measures did not stop the transmigration, but it interposed great obstacles. Tatamagouche was the chief port of embarkation, because of its location directly opposite Port la Joie, from which it was distant less than twenty miles.

At certain seasons of the year, when the British cruisers were patrolling the length of the coasts, the crossing over the strait, by the refugees, was accompanied by difficulties and not a little risk. It was often necessary to wait for some time for a favourable opportunity, such as a dark night with a good wind, or during a fog.

A census taken in 1748 showed that the population of the Island had increased to one hundred and twenty-eight heads of families, making a total of seven hundred and thirty-five souls. In this total were included twenty-one settlers from Acadia, making thirty-two persons. This was the group brought over by M. Benoist. M. Desherbiers, Governor of Isle Royale, when reporting the census to the Minister, M. de Ronille, in November, 1749, intimated that the Acadians settled in the Island that year came to nigh upon nine hundred persons.

The total population would, certainly, have been greater, but for the waste caused by the ravages of 1745, of which it is impossible to estimate the extent, and which had compelled a number of the inhabitants to seek refuge elsewhere.

Four years had scarcely gone by since that event, when a new disaster befell the unfortunate colonists. It was said at that time that everything that bore the name, "Acadian," was shadowed by a kind of fatality. Wherever they looked for refuge, misfortune dogged their steps.

The harvest of 1749 gave splendid promise. Hope was at its brightest when, as it were in an instant, clouds of locusts hurled themselves on the fields and stripped them bare.

"We have just received," wrote the Intendant Bigot from Quebec, on 11th October, 1749, "despatches from M. de Bonaventure, Commandant at the Island of St. John, by the schooner sent thither, at the end of August, to carry food and supplies for the settlers, who have none. He informs us that the locusts have completely ravaged the harvest, that there is not a speck of grain in the Island for next seeding, nor flour to provide for the subsistance of the residents and refugees from Acadia."

## DE ROQUE.

In 1752, Compte de Raymond sent the Sieur de Roque to take a census of Cape Breton and then of the Island of St. John. He was to get full particulars of all the inhabitants, together with a complete description of the condition of the Island and of its people. He took the census of Cape Breton, then proceeded to the Island of St. John and entered the port or harbour of Port la Joie. He found that the population amounted to only nine families, comprising a total of thirty-eight persons. Port la Joie had suffered much and lost heavily of its population since, in 1720, St. Pierre had made his settlement there. From La Joie, de Roque visited the different settlements up the rivers and along the coasts. He took in the south shore as far as Fortune Harbour and East Point. On the north side he took in St. Peter's and the various settlements as far as Macpec (Malpeque). Crossing over from Malpeque to the south side again, he visited Bedeque and the settlements from Bedeque eastwardly to Port la Joie. He seems to have made a very full and accurate census and to have taken very complete details of the condition of the inhabitants, who, with few exceptions, were very poor. The population amounted to two thousand and fourteen souls.

One of the first cares of the Compte de Raymond, who had recently taken over the administration of Cape Breton, was for the Island of St. John, for which the French ministry was evincing a tardy solicitude. His visit, made shortly after that of Franquet, infused a general feeling of confidence among the settlers. He pleased them by his spirit of fairness. He put an end to boundary disputes, which kept the inhabitants in a state of turmoil, by sending thither surveyors to establish the lines of properties. The general impression which he brought back with him was most favourable and helped to corroborate that of Franquet. In 1753, the wealth of immigration, which continued to flow in from Acadia, had already so modified the conditions on the Island that it was deemed necessary to take a new census, which showed a population of two thousand six hundred and sixty-three souls.

## The Great Fire.

A great fire had, some years before, run through a large part of the eastern section of the Island, doing enormous damage. There is frequent reference to it. To its ravages were attributed the destruction of the deer which had been plentiful. The writer had no doubt that this fire did very much harm, but it could not have been as destructive as reported. It destroyed the settlement at East Point, but it seems to have confined itself to the eastern part of what is now King's County. As pointed out by Sir Andrew McPhail the date of the fire "may be fixed in 1738, since one Magdelaine Poitevin claimed, at the time of de la Roque's visit, that she held her land under a deed that was burned at the time of the fire fourteen years ago."* The size and abundance of the timber to be found in 1752 over the greater part of the Island effectually disposes of the story that the great conflagration had

*"Canada and its Provinces," Vol. XIII, page 309.

swept over the whole Island, destroying the deer and other animals in its course. It does not require a fire to account for the destruction of the deer. That may safely be assigned to the agency of man.

## PICHON.

The last of the French travellers who visited and reported upon the state of St. John's Island and its inhabitants, to whom I think it well to refer, somewhat at length, is Thomas Pichon. Professor Caven says of Pichon that he was a native of France, well educated, was secretary to Count Raymond, Governor of Louisbourg, and from 1751, Commissary of Stores at Fort Beausejour. Here he became intimate with the British officers at Fort Lawrence two miles distant, when he turned traitor and kept them informed as to everything connected with the fortress and garrison. He wrote an account of Cape Breton and St. John's Island, which were published anonymously in London in 1760. This is not the description of a very admirable character. Pichon, however, whatever may have been his relations with the enemies of his country, was a clever, observant and capable man. He makes an initial error in giving the size of St. John's Island, where he says that its length is twenty leagues and its circumference fifty; but that does not affect his observations with regard to the inhabitants and their settlements.

The voyage of Pichon to the Island, made in 1752, less than a year after that made by Franquet, of which he has left an account in his memoirs, gives interesting details. But he must be taken with reserve; because Pichon was one of the most dishonest and most vile men that appeared, at that time, in the region of the St. Lawrence. He was born in France of an English mother named Tyrrell, whose name he assumed in the second half of his life. He was intelligent, educated and a schemer. Protected by the Count de Raymond, successor of M. Desherbiers in the Government of Cape Breton, and become his secretary, Pichon has taken pleasure in traducing the Count in his writings. After having solicited, to no purpose, the position of sub-delegate of the Intendant at the Island of St. John, he, through Count Raymond's influence, obtained that of Commissionaire of Food at Fort Beausejour. He knew how to ingratiate himself with the Abbe Le Loutre, then very influential and quite taken up with the exodus of the Acadians from Nova Scotia to the French territories. Possessed of all the secrets of French policy, Pichon availed himself of this knowledge to make himself useful to the British as a spy. The proximity of Fort Lawrence to Beausejour made the traitor's work easy, and he kept the English well informed as to all that transpired in the latter. Ostensibly made prisoner in 1755, on the surrender of Beausejour, he was carried to Halifax, where he continued to spy on the French prisoners. In 1758 he sought refuge in London, where he published anonymously his *"Lettres et Memoires sur le Cap. Breton,"* in which he inserts the account of his journey through the Island of St. John. He pretends to have made the tour of the Island, staying over at the principal harbours, from Port la Joie to East Point, and thence along the north side of the Island to Malpeque, where he crossed over to Bedeque on the return journey to Port la Joie.

Pichon describes the Island of St. John as the largest of the islands in the Gulf of St. Lawrence and as having the advantage of Cape Breton in point of fertility. It has safe commodious harbours with plenty of wood. The French have been of late at great pains, he said, though not enough, to plant this Island. Having made a journey on the coast, Pichon gives, at first hand, a description of the country.

The Commandant of St. John's Island received his orders from the Governor of Cape Breton and administers justice conjointly with the sub-delegate of the Intendant of New France. They reside at Port la Joie where the Governor of Louisbourg supplies a garrison of fifty or sixty men.

In the beginning of 1752 Pichon's party ascended the river (East) to its source, thence they crossed over the land to St. Peter's, four leagues, through well cultivated lands abounding with all sorts of grain. After some stay there, they set out for the south side and, the same day, reached the creek at Matieu (Souris?) on the south side of the Island within three leagues of Three Rivers and six leagues of East Point. Matieu harbour has no plantations. Its channel has nine or ten feet at low water.

Fortune Harbour, situate farther up, runs a league southwest into the country, with seven feet at low water on the bar. The lands are exceedingly good. There were several sorts of trees with a prodigious number of foxes, martens, hares and partridges. The rivers abound in fish and are bordered with pasture lands that produce, in limited quantities, exceedingly good grass. The inhabitants, who came from Acadia during the last war, number about forty-eight. From Fortune they made for East Point, passing Souris harbour, the entrance to which is practicable for small boats. Continuing they arrived at the harbour of L'Esconssier, which is capable of receiving small boats. Its banks are covered with beautiful meadows. About two leagues farther they doubled East Point, which they found deserted, as a fire had obliged the inhabitants to abandon it and settle two leagues further up on the north side. These settlers, though in excessive poverty owing to the fire, have already begun to clear land. They number twenty-two in all.

Six leagues further on they reached Naufrage, so called from a French ship that had been cast away there. She was lost out at sea, but a few passengers were saved and were the first to settle at St. Peter's Harbour. The coast from Fortune to St. Peter's, where they arrived on 14th August, swarms with all sorts of game and with a variety of the very best fish, which was a great relief to the ship-wrecked people. The Indians, then the only inhabitants, became civilized and helped them to settle and maintain themselves. They even shared with them their game, which then consisted chiefly of otter and muskrats. The mouth of St. Peter's harbour was choked with sand. The channel north and southeast is quite safe at high water. It is fifteen or sixteen feet deep and navigable for vessels drawing ten or twelve feet. Pichon recommended a breakwater, such as in recent years the Government of Canada has placed there. The fishery is carried on here with great success. While the cod is larger here than at Cape Breton and caught in greater quantities, it is difficult to cure. It might answer as well to salt and barrel it directly, and send it to Europe. The plantation of St. Peter's Harbour is of great consequence as well to the fishery as to the commerce carried on in the interior points. But they should attend to the essential part, namely, agriculture, and pasture and all sorts of live stock, especially sheep. Then they would be beholden to strangers for nothing but salt, lines, hooks and fishing tackle. They have also a vast quantity of plaice, thorncods, carbels, mackerels and herrings. In several pools and lakes there are excellent trout and a prodigious multitude of eels. Also, as in other parts of the Island, a great plenty of game, ortolans and white rabbits of a most delicate taste. Consequently the country is more settled than other parts. In this harbour they reckoned three hundred and thirty-nine persons, though some of these ranked as of St. Peter's, have their plantations around Savage Harbour, about a league distant. Savage Harbour has a grist mill and grows the best wheat on the Island.

Thence they went three leagues to Tracadie. There they found the same conveniences for fishing and for agriculture. The inhabitants seemed very comfortable, the natural consequence of industry.

The channel of the harbour is sixteen feet throughout. At the south is a sand bar that prevents vessels, drawing more than eleven or twelve feet, from entering. The harbour is handsome and spacious. In the harbour there are seventy inhabitants.

From Tracadie they set out on 22nd August and, after an hour, found themselves in the harbour of Little Rasico (Rustico), which is practicable only for boats at high water and in fair weather. The country is well timbered and proper for culture. There are also facilities here for building large vessels, shallops and canoes. Bad weather drove them into the harbour of Great Rasico, the entrance of which is one hundred and twenty fathoms wide. It has two extremely rapid rivers running into it. Their banks are covered with timber and they might have saw and grist mills here. They left on 23rd August, but the wind rose so as to force them into the Little Harbour. Throughout there is a depth of eleven to twelve feet at high water. There are some remains of a settlement here.

The wind having changed, they started for Malpeque, arriving the same evening. They had a prospect of a charming coast with meadows and beautiful trees; but they were greatly inconvenienced with gnats (black flies), whose sting is worse than in any other part of the country. There were swarms of these insects and they bit with venom and fury.

Malpeque Harbour is within sixteen leagues of St. Peter's. It is very convenient for the cod fishery, having several small islands, as well as strands adapted for drying, and sharp air proper for the purpose. There are four entrances. In the deeper, vessels of from one hundred to one hundred and fifty tons can go up. At the west side they reached a kind of canal (The Narrows), which runs northwest as far as the harbour of Cachecampec (Cascumpec). It admits only of small vessels and forms a communication between the harbours, distant from each other six leagues. The lands about Malpeque Harbour are superior to those of St. Peter's and are the best in the whole Island of St. John. The river lands are covered with all sorts of beautiful trees. Pichon mentions a large grove of cedar between Malpeque and Cascumpec. He says there are two sorts of cedar, the white and the red. The wood distills a kind of incense. The fragrance of the red is in the wood. The Acadian women chew this incense, which preserves their teeth and makes them extremely white.* Nevertheless, the inhabitants, owing to unforeseen accidents, are reduced to great misery, and Pichon recommended that they be allowed the privilege of fishing. He said one advantage would be that the stock of dry cod, which they would keep by them, with milk, butter and cheese, would supply them in bad years and repair the damage done by locusts and field mice. These animals are the scourge of the country. Whenever there are plenty of beech nuts the field mice come out and devour whatever they can find, and after everything is consumed, they make headlong into the sea. In rainy weather, inundations of rivers or in thick fogs, the mice are succeeded by locusts. These misfortunes frequently reduce the inhabitants, who number two hundred, to great misery, which was their condition when Pichon visited them.

From Malpeque they set out in a canoe and, crossing a bay three leagues, were landed at a small rivulet, whence they directed their way for a league to the southward. The earth was covered with beech, a prodigious quantity of French beans and a kind of pine trees. At length they arrived at Bedeque. Bedeque Harbour is inhabited by eight families, making forty-four souls. It is on the south side sixteen leagues from Port la Joie. The soil is proper for cultivation and is adorned with beautiful meadows. After doubling the Isle of Bedeque (Holman's Island) the harbour divided into two branches. In both anchor can be cast in four or five fathoms at low water, but, for greater safety, it is better to move to the southwest side, which is thoroughly protected from the wind.

*Should not this be spruce? So far as the writer's knowledge goes, cedar does not grow east of Lot 17, and it does not produce anything to chew. The spruce does produce an excellent chewing gum, which was used to keep the teeth white.

From Bedeque they made the Traverse River, where they reckoned only twenty-three inhabitants, thence following the coast to the river Aux Blond (Tryon River) three leagues. This river runs up the country four leagues. The inhabitants number thirty-seven, settled on both sides for a league from its mouth. The cultivated land promises well; the untilled is covered with timber and in the river lands there is excellent pasture.

At Crapaud River thirteen inhabitants were found and farther on thirty. The coast is low and covered with plenty of timber. From Traverse to Port la Joie, the coast swarms with wild fowl, especially vast multitudes of bustards, crevans and teals. In the woods are vast numbers of foxes, martens and hares; but very few partridges. There are numerous flocks of woodcocks, very tame. Also plenty of shellfish, which are a good relief to the inhabitants.

Returned to Port la Joie, Pichon describes the bay. On the right side going in is Governor's Island with much timber and game. On the left is the island of the Count of St. Pierre, covered with pine and fir trees. Upon the bar and all along the banks of the Island are prodigious quantities of bustards, crevans and woodcocks. There is good holding at nine fathoms. Three rivers enter into the harbour here. The Northeast River runs nine leagues into the country. It is one of the best settled streams in the whole Island. The soil is light, somewhat sandy and suitable for cultivation. The south side of the bay of Port la Joie is well settled. The coast on this side is separated from the Northeast River by a very thick wood, in the middle of which is the royal road to Three Rivers. A very good settlement could be made here. Fine woods, pleasant meadows, fruitful lands, plenty of game and fish afford encouragement to settlers. The settlements increase every day by the arrival of Acadians and others. With a little care, this Island might be made as serviceable as Acadia. Flies and mosquitoes are a great inconvenience. They darken the air, but as the land is worked and the country peopled, their number diminishes. "But," adds Pichon philosophically, "granting they are very troublesome, I do not know what place in the world is exempt from all inconveniences."

## MICE.

Pichon, in his interesting narrative, tells us that, at the time of his visit to Malpeque, the people there were impoverished and suffering from damage caused by mice. In the days of the French regime and, though to a less extent, for some time after the Island passed under British rule, mice, almost periodically, were a terrible scourge to the settlers. Their raids upon the crops left nothing that was not destroyed. The name of Souris is commemorative of one of these plagues. This plague of mice was so terrible a menace to the settlers as to make necessary some description of them finding a place in any account of the French period in the Island of St. John.

They usually appeared at intervals of a few years. Their advent meant the utter destruction of crops and starvation for the settler. They devoured every vestige of crop. Not a blade or ear escaped them. Between 1724 and 1738 there were three of these awful visitations. They increased in the forests with marvelous rapidity. Every six weeks or so they produced litters of a dozen or more. Multiplying under shelter of deep snow and in mild winters, they became almost innumerable and consumed all the means of subsistance provided by their native woods. Prior to 1738 there had been ten years of comparative immunity from their attacks. Then they invaded the cultivated lands. "The manner," to quote Professor Caven, "in which these famished creatures swarmed from the woods and rushed upon the cultivated lands resembled more the action of some savage tribes, carrying out some pre-conceived scheme of vengeance, than the doings of irrational animals. Every field of grain, from Three Rivers to Malpeque, was made desolate by their ravages, and the settlers, all of a sudden, found themselves face to face with starvation. Animated by a spirit of destruction keener than they had ever been known to exhibit in former inroads, these invaders, when the cultivated fields were laid waste, swarmed down upon the grassy flats that lay along the estuaries and, after devouring these, the food for cattle, as they had devoured the food of man, hurried onward, as was their wont, over the protecting dykes, in search of further spoilation and so found a watery grave. So numerous were these destroyers, that vessels sailing along the Island shores encountered, more especially off the mouths of long inlets, huge masses of drowned mice."

The authorities of Louisbourg came promptly and generously to the relief of the people and provided them with means of subsistence and with seed for the following season. Even so, the winter of 1738 was one of misery for the settlers.

The Governor of St. John's Island at that time was M. de Pensons, an able man. He had planned the gradual transfer of the population of Acadia to the Island to settle there. The settlers were coming in rapidly and taking up farms. The prospect seemed bright, but the invasion of the mice destroyed all their hopes. Not even the seed was saved. The people felt that the land was under a curse and feared to settle on it. This feeling was bound to affect the policy of bringing in settlers from Acadia or elsewhere.

To dispel this feeling de Roma of Three Rivers made careful study of the habits of the destructive little animal and reported his conclusions to the French Government. Professor Caven condenses de Roma's report as follows:

"It (the mouse) is somewhat larger and stouter than the ordinary mouse, of a blackish colour, with short legs and flat paws, badly adapted for climbing. It lives in the forest, and feeds on herbs of different kinds. After the manner of the squirrel, it lays up stores of provisions against the winter; these consist of seeds, nuts, grasses and such like. Under stumps and rocks, in the hollow trunks of fallen trees, and sometimes in the fissures of standing ones, are found the dwellings of this destructive creature. Its provident habits enable it to maintain its body in a plump condition, affording thus a dainty morsel greatly prized and sought after by its enemies. These were many. The dog, the cat, the fox, the marten, and every species of hawk, owl and crow were unremitting in their attacks on the foragers, as they sallied forth in quest of stores; and frequently the fox, the marten and even the cat carried the war into their very dwellings, and left their homesteads desolate. The extraordinary fecundity of the animal, however, quickly filled up the gaps made in their numbers by such casualties. With the exception of the more severe months of winter, the females brought forth every six weeks a litter of ten or twelve. In seasons when their homes were kept warm and protected from the invasion of enemies by deep snow-drifts, the increase in the population was marvellous. Two or three consecutive winters of this description brought about those disasters to cultivated lands, which in years not long gone by spread desolation round the cabins of the settlers. It would appear, however, as if some feelings of a domestic character were interwoven with the nature of the mouse. He abandons his native haunts only when his numerous progeny fail to find sufficient support in the immediate neighborhood, and when starvation is sure to be his lot. In such an emergency the march in quest of food is conducted in a long narrow column which, turning aside for no obstacle, goes onward in a direct line, until the cultivated fields are reached. The column of march then becomes a line of attack, and in an incredibly short time energetic voracity converts rich harvest fields into barren wastes. This accomplished, the marauders resumed their route in quest of fresh pastures. Should a river, or the sea itself, cross the line of march the intrepid leaders plunged confidently in, followed by their devoted adherents, who fought to the death with the waves and currents. This in the early days of settlement was the usual termination of such incursions. In these times the cultivated lands generally lay along the seashore. or skirted the margins of navigable rivers, which might either protect the crops from these fell invaders, or overwhelm them in ruin on their departure for fresh depredations."

Many were the devices resorted to by the early settler in order to protect his pasture land and grain fields from the ravages of these dreaded enemies. The most effective remedy, however, has been the cutting down of the wood lands, which afforded them shelter until their voracity and numbers rendered them formidable.

### EFFORTS TO SETTLE ISLAND.

Let us now revert to the efforts being made by the French to settle St. John's Island from the main land, which for thirty years, even as late as 1756, were subjects for anxious thought by the governments of Nova Scotia and of the New England colonies.

During the war of 1745 to 1748, "many settlers in Cape Breton, while it was in the hands of the British, fled to the Island; and others came over from Acadia. It was in the three years war that seven or eight French families from Acadia began the settlement about Rollo Bay and Souris."*   .   .   .   The garrison and population (of Louisbourg and Cape Breton) imported the larger share of their provisions. They naturally looked to this Island for such cattle, vegetables and grain as could be obtained on it. They

*Rev. George Sutherland, History of Prince Edward Island, page 86. Charlottetown, 1861.

strove to force its agriculture, or prevent its fishing, by restricting the fishing to the two harbours of St. Peter's and Tracadie. Numbers of Acadians did leave Nova Scotia to make new homes in Cape Breton and in the Island of St. John. They suffered much hardship and privation in their new abodes, and were even in want of food, with which those already settled were little able to supply them. This can be gathered from a pregnant reference in a letter from M. Le Loutre, the missionary priest among the Acadian French and the Indians, whose name so frequently appears in Nova Scotian records of this time. Writing on 15th August, 1750, from Bay Verte to M. Bigot, commissary of New France, he says: "M. de Bonaventure is to write you by this opportunity, to ask you for provisions, not being able to get any from Louisbourg, for the subsistence of the refugee families. If the four vessels, that you promised, had arrived, we would have sent some flour to Isle St. John; but, for the present, we cannot do so." M. Le Loutre was a stormy petrel for the inhabitants of Nova Scotia, and much of the misery that fell to the lot of the French population was due to his machinations. He made his headquarters at Fort Beausejour, where,* Bourinot says: "The treacherous priest Le Loutre continued to pursue his insidious designs of creating dissatisfaction among the French Acadians and pressing on them the necessity of driving the English from the former possessions of France."

Mr. Hannay† describes Le Loutre as "a man whose name fills a large place in our Acadian annals, a missionary priest, who had been officiating among the Indians about the Basin of Minas. He was, probably, the most dangerous and determined enemy to British power that ever came to Acadia." Le Loutre, we learn from the same source, held the office of Vicar-General of Acadia under the Bishop of Quebec. He came to Acadia in 1737. He was the prime mover for the subversion of English authority, up to the fall of Beausejour. In 1749, he induced the inhabitants of Chignecto to take the oath of allegiance to the King of France and afterwards caused many of them to withdraw to Cape Breton and St. John's Island. He persistently thwarted Governor Cornwallis' efforts to keep the French inhabitants on their lands. He ever fomented strife and ill-will between the two nationalities in Nova

---

*Bourinot, "Canada," in "Story of the Nation," series.
†History of Acadia 332.

Scotia. Wielding vast influence over the Indians, he was able to cause much trouble by inciting them against the English, and he kept his own compatriots, who looked to him for guidance, embroiled in the same way. From the records published in Akins' Archives of Nova Scotia, it seems clear that, in the course he adopted in this respect, he was acting directly contrary to the wishes of his ecclesiastical superiors, if not against their express instructions, although M. Casgrain takes a different view. Though a hollow truce had been patched up in Europe, war never really ceased out here. The French had erected two forts, a strong one at Beausejour and a smaller one at Bay Verte. In 1755, these were captured by Colonel Monckton, after whom the city of Moncton is named, who attacked them with a force of regulars and colonials, principally the latter. A number of French Acadians were captured. Le Loutre was there, but, at the time of surrender, he effected his escape. "His career," to again quote Mr. Hannay, "as an agitator and political incendiary, was ended." He fled to Quebec, where, "after a fatiguing journey through the wilderness, he met with a cold reception from the Governor, and was bitterly reproached by his bishop for his unclerical conduct."* In August 1756, he sailed for France, but the ship on which he took passage was captured at sea by the British ship L'Ambuscade and he was made prisoner by the English, who sent him to the Island of Jersey, where he remained confined in the Chateau d'Elizabeth for some years until the Treaty of Paris in 1763, when he was released, and thenceforth does not appear in Acadian history.

Le Loutre stands out a sinister figure in the history of Acadia, and, to a less degree in that of the Island of St. John, during the central period of the eighteenth century.

Mr. Thomas O'Hagen, a writer not unfriendly to the Acadians, writing of Le Loutre, says: "There can be no doubt that this over-zealous and hot-headed priest did everything in his power to stir up the Indians against the English, and on this score his conduct is entirely reprehensible; but," he very pertinently adds, "the reader should remember that Le Loutre was never a missionary to the Acadians on *English territory.*"

He further says: "Le Loutre's attempt to coerce the Acadians into abandoning the English territory was wrong, and for this he

*It is right to note that, later, according to M. Casgrain, the bishop's opinion of Le Loutre was greatly modified.

was reprimanded by the Bishop of Quebec."* He first came to Canada in 1747. While on a voyage to revisit France, some years later, he was made prisoner by the English and carried to England, whence, after a short captivity, he returned to France. His superiors offered him positions where he might have lived in peace, after his years of missionary work, but he preferred to go back to his life among the Micmacs. After his return to Acadia (then British territory) in the summer of 1748, he had been given charge of the parish of Beaubassin, a large town or village on the English side of the River Missiquash, which the French contended was the boundary between the French and English territories.

Le Loutre acquired almost unbounded influence over the Indians, who were being continually incited to acts of barbarity against the British. His devotion to the French cause, of which he had given proof during the late war, had attracted the attention of the Quebec authorities and of the Court of Versailles. By them he was entrusted with the task of inducing the Acadians to forsake Nova Scotia and settle on the French side of the Isthmus, or to direct them to the shores of the Island of St. John. He was authorized to offer the emigrants compensation for their losses and three years subsistence in their new homes.

At this period the British policy was, and for a generation had been, to retain the Acadians in their old establishments, and they were opposed to this scheme of drawing off the settled population. The river only separated the two territories at Beaubassin, but the route to the Island of St. John was by the isthmus at Chignecto. Here the French in 1750 laid the foundations of a strong fort, Fort Beausejour, which was scarcely completed when five years later it was captured by the English.

In March, 1750, the British decided to erect a fort at Chignecto, where the French had already begun Fort Beausejour, and in April Major Lawrence, with a force of four hundred men, was sent to Chignecto for that purpose. Upon their approach to Beaubassin, which consisted of one hundred and forty houses and two churches, with a population of one thousand souls, the Indians, instigated by Le Loutre, reduced the whole place to ashes. The inhabitants were forced to cross the river to the French territory.

---

*"Canadian Essays," by Thomas O'Hagan, M. A., Ph. D., Toronto; Wm. Briggs 1901,— pages 144-5.

M. Edward Richard, in his "Acadia," tells us that "The first important settlements in this Island began only in 1749, when Beausejour was founded. Le Loutre had set fire to the dwellings of the inhabitants of Beaubassin, so as to force them to take refuge with the French and leave a wilderness around the fort which the English purposed constructing on the south side of the little river, Messagoutche. The half of this populous district was thus depopulated against the will of the inhabitants. The greater number of these passed immediately into Prince Edward Island, . . . Furthermore, after the events of 1755 (in Acadia), their number increased considerably by the addition of those who escaped the deportation. Until 1758 they were able to lead their former tranquil life without molestation, for they were protected by France, which still held possession of Isle Royale (C. B.), and kept a garrison at Fort La Joie in Prince Edward Island."

In October of the same year, Captain Edward How was murdered by the Indians, near the English fort. Both the burning of Beaubassin and the murder of How have been attributed to Le Loutre. How was an English officer, esteemed by French and English alike. He had conducted negotiations with both French and Indians, and was sent to Chignecto to try to bring about a peace with the Indians, and to procure from them the release of some English prisoners. In this connection he had frequent conferences with Le Loutre, La Corne (the French commandant) and other officers, under flags of truce. On 4th October, 1750, an Indian named Cope, dressed as a French officer, was sent under a flag of truce, when How, taking Cope for a French officer, came out to receive him; but as soon as he appeared, Indians in ambush fired at and killed him. There seems little doubt but that this foul deed was instigated and planned by Le Loutre.

Le Loutre's is a complex character difficult to analyze. To understand him one must bear in mind his environment and other circumstances. He spent so many of the most vigorous years of his life living among and managing the savage tribes that he seems himself to have become imbued with their characteristics. It must further be remembered that he flourished nearly two centuries ago. We are not justified in measuring men of the middle eighteenth century by the standards of today. Moreover, as Mr. Murdock in his history of Nova Scotia points out, our ideas as to Le Loutre's personality are formed from the reports and descriptions of men who were most hostile to him. French writers, Abbe Casgrain for instance, convey a very different impression of the man. Making every possible allowance for prejudices, friendly or hostile, he yet stands out as a cruel and treacherous man, absolutely unscrupulous and ruthless as to means to effect his purposes. His object, his motive, was from his standpoint a very laudable one. His impelling motive, throughout his career, was the restoration of Acadia to France, the land which his countrymen had worked for, fought for and died for. It was patriotism of the most earnest type. It is a motive that the chroniclers of his time seem to overlook. One is lost in horror of the ruthless methods to which he resorted to achieve his object. Yet it was surely the object to which he devoted his life; for which he stirred up savage warfare; for which he drove his countrymen from their settlements on British territory, consigning their homes to the flames to prevent their return, forcing them to start life anew on French soil; and for which he shrank from no crime. It was the one engrossing, overmastering motive, the overpowering passion that possessed him. In itself and for itself it was worthy of praise. But there can be nothing but reprobation for the inhuman means employed to forward his purposes. His motives were admirable, his methods damnable.

The English, in the spring of the same year, began the erection of Fort Lawrence, a strong fortress capable of accommodating six hundred men, at a distance of about half a league from the French stronghold. This commanded the route via the Isthmus.

Notwithstanding the erection of Fort Lawrence, the Acadians continued to make their way to the Island of St. John. The Abbe de L'Isle Dieu, in a memorial to the Ministry in 1753, said that there remained only 6510 inhabitants under British rule. Of 1200 souls who had lately composed the Parish of Cobequid, there remained not more than 300. The remainder had betaken themselves to the Island of St. John by the passage of Tatamagouche, which the English had not taken the precaution to guard. Five hundred inhabitants had left Pigiquit and 300 Grand Pre. The two parishes of Riviere Aux Canards and Port Royale had not lost so many because of their distance from the French boundaries. Of the two churches that were lately at Pigiquit, there remained only one, that of the Assumption having been destroyed and replaced by Fort Edward. The Court of Versailles, which had incurred heavy expenditures to settle the Island, thought this would be best effected by the clearing and cultivation of the soil. With this view it desired that all should be so employed, and consequently discouraged and even forbade the colonists from prosecuting the fisheries. The Intendant congratulated the Minister on the part he had taken in prohibiting fishing, as being the best course to encourage the cultivation of the soil, that every settler who became a fishermen no longer worked. Farming did not return so evident a profit, but it was permanent.

During the summer of 1751, M. de Bonaventure visited Louisbourg to give a report as to affairs in the Island. The Commissary General, on 28th November, 1751, writing to the Minister, summed up that the old colonists had more reason to complain than had the new, because they had not received rations, and the harvest having totally failed the greater number had no bread, and were not in a position for the coming year's seeding. There were among them many poor, whose great misery necessitated relief till the spring. M. de Bonaventure was directed, while using all practicable economy, and while endeavouring to help them in preparing for seeding, to make an effort for relief till the end of April, if the one hundred hogsheads ordered for them in New York would arrive in time.

The new settlers on the Island, including men, women, boys and girls, amounted to about 2,000 souls, while there remained there nearly 1,100 of the old. Those who first came from Acadia brought 2,209 head of horned beasts, such as oxen, cows, bulls, heifers and calves, much poultry, some sheep and 171 horses. This immigration would have been pushed on with greater energy could the immigrants have seen batteries or forts to safeguard them against the English whom they feared so much.

These families were so considerable in themselves, that, barring an epidemic of sickness, they might be expected, in a few years, to provide population to increase these hamlets, which they were always clearing, by means of the divisions which parents were obliged to make when settling their children, or those made between collateral and elder stems.

On his journey to the Island of St. John, the engineer, Franquet, was not less astonished than the Commissary General of Louisbourg at the prodigious numbers of children which he saw in nearly all the families. That fruitfulness of the Acadian race which, in the eighteenth century, struck the observer, still attracts the attention of scientific men. Few similar examples among other peoples are to be found. In the present day, the only one is that of the Boers of the Transvaal, a pastoral people, whose mode of life has analogies with that of the ancient patriarchs. The Acadians, those of today, equally with those of the past,— because the sons have not degenerated from their sires — somewhat recall the Biblical ages by their moral virtues, of which the numerous families who gather round their firesides are the result.

The causes which brought about a great increase of population in the Island of St. John, starting from the year 1750, have been pointed out. It was an advantage for the future, as M. Casgrain points out, but a present danger, because the means of subsistence provided by the Government were not sufficient to prevent destitution from increasing.

The Intendant, Bigot, writing to the Minister in October, 1750, reports that they had done what they could to induce the Acadians to withdraw from the British territory into the French, and that 600 or 700, as he was informed by M. de Bonaventure, Governor of the Island of St. John, had crossed over to that Island. They were passing over every day, but not with the energy they would have displayed but for the British cruisers. M. Bigot says that sufficient flour had been sent them, also implements and tools of various kinds and some clothing. The great part were naked and had escaped from the main land as they could. At the opening of navigation next year, he said, more meal and vegetables would be sent. This autumn he had not been able to get vessels to take supplies to them and had them sent to Louisbourg, whence they might be forwarded.

It was truly heartrending, that the families who, pursued on their departure from the Isthmus by the English patrol, and during the passage of the Strait by armed cruisers, were unable to bring with them either clothing or provisions. Abbe Girard, in a letter dated 24th October, 1753, to the Commissary-General Prevost, draws a sad picture of these unfortunates. He describes them as in a state of lamentable destitution, the children quite naked, without shoes, without socks, without shirts, absolutely nothing to guard against the cold by night or by day. When he visited them, he found them huddled about their fireplaces, from which, at his approach, modesty compelled them to flee.

It must not, however, be overlooked, in order to give an account of the condition of the Islanders, that this excess of misery was a passing phase of their existence, because the Government, as has been seen, sent periodically from Louisbourg and from Quebec cargoes of clothing and of provisions, which, judiciously distributed, served their immediate needs. At the moment when Abbe Girard wrote, the general state of the Islanders, other than the fugitives, far from being desperate, was even satisfactory. On 31st October, 1753, just a week after M. Girard's letter, the Commissary-General of Louisbourg reported to the Minister the success of farming operations on the Island of St. John, and on 27th September of the following year, the Count de Raymond extolled the prosperous condition of the Island. The real misery, as already pointed out, was restricted to the newcomers, whom the government relieved by more or less regular distributions.

All thought at Beausejour and Bay Verte on the mainland and at the Island of St. John turned to Louisbourg, whence the inhabitants implored re-inforcements to resist invasion, should the English, who had advanced as far as the Bay Verte and were masters of Fort Gaspereau, attempt to push their conquests further. The war, which was not formally declared until the following year, kept the Islanders in continual alarm. But three years were yet to go by before the culmination of their misfortunes.

The news of the deportation, *en masse*, of the Acadians from Nova Scotia was brought by a crowd of fugitives from all points of the coast. Some escaped from Beaubassin, from Memramcook, from Petitcodiac, from Chepudy; others from Cobequid, from Pigiquit and even from Port Royal. In the course of the autumn and the following spring there arrived not less than fourteen hundred, destitute of everything; famished and in a state of indescribable despair. Families had been broken up, children separated from parents, wives from husbands. These broken crowds wandered from house to house seeking an asylum, happy when a family found a lodging, a barn, a shed, to shelter them;

because almost all the dwellings were already filled by previous arrivals. The inhabitants had taken no part in the war which ended so grievously for them.

M. de Villejoin, who governed the Island, did not await the relief sought from Isle Royale before putting to use the few means of defence he had at his hand. He began by placing his supplies in shelter, sending them up the Northeast River. He caused women and children alike to go inland from the sea coasts. Then he distributed his limited supply of firearms (about 200 muskets) among the young men who seemed most reliable and stationed them by squads at the points of the coast most exposed to descents of the enemy. All his artillery consisted of three pieces, which were not even mounted in batteries, and which would only serve for signalling purposes.

The significance of these means of defence betrayed the carelessness of the Government and the absolute lack of protection in which these unfortunate colonists had been left, and whom that same Government had invited to populate the Island in the interests of France. M. Rousseau de Villejoin was Governor or Commandant of the Island for the three years immediately preceding its surrender to the British, shortly after the fall of Louisbourg in 1758. In a despatch to the Minister in France he says that "it was then three years since the last refugees arrived on the Island. They had to endure great loss and much fatigue to get there, and after arriving they found themselves, so to say, destitute. Shortness of food and clothing accompanied them to the Island. I had very little to give them, my contributions were necessarily meagre, and it was only by giving frequently that I did not see any of these people die." These refugees were the inhabitants of the neighbourhood of the captured forts, who retired to the Island of St. John for safety and as offering a basis for continuing or renewing the struggle. The French authorities in Cape Breton had now, for a long time, recognized the importance of their Island colony as a source of supplies for Louisbourg and their forces in Cape Breton. The great fertility of the soil, its adaptability for raising wheat, vegetables, cereals, cattle and other live stock would render the Island invaluable as a place whence supplies of provisions could be procured. Mr. Stewart informs us that, at this period, the garrison of Louisbourg drew a great part of its subsistance from the Island of St. John. The French maintained an officer there, who was called the Governor, and, in addition, they had two officials or commissaries, whose duty it was to procure food for the forces in Cape Breton. These officials themselves fixed the prices which the people were obliged to accept, and we are told by the same excellent authority that they generally put the price of a fat ox at eight to ten dollars.

In April, 1757, the Marquis de Vaudreuil, Governor of Canada, whom M. de Villejoin kept informed of his position, informed the Minister of Marine, M. Peirenne de Moras, that M. de Villejoin had attracted the settlers who came from Cobequid, Tatamagouche and the Mines. He had forwarded more than five hundred beeves to Louisbourg and had neglected no means of saving the cattle from the enemy. He went on to say that the harvest on the Island was very bad, besides which M. de Villejoin had not received any considerable supplies from Louisbourg. Pursuant to instructions from M. de Dracour he has rid his post of useless mouths, yet there remain some thirteen hundred who live in a very wretched way. It is to be hoped that he may not be obliged to destroy his live stock, as in that event the Island would become almost wilderness. Moreover, at the outside, M. de Villejoin had only six weeks provisions to give the refugees, while several of the old inhabitants had not the wherewith for subsistence or seed for the spring seeding. The women and girls could not stir out as they had no means of covering their nakedness and the same was true of a number of the older settlers. The Island of St. John, he continues, deserves attention. Its loss would be a very serious one, as there are actually better than six thousand head of horned cattle there. "It is, then, very important, Monsigneur, that the king should appropriate some frigates for that Island, and even that they winter there; without that, the English could very easily pillage and burn the habitations."

During the same year (3rd October, 1757), the Bishop of Quebec joined the Marquis de Vaudreuil in arousing, if that were possible, the Court of Versailles from its apathy with regard to the imminent danger to which the colony was exposed, a colony whose progress he had watched from year to year and whose development he had hastened by the religious organization which he had created.

Their representations were no more listened to than preceding ones. The assistance from Louisbourg was reduced to very small limits. This abandonment, however, did not weaken the zeal nor impair the activity of Governor de Villejoin, who prepared, abandoned though he was, to offer all the resistance of which the Island was capable.

In the early spring of 1758 the Governor of St. John learned a formidable English fleet had sailed from Halifax to lay siege to Louisbourg. The difficulties of a landing in the neighbourhood of that fortress raised the hope that a repulse would save it; but that illusion soon vanished. With the knowledge they had of the weakness of the fortress the issue of the siege might be readily foreseen. It is easier to imagine than to express in words the anxiety in which, during the siege, the population of the Island of St. John lived. Before the end of June they had learned of the progress which the enemy had made, the destruction of the Royal Battery, which the Chevalier Drucourt had been compelled to evacuate, the abandonment of all the outer posts, except Entry Island, and, three weeks later, the burning of the French fleet cooped up in the roadstead; finally the open breach and the capitulation expected from day to day.

The population of the Island of St. John, almost entirely Acadian, increased, as we have seen, by a great number of refugees from Acadia, come in the train of the great disaster, got a glimpse, from the fall of Louisbourg, of the lot that was in store for them, but they refused to believe. They could not grasp the idea that there would be a new break-up of the lands they had opened up to cultivation, and which were to gain for them competency and prosperity.

They could not realize that the scenes of Acadia, when the settlers there had been deported, would be renewed. They were still uncertain as to their fate when the Abbe Maillard, Vicar-General of the Bishop of Quebec, and missionary to the Micmacs of Cape Breton, arrived at Port la Joie. He had been at his mission on the Bras-d'Or Lake before the siege. He had sought, to no purpose, to arouse the courage of M. de Boishebert, who, with the force of Canadians, Acadians and Indians, which he commanded there, might have reached Louisbourg in time, possibly, to have prevented the descent of the English. In despair from this officer's cowardice, and knowing that henceforth his presence in the Isle Royale would be of little use, he had taken the route by Miramichi where his confrere in the mission, Abbe Manach, awaited him. There they found themselves at the head of a large number of refugees, who knew not where to turn and were perishing from hunger. Under these circumstances he arrived at Port la Joie where he could give a report of the situation.

The inhabitants of the Island of St. John, he says, are all very determined not to leave their Island, preferring to support themselves there, as well as they could, rather than go to certain death by hunger in Miramichi. Their commandant, M. de Villejoin, had put the Island into very good shape. The gardens were fine and the crops good. Three months after their capture of Louisbourg the English had not yet arrived in Port la Joie. The inhabitants wanted to make terms with them or to flee to the woods should the conquerors treat them harshly; but not to leave the Island, where they much preferred, if it could be, to end their days than, going further, to perish wretchedly in Miramichi.

After the fall of Louisbourg, Admiral Boscawan detached a portion of his fleet with orders to burn and destroy the French settlements on the Islands Royale and St. John and of all the coasts of the Gulf of St. Lawrence. One of the principal officers of this expedition, Lord Rollo, was charged with the execution of this task in the Island of St. John. On his arrival at Port la Joie, he sent to the commandant the articles of the capitulation of Louisbourg, with a letter from the Chevalier de Drucourt instructing him to conform to them. The Island of St. John, being a dependency of the Isle Royale, was embraced in the capitulation.

The leading men of the several parishes met together and addressed a memorial to the English commander, asking that they be suffered to remain on their lands. Lord Rollo could not act contrary to his orders, but he allowed MM. Cassiet and de Biscaret, who were the bearers of the memorial, to submit it to the commander-in-chief. Amherst and Boscawen remained inflexible, doubtless inspired by Lawrence, the Governor of Nova Scotia, then at Louisbourg, the same who had removed the people of Acadia and made a wilderness of their settlements. The Chevalier de Drucourt, being unable to secure any guarantees for the inhabitants of Islands Royale and St. John, they were completely in the hands of the conquerors. Their fields, covered at this season with beautiful crops, were to be laid waste, the animals killed or carried off, the houses given to the flames. A crowd of Acadians from Nova Scotia, witnesses and victims of such spectacles three years before, were to see them renewed before their eyes.

It is impossible to arrive at even an approximate estimate of the quantities of wheat and other cereals as well as of vegetables that were produced, or of what surplus the settlers would have to send to Cape Breton to supply the French forces there. That they had raised good crops is evidenced by the accounts already set out. But the reports of De Rond, Franquet and Pichon testify to the quality of the crops raised rather than to their quantity. To the writer's mind the quantity of wheat and other grains said to have been produced by the French settlers of the Island of St. John has been greatly exaggerated. Mr. Edward Richard, in his history of Acadia, quotes, and apparently accepts as correct, the statement said by Admiral Boscawan to have been made to him by many of the inhabitants that "they each harvested over twelve hundred bushels of wheat a year." This seems to the writer to be utterly absurd. The French had only some ten or eleven thousand acres of cleared land with a population on the Island of four thousand or more to feed. Lord Selkirk, a shrewd observer, writing in 1805, says that the crop of wheat was about fifteen to sixteen bushels to the acre. Allowing twenty bushels to the acre, it would have required sixty acres on each farm to raise so large a quantity. Moreover, in referring to the area of cleared land on the farms, the highest mentioned was of one man who had land sufficient to take twenty-eight bushels of seed grain but he could procure only nineteen bushels to put in it. That included all sorts of grain. Again, if such splendid crops of wheat were harvested, how was it that refugees, who came from the mainland, were on the verge of starvation and efforts were made, as Le Loutre stated, to procure flour for them out of shipments from Quebec? Villejoin, in his letter already referred to, tells of the destitution and lack of food suffered by these poor people. With the primitive implements of husbandry of that time, it is very doubtful if the farmers could have prepared the land, put in the seed and harvested so large a crop.

The French had farming settlements along the coast from Port la Joie to Point Prim, taking in Orwell and Pinette. They were not good farmers. When, nearly fifty years after the deportation, Lord Selkirk planted his settlement in that section of the Island, the old French farms were grown up with a young growth of wood, but the land, having been cultivated, was supposed to be the best for farming purposes, and as such was given out among the newcomers. As a fact, the crops on these lands were poor. The soil had been "cropped out" by the former owners.

With regard to cattle and other live-stock, the Island of St. John was probably better able to supply these to Louisbourg and the troops in Cape Breton than it was to supply wheat or other grain. Villejoin, writing in the autumn of 1758, says that three years before "the Island was stocked with cattle in the hope of its being able to supply efficient and annual help to Louisbourg" and that "there will remain over six thousand (cattle) at the disposition of the English." The settlers, also, had always kept large numbers of pigs. Hence considerable supplies of meat might readily be furnished. In this respect the Island of St. John might well be styled the storehouse of Cape Breton. It was less difficult to keep and supply cattle and pigs than wheat or other grains, because they, during a great part of the year, could find subsistance for themselves in the woods.

### Dykes.

The French settlers had dyked the marsh lands along their settlements and, consequently, had abundance of pasture and grass to feed their live stock in winter. Remains of these dykes are still to be seen. The Rev. Wm. H. Warren, writing in the Prince Edward Island Magazine in an interesting article on "Remnants of Acadian Dykes," among other things says that "along the margin of some of the Prince Edward Island marshes may be noticed an occasional mound, of greater or less dimensions, bearing unmistakable evidence of an artificial origin. In some cases the mounds are so well extended and well defined that little doubt can be entertained as to their original design.

"In view of the difficulty of clearing the upland, the Acadian settler cast up sea walls. It was hard work, but he soon formed a smooth area from which he could make a living, and later he could clear the uplands and so make his farm. The English neglected the dyke-lands and the embankments gradually broke down and disappeared." These marsh lands, together with the uncleared forest lands, enabled the Acadian settler to raise cattle and pigs at a minimum of cost.

Upon the fall of Louisbourg in 1758, the Island of St. John, the storehouse of Cape Breton, became a part of the British Empire, although the formal cession did not take place till five years later. It is outside the writer's purpose, in writing these pages, to discuss the siege and capture of Louisbourg or to digress upon the brilliant feat of arms which resulted in the overthrow of that fortress. He has to do with it only as far as it affected the Island of St. John. The articles of capitulation covered this Island as well as other French possessions. They are as follows:

*Articles of Capitulation between their Excellencies, Admiral Boscawen; Major General Amherst, and his Excellency, Monsieur Drucourt, Knight of the Order of S. Louis, Governor of the Royal Island, of Louisbourg, of the Island of St. John, and their dependencies, etc., etc., etc.*

*Article I.* The garrison of Louisbourg shall be prisoners of war, and shall be transported to England in his Britannic Majesty's ships.

*Article II.* The whole of the artillery, warlike stores, and provisions, as well as arms of all kinds, which are at present in the town of Louisbourg, Isle Royale (Cape Breton), and Island of St. John, and their dependencies, shall be delivered, without the least waste, to the Commissaries, which shall be appointed to receive them, for the use of his Britannic Majesty.

*Article III.* The Governor shall give orders that the troops, which are on the Island of St. John and its dependencies, shall repair on board such ships of war as the Admiral shall send to receive them.

*Article IV.* The Porte Dauphin shall be delivered up to his Britannic Majesty's troops at eight o'clock tomorrow morning, and the garrison, comprehending all those who have carried arms, shall be drawn up at noon upon the esplanade, and lay down their arms, colours, implements and ornaments of war; and the garrison shall be embarked to be sent to England in a convenient time.

*Article V.* The same care shall be taken of the sick and wounded, which are in the hospitals, as those of His Britannic Majesty.

*Article VI.* The merchants and their clerks, who have not borne arms, shall be transmitted to France, in such manner as the admiral shall judge proper.

Done at Louisbourg the 26th of July, 1758.

(Sgd.) DE DRUCOURT.

Admiral Boscawen, in his report to the Home Government states that "it (the Island of St. John), had been an asylum for the French inhabitants from Nova Scotia, and from this Island has been constantly carried on the inhuman practice of killing the English inhabitants of Nova Scotia for the sake of carrying their scalps to the French, who pay for the same. Several scalps were found in the Governor's quarters when Lord Rollo took possession."

Mr. Stewart, in his work already referred to says, in this connection:

"In 1758 the Island was surrendered to Great Britain by the capitulation of Louisbourg and a detachment, under the command of Lieutenant-Colonel Lord Rollo, was sent by General Amherst to take possession, on which occasion, it is said, that a considerable number of English scalps were found hung up in the French Governor's house; the Island having been, for the two preceding years, the headquarters of the Micmac Indians, and it is not denied by the old Acadian French still residents of the Island that they were very partial to this savage practice of their Indian neighbors, with whom, indeed, they were very much assimilated in manners and customs."

It is extraordinary how, once started, a report of this kind grows. Boscawen says several scalps were found. Stewart has "a considerable number," but, careful not to commit himself, prefaces his statement with "it is said." McGregor, twenty-two years after Stewart wrote, says that "Lieutenant-Colonel Rollo was sent from Louisbourg by General Amherst to take possession of it (Island of

St. John); and to the eternal disgrace of the French Governor, a *vast* number of English scalps were found "hung up" in his house."

Sir Andrew McPhail denounces Boscawen's statement as the "grossest misrepresentation." "There is no evidence," he writes, "that Rollo, who, with the 35th Regiment and two companies of the 60th was sent to take possession, made any such charge, or, if he did make it, that it was true."* The writer entirely agrees with McPhail. No evidence of any kind justifying such a charge, has been produced. Villejoin's (the French Governor) letter to his Minister is the letter of a generous and humane man. It is unbelieveable that the writer was either a scalp hunter or a scalp buyer. As there is no evidence that he was, so foul a charge should not be fastened on his memory.

## Population.

There is much difference in the estimates of the population of the Island of St. John at the close of the French regime. Mr. Stewart tells us that there was said to be nearly ten thousand people on the Island in 1758, but that, from the appearance of the remains of their improvements, the greater part could have been but a few years settled. This would bear out the statement that there had been a considerable recent influx from the mainland. But, from the non-committal way in which Mr. Stewart writes, it may be assumed that he, though writing less than half a century after the event, was doubtful as to the correctness of this estimate.

Sir John Bourinot, whose extensive researches and painstaking accuracy of investigation entitle whatever he says to the greatest weight, places the population at about four thousand souls engaged in fishing and farming and composed principally of Acadians, who had commenced to cross from Nova Scotia after the Treaty of Utrecht in 1713, and who were able to supply Louisbourg with provisions, as no agricultural operations of importance were carried on in Cape Breton. He also tells us that there were several prosperous settlements at Port la Joie, St. Pierre and on the bays of the low lying coasts.

M. Rousseau Villejoin, who was Governor of the Island of St. John at the time of the capitulation, and had filled that position for three years preceding that event, in his letter to his Minister

*Canada and its Provinces, Vol. XIII, page 324.

says that although Lord Rollo made about seven hundred persons embark at the same time as he (Villejoin) did, and who were then actually in the roadstead, there remained about four thousand souls on the Island. This estimate by the French Governor of the Island seems to me more likely, than any other, to be correct. Surely if any man knew the number even approximately, it would be the head of the government system of the colony. Adopting Villejoin's estimate, the writer would put the population, at the time of the surrender in 1758, at four thousand five hundred or a little more.

The French had no fortifications of importance on the Island of St. John. They had a few guns mounted at the mouth of Port la Joie harbour, at the north side of the Hillsborough River, opposite what is now McNally's Island, and at St. Peter's. Franquet had prepared elaborate plans for fortifying the different centres. "But," to again quote Professor Caven, "they never rose in stone or mortar on the heights of La Joie; they found a more peaceful resting place in the archives of the Marine and Colonies in Paris."

There was a fine settlement from the mouth of the harbour of Port la Joie round to Point Prim. St. Peter's had long been settled. It was the commercial capital of the Island of St. John. There the great fishing industries were carried on. In Prince County they had settlements along the Dunk River and on the present townships Twenty-seven and Twenty-eight. They had also settlements on townships numbers Thirteen and Fourteen, as well as around Richmond Bay. A considerable settlement flourished near Bedford Bay, where the pursuit of both agriculture and the fisheries could be protected. There was a small settlement between the Montague and Brudenell Rivers, said to have been founded by the French Government. The splendid harbour of Three Rivers, after the destruction of de Roma's settlement, doubtless owing to difficulties as to procuring titles to the lands, which were still vested in his company, seems to have been touched. The principal agricultural settlements were in the neighbourhood of marsh lands, whence the settlers could procure food for their cattle. They also possessed many boats and some small vessels, with which they engaged in fishing, in trade with Cape Breton and the mainland, possibly they engaged to some extent in privateering.

The lot of the settler on the Island of St. John could not have been an easy one. Ever disturbed by war or the threatenings of war; called upon to supply the needs of the great Cape Breton fortress and of his country's armies and fleets, and that almost within sight of his British foes, his was a trying life. Mr. Stewart says that some of the settlements were fine, but the refugees, who sought a resting place there in the later years had little chance to found new homes. Le Loutre's desire to supply them with flour, in itself shows to what straits they were reduced. Rev. Mr. McMillan, in the work already referred to, tells us of their awful destitution, that some of them had not even sufficient clothing to work out in winter, or to cover their nakedness in public. The greater the number of refugees, the more appalling must their condition have become.

The struggles between Great Britain and France for supremacy in North America continued fitfully for a few years longer; but, with the fall of Louisbourg, French power, in what are now the Maritime Provinces of Canada, was broken. The Island of St. John, as already pointed out, was taken possession of on behalf of Great Britain, by Lord Rollo in 1758. In 1763, the Treaty of Paris confirmed to Great Britain what her victory had won. With the rest of France's possessions in North America, save some small islands and some fishing rights, destined to breed much trouble in the future, the Island of St. John became, as it is today, part of the British Empire.

The long struggle for supremacy was at an end. A halo of romance invests the wondrous story of French performance in Canada. The record of France's achievements in the field, on the flood, in the forest; the tale of her pioneers; the deeds of her soldiers; the wanderings of her voyagers; the self-sacrifice and indomitable resolution of her explorers, of her priests and of her people; the whole legend of French dominion in the New World is one that has in it much of sadness, much of toil, much of heart-burning, much of sorrow; but a thousand times more has in it that in which all these things and more are combined. It has in it the memory of noble purposes, of high resolves, of great and gifted men, of mighty struggles, a story worthy of the great people whose sons are its theme and whose Canadian sons were worthy of the wonderful fatherland from whose loins they sprang.

We rejoice that we live under the folds of the three cross flag. We must, also, feel a just and generous pride in the men of French blood who first made Canada, whose deeds and whose glories are now the common heritage of the two races, those ancient foes; who are, today, pressing forward as one, in the building up and consolidating of this North American Dominion, whose united efforts will result in a nation as great as the world has seen. Yes, there is a common heritage, because it belongs to one common Canada, to our common country.

## PART III.

## THE DEPORTATION.

THE troubles of the French settlers in the Island of St. John culminated with its occupation by the British. Their compatriots had already been expelled from Nova Scotia, many of them having sought a refuge in the Island. Instructions were given to remove the inhabitants, and great numbers were sent away. Some found their way to Quebec, where they were but coldly received, others were sent or found their way to the English colonies further south. Many more sought or were transported to their motherland. Some of these never reached their haven, and to those who did, we are told by Mr. Stewart, France accorded a poor welcome, and blamed them much "for their obstinate hostility to the British government." Of those who went further south, the writer has been unable to obtain reliable information. He has heard vaguely that they prospered in their new homes. A good many families concealed themselves in the woods until the storm had passed, and thus avoided deportation. They were afterwards allowed to remain. This was more particularly the case with those who were settled in or about Malpeque. Their remoteness from the central settlements stood them in good stead in this respect, as they were not in view of the authorities and thus were enabled to avoid the deporting force.

An English writer, treating of this subject, makes the statement that: "In consequence of the determined hostility manifested by the Acadians of Prince Edward Island, they were included in the order for the removal of their countrymen from Nova Scotia and a large number were shipped off to the neighbouring continent and to the southern colonies. Some were sent to France, where they were ill received and upbraided for the systematic aggression which had so materially conduced to undermine the Dominion of France in North America."*

---

*"The British Colonies, their History, Extent, Condition and Resources," by R. Montgomery Martin, page 274.

## HISTORY OF PRINCE EDWARD ISLAND.

The writer takes exception to this statement. The French settlers in St. John's Island, as already seen, agreed, after the fighting which took place at Port la Joie in 1745, not to again bear arms against the British and to supply them with provisions, if they were left undisturbed on their lands. They agreed to give hostages to guarantee the carrying out of this agreement. There is nothing to show that they, after that agreement, ever bore arms against the English. In fact, they became neutrals. Whatever justification there may have been for the expulsion of the Acadians from Nova Scotia in 1755 (and the writer thinks there was some) there was none for the deportation of the settlers in St. John's Island in 1758.

McPhail,* on this point says: "Whatever causes existed in Nova Scotia for the deportation of the Acadians in Isle St. John, there were none associated with the conduct of the inhabitants. They were 'an inoffensive people.' They had molested no one, either by themselves or in conjunction with the Indians, and the Indians also kept their hands free from blood." The writer agrees with McPhail in this view.

The settlers' lot was indeed a hard one. Our sympathy must go forth for these poor people. At this time little is to be gained by discussing their expulsion. Such a measure would not be thought of in our day, but we cannot judge the middle of the eighteenth century by twentieth century ethics. That the authorities in Nova Scotia had some reason for stern measures is evident to an unprejudiced student of this period subsequent to the Treaty of Utretch in 1713 who considers the circumstances and conditions of that time. That even these conditions justified the appalling treatment meted out to these unhappy people will not be asserted. It is inconceivable that a more humane policy would not have accomplished the purpose desired, namely, to make of them peaceable and loyal subjects of the British Crown. The expulsion furnishes a very gloomy page in the history of Nova Scotia and Prince Edward Island, a page over which it is not a pleasure to linger. That these people were unwise goes without saying, that they were ignorant was inseparable from their surroundings; they had doubtless their faults; their conduct towards their new rulers may not have been that of wise men, or men of the world. The

---
*"Canada and its Provinces," Vol. XIII, page 323.

penalty they paid infinitely outweighed their offence. And yet we wonder at the treatment they received when they went back to their own kin. The spirit, after all, which actuated the poor French settlers was the same spirit, which, not so long afterwards, impelled a far more enlightened, educated and wealthy class of men to abandon their homes in New England, when the revolting colonies had achieved their independence, and to seek homes in these more northern lands, where they could still be under their old flag. Love of the Empire in which he had been born and spent his life was what sent the United Empire Loyalist a wanderer from his home. It was the same deep-rooted loyalty to his race and his King that influenced the poor settler in Nova Scotia and the Island of St. John. The one left a country where he had long been a dweller, but which had become to him a foreign land, to seek a new home in old Canada, Nova Scotia, New Brunswick or the Island of St. John. He was honoured and rightly honoured, for his noble resolve; and, to this day, to be the descendent of an United Empire Loyalist is in itself a claim to distinction. The other, poor and ignorant, driven from his home, went to his own and his own received him not. To him no kindness was shown, no reverence or honour extended; truly his was a hard lot.

The expulsion of the Acadians from Nova Scotia has been made the subject of endless prose and verse. Over it historians have exhausted their powers of research. Discussion embittered by religious and racial feeling has been kept up for a century and more. Opinions in regard to it, limitless in number as in variety and usually worthless, have been propounded. The policy of expelling those poor people from their homes has, and will continue to have, its supporters. It has, and will continue to have, its opponents. At times, and not unnaturally, much acrimony has been displayed. Most frequently, perhaps, commiseration for the sufferings of the exiled Acadians has been the rule. Longfellow's great poem, "Evangeline," has been the most potent influence in perpetuating and spreading the world over the tale of the banished Acadians. Readers look only through the eyes of the poet and see only the idyllic scenes his muse has created. Speaking from the prosaic view point of the twentieth century, it is safe to say that, despite provocations, despite the supposed demands of policy, despite more or less imaginary dangers to British supremacy, such a deportation might well have been spared and could not now take place. But we are living in the twentieth century and these scenes transpired in the middle years of the eighteenth. While the genius of the poet has cast a halo of romance around the expulsion from Acadia, that from the Island of St. John has not been so commemorated, and consequently it is but little familiar to the general public. The expulsion from Nova Scotia has so monopolized attention, has been the subject of so much research and controversy, that few ever think — even if they know of it, — of the later yet great deportation from the shores of the Island of St. John. It is referred to in a few lines by writers on the history of this Province and dismissed with brief notice. Yet it was an important matter. In its way it was as important as the earlier expulsion. In its details it was more tragic.

Upon the fall of Louisbourg in 1758, St. John's Island, the storehouse of Cape Breton, became part of the British Empire and ever afterwards has remained subject to the British Crown, although the formal cession did not take place until 1763.

Immediately following the capitulation of Louisbourg, General Amherst sent Colonel Lord Rollo, with a detachment of five hundred men to take possession of the Island of St. John. His name is perpetuated in that of Rollo Bay in King's County. Amherst's instructions to Colonel Rollo were as follows:

"Sir,—You are to take on you the command of three hundred men, and two hundred light infantry and Rangers, in the whole five hundred ordered to parade this day at twelve o'clock at the head of the artillery, and you will march to the Barasoy, where there will be boats to embark you in the following disposition:

| | |
|---|---|
| On board the King of Prussia | 140 |
| Dunbar | 140 |
| Bristol | 130 |
| Catherine | 90 |

"The ships will be victualled for three months for the number of 500 men, and Admiral Boscawen will order a proper convoy, to proceed to the Island of St. John, Lieutenant Spry, engineer, will embark with your detachment, and will have tools that three hundred men may work, and a thousand palisades, to build a redoute round the barracks if practicable, or in such a manner and on such ground as you will judge best, that one hundred or about that number, which I propose leaving at Fort la Joie, on the Island of St. John, may be sufficiently covered and secured to defend themselves against any attacks the enemy can possibly make against them. An engineer and ten carpenters will embark with the said detachment, who have orders for carrying boards, spikes, nails and whatever may be wanted to make cover for the intended garrison and palisading the redoute.

"Monsieur Drucourt will send two or three officers from Louisbourg to inform the garrison and the inhabitants of the Island of St. John's of the Articles of Capitulation, in which they are included, who are to lay down all their arms and surrender themselves. The garrison at Fort la Joie, consisting of one company of marines, are to be disarmed and you will embark them as soon as you think proper.

"A copy of the Capitulation is herewith enclosed for your farther information. The officers ordered by Monsieur de Drucourt may be sent in boats to the different places in the Island (keeping always with you one hostage) to order the inhabitants to bring in their arms, and if after the Articles of Capitulation are made known, the inhabitants should make any opposition, or be found in arms, they should be treated as rebels and destroyed, that we may remain in quiet possession of the Island.

"All the inhabitants who surrender, or who may be taken alive, are to be brought to Louisbourg, and if the number should be so great as not to leave room for the troops in the ships, you will, in that case, send away the inhabitants immediately, and the ships will return to you to bring the detachment back.

"When you have called in the inhabitants of the Island and have settled everything in the best manner you can, that the redoute or work that you and the engineer may think proper to erect for the security of the garrison is finished, the barracks properly covered, and the provisions laid in, which you will do from the three months ordered on board the ships, you will then leave a captain and three subalterns with one hundred, or twenty or thirty men more or less than that number, as you on the spot will judge best for the intended service, with the necessary orders for executing it, and you will then, with the remainder of your detachment, return to Louisbourg, and if I should be gone from hence, you will report to Brigader-General Whitmore or the officer commanding at Louisbourg, and you will receive your further orders from him.

"Given at the camp before Louisbourg, August 8th, 1758.

"JEFF AMHERST."

### LORD ROLLO.

Andrew Fifth Lord Rollo distinguished himself at the siege of Louisbourg and co-operated with General Murray in the reduction of Montreal. After the conquest of Canada he was sent to New York. In June, 1761, he was detailed for the West Indies, with the command of a large force of troops. After an assault of two days' duration, he drove the French from Dominica and took possession of the Island. He took part in the reduction of Martinique in the following year, and then joined Lord Albermarle, who was besieging Havana. Before its surrender, his health obliged him to sail to England. He died in 1765.*

On 28th August, 1758, General Amherst appointed Brigadier-General Whitmore to the governorship of Louisbourg, the islands of Cape Breton and St. John and all the dependencies thereunto belonging. His orders to General Whitmore, dated 28th August, 1758, were, in part, as follows:

"In obedience to His Majesty's orders to me I do hereby appoint you to be Governor of Louisbourg, the islands of Cape Breton and St. John, and all dependences thereunto belonging.

"As this government is one of the most important trusts to be given to any officer in this country, I believe His Majesty has fixed on you for it, and I have ordered the regiments of *Whitmores, Braggs, Hopsons and Warburtons* to remain here under YOUR COMMAND, and I have named these four regiments as a strong and sufficient garrison for this place. I shall add to it a company of Rangers, which will be of use in patroling constantly in the adjacent parts, and for taking up any people that may be struggling or lay hid in the more distant parts of the Island." . . .

Accompanying these orders and of the same date was a private letter of instructions from Amherst to Whitmore. In its words it

---
*Kimball, correspondence of William Pitt, Vol. II, note page 440; Knox's Historical Journal, page 399.

refers only to Cape Breton, but in the light of the events that transpired in the Island of St. John, it must be taken to apply also to that Island. It is of interest as showing the stern policy adopted by the conquerors of Louisbourg and the islands of Cape Breton and St. John. Amherst writes:

"As the last of the regiments will be on board today, and that I shall sail for Boston the first moment that offers, I enclose you herewith, in obedience to His Majesty's orders, an appointment as Governor of this place.

"My intention is that every German inhabitant of this Island (most of them are on board) should be sent to Lunenburg, those, the few who don't like to go, to be sent to France. The French inhabitants all to be sent to France, except such as you may like to continue in the town of Louisbourg. Some may be of service.

"I would have the settlement in the different parts of this Island absolutely destroyed. It may be done in a quiet way, but pray let them be entirely demolished, and for these reasons, that in the flourishing state this Island was growing to, many years would not have passed before the inhabitants would have been sufficient to have defended it. If it is to be given up, the destruction of the settlements at this time will insure His Majesty's subjects in Nova Scotia from any danger of the inhabitants of this Island for some years to come, as it must be the work of many years for the French to bring it into its present state. If they are not destroyed, they will re-establish it easily and may be too powerful. This is on a supposition that this Island may be given up; but if we are to keep possession of it, the present inhabitants are not to be trusted by us in their settlements. The produce of the settlements are not so necessary to an English garrison as to a French; we can very well live without it, and a French garrison would starve for want of it.

"The above reasons have fixed me in this determination, which you will be so good as to have executed, and as I do it for the best, I hope it will meet with approbation in England. . . .

"JEFF AMHERST."

Lord Rollo lost no time in carrying out his instructions. He proceeded at once to the Island of St. John, which on receipt by M. de Villejoin of the capitulation and of the orders from M.

de Drucourt, was surrendered to him by the French. Measures were forthwith taken to gather in the inhabitants, placing them on board ship for removal to Louisbourg. By 8th September, just one month from receiving General Amherst's orders, M. Villejoin, the Governor of the Island, with some seven hundred of his compatriots, had been placed on board ships in the harbour. Of that date we have a despatch from M. Villejoin to his Minister, briefly describing the condition of the Island, the measures he had taken for defence and for the year's cropping, the surrender and the present condition of the Island and its inhabitants. The writer has already, more than once, referred to this letter, but it gives so clear an insight into the conditions on the Island, that it is here inserted in full.

"PORT LA JOIE, 8th September, 1758.

"MONSEIGNOR:

"I received the letter you honoured me by writing to me last spring and have used the seeds which reached me by the King's boat, the only one to come to our Island. Although not quite enough, that quantity of seeds added to those I had in store since last autumn was almost sufficient to seed all the prepared land, and I see myself, this autumn, in the situation, with a little help, of being able to provision all the Island. A great satisfaction to me, Monseignor, after having endured three years of scarcity without intermission. Three years ago, the Island was stocked with cattle in the hopes of its being able to supply efficient and annual help to Louisbourg.

"Following your instructions, Monseignor, I took every practicable precaution, in the unfortunate situation in which I was placed, for repulsing the enemy should he have approached our shores before the surrender of Louisbourg. This did not occur, and the Capitulation of Louisbourg necessarily included our loss.

"Three weeks after that expedition the English came to the Island of St. John, and through two officers whom Monsieur de Drucourt had put on His Britannic Majesty's vessels I received his letter in which he enjoined me to conform to the Capitulation he had made with the English generals for Louisbourg and all its dependencies. There only remained for me, Monseignor, to do what I could. Knowing that Louisbourg had surrendered, I could not persuade the colonists to take up arms, without exposing them to the fury of the conquerors, neither could I, without arms or on my own initiative, abandon the inhabitants and proceed to Canada.

"Without superior orders this action on my part would have seemed heartless, exposing the people committed to my care to all the horrors of war should all roads have been closed to me; the enemy would have given me, Monseignor, time to evacuate the country; but that was impossible. Miramichi, the nearest refuge, was without provisions and still is, so that some of our people who went there have had to retrace their steps, preferring rather to abandon everything than to die of hunger.

"A request was presented, Monseignor, to Colonel Rollo, who had come to take possession of the Island in the name of His Britannic Majesty by the colonists, begging that they might be allowed to remain on their lands. Colonel Rollo even allowed them to send the same request by Messieurs Viscara and Cottier to the generals at Louisbourg. These gentlemen did not agree to their petition and the English generals appeared to desire the complete evacuation of the inhabitants. I do not think, Monseignor, that they will succeed this autumn, for although they have made about seven hundred people embark at the same time as I did, who are actually in this roadstead, there remain about four thousand souls on the Island. No one is to blame, Monseignor, that a greater number did not embark or that more did not surrender at Louisbourg, for the treatment by the English, Monseignor, does not make one wish to be under that rule, neither are officers kindly treated.

"In short, Monseignor, I believe all these unfortunate people will return to France. I take the liberty of representing their sad case to you. It is three years, Monseignor, since the last refugees arrived on the Island, they had to endure great loss and much fatigue to get there, and after arriving they found themselves, so to say, destitute. Shortness of food and clothing accompanied them to the Island. I had very little to give them, my contributions were necessarily meagre, and it was only by giving frequently that I did not see any of these poor people die. Returned to France, Monseignor, unless you have the goodness to consider favourably their misery and want, I see them plunged in worse poverty than they have suffered yet, or than I can describe, it will be so great. These poor people will be without food or clothing and unable to find lodging, or wood for heating, in a new world and not knowing to whom to address their requests, being naturally timid.

"Messieurs Viscara and Cottier will be necessary to them as guides. They are capable men, Monseignor. For my part, I hope when I am free to return to France, that you will allow me to join these people. I think, Monseignor, in order to avoid sickness they should go far from a seaport; and if you have confidence in me, I offer to follow them to the destination it may please you to decide on for them.

"It will be, I think, Monseignor, a great mistake if the English do not permit a certain number to remain on the Island. It will be very difficult to re-stock it with cattle. There will remain over six thousand at the disposal of the English.

"My family, Monseignor, goes to Rochefort and it is by that means I have the honour of writing to you. The scattering of our families increases greatly our expenses, and we find ourselves unable to support them. I myself have lost greatly both at Louisbourg and the Island of St. John, and that Island has been the cause of great trouble and expense to me during the four years I have managed it, without having had any remuneration. You have appeared, Monseignor, satisfied with my management, so I beseech you not to abandon my family during my residence in England. On my return, if my means permit, I purpose seeing you personally and giving a more detailed account of my conduct. I hope, Monseignor, that it will meet with your approval and be worthy of the honour of your protection. This is the favour I beg you will accord me.

"(Sg'd.)    ROUSSEAU DE VILLEJOIN."

Lord Rollo, on 10th October, 1758,[*] replying to a communication from Admiral Boscawan of the 17th September, endorses an opinion given by the Admiral, as to the advisability of establishing a fort near the heads of the Rivers Grand (Hillsborough), St. Peter's and Tracadie, all within ten miles of each other. He named Tracadie, as he had been told that it was a better harbour than St. Peter's. The country betwixt these rivers is plain and there is a ready-made road and small rivulets, so that a suitable ground could be readily fixed upon. It would divide the Island in two and enable a

[*] Archives, Chatham M. S. Vol. 96; pages 94 and 96.

commanding officer to detach commands to either side by the heads of the rivers without the necessity of boating, and might even cut off any communication between the two sides by lines and small redoubts, the distances being small, that between the Grand River and Tracadie is only three miles, so that if Britain intended to settle and secure it that was the place he had intended to recommend.

He goes on to say, with regard to population, the number reckoned for this Island when he landed was five thousand, which he did not doubt. He had sent away six hundred and ninety-two, and cannot say how many he shall send now, as numbers had fled to Canada, carrying off great quantities of cattle by means of four schooners which plied between Malpeque and the continent.

He adds that, with the assistance of Captain Spry, engineer, he has put the fortification in such order that, with one hundred and fifty men, then, it could not be taken without cannon and mortars, but that it must receive early attention in the spring.

The number of the population was due to refugees from Nova Scotia, and it is such good land and so fine a climate, being free of fogs, and so many rivers that it must invite settlers and would soon have become a granary for the French settlements, as it abounds in wheat, barley, rye, oats and some Indian corn, and all sorts of garden stuff. Musk melons he had picked in the open garden and used the tobacco which grows in plenty. Cattle, hogs, sheep and fowl in great quantities have been destroyed by them and by us, and many, now in the woods, will perish in the snow.

The inhabitants, being in no fear of the Indians, built on their farms so that there are no villages. There are five parishes under five priests, namely, Point Prim, St. Louis, St. Peters, Malpeque and Parish of Port la Joie, now Fort Amherst. The priest of Fort Amherst had gone, as had the most valuable of the officer's effects, the day before he landed. The priests of St. Peter's and St. Louis he had sent in the first transports, those of Point Prim and Malpeque he expected to go now.

This part of the Island, although the seat of Government, has no fishery, only plenty of oysters. The coast of St. Peter's and Malpeque is a noble fishery, but has not been brought to the perfection which it soon would have been, for they had begun in fitting out privateers, which in time of peace would have carried on the fisheries.

He writes that there are now one hundred and fifty Indians in the northernmost part of the Island. What they would attempt he could not say. There had been a large number of young men in the woods plundering their neighbours and sending their cattle to the continent. Whether they themselves go, he cannot say, but if they stay they may prove troublesome neighbours.

The year was so advanced when Rollo came, being the 17th August, and there being so much to do to get up the fort, as there was not the smallest trace of fortification here, he could not spare any of his five hundred men to chastise them. A fort where the admiral proposed would remove the difficulty in case any remain contrary to orders given them.

At midsummer, 1758, a fleet of transports carrying troops from Cork arrived in Halifax, whence they carried the soldiers to Louisbourg. On the reduction of that fortress, a number of these ships were ordered to the Island of St. John to convey the inhabitants to France. Of these ships the Duke William was the largest. As the tragic story of the departed people largely centres round this ship, a sketch of its career in the early part of the year 1758 may be of interest. In the spring of that year the Duke William, having been ordered to Cork, under convoy of the York man-of-war, to take in soldiers for America, lost the man-of-war and the other ships in a fog which thickened as they approached the Irish coast. Captain Nicholls, who commanded the vessel, stood in as near as prudence would permit. Just as he neared the land it cleared and the wind blew off the coast so that the ship was away to leeward.

In the morning he made all sail, and just as the man-of-war had got its pilot on board, the Duke William had gained so much that the pilot-boat came directly to her and put a pilot on board, but the flood-tide having come away Captain Nicholls could not weather the entrance of the harbour.

The succeeding night it blew so hard the transport was driven as far as Bellerotten Island, and the next day was obliged to bear away for Waterford. Off Credenhead several guns were fired for a pilot; but none coming they brought the ship up. At last a pilot assured the captain that he could carry the ship in safely. They ran for some time and could just see the land.

Finding the water shoaling very fast Captain Nicholls brought up, and when daylight appeared, to his great surprise, he found high rocks astern of him so very near that it was impossible to veer away a cable.

At last a boat came out and a pilot in her agreed to come on board for fifty guineas, but when he came on deck and found how near the rocks were he declared he would not stay on board. The captain then cut his boat adrift. The pilot appeared in the greatest confusion. He assured the captain he could not take charge of the vessel, nor could he venture to carry her in, for he was afraid she would be on shore and all to pieces against the rocks before she could veer.

The ship rode very hard; and it being Sunday, there was a great number of people ready to plunder her should she strike. There were two frigates in the harbour, which, as soon as the weather became more moderate, sent their boats to assist them.

They lay there for three weeks before they could get out to proceed to Cork. They got off Cork in the evening and, it being fine weather, came immediately to anchor. On the succeeding morning the York with the transports came out and put the soldiers on board the Duke William. They sailed the day after and saw two ships, the America of sixty-four guns, and a frigate cruising off Cape Clear.

The Duke William, having proceeded to Halifax, arrived there safely, and from thence went to besiege Louisbourg.

On the reduction of Louisbourg, the Island of St. John fell by capitulation and the inhabitants were to be sent to France. Lord Rollo with his force, as already mentioned, was sent on board the transports which were ordered to the Island to remove the settlers. The transports were nine in number, of which the Duke William was one.*

They proceeded under convoy of the Hind sloop of war, Captain Bond, but meeting with contrary winds and bad weather had a long passage.

---

*Reports vary as to the numbers of the transports sent to the Island. On 5th November, 1758, Admiral Durell, writing to Lord Cleveland, says: "I have just received a letter from Captain Bond, who was sent to Fort la Joie in the Island of St. John, with sixteen transports to embark the inhabitants there. He informs me that he has embarked two thousand which he has distributed in the above mentioned transports and sent them as cartel ships to France." (Archives of Canada).

Having brought the fleet up off a cape called St. Louis, nine leagues distant from the Gut of Canso, and it blowing strong in the night, the Duke William's cable parted. In the morning the man-of-war signalled to bear away to the Gut again. Captain Nicholls, however, resolved to stay and endeavour to recover his anchor and cable. The ships left the Duke William riding, and the next day the weather became fine. They weighed and dropped the ship at the buoy, took the buoy-rope in the hawser and hove the anchor up; but by the time they got the anchor into the bows it came on very bad weather,— wind, hail and rain, with terrible claps of thunder and severe lightning. A long winter's night was approaching, and as they were on an unknown coast (for their charts were very erroneous) their situation was extremely unpleasant. The fleet were much afraid that some misfortunes had befallen them, for though the weather was very bad with the others it was not so severe as with the Duke William.

Captain Bond in the morning signalled all masters of transports and desired they would man their boats, as he thought he had heard several guns fired in the night which he supposed to be signals of distress from the Duke William, which, he apprehended, was driven on shore, and the crew consequently attacked by the Indians. Accordingly, when their boats were manned, they were desired to row as far as it was prudent to venture. As the weather was still bad, and they could see nothing of Captain Nicholl's vessel, they returned, giving her up as lost.

In the meantime, the weather being very stormy, the captain kept the ship under a pair of courses, and in the morning bore away; but it coming on dark he was obliged to lie to; and as it did not clear until late in the afternoon he had a narrow escape in getting in, the Gut being very narrow, and, in consequence of the trees, very difficult to find. They shortly afterwards sailed out of the Gut, and got to St. John's. In the passage, Captain S. Hurry, in the Yarmouth, was run ashore by the ignorance of his pilot and was near being lost, but fortunately got his ship off without any damage.

A large party of soldiers having been ordered up the river to bring the inhabitants down on board the different transports, as the Duke William was the largest, the missionary priest M. Girard, cure of Point Prim (who was the head man of the country), with the principal inhabitants, were ordered by Lord Rollo to go to

France with Captain Nicholls. The priest requested permission for the other people, who wished it, to come on board to mass and to be married. Many marriages were celebrated. The special reason why the people, just then, were eager to get married was that they believed single men, when they reached France, would be compelled to become soldiers, and that they wished to avoid.

M. Richard says that "Three or four thousand of these unfortunate Acadians were thrown pell-mell into the holds of ships hastily collected, without any regard to their destination or their condition, and were consigned to England.

"What was their fate? We have not, or rather we can merely form more or less satisfactory conjectures. Their destination was probably England and not France, since the war between the two nations was at the height of its intensity. However, from statistics collected in England, after the Peace, by M. de la Rochelle, we have reason to think that many of them were transported directly to France. We know that M. de Villejoin, who commanded at Port la Joie before the surrender of the Island, was able to take away with him seven hundred, whom he put ashore at La Rochelle in France. On the other hand, one of these vessels, containing one hundred and seventy-nine persons, was driven by a storm into the port of Boulogne-sur-Mere."

The writer takes exception to parts of this statement. The total number sent away in ships did not much, if at all, exceed two thousand. There is no ground for the statement that they were thrown pell-mell into the holds of ships, hastily collected. They, so far as can be learned, were not unkindly treated. The writer agrees that the deportation in itself was a harsh act, but outside of hardships inseparable from such a measure there is nothing to show bad treatment of the prisoners. Their destination was France, not England. The ships carrying them sailed under cartels and were secure from capture by the enemy.

Admiral Boscawan, on 13th September, 1758, writing from Louisbourg Harbour, to Pitt, reports that the Hind had returned from St. John's Island with an account of the number of inhabitants there. Lieutenant-Colonel Lord Rollo wrote that "they have, most of them, brought in their arms and will embark for Europe. I am preparing transports for that purpose and hope to get them all from thence this season. By the number of the inhabitants on this Island and the plenty of corn and cattle they have, you will see the great importance of it to the French. By the best accounts I can get, they have been the only supply of Quebec for corn and beef since the war, except what has been brought from Europe, having, at present, ten thousand head of cattle. . . . This Island hitherto has been thought of small consequence and not to have above four or five hundred inhabitants. M. Drucourt informed me there might be near fifteen hundred at the surrender of Louisbourg to his Majesty. Last war this Island was included in the capitulation as it now is, but for want of proper methods it never was in his Majesty's possession, the inhabitants standing to their arms, and destroying those coming to take possession of it. At that time the French had no regular troops in it."

General (Governor) Whitmore, writing to Pitt in the late autumn of 1758, says that "Lord Rollo having settled a garrison on the Island of St. John's, returned here in November with the remainder of his detachment. One of the transports having part of his people on board was stranded and lost on the Island. The officers and men were taken up by one of the cartel ships and sent here. On the 14th November a sloop sailed from hence for St. John's with stores. She is not yet returned nor have we advices from that place." Writing again, Whitmore said: "There are about two thousand two hundred of the inhabitants of St. John's Island, already embarked, but Lord Rollo, who was sent there with a detachment of five hundred men to see them all embarked, writes me that, much against his inclination, he is compelled to leave the inhabitants of a whole parish behind. They live at a distant part of the Island, about one hundred miles by land, which is impracticable for them to march. . . . Lord Rollo reports the Island to be a rich soil, a fine country and well worth being settled, for which reasons he has not destroyed the houses. When the French are embarked he is to leave one hundred and ninety men in garrison and return with the rest of the detachment."

The people whom Lord Rollo was compelled to leave behind were probably the inhabitants of Malpeque. The French there took refuge in the woods and subsequently, when they returned to the settlements, the deportation had ceased and they were allowed to remain undisturbed. The writer believes that a great part of the present French population of Prince Edward Island are descended from these settlers.

Having got a great abundance of stock, they all sailed from St. John's together; Captain Wilson, with Lord Rollo and some soldiers on board, and Captain Moore with soldiers under convoy of the Hind. The other vessels being cartels did not require convoy. Captain Moore's vessel was lost going through the Gut, by striking on a rock under water and the soldiers were put on board Captain Wilson, bound to Louisbourg. Captain Moore, his son, mate and carpenter, took their passage in the Duke William. Another of the transports, the Parnassus, was lost here. The Narcissus went on shore, but seems to have been floated off, and most of the others were damaged before they got clear of Canso. All the prisoners on the Parnassus got on shore, where Captain Nicholls found them and, next morning, embarked them on the Duke William.

As the wind was contrary, they lay in the Gut of Canso some time. The French used frequently to go on shore and remain there all night, making fires in the wood to keep themselves warm. Some of them desired that they might be allowed muskets to shoot game, as they were not afraid of meeting with the Indians, which Captain Nicholls granted. About three hours after they were gone, one of them came running, and begged that the captain with his people would go immediately on board as they had met with a party of Indians who were coming down to scalp them. Accordingly, Captain Nicholls, with the other masters and sailors, went off and had but just got on board before the Indians came down; but finding only Frenchmen they went away directly.

November 25th, they sailed out of the Bay of Canso, with a strong gale at northwest. Captains Nicholls, Henry, Beaton, Dobson, Sagget, Whitby and Kelsy, agreed to make the best of their way to France with the people and not go to Louisbourg, as it was a very bad time of the year to beat upon the coast. Captain Nicholls was appointed to lead the fleet. They took leave of the agent, who was bound for Louisbourg.

The third day after they had been at sea it blew a storm in the night, being thick with sleet and very dark. The transport parted company with three ships of the fleet. The storm still continuing, in a day or two she parted with the others. The Duke William continued in very good order, and though the sea ran mountain high, went over it like a bird and made no water.

On the 10th of December, they saw a sail which proved to be the Violet, Captain Sagget. On coming up, Captain Nicholls inquired how all on board were. He replied, "In a terrible situation." They had a great deal of water in the ship, her pumps were choked and he was much afraid that she would sink before morning. Captain Nicholls begged of him to keep up his spirits and he would, if it were possible, stay by him and spare him a pump which he got out of the Parnassus. He also told him that as the gale had lasted so long he was in hopes that it would moderate after twelve o'clock; but, unfortunately, it rather increased.

At changing the watch at twelve, Captain Nicholls found that they went fast ahead of the Violet, and that, before morning, if they did not shorten sail they would run her out of sight. While scudding under the foresail and treble reefed mainsail, he consulted with Captain Moore and their mate, what was best to be done, and it was unanimously considered that the main-topsail should be taken in, as the only way to save their lives was by keeping them company till the weather should moderate. Accordingly they took in the main-topsail and got their three pumps ready in case of necessity. They had forced the spare pump down the after-hatchway, and shipped into an empty butt, of which the French had brought several on board for the purpose of washing. They aired them with spun yarn, to bail in case of need. They now thought that the Violet gained on them; at four o'clock, to their great satisfaction, they saw her very plainly.

On changing the watch they found the Duke William still very tight and going well, the carpenter assuring the captain there was no water to strike a pump. Being very tired with walking the deck so long, Captain Nicholls thought he might go down and indulge himself with a pipe of tobacco; he told the mate to acquaint him immediately should there be any alteration. They had driven the board next the lower part of the pump to see how much water was in the well; and every half hour, when the bell was struck, the carpenter went down. As he had yet found no water Captain Nicholls entertained no apprehensions of the safety of the Duke William, he was only concerned at present for the Violet.

Soon after the captain had filled and lighted his pipe, while sitting in the state room, he was thrown from the chair by a blow which the ship received from a terrible sea. He sent the boy to ask the mate (Mr. Fox) whether anything was washed over. The mate sent word that all was safe and that he saw the Violet coming up fast.

Being still very much fatigued, the captain thought he would try to get a little sleep to refresh himself; and without pulling off his clothes he threw himself on the side of the bed. Before he had closed his eyes Mr. Fox came and told him that the carpenter had found the water above the keelson and the ship must certainly have sprung a leak. The captain immediately arose and took the carpenter with him into the hold, and to his great surprise found the water roaring in dreadfully. On examination he found it was a butt started and the more they endeavoured to press anything to stop it the more the plank forsook the timber. They then went on deck to encourage the people at the pumps. Captain Nicholls had made a mark with a piece of chalk to see how the water gained on them. Finding their case desperate he went to all the Frenchmen's cabins and begged of them to rise; telling them that though their lives were not in danger their help at the pumps was highly essential. They immediately got up and cheerfully assisted.

By this time it was daylight, when, to their great surprise and concern, they saw the Violet on her broadside a little distance from them; the foreyard broken in the slings, the fore-topsail set, and her crew endeavouring to free her of the mizzenmast, as it appeared she had just then broached to, by the fore-yards giving way. It came on a most violent squall for ten minutes, and when it cleared up, they found, to their great and deep concern, that the poor unfortunate Violet, with near four hundred souls, was gone to the bottom. This fatal disaster shocked even the stoutest on board the Duke William; especially as a similar fate was now threatening them.*

All the tubs before mentioned were now got together and they made gangways, the Frenchmen and women, who behaved with uncommon resolution, assisting. They then opened all the hatches

---

*According to Admiralty, Adjt. General, Misc. Various, Vol. 1, the Violet was "supposed to be lost on 12th December, 1758, while the Duke William was lost 13th December, 1758." (Archives).

and, as the water flowed fast into the hold, they filled the tubs, hauled them up, and turned them over the combings on the upper deck, which, with three pumps constantly at work and bailing out of the gun-room scuttle, must have vented a large quantity of water. A seam would not have hurt them, but a butt's end was more than they could manage; however, every method was tried which was thought of service. They quilted the sprit-sail with oakum and flax, with one of the top-gallant sails in the same manner, to see whether anything would suck into the leak to stop it, but all in vain.

They continued in this dismal situation three days; the ship, notwithstanding their endeavours, full of water and expected every minute to sink. The captain had given all the liquor that was left on board to the people, and all the provisions; the hold being full of water, and the ship swimming only by the decks being buoyed up with empty casks.

About six o'clock on the fourth morning, the people came to the captain and declared they had done all in their power; that the vessel was full of water; and that it was in vain to pump any more. The captain told them he was convinced that what they said was too true, and complimented them upon their attention and exertion. He then acquainted the priest with their situation, assuring him that every method for saving the ship and the lives of the people had been resorted to in vain and that they expected the decks would blow up every minute. The priest appeared confused, but immediately went to give his people absolution; and a melancholy scene ensued. Strong, hearty and healthy men were looking at each other, with tears in their eyes, bewailing their unhappy condition and preparing for death.

Captain Nicholls now walked upon the deck with Captain Moore, desiring him to think, if he could, of some expedient to avert their destruction. Captain Moore, with tears in his eyes, confessed that he knew of no method. Captain Nicholls proposed hoisting out the boats, that in case a ship should appear they might save their lives, as the gale was more moderate. Captain Moore thought it would be impossible, as every one would endeavour to get into them. The former captain, however, called his mates, carpenters and men, and proposed getting their boats out, at the same time acquainting them that it was to save, if possible, every soul on board, and that in case any person was to be so rash as to insist upon going into the boats, besides those whom he should think proper, he would immediately punish such person. They all solemnly declared that his commands should be as implicitly obeyed as if the ship were in her former good condition — a rare instance of obedience and submission.

The captain then went and acquainted the head prisoner whom they had on board with what they were going to attempt. He was a hundred and ten years old, was the father of the whole Island, and had a number of children, grand-children and other relatives on board. He assured the captain that he and his fellow-prisoners would assist him in anything he proposed, and the captain in return assured them that he would run the same chance with them and never desert them.

Captain Nicholls now asked Mr. Fox and the carpenter if they were willing to venture in the long-boat; they answered bravely that they were; for whether they died in the vessel or a mile or two farther was a matter of very little consequence; and as there was no prospect but death if they stayed they would willingly make the attempt. The captain then proposed to Captain Moore, the carpenter and mate, their going into the cutter, which they also agreed to. As the sea was too high to lower the boats into the water with runner and tackles, the captain told them his people should get the cutter over the side and have a proper painter made fast to her before she dropped into the water; and that they should have two axes to cut the runners and tackles when they should think the most convenient time. They accordingly got the cutter over the side, and the ship lying pretty quiet they cut the tackles and she dropped into the water very well and the painter brought her up.

They went to work then with the long-boat. Daylight now raised their spirits, and the weather was tolerably moderate. The mate and carpenter cut the runners, and the long-boat fell into the water as well as the cutter had done; and having a proper painter made fast she brought up extremely well.

There were people at the fore and main-topmast heads to look out for a sail when, to their unspeakable joy, the man at the main-topmast head cried out that he saw two ships, right astern, making after them. Captain Nicholls went and acquainted the priest and old prisoner with the good news. The latter took him in his aged arms and cried for joy. The captain ordered the ensign to be hoisted to the main-topmast shrouds, and to get the guns all clear to fire. It was very hazy and the ships were not far from them when they discovered them first.

As soon as Captain Nicholls hoisted his signal of distress they hoisted English colours, and seemed to be West Indiamen of about three or four hundred tons. They kept loading and firing as fast as possible, when they perceived that the two ships spoke each other; and setting their fore-sail and top-sails hauled their wind and made from them. Captain Nicholls imagining that the bigness of the vessel, and her having so many men on board, it being war time, might occasion a distrust, ordered the main-mast to be cut away to undeceive them. They had people all the time at the shrouds to cut away in case of necessity. One of the shrouds, not being properly cut, checked the main-mast and brought her up right athwart the boats. Captain Nicholls ran aft himself and cut both the boats' painters, or else they would have been stove to pieces and sunk immediately. A dismal thing to be obliged to cut away the only thing that could be the means of saving their lives, and afterwards to see the ships basely desert them. Driven from the greatest joy to the greatest despair, death now appeared more dreadful. They had only the fore-sail hanging in the brails, and the braces of both preventers being rendered useless by the falling off of the mainmast, and the yard flying backwards and forwards by the rolling of the ship, they were fearful she would overset entirely.

They ran from the boats till they could but just see them; and finding that they did not endeavour to join them, though they had each oars, fore-mast, and fore-sail, Captain Nicholls consulted with the boatswain on the best measures to be adopted in their deplorable situation. The captain thought that at all events they should bring the ship to, though he confessed it a terrible attempt to hazard her up-setting. The boatswain said it appeared too hazardous, as the vessel steered very well. However, finding that the men in the boats did not attempt to join them, the captain called all the people aft and told them his resolution. They declared it was desperate, but so was their condition, and that they were ready to do whatever he thought best. Captain Moore disapproved of the measure. Captain Nicholls then acquainted the priest, the old gentleman, and the rest of the people, with his intention and the motives for them. They were all pleased to say, let the consequence be what it would, they should be satisfied that he had acted for the best, they were therefore resigned to what might happen. This was a dreadful crisis; and great were Captain Nicholls' feeling when about doing that which, though in his own judgment was right, might be the means of sending four hundred persons to eternity. His resolution, however, did not forsake him.

He persevered, and gave orders to bring the ship to. In hauling out the mizzen, which had been greatly chafed, it split. Then they got a new stay-sail, and bent it to bring her to, which had the desired effect, though it was a long time before this was accomplished, and they were once afraid that they should be obliged to cut away the foremast, by a large sea striking on her starboard quarter. The next sea hove her to, and she stayed very well. When those in the yawl saw that she was lying to for them, they shipped their foremast, and ran them on board. As there was too much wind and a large sea, to sprit the sail, they came on board, holding their sheets in their hands. As soon as she came, Captain Nicholls sent some men into her to row and fetch the long-boat. They soon joined her, got her foremast up and set sail, as did the cutter; and to their great joy came safe to them.

Just as they had joined them, the people from the fore-topmast cried out, "A sail! a sail!" The captain thought it better to let the ship lie to, as, by seeing the mainmast gone they might be certain they were in distress. It was hazy weather and they could see at no great distance; but the strange ship was soon near enough to see and hear their guns. Just after she had hoisted her colours (which were Danish), her main-topsail sheet gave way, which, when Captain Nicholls saw, he concluded that the other captain was going to clew his main-topsail up, to bend it, and to come to their assistance, which good news he immediately communicated to the priest and others. In transports of joy they embraced him, calling him their friend and preserver. But, alas! poor mistaken men, this momentary joy was changed into many hours of despondency by a second disappointment; for as soon as the strange captain had knotted or spliced his topsail sheet, he sheeted it home, and hauled from them. This was about three in the afternoon. Gloomy despair then reigned in every countenance, and lamentations echoed in the air. Captain Nicholls now wore the ship, which she bore very well, and steered tolerably before the wind.

About half an hour later, the old French gentleman came to Captain Nicholls, and affectionately embracing him, said that he and his countrymen requested that the captain and his people would endeavour to save their own lives in the boats, and leave them to their fate, as it was impossible the boats could carry all. The captain replied that there was no hopes of life for any, as they had all embarked in the same unhappy voyage they ought all to take the same chance. Urged by their further solicitations, he mentioned their proposal to Captain Moore and his people, who said, as nothing further could be done, they should comply with their request. They took leave of each other with tears in their eyes, and the captain requested his people to keep the boats near the ship, which he was determined not to quit himself until it was dark. They all assured him that they would not leave him and hastened down the stern-ladder. As the boats ranged up by the sea, under the ship's counter, those that went last hove themselves down and were caught by them in the boat.

Captain Nicholls had a little Norse boy on board, whom no entreaties could prevail upon to go into the boat until he did. When it grew dark the captain insisted upon his going, saying he would follow him immediately. He got on the stern ladder, when a Frenchman whom the fears of death had induced to quit his wife and children, unperceived by any, got over the taffrail, and treading upon the boy's fingers made him shriek out. Imagining somebody was in danger, the captain went to see what was the matter, the old Frenchman following him; when the latter, perceiving the man and his intentions, called him by his name and said he was sorry to find him so base as to desert his family. The man seemed ashamed of what he had done and came over the taffrail again. The people in the boat begged the captain to come in, as the blows, which she took under the ship's counter, were likely to sink her.

Seeing the priest, the captain asked him if he were willing to take his chance with him. He replied, yes, if he had room for him. The captain told him he had. Immediately the priest went and gave his people his benediction; then after saluting the old gentleman he went into the boat.

As soon as the captain was in the boat he bade the sailors cast them adrift. It was very dark; they had neither moon nor stars to direct them. Dreadful situation! Twenty-seven in the long-boat and nine in the cutter, without victual and drink, and wholly ignorant how far they were from the English coast. It began to blow very fresh, with sleet and snow, and they agreed to keep as close to the ship as it was possible. The people from their long exertions at the pumps were very much fatigued; and after sitting a while in the wet and cold they began to wish they had stayed in the ship and perished, as now they might endure a lingering death.

The boats now began to make water, and the men being so exhausted became indifferent of their fate and refused to bail them. The captain, however, prevailed upon them to heave the water out of the long-boat. Having a brisk gale, they had run a great way from the time they had left the unfortunate ship; but at ten a. m., to their great sorrow, it fell calm, which threw the people into absolute despair. Captain Nicholls observed that the water was coloured; and asked for twine. One of the men gave him a ball which he had in his pocket. They then knocked out the bolts of the long-boat to make a deep sea lead with, and, when sounded, to their great joy they found but forty-five fathoms water.

The people now began to complain of hunger and thirst, when the captain showed that as they had nothing to eat or drink it was useless to complain. He was certain by their soundings that they were near Scilly, and did not doubt, if it cleared away, but they should see land. He begged them then to hope for the best, and bear up with manly resolution. His little Norse boy (who always kept close to the captain) now told him that he had some bread in the bosom of his shirt, but when he took it out it was like baker's dough. It was, notwithstanding, very acceptable, being about four pounds. The captain put it into his hat, and distributed it equally, calling the yawl to have their share. This, instead of being a relief, increased their troubles; for, having been so wet and clammy, it hung to the roofs of their mouths and they had nothing to wash it down. Mr. Fox had some allspice which was of very little service. One of the sailors, having a pewter spoon, they cut it into junks, and by forcing them down their throats, created a saliva, and by this means they swallowed.

A light breeze sprung up about noon at southwest. By the boats being foul of the mainmast, etc., the oars were all washed out except two in each boat. The captain, hearing a noise among the crew, inquired the reason; and having been informed that two sailors were disputing about a couple of blankets, which one of them had brought from the ship, he observed that the present was not the time for contentions, and ordered the blankets to be thrown overboard. On recollection, however, he desired them to be brought to him, as he would convert them to a purpose that would be serviceable to all. On asking for a needle and twine, which he was presently furnished with, he told them that he designed to make a mainsail of them, and requested the mate to take the remainder of the painter and unlay it; as, it being a three-strand rope, it would make them shrouds and a stay. They erected one oar for a mainmast, and the other they broke to the breadth of the blankets and made a yard of. The people in the cutter, seeing what they had done, and having a hammock with them, made a mainsail of that.

At four p. m. it cleared up, and they perceived a brig about two miles from them. Captain Nicholls now ordered the cutter to give chase and let them know their distress; for, being lighter than the long-boat, he thought that she would soon overtake them. The brig, seeing them alter their course, stood from them directly. In consequence of their strange appearance, and it being war time, she probably took them for one of the lug-sail boats which the French privateers used to frequent the islands of Scilly with. The cutter, however, gained on the brig very fast, but to the great mortification of those in the long-boat, by the time they supposed her midway, a very thick fog came on and they saw neither the brig nor the cutter any more.

Night now coming on, and it being still very foggy, the people nearly dead for want of sleep, reposed themselves, sitting half way in water, for it was impossible for so many to find seats. Captain Nicholls, anxious for the preservation of his people, endeavoured to keep his eyes open, though this was the fifth night that he had taken no rest. About eleven it cleared up. The captain thought he saw land. Everybody was asleep but the man at the helm and himself. The captain, however, was determined not to call out "land" till assured it was so. Again he thought he saw land. The man at the helm had by this time dropped asleep, and Captain Nicholls took the tiller. After some time he awoke Captain Moore and told him that he thought he saw land; but Captain Moore only answered in a tone of despondency that they should never more see land, and dropped to sleep again. Captain Nicholls then awoke Mr. Fox, who had a good sleep, and seemed quite refreshed. Mr. Fox immediately cried out that they were near land and close in with the breakers. Thus it was fortunate that Mr. Fox was awake, for in all probability they would all have perished by running on the breakers, as Captain Nicholls was totally unacquainted with them. At the word "land" everyone awoke, and, with some difficulty they cleared the rocks.

At first they could not distinguish what part of the English coast it was; but it clearing more and more every moment, Captain Nicholls looked under the lee-leach of the blanket mainsail and discovered St. Michael's Mount in Mount's Bay. The boat would not fetch the land near Penzance, and as they had no oars it was determined not to endeavour to run round the Lizard, but for Falmouth, and whatever she might chance to fetch, to run her boldly on shore. It was a fine night; and after they got round the point they found the water was smooth. They kept the boat close to the wind, and fetched between Penzance and the Mount. The joy in finding themselves in such a happy condition is not to be described; it gave them new life and strength. The people called out that there were two rocks ahead. Captain Nicholls jumped up and carried the boat between them without ever touching ground. In a little time after she ran ashore on a sandy beach.

The sailors immediately jumped into the water, and carried Captain Nicholls and the priest ashore. They left the boat as she was, making the best of their way to Penzance. Some of the people, with sleeping half way in the water, by which they were wet from head to foot, found themselves so benumbed that they with difficulty went along.

On the road, as they marched to Penzance, they fell in with a river of fresh water, of which they drank heartily and were thereby greatly revived. They got into town about three o'clock in the morning, and seeing a light in a tavern made up to it. Having been market day, the people of the inn were all gone to bed, but the mistress of the house was up. She was terribly alarmed at the sight of the strangers, and indeed their shocking appearances, together with the unseasonable hour of their visit, were sufficient cause for apprehension. On hearing their story the master of the inn got up and called his servants, who soon got for them what provisions the house afforded. After drying and refreshing themselves, as many as could find beds, went to them, and the rest slept on the floor by the fireside.

The next day Captain Nicholls went, with the priest, to the mayor of the town to make a protest before a notary, in order to get credit for the people as well as for himself, who were in want of everything necessary. Having been referred to a Mr. Charles Langford, a merchant, the captain went to him. This gentleman received Captain Nicholls very politely and asked him to breakfast with him, when the captain declined, saying he wished to breakfast with his people at the inn. The captain requested that he would furnish him with credit; but Mr. Langford declined complying with his request, as the captain was an entire stranger to him and he had already suffered from having been lately imposed upon.

Captain Nicholls finding that the master of the inn refused him credit, applied again to Mr. Langford for some money on his ring, watch, buckles, etc.; but as he was going to take his buckles out of his shoes, Mr. Langford, perceiving his tears, and believing him, he said, an honest man, told him he should have what credit he pleased. He then gave him the money he required without any deposit.

During this the second mate and eight men from the cutter arrived. They informed Captain Nicholls that in consequence of fog they could not come up with the brig; that, when it cleared, they saw the Land's End and got on shore. They had left the cutter, as nobody would buy her, and had inquired the way to Penzance, where, as they were in great distress, they were happy in having met their fellow-sufferers.

Captain Nicholls went to the inn, paid what was owing, and for their unkindness went to another house to breakfast. After this he got what necessaries the people wanted. They stayed a day longer at Penzance in order to rest themselves. The captain then having procured a carriage for himself, Captain Moore and officers, set out for Exeter. The rest of the people, who had procured a pass from the mayor, walked. At Exeter Captain Nicholls was entertained by a worthy friend of his, Samuel Kellet, Esq., collector of the customs, who sincerely sympathized with him on account of his misfortunes and the loss of the Duke William with three hundred and sixty souls. Mr. Killet provided a house, a good supper and beds for them at his own expense. They stayed in Exeter two days and then set out for London.

What is very remarkable, when Captain Nicholls and his party left the Duke William in distress, there was a small jolly-boat on board; and just before she went down, four Frenchmen threw her, with two small paddles, overboard and swam to her. They got into Falmouth soon after Captain Nicholls landed. They were no seamen, nor had ever seen the English coast, so that their's, like that of the long-boat and cutter, was a most miraculous escape. The Duke William (according to their report) swam till it fell calm, and as she went down her decks blew up. The noise was like the explosion of a gun, or a loud clap of thunder. The Frenchmen had just left her when she was seen no more.

### M. Gerard's Letter.

In addition to the account above set out, regarding the loss of the Duke William, there is a letter from M. Gerard, the former cure of Point Prim, who was on board that ship and left in the long-boat with Captain Nicholls. His letter, dated 24th January, A. D. 1759, was written on board the packet, The Canadian, in the Port of Brest. It is addressed to M. the Rev. L'Isle Dieu, Vicar-General of the Colonies of New France in Canada. Considering the terrible experience he had gone through the priest's account is singularly meagre, but so far as it goes it bears out the story of the loss of the transports with the prisoners on board. He wrote:

"Here I am, sir, resting at Brest, after having been preserved and rescued from a wreck where I nearly perished, and where three hundred persons lost their lives in an English ship which was carrying us from the Island of St. John to St. Malo after the capitulation of Louisbourg.

"I went aboard the 20th October with a fair number of inhabitants from my parish. I started from Port La Joie where the English have built a small fort and where they have left a garrison of one hundred and fifty men.

"On the 4th November we very nearly perished, but on the 13th December the ship was making water that it was impossible to keep down with four pumps and three wells. The crew were saved and I also with four of my parishioners, Acadian passengers, of whom two are married and two single.

"All the others have been buried in the sea, and that in the channel at twenty or thirty leagues from land. We happily and miraculously reached the shore of England, where we did not receive any assistance, neither from the King of England nor from the King of France, during one month and some days (not being prisoners). . . . At last we were put on board a pacquet boat for Rochelle.

"We are now resting at Brest, where we had disembarked to await the honour of your reply and your advice, but being without means we have been compelled to remain on board to live, as we have saved nothing except our body very badly clothed (books, papers and other effects lost).

"We are now unable to work, unless the Court takes notice of our sorrowful condition, after more than twenty years of service as well in Acadia, under the English, as in the Island of St. John.

"There perished in that wreck those that were the leaders in my parish, after three months in prison at Halifax.*

"You see my condition, sir, and my pitiful position. I shall not take a step until I have the honour of your reply in order to induce me to follow entirely the vocation given to me by God and which shall sufficiently appear from the wishes of my superiors concerning me, . . . persuaded always that God saved my life in order that I shall devote to Him what shall remain thereof, and wheresoever my superiors shall direct.

"I cannot give any further details for the present, sir, as I must depart from here at the first fair wind, for Rochelle, where I expect to find more assistance, but I cannot say when the wind shall be favourable, as it is very often contrary here. . . .

"(Sgd.) GERARD.
"*Missionary of the Island of St. John.*"

---

*The three months in prison, of which M. Gerard speaks above, are those which he spent in Halifax with four of his principal parishioners before leaving the parish of Cobegie aux Mines, in Acadia, under the English government. There can be seen on that point the Journal of 1753, of which a copy is in the Marine Archives. (Anonymous Note).

In the collection of the Nova Scotia Historical Society, Vol. II, p. 148, there is published "A Remarkable Circumstance respecting the French Neutrals of the Island of St. John, related by Captain Pile, of the Ship Achilles." It is as follows:

"A Captain Nicholls, commanding a transport belonging to Yarmouth, was employed by the Government of Nova Scotia to remove from the Island of St. John about three hundred French neutrals with their families. He represented to the agent before he sailed the situation of his vessel, and the impossibility there was of his arriving safe in Old France at that time of the year.

"He was nevertheless compelled to receive them on board and proceed upon the voyage. After getting within one hundred leagues of Scilly he found the ship so leaking that, with all hands employed, they were not able to prevent her sinking. Finding that she must, in a few minutes go down, and that all on board must perish if the French did not consent to the master and crew taking to the boats, by which means a small number had a chance of being saved.

"Captain Nicholls sent for the priest and told him the situation, and pointed out to him the only probable means of saving the lives of a few, of whom the priest was one.

"He accordingly harangued the Frenchmen for half an hour on the ship's deck, and gave them absolution, when they, with one consent, agreed to the master, crew and priest taking the boats and themselves to perish with the ship. One Frenchman only went into the boat, on which his wife said, 'Will you thus leave your wife and children to perish without you?' Remorse touched him, and he returned to share their fate. The ship, in a few minutes, went down and all on board perished. . . .

"The boats, after a series of distress, arrived at the port of Penzance in the west of England, Captain Nicholls afterwards commanded one of the Falmouth packets."

This, if true, imposed a most serious responsibility upon the then Government of Nova Scotia and the agent. Was it true? The writer has very grave doubts as to its truth. It is inconsistent with the facts concerning the Duke William already set forth at length. The ship was employed by the British authorities and not by the Government of Nova Scotia. She was one of a fleet of transports sailing from Cork, early in the summer of 1758, for Halifax and Louisbourg, carrying troops for the siege of the great French fortress. Her crew were landed and took part in the siege. After the capitulation she was sent, with a number of other ships, to remove the French population of over four thousand from the Island of St. John. After taking on board a number of prisoners at Port La Joie she sailed for Canso. There she took on board the prisoners who had embarked in the Parnassus, which had been lost. She sailed on 25th November, in company with six other transports, for France. They had very stormy weather and parted with the other vessels. The Duke William continued in very good order and though the sea ran mountain high, went over it like a bird and made no water. On December 10th, fifteen days after leaving Canso, they saw the Violet, which was in great distress, when they decided to stand by her till the weather should moderate. The Duke William was still "very tight and going well." Shortly afterwards the ship was struck by a terrible sea, and a plank butt started. This it was that caused the ship to go down, which she did not do for several days. It seems clear from this statement that the Duke William was in good condition when she took the prisoners on board and left Canso. The starting of the plank butt by a terrible sea could not have been foreseen or guarded against. To the writer's mind Captain Pile's story as to the condition of the Duke William is not warranted by the facts as we have them.

Some of the inhabitants were deported the following summer. Vice-Admiral Saunders, writing from the Neptune off Scatari, on 16th June, 1759, says:

"There are still at Louisbourg a number of French prisoners and inhabitants that have been maintained at great expense and have taken up much room in the hospitals that has been wanted for our own people. I have, therefore, ordered one of the victuallers which I have discharged of her prisoners, to take in such of them as Governor Whitmore may appoint and carry them to France, taking from them such English prisoners as he may be able to obtain."

Governor Whitmore, writing from Louisbourg to Mr. Pitt on 7th July of the same year, said: "There was remaining in this garrison all winter about one hundred and forty French inhabitants and a whole parish of the inhabitants of the Island of St. John, that could not be got in time to send home last fall. Early in the spring I chartered a ship to go to St. John's, together with two armed sloops, with a command of men to relieve that garrison and bring back all the French that were there, that, together with these here, they might be all sent to France according to the capitulation. And as I imagined there would be more altogether than that ship could transport, I applied to Admiral Saunders for another, that so we might get rid of all together and the public be eased of the expense of their maintenance. But on the 30th ult., the ship and one sloop returned from St. John's, and Captain Johnson, who commanded there during the winter, informed me that all the French were gone off to Canada just before our sloops got round to that part of the Island, so that I have only despatched one ship, a cartel, to Rochelle or Rochefort, viz., the William and Ann, David Wardroper, master, with ninety-six persons, and directed him to apply to the French Government for English prisoners to be brought and landed at Portsmouth or any other port in England, agreeable to Admirable Saunders' instructions to him. There are yet remaining in the hospital and of the families of some carried up the river as pilots, about forty French people in this place."

Of those who remained on the Island, there is little more to be said. From a memorandum, dated 22nd March, 1764, relating to the number of French families then remaining in Nova Scotia, who had agreed to take the oath of allegiance, we learn that "In addition to the above (*i. e.*, the families in Nova Scotia) there are three hundred on the Island of St. John's, who have lately in a solemn manner, declared the same intention as those mentioned, to the officers there in command."

Colonel Haldimand, after whom Haldimand County in Ontario is named, wished to take them to his property there. On the 2nd of December, 1765, Governor Wilmot wrote from Halifax to Captain Williams, that "Colonel Haldimand having applied to me for leave to take the Acadians on St. John's Island to settle them on his lands in the province of Canada, I very readily give my consent for so good a purpose, as under his care and inspection there's great reason to hope that they will soon be brought over to their duty and allegiance.

"Captain Haldimand's undertaking being a public good, in order to enable him to succeed more effectually, it will be necessary that the people shall be at liberty to take with them a proportion of their cattle, and that they may build as many shallops as may be sufficient to carry them up the River St. Lawrence."

This design was not carried out, and thenceforth the remaining French settlers were allowed to dwell there in peace.

On the conclusion of peace in 1763, the Island of St. John was annexed to Nova Scotia, and continued to form a part of that province until 1769, when it was erected into a separate government.

## PART IV.

## ANNEXED TO NOVA SCOTIA.

In a sense the fair appearance of the Island and the known fertility of its soil were not unmixed blessings. Scarcely was the ink on the Treaty of Paris dry when persons of influence in Great Britain, or who had claims, real or supposed, upon the government, began to petition for grants of the Island. Of these, the first and most quixotic was John, Earl of Egmont, who, in December, 1763, put in a memorial to His Majesty the King, in which he modestly states that he "desires from His Majesty a grant of the whole Island of St. John, estimated at two million acres, with all rights, royalties, privileges, franchises and appurtenances, with all civil and criminal jurisdiction." The jurisdiction was not to differ from the known rules of the common and statute law of England. Fifteen thousand two hundred acres of land were to be reserved for a capital town and for principal places of trade.

The Earl, whose name is preserved in that of Egmont Bay, was then first Lord of the Admiralty. He proposed to introduce the feudal system into the Island, where he was to be Lord Paramount. His memorial, which is of great length and detail, sets out the various tenures he proposed to establish, and the gradations in rank which were to be introduced. He summarized his proposition as follows:

### SUMMARY OF LORD EGMONT'S PROPOSALS.

Tenure for the service — one earl of the whole country; forty capital lords of forty hundreds; four hundred lords of manors; eight hundred freeholders; 800,000 acres.

Tenure for burgage, for the establishment of trade and commerce in the most proper parts of the Island — one county town, 15,200 acres; forty market towns, 20,000 acres; four hundred villages, 40,000 acres; 75,000 acres. Tenure at large in common soccage —left (at large) in common soccage, as a fund to enable the undertakers and for their encouragement to complete this plan, 1,124,800 acres; making a total of 2,000,000 acres.

Among other things he asked to have certain lands in Dominique, West Indies, annexed to the tenures of the Island of St. John. He points out how he and his adventurers might employ their capital "To purchase three thousand negroes, clear and plant at least ten thousand acres with sugar, indigo, coffee, etc., in seven years, which ten thousand acres would ever after add a produce to the trade of England of at least two hundred thousand pounds per annum, etc., etc.*

Lord Halifax (then one of His Majesty's principal Secretaries of State) on 18th January, 1764, transmitted Lord Egmont's memorial to the Lords of Trade and Plantations for their consideration and report. On 13th February that body submitted their representation back to Lord Halifax for submission to His Majesty. In their report they say: "That we have examined his Lordship's memorial with the greatest care and attention and observe that the constitution of government and plan of settlement are formed with great ability from an accurate knowledge of the ancient tenures of this kingdom, which, as they appear to have been calculated more to answer the purposes of defence and military discipline than to encourage those of commerce and agriculture are, we conceive, totally and fundamentally adverse, in their principles, to that system of settlement and tenure of property which have of late been adopted in the colonies with so much advantage to the interests of this kingdom, and, therefore, we do not see sufficient reason to justify us in advising your Majesty to comply with his Lordship's proposal." The Board recommends that the Island be settled upon the same plan with Nova Scotia to which it is annexed.

On the 23rd February, 1764, the Lords of Trade reported, recommending that Lord Egmont's prayer be not granted.

He sent in a second memorial, to which no official answer was made, and in February he sent in a third memorial, which is undated but must have been immediately after the unfavourable report by the Lords of Trade on his first petition. In this he asks on behalf "of himself and his nine children, and of a great number of land and sea officers, whose names are inserted on the other side hereof, with many persons of distinction, officers of rank in the navy and army, and others . . . to undertake the complete settle-

*Can. Archives, series M., Vol. 404, page 1.

ment of the Island of St. John's, in the Gulf of St. Lawrence, in the province of Nova Scotia, . . . prays a grant in fee of the said Island, with is appurtenances, . . . the land of the said Island to be surveyed and divided by your Majesty's surveyors, and to be parcelled out by him, the said Earl (for himself and his nine children), and the other intended adventurers, in such proportions and divisions, and upon such conditions, as have been already declared and agreed . . . to be held of your Majesty in free and common soccage, and as part of your Majesty's province of Nova Scotia, on such terms of settlement and payment of quit rents, after ten years, to Your Majesty as Your Majesty shall think fair, provided the same be no more burthensome or take place sooner than as required by any grant already made in Your Majesty's province of Nova Scotia."

On 23rd March, 1764, the Board of Trade reported, pointing out objections to his Lordship's proposals, which were not approved, and were rejected by Order-in-Council on 9th May, 1764.

But the authorities in London, whether moved by Egmont's persistent applications, or for some reason the writer has no means of knowing, now took the case of the Island into their serious consideration.

As early as November, 1763, Lord Halifax wrote to Montague Wilmott, then Governor of Nova Scotia, giving very explicit instructions as to the Islands of St. John and Cape Breton. He said:

"The Islands of St. John and Cape Breton, being annexed to the Government of Nova Scotia, are now become pressing objects of your particular care and attention. Their advantageous situation, in respect to the fishery, renders them of the greatest importance to this country and no measures should be left untried that may tend to promote and encourage the carrying on the fishery to the utmost extent it is capable of. We must desire, therefore, that you will forthwith cause an actual survey to be made of these Islands, reporting to us, in the meantime, every circumstance you can collect, which may furnish us with any information on the true state of them, in respect to their extent, the nature of the soil, the rivers and harbours in each of them, and their particular productions and advantages, with your opinion, in the fullest manner; not only what establishment may be necessary for effectually uniting them to the Government of Nova Scotia, but also what place of settlement will be the most eligible and advantageous, with respect to their situation in general and the advancement and convenience of the fishery in particular, and until this is done and you shall have received particular orders from home, you are, on no account, to make grants in these Islands to any particular persons whatever, but as much as possible to encourage and protect all temporary establishments for carrying on the fishery, taking care that such establishments, in respect to extent of coast, are within the bounds of moderation; and to discourage every attempt that may, in its natural consequences, operate as a monopoly, or as a means of establishing any undue preference whatever."

On 13th March, 1764, the Lords of Trade recommended that the Island be forthwith surveyed, and divided into counties containing, so near as the natural and proper boundaries would permit, five hundred thousand acres each. The counties were to be laid off into parishes of about one hundred thousand acres each, and each parish was to be subdivided into townships of twenty thousand acres each. Care was to be taken that each county, parish and township should be laid out so as to partake, as much as possible, of the natural advantages of the country, especially those which arise from the sea coasts, and from the sides of the navigable rivers. In each county sufficient land for a town site was to be laid out, and in each parish a proper site for a church and a sufficient quantity of land for a glebe for a minister. It was recommended that, when the survey was made and returned to the Governor of Nova Scotia, regular grants of such divisions and sub-divisions should be made, under the seal of the province, to the Earl of Egmont and his family and to each of the other memorialists, under the like regulations and conditions of cultivation and settlement as are prescribed in his Majesty's instructions in respect of grants of land in other parts of said province. And it was also recommended that, with the exception of the Earl and his nine children, no one person should get more than twenty thousand acres.

They go on to say that the Island is particularly valuable for its soil as well as situation, and that they had the design to raise a higher revenue of quit rents from this Island than from other parts of Nova Scotia, and that certain merchants had agreed to accept grants at three shillings a hundred acres, being an addition of one shilling. They further state to His Majesty that they have been informed that there are cleared lands consisting of many thousand acres in the most fertile parts. They recommended that out of any grants there should be reserved all mines of gold, silver, copper, lead and coal, and a sufficient breadth on the sea coast from high water mark for the accommodation of all his Majesty's subjects carrying on the fisheries, for which the coasts of the Island are so advantageously situated, together with proper accommodation for the fishing of sea-cows, which, they understand, abounded on some parts of the coast.

In the following May, Admiral Holmes and his associates memoralized His Majesty, praying that, inasmuch as Lord Egmont's proposal had not been approved, the whole Island of St. John should be granted, in lots of twenty thousand acres each, to them, and they would engage to complete the settlement of the Island within ten years.

The following from a diary kept by one Smethurst in 1763 is not without interest. He says: "I was the first Briton who attempted a fishery on the Island of St. John. I had raised two storehouses at St. Peter's, and had employed most of the people on the Island in the fishery; I had likewise brought a crew from Marblehead in New England to cause an emulation. . . .

"The land (on the mainland) from Bay Verte to Pictou, along the sea coast, is very good deep, red mould; better land than on the Island of St. John, which is opposite it. The land on this Island is in general very light land; will sooner make a show of vegetation, but is not so strong and deep as the land upon the continent, which will last longer. There has been a fire about seventy years ago which passed almost through the whole Island and burnt up a great deal of the soil, so that you soon come to the gravel; and their salt marshes are good for little, being spungy, mossy ground. Up some of the rivers and in some of the bays, the land is better and the soil deeper.

"I was called to this Island to examine and put a stop to depredations made in the white pine timber, at a place called 'Three Rivers.' I found them destroying the finest groves of white pine that America could boast of."

He then presents affidavits that several Acadians had been employed to cut down white pine timber at Three Rivers on the

Island of St. John, that they had cut down and felled upwards of twelve hundred white pine trees; and that more than two hundred of the said trees were more than two feet through at the butt where they were cut, which was about two and one-half feet from the earth; and that *all the said pine trees*, so cut and felled, grew within less than one hundred and fifty yards of high water mark.

This shows the excellent pine that formerly grew on the Island, and incidently shows that the great fire could not have over-run the Three Rivers section of country, as the pine, in the period that had elapsed since that fire, could not have grown to the size described by Smethurst.

By a Royal proclamation dated 7th October, A. D. 1763, of His Majesty King George III, the Islands of St. John and Cape Breton were annexed to Nova Scotia. Up to this time no plan of settlement had been adopted. But now, 1764, a general survey of British North America was ordered, and Captain Samuel Holland was commissioned as Surveyor-General "for making an accurate survey of the northern district upon the continent of America." This district was to embrace, "All His Majesty's territories in North America which lie to the north of the Potomac River and of a line drawn due west from the head of the main branch of that river, as far as his Majesty's dominions extend."

Cape Breton, the Island of St. John and the Magdalens, being of greatest importance, on account of the fisheries, were to be surveyed first, beginning with the Island of St. John and the Magdalens.

A full report giving a careful description of the country and its capabilities, was to accompany the map. It was pointed out how the Island was to be divided, and what should be the areas of the townships, parishes and counties. A staff of assistants was appointed to accompany him, and as soon as the vessel assigned for the service was ready he was to enter upon the survey. This was a merchant vessel named the Canceaux, of two hundred tons, armed and manned with forty men. They probably sailed from Plymouth. On 11th July, near Scatari, Cape Breton, in a thick fog, they narrowly escaped shipwreck. Holland landed and went over land with despatches for General Murray, arriving in Quebec ten days ahead of the Canceaux. After making repairs the Canceaux sailed on 14th September and arrived at the northwest part of the Island on 5th October,* (1764) Holland began the survey the same autumn and completed it in 1766.

The following description of the Island is taken from a letter written by Captain Holland, at the time of its survey in 1765.

"The woods upon the north coast, from the East Point as far southward as the Hillsborough River, and to Bedford Bay on the west, was entirely destroyed by fire, about twenty-six years since. It was so extremely violent, that all the fishing vessels at St. Peter's and Morell were burned. In many parts round the Island is rough steep coast, from forty to sixty-feet high — in some places a hundred — composed of stratas of a soft red stone, which, when exposed to the air for some time, becomes harder, and is not unfit for building. Wherever this sort of coast is, it diminishes considerably every year upon the breaking up of the frost, which moulders away a great part of it. It may probably be owing to this cause that the sea betwixt the Island and the continent is frequently of a red hue, and for that reason by many people called the Red Sea; on the north and southeast side, it has received some addition by the banks of sand which the sea has thrown up.

" . . . The rivers are properly sea creeks, the tides flowing up to the heads, where generally streams of fresh water empty themselves. In most parts of the Island the sarsaparilla root is in great abundance and very good. The mountain-shrub and maiden-hair are also pretty common, of whose leaves and berries the Acadians and soldiers frequently make a kind of tea.

" . . . . With proper care, it produces most kinds of grain, wheat, barley, oats, peas, beans, etc.; also cabbage, cauliflower and potatoes, very good in great abundance; carrots, turnips, etc. In those places which have been settled, and are still tolerably cleared, is very good grass; but a great part of the lands formerly cleared are so much over-grown with brush and small wood that it will be extremely difficult to form a true estimate of the cleared lands, or to make it fit for the plough again. It may be proper to observe here that very few houses . . . are good for anything, and by no means tenantable, except one or two at St. Peter's kept in repair by the officers, and one built by me at Observation Cove.

---

*H. J. Cundall, Prince Edward Island Magazine, Vol. 1, page 250.

## Timber.

"Red and white oak, neither of which are in plenty, or of large growth; beech and maple very good; black and white birch, the former of which is a useful and handsome wood. The pine is extremely large and fine. In some places is found the curled maple, which takes an excellent polish. Spruce of many kinds is the universal produce of the whole Island; from one species of which is got the balsam of Canada, which the Canadians hold in great repute. . . .

## Best Harbours for Trade and Fishery, and Why.

"Port Joy, Cardigan and Richmond Bay are without dispute the only places where ships of burden can safely enter, and consequently the most proper to erect the principal towns and settlements upon. In point of fishing, Richmond has much the advantage of situation; the fish being in great plenty most part of the year, and close to the harbour. Ships outward bound from any of the above ports have their choice of two passages out of the Gulf of St. Lawrence, viz.; the Gut of Canso, or round the North Cape of the Isle of Cape Breton, either of which they prefer, as the weather, season of the year, or port bound to, may make it most advisable. Such parts of the Island on the southwest coast, or the places inland, not conveniently situated for fishing, may and undoubtedly will turn to a general good account, if proper encouragement be given to settlers, whose business is the cultivation of lands only — and upon the settling of the Island I would humbly recommend that this particular branch of people should receive the utmost encouragement; the great length and severity of the winters making it extremely expensive and difficult to provide for their stock, as that season is of very little use to them; besides the very short time they have for ploughing, sowing, reaping and making hay of, will take up their attention so closely while the good weather continues that it must of course make the great point of clearing the Island go on but slow.

## Reasons for Location of Chief Towns.

"The capital, called Charlottetown, is proposed to be on a point of the harbour betwixt York and Hillsborough Rivers, as being one of the best, and nearly a centrical part of the Island; has the advantages of an immediate and easy communication with the interior part of the Island, by means of the three fine rivers of Hillsborough, York and Elliot. The ground designed for the town and fortifications is well situated upon a regular ascent from the water-side; a fine rivulet will run through the town; a battery or two, some distance advanced, will entirely command the harbour; an enemy attempting to attack the town cannot do it without great difficulties, viz., having passed the batteries at the entrance of the harbour, they must attempt a passage up Hillsborough or York Rivers, the channels of both of which are intricate, and the entrance of the respective channels will be so near the town that it must also be attended with the greatest hazard. Should they land any troops on either side of the Bay of Hillsborough, they must still have the river of the same name on the east, or Elliot and York rivers on the west, to pass, before they could effect anything of consequence, As this side of the Island cannot have any fishery, it may probably be thought expedient to indulge it with some particular privileges; and as all judicial and civil, as well as good part of the commercial business will be transacted here, it will make it at least equally flourishing with the county town.

## Georgetown.

"Recommended to be built upon that point of land called Cardigan Point, there being a good harbour for ships of any burthen on each side of Cardigan River on the north, or Montague River upon the south side; but the latter, though a much narrower channel upon coming in, is preferable, as the bay for anchoring will be close by the town. Immediately upon entering the river, and going around the Goose Neck, a long point of dry sand running half over the river, and forming one side of Albion Bay, the place for anchorage on the Goose Neck, may be erected a pier with great ease and at a small expense, where goods could be shipped and unshipped with facility and convenience."

"The place proposed for the town is so situated as to require very little difficulty in making it secure, as well as the entrance into the two respective harbours. It ought not to be omitted mentioning the advantage it has of a communication inland by means of Cardigan, Brudenell and Montague Rivers, from the top of which last to the source of Orwell River is not quite ten miles; and Orwell River, emptying itself into the great Bay of Hillsborough, makes a safe and short communication betwixt two of the county towns both winter and summer."

Mr. John McGregor, writing in 1828, sixty years later than Holland, describing Georgetown, says:

"Very little has been done, as yet, towards forming a town in this place, although it has often been pointed out as better adapted for the seat of government than Charlottetown. It has, certainly, a more immediate communication with the ocean, but is not so conveniently situated for an intercourse with many parts of the Island."*

### PRINCETOWN.

"Besides the advantages mentioned of Richmond Bay, it is proposed to be built on a most convenient spot of ground as well for its fisheries as fortifications, being situated on a peninsula, having Darnley Bay on the northeast, which is a convenient harbour for small vessels, and where they may be laid up to winter; lying at the entrance to Richmond Bay, with all the convenient grounds of curing and drying of fish about it, and ships of burthen can anchor near in the bay. For its fortifications the neck of land can be strengthened with little expense, and some batteries and small works erected along the shore will entirely secure it."

### ANIMALS, FISH AND FOWL. (†)

Captain Holland was an observant man, and it is of interest to compare his account of the birds, game and fish of the Island with that of the French travellers who preceded him. He tells us that "here are bears, otters, martens, foxes, red, black and grey, lynxes or wild cats, minks, muskrats, and some, though very few, caribou, a kind of a deer; hares extremely good, but in the winter are white. Of birds, may be accounted the eagles of their several species, though not very common; hawks, partridges, a kind of a thrush called robins, in great abundance, who sing very agreeably; of birds of passage there are a great variety, as doves, which come

---

*McGregor, Historical and Descriptive Sketch of the Maritime Colonies of British America, London, 1828. Account of Prince Edward Island, pages 6 and 7.
†P. E. I. Mag. Vol. III, p. 169, 170.

in July and August, corbejeaux, a kind of a woodcock, which fly together in large flocks; plover, snipes, curlews, outards, a large and fine sort of wild goose; the brant goose, a smaller sort but of excellent flavour; ducks of many kinds, teal, moyagues, cacois, marchaux, cacoas, carmes de roche, goilans, esterlets, margotts, godes, sea pigeons, perrigains, etc., many of which are peculiar to this climate. Several of these, as well as the caribou, are no longer to be found in the Island, and not even their names are now known. In the winter there is scarce a bird to be seen except partridges and some few straggling wild fowl, who either wait to breed or are else crippled, and are disabled from accompanying the rest upon their return. Fish — both sea and river fish there is in great abundance, and extremely good, viz., cod, turbot, hollybut, thomback, sturgeon, plaice, flounders, mackerel, and gaspereaux, a kind of a mackerel, but smaller, and often used as bait for codfish. In the rivers and lakes are also very fine trout and eels, smelts; also in Morell River are some salmon; along the coast and in the rivers are lobsters, oysters and mussels extremely good and in great plenty, besides a shellfish they call clams, and another named razor-fish — in short for beasts, birds and fish, no place can wish to be more plentifully stored, though the chase of them is attended with difficulty and trouble, and require much patience."

McGregor, with whose account it is interesting to compare the older descriptions of Holland, says: "The principal native quadrupeds are bears, loup-cerviers, foxes, hares, martens, otters, musquashes, minks and squirrels.

"The bear is jet black in colour. For many years after the settlement of the colony they were extremely mischievous and hurtful to the inhabitants, destroying black cattle, sheep and hogs. Their numbers are now much reduced and a bear is rarely met with.

"Foxes are numerous. . . . Hares are in great abundance — their flesh very fine, at least equal to that of the English hare. The marten is a beautiful animal. . . . Otters are the same species as in Europe, but the fur is rather finer." . . .

"Wild pigeons arrive in great flocks in summer from the southward and breed in the wood.*

"The oysters are considered the finest in America, and equally as delicious as those taken on the English shores. There are two

---
*The wild pigeon is now extinct.

or three varieties, the largest of which is from six to twelve inches long.*

CLIMATE.

"The time of setting in of the frosts in winter and their breaking up in the spring is very uncertain, sometimes being a difference of three or four weeks. In general it is observed that about October there usually begins to be frosts morning and evening, which gradually increase in severity till about the middle of December, when it becomes extremely sharp; at this time a northwest wind, with small sleet, seldom fails. In a little time the rivers on the Island are frozen up, and even some distance from the land, upon the sea coast, the ice soon becomes safe to travel upon, and is at least from twenty-two or twenty-four to thirty inches thick. The snow upon the ground and in the woods is often a surprising depth, and no possibility of passing except upon snow shoes. The Acadians now have recourse to little cabins or huts in the woods, where they are screened from the violence of the weather, and at the same time have the convenience of wood for fuel so near them. Here they live upon the fish they have cured in the summer, and other game which they frequently kill, as hares, partridges, lynxes, or wild cats, otters, martens or muskrats, none of which they refuse to eat, as their necessity presses them. In the spring the rivers seldom break up till April, and the snow is not entirely off the ground till the middle of May. It ought to be observed here, that as St. John's is fortunately not troubled with fogs as the neighbouring Islands of Cape Breton and Newfoundland, neither is it so settled and constant a climate as Canada; here is quick and frequent change of weather, as rain, snow, hail and hard frosts, which sometimes succeed each other in a very small space of time.

"The respective divisions of the Island are as near as possible, agreeably to my instructions; the divisions of the counties, parishes and townships, bounded by the magnetic north and south, or east and west lines, being the most easy way of running the lines for the surveyors that will be employed on this service, the natural situation of the Island having favoured this method. It is not possible to divide the counties or parishes into more equal parts, as the lines

*McGregor, pages 24 and seq.

would otherwise have been too much confounded and confused; it has also been observed in dividing the townships to give them a share of what natural advantages the Island afforded. The two lots that could not be brought to any township are left undetermined. There are 520 acres reserved for the first lot, having 1,000 yards to the north, south and west from the centre of Fort Amherst, and to the east as far as the water side; but it must also be remarked that the first lot takes up almost all the cleared lands of Fort Joy.

"The scale proposed to work with I was obliged to alter to that of 4,000 feet to a yard, as we found that sufficiently large and expressive; but should any part be required to be of a still larger scale, it shall be done whenever ordered. . . . Throughout the whole survey has been observed the greatest exactness; and all rivers and creeks are surveyed as far as a boat or canoe would go, or the chainman penetrate, but sometimes we were compelled to stop by inaccessible woods and swamps."*

(Sgd.) SAMUEL HOLLAND.

Island of St. John's, Observation Cove,
    October 5th, 1765.

McGregor writing of the climate says: "It is said in Pennsylvania that it is a compound of all the countries in the world. In Lower Canada, the houses cannot be kept comfortable without stoves. In Prince Edward Island, a common English fire-place is sufficient to keep a room warm, and stoves are by no means general."†

The survey being made, the plan, already outlined, of granting the Island to persons applying, was then carried out, but owing to the number of such applicants it was decided that the townships should be drawn in a lottery, which was done before the Board of Trade in London, and in this way all the townships, except numbers 40 and 59, were allotted to different persons, and thus was foisted upon this Island that proprietory or landlord system which was the cause of continual turmoil and agitation until it was finally abolished in 1877.

The method of granting the lots was as follows: The Board of Trade ordered all petitioners for grants to appear before them personally or by deputy, on the 17th and 23rd of June and 1st July,

---
*Prince Edward Island Magazine, 1901, Vol. III, 121, 169.
†Account of Prince Edward Island note.

1767, in support of their respective claims. During these days, after hearing parties, they selected those whose claims seemed preferable, and on the 8th July the list was completed and finally adopted. The balloting took place on the 23rd of July, 1767, in the presence of the Board. The name of each applicant was written on a slip of paper or ticket and put in the balloting box, the lots being granted in running numbers, as they were drawn.*

The Report of the Lords Commissioners of Trade and Plantations and His Majesty's Order-in-Council approving the same, dated 26th August, 1767, after reciting former petitions and orders, went on to say:

"The Lords Commissioners of Trade and Plantations having proceeded to carry into execution the plan approved of by Your Majesty on 9th May, 1764, according to what they conceived to be the spirit and intention of that plan, they begged leave to annex to their report a copy of the proceedings upon the whole of this business, containing the names of the persons to whom the several townships in the said Island as laid out upon the survey are granted, the particular townships (expressed by numerical figures), referring to the survey itself annexed to their proceedings, which in consequence of a *ballot* taken before the Lords Commissioners are to be granted to the several proponents; the conditions and reservations on which the lands are to be held, and the manner and form in which the town lots, reserved on the said survey, are to be laid out and granted. And the Lords of the Committee, having this day taken into consideration the report of the Lords Commissioners for Trade and Plantations, together with their proceedings on the whole of their business, do agree humbly to report as their opinion that it may be advisable for Your Majesty to approve and confirm the same, and to order that a copy of the minute of the Lords Commissioners for Trade and Plantations should be transferred to the Governor or Commander-in-Chief of Your Majesty's Province of Nova Scotia, with directions to him to carry the several regulations therein named into execution, and to pass grants of the several townships to the several persons who are entitled thereto, upon they or their agents producing an order from Your Majesty in Council for that purpose.

---

*Campbell, page 18, note.

"His Majesty, taking the said report into consideration, was pleased, with the advice of his Privy Council, to approve thereof, and also to approve and confirm the said proceedings of the Lords Commissioners for Trade and Plantations, and to order, and it is hereby ordered that a copy of the said proceedings be transmitted to the Governor or Commander-in-Chief of his Majesty's Province of Nova Scotia, who is hereby required to carry into execution the several regulations therein, and agreeably thereto to pass grants of the several townships in the said Island of St. John to the respective persons who are entitled thereto, upon they or their agents producing an order from His Majesty in Council for that purpose. And the Governor or Commander-in-Chief of the said Province of Nova Scotia, for the time being, and all others whom it may concern, are to take notice and govern themselves accordingly."

Writing from Whitehall, on 26th February, 1768, to Lieutenant Governor Francklin of Nova Scotia, Lord Hillsborough, one of His Majesty's Secretaries of State, says:

" . . . With this letter you will receive His Majesty's Order-in-Council for carrying into execution a plan for the settlement of the Island of St. John. His Majesty considers this as a service of very great importance, and as such I have it in command from His Majesty to recommend it to your care and attention.

"The directions contained in the resolution of the Lords of Trade annexed to this order are so full and precise as to render any further instructions unnecessary. His Majesty trusts that the zeal and fidelity of his officers in Nova Scotia, in carrying this useful plan into execution, will be found to correspond with the attention which has been given to it by his servants here.

"His Majesty is sensible that in order to render this plan of settlement effectual and productive of those public advantages which are the special objects of it, it will be necessary that it should be accompanied with such civil establishment as shall correspond with the policy which is adopted in the distribution of the property. You will, therefore, give the fullest attention to this important consideration and report to me for His Majesty's information what shall occur to you as necessary to be finally and permanently established in this respect; taking care, in the meantime, to make such temporary regulations as that His Majesty's subjects, who shall become settlers in consequence of the grants now to be issued, have a full and complete participation of those benefits enjoyed by His Majesty's other subjects in the continental parts of Nova Scotia under the present form of government established therein."

A term of the grants was, that quit rents of six shillings per hundred acres should be paid on some townships, four shillings on others and two shillings on the remainder, payment on half to begin in five years from the date of the grant and on the whole at the expiration of ten years. The proprietors were also to settle their townships within ten years, in the proportion of one person for every two hundred acres, and if one-third were not settled within four years, then the whole was to be forfeited to His Majesty. In 1767, a mandamus for each township or section of a township was issued to the grantee by whom it was drawn.

There were other conditions, but the two relating to quit rents and settlement were the most important, and were the ones which were the cause of trouble for the next century. During this long period the proprietory system, or the "Land Question," as it was usually called, was the burning question in Prince Edward Island politics. It will be referred to again, when treating of the Island after its separation from Nova Scotia.

## Charlottetown, Georgetown, Princetown.

In May, 1768, Lieutenant-Governor Francklin took measures for laying out the sites of the proposed towns in the Island of St. John. He directed Hon. Charles Morris, Chief Surveyor of the Province of Nova Scotia, to proceed immediately to Charlottetown with officers of Government, artificers, etc., where Captain Williams or the officer commanding at Fort Amherst was instructed to assist him with the troops under his command, whether as pioneers, boatman or otherwise. As soon as he had examined the ground and determined on the site upon which Charlottetown was to be located, the town plots and house lots are to be laid out, he was to give directions to the proper officers to land the lumber, stores and provisions for the erection of a shed sufficient to lodge himself and the other officers of Government, conformably to plan furnished.

He was directed in laying out the town to conform to His Majesty's instructions, an extract from which was given him. In addition to the several public buildings directed to be laid out by him, parcels of land were to be reserved for the following public uses, viz., for an ordnance yard and for King's stores situated conveniently for the water; for building barracks for the lodgment of troops; for a Province House and Gardens; for a burying ground; for a parsonage house; for a court house; and as the houses will, for many years to come be composed of wood, subject to fire, and as the breadth of the streets may, in a great measure, prevent its spreading when these accidents happen, I am to desire that the centre or main street be one hundred feet wide and that all the other streets be not less than eighty feet wide. If the ground would permit, one thousand feet all round the house lots was to be reserved.

When he laid out the pasture lots one hundred acres were to be reserved for the Province House. Mr. Franklin also recommended that all the pasture lots be laid out between the reserve at the back of the town and the common, and that the common consist of five hundred acres.

The Chief Surveyor was further instructed, immediately on his arrival, to despatch one of his assistants to lay out such township or townships as may be desired by the agents of the proprietors, always preferring those who have settlers arrived ready to go on the land.

Captain Holland was desired to be ready to repair to Charlottetown to give what information he could, if he should be required.

After having laid out the town plot of Charlottetown the Chief Surveyor was ordered to proceed, in like manner, to the laying out of Georgetown and Princetown, conformably to His Majesty's instructions.

Mr. Deschamps, who was appointed first magistrate of the Island and was to superintend the settlement, was instructed to proceed thither by way of Tatamagouche.

Francklin, who was clearly a very energetic administrator, writing to General Gage on 18th May, 1768, says that he was then despatching the necessary civil officials to the Island, and as they would need the assistance of the troops posted at Fort Amherst, to act as artificers, pioneers or otherwise, together with any craft there belonging to the King, he asked for the General's orders to the commanding officer for the purpose. He further requested that Lieutenant Marr, the engineer, survey the road from Halifax to Tatamagouche, distant about eighty miles, where he had required a subaltern's command to be posted and a vessel directed to transport the detachment, with the necessary artificers and material to build a block house there, covered by a redoubt, which would be an effectual check to the savages of that coast, as they rendezvous in that neighbourhood. Some of whom, no longer than last fall menaced the inhabitants of Pictou, who were lately settled there, saying the lands were theirs and they would not allow any settlement to be made. The distance from Tatamagouche to Cobequid, the head of the southeast branch of the Bay of Fundy, is in all, about twenty-two miles, where are upwards of one hundred families well settled, who will be capable of furnishing many supplies and refreshments to the new settlers of Charlottetown, it being the nearest port and distant about ten leagues only, so that, on the whole, we shall not have more than one hundred and ten or twenty miles by land and water from Halifax to Charlottetown.

## Isaac Deschamps, First Justice of the Court of Common Pleas.

On 20th May, 1768, Francklin wrote Isaac Deschamps that he had "thought fit with the advice of His Majesty's Council to appoint him the first Justice of the Court of Common Pleas for the Island with a salary of £200 per annum." At the same time the new Justice was appointed superintendent of the settlement to be carried on there, with orders to forthwith proceed to the Island. As he would be put to considerable expense in carrying on this service he was to be allowed an additional seven shillings and sixpence per diem, during such superintending.

As he went from Windsor, where he had resided, by way of Cobequid and Tatamagouche to Charlottetown, the capital of the Island of St. John, Deschamps was ordered, on his arrival at Cobequid, to apply to the magistrate, whose residence is nearest the road designed to be carried from Halifax to Tatamagouche, and fix a permanent plan with him for his forwarding all public despatches and expresses to and from Halifax which may be sent to him. Acadians on the Island might be employed as men to clean the streets of wood, etc.

He was instructed to show all the countenance possible to intending settlers, seeing that they met with as little delay as possible in being placed on their lands; and, where it could conveniently be done, call upon them at their habitations, which never fails to greatly encourage new beginners in a strange country. He was also to give all possible encouragement to the fishery and to those who are inclined and intend to carry it on. He was, without fail, to report the number of people on the Island, what they are about and by whom they are employed. Particular instructions were given him to receive the oath of allegiance to the King from such of the Acadians, who are on the Island, as choose to take it, to whom he should signify His Majesty's most gracious assurance of favour and protection, in the same manner as done by those of Kings County and Windsor, the place of his former residence. Those taking the oaths might have lots in either of the towns on the Island with pasture lots in the same manner.

On the other hand the Acadians who remained obstinate and adhered to their old prejudices and attachments to the French King are to be told they would not be allowed to remain on the Island.

In 1770, Deschamps was appointed assistant justice of the Supreme Court of Nova Scotia, in place of Mr. Duport, appointed Chief Justice of the Island of St. John.

### DETAIL OF FRANCKLIN'S MEASURES.

On receipt of the Secretary of State's despatch Lieutenant-Governor Francklin directed the Chief Surveyor to prepare for his departure to the Island. He called the Council together, to whom he communicated the orders he had received respecting the settlement of St. John's Island. After mature deliberation the Council advised that Charlottetown be the capital. A commission for holding a Court of Common Pleas and a General Session of the Peace at Charlottetown was issued, which Court should have jurisdiction over the whole Island, subject to appeal to the Supreme Court at Halifax as had been the practice, hitherto, by the other County Courts. Officials of government, with salaries conformable to an estimate made, should forthwith be sent to reside in Charlottetown, where temporary sheds were to be built to lodge them. A vessel was to transport the Chief Surveyor and the other officers with the necessary stores and materials for building the sheds. The Council advised that an exact survey of the road from Halifax to Tatamagouche be made, and that the Colonel commanding His Majesty's troops be applied to for a detachment to be posted at the latter place.

On 21st May, the Chief Surveyor with two assistants and several other civil officials sailed for Charlottetown with the artificers and materials for erecting the temporary sheds, to whom the Lieutenant-Governor gave the necessary instructions. The same day the first magistrate set forth from Windsor, whence he was to repair to Tatamagouche to embark for Charlottetown.

Francklin also despatched Lieutenant Marr of the Engineers to make a survey of Tatamagouche road, with directions to frame an estimate of the expense of building it. To General Gage he wrote desiring him to order the officer commanding the troops at Fort Amherst to assist the civil officials of the government. He also applied to Commander Hood to station one of the King's ships in the neighbourhood of Charlottetown, with orders to render any assistance that may be required. He further proposed to advertise on the continent of America, setting forth the advantageous situation of the Island for the fishery, that house and pasture lots would be given to settlers in any one of the three towns and that temporary licenses of occupation would be given to all persons to make and cure fish on the sea coast.

On 29th May, 1768, Francklin submitted to Lord Hillsborough an estimate (No. 3) of the expenses conceived to be necessary for the erection of several public buildings at Charlottetown and for the purchase of a vessel and a boat for the use of the Island. Another estimate (No. 4) also submitted showed what would be, finally and permanently, the establishment of the Island, as there are several appointments not included in the temporary establishment. He proposed that the supreme magistracy, or command of the Island of St. John, be in the Lieutenant-Governor of Nova Scotia for the time being, who should constantly reside upon it while the Governor-in-Chief remained in the province, in whose absence the Lieutenant-Governor must repair to the provincial seat of government during the time of such absence.

He pointed out that it was highly expedient that a clergyman of the Church of England be established there as soon as possible, that the persons to become settlers may perceive that His Majesty pays the earliest attention to their religious as well as their civil concerns.

A small decked schooner or boat was extremely necessary, together with a row boat, to be on the establishment of the Island to answer the purpose of carrying expresses and despatches on emergent occasions of His Majesty's service, from the Island of St. John to the continent, as well as to transport the Lieutenant-Governor from one settlement to another, until there are proper roads of communication, as no one measure contributes to give life and spirits to new settlers more than their being visited and enquired after by the officer of government who is in command.

He suggested that a respectable body of troops should be stationed on the Island at such places as may be thought proper, whose headquarters should be in Charlottetown, for which the small detachment of two companies at present posted at Fort Amherst would, in no wise, be sufficient to prevent the mistrusts and fears of safety, however groundless, that people are generally possessed of on their first coming into a new uncultivated country. And for the same reason, if a small ship of war from the fleet in North America was stationed for the whole year about the Island, to have her general rendezvous and winter quarters at Charlottetown, it would not only give spirits to the settlers and assist to establish the capital, but would also be a means of preventing an illicit trade with the Islands of St. Pierre and Miquelon, whose vicinity will be a great temptation to carry on a smuggling trade.*

---

*Enclosed in the despatch from which the above is abstracted, Francklin sent these four estimates to Lord Hillsborough: "Island of St. John.

"ESTIMATE No. 1, 29TH MAY, 1768.— Temporary Establishment, which the Lieutenant-Governor has now carried into execution and granted commissions accordingly:

| | |
|---|---:|
| "Isaac Deschamps, Esq., the first Justice, per annum | £200.00.0 |
| "Jonathan Binney, Esq., Naval Officer | 136.17.6 |
| "Thomas Proctor, Provost Marshal | 91. 5.0 |
| "Lauchlan Campbell, Registrar of Deeds | 91. 5.0 |
| "John Moreau, Clerk of the Crown | 50. 0.0 |
| "Alexander Morris, 2 Assistant Surveyors at £91.5.0 | 182.10.0 |
| "Samuel Morris, Chairman for Do | 48. 0.0 |
| "The First Justice, as Superintendent for table money during his Superintendency at " 7/6 per diem | 136.17.6 |
| "Michael Head, Surveyor, 5s. per diem | 91. 5.0 |
| | £1,028. 0.0 |

## HISTORY OF PRINCE EDWARD ISLAND. 139

In 1768 the proprietors petitioned the King to erect the Island into a separate government, and proposed to provide for the expenses of the establishment out of the quit rents, one half of which they expressed themselves willing to pay, from the first of May, 1769, the other half to be deferred for twenty years. In their memorial, the proprietors expressed their desire to fulfil the Royal intentions in the grants His Majesty had been pleased to make of the Island, by the most speedy and effectual settlement of the same. If properly encouraged the Island must become a place of great advantage both to Great Britain and the colonies, as well from its position with regard to the fisheries and the fertility of the soil so well adapted to the production of corn, hemp, masts and naval stores; as from the excellence of its bays and harbours. Yet

REMARKS RE ABOVE.— "Isaac Deschamps, Esq., first Justice and Superintendent, has been years Justice of the Court of Common Pleas in King's County and has generally transacted the Public Business concerning the new settlements in that County and has been greatly serviceable on many occasions."

"Jonathan Binney, one of the Members of His Majesty's Council, Collector of His Majesty's Customs and Collector of the Provincial duties at Canso."

"Thomas Proctor, son of Charles Proctor, Esq., many years an officer in the Army and a settler in the Province with a large family."

"Lauchlan Campbell, a young man of good character particularly recommended to the Lieutenant-Governor by Lord William Campbell."

"John Moreau, son of the worthy Missionary at Lunenburg, brought up in the Secretary's office, and who understands the French language."

"Alexander Morris and Samuel Morris, sons of Charles Morris, Esq., Chief Surveyor, young men of good character brought up to that business in his office."

"Michael Head has been for some time Assistant Surgeon at Lunenburg upon the establishment now required to be struck off."

ESTIMATE NO. 2.— Of expenses to be immediately incurred for carrying on the Settlement Enclosed in Lieutenant-Governor Francklin's letter of 29th May, 1768, to Lord Hillsborough:

"Hire of the vessels, the one to carry the Officials of Government, artificers and part of the materials for building the sheds, with tools, etc., and the other to carry the troops to Tatamagouche with the artificers and materials for erecting a Block-House, etc., supposed to be.............................................. £250.0.0
Cost of material for building, tools, etc........................................ 400.0.0
Provisions and Stores........................................................... 100.0.0
Allowances to Overseers, Artificers and Labourers, employed to erect buildings, cut down timber, clear streets, etc............................................ 500.0.0
The expense of boats and other small craft, supposed to be.................... 100.0.0

£1,350.0.0

ESTIMATE No. 3.— Enclosed in same letter. For public buildings, Charlottetown, and for small vessels and a proper boat, House for the Lieutenant-Governor and officers................................................................... £1,000.0.0
Ditto for a Church............................................................. 500.0.0
Ditto for Court House and Prison............................................... 500.0.0
A vessel of about 40 tons...................................................... 200.0.0
For a boat for the Lieutenant-Governor......................................... 50.0.0

£2,250.0.0

the settlement of this Island will be retarded by its dependence on Nova Scotia, as no legal decisions can be obtained nor any matter of property determined without a voyage to Halifax (where the superior courts and the public offices are held), which, in winter, is impracticable on account of the ice. This is attended with great detriment both to the trader and planter. That settlers are deterred from coming to a place so circumstanced. These inconveniences would be renedied and settlement become speedy and certain if this Island were formed into a separate government.

The memorial having been referred to the Committee of the Privy Council, that Committee on 28th June, 1768, took it into consideration. They were of opinion that under proper restrictions and conditions, the carrying of the proposition into effect might be of public advantage and promote the settlement of the Island. They ordered it to be referred to the Lords Commissioners for Trade and Plantations, and in case their Lordships could suggest

(Enclosed in same.) ESTIMATE No. 4.— Island of St. John.

"An estimate of a final and permanent Civil Establishment for the Island of St. John.

"For the Lieutenant-Governor of the Province of Nova Scotia for the time being, whatever salary His Majesty shall be graciously pleased to appoint.

| | |
|---|---|
| "For the first Justice and Custos Rotulorum of the Island...................... | £200. 0.0 |
| "For a King's Attorney..................................................... | 100. 0.0 |
| "For a Secretary to the Lieutenant-Governor and Clerks........................ | 200. 0.0 |
| "For the Naval Officer..................................................... | 136.17.0 |
| "For the Registrar of Deeds................................................ | 91. 5.0 |
| "For two Assistants Surveyors of land and Chainman.......................... | 230.10.0 |
| "For a Provost Marshal..................................................... | 91. 5.0 |
| "For the Clerk of the Crown................................................ | 50. 0.0 |
| "For a Surgeon............................................................ | 136.17.6 |
| "An Assistant to ditto..................................................... | 91. 5.0 |
| "For a Clergyman for Charlottetown......................................... | 70. 0.0 |
| "For a small vessel and men................................................ | 250. 0.0 |
| "Fuel Money for the Lieutenant-Governor's house and public offices............... | 150. 0.0 |
| "Barge and Bargemen...................................................... | 250. 0.0 |
| "Messenger to the Lieutenant-Governor..................................... | 27. 6.0 |
| "Stationery for the Public Offices and other unavoidable contingencies............ | 100. 0.0 |
| | £2,175. 6.0 |

REMARKS.— "The two Assistant Surveyors, necessary only for a certain time, surgeons the same."

Francklin to the Commissioners for Trade and Plantations, 12th June, 1768.

"I think it necessary to mention to Your Lordship in addition to what I have already said to the Earl of Hillsborough on the subject of the Permanent Establishment for the Island of St. John that after a certain time it will be necessary to have more clergymen than one, that the expense of building a church, court-house and prison, for each of the other two counties must be provided for, and that a sum of money will also be necessary for such contingencies as may happen conformable to the plan His Majesty shall be pleased to adopt."

any method of defraying the expense attending the execution of the measure, without any additional burthen upon the English Government, and that their Lordships shall, in that case, lay before this Committee such a plan for a separate government in the Island of St. John as they should judge expedient, together with an estimate of the expense and the ways by which it may be defrayed.

The report of the Commissioners of Trade and Plantations in reply to this reference was made to the Committee of the Privy Council on 30th May, 1769. It points out that under the terms of the Committee's reference, "the means of obtaining such a fund as would be adequate to the purpose of a proper civil establishment necessarily became the first object of their attention." Some of the principal proprietors, on being consulted, suggested to the commissioners "that they were ready and willing, as far as concerned themselves, that the payment of the moiety of the quit rents reserved upon each of their lots respectively, and which by the original condition of their grants was to commence at the expiration of five years from these dates, should commence and begin to be paid from the first of May, 1769, provided His Majesty should think fit to accept the same as a fund for defraying the expense of a civil government, and would be graciously pleased to consent that the payment of the other moiety, which was to take place at the expiration of ten years, should, in consideration thereof, be postponed for ten years longer, so as not to take effect till the expiration of twenty years from the dates of the grants."

This proposal appeared to suggest the only method for carrying out their Lordship's intentions, but as it only carried with it the consent of a small part of the proprietors, it became necessary to consult the whole upon it "and that their sentiments should be known before any proposition could be made to your Lordship."

After several meetings of the proprietors, the proposal was, at length, concurred in by all except eight, and they have now declared their willingness to take out fresh grants from the Governor of St. John's Island, when appointed, in exchange for those already taken out from the Governor of Nova Scotia, pursuant to His Majesty's Order-in-Council, provided such grants were made out to them without fee or reward.

As the main object sought in this business was the attainment of such a fund for defraying the civil government in the Island of St. John as, without bringing any burthen upon this Kingdom or charge upon His Majesty's Treasury here, would be sufficient for the present and until the Island be able to provide for its own establishment, it became necessary for the Lords Commissioners to fully explain to the proprietors that they would not think themselves justified in laying this proposition before their Lordships unless it was understood and acquiesced in by them that this appropriation of His Majesty's quit rents to the support of the civil establishment should be only for a limited time, namely, not to exceed ten years; and that should the amount of them fall short of the intended establishment, either by a failure of consent, in any number of the proprietors, to the alteration now proposed in the condition of their grants, or hereafter, by any other accident or defect whatsoever, the salaries and all money to the officials should be diminished in proportion, and no demand, whatever, brought either upon Parliament or upon the Treasury, to make good such deficiency.

To these conditions the proprietors readily assented, and it was under this explanation, fully acquiesced in by them, that the Commissioners laid this proposition before their Lordships for such advice thereupon to His Majesty as their Lordships should think fit, and submitted it to their Lordships as a measure that would not only facilitate the settlement of this Island for the public advantage, but would also thereby promote the interest of the Crown by more effectually securing the payment of a very considerable quit rent, which would, after a short period, revert to His Majesty's treasury.

The Commissioners, in further conformity to their Lordship's directions to add an estimate, not only of what will be the amount of the fund that will by this measure be created for supporting for the present the civil establishment (of which fund, the rents proposed to be reserved upon town and pasture lots, hereafter to be granted, ought to make a part), but also of what the expense of such an establishment may reasonably amount to in the present state of this Island, which, being almost wholly unsettled and void of inhabitants, does not appear to require, at least until an Assembly or House of Representatives can be formed upon the plan and constitution of the other American colonies, more establishments than are necessary for the administration of government by a Governor and Council, and of Justice in civil and criminal matters by a Supreme Court exercising the authority of the Courts of King's Bench, Common Pleas, and Exchequer in Westminster Hall, under the laws of England, as far as they apply to the situation and circumstances of that Island, for the forming of which Courts, as well as for all other necessary rules of government, under such a limited plan as is now submitted, the example of the several new colonies lately established under similar circumstances furnish every useful and necessary precedents; but as the Commissioners wish, in the course of this business, to adhere as closely as possible to the opinion so justly adopted by their Lordships that no new establishment of this nature ought to be undertaken, either at the expense of the King or by charges upon the peculiar revenues of the Crown, so they cannot close this report without suggesting that the Governor of this Island should in their opinion (in which opinion the proprietors concur) be fully instructed that so soon as a House of Assembly shall be formed, and the circumstances of the people will admit of it, he shall make the strongest requisition, in His Majesty's name, for the establishment of such a permanent revenue by proper duties or taxes as may amount to all the expenses of Government upon some certain estimate.

The Committee of the Privy Council recommended the King that the Commissioners of the Treasury and Lord Hillsborough, one of His Majesty's principal Secretaries of State, receive His Majesty's pleasure for the appointment of the several officers proposed as necessary for the administration of government, so far as related to their respective departments; "and that the Lords Commissioners for Trade and Plantations should prepare drafts of a commission and instructions for such person as Your Majesty shall be pleased to appoint Governor of the said Island, conformable to the plans before mentioned, and likewise consider of and prepare the form and device of a new seal for the said Island, and lay the same, together with the said drafts of a commission and instructions, before Your Majesty's Council."

His Majesty, in Council, approved of the proposition and ordered that the same be carried out. The following estimate of the annual expense of the said establishment, and the amount of the fund for defraying the expenses thereof, were also approved.

ESTIMATE OF THE ANNUAL EXPENSE OF THE PROPOSED ESTABLISHMENT FOR THE ISLAND OF ST. JOHN.

| | |
|---|---:|
| The Governor | £500.0.0 |
| Chief Justice | 200.0.0 |
| Secretary and Registrar | 150.0.0 |
| Attorney-General | 100.0.0 |
| Clerks of the Courts and Crowns | 80.0.0 |
| Provost Marshal | 50.0.0 |
| Minister of the Church of England | 100.0.0 |
| Agent and Receiver of Quit Rents | 150.0.0 |
| Contingent Expenses | 140.0.0 |
| | £1,470.0.0 |

Estimate of the amount of fund for defraying the expenses of the intended establishment of the Island of St. John, according to the proposals of the proprietors:

| | |
|---|---:|
| Twenty-six lots, at 6s. per hundred acres, a moiety of which is | £780.0.0 |
| Twenty-nine lots as 4s. per hundred acres | 580.0.0 |
| Eleven lots at 2s. per hundred acres | 110.0.0 |

Rent of town and pasture lots uncertain.

On 30th June, 1769, Lieutenant-Governor Francklin, of Nova Scotia, writing from Westminster to John Pownal, Esquire, enclosed a return of the provisions and stores at Charlottetown received from Mr. John Moreau, in whose charge they were, and also a description, signed by Mr. Moreau and Engineer Ness, of Tatamagouche, dated October, 1768, of two buildings at Charlottetown. As these are the earliest buildings in Charlottetown of which we have a report, their description is of interest. They were: "A dwelling-house, fifty-six by twenty-six, one story, with a pitched roof shingled and clap-boarded, and filled in between with stone laid in rough mortar, two stacks of chimneys, with two ovens and six fire-places, two parlours, two kitchens and lodging rooms, a cellar, stoned, under one-half of the house." "A house intended for a dwelling-house, of the same dimensions, clap-boarded and shingled, now used as a store, but partitions fixed up for the same number of rooms as the above house, a cellar, stoned, under the whole house and a stone pier at one end of it for a foundation for a chimney. A wharf head next the shore of Hillsborough River fifty feet wide, carried out thirty feet, solid with stones and timber. Several of the streets of Charlottetown entirely opened."

In the meantime Lieutenant-Governor Francklin of Nova Scotia was actively engaged in carrying out his instructions, as he understood them, with regard to the Island of St. John. On 31st July, 1768, he wrote to Lord Hillsborough from Halifax that "Mr. Morris, the Chief Surveyor of this Province, and Mr. Deschamps, the first magistrate of the Island of St. John, arrived, without accident, there, together with the other officers of Government, and that on the 22nd of June the Courts of Common Pleas and General Sessions of the Peace were opened at Charlottetown when the magistrates and civil officers of government took the State oaths and those necessary to qualify them for their respective offices.

"Mr. Morris," he writes, "has laid out the ground on which the Town of Charlottetown is to be built on Hillsborough River at the extremity of the lands reserved for that purpose, which he found to be the most proper place, the land being level, dry and healthy, rising with a small ascent, which makes it a pleasant situation, and there is also plenty of good water to be had by sinking wells; but I am concerned there is not that depth of water near the town which I could wish, as Your Lordship will perceive by the plan which I have the honour to enclose, and yet Mr. Morris tells me that there is no other part of the lands reserved for the town which has a greater depth on which the town could possibly be placed, the whole front of it being so extremely shoal.

"All officers of the Government have been hutted on the spot from the commencement of their arrival and are now building a little house marked on the plan to contain them during the winter, some of the streets are opened, which will be attended with an expense to Government, but it cannot be avoided, and some few house lots have been taken up."

"I also enclose a return of the inhabitants on the Island of St. John to the 21st instant, since I have letters from Mr. Deschamps of the 26th who advised there are a few more families arrived and several persons from New York, the Jersey and Pennsylvania Governments, who are come to view the land, but I have not, as yet, had more than two of the orders of His Majesty in Council presented for grants.

"Mr. Morris has, by this time, completed the laying out of the town plotted for Georgetown, whence he will proceed to Princetown to do the same, in each of which an overseer will be left to execute any orders that may be given. . . .

"The post of Tatamagouche I find very necessary and convenient and will be of the greatest utility, as all the advices from Charlottetown now come that way, which the couriers generally perform in four days with great ease." . . .

In his despatch of 31st July to Lord Hillsborough, Francklin enclosed two returns of the inhabitants, one of the English-speaking inhabitants of whom he gives the names, and the other of the Acadians. They were as follows:

No. 1.—"Return of the number of persons residing on the Island of St. John, July 21st, 1768, with the number of the townships on which they reside:

| NAMES | Townships | Men | Women | Boys | Girls | Total | Vessels |
|---|---|---|---|---|---|---|---|
| John Urguhart | No. 39 | 2 | 1 | 1 | 1 | 6 | 2 Schooners |
| John Hamilton | No. 39 | 3 | 3 | 1 | 1 | 8 | 1 Schooner |
| Joseph Moss | No. 39 | 1 | 1 | 2 | 3 | 7 | 1 Schooner |
| ———— Ayres | No. 39 | 1 | 1 | 2 | 1 | 5 | 1 Shallop |
| †Wm. Lavingston | No. 59 | 2 | .. | .. | .. | 2 | 1 Schooner |
| †James Davidson | No. 59 | 2 | .. | .. | .. | 2 | 2 Schooners |
| †William Creed | No. 1 | 1 | .. | .. | .. | 2 | 1 Schooner |
| Michael Molineaux (Prince Town) | ...... | 1 | 1 | 2 | 2 | 6 | 1 Schooner |
| †Wm. Coffin | No. 37 | 1 | .. | .. | .. | 1 | 1 Sloop |
| †John Coffin | No. 37 | 1 | .. | .. | .. | 1 | .......... |
| †Dr. Fergus | No. 53 | 3 | 3 | .. | .. | 6 | .......... |
| †———— | No. 58 | 6 | 3 | 7 | 6 | 22 | .......... |
| | | 24 | 15 | 14 | 15 | 68 | |

N. B.— Of the above only those marked (†) are settlers on the lands in behalf of the grantees. The others are on sufferance.

Charlottetown, July 21st, 1768.

(Sgd.) J. Deschamps.

No. 2.— The second return was of "Acadians all employed in the fishery, the greatest part in the aforementioned vessels."*

| WHERE LOCATED | Men | Women | Boys | Girls | Total | Vessels |
|---|---|---|---|---|---|---|
| At St. Peters....................... | 15 | 13 | 26 | 17 | 71 | ........... |
| At Harris Bay, called by the French "Restice"........................ | 5 | 5 | 10 | 5 | 25 | 2 Shallops |
| At Bedford Bay, called by the French "Tracadie"....................... | 10 | 10 | 17 | 20 | 57 | 1 Sloop and 2 Shallops |
| At Bay Fortune..................... | 1 | 1 | 2 | 1 | 5 | 1 Shallop |
| At Richmond Bay, called by the French, "Malpec"........................ | 10 | 10 | 13 | 12 | 45 | 2 Schooners |
|  | 41 | 39 | 68 | 55 | 203 |  |

"The greatest part of these Acadians have taken the oath of allegiance and fidelity and the others will take them as soon as they return from the fishing."

(Sgd.) Isaac Deschamps.

Charlottetown, 21st July, 1768.

Lieutenant-Governor Francklin in carrying out his instructions as he understood them, with regard to the plan of settlement of the Island of St. John, incurred expenses considerably in excess of what was intended by the authorities at Downing Street, who expressed their disapproval of his conduct in this respect. Lord William Campbell, or the Governor of Nova Scotia, on his arrival in Halifax, in 1768, ordered the work being carried on by his Lieutenant-Governor to be discontinued. In the meantime Francklin had drawn bills on the London Agent of Nova Scotia to meet his expenditure. Part of these were paid, while others, amounting to £2,210.12.10½, were about to be dishonoured.

Francklin, on 6th March, 1769, memorialized the Lords Commissioners of the Treasury setting out the facts as understood by him. In substance he said that in the previous May he had received His Majesty's commands for carrying out a plan of settlement of the Island, and that with the advice of His Majesty's Council he had undertaken the following measures, viz.: (1) To cause the three county towns to be surveyed and laid out in lots,

*The writer has great doubt as to the accuracy of this return, as the Acadians, a prolific race, who had now been undisturbed for a decade since the Deportation, surely amounted to more than the number given in this return.

and to place boundaries to the several townships throughout the Island. (2) To build a block-house at Tatamagouche for securing a communication between Charlottetown and Halifax; (3) To establish a Court of Common Pleas and appoint officials to prevent any delay of justice or of public business; (4) To build such temporary sheds or houses at Charlottetown as might be necessary for the lodgment of the officials of Government. (5) To hire such small vessels as might be thought necessary to attend the surveyors and for transporting the officials of Government with the materials for temporary buildings.

These measures were unavoidably attended with an expense for which he was under the necessity of drawing Bills of Exchange on the Agent of the Province of Nova Scotia, part of which have been paid out of the contingent money granted by Parliament, but there yet remains unpaid a balance of £2,210.12.10½ for which no provision has been made and the bills for the same are now about to be protested, and he prays their Lordships to provide for payment of this balance.

John Pownal, Secretary of the Board of Trade and Plantations, on 24th April, 1769, in a letter enclosing correspondence on this subject to the Secretary of the Privy Council, writes that he has been directed by Lord Hillsborough to add that it is his opinion, founded upon the general good character of Mr. Francklin, that if his conduct, upon this occasion, has been reprehensible, it has probably been the effect of a mistaken zeal for His Majesty's service, and that, therefore, his case is an object for their Lordships' favourable consideration.

On the 7th, 1769, Lord Hillsborough having learned that Mr. Higgins was about to embark for the Island of St. John, informed him of the intention to erect it into a separate Government, and appointed him store-keeper.

On the 10th July, the Lords of Trade and Plantations submitted to His Majesty a draught appointment of Walter Patterson as Governor, also a description of a plan and device for a new seal. On the 13th, Lord Hillsborough wrote the Lords of the Admiralty, reciting the appointment of Walter Patterson to be Captain-General and Governor-in-Chief over the Island, and that "it is His Majesty's pleasure that your Lordships should grant him such powers as have been usually granted to the Captain-General of the rest of His

Majesty's Colonies and Provinces in America." He also wrote to the Lord Chamberlain to give the necessary orders for the new governor to have the allowance of plate and other things which are customary on the like occasions.

On the 14th July, an Order-in-Council under the great seal was made, passing on the draft of Mr. Patterson's Commission as Governor, and also an order approving of the new seal and ordering the chief engraver to prepare a draft of it.

On the 4th August, an Order-in-Council was passed approving of the instructions to Mr. Patterson, who, the same day, took the oaths required to be taken by Governors of Plantations. On the same date an order was made authorizing the Lords of the Admiralty to appoint a Vice-Admiral and officers of a Court of Admiralty for the Island of St. John.

On 4th December of the same year, the proprietors petitioned the Lords Commissioners of the Treasury, setting out, in order to encourage settlers to repair thither, to secure their property there, and to recommend and enforce obedience to the laws, it was absolutely necessary that there be, as soon as possible, a church, a court house and a jail erected in Charlottetown, which is appointed to be the seat of Government, and praying as there is no fund belonging to the Island, that their Lordships should take the premises into consideration, and grant such relief as to their Lordships should seem proper.

# PART V.

## SEPARATE GOVERNMENT.

### CHAPTER I.

### GOVERNOR PATTERSON.*

Although appointed to the governorship in 1769, and sworn in on 4th August of that year, Mr. Patterson did not arrive in the Island until 30th August, 1770, when he at once entered upon the duties of his office. He seems to have been a man of very fair ability and of a sanguine temperament, perhaps too sanguine. Unfortunately for his memory, the accounts we have of him have been largely handed down by his enemies, of whom he managed, particularly in the latter part of his governorship, to acquire a great number.

"Patterson was an Irishman, son of William Patterson of Foxhall, County Donegal. He had seen service in the 8th Regiment, in America."† He evidently had the utmost faith in the future of the Island, in which he invested the greater part of his fortune, and where he acquired much property, all of which he subsequently lost. He died in England, a broken and ruined man.

According to Mr. Stewart when, in 1770, the Governor and the other officers arrived on the Island, "there were not more than one hundred and fifty families thereon, and only five proprietors, and it soon appeared that, having succeeded in procuring the establishment of the separate government, many of the proprietors relied on the operation of that measure for the settlement of the colony, as few of them made any attempt to comply with the terms of settlement on which their lands were held; and the payment of the quit rents was as little thought of, for in five years after the arrival of the officers on the Island, the receipts of the Receiver-

---

\* Patterson's portrait is from a photograph of a miniature owned by the Rev. C. W. S. Patterson, Chersey Vicarage, near Stafford, England. He very kindly sent the photograph to the writer with permission to insert it in this volume. The miniature is the only known likeness of Governor Patterson. It would be a very desirable addition to the Dominion Archives.

†Carlyle's First Love, page 6.

GOVERNOR WALTER PATTERSON

General amounted to little more than would discharge two years salary to the establishment, which, as may easily be conceived, brought the officers into great distress and materially retarded the progress of the settlement."

"Shortly after his arrival, Patterson planted a number of Acadian French along the front of Lot 17 (St. Eleanors), and the proprietor of Lot 18 (fronting on Richmond Bay) brought several families from Argyleshire, who were settled there in 1770 and 1772. The settlement of New London, Rustico and Elliot River commenced in 1773; and Cove Head and Lot 59, at Three Rivers, were settled early by the late Sir James Montgomery, who did more than any other proprietor for the settlers. Tracadie was planted with about three hundred Highlanders, by the late Captain MacDonald, between 1770 and 1773; and a few other places were partially settled about the same period."*

It can be gathered from his correspondence, and from that of other residents contemporary with him, that, at least in the earlier part of his time here, he worked hard to improve the country and to promote its interests. There can be no doubt but that very material advances in prosperity were made. When he arrived the Island was a wilderness. There were very few English people. The Acadian inhabitants were much more numerous. They were extremely poor and their loyalty was very much questioned, the writer thinks unjustly. There were no roads, and the means of traversing the country were of the rudest kind. The routes of travel over the Island were by water or by paths blazed through the woods. There were no public buildings, very few private ones, and these of a most indifferent kind. When he was dismissed from his office, the population had materially increased, the inconveniences referred to were to some extent overcome and the most pressing wants largely supplied.

In his first despatch to the Earl of Hillsborough, dated 21st October, 1770, only seven weeks from his arrival, he gives an interesting description of the Island, so far as he was then able to form an opinion. Ever since his arrival he had been engaged in furnishing one of the houses in such a manner as he hoped would keep out a little of the approaching cold, and in sending to different parts of the continent for provisions to maintain his family during

*McGregor, Account of Prince Edward Island, 88.

the winter. Owing to the bad communications, he was able, at that time, to furnish a very indifferent description of the Island, though, so far as he could see, the soil seemed good and easily cultivated, and he was of the opinion it would produce every kind of grain and vegetable, common in England, with little or no trouble; and such as he had seen of the latter were much better of their kind than those in England, though raised in a very slovenly manner. The various woods near Charlottetown he describes as of very little use, except for firing, but in other parts of the Island there were some oaks and large pine trees in plenty. He mentions the different wild fowl, and describes the geese, brant and ducks, as of as good of their kinds as he ever met with. The beasts were principally bears, foxes, otters, wild-cats of a very large size, martens, squirrels and mice. That year the mice were so numerous that, in some places, they had devoured the little that was attempted to be raised. The inhabitants said they appeared every seven years. He adds, as to the mice, which were a plague to the early settlers: "My opinion is, it depends entirely on the sort of winter we have, as I am informed the last was an uncommon one, the snow falling before the frost came on, by which means the ground was kept soft, and the mice, instead of being partially destroyed by the frost, as is commonly the case, bred under the snow; they are, in size, something between our rats and mice in England."

As for fish, he says: "This side of the Island is but indifferently off for fish, except in the spring, when, I am told, we may have a small kind of cod, mackerel, trout, bass, smelts and several sorts of flat-fish pretty good. At present there are only lobsters and oysters, neither very good." He had only been here a few weeks, and had evidently not learned much about the fisheries of this Island.

He speaks highly of the climate, and says that, in the winter season, the inhabitants "make all the frames for their houses, saw boards and do almost all their woodwork." The French inhabitants were mostly employed by a few British subjects in the fishery, and had been paid their wages in "clothes, rum, flour, powder and shot." Owing to this, "agriculture has been so much neglected there is not one bushel of corn raised by all the French inhabitants on the Island."

He reports that "about one hundred and twenty families had arrived that summer, part sent by Mr. Montgomery, the Lord

Advocate of Scotland, the rest by a Mr. Stewart, of the country; the last arrived about three weeks ago at Princetown, but very unfortunately, for want of a pilot, their vessel ran on shore at the entrance of the harbour and is entirely lost and part of her cargo, but no lives".*

As soon as possible after his arrival the Governor convened some of the principal inhabitants at Charlottetown, and caused his Commission to be read, Mr. Phillips Callbeck, Mr. John Russell, Mr. Thomas Wright and Mr. Patrick Fergus were appointed to the Council. Mr. Wright was not a resident, only wintering here, but was willing to become one, if appointed Surveyor-General of the Island, which Patterson recommended. Lieutenant-Governor DesBrisay had not yet arrived. The Governor was sworn in on 19th September, and the same day the proper oaths were administered to the officers of the government who were present; the Chief Justice (Duport) was given a commission for holding the Supreme Court, which was opened on the 24th.† Acting upon instructions the Governor made enquiry into the sea cow fishery, which he feared would be rendered useless, owing to the operation of a Mr. F. Gridley from the Magdalen Islands, and of some New England fishermen, who often landed for a few days to kill these

---

*These emigrants came out in the barque Annabella from Campbellton, Scotland, in 1770. The emigrants, it seems, thought they were to go to North Carolina, where they had friends and whither the trend of Scotch emigration was then directed. The Annabella was cast away on the sandhills at the entrance of the harbour in October, in a snow storm, and the emigrants lost all their provisions and much of their clothing. Some French fishermen had houses on the Malpeque Point, where some of the castaways found shelter. The wrecked emigrants nearly starved that winter. Robert Stewart, one of the proprietors, came out in the Annabella. Among the emigrants was John Ramsay with six sons and two nephews who came out with him. They were the forefathers of the Ramsays of Prince County, so prominent in the life of that county. One of the sons was Malcolm, who became agent for Governor Patterson. He was a member of the House of Assembly and was called "Moccasin" Ramsay, because he wore moccasins when he came to Charlottetown to attend the Sessions. Other emigrants were McGougan, McKenzie, McIntosh, McArthur, English, McDougall, Sinclair, Murphy, McKay. Part of these settlers later left Malpeque and settled at Low Point, Lot 13, where there had been a French settlement. There is a tradition that some three or four years after the coming of the settlers in 1770, another ship, on which a family named Montgomery, were passengers, called at Malpeque on her voyage to Quebec. Mrs. Montgomery had been very ill on board and wished to land. On getting on shore, she positively refused to again go on board the vessel. Her husband and family had also to land. They settled there and founded a family, which became very prominent in the public affairs of the colony. Hon. Donald Montgomery, a descendant (commonly called "Big Donald" because of his commanding stature), was one of the first four Prince Edward Islanders appointed to the Dominion Senate when the Island became a Province of Canada in 1873. Although he has been unable to positively verify this tradition, the writer yet believes it to be well founded. Louise Maud Montgomery, the well known authoress, is also a descendant.

†For Duport, see Part VI, "Miscellaneous."

animals, and of the inhabitants of the Island, who had been endeavouring to carry on this fishery. In consequence, by the advice of Council, he had an Act passed for regulating it, which was submitted for approval. This appears to have been the first enactment after the erection of the Island into a separate Government. The sea cow fishery was of much importance, and in these early days there was much correspondence and legislation affecting it. The animals were of great size, said to weigh as much as four thousand pounds. They frequented the waters of the Gulf, and abounded about the Magdalens and north shores of this Island. Cartier mentions them. They were numerous for some years after Patterson's arrival, but were ultimately exterminated or driven from these waters. Even in 1806, when Stewart wrote, there were very few remaining, though they were not yet extinct, and he calls attention to the matter. Their oil was of a very fine quality, the flesh was used by some of the inhabitants, the skins were of great value for harness and other purposes, and as an article of trade. It was sometimes an inch and a half in thickness. By some the sea cow is said to be extinct. It is certainly no longer seen around the shores of this Island, but it is likely the same as the walrus still found in Hudson's Bay and possibly in other northern waters.

On 18th July, 1783, after the termination of the war with the revolted colonies, Patterson again took up the matter with the Secretary of State. Writing on that date, he says that "since the Peace, the New England fishing vessels have again begun to frequent the Gulf and are in a fair way to destroy the sea cow fishery if there are not some steps taken very soon to prevent them. The great resort of these fish is about this and the Magdalen Islands.

"The fishery during the last Peace was carried on upon one of the last mentioned Islands by a Mr. Gridley. But two or three years ago he fled to Boston, as I have been told, to avoid being taken up by General Haldimand. He pretended to have an exclusive right to the fishery given him by General, now Lord, Amherst, soon after the conquest of Canada. While he held it, with the assistance of His Majesty's ships, he preserved the fish pretty well from the New Englanders. At present they are under no restraint. They come to fish in the Gulf as early in the spring as the ice will permit them, at which season the females are bringing forth their young, two of which they have most commonly at a time.

"Their attachment to their calves is wonderful. If a calf is taken the mother will stay by it till she is killed. There have been many instances of their receiving several wounds and still, on hearing the calf, they return, endeavouring all in their power to get hold of it. If the calf be killed and the dam gets it afterwards, she will keep it under her fin or flapper, till it decays to pieces. The fishermen are well acquainted with this fondness of the female and turn it to their destruction. The fishermen are seldom without a calf on board their vessels, and on causing it to make a noise, the females, whether mothers or not, come directly on hearing them. By this means the mother fish are destroyed and their young perish. I am credibly informed there is not a male to be met with just at this season. They are separated from the cows and keep in deep water. The others, on account of their young, stay near the shore.

"Mr. Gridley killed all his fish upon land, but I do not believe he was so attentive, as he ought, to the killing them at a proper season. By the best accounts I have, it appears they should only be taken in the autumn. At that time they will yield much more oil. Both sexes are together and the young can provide for themselves. The manner of taking the fish is curious, but I dare not intrude on Your Lordship's time so much as to give an account of it. I shall only say it is done so cautiously as not to alarm those that escape.

"The New Englanders, by harpooning and pursuing the fish, frighten them from their usual haunts and scatter them so much, that they are not worth attending to, even by themselves. Mr. Gridley has told me that he used to kill, on his first establishing the fishery, from seven thousand to eight thousand of these animals in a season, and in the autumn they will yield, one with another, thirty gallons of oil. Their hides make excellent traces for any kind of labouring work and will answer for the heaviest draughts.

"A large hide will cut into twenty pairs of traces, and they only require being dried in the sun to render them fit for use. They would soon find their way into England and would, most probably, save both iron and other expensive articles.

"I have thought it my duty most humbly to mention the matter to Your Lordship, as the intercourse between the Magdalen Islands and this is much more frequent than with either Quebec or

Newfoundland, consequently my intelligence is better than can be had at either of these places. The Islands of Magdalen lie only twelve leagues to the northeast of this Island, and I beg leave humbly to submit whether it would not be advantageous to them if they were dependent on it in matter of Government."

## Church, Court House and Jail.

Almost immediately after his arrival in Charlottetown Patterson began to urge upon Lord Hillsborough the necessity there was for a church, a jail and a court house, which he estimated would cost about three thousand pounds, but which the Island could not itself build. There was not even a barn or other place to assemble the people for worship, and a jail and court house could not be done without, "unless we are left to submit to all manner of injustice and violence. At present this is only the shadow of a government without the substance, for there is not one house or place in or near this town that would confine a man contrary to his inclination."

The Governor expressed the hope that His Lordship and the rest of His Majesty's ministers would take their situation into consideration and grant such aid as would be sufficient for the above purpose. He had had no time or opportunity to get a draft made of such buildings as would be proper, nor any estimate of what they would cost. He could only inform His Lordship that the price of labour was then very high, which made him imagine that they could not be built, as they ought to be, of proper materials for less than the sum mentioned. He estimated the cost of the church at one thousand pounds, of the jail at fifteen hundred, and of the court house at five hundred pounds. This, he impressed upon His Lordship, was only his own opinion and that of other people. He pointed out that there were proper people belonging to the public offices at home from whom His Lordship might have drafts made to his satisfaction, and if the money were granted he would undertake to have the work executed, by contract, with all their disadvantages, at a much cheaper rate than anything of that sort was ever done in this country, and, he hoped, to His Lordship's satisfaction.

Lord Hillsborough replying on 2nd January 1771, expressed himself as sensible of the propriety and necessity of the colony having a church, a court house and a jail, and promised to endeavour, so far as depended upon him, to obtain some provision for erecting those buildings as well as for making such roads as were necessary for opening such communications as may contribute to improve the commerce and promote the settlement of the Island, but whether this provision could at present be obtained depended upon considerations that belonged to another department.

On 6th March, 1771, Lord Hillsborough again wrote, enclosing a copy of the estimate for Nova Scotia, giving the sum granted by Parliament for building the church, court house and jail, but advising the Governor not to go on with the work till he heard further from His Lordship.

In acknowledging on 24th July, 1771, receipt of His Lordship's letters of 22nd January and of 6th March of that year, the latter containing an estimate of the charge for maintaining the civil list of Nova Scotia, Patterson expresses the great pleasure with which he saw there were fifteen hundred pounds granted by Parliament, in part of three thousand pounds for building a church, a court house and a jail in this town. From this it is evident that only half the sum asked for was then granted. The other half was granted the following year. He expresses his opinion that this sum would not only answer the purpose for which it was granted, but would, also, "make us a little respected by the other provinces, in some of which people were kind enough to say publicly that this government was formed rather by way of experiment than with any fixed intention of being supported or carried into execution, and as the payment of the establishment depended upon the proprietors it would fall through. These reports, however groundless, deterred many people (who otherwise intended it) from coming to settle here."

The Governor assured His Lordship that he might rely on his carrying this service, and every other with which he was entrusted, into execution, with the strictest economy and, he hoped, in such manner as to give satisfaction. He would not, nevertheless, take any step towards it until he received His Lordship's further commands, together with the plans and estimates promised him.

## £3,000.— How Expended.

The actual disposal of this three thousand pounds was for many years a matter of enquiry in the House of Assembly and in the country. In the session of 1784, the question was brought up and an address presented to the Governor praying for an account of this money. This House seems to have been hostile to Patterson. He sent a written reply in which he stated that the money had been spent in payment of salaries due officials, including himself, who had received no pay owing to the default of the proprietors in paying their quit rents, from which the salaries should have been paid.

He dissolved this House, and at the first session, in March, 1785, of the new House, which was friendly to the Lieutenant-Governor, the matter was again brought up. It was charged against John Stewart, speaker of the former House, and his friends, that they kept the Journals of that Assembly and mutilated them, suppressing part of Patterson's reply to their address. The House ordered that the Journals, and Patterson's answer to the Address of the former House, be sent for, which was done, and after the messenger was sent a second time to the late speaker's house for the Journals of the last Assembly, he found them in the Chief Justice's house. The messenger, Captain Stewart, being sworn, said, "I found the Journals now before the Committee in the Chief Justice's house. They were brought from the Chief Justice's bed room. He brought them in, in his hand, and laid them on the table, from which I received them."

William Craig, one of the members of the new House who had been clerk of the old, being sworn, said in substance: "I know the papers now presented to me and appearing to be the Journals of the last Assembly. They are in my handwriting, except some alterations and interlineations. They are in my writing as part of my duty. They are *not* the original Journals kept by me. They are not an exact copy. They have been altered since my copying them, as seen by several interlineations in different handwriting, and parts struck out. I copied them first week in July, about ten weeks after the Assembly was dissolved on 13th April. The copy was made at the house of Lieutenant John Stewart, the late Speaker, and by his direction. I left the original Journals with him. I delivered the original to him in July last and this copy, as well as another copy to him, sometimes in the beginning of September following. There were then no alterations until I delivered them, nor in the copy.

"The whole of Governor Patterson's answer to the Address is not entered in the copy of the Journals now produced to me. I left it out by direction of the late speaker, John Stewart, and inserted the partial report by his direction also. I know of no other reason why it was omitted from the Address to His Majesty from the late Assembly. The answer of Governor Patterson was not introduced in the original Journals. Blanks are always left for the purpose of inserting speeches, addresses, answers and other lengthy papers, of which copies are kept, and are wholly introduced in fair copies for lodging and transmitting."

A committee of the House on 28th March, 1785, was appointed to request the Lieutenant-Governor to furnish the House with a copy of his answer to the Address of the last House of Assembly relating to the three thousand pounds granted by the Parliament of Great Britain. The Lieutenant-Governor promised to acquiesce, without delay, to the House's request. The next day he wrote the Speaker as follows:

"Agreeably to the request of your House, I shall herewith enclose an exact copy of the answer I gave to the request of the last House of Representatives, concerning the sum of £3,000, granted by the Legislature of Great Britain, for the purpose of erecting a church, a court house and a jail in Charlottetown, and I shall also accompany it with the original Treasury minute from which I have sent an extract."

PATTERSON'S ANSWER TO ADDRESS OF LATE HOUSE.

"The Governor's answer to the Address sent by the Assembly, yesterday, requesting him to lay before them the state of the fund of £3,000, granted by the Parliament of Great Britain for the purpose of erecting a church, a court house and a jail in this Island.

"There was £3,000 undoubtedly granted for the above purposes by the Legislature of Great Britain, therefore the Assembly can have no cognizance of the matter, nor will His Majesty's Ministers permit any other to enquire into the expenditure thereof, but themselves, or such as derived authority from them.

"This renders it incompatible with his duty to lay such a state of the matter before them as they may expect,— which, he supposes, is an account. But, as it will give him pleasure on all occasions to give every satisfaction in his power to the people entrusted to his care, he will explain, not as to a part of the Legislature, but as to so many inhabitants, why a church, a court house and a jail have not been built agreeably to His Majesty's most gracious intentions.

"At the time the £3,000 was granted, any man, who was then here, knows there were not workmen on the Island capable to undertake such buildings. The Governor, therefore, caused advertisements to be published in Boston and other parts of the continent, desiring plans and estimates of them, but to no purpose. This want of artificers prevented the work being begun,— and before any could be obtained, the distress brought on the officers of government by the failure in the payment of their salaries obliged him to share a part of the public money for their support. A small part of it has been laid out on public uses. The remainder was expended to support his own family and himself, as became his station — an account of which he laid before the Treasury when last in England, in consequence of their Lordships' order — and he shall send herewith an extract from a Treasury minute, by which it will appear the public buildings cannot be undertaken until the officers are paid their arrears due from the quit rents, and he can assure them that such has not been done with any of them, except the present Chief Justice.

"The Governor believes he may safely say there is no man feels so much as he does the real want of those necessary buildings; nor the disgrace which attends it, and he is very sorry to say he does not see any prospect of their being undertaken for some time, as he is ordered to desist enforcing the further payment of quit rents for the present, by which all chance of the arrears being paid is prevented.

"Dated Charlottetown, 16th March, 1784."

At this time a most bitter feud prevailed between the Governor and the Stewarts. It is not necessary to enquire into the reasons for this feud. It is sufficient for present purposes to know that it existed. The Stewart faction, lead by John Stewart, with the Chief Justice taking an active part, had carried the elections for the last House, but in the new House of 1785 the Governor's supporters dominated. They attributed the mutilation of the Journals and of Patterson's answer to their Address for 1784 to their opponents, and they were probably correct in this. Very strong opinions were expressed in the House on the subject, and it was moved, "That so far as we can, such conduct shall be stigmatized as it deserves, and that we shall have our sentiment of it on record in the Journals of this House." This was not seconded, but resolutions expressive of the opinion of the members were unanimously passed. They were, in part, as follows:

. . . 2nd. "That the proceedings of the Speaker and eight members of the late Assembly (not being a quorum), who met in April, 1784, are unconstitutional and every way illegal.

3rd. "That the address of the late Assembly to His Majesty (in which only a part of the Governor's answer to their requisition relative to the £3,000 was inserted) was unfair and ungenerous and clearly discovers that private pique and party prejudices totally governed their proceedings, and that the efforts of an united faction were exerted to injure a Governor whose public conduct has ever merited the gratitude and esteem of the inhabitants of this Island, and whose candour in the instance before us reflects honour on his character.

4th. "That the House from their hearts do sincerely and avowedly disapprove of and condemn the proceedings of the influenced majority in the late General Assembly and their abettors; as highly repugnant to the sentiments of public spirit which should ever regulate the conduct of an House of Representatives."

On April 4th, 1785, the House addressed the Lieutenant-Governor on the propriety of his joining with the Council and this House, "in a memorial to the Secretary of State or the Lords of the Treasury, respecting the appropriation of the sum of £3,000 granted some time ago by the Parliament of Great Britain for the purpose of erecting public buildings in this Island."

The following day the Lieutenant-Governor replied in part that;

. . . "As to the desire of adopting some plan to procure the £3,000 to be laid out as intended: I approve of it highly and shall join in it with all my heart, and it will undoubtedly add much to the weight of such a measure to have it the act of the whole Legislature.

"In my opinion, the most likely way to accomplish will be by a memorial to His Majesty's Secretary of State, stating the great want there is of a proper church, court house and jail, and also mentioning how the money has already been disposed of and the impediments which are, at present, in the way of re-placing it. And praying his Lordship to recommend to the Lords of the Treasury that orders may be given for the immediate enforcement of the quit rent laws,— or that there may be such other methods adopted as shall appear proper for having the above sum appropriated, agreeable to His Majesty's gracious intention."

*Extracts from Memorial of the Lieutenant-Governor, His Majesty's Council, and the House of Representatives to Lord Sydney, Secretary of State:*

. . . "That in the years 1771 and 1772 there was £3,000 voted by Parliament for the purpose of erecting a church, court house and jail in Charlottetown, but before the money could possibly be disposed of as intended the very distressful situation the officers of the civil establishment were brought into by the proprietors failing in the payment of the quit rents obliged the Governor to expend the above sum in supporting his own and the families of his brother officers, knowing it would again be replaced as soon as the quit rents could be collected.

"That there are still arrears to a large amount due to the officers from that fund, the payment of which cannot be, at present, enforced, as there are orders to the contrary from your Lordship's office.

"That it appears by the copy of a minute of His Majesty's Treasury, the money lent for the support of the officers cannot be demanded of them until they shall be paid what is owing to them from the quit rents. Consequently, till then, the country must continue to suffer for want of these very necessary buildings.

"That the memorialists most humbly conceive the most effectual remedy for the above mentioned evils will be the enforcement of the payment of the quit rents, that the money may be again replaced, so as to be applied to the purposes for which it is granted."

Nothing came of this memorial. The matter of the £3,000 was repeatedly brought up to no purpose, until eventually it was abandoned. The question is of interest as showing how the proprietors shirked the carrying out of the terms upon which they procured the separation of the Island from Nova Scotia and its creation into a separate province.

## ROADS.

Patterson, on his arrival here in 1770, at once saw the need of roads to connect the principal settlements. At the same time that he was asking for means to erect public buildings he called Lord Hillsborough's attention to the badness of the communication between Charlottetown and the out-lying sections, "almost the whole depending on water carriage." To reach Prince Town involved a journey by boat to the head of the Hillsborough River, thence by land to St. Peter's, and there a greater or less detention waiting for a chance boat in which to get a passage by water to Richmond Bay. This sometimes took two weeks. The route to Georgetown was the same as far as St. Peter's, thence the traveller had to be ferried over the bay, take the land to Fortune and there wait a chance by water to Georgetown, a long round-about journey. The Governor pointed out how "easy, short and certain it could be made by cutting a road from the south side of the Hillsborough River to the head of either Cardigan, Brudenell or Montague rivers." He urged the need of a road to Prince Town and to St. Peter's. These three roads would give good communication to the principal parts of the Island. He pointed out that few things help more to make a country prosper than good roads. The whole could be made for five hundred pounds. Patterson persistently pressed for roads and eventually obtained them. He even risked some of his own means in procuring them.

At the same time, also, he asked that five companies of soldiers be sent here, who could, without harm, be employed on public works. They would also keep the French inhabitants peaceable, in case of war, protect the place from privateers and guard against attacks of the Nova Scotia Indians.

In July, 1771, the Governor writes Lord Hillsborough that he has ventured, at his own risk, to have a road laid out from Charlottetown to Prince Town, and although the surveyor avoids, by his instructions, all swamps, difficult rivers and steep hills, the road, as measured, was only three-quarters of a mile more than if it were on a straight line, and is only thirty-three miles. His reason for undertaking it was that a Mr. Blaskowitz, one of Captain Holland's surveyors, wintered here, and, being detained in the spring, the Governor induced him to undertake it, on much easier terms than otherwise he could have done.

## Town Plan.

In the same report he explains changes he has made in the plan of the town which had been laid out by Mr. Morris, surveyor-general of Nova Scotia. As this may be of interest, the passage is quoted, as follows: "I have taken the liberty to alter the plan of this town, and have the honour to send that which I have adopted for Your Lordship's approbation. I think it the best calculated for a northern climate of any I have met with, as every house will have a southern aspect; there being but one row of houses on each range; by which means, likewise, there will be a communication from every back yard into a street, which I look upon as a great convenience.

"I have enlarged the town lots by adding twenty-four feet front and twenty feet in depth each, as they were too small to admit of all the conveniences necessary for a man in business in a country where snow, in a great measure, prevents one building houses with double (?) roofs.

"I do not mean to give to every person, who may apply, a whole lot, nor to some not more than one-third, according to their abilities. And, as in the first settling of a town, every man must be something of a farmer to supply his family with milk, butter, roots and all other vegetables, until there be a market, which we cannot expect will be the case soon, I have doubled the quantity of land in each pasture lot, as will appear by the plan. They were in the original only six acres each; besides which, there is a large common left for the purpose of extending the town whenever that is necessary. I think it, upon the whole, the best calculated plan, both for usefulness and regularity, I have seen, and shall be highly flattered if it be approved by Your Lordship."

The plan accompanying this despatch gives the area of the whole as 7,300 acres, of which the town proper embraced 270, and 565 acres were reserved for the common. The roads to St. Peter's and Prince Town were thirty feet wide, and those to the pasture lots twenty feet. The roads covered sixty-four acres. The remaining 6,401 acres were divided into pasture lots of twelve acres each. The town lots were eighty-four by one hundred and twenty feet. The five principal streets fronting on the river were to be one hundred feet in breadth, and the others eighty feet. The present sites of the market house and St. Paul's Church were reserved for a church, court house and jail. What is now Dundas esplanade was reserved for an ordnance yard. The land along the shore, from Prince street to Pownal street, was set apart for store houses and a market place.

The square corresponding to our jail square was named Fitzherbert square, but was farther east than the jail square, faced Queen street, and ran back to Pownal, and lay between Sydney and Dorchester streets. King's square was called "North square;" the others bore their present names. Great George street was the only street named on the plan. Considerable changes have since been made in this plan of the town, as well as in the roads leading from it, but that of the Royalty seems to be still the same, except in the widening of the roads.

In September, 1771, Chief Justice Duport wrote Lord Hillsborough that no settlers had yet arrived this summer; except Mr. Burns and his family and about seventeen brought out by one Mr. MacDonald, who is come to settle on Lot 36. Mr. Stewart says that he expects five hundred to his lot at Malpeque, but should they arrive he feared they will be exposed to great inconveniences, as it is so late in the year, an error which he hoped the proprietors would be convinced of and send out their settlers earlier in the future.

Since the Chief Justice's arrival, the Governor and Council established the terms for the sitting of the Supreme Court to be twice a year, viz.: On the third Tuesday in February and the first Tuesday in July, which, upon consulting the gentlemen in the Island, appeared to be the most convenient times for the inhabitants and would the least interfere with their business, both in the fishing and in farming. The Court had been held and three persons, being convicted of petty larceny, were sentenced to be whipped, and the Court was adjourned to the third Tuesday in February agreeable to the resolution before mentioned. A resolution also passed the

Council for opening the roads from Charlottetown to Malpeque, Three Rivers, and St. Peter's, the last of which is to be set about immediately, under the encouragement of the Governor and some other public-spirited gentleman, who proposed to be in advance for that purpose. Duport imagined nothing would be done till next spring.

Writing again on the 18th October, 1771, Patterson reported the loss of Mr. Fergus, one of the Council, who had sailed the previous November in a small vessel from Three Rivers to Charlottetown. She was lost with all hands, in a snow storm, on the coast of Nova Scotia. He had been missing until May, when the news of his loss was confirmed, but the Governor had omitted to report the accident. In the same letter he again gives Lord Hillsborough an account of the Island and of its productions as follows:

### PATTERSON'S DESCRIPTION OF THE ISLAND.

"I promised Your Lordship some further accounts of the Island this autumn, and from everything I have tried, both in husbandry and in gardening, my expectations are fully answered, and in many surpassed, such as the raising of Indian corn, which I have done this year myself, and very good too, though it was not planted by more than a month so early as it ought to have been. In every other part of America where I have been, grain, in general, deteriorates, especially oats and barley; but here I have raised both this year to the full as good as the seed sown, which was the best I could purchase in London. The oats were of the Polish kind, as I judged our summer might resemble theirs in Poland, more than that of England, and believe we would be right if we used more of the continental seeds of Europe than we do. I never met with or heard of such an increase of potatoes as I was told of yesterday by two servants belonging to Captain Holland. One of them planted six bushels and has from them raised two hundred bushels; the other had a hundred and sixty bushels from three. This they offered to take their oaths of. Wheat has not had a fair trial yet, but I have every reason, from what has been done, to think we may have it as good as anywhere, and as to garden stuffs, there is no country produces better. In short, my Lord, if only the proprietors will exert themselves, this Island will, in a short time, be the garden of America."

## IMMIGRATION.

The British population in 1770, on Patterson's arrival, numbered only about a hundred and fifty families, but immigrants were beginning to come in, some coming of their own accord, but the greater part being sent to the Island by the few proprietors who were honestly trying to fulfil the conditions of their grants. We learn, from a letter of Chief Justice Duport to Lord Hillsborough, dated 15th October, 1771, that "since my last letter, dated the third ult., nine families are arrived here, sent by Lieutenant-Governor DesBrisay, to settle on his Lot near Charlottetown. About seventy persons are also arrived at Malpeque, who are come on their own account to seek a settlement on this Island, and I hope they will be accommodated to their satisfaction as it will be an encouragement to others to follow them on the same lay."

But it would seem that some of those coming to the Island were inclined to stray away, so, to offset the effect of this tendency, it was required that masters of vessels carrying passengers away from this Island must have a license to do so. In 1771, Mr. David Higgins was appointed a commissioner at St. Andrews Town, in King's county, to keep a "Public Pass Office," agreeable to an ordinance of Council "for prohibiting masters of vessels, or any other persons, from transporting or conveying away any persons out of this Island, without a license or pass." Offices, in consequence thereof, were established at the three capital towns in Queen's, King's and Prince counties.

The policy of His Majesty's Government, with regard to the settlement of these colonies, was decidedly opposed to their being peopled by emigrants from other parts of the empire. The home authorities were afraid of loss of population, and the landholding class also were afraid of their tenants becoming emigrants; this was probably the real reason for the objection to settling the colonies with people from Great Britain and Ireland. A provision of the grants was, "That the settlers so to be introduced be Protestants from such parts of Europe as are not within His Majesty's dominion." In this connection, Lieutenant-Governor DesBrisay, who was in Ireland, incurred the displeasure of the authorities by advertising for emigrants from that kingdom, to his lands in St. John's Island. On 9th November, 1773, J. Pownal, Under Secretary of State, wrote him a peremptory letter on the subject. After stating that, when in conversation with him, he had stated in strong terms his sense of the impropriety of the encouragement held out by these advertisements of Mr. DesBrisay's to emigration from Great Britain and Ireland to the Island of St. John, he had trusted that his arguments to dissuade from such a proceeding would have had their effect, but it appeared that they had not been discontinued, and land owners, whose estates have suffered extremely by the emigration of their tenants, have made public complaint of the ill effects of these advertisements. That those complaints have been laid before the King, together with a copy of the advertisements, from "which it appears that you have not only held out encouragements to emigration, as proprietor of lands in the Island of St. John, but that you have unwarrantably presumed to recite, in the preamble of those advertisements, the offices which you hold under the King's Royal Commission, evidently with a design to give the greatest colour of authority to your proposals.

"I am commanded, therefore, by the Earl of Dartmouth, to acquaint you that all such publications must be immediately suppressed, and that, if it shall appear that any of the King's subjects in Great Britain or Ireland shall have emigrated from these kingdoms in consequence of any encouragement you may have offered, you must expect to receive the strongest marks of His Majesty's displeasure."

In reply, Mr. DesBrisay expressed his concern that his advertisements should have given offence; he had never taken a tenant from the north of Ireland without the consent of the proprietor or agent of the lands, and has now withdrawn his advertisement.

## Captain John MacDonald.*

We learn from Chief Justice Duport that in 1771 Captain John MacDonald, of Glenaladale, came out with about seventeen emigrants to settle on his Tracadie estate, Lot 36. He was one of the very few proprietors who tried to fulfil the terms on which the original grants were given.

In the following year (1772), he and his brother brought over three hundred persons to settle on Lot 36.† These emigrants

---

*Prince Edward Island Magazine, Vol. VI, 99-100.
†Captain MacDonald did not personally come out in 1772. He came the following year.

came out that year in a ship named the Alexander, from which they were landed near Scotchfort on the Hillsborough river. MacDonald furnished them with a year's provisions, besides subsistence for the passage and with clothing and implements. During the first two years he was here there was a shortage of provisions, and but for Captain MacDonald's exertions in importing provisions and necessaries they must have suffered. He seems to have assisted, not only his own people, but some of the Acadians and British settlers other than his own as well. For this purpose he chartered a vessel in Boston, loaded her with supplies and brought her to this Island. His brother had in the meantime gone to Quebec, and there purchased a vessel load of provisions for the settlers, and by these vessels all wants were supplied. This body of immigrants was much the largest that had yet arrived in the Island.

Before these arrived the settlers suffered much privation. The crops planted the previous year had failed. The people were disheartened and wanted to leave. MacDonald set them to work under his own direction, he undertaking to support them until they could raise crops enough for their own subsistence, and if crops would not ripen he promised to transport them elsewhere. "But if they refused to work, he would supply them until spring and then land them in a settled country to shift for themselves." They agreed to work. He then imported cattle, horses, sheep and swine for them. On the outbreak of the American Revolution he joined the British forces and was eight years absent from the Island. On his return in 1783 he found that his property had been sold, in 1781, by the Provincial Government for quit rents. He then memorialized the King, praying for the remission of the quit rents. The memorial sets out the circumstances clearly. It is in part as follows:

*Petition of Captain John MacDonald, of the 2nd Battalion of the 84th Regiment of Foot.*

. . . . "That in the year 1772 Your Majesty's petitioner and his brother had placed upwards of three hundred persons upon an allotment of twenty thousand acres of land purchased in this infant colony of St. John's Island, under articles by which they were to pay a yearly rent, increasing gradually to

£300 sterling in the year 1788, for about a third of the said lands upon perpetual leases. The foundation of settlement thus laid, every subsequent year would add an accession of value to the estate, and the whole could not fail thereby and by the great growth of the colony to become a considerable property even in the probable course of the petitioner's life. . . .

"In the spring of 1775 . . . petitioner was asked to go to the mainland, on the outbreak of the war (American Revolution), to help prevent the Scots Highlanders, settled in the revolted colonies, being seduced by the Congress, and for raising the 84th Regiment, in which it was proposed to give commissions to gentlemen of that description best known and respected.

"Petitioner went and was away on active service eight years. His brother also went and was killed in action. Petitioner had no power to pay the least attention to his interest in the Island.

"As a result, the settlers, despairing of his return and not receiving their location of land, and threatened by American privateers, removed to the estates of other proprietors who were not so obnoxious (to the Americans). . . .

"Not only was all this expenditure lost, but the lands were taken in execution for quit rents accruing to Your Majesty, when he was absent on service as above, and cannot be restored until the sum in arrears shall have been paid up or remitted by Your Majesty."

Then follows the usual prayer to have the quit rents remitted. Captain MacDonald ultimately recovered his lands.

Captain MacDonald lived on his Tracadie estate and made successful efforts to perform the conditions of the grants. It is said that he would not allow the spruce trees along the north shore of his property to be felled or the sand-hill grass cut, as he considered them to be a natural protection against the encroachment of the sands from the sea. In this he displayed foresight in advance of his time. After his death the woods were allowed to be removed, with the result of the encroachment of sand on the arable fields now to be seen on that shore. It is to be regretted that his practice has not been continued.

Captain MacDonald seems to have been possessed of an exceedingly hot temper, and also had the faculty of making very strong enemies and equally strong friends. Illustrations of the very opposite opinions held of him are found in the Assembly Minutes for the Session of 1797 and 1806 respectively. On 14th July, 1797, he wrote Lieutenant-Governor Fanning a letter "containing matter of the most alarming nature to the peace and good order of the Island at large; which being read with leave of the House was ordered to be entered upon tomorrow."

On 22nd July, the House, after summoning Captain MacDonald to attend at the Bar, which he refused to do, passed several resolutions in part as follows:

"Captain MacDonald has manifested a wanton and wicked attempt to impress by a torrent of the most shameless scurrility, mis-representation and falsehood, a belief in the Lieutenant-Governor that there actually existed a levelling party in this Island who were busily employed in disseminating principles analogous to those which led France to her disastrous internal calamities, and which assertions, upon a deliberate examination made by the House, appears to be false and groundless, and therefore an unprovoked slander on the good people of this Island.

"He has discouraged the success of His Majesty's recruiting service in the corps ordered to be raised . . . by menaces and threats to several of his tenants and dependants, prevented them from entering into the Independent Volunteer Militia Company embodied for the defence of this colony. . . .

"Has used unremitting industry in exciting factions and dissentions therein . . . particularly aiming at bringing the officers of this government into general contempt . . . to weaken the hands of government. . . .

"Being of such turbulent, restless and factious character and disposition, proceedings to enforce his attendance at the Bar of this House . . . would prove highly gratifying to him and might tend to raise him into a degree of consequence and importance before unknown among the few weak friends his baneful and pernicious endeavours have in any manner influenced, which appears to be his only object. . . . Therefore this House dispenses with his attendance."

In the Session of 1806 the Assembly expressed a very different opinion of MacDonald. On 16th December of that year the Assembly

172     HISTORY OF PRINCE EDWARD ISLAND.

passed an Address to the Lieutenant-Governor (DesBarres), in which they say:

"We, the members of the House of Assembly convened, beg leave to represent that Captain John MacDonald, proprietor of Lots 35 and 36 in this colony, has been particularly active in endeavouring to settle and improve the above Lots at a period of time so far distant as thirty-five years. That for this purpose he sold an estate in Scotland which now yields a large yearly income, and was unremitting in his personal exertions to bring out settlers and supply them with various necessaries at an expense altogether of several thousand pounds.

"We further beg leave to state that Captain MacDonald had by such expenditures involved himself in difficulties at the very time that he was benefiting the estates of sundry dormant proprietors. And we do humbly beg leave to represent him as a gentleman deserving the consideration of our beneficent Sovereign and his kindness, to the end that he may obtain either the remission of the sum now due for arrears of quit rent on Lots Nos. 35 and 36, or in case it shall not be thought advisable to grant such remission, then that His Majesty may be graciously pleased to order a like sum to be paid to Captain MacDonald out of the quit rent fund as a reward for his eminent and patriotic services.

"May it, therefore, please Your Excellency to lay before His Majesty's Ministers, this, our humble representation, together with such recommendation on the subject as may tend to promote the furtherance of our wishes."

(Sgd.)  ROBERT HODGSON,
*Speaker*.*

Assembly Room, December 16th, 1806.

---

*From a rare pamphlet — "Sketches of Highlanders, etc.," by R. C. MacDonald, Lieutenant-Colonel of the Tioram Regiment of Highlanders, Prince Edward Island, Chief of the Highland Society of Nova Scotia; paymaster of the 30th Regiment, published in 1843 by Henry Chubb & Co., Market Square, St. John, N. B., pages 44 and 45, the writer has gathered the following information with regard to Captain John MacDonald, "Chief of Glenaladale."

"At the commencement of the revolutionary war he (being offered the rank of Captain by the British Government) successfully used all his influence to induce his followers to join the Royal Standard. With Major Small he formed the 84th or Royal Highland Emigrant Regiment in Nova Scotia.

"During the American Revolution an American ship of war came to the Nova Scotia coast, near a port where Glenaladale was on detachment, with a small party of his men of the 84th Highland Emigrants. A part of the enemy's crew having landed for the purpose of plundering the people of the country, Captain MacDonald with his handful of men boarded the vessel, overcame

## THE STEWART IMMIGRANTS.

In December 1774, the Earl of Warwick, recommending Mr. Peter Stewart, as successor to Chief Justice Duport, wrote that "Mr. Stewart was bred to the law and upwards of twenty years in the practice of it; is a large proprietor and has sent near two hundred people thither, who have been settled upwards of two years." If this is correct, these settlers were a second lot sent out by Stewart and arrived the same year (1772) in which Captain John MacDonald brought out his immigrants in the Alexander to Tracadie. The writer thinks that the settlers mentioned by the Earl were really part of the hundred and twenty families brought out by Mr. Stewart and Sir James Montgomery in 1770. If so, they were two years earlier than those brought out by MacDonald in the Alexander.

---

those who had been left to take charge of her, hoisted the sails and took her in triumph into the harbour of Halifax. He then returned with a reinforcement and took the crews of Americans and French all prisoners."

Glenaladale died in 1811. In relation to his military abilities the following opinion was given by General Small in an address to the Government:

"The activity and unabating zeal of Captain John MacDonald of Glenaladale in bringing an excellent company into the field is his least recommendation, being acknowledged by all who know him to be one of the most accomplished men and best officers of his rank in His Majesty's service."

Another equally rare pamphlet,—"A Knight of the Eighteenth Century," a short account of Captain John MacDonald, Laird of Glenaladale and Glenfinnan, by Miss Anna MacDonald, confirms the foregoing, and adds: "Alexander MacDonald of Glenaladale in Scotland, was one of the first to join Prince Charles Stewart in the Rising of 1745. On 17th August, that year, the standard of the Stewarts was raised on Alexander's Estate of Glenfinnan." His son, the future Captain John, of Prince Edward Island, was then three years of age. At the age of twelve, he was sent to the Jesuit university of Ratisbon in Germany. He completed the course there, taking his degree, and was a very accomplished linguist.

Owing to religious troubles, Captain John and a number of his co-religionists determined in 1770 to emigrate from Scotland to Prince Edward Island. In 1771 he bought the "Tracadie Estate" of forty thousand acres on the Island. The intending emigrants, not having the means to pay their way out, funds to assist them were raised in the Roman Catholic churches in London. MacDonald mortgaged his own estates for the same purpose.

Through his exertions, in 1772, the Alexander, with a year's provisions, sailed from Scotland with two hundred emigrants. MacDonald came out the following year. In 1773, with another cargo of provisions and farm implements, he joined the settlers at what has since been called Scotchfort. He himself journeyed by way of Philadelphia and Boston.

The foregoing is confirmed with additional details, in "A Chapter in our Island History, 1772," a lecture by the late Rev. Dr. MacDonald, published in the Charlottetown Herald of 9th February, 1882.

Dr. MacDonald said: "Alexander of Glenaladale (Captain John's father) accompanied Charles Edward in his advance into England and fought with him at the battles of Preston Pans and Falkirk and finally at Culloden Moor."

Early in May, 1772, two hundred and ten emigrants sailed from Arisaig and South Uist for the Island of St. John, one hundred from Uist and one hundred and ten from the mainland. Rev. James MacDonald, a secular priest (See infra, Part VI, Miscellaneous, "The Roman Catholic Church) and Dr. Roderick McDonald, a medical man, accompanied them."

Immigration was a vital question, and various means were devised to answer it. Settlers were, from time to time, brought out by the proprietors, and others found their own way to the Island. Proposals from one Emmanuel Lutterlot to Lieutenant-Governor DesBrisay and the other proprietors of the Island of St. John, to furnish four thousand families as tenants and settlers on their respective estates in the said Island were enclosed to Lord Dartmouth by Mr. DesBrisay, in May, 1773.

The proposals, which came to nothing, are interesting as illustrating the means taken to settle these new possessions, and also the light in which the German princes looked upon their subjects as a species of negotiable commodity. They hired them out as mercenaries in war, and they were willing to dispose of them to supply population for new lands over the ocean.

Lutterlot's proposals were:

1. To procure four thousand families in three years from 20th March, 1773, or sooner, as can be ready, to be shipped in any ship or vessel from abroad, proper for that purpose, under inspection of agents of the proprietors and Mr. Lutterlot, said families to be delivered to the proprietors' agent at Port Joy, Richmond Bay or Cardigan Bay (death, etc., excepted).

2. Mr. Lutterlot to bear all expenses of the families, from the time of perfecting their leases (which is to be done before they embark), until landed in the Island of St. John. . . .

3. Major Lutterlot agreed to provide six months provisions for each family, consisting, at least, of four persons, three of whom to be capable to labour, the voyage to be included in the six months provisions.

4. Each proprietor is to contract for not less than fifty families, and not to lease to each family less than one hundred acres.

5. The proprietor to give security at the rate of five pounds for each family.

Mr. Lutterlot was to get the fifth year's rent at one shilling an acre. Rents to be one penny an acre for the first four years, and one shilling the fifth year, and thenceforth two shillings an acre.

On second best lands, one penny an acre for the first four years, and one shilling for the fifth year, and one shilling and sixpence thereafter.

On the third best lands, one penny an acre for the first four years, one shilling for the fifth year and forever thereafter.

Mr. DesBrisay, in a postcript, says:

"Mr. Lutterlot is a gentleman of the strictest probity and honour. He is a Major in the German service, and resident agent at London to Prince Ferdinand and other German princes, and is empowered by them to make the above proposals."

## HOUSE OF ASSEMBLY.

A time had now arrived when the Governor concluded that it would be practicable to establish a House of Assembly, In a despatch of 17th February, 1773, to Lord Dartmouth, he said that the increase of inhabitants during the previous summer enabled him to call a House of Representatives, as in the manner resolved upon by Council, namely, "by taking the voices of the whole people collectively, as belonging to one county, and waiving all kinds of qualifications, except their being Protestants and residents; it is impossible to have any other terms, owing to the unequal distribution of the inhabitants over the Island, and the small number of freeholders there are among them.

Wishing to have the representatives as respectable as possible, their number was limited to eighteen, as he knew there were about that many who would make a tolerable appearance. They were to meet in July. The Council, whose opinion the Governor asked as to calling a House of Assemblymen or Delegates, met on 17th February, and consisted of Mr. President (Wright), Mr. Attorney-General (Callbeck), Mr. Allenby and Mr. Spence. It resolved unanimously: "That it is the opinion of this Board that it would be conducive to the interests of this Island for an Assembly of Representatives to be called, and that, in their opinion, the Island is in a situation to admit of the calling thereof." In the afternoon meeting, the Governor and Chief Justice (Duport) being present, it was resolved "That a House of Representatives or General Assembly of the inhabitants of this Island be forthwith called."

This first House of Assembly held only one session, Robert Stewart was speaker. It passed thirteen Acts, the most important of which was, "An Act for the effectual recovery of certain of His Majesty's quit rents in the Island of St. John."

The Council was not only the executive body, it was also the Legislative Council or Upper House. It was quite irresponsible. Long and bitter were the struggles between the popular Assembly and the autocratic Council.

On 24th September of this year (1773), the failure of the proprietors to pay their quit rents and the distress occasioned the public officials, whose salaries were dependent thereon, were forceably brought to the attention of the English government by Chief Justice Duport, Attorney-General Callbeck, Provost Marshal Allanby and John Budd, Clerk of the Crown and Coroner for the Island, who, in a memorial to the Earl of Dartmouth, one of His Majesty's principal secretaries of state, submitted the facts to His Lordship. The memorialists in substance shewed: That the major part of the proprietors had petitioned His Majesty that the Island might be formed into a separate government, and in order to defray the charges of said government they engaged to commence the payment of half their alloted quit rents on the first day of May, one thousand seven hundred and sixty-nine.

That His Majesty thereupon ordered that the Island should be formed into a separate government, the expenses of which should be paid out of the quit rents as proposed by the proprietors.

That the memorialists were appointed to their offices by Royal Warrant and repaired to the Island in 1770, where they still continue officiating in their several departments.

That the Governor and the memorialists are the only officers that are or have been resident on the Island.

That the memorialists have suffered the greatest hardships, even to almost the total want of every necessary of life, for want of the regular payment of their salaries, there not having been quit rents enough received as yet to pay the memorialists one year's salaries, though they have held their offices upwards of four.

That there was not, on their arrival, a house fit to shelter them and they were obliged to expend all the small funds of cash which they brought with them, as also to strain their utmost credit to make habitations fit to live in, and they have been for above three years past, and are still, living upon a very scanty allowance of the worst kinds of provisions as they cannot afford to purchase a sufficiency of such as are good, nor could they have procured even such had not the Governor advanced more money than their dividends of the quit rents amounted to.

They submitted to His Lordship that their salaries are not adequate even if paid regularly, not being equal to any of those annexed to similar offices upon the continent, though every necessary is much cheaper there than here, all they get of every kind being imported from thence.

And they ask for payment of their arrears of salary and other relief. Thus early did this baneful question protrude itself into the Island legislation. This Act will be further referred to when the Land Question is being discussed. On 12th July, Patterson consulted his Council, whether to continue or dissolve the House of Representatives. Their opinion agreed with his, that it was better to dissolve, as there was advice of many respectable people coming to the Island this summer, who, on a new election, would give a greater choice of men, and the number might be increased.

## Public Roads.

From the day of his arrival in the Island, Patterson took much interest in the building of roads to connect the more important centres or settlements. He saw that without public highways, the progress of settlement in the colony must be slow. In November, 1774, he consulted his Council as to the enactment of a law for the building and carrying on of public roads. He proposed to find provisions for the people who worked on them, and required the Council to furnish an estimate of the time that each resident should work on them. In short he proposed to introduce the statute labour system.

Council were of opinion that all persons above the age of twenty-one, residing on the Island, should be looked upon as proper to be assembled for the making of the said roads, except actually indented servants. The inhabitants were divided into classes, whose respective periods of time to be given to the road work were as follows:

| | |
|---|---|
| Housekeepers, 1st Class | 18 days |
| Housekeepers, 2nd Class | 12 days |
| Housekeepers, 3rd Class | 6 days |
| Tradesmen | 9 days |
| Labourers | 6 days |

The Board were also of the opinion that the "properist" season of the year to commence operations would be the beginning of October in each year. The writer has not met with any report of the results from these proposals.

## Assembly of 1774.

In 1774, the House passed a number of Acts, of which one, "An Act entitled an Act for laying an Imposition on Retailers of Rum and other Distilled Spirituous Liquors," which passed its third reading by the Council, and was agreed to on the 11th October, is of interest, as being the first Act, other than a license Act, to regulate the liquor business, and also as being the first attempt to raise money for public purposes by a law. Only twenty pounds a year was expected from it, and the Governor's reason for assenting to it was the absolute necessity for a little money to answer the common exigencies of government and to pay off some small debts already contracted.

## Winter Mail Service.

In February, 1775, owing to the vessels in which his despatches were to have gone to England having been frozen into the harbour on the 21st December, when there happened severe frosts (remarkable as being uncommon so early in the season), Patterson determined to attempt a winter mail service. He endeavoured to persuade some men to attempt a passage, in a small canoe, to Nova Scotia. He points out that, if successful without great difficulty, it would remove an objection made by many people against being here, namely, being shut out from intercourse with the rest of the world for so long in winter, and if successful, he would have rendered an essential service to the Island. The attempt was made from Wood Islands and succeeded. Thus Patterson is entitled to the credit of inaugurating the winter mail service.

On 2nd August, the Governor, who had been granted a year's leave of absence, sailed in the ship, Two Friends, for England, and, in the absence of the Lieutenant-Governor, Mr. Callbeck, as the oldest councillor, assumed the administration of the government.

## Rape of the Government.

November, 1775, was an eventful month in the history of Prince Edward Island, then the Island of St. John. The population at that time was very small, and there was not, as a rule, much to disturb the even tenor of the ways of the few who were there. While its population was small, the Island was blessed with the machinery of a big government, one which was evidently devised with a view to future growth and development. It had a Governor, a Lieutenant-Governor, a Chief Justice, Assistant Justices (unpaid); an Executive Council of seven members (who were also the Second House or Legislative Council), nominally appointed by the Crown, but practically the creation of His Excellency, the Governor; an elective House of Assembly of eighteen members, some of whom were not at all particular about attending to their legislative duties, and had, on occasion, to be haled to the House by the Sergeant-at-Arms, duly authorized for this duty by the warrant of Mr. Speaker.

The Island had, also, an Attorney-General, a Solicitor-General, a Surveyor-General, a Provost Marshal, and other officials of greater or lesser rank. The officials, with the exception of the Lieutenant-Governor, who was not salaried, and who, though appointed some time previously, had not yet put in an appearance in His Majesty's Island of St. John, looked to the Old Country and the quit rents supposed to be levied on and collected from the large proprietory estates into which the Island had been parcelled out. The latter was a very precarious source, and those relying on it more often than not found that they were trusting to a broken reed.

The Imperial Government dealt liberally with the officials and paid salaries to the most important. Patterson filled the gubernatorial chair when he happened to be in the Island, but at this time he had obtained leave of absence for twelve months in England, leaving the Island in August of this year, which leave he extended till 1780, or over five years, and so was out of harm's way. The Lieutenant-Governor, Major DesBrisay, had not yet made his appearance in Charlottetown. Hon. Phillips Callbeck, the Attorney-General, was administering the government, assisted by the Council. He was, evidently, a man of ability, though the scope for its exercise was limited. His descendants have been numerous, the name being a prominent one to this day in Prince Edward Island.

The year 1775 was not only marked by the inception of the winter mail service, and by the Governor's departure for England, but is notable for the descent of American privateers upon Charlottetown, who plundered the place and carried away the leading members of the government, prisoners, to General Washington's headquarters.

A valuable article by Mr. John Calder Gordon, Secretary-Registrar of the Scottish Historical Society of North America, appeared in "Americana" for September, 1913, on this subject.* He writes of the conduct of Broughton and Selman, Commanders of the two privateers, in terms of the sternest indignation. Much of the following account is taken from Mr. Gordon's article. Mr. Gordon writes:

"The pillaging of the place, by Broughton and Selman, was not an act of war (though done in time and colour of war), but of plain unvarnished piracy, and one which ranks with the most contemptible, cowardly, cruel, dastardly, unjustifiable, unnecessary and wanton acts recorded in history, since the laws of war have existed. It was particularly atrocious, because it was done not only without orders, but in open defiance and contempt of orders, and for the purpose of private personal profit."

In October, 1775, Congress learned that two brigs had sailed from England loaded with arms and stores for Quebec. Instructions were sent to Washington to fit out two armed vessels to sail to the St. Lawrence to intercept them. He equipped two schooners, the Lynch and the Franklin, the former of six guns, ten swivels and seventy men, commanded by Captain Nichols Broughton; the latter of four guns, ten swivels and sixty men, commanded by Captain John Selman, both of Marblehead, Massachusetts. On 21st October they sailed from Beverly, Mass., for the St. Lawrence. Their orders were, in part, as follows:

HEADQUARTERS, October 16th, 1775.

"To make all possible despatch for the River St. Lawrecne, and there take station to intercept the two vessels. . . . To seize and take away any other transports laden with men, ammunition or other stores and secure them in such place as may be convenient." They were to receive one-third part of the value

---

*"Discovery, Early Descriptions and first Settlements of Prince Edward Island." The first chapter treats of the Discovery. The second treats of the raid by the two American privateers in November, 1775.

of any prizes they might take, the wearing apparel and private stock of the captain and other officers and passengers to be exempted.

The eighth paragraph was explicit: "Should you meet with any vessel, the property of the inhabitants of Canada, not employed in any respect in the service of the ministerial army, you are to treat such vessel with all kindness, and by no means suffer them to be injured or molested.

(Sgd.) GEORGE WASHINGTON.

They captured some prizes but never reached the St. Lawrence. They arrived at Charlottetown on 17th November. Phillips Callbeck, the Attorney-General, was acting as Governor, and he has left us a very complete and lucid account of the doings of these marauders on that day. This narrative of his, which is his memorial to Washington, and the one on which the latter acted, may be taken as true, as neither Broughton or Selman made any answer to it.

"That on Friday, the 17th November, two privateers arrived at Charlottetown, the capital of the Island; and immediately after, Captains Broughton and Selman, who commanded said vessels, landed with two parties under their command.

"That Mr. Callbeck met Selman on his landing, who, notwithstanding a very civil reception, instantly ordered him on board one of the vessels, without permitting him to return to his house, though requested so to do; and as he was going on board, one of the party insolently, without any provocation, struck him.

"That as soon as Mr. Callbeck was conveyed on board he received a message from Selman to send the keys of his house, stores, etc., otherwise he would break the doors open.

"On the receipt of the message, Mr. Callbeck sent the keys with one of the clerks (who was detained a prisoner), that he might attend and open the doors of such places as should be required to be inspected into. Upon the clerk informing Selman of Mr. Callbeck's directions, he told him he did not want his assistance, and desired him to deliver the keys, which he accordingly did.

"That Broughton and Selman, with their party, immediately proceeded to a store, in which there was a very large and valuable assortment of goods, all of which, except some very insignificant articles, they sent on board Selman's vessel. After which, although they had the keys of the doors, they broke open two other stores, out of which they took the most valuable articles, together with the entire stock of provisions that Mr. Callbeck had provided for his family's winter support, and the inhabitants immediately about him. That they next went into Mr. Callbeck's dwelling house, where they examined all his household papers, broke the bed chambers, closets and cellar doors open. In Mrs. Callbeck's bedroom they broke open her drawers and trunks, scattered her clothes about, read her letters from her mother and sister, took the bed and window curtains, bed and bedding, Mrs. Callbeck's rings, bracelets and trinkets, also some of her clothes. They then took the parlour window curtains, carpets and several articles of plate and household furniture, etc., etc., also all the porter, rum, geneva and wine (except one cask which they stove the head into and drank the whole out). At the same time they plundered the whole of Mrs. Callbeck's little stores of vinegar, oil, candles, fruit, sweetmeats, bacon, hams, etc.

"Not yet satisfied with wanton depredation, they next went to Mr. Callbeck's office, from which they took some of his clothes, etc., the Provincial silver seal, Governor Patterson's commission, two trunks full of goods, his clerk's desk and wearing apparel; opened Mr. Callbeck's bureau and desks, read all his papers, which were of great importance in his private connections.

"That after they had ravaged Mr. Callbeck's house and outhouses, they broke into Governor Patterson's house (in which no person resided), out of which they took the window curtains, carpets, looking glasses, cases of knives and forks, silver spoons, table linen, sheets, bedding, his wearing apparel, and the Church furniture, which was deposited in his house, etc., etc., broke a quantity of his china and drank what liquors were in the house.

"That after they had accomplished thus far of their cruelty, they made Mr. Wright a prisoner, and, with insulting language, laughed at the tears of his wife and sister, who were in the greatest agony of distress at so cruel a separation from their husband and brother.

"That after Mr. Wright came on board where Mr. Callbeck was confined, they represented the treatment they had received, and the confidence they had that Broughton and Selman had no orders to commit such outrages, they, for the purpose of justifying themselves, read their orders, by which it appeared that they were in no way directed to go to the Island, and that they were particularly cautioned not to abuse private property; upon which Mr. Callbeck and Mr. Wright laboured, all in their power, to convince them of their not having, in any respect, conformed to their instructions or orders. They urged the cruelty of taking them away, and, although it was probable they would be immediately dismissed, yet it would be almost impossible for them to get back to the Island before winter set in, the season being so far advanced. Notwithstanding the reiteration of every argument that could be offered, they were deaf to every feeling and sensation of honour, and determined to take away Mr. Callbeck and his effects with Mr. Wright. Mr. Callbeck supposes that they have in their custody, of his property, to the amount of £2,000 sterling. To exaggerate the cruel treatment he has received, is impossible; and it is equally so even to give an exact detail of the injuries that have been offered to him and his property. All his papers read, some of which were of a very private nature; although they had all his keys, his doors broken down; his effects, and the provisions and necessaries he had provided for his family's support taken away and wantonly destroyed, his wife left destitute of every support; not so much as a candle to burn.

"Also, between seventy and eighty people, who were lately arrived on the Island, and depended on him for their support during the winter, are left without any sort of provisions; some of whom, if not all, will inevitably perish for want, which would have been prevented had Mr. Callbeck been permitted to stay. Of this both Broughton and Selman were informed by him, as well as others. Not to add the further disadvantages that Mr. Callbeck suffers by being taken away, he is debarred from assisting Mrs. Callbeck in her distressed condition, and taking the necessary care of what remains of a shattered fortune. What has been left of his property in the Island is in the hands of servants, who, doubtless, will be neglectful, and perhaps avail themselves, under the depredations that have been committed on his property, by alleging several of his effects, which they will choose to plunder, were taken by Broughton, Selman and party. They, by their conduct, have left Mrs. Callbeck open to these apprehensions; for, although it was urged and requested by his clerks, that an inventory should be taken of the effects they took away, they would not permit it, nor would they suffer the clerks to stand by while they were sending the things away, which were sent in utmost disorder.

"To make it still more doubtful, and to give the inhabitants an opportunity to plunder, Broughton and Selman, after they had made a prisoner of Mr. Wright, suffered some of their people to remain on shore (without an officer), who broke down the doors and windows of Governor Patterson's and Mr. Callbeck's houses, and a second time lawlessly entered and took out what they pleased, and finished what liquor had been left in both houses."

After leaving Charlottetown, they took a vessel from London having on board J. R. Spence, Mr. Higgins and the chaplain, Mr. DesBrisay. Spence, his wife and servants, and Mr. DesBrisay were released, but all their effects were kept with the exception of their clothes and bedding. They subsequently reached the Island.

Washington was indignant at the conduct of the two captains.

"The plague, trouble and vexation," he wrote, "I have had with the crews of all the armed vessels, are inexpressible. I do believe there is not on earth a more disorderly set."

On 7th December he wrote the President of Congress:

"My fears that Broughton and Selman would not effect any good purpose were too well founded. They are returned and brought with them three of the principal inhabitants of the Island of St. John. Mr. Callbeck, as president of the Council, acted as Governor. They brought the Governor's commission and the Province seal. As the captains acted without any warranty for such conduct, I have thought it but justice to release these gentlemen, whose families were left in the utmost distress."

On his release, Callbeck wrote to Washington:

"I should ill deserve the generous treatment which your Excellency has been pleased to show me had I not gratitude to acknowledge so great a favour. I cannot ascribe any part of it to my own merit, but must impute the whole to the philanthropy and humane disposition that so truly characterizes General Washington. Be so kind, therefore, as to accept the only return in my power, that of my most grateful thanks."

Broughton and Selman, on this cruise, besides sacking Charlottetown took ten prizes, which, Mr. Gordon says, were released. The two captains were severely reprimanded by General Washington, who told them, in their own style, "that they had done those things which they ought not to have done, and left undone those things which it was their duty to have done." They were dismissed from their commands and never afterwards entered the Continental service. Mr. Gordon indignantly adds, "The conduct of the two captains is beyond the saving grace of an excuse." We are told that Broughton, the ranking officer, was "a prominent and active member of the First Church at Marblehead until the time of his death." With fine sarcasm Mr. Gordon says: "If there be now alive any descendants of the men whom he plundered they may be interested to know that the inscription on his tombstone describes him as 'a man, whose life and conversation shed lustre on his religious profession and furnished an example every way worthy of imitation.'"

Mr. Stewart, who treats but briefly of this episode in our Island story, says: "Upon the arrival of these gentlemen (that is Messrs. Callbeck and Wright) at the headquarters of the American army, then at Cambridge in New England, it appeared that the rebel officers had acted in this manner totally without any orders from their superiors; . . . their prisoners were immediately discharged with many polite expressions of regret for their sufferings, and the plundered property was all honourably restored." This from the well-known character of Washington, and also from the fact that it was not the policy of the revolting colonies to antagonize the other colonies which had not joined in the revolt, is what might have been expected.

It is not, however, what the victims of the raid themselves say. Mr. John Russell Spence, a member of the Council, writing from Canso on 23rd November to Lord Dartmouth, informs him that while waiting there for a wind to take him to the Island of St. John's, he was, on the 20th, captured by the schooners which had on board Messrs. Callbeck and Wright. He adds that, upon applying to the commanders, they released him and his wife and servants, giving them only their clothes and bedding, but that the rest of his effects they carried off. The Rev. Mr. DesBrisay was released with him. This is the only intimation of the latter's having been captured that the writer has seen.

"Various writers, including Jared Sparks, a former president of Harvard, have sought to excuse these men, but no valid excuse can be offered for them. They were really pirates. Their orders were explicit, and they contravened them. They were men of experience. Broughton was fifty-one years of age and had been a master mariner for twenty years, part at least of that time in the foreign trade. Selman was considered old enough and experienced enough to receive commissions. As ranking officer, Broughton was most to blame."

For a great part of the foregoing, the writer is indebted to Mr. Gordon's excellent article in Americana. Mr. Gordon, as appears from the article itself, based it upon General Washington's orders, his reports on the piratical doings of Broughton and Selman, and upon Mr. Callbeck's memorial and letter to the American commander.

Mr. John Budd, clerk of the Courts, writing on 25th November, mentions the plunder of supplies that had been collected for one hundred and three souls who had arrived late in the fall and settled on Lot 5, belonging to Messrs. Smith & Co. He had himself been seized and kept prisoner for forty-eight hours and then discharged, and, on being discharged, at once notified Robert Stewart, senior councillor, requesting him to take command of the province.

Messrs. Wright and Callbeck, the principal sufferers, after they had reached Halifax on their return from General Washington's headquarters, themselves made very full reports to Lord Dartmouth. Writing on 15th December from Halifax, Mr. Wright, after shortly relating their capture by "a number of armed men from two New England schooners, then at anchor before the town," goes on to say that "they plundered Governor Patterson's, Mr. Callbeck's and other houses, of almost every article which they thought worth carrying off . . . even the Church furniture, provincial seal, etc., . . . From the reception we met with at the headquarters at Cambridge, and particularly from General Washington, I have reason to believe that these transactions were not intended, but proceeded from a spirit of revenge, in the commanders of these vessels, on their having been informed that recruits had been raised on the Island and sent for the defence of Quebec; of this they accused us with, to the General, and particularly that I (although it was my duty as a magistrate) had been very active thereto in having attested them. We were released from our captivity to make the best of our distressed situation, without the least offer of redress for the injuries we had sustained to almost the inevitable ruin of my family."

Writing at great length, on 5th January, 1776, Mr. Callbeck prefaces his despatch with a recital of his efforts to assist a recruiting party sent to the Island by General Gage, and of the success which had attended his efforts. He goes on to say that the privateers made preparations to fire on the town, and their commanders, with armed parties, landed. To save the town from being burned, he resolved, having no force, to face them singly, when one of the parties made him prisoner and instantly conveyed him on board of one of the privateers, after which they proceeded to commit the most wanton and flagrant outrages on Governor Patterson's interests and his house. They possessed themselves of his (Callbeck's) property to the amount of upwards of two thousand pounds sterling, and then sailed with him and Mr. Wright, whom they also made prisoner. Previously to attacking Charlottetown, they had been in the Gut of Canso three weeks and captured five vessels loaded with fish, and on their return captured three more, without the least opposition. Not satisfied with their flagitious depredations on the whole of his property and the common rights of mankind, these monsters, blood-thirsty, sought out Mrs. Callbeck for the purpose (to use their own words) of cutting her throat, because her father, a Mr. Coffin of Boston, is remarkable for his attachment to the Government. She was, fortunately, out at his farm, four miles distant, and escaped, but "these brutal violaters of domestic felicity have left her without a single glass of wine, without a candle to burn, or a sufficiency of provisions of the bread kind, most of the furniture of her house taken away and, for what I know, all her clothes. They have certainly taken away her best things, together with her rings, bracelets, etc., etc., none of which have been restored, although some of them have been seen worn by the connections of these villains."

After a passage of fourteen days, the prisoners reached Winter Harbour, one hundred and ten miles east of Cambridge. They were received by Washington very politely. The relation of the barbarities inflicted on them affected the authorities so much that they were shortly afterwards liberated. "Fearing a change in their favourable resolutions, which I had a right to expect, the corporal (who was employed on the Island recruiting) being a prisoner with us, and having accounts in his pocket of the money I advanced to carry on the service, I hastened away, after three days stay, and at a considerable expense have fortunately got thus far, having been brought in a state of captivity six hundred miles by sea, and travelled one hundred and twenty miles by land, all of which I have repeated on my return."

Mr. Callbeck then went on to give a lengthy statement of the state of the rebel forces, and of the condition of affairs in the New England provinces. On the 15th January he again wrote at length, urging that measures to provide for the future defence of the Island be taken. Considerable further correspondence took place between Callbeck and the home authorities, and also with General Howe, on the same subject. Mr. Callbeck did take very active measures to put the Island in a posture of defence.

In October, 1776, the Council and House of Representatives jointly memorialized Lord Howe, praying for a vessel of defence to winter here, and proposed that Lieutenant Edmund Dodd, commander of His Majesty's armed brig, the Dilligent, be granted them as their future safeguard. In February, 1777, the Grand Jury addressed Mr. Callbeck, President of the Council and Acting Governor, setting out the dangers to life and property in which the inhabitants were, by reason of their firm attachment to their sovereign and the laws of their country, and pray "that every possible means may be put into execution for the immediate protection of this province."

The Dilligent was stationed at Charlottetown during the summer of 1776 for the protection of the Island, and was relieved in November by the Hunter, sloop of war, Captain Boyle, who wintered and spent the following summer, and until November, here for the same purpose. In December, the Hunter brought from Halifax fifty stand of arms, one hundred weight of gunpowder, and musket balls in proportion, for a company being raised by Callbeck.

This company the Secretary of State for the Colonies had, in 1777, directed Mr. Callbeck to raise for the defence of the Island. Most of those fitted to be soldiers had already enlisted in two new regiments commanded by Colonels McLean and Goreham, hence the company could not be completed.*

The following year, however, four provincial or independent companies were sent from New York under the command of Major Hierlehy, and the commanding engineer of Nova Scotia was directed to erect barracks for them and also such works of defence as were necessary. From this time, excepting a few sheep taken at distant parts of the Island by privateers, and the robbery of valuable property from the harbour of Georgetown, the Island was undisturbed during the remainder of the war. The frigates, which annually brought out the Quebec convoys, usually spent part of the summer here. They and other ships, cruising in the Gulf, captured several of the enemy's armed ships in this neighbourhood and brought them to Charlottetown, where their crews were landed and afterwards sent to Nova Scotia and marched through the woods to Halifax, under escort of detachments from our garrison.†

In 1794 two provincial companies were raised for the protection of the Island. In addition to these, two companies and a small detachment of the royal artillery; three troops of volunteers horse and a light infantry company were formed among the inhabitants, handsomely clothed and mounted at their own expense; the arms and accoutrements being given by the government.‡

Mr. Benjamin Chappel entered in his diary a note of privateers appearing off New London and Malpeque. Under date of 6th June, 1778, he notes that two privateers appeared off the Bar (New London) plundering Malpeque. On 7th June the privateers were in Malpeque. On the 8th they "chase a vessel and seem to stand for us. In the afternoon the privateers disappear at the west, a vessel stands for us." The attitude of the people, was "watching and warding."

On the 18th August, 1778, Callbeck reported to Lord George Germain that the Island had again been invaded by two rebel privateers, who landed at St. Peters and "began their accustomed wanton depredations by shooting, with grape shot, oxen and sheep, and taking but very few of them away for use." He ordered a detachment of his own company, and Colonel Hierlethy's independent companies, who had been sent from New York by

---
*Stewart.
†Id.
‡Id. page 244, 245.

General Howe, to march against them, but the rebels had notice and got away. They took two schooners belonging to the Island. His Majesty's brigantine Cabot, Commander Edmund Dodd, which was lying in the harbour, started in quest of the marauders but could not come up with them.

About this time some of our neighbours in Cumberland, Nova Scotia, who were disaffected, on the arrival among them of two whale-boats from Machias, Massachusetts, rebelled and laid siege to Fort Cumberland, then garrisoned by a newly raised provincial corps under Colonel Goreham. They planned a second raid on Charlottetown, but not having any craft to carry off a number of dismounted cannon at Fort Amherst, which was one of their objects, they first visited Pictou, where, joined by several of the inhabitants, they seized a valuable armed vessel then loading for Scotland. Not knowing the Island's state of defence, they went to Bay Verte to procure reinforcements from those besieging Fort Cumberland. Just then the Hunter arrived on her way to Charlottetown, having retaken a sloop which was one of their prizes captured at Pictou. She was fitted out by Captain Boyle and sent, under command of Lieutenant Kippie, after the ship. The sloop came up with her the next day and found that, in consequence of the defeat of the rebels at Fort Cumberland by the arrival of re-inforcements from Halifax, she had been given up to the mate, the rebels escaping on shore. She was brought into Charlottetown and given up to her commander, who, thinking it unsafe to return to Pictou, wintered in the Island.*

In November, 1775, shortly after the raid by Broughton and Selman, "a ship valuably loaded from London, with a number of settlers on board, suffered shipwreck on the north shore of the Island; the people were saved, but their effects and the cargo were almost totally lost." Chief Justice Stewart who, with his ten children were passengers in this vessel, lost nearly everything they possessed.

---

*Mr. Benjamin Chappel for many years kept a diary in his business day-book. In addition to his business entries, he each day made very brief notes of the day's happenings. The business entries and the happenings are mixed together so that one has to read both to get at the latter. The happenings were very numerous and the volumes of the old day-book diary are very valuable and interesting.

## LAND DEFENCE.

Immediately after again setting his feet on British soil, Callbeck addressed himself with persistent energy to the task of having the Island fortified against future attack. In his despatch of 15th January, 1776, to Lord Dartmouth, he laid before his Lordship the very defenceless state of the Island and what, in his opinion, might be done for its defence. At present, he said, the Island was "without any militia, arms or ammunition," in consequence of which state of affairs His Majesty's servants, as well as the settlements and tenantry of some gentlemen, who, stimulated by their loyalty to their Sovereign, "had, on the outbreak of war, left their habitations and entered His Majesty's service, all of whom are now on duty in different parts of America, would be in a very disagreeable and precarious position. The officers of government are apprehensive of danger, owing to their defenceless state. He had written Admiral Shuldham, requesting him to send a frigate to be stationed at the Island early next spring. He also wrote General Howe, asking him to send two companies to be quartered at Charlottetown. He thought these would be sufficient to oppose the landing of a considerable number of the enemy. He suggested that there should be erected a work on a crescent shaped piece of ground on the shore, at the beginning of the town, which from its eminence and natural advantages would command the entire harbour and all the rivers, so much that no vessel that may be employed in the rebel service could pass it. There were some cannon lying near the place that could be mounted on the work, and this fortification and small armament, there was not a doubt, would protect the capital and other parts of the Island.

Should General Howe be unable to spare so many troops, Callbeck proposed himself to raise, on the Island, an independent company of one hundred men or more, to continue for such time as might be thought proper. If this proposal should be approved, and Callbeck himself should be appointed, or whoever should be appointed, such person should be ordered immediately on the service. To carry it through it would be necessary to be assisted with enlisting money, provisions, arms, ammunition and other necessaries usually allowed troops while raising or on service. In the present state of the Island it could not itself supply these things. Should it be determined that the Island is not an object to be defended, he pointed out that it would be necessary to remove or destroy sixteen nine-pounders, most of which are fit for service, one eight-inch mortar, a number of cannon ball and grape-shot, all of which are at Fort Amherst.

The barracks are entirely down, everything about the fort is in ruins, and if the cannon are not some way disposed of they will be a temptation to the rebels to make a second raid.

Lord George Germain, who had succeeded Lord Dartmouth in the Colonial Office, replying, on 1st April, 1776, said that in view of the descent at Port la Joie, it was thought advisable to augment the Newfoundland fleet, to order it to be ready to proceed to its station at the latter end of the month of February and to give particular instructions to the admiral to be attentive to the security and protection of His Majesty's possessions in every part of the Gulf of St. Lawrence, and that it was from the vigilance of that fleet that St. John's Island is to expect security. At the same time he did not disapprove of the applications made to General Howe and Admiral Shuldham, and would be glad if His Majesty's service will admit of their sending the force asked for, but warned them not to depend upon this relief, at least not so far as to neglect the pursuit of every means to induce the inhabitants to keep watch where the rebels could expect any disadvantage from a descent, and to rely on themselves for defence in case of any sudden insult like that of the 17th November.

Writing again, on 2nd March, 1776, Callbeck, says that he had determined immediately to leave Halifax and attempt returning to the Island, where, in order to carry on recruiting, re-victualing, clothing, etc., of the hundred men he had set about to raise, he had, that day, drawn on the Lords of the Treasury for £824 2s. 4d. sterling, and had taken the liberty of advising them thereof, and assures His Lordship that in less than three months he will raise one hundred unexceptionable men. He adds that he has got from Captain Spry, Chief Engineer of this province, two plans of a work to be erected, also estimates, which he sends to His Lordship for his approbation of one of them; after which he proposes drawing on the Lords of the Treasury for the amount of the one approved of; and in the meantime would erect a temporary log breast-work.*

---

*See plans printed herein

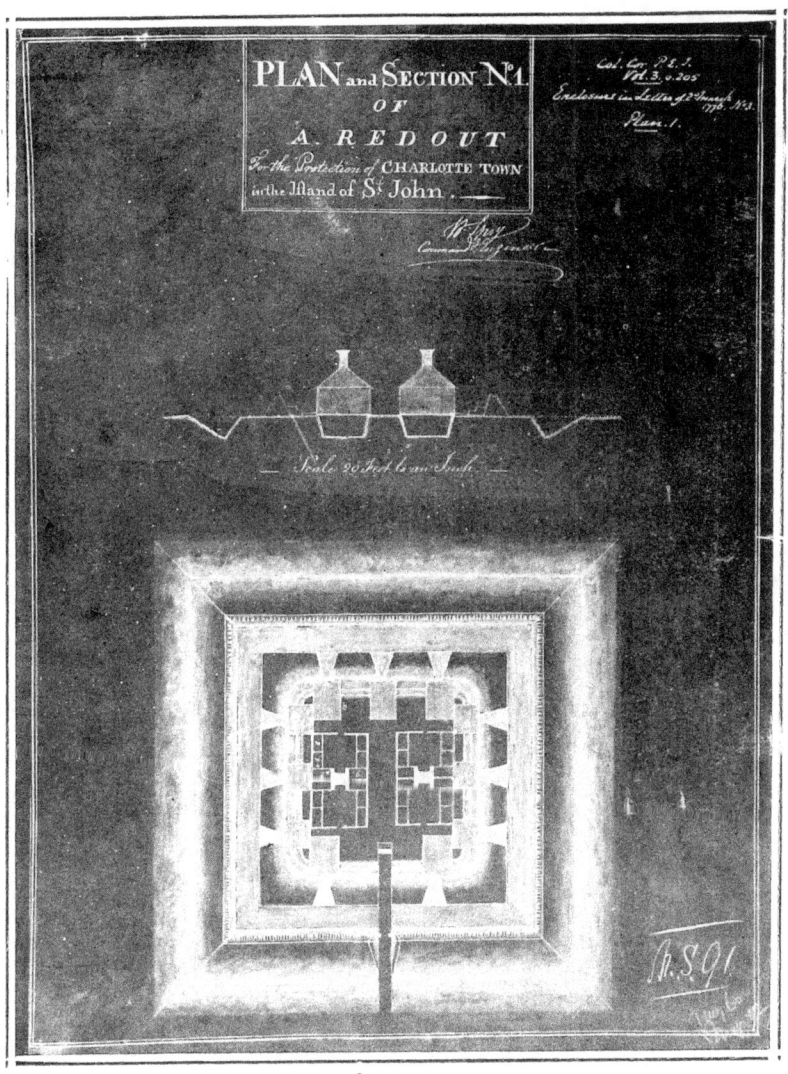

PLAN AND SECTION No. 1 OF A REDOUBT FOR THE DEFENCE OF
CHARLOTTETOWN PREPARED BY CAPTAIN SPRY,
CHIEF ENGINEER OF NOVA SCOTIA, FOR
PHILLIPS CALLBECK, A. D. 1776.

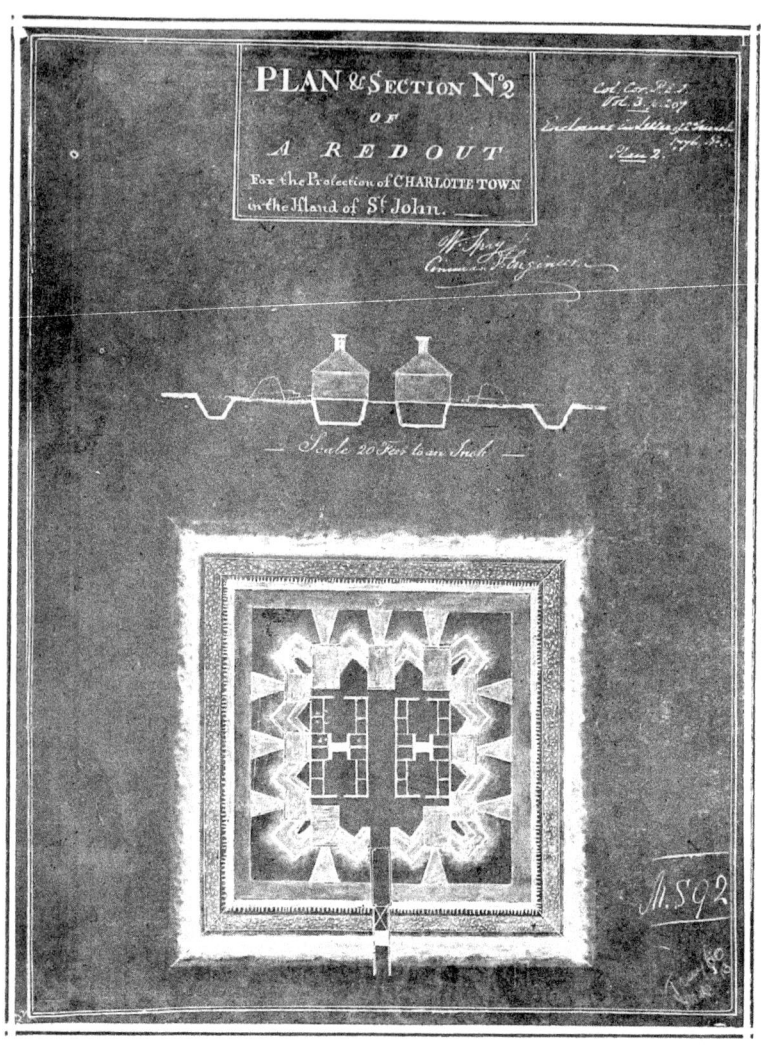

PLAN SECTION No. 2, FOR THE DEFENCE OF CHARLOTTETOWN, PREPARED FOR MR. CALLBECK BY CAPTAIN SPRY, CHIEF ENGINEER OF NOVA SCOTIA, A. D. 1776.

General Howe, replying on 6th February, 1776, to letters from Callbeck of 5th and 10th January, approves of the latter's intention to return as soon as possible, to his duty, and informs him that: "The admiral proposes to send a ship-of-war in the spring for your protection, by which you will, probably, be freed from future insults in the same way, and as you seem to think that one hundred men will be sufficient for the defence of your capital when a ship is stationed there, I would advise your raising a company upon the Island to consist of that number, putting yourself at the head of it, and commissioning officers in proportion, the whole to be paid at the full rate allowed for the King's troops. I would also recommend your constructing the work proposed upon the eminence near Charlottetown, erecting only a shed barrack within to contain your company for the present. It will also be necessary to appoint signals and place beacons for assembling the militia in case of an invasion.

"With regard to the expenses that must attend the raising of these works and payment of the company, the Island not being immediately within the district of my command, I can give no positive orders, but I have not a doubt that government will defray all charges upon your representation, and I should expect that the inhabitants, on this emergency, will readily exert themselves in defence of their property, more especially as by quitting it, which you seem to apprehend may be the case, they must lose all the advantages they would otherwise reap by supplying the army with the produce of their estates. However, if they should decline to act in the spirited manner that is necessary, I shall advise the admiral to remove the ordnance stores, which, by your information, are upon the Island.

"At all events, I shall send arms for your company by the man-of-war, with ammunition in proportion for them and six nine-pounders with proper carriages for the last, which will probably mount as many guns as you will find fit for service." He then goes on to express "my fullest approbation of your proposals for the defence of the Island, in which I heartily wish you success and an adequate reward for your sufferings and services."

Soon after his return from Halifax, on 26th June, 1776, Callbeck, as administrator of the government, convened the General Assembly in its second session. In his opening speech he informed the House that, during his absence, he had exerted himself assiduously to secure protection against future wanton depredations, such as he had "woefully" experienced. "In consideration of our sufferings and defenceless state the fleet on the Newfoundland station had been augmented and its commander-in-chief had been instructed to look to the security and protection of this Island and other possessions in the Gulf of St. Lawrence. For this we are indebted to the unwearied zeal of our excellent Governor, whose attention to the prosperity of this Island cannot be too gratefully acknowledged." Admiral Shuldham, on Callbeck's application, had sent the armed vessel now stationed here to remain until the arrival of a frigate from Quebec. He suggested, in closing, a conference between both Houses "to devise some salutary measure for securing ourselves against future invasion."

Three years later, on 30th July, 1779, in opening the first session of a new House, Callbeck declared his confidence that they had come together with the justest sentiment of duty to our excellent Sovereign, "who has gratified the earnest wishes and entreaties of his faithful subjects of this Island by directing a part of his army to be quartered here, and also giving orders for fortifications to be carried on when judged necessary for the Island's defence. . . . We cannot express our gratitude in a more acceptable manner than by adding to that force which has been sent for our protection at this critical and alarming conjuncture, when our natural enemies, the French and Spaniards, allured by the continuance of our deluded brethren's unnatural rebellion, have meditated the destruction of the British Empire. To effect which and an internal security a well-regulated militia is essential."

## WINTER CROSSING.

In February, 1777, Callbeck wrote to Lord George Germain that he was endeavouring to persuade a man or two, with a Mr. Stewart, one of his officers, to attempt a passage in a small canoe to Nova Scotia, and hoped to succeed if the weather proved the least favourable.

"The same was effected by Governor Patterson, and, if this second attempt succeeds, it will be a means of removing an objection which many people have made against living here, they being so long shut up from any intercourse with the rest of the world."

In April, 1777, Lord George Germain informed Patterson, in London, that a vote of three thousand pounds had been given for the civil establishment of the Island, and added that it was His Majesty's pleasure that he return to his government on the first opportunity of safe conveyance, which, however, the Governor did not do until three years later. Accompanying Lord Germain's despatch was an estimate of the civil establishment and incidental expenses attending the same, from the 1st of January, 1777, to the 1st of January, 1778, as follows:

| | |
|---|---:|
| To the salary of the Governor-in-Chief | £1,000 |
| To the salary of the Chief Justice | 400 |
| To the salary of the Attorney-General | 200 |
| To the salary of the Secretary and Registrar | 300 |
| To the salary of the Surveyor of Lands | 180 |
| To the salary of the Minister of the Church of England | 150 |
| To the salary of the King's Agent | 150 |
| To the salary of the Clerk of the Crown and Coroner | 120 |
| To the salary of the Clerk of the Council | 80 |
| To the salary of the Naval Officer | 100 |
| To the salary of the Sheriff or Provost Marshal | 100 |
| To the salary of a Schoolmaster | 50 |
| To an allowance for a Private Secretary, and for despatch boats to and from the Continent, and also for stationery, firewood, etc., etc. | 170 |
| | £3,000 |

In May, 1778, Lord George Germain again informed Patterson that he had received the King's commands to signify to him His Majesty's pleasure that he immediately return to his government and avail himself of the opportunity of a safe conveyance thereto. Patterson did not leave till the next year, when he was eight months on the way, having wintered, according to Lieutenant-Governor DesBrisay, either in Georgia or New York. He arrived in Charlottetown on 28th June, 1780, having been, he writes, six months of the eight at sea. His leave of absence for twelve months had been stretched out to five years; but he seems to have been working in the Island's interests during his long absence. Writing to Lord George Germain, on 6th July, he says: "I arrived here on the 28th ult. . . . My voyages (for I have had several) have all been uncommonly long, and considering my anxiety to be here they were to me extremely tedious. I was eight months from the time of my sailing till my arrival, six of which I was at sea." He also speaks most highly of Mr. Callbeck's management of affairs during his absence. The colony had improved, he believes the population had doubled, and says, "They are comfortable in their situation, have large stocks of cattle, and abound with all the necessaries of life as far as they regard the table."

The previous month (May) Mr. DesBrisay wrote, stating that he could not be happy under the command of Patterson, and asked to be appointed Lieutenant-Governor of Nova Scotia, or, if he had to remain here, that he be given a salary as Lieutenant-Governor, as his present salary of three hundred pounds as secretary is but small, owing to the high prices here. He enforced his request by giving the prices of various articles, which, as they may be of interest to present-day householders, are here produced. It will be remembered that these prices were in sterling. They were:

| | |
|---|---|
| Beef, per pound | 7d. = 14c. |
| Mutton, per pound | 7d. = 14c. |
| Veal, per pound | 10d. = 20c. |
| Pork, per pound | 6d. = 12c. |
| Fresh Butter, per pound | 1s. 3d. = 30c. |
| A loaf of Bread weighing three and one-half pounds | 1s. 3d. = 30c. |
| Lump Sugar, per pound | 2s. 6d. = 60c. |
| Milk, a quart | 0s. 6d. = 12c. |

"And all other articles, wearing apparel, etc., etc., as dear in proportion."

### CHANGE OF NAME.

The Assembly was to have met the day of Patterson's arrival, but as a sufficient number to form a House did not attend, it was adjourned for five days, when curiosity brought every member to town who had heard of his arrival. They passed several Acts, particularly one to change the name of the Island to "New Ireland." In urging its approval, the Governor pointed out that the Island is mistaken for a variety of places of the same name with which it is surrounded; that "St. John's, Newfoundland, is the place longest known by that name to the majority of the mercantile and common people at home; and since ever it has been known the ideas of fogs and barrenness have been annexed to it. We are so much confounded with this part in particular that people have even sailed for Newfoundland, thinking they were coming hither." He adds that the confusion occasioned in their correspondence was inconceivable. The home government, however, would not assent to this name, as it was already appropriated, and suggested New Guernsey or New Anglesea.

Mr. John Stewart, the colony's agent in London,* writing to Patterson gave other, and doubtless correct, reasons for the disallowance of this Act. This, he wrote, was regarded as an unprecedented irregularity, and that the Assembly should have set out reasons for the change which were admitted to have weight, by petition to the King, "instead of passing a presumptuous Act which is neither warranted by law or usage." Their Lordships of the Privy Council stood upon their offended dignity and disallowed the Act. In 1794, Prince Edward, Duke of Kent, arrived in Halifax. That year two provincial companies were raised for the protection of the Island. When the Duke became Commander-in-Chief in British North America he ordered new barracks to be erected in Charlottetown as well as defensive works for the harbour. He never visited the Island; but because of his interest in its welfare and of the intense loyalty of its people, and of its having been decided to change the name of the Island, a local Act was passed in 1798, assented to 1st February, 1799, changing its name from St. John to that it has ever since borne, namely, "Prince Edward Island."

In March, 1781, the Governor forwarded a number of Acts for approval, among which it seems strange to find one thus entitled, "An Act declaring that Baptism of Slaves shall not exempt them from Bondage." Slavery did exist here for some decades, but the number of slaves was very small, and those mostly domestic servants. A few were brought in by refugees from the United States, and as late as the opening years of the nineteenth century transfers of slaves were registered in the registry office in Charlottetown.

―――――
*Not to be confounded with John Stewart of Mount Stewart.

## PRIVATEERS.

At a meeting of Council held 11th June of this year (1781), "His Excellency informed the Board that he had information that there are two small privateers cruising for some days past between the continent and this harbour. And that the largest of them, from report, has about eight or ten swivels and from thirty to forty men; and that the other is much smaller."

## MILITIA.

On 13th September, Patterson laid before the Council a letter received by him from Halifax regarding the removal of the troops from this Island. The writer, Brigadier Campbell, mentioned that the commander-in-chief had granted a warrant to Captain Callbeck to complete his company to one hundred men for the defence of the Island, and that when his Excellency thought it sufficiently strong he was to order the independent companies to quit the Island for Halifax and be incorporated with the Nova Scotia volunteers. . . . General Campbell added that Patterson had his permission (should he think it necessary) to detain two subaltern officers, two sergeants, one drummer and forty rank and fyle from the independent companies.

A long discussion took place when it was resolved that as no block-house had yet been erected, no arms or ammunition supplied as promised, and many other things not done as promised, it was not advisable that the companies leave here until these things have been performed.

## QUIT RENTS — ESCHEAT.

When, on the petition of the proprietors, the Island of St. John was, in 1769, separated from Nova Scotia and formed into an independent province, they agreed to pay quit rents each year to an amount sufficient to cover the cost of the civil government. With a very few honourable exceptions the proprietors failed to comply with this part of their agreement. A result was that government officials who depended upon these quit rents for payment of their salaries went unpaid and were reduced, in some instances, to great distress. John Duport, the Chief Justice, drawing for his pay on the Governor's London agent in the spring of 1771, had his drafts dishonoured and was reduced to want, because the proprietors had not paid their quit rents. This was little more than a year after their undertaking. Their arrears continued to accumulate without any effort, as evidently with no intention, on the part of the proprietors to make payment. So distressed became the position of the officials that the Governor was compelled to appropriate the sum of £3,000, granted by the Home Parliament for public buildings, to the support of himself and the other officers.

In 1773, a law was enacted by the Island Legislature, "for the effectual recovery of certain of His Majesty's quit rents in the Island of St. John," which had received the Royal assent. Patterson went to England in 1775. While he was there, the British government, by minute of Council of 7th August, 1776, ordered that the arrears of quit rents due should be enforced by legal proceedings, and that the sum thus obtained should be devoted to the refunding of the amount expended in a manner incompatible with the object for which it was voted. This refers to the £3,000 voted for the erection of public buildings and which had been applied in payment of official salaries.

After his return to the Island in 1780 the Governor determined, in conformity with the Treasury minutes of 7th August, 1776, to enforce the Act of 1773, which had received the Royal assent. Early in 1781 proceedings were commenced against the townships in arrears, as enumerated in the Act of 1773, and the sale of several effected. Complaint was made to the British Government and powerful influence was brought to counteract them. As the Act of 1773 only applied to part of the lands, another Act was passed in 1781 to render the sale of all lands in arrears legal. This Act had a clause suspending its operation till the King's pleasure should be known. Counsel for the Board of Trade and Plantations reported that in point of law no objection could be taken to this Act.

Petitions were presented by proprietors complaining that many of the allotments in the Island were sold under the Assembly Act of 1773 and the Treasury minute of 1776, *to officers resident* in the Island, for little more than the arrears and charges of confiscation. They further prayed for the remission of the quit rents in arrears. The Council took these matters into consideration, and agreed: "That all such as, on or before 1st May, 1784, should have paid up all the arrears of quit rents upon their respective Lots to the

1st of May, 1783, should, from the said 1st of May, 1783, until 1st May, 1789, be exempted from the payment of more than the quit rents now payable upon each of their Lots, and that, for and during the further term of ten years, to commence from the said 1st of May, 1789,— the same quit rent, only as is now payable on each of their Lots, should continue to be paid in lieu of the advanced quit rents, which, by the terms of their grants, would have become due and payable from the said 1st of May, 1789."

Accordingly a Bill was prepared not only granting the redress specified, but also disallowing the Act of 1781 and repealing that of 1773, rendering all sales under it voidable on payment by the proprietors of the purchase money, interest and charges incurred by the present holders, compensations being also required for any improvements made since the date of the sale. This draft Bill was sent to Patterson in 1784 to be submitted to and adopted by the Assembly. But the Governor assumed the responsibility of postponing action in the matter, on the ground that the British Government was mistaken as to facts connected with the sale of the land, and, on consultation with the Council, it was resolved to send to the Home Government a correct representation of the circumstances under which the confiscation took place in justification of delay in submitting the Bill to the Assembly for approval.

The preamble to this Act stated that the Governor-in-Council on 1st December, 1780, unanimously resolved, in order to give absent proprietors an opportunity of relieving their property, that no sales should take place until the first Monday of November following; that in the meantime the Colonial Agent in London should be instructed to inform the proprietors of the proposed sale; and, "whereas," runs the Bill, "notwithstanding such determination and resolution, no such notice was given . . . it seems reasonable that they should obtain effectual relief in the premises."

Writing to John Stuart, the Colonial Agent in London, Patterson, in reply to complaints against himself, says that, in the matter of the sales, he sought to benefit the proprietors. For that reason he advised "sending the advertisement to England, which the law did not require." That, by advice of Council, he postponed the sales from time to time in hopes the proprietors would take some steps, in consequence of the advertisements; and he prevented the sales taking place until the end of November, when every hope was over. This the law did not require, and it was not his fault that the advertisements did not reach England in time, as the resolution of Council to send them was made on 26th November, 1780, and the sales did not take place for a year afterwards. He prevented sales of Lots, the proprietors of which were inclined to improve their lands. He also saved others, taking the debt upon himself. He prevented any further sales taking place. This he did for the benefit of the proprietors, knowing the lands would not bring their value; and did it at the risk of his commission, as he did it in the face of a positive order from the Treasury. So far he contends he was not to blame. He was not responsible for the regularity or legality of the proceedings in other respects. The lands were seized and sold under a law passed ten years ago and the proceedings conducted by the law officers, he had no doubt, properly.

Patterson asserted that there had not been a Lot sold on which a single shilling had been spent by way of settlement, nor upon which there had been a settler placed; hence those proprietors who had spent money in making settlements have no cause of complaint. Complaints were made that much of the land sold had been bought for small sums by the Governor and other officials. This was true, but he contended that he was quite within his rights in this.

In the Act of 1773 and the minute of Council of August, 1776, Patterson had full authority to sell the lands. The defaulting proprietors richly deserved that their lands should be sold. But the Governor was indiscreet in allowing the sales to take place before he knew that the advertisements (even though they were not required by law) had been published in England or brought to the notice of the proprietors whose lands had been taken. As a fact they do not appear to have reached England at all. Also the sales were made at a very bad time, in the midst of war, when the chance of getting fair values would be slight. As Mr. Campbell says: His conduct "seems to import that the Governor had, in the conduct of the business, consulted his own interests rather than those of the proprietors."

Knowing that the present Assembly, which was not friendly to him, would pass the Act if submitted to the House, he dissolved it. In March, 1784, a general election took place and the Legislature met soon after. But the new House, instead of approving of his conduct, was actually preparing complaints to the King against him, when he again resorted to a dissolution.

At this time a large number of disbanded troops and Loyalists were leaving the United States to settle in Canada. Patterson made efforts,— and with a measure of success,— to bring some of them to the Island of St. John.

He gave much attention to them and received their support at the election for a new House. The Governor was directed to apportion part of the land to the Loyalists. Many of the allotments to the refugees he caused to be located on the lands sold in 1781, thus further complicating matters.

At the new election in March, 1785, a House friendly to his interests was secured. This result, Mr. Stewart says, "was not accomplished without a severe struggle, much illegal conduct, and at an expense to the Governor and his friends of nearly two thousand pounds sterling."

In his speech opening the session on 22nd March, 1785, Patterson says, referring to the Loyalists:

"There hath been no honest means left untried, on my part, both to invite the suffering Loyalists to the Island, and to have justice done them when here; but I am sorry to observe that the effect of my efforts have been much lessened by the malicious machinations of some noisy and pretended patriots, who, to gratify their own private resentments, oppose the interest of the public.

"The prospect, however, is yet flattering, and if these baneful practices are not still pursued the ensuing summer will, in all probability, add greatly to the numbers of our inhabitants."

In the following session, in his speech opening the Assembly, on 15th March, 1786, he again takes up the matter of the refugees, and says:

"In the year 1783, a number of the proprietors signed a paper declaring their intention to give up a fourth part of their property in this country for the benefit of Loyalist emigrants and disbanded soldiers.

"The paper was delivered to and approved of by His Majesty's Secretary of State for America, and a copy of it was forwarded to me by the Colony Agent of the Colony. On receipt of it a proclamation was issued giving notice thereof, and offering all who choose to become settlers in this Island the same encouragement as should be given in the neighbouring colonies of Quebec and Nova Scotia, and some, depending thereon, have taken refuge among us, all of whom have been, with as much expedition as possible, put in possession of the lands allotted them, but several are without any other title; for though the proprietors, by the paper I have mentioned, have empowered the Governor-in-Council to lay out and give possession of their lands, they have not thereby vested a sufficient authority to give proper deeds, thereof, and only a few of them have, as yet, sent letters of attorney for the purpose.

"To remedy this inconvenience, as far as in my power, I shall recommend to your consideration a law to vest in His Majesty, for a certain time to be therein mentioned, all the lands so signed for, and which shall empower His Majesty to direct their being granted agreeable to the intention of the proprietors."

This Assembly, on 27th March, 1786, appointed a committee to consider the original and authentic sales of lots of land in this Island in November, 1781. This committee, on the 31st March, brought in their report in which they say:

"Your Committee have read and considered the papers referred to them, as well as the proceedings heretofore had in this House, together with the suspicions evidently possessed by persons who have lately emigrated to this colony, many of whom have clamourously expressed their apprehensions that they will not get any titles or grants to the lands which have been located to them upon the tracts of land purchased in 1781. These apprehensions have fomented much discord and uneasiness in those Loyalists who have remained on the Island. The settlement of the Island has been much retarded by the reports, which have been industriously propogated respecting the situation of the Loyalists located there.

"Your Committee are of opinion that a Bill should be passed confirming the sales of lots in November, 1781. Agreeably thereto, they have, with every deference, prepared the heads of a Bill, entitled, "An Act to render valid in law all and every of the proceedings in the years 1780 and 1781, which, in any respect, related to or concerned the suing, seizing, condemning or selling of the lots or townships hereinafter mentioned, or any of them, or any part thereof."

The report was unanimously approved by the House, and on 20th April, 1786, the Bill, confirming sales made in 1780 and 1781, was read a third time, passed and sent to the Council. It was also ordered that the Lieutenant-Governor be asked to assent to this Bill without a suspending clause. It received his assent accordingly on 22nd April, 1786. The Bill was adopted by the Assembly, but was disallowed by His Majesty and led to Patterson's dismissal.

In the session of 1786, he was commanded to submit to the Assembly the Bill rendering the sales of 1781 voidable, which he did.

This session of the Assembly was held in November, 1786, and extended from the 8th to 10th of that month. In opening the session Patterson said:

"My reason for calling you together at present is that I may, in obedience to His Majesty's commands, lay before you a Bill intended to regulate in future the receipt and mode of recovering the quit rent of this Island — and for setting aside and annulling the sales of lands which took place in the year 1781. And I do it thus much earlier than I proposed at our last meeting that I may have an opportunity of transmitting the result of your proceedings before the winter shall have shut up our communication with the continent.

"The same Bill was sent to me in 1784, but as it contained some injurious and ill-founded reflections on myself and the members of His Majesty's Council it was judged proper at that time to withhold it from the Assembly, that we might lay our humble representations on the subject before His Majesty's Ministers. This has taken place and I have received permission to leave these reflections out. Thus altered I shall send it for your disposal, with my most hearty wishes that it may pass into a law, not on the principle of illegality, but because it appears very much the desire of His Majesty's Council to have it so.

"From the long and careful investigation which took place last session, it appeared both the confiscation and the sales had been conducted in all respects agreeably to the law as far as possibility,

humanity, and good policy would admit, and that where there was the least deviation, it was obviously intended for the benefit of the proprietors and of the country. This, and to quiet the minds of the Loyalists who are settled upon those lands, induced you to pass a law last session confirming and legalizing that whole transaction. You judged on that occasion, as I then did, that His Majesty's ministers had seen fit to drop the Bill, and this idea was evidenced by your passing and my consenting to the law. .
. . "In rescinding the law I must recommend a clause securing to the Loyalists and others the parts in those purchases which they hold of the present possessors. The justice of this measure calls loudly for attention and such a clause must meet with approbation everywhere."

### THE REPEALING ACT.

The Repealing Act went before the Committee of the whole House, from which it received summary treatment. The chairman reported that "the committee had gone through and considered the Bill, and that the same appeared to them to be highly detrimental to the settlement of the colony . . . and that it also appeared to them that it was founded on misrepresentation."

They, therefore, with all due deference, had come to a determination that it should lie, for the present, upon the table.

The Bill received its first and second reading in November, but was subsequently turned down by the House. The Governor then caused a private Bill to be introduced providing for the restoration of the escheated lands to the proprietors but subject to such heavy payment as outweighed any benefit that could come from its adoption. When the measure became known to the proprietors, they brought a "criminating complaint" against Patterson and the Council, which, on being investigated by the Committee of the Privy Council, led to the dismissal of the members of Council implicated, as well as that of the Attorney-General. No further action against Patterson was deemed necessary as he had already been dismissed.

### LEGAL TENDER, DEBENTURES, ETC.

Even at this early stage in the Island's story, great inconvenience was experienced from the scarcity of currency. Patterson, in his speech to the House on 8th November, refers to it, and makes a crude suggestion for remedying the inconvenience. "The scarcity of specie," he says, "subjects people in the payment of small debts to many hardships. And until our exports shall be more extensive I see no means to remedy the evil — unless you should think it proper to enact a law making certain produce of the Island — such as fish, grain, lumber, etc., among ourselves a legal tender under certain well-guarded restrictions."

In November, Lieutenant-Governor Fanning of Nova Scotia arrived to assume the Government. Patterson refused to give over the reins on the ground that the season was too far advanced for his return to England. Though a most unwise proceeding, Patterson had some ground for this, as Lord Sydney, in his despatch of 30th June, 1786, notifying Fanning of his appointment, said: "The King having thought it necessary to recall Lieutenant-Governor Patterson . . . that an enquiry should be made into his conduct . . . has been pleased to appoint you to carry on the public service of the Island *during Lieutenant-Governor Patterson's absence.*"

As generally anticipated, in the spring Patterson was reprimanded by the Home Government and per-emptorily ordered to transfer the permanent command to Fanning.

Lord Sydney wrote to Fanning on 5th April, 1787, that "His Majesty, from the very extraordinary conduct of Lieutenant-Governor Patterson, has thought it advisable to dismiss him at once from office, and has been graciously pleased to fix you in the government of that Island."

On the same date he wrote Patterson: "Sir,— I have received your letter of 5th November, in answer to mine of 30th June, wherein you have stated certain reasons which have induced you to delay the carrying into execution His Majesty's commands. . . . "Without, however, entering into the grounds upon which you have proceeded to justify disobedience of His Majesty's orders, I must acquaint you that I have received his Royal commands to inform you that His Majesty has no further occasion for your services as Lieutenant-Governor of St. John.

"Colonel Fanning, who has been appointed your successor, will receive from you all the public documents in your custody, and such orders and instructions as have been transmitted to you which have not been fully executed."

Patterson soon left the Island for Quebec, but, returning shortly, exerted himself to the utmost in obstructing the operations of the new government, but, after two years residence and bitter opposition to Fanning's administration, he returned to England.

The second Assembly elected in the opening years of Fanning's term as Lieutenant-Governor met on 22nd March, 1790. Patterson, who was then in England, was elected a member of this Assembly, in which, however, his old opponents were in the ascendant. The day following the opening a motion passed that "counsel may be heard to examine the qualification of Walter Patterson, Esquire, relative to his election as a member of this House."

The same day it was resolved "that Walter Patterson, Esquire, is a disqualified person to be elected a member of this House, he being resident in London, in the Kingdom of Great Britain, and not a resident nor inhabitant of this Island."

When Patterson arrived in London he found his means extremely straitened. Pressed by his creditors, his extensive and valuable properties in the Island were sold at nominal prices. He died in great poverty in London, September 6th, 1798. His widow was unable to recover anything from the wreck of his fortune.*

After they had established their claims, no determined effort was made by the original owners to obtain the property. The Assembly did pass an Act in 1792, by which they were permitted to take possession of their property; but eleven years having passed since the sales, and complications having, in consequence, ensued, the Home Government deemed it expedient to disturb the present holders, not a few of whom had compromised with the original grantees, entitling them to permanent possession. Hence the Act was disallowed and little more was heard of the subject.†(2)

### Reversion to Lieutenant-Governorship.

In 1784 an important constitutional change was made in the Island Government. In 1769 it had been erected into a government separate from Nova Scotia, and having a Governor and Lieutenant-Governor of its own. The Island was now to be annexed to Nova Scotia and administered by a Lieutenant-

†McPhail.
*(2)Campbell

208    HISTORY OF PRINCE EDWARD ISLAND.

Governor. The Legislature was to be preserved intact, and every act of the government was to be executed by the Lieutenant-Governor, except when the Governor-in-Chief was in person on the spot. A commission as Lieutenant-Governor was sent out to Patterson, which he read to the Council, and took the prescribed oaths.* He appointed a new Council, which was the same as the old, except that Mr. Townshend, collector and naval officer, was added, and Mr. DesBrisay, who had been Lieutenant-Governor, was left out. In a despatch to the Secretary of State (Sydney), Patterson mentioned his successful efforts, largely at his own expense, to bring the Island out of chaos to order; referring to the enmity of Nova Scotia against the Island on account of the Island's superiority in natural advantages. He referred to premature attempts at settlement, from Ireland and Scotland, injudicious efforts to carry on the fishery and trade under incompetent agents which had been made. These and other difficulties, he says, were overcome, when the annexation of the Island to Nova Scotia did more harm than all other causes put together. But for this, and the influence of the Governor of Nova Scotia (Parr), who threatened the Loyalists and refugees that, if they went to the Island, he would not furnish them the supplies which the government had provided for them, there would have been two thousand more inhabitants than there are. He did not complain of the change on his own account, but did so on account of the officials. This arrangement, however, was of short duration. The Island of St. John, in common with Nova Scotia and New Brunswick, was soon affiliated with Canada, the Governor-General being Lord Dorchester, better known in Canadian history as Sir Guy Carleton.

LOYALISTS.

At the close of the war for independence in the United States great numbers of Loyalists left the Republic and sought new homes in the remaining British provinces. A small number came to this Island and settled. They formed a most valuable addition to the population. Greater numbers would undoubtedly have come had the conditions of settlement been more favorable. It is true that, in 1783, a number of proprietors offered to give one-fourth of their lands, aggregating one hundred and nine thousand acres, for settlement, to the Loyalists, but comparatively few availed

*Appendix E. Infra

themselves of the offer. In fact the proposition was so clogged with conditions as to deter many of this most desirable class from coming to the Island, rather than to encourage them to seek homes here. Energetic measures do not seem to have been taken to bring them here in greater numbers. Patterson himself saw the importance of getting such a class of settlers, and put forth efforts to secure them, as also did his successor, later on; but they do not seem to have been seconded in this by the other proprietors, although they had proffered the lands. Still, those who did come were a most valuable class of settlers and their descendants are yet to be found throughout the Island. A considerable number of settlers came from Rhode Island, and we learn from Mr. Walter Johnston in a series of letters published by him in Aberdeen, about 1821-1822, that many of their children were, at the time he wrote, settled in King's county. Writing to the Secretary of State, in January, 1786, Patterson says that the influx of settlers was not up to expectation. Only about two hundred had arrived, and some families from Rhode Island, who expected more to come, who were leaving the United States on account of heavy taxes and want of trade there.

As in the case of the quit rents and the agreement to pay them for the support of the civil government by the proprietors, faith was not kept with the refugees. Time and again the Loyalists endeavoured to have the promises made to them carried out. It is unnecessary to enumerate, in their wearisome sameness and detail, the efforts made by the Loyalists and their descendants during half a century. Their grievances were pretty fully and clearly set out in a petition to the House of Assembly in 1832 and the reports of a committee to which it was referred made in that and the two following years.

The Journal of the House of Assembly for 1832 has a minute that on the 17th March of that year:

"A petition of divers persons styling themselves 'American loyal emigrants, or their heirs and representatives, whose names were subscribed thereto . . . set forth' — that in the year 1783, when the United States were separated from the British Crown, the petitioners or their ancestors, desirous of being under the British government, were induced to settle on this Island, on the invitation of Governor Patterson, and by the offer of certain grants of land by the government, as a compensation for the losses they had sustained for their loyalty and adherence to the cause of Royalty; that petitioners had to complain that they have been unlawfully deprived of the lands granted to them; and they confidently expect, should the House institute an enquiry, that it will appear that the lands in question ought, in justice and equity, to be awarded to them — and praying that the House take the subject into consideration and grant such relief as may appear just and proper."

This petition was referred to a special committee who, on 19th March, reported, regretting "that, from the late period of the session at which the said petition was introduced, and from the pressure of business now before the House, they have not been able to give the subject matter of the petition that attention and consideration which its importance and (as the committee conceive) the claims of the petitioners are entitled to.

"On reference to the statute book of this Island, it appeared to the committee that, in an Act passed in the thirtieth year of the reign of His late Majesty King George III, it is recited that certain proprietors of land in this Island, or their agents, had, in the year 1783, signed and delivered a paper to the Right Honourable Lord North, at that time one of His Majesty's principal Secretaries of State, binding themselves to grant in certain proportions to such loyal American emigrants as should settle in this Island, and who should apply to the Governor and Council for the same, one-fourth part of the lands placed opposite to their respective names on the same terms as they, the said proprietors, held the said lands of the Crown, which lands amounted in quantity to one hundred and nine thousand acres.

"It also appeared to the committee, by a provision of the said Act, that the Governor, Lieutenant-Governor or Commander-in-Chief for the time being, is authorized to give grants under the Great Seal of this Island of such proportions of the said resigned lands as were then in the possession of such Loyalists and who had not received deeds or grants from the said proprietors.

"The committee were therefore of opinion and respectfully recommended that a committee be appointed to examine into and investigate the allegations contained in the said petition and report thereon to the House at an early period of its next session."

The report was ordered to be accepted. The committee appointed in pursuance of such recommendation reported during the next session, that of 1833, "that in the year 1783 a number of the proprietors of lands in this Island, or their attorneys for them, in order to induce American Loyalists, who at that period, from a principle of loyalty and attachment to the British government, were abandoning the country now called the United States in great numbers to settle in this Island, and also with a view to have some indulgence extended to them in the payment of their quit rents, bound themselves to grant to such persons, on their arrival here, in the same proportions to each family as were received by loyal emigrants in the neighboring province of Nova Scotia, and on the same conditions as they, themselves, held of the Crown, one-fourth of the quantity of lands placed opposite to their names in a document signed by them and delivered to the Right Honourable Lord North, at that time one of His Majesty's principal Secretaries of State.

"This engagement having been acquiesced in by His Majesty's government, Lieutenant-Governor Patterson issued a proclamation, under his hand and seal, signed by Thomas DesBrisay, Provincial Secretary, dated the 13th October, 1783, in which the foregoing facts were briefly recited, and notice given 'to all such of the refugees, provincial troops, or other American emigrants, as wish to become settlers in this Colony, that in a few days after their arrival in Charlottetown they shall be put in possession of such lands as they shall be entitled to, free of every expense. That they may depend upon the land being good; neither mountainous, rocky nor swampy; contiguous to navigable harbours; many parts convenient for the fishery, and in every respect preferable to any at this time unoccupied throughout His Majesty's American dominions.'

"A number of loyal emigrants repaired hither in the confident expectation of obtaining lands of a superior quality; while several officers and a number of soldiers, who were disbanded on this Island, were induced to remain on it by the same flattering prospects. It appears by the Council books that several of these persons were put in possession of the lands laid out and allotted to them, and that they also made considerable improvements thereon; notwithstanding which, and that several years had elapsed since the aforesaid proprietors covenanted and agreed with government to make conveyance of the lands so allotted and laid out to the individuals respectively settled thereon, no disposition was evinced by the said proprietors (with one or two exceptions) to fulfil their engagements — in consequence of which a great proportion of the emigrants left the Island. Of those who remained, some accepted of grants clogged and loaded with such impracticable conditions and covenants as to make the tenure of them, in effect, to be merely at the will and pleasure of the grantors, the same being altogether contrary from the grants from the Crown to the original proprietors; and the minds of those who had no grants or deeds of any kind were kept in a state of constant disquietude by reason of the uncertainty of the tenure by which they held their lands. In consequence thereof, an Act was passed by the Colonial Legislature, in the year 1790, intituled 'An Act to empower the Lieutenant-Governor to give grants of lands under the Great Seal of this Island to such Loyalists and disbanded troops as are in the occupation thereof, by virtue of locations formerly made by the Governor and Council.' The same Act provides 'That from and after the publication hereof it shall and may be lawful to and for the Governor, Lieutenant-Governor, or other Commander-in-Chief for the time being, to give grants, under the Great Seal of this Island, of such proportions of the aforementioned resigned lands as are now in possession of such Loyalists and reduced officers and soldiers, by virtue of, and under the authority of the Governor and Council of this Island, as have not received deeds or grants from the said proprietors."

The Royal assent was signified to this Act in 1793.

Notwithstanding the power vested in the Lieutenant-Governor by the before mentioned Act, very few of the Loyalists were able to obtain their grants. Whereupon those who were settled in Township Number Fifty resolved on forwarding a remonstrance to government on the subject, and one of their number was selected to be bearer thereof, who, from having been personally known to Lord Cornwallis in the course of the war, hoped through his means to obtain redress, and was preparing to visit Europe with that view. This individual made known his intentions to the then Lieutenant-Governor Fanning, at that time an extensive proprietor on that Lot, and to other officers of the government here. The consequence was that nearly all the Loyalists who had lands located on that Township received their grants within a week afterwards. The great majority, however, less fortunate, disgusted and worn out by repeated disappointments and delays, abandoned their improvements and either became lease-holders in other parts of the Island or left the colony, and a few still retain possession of their allotments, notwithstanding the want of deeds — but such lands, it is understood, generally remain in a wilderness state, the occupiers thereof being deterred from cultivating the same from an apprehension that they might, one day, be deprived of them. A case brought under the notice of the committee, on affidavit, was that of a disbanded soldier, who had drawn one hundred acres on Lot Number Thirty-two, which were duly laid out and located to him, and of which he took possession in the following spring and built a house thereon in which he lived two winters, and was often promised and expected to obtain his grant but never could procure it. But, being necessarily absent from his place for a few months only, when his house was accidentally burnt in his absence, the then Governor of this Island (Patterson), then also claiming to be proprietor of the said Township Number Thirty-two, informed him that he should not have the land so located to him, in consequence of his said absence therefrom, and he was, therefore, obliged to abandon it and his improvements.

The committee also stated the Loyalists and disbanded troops "appear to have been persecuted in every possible way. In one instance a Council book, containing entries from the year 1784 to the year 1787, was designedly suppressed or destroyed and could never since be found; in which book were contained the locations of numerous Loyalists, which was, in fact, their only title, as they had not, and never could obtain, their grants, and it appeared to the committee that the last time this book was seen was in the year 1803, when it was handed into Court by the late General Fanning to be produced as evidence in an ejectment cause, wherein his son was plaintiff and Messrs. Laird and Young were defendants; and that in a few hours after it was returned to General Fanning or his servant, all of which will appear on reference to the Journals of this house for the year 1810."

In fact, the committee felt compelled "to state, from the examinations of several Loyalists and their representatives who have attended before them, a few of which examinations are subjoined to their report, and from the statements of many others, all nearly to the same purport, that the unhappy situation of many of the Loyalists still remains as stated in the second preamble of the Act of 1790, and also from an examination of the minutes of Council it appeared to the committee that numbers of Loyalists and disbanded soldiers have had lands located to them, but have not yet received any grants or title deeds of the same."

### ADDITIONAL ROYAL INSTRUCTIONS AS TO GRANTS.

On 24th July, 1783, additional Royal instructions relating solely to the terms on which grants be given Loyalists were issued to Governor Patterson. "The grants contained many and drastic conditions which it is unnecessary to enumerate, which were not authorized by the Royal instructions, upon which the committee observed 'that it appears to them all these conditions were contrary to the true intent and meaning of the said Act (of 1790), and entirely unauthorized by the said instructions, which direct a grant in fee to be made and registered and the grantee to be put into possession of his land, free of any expense whatever. He is thereby only required to take certain oaths and make a declaration as therein provided.'"

The committee further stated that "J. P. Collins, Esquire, the Clerk of His Majesty's Council, has produced to them a few sheets stitched together and without a back or cover, which appear to contain the original entries or rough minutes of the proceedings of His Majesty's Council for the period between the 22nd February, 1785, and 1st March, 1786, both inclusive; and Mr. Collins has assured the committee that the same was given him on his entering into office, sewed up with other loose papers in a bag, which he first examined in the presence of two of the committee and immediately produced the same on request to the committee. These are supposed to be the minutes of Council before stated to be lost, and, on referring to the regular, fair-copied Council book of that period in possession of Mr. Collins, it appeared that these minutes were omitted to be copied into it, and on looking at the entry in these rough minutes of several applications from Loyalists for lands on Township Number Fifty-five, there appeared some remarkable erasures and interlineations, in which different ink appears to have been used. Mr. Collins also informed the committee that many of the old Council entries or minutes appear to be lost and not copied and that he had found several sheets, apparently being original rough minutes, which have never been transcribed into the Council books or records. This the committee considered a serious grievance justly complained of by the Loyalists and others, whose interests have been much injured thereby."

The committee then directed their chairman to report a Bill for the relief of the Loyalists and disbanded troops, as prepared by them, in obedience to the order of the House.

This report and the Bill founded upon it took considerable time, so that it did not reach the Legislative Council until late in the session. By minute of that Council of 3rd April, 1783, it was resolved: "That the advanced period of the session at which the Bill intituled 'An Act for the relief of the Loyal American emigrants and disbanded troops in this colony,' was brought up from the House of Assembly, precludes the possibility of its receiving that consideration which the importance of the subject and the difficulties connected with it require, as regards the remedies proposed, and the private rights thereby involved."

Little came of the efforts of the committee, and the Loyalist question, like so many others, continued to be a blot on the fair name of the colony.

## LAND COMMISSION, 1861.

In 1861 a Royal Land Commission was granted by His Majesty to investigate the several grievances that had persisted for so long. It consisted of the Hon. John H. Gray, of New Brunswick, representing the Crown; Hon. Joseph Howe, Provincial Secretary of Nova Scotia, representing the tenants, and Matthew Ritchie, of Halifax, representing the proprietors. In August of the same year they made their report.

With regard to the Loyalists they found as follows:

"Loyalists,— 'These are professedly the descendants and heirs of men who remained true to the Crown of Great Britain at the time of the revolt of the American colonies. Some of these Loyalists, as they were termed, came to this Island from the revolted colonies and several of the proprietors offered large portions of their Lots as lands which might be granted to them in reward for their fealty to the Crown, and as some amends for the losses they had sustained. The Commissioners have come to the conclusion that, at this late period, the present owners of the lands claimed by certain Loyalists' descendants cannot be dispossessed, but recommend to the Government to consider any special claims, and if supported by satisfactory evidence, to apportion some public lands to such claimants.'"

## ESCHEAT.

Agitation for the escheat of lands of proprietors began at an early date and continued for many years. On 28th March, 1783, the House of Assembly addressed a humble memorial to the King praying for a Court of Escheat. It recited the original grants and quit rents reserved, and the conditions to be observed by grantees, the erection of the colony into a separate government; the terms of same, and the agreed payment of the cost of government out of quit rents voluntarily pledged by the proprietors, and their breach of these terms.

The address went on to state that: "From the almost total neglect, however, on the part of the original grantees, settlement was so much impeded and the liability to escheat or forfeiture became so evident, original grantees, with a few exceptions, disposed of their large tracts for a mere trifle (in numerous instances for less than one penny an acre), to speculators, who have, by false representations at the Colonial office, prevented the remonstrances of the loyal inhabitants of this Island from reaching the ear of the Government, and have prevented laws, passed by the Local Legislature and sanctioned by the King's representative here, from going into operation, whereby the inhabitants of the Island have been virtually deprived of the benefits intended from a Local Legislature, . . . In no instance have the grantees or proprietors of the lands contributed towards the improvement of the colony, . . . but are indebted to the industrious classes of the community for making their lands valuable. . . .

"Your Majesty's Royal Father was graciously pleased by his Secretary, Lord Hobart, to sanction the establishment of a Court of Escheat here, and directed an Act to be passed to regulate the form of proceedings, which was enacted in the following year; from which the colonies justly expected the most beneficial results, as nearly all the lands in the colony were then liable to forfeiture and would, inevitably, have reverted to the Crown; but the said Act, being reserved for His Majesty's pleasure, was forwarded to England and no account has been since heard of it in the Island.

"That an Act, similar in effect, was passed at last session and assented to by Your Majesty's representative, who could not avoid seeing the justice and necessity of such a measure; but from a despatch received from Lord Goderich, Principal Secretary for the Colonies, it appears that a further mis-statement has been made at the Colonial office, whereby His Lordship had been led to believe that injustice would be done to some proprietors by such a measure, who, it is stated, have sent out settlers to settle their lands, and that those intended for their lands have removed to the lands of others. The House of Assembly, however, most respectfully state to Your Majesty, that, with the exception of one or two individuals, none of the proprietors ever brought persons to the colony for the purpose of settling on their lands, who, after being placed thereon, left the same to settle on the property of others, except in cases where they were refused titles on the terms promised before they left their native country, or where they could only obtain leases of forest or wilderness lands for the short term of forty years or thereabouts.

"That Courts of Escheat are established and in active operation in the other North American provinces, and the benefits therefrom are evinced by the general settlement and rapid improvement of those colonies and by the certainty of tenure by which the agriculturalists hold their lands; and as there are many large tracts in this colony liable to forfeiture and escheat the House most humbly intreats that Your Majesty may not grant to any of the proprietors of lands in this colony a further waiver of any of the conditions in the Crown grants, to the continued injury and disappointment of Your Majesty's loyal inhabitants therein; and that Your Majesty will be graciously pleased to direct that a Court of Escheat be established and go into operation, in order that the settlement and improvement of the colony may not be further retarded, and that the Island may no longer remain a burthen to the government of the Mother Country."

That in only ten of sixty-seven townships were the engagements entered into by the proprietors carried out within ten years of their grants showed their utter indifference to their undertakings.* In forty-eight townships no attempt at settlement had been made. In 1797, thirty years after the grants were made, the House of Assembly passed a series of resolutions, founded on most careful investigations of all the townships, which were embodied in a petition to the Home Government, praying that measures be taken to compel the proprietors to fulfil the terms of the grants. They showed that on twenty-three specified townships of four hundred and fifty-eight thousand five hundred and eighty acres, there was not one resident settler; that on twelve townships, containing two hundred and forty-three thousand acres, there were only thirty-six families, or, allowing six persons to a family, an aggregate of two hundred souls. It was shown that the failure of so many proprietors to comply with the terms of their grants was highly injurious to the growth and prosperity of the Island, ruinous to its inhabitants, and destructive of the just expectations of its settlement. The Government's long forbearance towards defaulting proprietors had no other effect than to enable them to speculate on the industry of the colony. If fully settled the Island could maintain half a million inhabitants, and the House prayed that the proprietors should either be compelled to do their duty or that their lands should be escheated and granted to actual settlers.

The petition was forwarded to the Duke of Portland, Colonial Secretary, and seems to have impressed the Government, as a despatch was sent to Lieutenant-Governor Fanning, intimating that measures would be taken to rectify the evils complained of. . . . In comformity with this despatch, Fanning, in his speech to the Assembly in November, 1802, informed them on the highest authority that the affairs of the Island had been brought under the consideration of His Majesty's ministers in a manner highly favourable to the representations lately made, respecting the many large, unsettled and uncultivated tracts of land in the Island. . . . It would be necessary that the Government of the Island should be prepared to adopt, when advisable, the requisite steps for re-vesting such lands in His Majesty, as might be liable to be escheated. . . . The House asked for more

---
*Campbell.

explicit information, which they were unable to obtain. . . .
The local Government prepared a Bill entitled, "An Act for effectually re-vesting in His Majesty, his heirs and successors, all such lands as are, or may be, liable to forfeiture within the Island," which passed and was assented to by the Governor on 2nd April, 1803. This Bill, contrary to all expectations, was disallowed by the Home Government without any reason assigned. A committee of the Local House then drew up a strong remonstrance in which they said: "It appears to this committee, and they have the strongest reasons to believe, that the royal *assent* to the said Act for re-vesting His Majesty with such lands as are or may be liable to forfeiture within this Island has been graciously approved by His Majesty." They then expressed their conviction, which was well founded, that the formal royal allowance had been withheld by means of unfounded representations of interested individuals in England. . . . The Assembly also presented an Address to the Lieutenant-Governor complaining of the efforts to render His Majesty's intentions abortive, and requesting him to transmit their petition and resolution to Lord Castlereagh and to Lord Liverpool, President of the Committee of the Privy Council for Trade and Plantations. A committee was also appointed to draw up a new Bill similar to the former, which was duly passed. The Assembly did all that could be done to neutralize the back-stair influence used in London to thwart their intentions. Lord Hobart, through whom the promise to rectify the evil had been made, had given place as Colonial Secretary to Lord Castlereagh, and the British Government did not, on this occasion, maintain its character for consistency and adherence to principles. As Mr. Campbell well says: "It would be difficult to point out in the history of the British Colonial administration another instance when the dictates of political consistency and honour were as flagrantly disregarded as in the case under review."

The proprietors' influence at the Colonial office seemed invincible. This was largely due to their being, as a class, in intimate social relations with parties in office, and mainly consisted of officers and others who were supposed to have rendered good service in time of war and who, therefore, commanded consideration and sympathy. The proprietors also cultivated the good-will of Under Secretaries and other government officials. This back-stairs influence was, probably, their strongest lever in thwarting the efforts of the Assembly. Not only did they succeed in preventing the resolution commended by the Duke of Portland from having any effect, they also obtained an important reduction in amount of quit rent arrears, which now totalled £59,162 0s. 0d. sterling, or nearly $300,000, — an enormous sum at that time, a fraction of which would have immensely improved the condition of the province. In fact, the arrears in some cases amounted to more than the lands would sell for at auction, hence these proprietors had now no inducement to fulfil the other terms of the grants and settle their lands. Purchasers who would buy the lands subject to this burden of arrears were not to be had. The matter was referred to a committee of the Council for Trade and Plantations, who recommended that a composition should be accepted, which was decided upon, the composition being smaller in proportion to the efforts made by the respective proprietors to settle their lands. They were divided into five classes.

The first consisted of those whose lands had the full number of settlers required by the terms of settlement. From these only four years quit rent was demanded in lieu of the full amount from 1769 to 1801.

The second class consisted of those whose lands had one-half the required number of settlers. Five years quit rent was demanded from them.

Those whose townships had from one-fourth to one-half the required population were to be charged nine years quit rent in lieu of the arrears.

Those who did not possess one-fourth the required number were charged with twelve years quit rent.

Those whose townships had no settlers were charged with fifteen years arrears.

The defaulting proprietors were certainly not entitled to such generous treatment, but the effect of this arrangement was good, as, in a short time, nearly one-third of the lands were sold and settlement received a great impetus. Those who retained their lands in some cases did not even pay the composition, and again let the arrears accumulate, and when efforts were made to escheat their lands they always had sufficient influence in London to procure the disallowance of Acts of the local Legislature, having that object in view, and again effected compositions reducing the amounts of the new arrears. Even the reduced amount was not paid, making it clear (if there ever was any doubt about it), that many of them had no intention of carrying out their undertakings. It was mainly owing to their long continued and repeated breaches of faith that the people from time to time were driven to seek relief in the establishment of Courts of Escheat.

Sir John Harvey was appointed Lieutenant-Governor of the Island in February, 1836, and arrived in Charlottetown in August. He visited various parts of the Island and expressed himself as highly gratified by the hospitality of the people and the evidence of progress manifested. In March of the following year he was appointed Lieutenant-Governor of New Brunswick and left the Island in May. Sir Charles Augustus Fitzroy, who succeeded him, arrived in June, 1837. He visited all the principal parts of the Island, and, as a result of enquiries made by him, addressed a circular to the proprietors, advocating the granting of important concessions to the tenantry to allay the agitation for escheat and removing just grounds of complaint. He put the case of the tenant in a clearer light than has been set out by others. His remarks are those of a shrewd observant man.

Sir Charles stated that no one unacquainted with the circumstances of a new colony could form a correct estimate of the difficulties and privations a settler had to encounter. For many years he could only make a bare subsistence. . . . He might be able to pay a fair equivalent in rent or otherwise for the land he occupied but would be dismayed at the thought of being deprived of the fruits of the labour of his manhood, whether from heavy arrears of rent, which he was unable to pay, or from the proprietor's refusal to grant a sufficiently long tenure to ensue to his family the profits of his labour, when, probably, in the decline of life. It could not be a matter of surprise if he became soured and lent a ready ear to any proposals for relief. . . . Long leases should be granted at the rate customary in the colony, the rent to be paid in produce at the market price. . . . Where long leases were objected to purchase in fee at twenty years purchase should be allowed, or that payment for improvements, at a fair valuation, should be ensured at the end of their terms. The Lieutenant-Governor forwarded a copy of this circular to the Secretary of State for the Colonies.

The Colonial Secretary, Lord Glenelg, transmitted to the Lieutenant-Governor a copy of a memorial from the proprietors protesting against the Royal assent being given to an Act of the Island Legislature for levying an assessment on all lands, and demanding an opportunity of stating their objections before the Judicial Committee of the Privy Council. This memorial was referred to a joint committee of the Legislature, who, in 1838, submitted a report justifying the law. Among other things the report showed the local expenditure of the Government for the last twelve years to have been £107,643 of which £36,506 had been spent on roads and bridges to the great advantage of the memorialists' property; £13,556 on public buildings and wharves; and £56,562 for other local purposes. Of this, the whole amount paid by the proprietors had been only £7,413, leaving over £100,000, to be borne by the resident consumers of dutiable goods.

It appears that Lord Glenelg forwarded this report, together with Sir Charles Fitzroy's circular and other documents bearing on the subject of escheat, to Lord Durham, then Governor-General, in September, 1838, for his special opinion on the subject for the guidance of the Home Government.

Lord Durham's reply, which follows, entirely sustains the opinion of the Islanders.

"CASTLE OF ST. LEWIS, QUEBEC,
8th October, 1838.

"MY LORD,—

"I have had the honour of receiving your despatch of the fifth September, whereby you desire that I will express to you my judgment on the whole subject of escheat in the Island of Prince Edward. After perusing the voluminous documents with Your Lordship's despatch, I do not feel that it is in my power to add anything to the very full information on the subject which these documents comprise. The information before me is now so ample that upon no matter of fact can I entertain a doubt. Nearly all the Island was alienated in one day by the Crown in very large grants, chiefly to absentees, and upon conditions of settlement which have been wholly disregarded. The extreme improvidence — I might say the reckless improvidence— which dictated these grants is obvious; the total neglect of the Government as to enforcing the conditions of the grants is not less so. The great bulk of the Island is still held by absentees, who hold it as a sort of reversionary interest which requires no present attention, but may become valuable some day or other through the growing want of the inhabitants. But, in the meantime, the inhabitants of the Island are subjected to the greatest inconvenience,— nay, the most serious injury — from the state of the property in land. The absent proprietors neither improve the land themselves nor will let others improve it. They retain the land and keep it in a state of wilderness. Your Lordship can scarcely conceive the degree of injury inflicted on a new settlement hemmed in by wilderness land, which has been placed out of control of government, and is entirely neglected by its absent proprietors. This evil prevades British North America and has been for many years past a subject of universal and bitter complaints.

"The same evil was felt in many of the States of the American Union, where, however, it has been remedied by taxation of a penal character,— taxation, I mean, in the nature of a fine for the abatement of a nuisance. In Prince Edward Island this evil has attained its maximum. It has been long and loudly complained of, but without any effect. The people, their representative Assembly, the Legislative Council, and the Governor have cordially concurred in devising a remedy for it. All their efforts have proved in vain. Some influence — it cannot be that of equity or reason — has steadily counteracted the measures of the Colonial legislature. I cannot imagine it is any other influence than that of the absentee proprietors resident in England; and in saying so I do but express the universal opinion of the colony. The only question, therefore, as it appears to me, is whether that influence shall prevail against the deliberate Acts of the Colonial Legislature and the universal complaints of the suffering colonists. I can have no doubt on the subject. My decided opinion is, that the royal assent should no longer be withheld from the Act of the Colonial Legislature.

"At the same time, I doubt whether this Act will prove a sufficient remedy for the evil in question. It was but natural that the Colonial Legislature — who have found it impossible as yet to obtain any remedy whatever — should hesitate to propose a sufficient one. Undeterred by any such consideration — relying on the cordial co-operation of the government and Parliament in the work of improving the state of the colonies,— I had intended, before the receipt of Your Lordship's despatch, and still intend, to suggest a measure, which, while it provides a sufficient remedy for the evil suffered by the colonists, shall also prove advantageous to the absent proprietors by rendering their property more valuable. Whether the inhabitants of Prince Edward Island prefer waiting for the now uncertain results of a suggestion of mine, or that the Act which they have passed should be at once confirmed, I cannot tell, but I beg earnestly to recommend that Her Majesty's Government should be guided by their wishes on the subject; and in order to ascertain these, I propose to transmit a copy of the present despatch to Sir Charles Fitzroy, with a request that he will, after consulting with the leading men of the colony, address Your Lordship on the subject.

"With respect to the terms proposed by the proprietors, I am clearly of opinion that any such arrangement would be wholly inadequate to the end in view.

"I am, etc.,

(Sgd.) Durham."

Lord Glenelg.

This very decided opinion of Lord Durham's caused the confirmation of the Act of 1837 for levying an assessment on all lands in the Island, which confirmation was effected at a meeting of the Privy Council held 12th December, 1838. Strange to say, Durham's despatch was not communicated to the Assembly by the Lieutenant-Governor. It was first published by Mr. Campbell in his history, from which the writer has taken it.

Escheat and the land question would not down. In 1839, Mr. Cooper, then speaker of the House of Assembly, was sent as a delegate to London to take up the whole land question with the Home Government. He proposed the establishment of a Court of Escheat, the resumption by the Crown of the rights of the proprietors, and a heavy penal tax on wilderness lands. The Home Government rejected the project of escheat and did not feel like drawing on the Treasury to buy out the lands.

With regard to taxing wilderness lands, which was the only way the proprietors could be reached, an Act for raising a fund by an assessment on land, for the erections of a Government House and other public buildings had been enacted in 1830. During its continuance the collection of quit rents was suspended. This Act, or others similar to it, was still in force. Lord John Russell, the Colonial Secretary, was unwilling to adopt the new proposal, until it had been clearly proved that no remedy was to be expected from the Act of 1830, so nothing was done. It is not the writer's intention to discuss at length the further efforts made in connection with escheat. Suffice it to refer, in this connection, to the doings of the Land Commission of 1861. That Commission held that: "Previous to the cession by Her Majesty in 1851, of the Crown and territorial revenues in the Island to the local government, the Crown had, by repeated declarations, denuded itself of the power of escheating the original grants, and declared any measure of that character impracticable,"* and give their decision in a few words as follows: "The Commissioners therefore report and award, that at the present time there should be no escheat of the original grants for non-performance of conditions as to settlement." And so we part with our old friend, "Escheat,"† but shall, however, have occasion to refer to it again.

## THE LAND QUESTION.

Almost at once, on Patterson's arrival in 1770, trouble began over the non-payment of the quit rents, and over the non-observance by the proprietors of the other condition of the grants. Some few of these gentlemen honourably endeavoured to fulfil their obligations, but the great majority quite ignored them. Bills drawn on the proprietor's agent by the officers of government who depended upon the quit rents for their pay were dishonoured. Those who were without private resources were, for long periods, left without means of support. Year in and year out, there is the same story of these men's shameless breach of the conditions upon which they held their lands, and of the undertaking they had entered into when they procured the establishment of a separate government. Many of them held their lands simply for the purposes of speculation, without the slightest intention of performing the conditions of their grants. Unfortunately they possessed sufficient influence with the authorities in England to thwart the efforts of the local government

*Campbell's History, Chapter 3.
†Commissioners Report page 40.,

and legislature to compel them to discharge their obligations, or to re-vest the lands in the Crown. Patterson doubtless had his faults, and much obloquy has been heaped upon him, but this was largely due to his attempts to remedy the grievous wrongs under which the people of the Island laboured. Mr. Stewart denounces Patterson and lauds his successor, Lieutenant-Governor Fanning; but, while the measures, and more particularly the methods of enforcing them taken by the former, may have been indiscreet, and brought him under the displeasure of the Colonial office, the course he tried to pursue was quite as much or more in the interests of the people than was that of the latter.

In 1853 was enacted "An Act for the purchase of lands on behalf of the Government of Prince Edward Island, and to regulate the sale and management thereof, and for other purposes therein mentioned." Under this Act the Worrell and Selkirk estates were purchased, under voluntary agreement by the government of the Island, at a reasonable price. Together they contained 140,000 acres.

The Land Commission appointed in 1860 suggested that the most simple remedy for the evils which then existed would be under the operation of that Act. Besides the Worrell and Selkirk, some smaller estates were purchased. There were, however, insurmountable difficulties in the way. It involved the raising of a large loan, which could only be done with the guarantee of the British Government, which it declined to give.

The Commissioners made a very thorough investigation of the question in 1861, and their report was a valuable one. They say: "After mature consideration of the subject in all its bearings the undersigned have unanimously agreed to recommend the application to the whole Island of the principles embodied in the Land Purchase Act, under certain guards and modifications which would appear to be essential to their more extended adoption. It is clear that the local government cannot generally apply the principles of the Land Purchase Act without the assistance of the Imperial Parliament. To complete the purchase already made their resources have been strained. . . . But if the Imperial Parliament would guarantee a loan of £100,000 sterling the money could be borrowed at a very low rate of interest. . . . The advantages of this mode of converting the tenures are so obvious, the objections to it so few and so trivial, that the undersigned beg to submit to Her Majesty's Government the propriety of guaranteeing a loan, which they have no doubt would be gladly accepted by the Island authorities." But it was clear that the Imperial Parliament would give no such guarantee, and it was certain that the colony could raise no such sum upon its own credit and resources, and this the Commissioners recognized. They go on:

"Driven, after mature reflection, to abandon all hope of a solution of their difficulties in this direction, the Commissioners have finally decided to adopt two simple principles.

"1st. To give to every tenant of township lands, not coming within the fourth and fifth provisions hereinafter made, the right to purchase the land on which he lives.

"2nd. To give the landlord and tenant the security of a fair valuation of the land in case of difference." . . . . . .

"In the case of the tenants of Prince Edward Island, it is not more the price at which they may obtain their holdings, than it is the *compulsory power of purchase at some price* that is wanted.

"The commissioners, therefore, report and award:

"1st. That tenants who tender twenty years purchase to their landlords, in cash, shall be entitled to a discount of ten per cent and a deed conveying the fee-simple of their farms. Where the tenant prefers to pay by installments, he shall have the privilege, but the landlord shall not be bound to accept a less sum than £10 at any one time; nor shall the tenant have a longer term than ten years to liquidate the debt.

"2nd. That tenants whose lands are not worth twenty years purchase, and who, therefore, decline to pay that amount, may tender to their landlords what they consider the value of their farms. If the landlord declines to accept the amount offered the value shall be adjusted by arbitration. If the sum tendered is increased by the award, the tenant shall pay the expenses; if it is not, they shall be paid by the landlord. If the sum awarded is tendered in cash a discount of five per cent to be allowed; if not, payment to be made by yearly installments of not less than £10, the term of payment in no case to exceed ten years.

"3rd. That the rent shall be reduced in proportion to the installments paid, but no credits shall be allowed for any such installment until three years arrears (if there are arrears) have been paid, nor while any rent accruing after the adjustment of the value of the farm remains due.

"4th. That proprietors, who hold not more than 1,500 acres, or those who desire to retain particular lands to that extent, shall not be compelled to part with such under this award.

"5th. That leases under a term of less than forty years shall not be affected by this award.

"The commissioners cannot close this branch of their report without again expressing their conviction, that the purchase of the estates, by the negotiation of a loan through the Imperial Government, presents advantages so manifest that they cannot too strongly recommend its adoption in preference to all other plans for the settlement of these unhappy disputes."

The award of the Commissioners, however, did not settle the land question. It still remained a vexed question on the Island, keeping the people in a state of unrest. It was not finally disposed of until the estates, not previously purchased, became vested in the government, under the compulsory provisions of "The Land Purchase Act, 1877."

## Fishery Reserves.

At the time, in 1767, of the granting of the townships of the Island to various persons, it will be remembered that certain reservations were made. One of these was of a strip 500 feet in width round the shores of the Island reserved for fishery purposes. Presumably it was supposed that a vigorous fishing industry would spring up along the Island coasts. As a fact these reservations were practically useless for the purpose for which they were retained. The shores of the Island, being indented with numerous harbours and "runs," which were much better adapted for fishery purposes than the reservation along the coast, afforded all the facilities necessary for the prosecution of the fisheries, and the reservations became, or always were, of little or no use. They were gradually taken possession of by the tenants or owners of adjoining lands and merged into their holdings. Moreover, while the fishing industry has always been and still is very important, and might readily be made more so, the people of the Island have not given the attention to it which has been given by the residents on the sea coasts and harbours of Nova Scotia and Newfoundland. The reason for this is a very simple one. The soil of Prince Edward Island is a fertile soil, much more responsive to the labour of the husbandman than is the soil of the neighbouring provinces, consequently its people are attracted to agriculture rather than to fishing.

To settle any complications that might arise the Land Commission in 1861 recommended that where the original grants passed the entire fee of the township, reserving an easement over the five hundred feet, the lands covered by such reserve should henceforth be held by the owner freed from the easement. "The commissioners, therefore, reported and awarded that the reservations for fishery purposes contained in the original grants of the townships of Prince Edward Island, abutting on the seashore, be abandoned."

## Church and Glebe Lands.

When the original grants of the townships were given reservations were made, in each, of one hundred acres and thirty acres respectively, for Church glebe purposes and for school masters. On several occasions it was proposed that these lands should be sold and the proceeds applied for educational purposes.

"In March, 1834, the Assembly passed an address to His Majesty, referring to similar addresses transmitted in 1830 and in 1832, praying that the lands reserved in the several grants for Church and glebe purposes, and for school masters, might be sold, and the proceeds appropriated exclusively for the purposes of education. To this address His Majesty's assent was conveyed in the month of October, and in the following session of 1835, an Act was passed, "to authorize the sale of lands in the Island, reserved as 'sites for churches and for glebe and school lands.' "

"This Act recited the reservation in the original grants and His Majesty's assent directing the sales, and then proceeded to declare the mode in which such sales should be conducted, and the titles given. In October and November, 1836, sales of these reserves were made under this Act, and due returns thereof laid before the Assembly by the Lieutenant-Governor in February, 1838. It does not appear that any objections to these proceedings were ever raised by the proprietors, or any person claiming under them; no preliminary steps by escheat or otherwise were deemed necessary, nor was any doubt raised by any party that the fee in such reservations had not remained in the Crown."*

The land question in its many aspects was really the history of the Island for the first century of its existence as a British possession. It was a tangled skein, the many threads of which were most difficult to unravel. The report of the Land Commission for 1861 is most valuable in this connection. Every claim, or shadow of a claim, from any quarter, seems to have found means for getting a hearing. Of several, little was heard until the Commission was created. One of these was a long unheard of claim of the descendants of the original French settlers for the lands which their forefathers had held before the surrender to Great Britain of the Island. The claims of the descendants of these people was strongly urged upon the Commission.

### Claims of Descendants of the Original French.

"It was alleged that the French settlers, who were in the Island prior to the Treaty of 1763, were, by that treaty, confirmed in the rightful occupancy of their lands, which were subsequently granted away in 1767; and that those grants of the whole Island must have been made in ignorance of the occupancy, or in violation of the rights of the French. This subject was not specially referred to the Commission of 1861, yet it appeared very desirable that it should be disposed of, as it seemed to interest a large class of the inhabitants whose forefathers had been driven from lands they thought their own, and who had themselves suffered a good deal, either from ignorance of their rights, or, assuming that they had any, from their practical invasion.

"Having examined the subject in all its bearings, the commissioners deemed it their duty to report, that assuming the statements made by the French to be true, and that these rights were not compromised by the facts of history, they would seem to have been

---
*Commissioner's report, page 40.

harshly treated. But upon the proprietors, who have been in undisturbed possession of their lands for nearly a century, no legal claim can now be established, and it is clear that the Island government, which was not organized till long after the wrong complained of was done, cannot be expected to make atonement."

### INDIAN CLAIMS.

The Micmac Indians, that doughty race of warriors, the fear of whose raids had kept the English settlers in Nova Scotia in a state of alarm, were no longer to be dreaded.

As far back as 1806, the Abbe de Colonne interested himself in the Indians and memorialized the British authorities on their behalf. He pointed out that he had resided in Prince Edward Island for six years past and had been resorted to, in line of his clerical profession, by the Micmacs of the Island and of Nova Scotia, who, before the war of 1755, when the country belonged to France, had been converted to Christianity.

A harmless and inoffensive people, subsisting by the chase, they were over-looked at the locating of lands, when settlement commenced, though as aboriginals they had a right to a share. Now, owing to increasing population, wild animals (their food) are becoming scarcer. The river fisheries have been appropriated and regulated, consequently the Indians are in a starving condition. The Abbe, as their pastor, had sought to induce their betaking themselves to manual labor. . . . Some have attended to his directions and made attempts at horticulture, and raising a little maize have exceeded his expectations. But to change long habit may be the work of a whole generation. . . . That is not enough unless they are fixed near the shore, in a situation near the coast, favourable for obtaining water, sea-fowl and fishing. Besides from the danger of spirituous liquors and peculiar ways of living, it is advisable to keep them so far isolated from the other inhabitants as to render the introduction of intercourse gradual.

They had applied to Lieutenant-Governor Fanning for a suitable location, but as all the lands were granted without reservation, he could only procure the consent of the agents of the proprietor of Lennox Island, containing a thousand acres of land, for them to reside on. Thinking this sufficient, they built a very neat chapel and cleared spots for small gardens and patches of maize.

The Abbe told them, as the Island was private property, they could not continue to possess it without the explicit consent of the proprietor himself. Therefore, as he was returning for a short time to England they requested him to mention their loyalty, and pray that His Majesty would be pleased to buy and grant the Island to them. . . .

He further submitted "the necessity of vesting in the government of the Island, in trust for the security and benefit of the Indians, this or whatever portion of land Your Majesty may be pleased to advise being set aside for them, so as to render void any purchases which individuals may in future attempt to elicit from their inexperience and improvidence."

The memorial was signed, "De Colonne, Missionary." A certificate from General Fanning, dated Cavendish Square, 14th July, 1806, in support of above memorial was annexed. Their case also came before the commissioners who reported that: "The Indian claims are limited to Lennox Island and grass lands around it, and as it appears by evidence that the Indians have been in uninterrupted occupancy of their property for more than half a century, and have built a chapel and several houses upon the same, the commissioners are of opinion that their title should be confirmed and that this very small portion of the wide territories their forefathers formerly owned should be left in the undisturbed possession of this last remnant of the race.*"

It was inevitable that, under the conditions that existed, there would be unrest and discontent. For decades the agitation for escheat was kept up. Organizations to resist payments of rent were formed, the last being the "Tenant League" in the "sixties" of last century. At times, also, force had been employed to prevent the collection of rents. But on the whole the people were orderly and law-abiding. Those of the proprietors who lived on the Island, who knew their tenants and were known by them, were not unpopular. But the greater number of the proprietors were absent, living in England out of touch with the tenants on their estates. These were represented by agents. The great majority of these agents were excellent, humane men. Among them were the

*Report of Land Commissioners, 1861.

leading professional men of the Island. But they were not, by any means, all of this high type. Some of the absentees placed the management of their estates in the hands of agents who were utterly unfitted for the position, — a delicate one at best,— and who were themselves greedy and unscrupulous men. It was through these men that acts of oppression and wrong usually took place, and to whose conduct reprisals were due. A very tragic case took place in 1819, on Lord Townshend's estate near Rollo Bay in King's county. The following account is taken verbatim from the Prince Edward Island "Register" of Friday, September 3rd, 1919, volume II, No. 19: "Died,— On Saturday last at the Bay of Fortune, *Edward Abell, Esq*. His death was occasioned by the stab of a fixed bayonet through the lower part of his body, inflicted by a man residing in the same neighbourhood, named *Richard Pearce*. The circumstances which produced this lamented catastrophe, as far as we have been able to ascertain them, were as follows: On the Tuesday preceding, Pearce (who is a tenant on Lord Townshend's land), called upon Abell, who is His Lordship's agent, to pay £5 sterling, his last year's rent. Some portion of the money tendered, being three shillings and four pence pieces (a money current in the Island) was refused to be accepted by Abell, who, at the same time, told Pearce that if the whole of the money was not immediately paid, he would distrain and take his horse.

"Pearce immediately went among his neighbours and changed the money into Spanish coin, except some small change amounting to about two shillings and six pence. When this second tender was made it appears Abell had proceeded with his bailiff to Pearce's house, distrained and taken possession of a horse which was tethered in the field. After the exchange of the small sum had been adjusted, Abell exacted six shillings more from Pearce for quit rent. Pearce again went to one of his neighbours and obtained two three shillings and four penny peices, which were tendered but refused, and the horse retained. Abell then seated himself on some timber close to Pearce's house and sent his bailiff to some person living in the settlement to witness his proceedings; and the bailiff, upon his return, heard a loud altercation between Abell and Pearce, and saw the latter enter his house and take down a musket and fixed bayonet which he placed upon the floor, and then taking off his jacket, took up his gun and proceeded to the spot where Abell was seated and made a lunge which pierced Abell's arm, and immediately making a second charge the bayonet passed through the back part of the thigh into the intestines. He was then seized by the bailiff, who wrested the gun from him and held him fast, while Abell crawled to the next house. The bailiff (who is also a servant to Abell) was sent for to attend his master and Pearce absconded. This account has been received from an undoubted source; and while we record it, we deeply lament the coercive measures which produced the tragical event, and much more so the unguarded passion and misguided redress which an individual usurped with his own hands to the destruction of his fellow creature. We understand the greatest activity has been pursued for the arrest of Pearce, but without success."

The local government offered a reward of £20 sterling for the arrest of Pearce, but without success. He was never arrested. The fact was that the sympathy of the people in his neighbourhood was strongly with Pearce, and they were certain to assist him in making his escape.

The promontory on the west side of Bay Fortune still bears the name of the ill-fated agent, though the writer has found few who know whence the name of "Abell's Cape."

LIEUT.-GOV. FANNING

## PART V.

## CHAPTER II.

## FANNING, LIEUTENANT-GOVERNOR

The position in which Lieutenant-General Fanning found himself, on his arrival in November, 1786, was an anomalous one. It has already been pointed out that Patterson refused to surrender the government until the following spring, when peremptory despatches arrived, dismissing and ordering him to transfer the government to Fanning. There can be no question but that the latter was in a most awkward situation, during the period between his arrival and Patterson's departure the following year. He evidently bore himself with dignity under trying circumstances, while Patterson weakened himself by the extraordinary ill-advised course he saw fit to pursue.

Fanning was Lieutenant-Governor and member of the Council of Nova Scotia at the time of his appointment to the Island of Saint John.* He was a native of America, having been born in the Province of New York, on the 24th April, 1739. He was a son of James Fanning, a captain in the British Army, and of his second wife, who was Mary Smith, a daughter of Colonel Smith, who for some time administered the government of New York, and was sole proprietor of Smithtown, in Long Island. The paternal grandfathers of General Fanning came to America from Ireland, with the Earl of Bellemont, in 1699. Captain James Fanning having disposed of his commission, while in England, returned to New York in 1748, when his son, then in the ninth year of his age, was sent to a preparatory school, and thence removed to Yale College, New Haven, where, after going through the regular course of collegiate studies, he received the degrees of bachelor and master of Arts; and in 1774 he was honoured by the University of Oxford, England, with the degree of Doctor of Civil Law. From college he proceeded to North Carolina, where, after studying two years under the Attorney-General of that province, he was, in 1762, admitted to the Bar. He was successful in his profession, but the

---

*The account of Fanning is largely derived from an article published in the Halifax Herald, of the 13th November, 1920.

troubles of that eventful period in America, which followed the passing of the Stamp Act by parliament, induced him to enter the civil and military service of his country. In 1765, he was appointed by Governor Tryon of North Carolina, one of the judges of the Supreme Court in that province, in the room of Mr. Justice Moore, who was dismissed from office upon the supposition of his favouring the public commotion at that time existing in North Carolina. In 1768, he raised a corps of eight hundred provincials to oppose and put down a body of insurgents, who styled themselves Regulators; whose object was to rescue leading rebels from trial and punishment. In 1771 he was again called upon by Governor Tryon to raise and embody a corps of Provincials to suppress an insurrection in North Carolina, and was second to Governor Tryon at the battle of Allamance, in which action the insurgents were totally defeated.

In the year 1773, Fanning went to England, strongly recommended to His Majesty's Ministers for his services in North Carolina. Having applied for the office of Chief Justice of Jamaica, he received a letter from Lord Dartmouth, then Secretary of State for the American Department, stating that in this case it was impossible to comply with his wishes, but that he should have the first vacant post that might be deemed worthy of his services. Having received this assurance he returned to America. Two months after his arrival in New York he was appointed to the office of Surveyor-General of that province, the annual fees of which were said to be worth £2,200 sterling. But in the following year Fanning was driven from his house in New York, and took refuge on board the Asia ship of war. He afterwards served in the army, having raised a regiment called "The King's American Regiment." During the war he was twice wounded. There is ample proof that he discharged his military duties with courage and ability.

On the 24th February, 1783, Colonel Fanning was appointed Lieutenant-Governor of Nova Scotia, an appointment which he accepted with a promise from Lords Sydney and North that it should lead to something better.* Subsequently, John Parr, who had been Captain-General and Governor, was reduced to the

---

*He was also Lieutenant-Governor of Annapolis Royal with pay of 10s. a day, which he lost on coming to the Island of St. John.

position of Lieutenant-Governor on Lord Dorchester being appointed Governor-General in British North America. Upon this Fanning was ordered to relieve Lieutenant-Governor Patterson, in the Island of St. John, which he did in the confident expectation that he would succeed to the government of Nova Scotia on the retirement or death of Parr. In 1791, Fanning was informed of the death of Parr by a letter from Richard Bulkeley, President of the Council of Nova Scotia, who concluded by saying: "As the government of this Province, by his Majesty's late instructions, devolves on you, as senior Lieutenant-Governor, I accordingly give you early notice of the vacancy." This information was received too late in the autumn to admit of Lieutenant-Governor Fanning's proceeding to Halifax, and while making preparations for going thither, he was informed that the position was conferred on Mr. Wentworth — intelligence which caused him great disappointment, as he had well-founded expectations of succeeding to the government of Nova Scotia. The Governor applied immediately for leave of absence, but was politely refused, on the ground that his absence might, in time of war, prove dangerous to the Island. After repeated application, he at last received a letter from Lord Hobart, dated 6th May, 1804, granting him liberty to return to England after the arrival of Colonel DesBarres, and informing him that His Majesty had directed that, in consideration of his long and faithful services, a provision at the rate of £500 sterling should be made for him yearly in the estimates of the Island.

In 1816, General Fanning closed his account at the Audit, when His Majesty's Ministers, to mark their approval of his administration of the government of Prince Edward Island, directed a retrospective increase of his salary from the period of his appointment to the colony, in 1786, to that of his retirement. General Fanning died at his residence in Upper Seymour street, on the 28th of February, 1818, in the seventy-ninth year of his age. His only son, a captain in the British Army, predeceased him.

The American view of Fanning's character, as detailed by Sabine, in his American Loyalists, is as follows:—"Among the public offices which he held was that of Recorder of Deeds for the County of Orange, and it is alleged that to his abuses in this capacity, the war or rebellion of the Regulators, in Governor Tryon's administration is, in a good measure, to be attributed."

The averment is that by his vicious character, nearly all the estates in Orange were loaded with doubts as to their titles; with exorbitant fees for recording new and unnecessary deeds, and high taxes to support a government which supported his wickedness. This charge rests on very high authority; and during the war of the Regulators against the Royal Government neither the person nor property of Fanning was respected. His losses were presented to the Assembly by Governor Martin, the successor of Tryon, but that body not only peremptorily refused to consider the subject, but administered a rebuke to the Governor, for thus trifling "with the dignity of the House." "It is not impossible," says Sabine, "that his unpopularity was greater than his offences deserved; since neither the Members of the Assembly, nor the people at large were, at this juncture, in a frame of mind to exact justice to opponents." Those who had intercourse with Colonel Fanning both in Nova Scotia and Prince Edward Island record the fact that, in every relation of life, he was a man of good principles, and of an agreeable disposition.

In the Annual Register for 1770, page 31, we get an account of an attack made by the mob in South Carolina upon his house. It is as follows:

"They (South Carolina anti-British mob), marched in a body to Colonel Fanning's house and, on a signal given by the ring-leaders entered the same, destroyed every piece of furniture in it, ript open his beds, broke and threw in the streets every piece of china and glassware in the house, scattered all his papers and books in the wind, seized all his plate, cash and proclamation money, entered his cellars and, gorging their stomachs with his liquors, stove and threw in the street the remainder, and, being now drunk with rage, liquor and lawless fury, they took his wearing apparel, stuck them on a pole, paraded them in triumph through the streets, and, to close the scene, pulled down and laid his house in ruins."*

Lord Selkirk, a shrewd observer, met Fanning in 1803, on two or three occasions. He refers to him as a man whose "politeness is rather burdensome. He is a man of no superabundant head."

---

*This is from a Memorial from Fanning for more pay, etc. It is of great length and a copy of it is contained in the Canadian Archives, "Colonial Correspondence" of Prince Edward Island, Vol. 18, pages 88-141 inclusive. The above extract is from page 104.

... "From his timidity and fear of losing popularity, he lets everybody do as they please, even those whom he has the most natural influence over. In this way he frequently cannot carry measures even in Council, though under his own nomination, and very improper people are allowed to remain in Council. The Chief Justice (Thorpe), who expresses himself as anxious for the improvement of the Island, seems to be so much disgusted at this style of proceeding that he says he will not attend Council. Sir Robert Chalmers and Mr. Townshend, both now absent, he speaks of as the best members of the Council, but lost in the crowd."

Opinion with regard to Fanning varied very much. John McGregor, who knew the Island and its people well, writing in 1828, says that "The administration of the late General Fanning was productive of no advantage to the Island, nor of any apparent injury to individuals.* . . .

"Governor Fanning's ruling passion, during his administration, was that of acquiring landed property in the colony, and he succeeded in securing to himself some of the best tracts without proceeding to any violent measures. He was brought up, and I believe born, in the United States and of very obscure origin. The Revolutionary War afforded him an opportunity of rising in the world; but as he was never actually engaged against the enemy, he owed his fortune to circumstances, the advantages of which he had the finesse to seize.†

"He possessed, also, a number of kind and generous qualities, but from the easy influence which designing men had acquired over him, he was led, perhaps more by them than by any deliberate principle of his own, to do a number of foolish things and some unjust ones."

On his arrival in Charlottetown in the autumn of 1786, an address dated 7th November, 1786, signed by Lieutenant-Governor DesBrisay, Peter Stewart (Chief Justice) and others, in fact by the faction hostile to Patterson, in which the Governor's conduct was denounced, was presented to Colonel Fanning, who was warmly welcomed to the Island. The address was enclosed by Fanning to the Secretary of State (Sydney) on the 9th November. At the same time Fanning forwarded to the Secretary a report of

---

*Account of Prince Edward Island, page 91.
†Part at least of this is incorrect. See account of Fanning *ante.*

his movements after receiving his instructions to proceed to the Island of St. John.

He says: "I left Halifax on 16th October and travelled to the harbour of Pictou, where I was detained for a fortnight by contrary winds, and after three attempts to cross, I, with great difficulty, and at imminent risk of being lost in a violent storm, arrived at the Island on the evening of the fourth instant. I immediately waited on Lieutenant-Governor Patterson and delivered to him the duplicate of Your Lordship's despatch to him of the 30th June last. At the same time I informed him I had come, in obedience to the King's commands, to carry on in his room, the public service of the Government of this Island, and requested he would convene the members of His Majesty's Council that I might lay before him in Council Your Lordship's letter to me and the Commission I was honoured with by His Majesty for that purpose."

A letter from Patterson was enclosed, which fully explained the steps taken by Fanning and the obstacles which prevented the King's commands from being executed. On Patterson's refusal to deliver over the government, and on receipt of his letter, Fanning conceived it advisable, for the preservation of the peace and public tranquility of the Island, to wait, without further controversy with Mr. Parterson, until His Majesty's pleasure should be further signified, at the same time earnestly recommending, as opportunity offered, that the party animosities and dissentions existing amongst the inhabitants should subside, and that unanimity and good order should be aimed at.

Patterson's letter to Fanning referred to, was dated 7th November, 1786. The following is an extract: . . . . "I am to inform you, I cannot think myself justified in complying with your request that you should be, at this time, admitted to the possession of the great seal and such papers and documents as should enable you to carry on the public services of this government, until I shall have it in my power to leave the country, of which circumstances I shall, in my public despatches on this occasion, make His Lordship fully acquainted, and I shall hope it will prove a perfect justification in this instance of your conduct and of mine."

During the summer of 1787, the Lieutenant-Governor made a journey around the eastern half of the Island and inspected the several settlements, upon which he made a report to the home government. This report is interesting as embodying the observations of a shrewd observer. He wrote to Nepean, Under Secretary of State, that:

"On the 6th June last I went on board a six-oared open boat, at Charlottetown, and proceeded down the Hillsborough River out of the mouth of the harbour (I write this on the supposition that you have a plan of the Island of St. John before you), taking my private secretary, my tent and marquees, canteens, two servants, and six hands to man the boat. The first day I passed several houses and in the evening encamped at Prim Village on Lot 57, where I remained three days, exploring the lands and old fields, which were delightfully situated and had formerly been well inhabited by the French, but at present not a house or family in several miles of it. I then went round Point Prim and encamped at Primit (Pinette) Village on Lot 58. Here, also, had formerly been a considerable French settlement. From hence I went to Wood Islands, Lot 58, and encamped two days. Thence to Georgetown at Three Rivers and Cardigan Bay. Not a soul living in all that coast and tract of country from Pinette to Cardigan Bay. Here I halted some days, being pleased beyond description with the harbour and country round it. I then went to Lord Townshend's Lot 56, on which, at the mouth of Grand River, live seven Loyalists or disbanded soldiers and no more. From thence I went to Fortune Bay, Lot 43, a small French village delightfully situated, having a beautiful harbour for small schooners and fishing vessels. From thence to the East Point not a single inhabitant. Near the Point, on Lot 47, I encamped three days. Here were large tracts of meadow lands. From thence round East Point, near Surveyor's Inlet, where I found settled three or four families of disbanded troops. From this settlement to Shipwreck Point, Lot 43, not a single family or inhabitant. Here were four Highland families; and from thence to St. Peters, not an inhabitant. At St. Peters is a well settled and fine country, where I remained a few days and then proceeded to Scotch Savage harbour; opposite to which is French Savage harbour, very pleasantly situated villages. There I had my boat, with all my baggage in it, put on a sled and drawn by four pair of oxen, across the portage, two miles and a half to the head of Hillsborough River, where I encamped one day and night. The day following I came down Hillsborough River to Charlottetown, from whence I had my departure; having been absent about four weeks, in which time I neither eat, drank or slept in a house, but devoted my whole time to going up and down the different creeks, rivers, bays and harbours, and exploring the coast. I can, therefore, speak with greater certainty respecting this circuit of the Island than, perhaps, any man on it. And confident I am that, had it been open to be granted by the Crown by Patents from the Governors, in the same manner as lands in Nova Scotia and New Brunswick were, at the evacuation of New York, that it would not, at this day, be equalled by any part of His Majesty's Dominion in America in proportion to the same extent of territory. As it is there are not above five hundred families, at the utmost, on the whole Island, including the French, Highland and all other inhabitants."

This must have been an underestimate. When Patterson came to the Island in 1770, there were one hundred and fifty British families. After the expulsion of the French, when Lord Rollo took possession of the Island, there remained, in 1764, a number of that nationality, amounting to three hundred, whom Colonel Haldimand wished to take to his lands in Canada. This was twenty-three years before Fanning wrote. The natural increase was most rapid, if reliance can be placed on the statements of Mr. Stewart, Patterson, and all who have referred to this subject. All writers on the early settlement of this Island and for the first quarter of the nineteenth century comment upon the large families that were the rule. Moreover, it may be laid down almost as a general principle, that wherever the conditions of life are hard, and there is a struggle to live, and luxury is unknown, it is the common experience that the birth-rate is high. And in this Island, in the early days, the life of the people was not, by any means, luxurious. They had a sufficiency of strong, wholesome food. They led, largely, an out-door life. In fact they lived nearer to nature than do the people of to-day. They had to labour for a subsistence. The charge of race-suicide can never be brought against the early settlers of any country. The first settlers in the Island of St. John were, certainly, not guilty of anything of the kind, and the meaning of the term was unknown to them. The natural increase must have been large. When Patterson returned from England, in

1780, he reported that the population had nearly doubled in the five years of his absence. And he had spent five years here before he went to England, during which there was a steady increase of population. Of the proprietors, Mr. Stewart, Captain John McDonald, Mr. Montgomery, Mr. DesBrisay and some others, had brought in a considerable number of settlers. Captain MacDonald alone had brought in over three hundred as far back as 1772. We have seen that as early as 1775, when the American privateers were on the coast, provision had been made, on Township Number Five, for a hundred and five settlers who had lately arrived. Some had come of their own accord, and at the time of Fanning's itinerary the Revolutionary War with the United States was over, and a number of Loyalists had come to the Island. Hence it seems that there must have been a larger population in 1787 than Fanning reported. It must be borne in mind, also, that all the early statements as to population were merely estimates. No census was taken.

## Captain Robert Gray.

Writing on 26th November, 1787, to Lord Sydney, Fanning acquainted his Lordship that he had appointed Captain Robert Gray, Receiver-General of Quit Rents in this Island. He goes on to say: "Captain Gray, My Lord, served the whole of the last war as an officer in the King's American Regiment of Foot, which I had the honour to command. He is a gentleman of superior merit and worth. He has been employed for three years past in the Province of Nova Scotia, in several stations, in all of which he has acquitted himself with the highest reputation and credit . . . and has a thorough knowledge of accounts. . . . The appointment of Captain Gray is a matter, in my opinion, of the first importance to the interest of His Majesty's revenue in this government."

The Gray family took an active part in the public life of the Island for a century after Captain Robert Gray's coming here. He himself was for many years an assistant Judge of the Supreme Court. On the death, at "Inkerman House," his residence in the Royalty of Charlottetown, of Colonel the Honourable John Hamilton Gray, towards the close of last century, the family ceased to make their home in Prince Edward Island.

## First Flagship and Squadron.

On 1st July, 1788, Fanning announced to Lord Sydney that Rear-Admiral Sawyer, with five ships of His Majesty's squadron under his command, arrived here the 23rd June, being the first visit of a flag officer and squadron of His Majesty's navy to this port. "The favourable opinion the Admiral has been pleased to express of the depth of water, the facility of entrance and the security of the harbour has afforded myself and all the inhabitants of this town infinite satisfaction."

## Smuggling.

Even at this early period of the Island's history, smuggling seems to have been carried on to quite an extent. On 14th August, 1788, Townshend, the Collector of Customs, wrote Lord Sydney:

"My Lord: . . . On 19th June last, I seized and forfeited a schooner of British plantation, built, owned and navigated, according to law. The causes of seizure were (1st), her cargo was imported direct from New York into this Island, contrary to the provisions of a late Act of Parliament, and (2nd) that bulk was broken before entry. The goods were landed in the night season at the farm of the late Lieutenant-Governor Patterson, near the entrance of this harbour, about three miles from Charlottetown. Having received information of an extensive smuggling trade intended to be carried on between the late Lieutenant-Governor, his brother, John Patterson and a wealthy resident of New York, to whose daughter John Patterson is married, and that this small vessel was to be followed by a large ship named the Kitty in the same disgraceful employ, I decided to seize this property and so stop the increase of so ruinous a traffic. Accordingly, in the night following, I obtained a party of soldiers from the commanding officers here, went to the farms, and in company with the constables made a seizure of part of the smuggled effects, but before we could get them to the boats prepared for this purpose, the servants of the late Lieutenant-Governor, aided by eight or nine other persons, who had been sent over the water by him to their assistance (being in all about twenty-five persons armed with various offensive weapons), wrested the property out of our hands. . . . We were made prisoners as well as the soldiers and detained several hours. Soon after I was informed of another quantity of goods being on the farm, part of the same cargo. . . . I obtained another party of men *fully armed*, and again went to the farm in company with the controllers and seized the goods in a very artful place of concealment. We conveyed them to town and have since libelled them and the schooner in the Court of Admiralty as forfeited."

The Governor asked the Secretary of State (Sydney) for instructions as to making grants to Loyalists. It is evident that the Island government hoped for a large influx of population from this source. Fanning called the Secretary's attention to the distinct grant of one-fourth of their lands, by the proprietors, for distribution among the Loyalists by the Governor-in-Council, and pointed out the onerous claims and conditions now annexed to the grants by the proprietors, who would not allow the grantees to hold direct from the Crown. He insisted that, unless the grants were made on as favourable terms as in Nova Scotia, disappointment to the Loyalists must result. He hoped that the proprietors would allow the governor and Council to sign permits for the one-fourth. If not, he said, settlers could not be expected, and some would go away to the lands of Nova Scotia and Cape Breton, which would be granted rent free, except for the quit rents. He reported to Nepean, Under Secretary of State, the terms offered by resident proprietors to Loyalists and disbanded soldiers, who had settled on surrendered grounds, but without a title. He enclosed a letter from a Mr. Edward Allen, who wrote on behalf of himself and others, refusing to accept the terms offered. The people of Bay Fortune had examined part of Cape Breton, and were now returned to this Island, but all were determined to leave. The proprietors had ruined all prospect of getting settlers. In different forms, the same wretched story is told time and again.

With the sanction of Lord Dorchester, the Governor-General, Fanning, in the autumn of 1787, cancelled the suspension of Mr. Wright from his office of Surveyor-General, and also those of Messrs. Callbeck, Wright and Burns from their seats in the Council, on their giving satisfactory assurances of future good behaviour. However, this did not save them, as they were dismissed by the Secretary of State in 1789. Mr. Callbeck died the following year.

## Death of Callbeck.

A committee was appointed to prepare a suitable monument and reported: "The committee appointed to ascertain the expense and to prepare a suitable inscription for a monument to the memory of the late Speaker, Lieutenant-Colonel Callbeck, report, that they had taken the matter into consideration, and are of the opinion that the expense ought not to exceed £20 sterling, and that the device or model should be left to the decision of the artist who may be employed to make the same; That Messrs. Cambridge and Bowley be requested to have it executed in London and to import it as soon as possible. And that His Excellency, the Lieutenant-Governor, be applied to and requested to issue a warrant on the public treasury for the amount."

The inscription they recommend to be nearly as follows:

"Sacred to the memory of Phillips Callbeck, Esquire, His Majesty's Attorney-General, Lieutenant-Colonel of the Militia, and late Speaker of the House of Assembly of this province; by whose Order this Monument is erected as a testimony of their esteem and a grateful tribute to a General Benefactor of this Island, who departed this life the 28th February, A. D. 1790, aged forty-six years." Unanimously agreed to.

The writer has been unable to ascertain if this monument to Callbeck was ever actually erected. He was buried in the "old" Protestant cemetery on Malpeque Road, where for very many years there was a stone to his memory, simply inscribed with the initials "P. C.", seemingly intended as a temporary monument to be succeeded by that voted by the Assembly, but there was no trace of the latter. Callbeck was a patriotic man of much ability, whose memory deserved to be perpetuated.

Previously to Fanning's arrival there had never been a printing press on the Island. In 1788 he induced a Mr. Robertson, a printer, to come to Charlottetown, and employed him in printing a complete copy of the laws. The Journals and Acts had never been printed, and some of the latter had been lost, and only imperfect manuscripts of others could be obtained. Fanning forwarded a memorial from the Council and Assembly to Lord Dorchester, asking to have Robertson appointed King's Printer, with a salary the same as that of the similar official in New Brunswick, as unless he had a salary, he must leave the Island, as the profits of his business here would not support his family. The Secretary of State, to whom Lord Dorchester referred the memorial, saw no objection to the appointment, but refused to attach a salary to the office. Robertson remained on the Island till 1798, when he printed the laws, a printed copy of which the Lieutenant-Governor forwarded to the Secretary of State. He then left the Island, which was again without a printing press.

Fanning had dissolved the Assembly immediately after assuming the government, and a new one was elected, being the fifth General Assembly convened on the Island. It met on 22nd January, 1788, when the members were sworn in and Phillips Callbeck elected Speaker.

The Lieutenant-Governor's speech opening the session contained little of importance. He submitted to the consideration of the House the public expediency of a revision and printing of the laws of this Island, in order that they might be more universally known and, of consequence, the salutary effect of their operations be more generally felt. Referring to the militia, he said: "Your own wisdom must dictate a due attention to the Militia Act, as important to your own security, and you will surely consider the time of peace as the fittest season to guard against the dangers and evils of a possible war." This House passed only one Act, being an Act in addition to two recited Acts relating to highways. The thanks of the House were voted to the Hon. Thomas Wright for nineteen years service as Surveyor-General . . . "and for his uniform, unimpeached integrity in the discharge of his duty as Assistant Judge of the Supreme Court and for upwards of three years as Senior Judge of that Court, the several duties of which he has performed without salary or other emoluments."

### AGRICULTURE AND FISHERY — GROWTH OF THE COMMUNITY.

On 15th July, 1789, Fanning made an interesting report to Lord Sydney on the state of the Island. He says: "Since my arrival in this government, not only the appearance of this town is much improved, by the addition of new buildings and the repairs of the streets and its vicinity, but that the state of agriculture in the Island and the fisheries on the coast are so greatly increased and extended. These favourable indications of the future growth and importance of this valuable Island, within the short space of two years and a half past, are undoubtedly justly to be attributed to a fortunate concurrence of a variety of circumstances, the principal of which appears to me that many industrious good farmers have lately come and settled in this Island and have, on trial, successfully experienced the benefits and advantages arising from sowing wheat, and rye and what is called "winter grain," in the fall season of the year, whereby the time for preparing the ground and putting in summer wheat, rye, oats, potatoes and the like, in the spring, is greatly enlarged, and the profits of husbandry much increased to the manifest encouragement of industry and agriculture." He then goes on to recommend the protection of our fisheries against the United States fishermen as is done on the Nova Scotia coast from Canso.

This proved to be a very refractory Assembly. The ill-feeling between the friends of the late Lieutenant-Governor and the supporters of the present one gave rise to much friction. Fanning thereupon dissolved the Assembly, and issued writs for a new one, which met on 22nd March, 1790. He reported to the Secretary of State that in this Assembly harmony prevailed. It certainly seems to have been a satisfactory one for the Governor, as it was in existence for twelve years, and held no less than nine sessions. It may fairly be called the "Long Parliament," of this Island. The Act changing the name of the Island from St. John to Prince Edward Island was passed by this Assembly at its seventh session in 1798.

On 30th March, 1790, the Lieutenant-Governor informed the Assembly that since the last meeting of the General Assembly he had bought a house, in one part of which he had appropriated for the performance of public divine service during the time he shall be continued in the government of this Island, whereby there is and will be a saving of £10 a year to the public, which sum has heretofore been annually paid for the hire of a room for a church.

In the public accounts for May, 1789, submitted to this Assembly we find the following entries:

"To cash paid Benjamin Chappel for repairing the Stocks," £0 15s 0d.

"To cash paid Ann Richardson for the use of her house for church from 6th November, 1788, to 6th November, 1789," £10 0s 0d.

## RUMORS OF WAR WITH SPAIN.

The second session of this Assembly met 10th November of the same year (1790). War with Spain was threatening. The Lieutenant-Governor, in his opening speech, placed the possibility of war fairly before the House. He spoke in part as follows:

"The rumour of a possibility of war with Spain has been heard by all, and that the discussion of the rights and interests of the two nations is not, as yet, finally adjusted, is what I can inform you from the highest authority. In this uncertainty of the event of peace or war, it is my duty, as well with regard to the security of this Island in general, as to the safety of the inhabitants of the particular towns and settlements in it, to recommend to your serious consideration the high importance it may be to each individual, his family and property, that a due and early attention be paid to embodying and equipping themselves with the means of defence in a manner as prescribed by the militia law of this Island, long since enacted with a view to the safety, protection and defence, of its inhabitants, their families and possessions in a time of war and in the hour of danger."

Turning from the things of war he referred to the great prosperity of the Island: "The herring and cod-fisheries in the bays, and all along the northern coast of this Island, I am told, have far exceeded whatever has before been observed, and that the harvests in general, but particularly that of winter wheat and rye, have been better than ever they were in this Island; and that in quality they have equalled, if not excelled, what has ever been known in any other part of North America."

In the autumn of 1790, when a war with Spain seemed likely to break out, the Governor offered his military services, and in the event of hostilities, suggested an attack on the south coast of Spanish America, which he thought would be successful. He had formerly served with the Creek and Cherokee Indians, of whose bravery and loyalty he had a high opinion, and with whom he would be willing to serve again. He urged the advantages that would result from the possession of the Floridas, and the ease with which they could be settled. Had they been retained by Great Britain they would have been settled by people now in the United States. Many Loyalists who came to Nova Scotia were forced by the cold to leave and go to the Southern States, some to the Creeks and Cherokees, and, if the Floridas were held by Great Britain, they would settle them. As the strained relations with Spain did not, at that time, result in war, the Governor had no opportunity of taking the field."

### Bishop McEachern — Highland Immigration.

The year 1790 was an important one for the Island of St. John. There was, about that period, a movement from the Highland clans to America. Reference will be made later to the causes of this movement when the Selkirk settlement comes under review. Many of the clansmen found their way to Canada. This Island had its share of these hardy immigrants. The McEacherns, the MacIntoshes and others came over the seas from Ardnamurchan in the Hebrides, to find homes at Savage Harbour. In 1790 also, the Coffins, Loyalists from Nantucket, settled at the same place, where many of their descendants still reside.

Soon after there came to these shores the great missionary priest, Rev. Angus McEachern, for so many years known as "Bishop McEachern," respected and beloved by all. He had been pursuing his studies in Spain, and, when finished, obtained permission to join his clansmen in the Island of St. John, which he did in 1790. He was a born leader of men. He gave an impulse to settlement and directed the people to co-operate in clearing the land, erecting dwellings and building boats. He had a roomy dwelling of red sand-stone built at Savage Harbour, whence he visited all parts of the Island as well as the Magdalens, Cape Breton and parts of the mainland. He was a man not only of great executive ability but also of tireless energy. He was equally respected by Protestants as by his own people. In 1821 he was ordained Bishop, his ecclesiastical title being "Bishop of Rosen." In 1831 he became Bishop of Charlottetown; in 1826 he purchased what is still known as the College Farm at St. Andrews and built a college there, where for many years young men received an excellent education. It was the precursor of the present fine University of St. Dunstan's. Bishop McEachern died in 1836. Like St. Paul he might have said he was "in journeyings often, in perils of waters . . . in perils in the wilderness, . . . in perils in the sea . . . in weariness and painfulness, . . . in hunger and thirst," but not, "in perils by his own countrymen."

### LACK OF CASH,— LEGAL TENDER.

The Lieutenant-Governor in opening the session, referring to the necessity for a circulating medium, said,— "But amid the general harmony of the country, and their sources of encouragement to industry and grounds of contentment among the inhabitants, the inconvenience of a want of *Cash*, or some circulating medium to facilitate the commerce of dealings among themselves, seems to be a difficulty very generally felt and lamented. I therefore think it a duty which I owe to the interest and convenience of the good people of this flourishing colony to recommend to your deliberation, in order to remedy the deficiency complained of, the expediency of framing a law for the emitting (for a certain limited amount), bills or debentures, which may be voluntarily accepted by creditors of the public, and made a legal tender to the public treasurer of this government, for the discharge of any Island duties, taxes or other debts, whatever, due and payable at the public treasury." The House in reply assured him of their concurrence in the matters mentioned in the Speech.

### LEGAL TENDER,— CURRENCY.

When the Assembly met for its third session on 6th November, 1792, it was found that the Act of the last session for emitting debentures or bills had not realized expectation. The Lieutenant-Governor grappled with the matter at considerable length. He said:

"The late Act of the General Assembly for emitting debentures or bills of public credit, not having afforded that relief, or proved that efficient substitute for the want of a circulating currency as was wished for and expected by the public and which the state of the Island required, and the term of their circulation approaching to an end, when the holders of them and government's warrants on the treasurer must be paid in cash, it becomes the duty of the present session to turn their attention towards the state of the public revenue, and to devise and adopt the proper ways and means for satisfying the demands of public creditors and supporting the public faith and credit of the government.

"The want of specie, or some circulating money, in this Island to facilitate the intercourse of traffic or dealings among the inhabitants, is not only a vast obstacle to trade and a great discouragement to industry, but is also in a great degree the occasion of that embarassment and heavy distress in which many individuals are, at the time, unhappily involved, although probably possessed of property sufficient to satisfy the demands of their creditors, and to extricate themselves and families from impending ruin, did not the want of a currency in this Island render it impossible for them to convert their effects into money.

"In cases of somewhat similar public exigency, the Legislatures of some of His Majesty's West Indian Islands have introduced foreign coin among them, such as Spanish milled dollars, half, quarter, eighths and sixteenths of dollars, and had these stamped, at the public expense, with the letters "G. R." on the face or dexter side, and a crown on the reverse or sinister side, which coin, when so stamped, has been by a law, to which the Royal assent has been obtained, declared and made a legal tender in such Islands in all payments whatsoever, and a heavy penalty inflicted on any person carrying or exporting any of the said specie or foreign coin, so stamped, out of the said Islands.

"And in order that the introduction and circulation of such a cash currency should not be opposed or obstructed, or any injury come to the merchant or trader, the sum to be stamped or introduced into circulation might be limited to the annual estimates, or sum voted by Parliament for the civil establishment of this government for one year; so that the officers of this government would, in each revolving year, find it both for their own benefit and convenience to give their bills for such money to the merchants to the amount of their respective salaries, which would effect an immediate circulation and secure a successive annual exchange of the whole money of the Island (besides what might be wanted for bills for the half-pay officers), to the mutual advantage and convenience of the officer, who might want to receive his pay, and to the merchant, who might be desirous of making his remittance in bills to England.

"Among the many public advantages which would attend such a measure, would be the removing of that weighty objection of the want of currency, which every stranger makes to becoming a settler in this valuable Island. It would fully answer all the exigencies of insular dealings among the inhabitants. It would enable the merchant to collect his debts, without distressing his customers. It would enable the tenant to pay his rent, and the farmer, the merchant and the labourer would thereby be excited to redoubled diligence, from a certainty of receiving, in cash, the reward of their labours and the fruit of their industry, to the infinite encouragement and universal benefit of all.

"I have dwelt the more largely upon this subject from a confident belief, in my own mind, that not anything whatever can immediately so successfully promote the interest or permanently advance the future prosperity of this Island as the procuring and establishing a circulating currency, without which every other expedient, I am persuaded, will prove a mere temporary relief, in a great degree defective, or altogether ineffectual."

As the trade and general business of the colony increase in value and in volume we meet with other crude financial schemes for providing permanent currency.

### LEGAL TENDER,— LEATHER NOTES.

In a recent valuable work* appears an interesting account of the fiscal difficulties with which the Islanders had to contend in this matter, and of some of the methods employed to remedy these difficulties. "Much difficulty," the author says, "was found in keeping coin in circulation. The authorities hit upon an interesting variation of the usual device of lightening coins to keep them in the country. The centre of a Spanish silver dollar was punched out so as to form a coin, which passed for a shilling, while the remainder passed for a five shillings or $1.00, in the Island currency, and was nicknamed 'The Holy Dollar.' At a somewhat later period, the continued scarcity of small change led to other experiments in the way of currency, one of the most curious of which was the leather notes issued by William Fitzpatrick, a shoemaker of Charlottetown. These were redeemed by Treasury notes of the Province." They

---
*"A History of the Canadian Bank of Commerce," by Victor Ross, page 27.

were for 2/6 and were dated in 1836. . . . "Prince Edward Island appears to have been a fertile field for currency experiments, no doubt partly on account of the fact that so small a community, devoted almost exclusively to agriculture and fishing, found unusual difficulty in devising any form of currency that would remain within its borders."

The Treasury note or bill, already referred to, issued in 1790, was made under the provisions of the statute, 31 George III, Cap. 8, passed that year. It was a legal tender, and was issued by three Commissioners appointed by the Lieutenant-Governor for that purpose. The form of the bill was as follows:

"*This Bill, shall be accepted as legal tender in discharge of any duties, taxes or other debts whatsoever, due to, and payable at, the public Treasury of this Island, in virtue of an Act of the General Assembly thereof, passed the          day of               1790.*"

*A.B., C.D., E.F.*

The total issue was limited to £500, in four different denominations, namely, 5s, 10s, 20s, 40s. Any person forging or counterfeiting any of said bills, or uttering and passing the same, knowing them to be counterfeit and thereof convicted, should be adjudged guilty of felony, without benefit of clergy, and suffer death accordingly.

Later on, in Lieutenant-Governor DesBarres' time, the House of Assembly took up the question of a paper currency to supply, in some degree, the deficiency of cash in the colony. This is a question that seems bound to come before every legislature at some time or other. Even our own Dominion Parliament has had on its floor advocates of paper money, or the "Rag Baby" as it was called. In the United States the silver free coinage nostrum of some years ago was not much better. There might have been some excuse for it in this Island, with its sparse population, where there was great inconvenience owing to the scarcity of a circulating medium. Various,— more or less crude,— remedies for this inconvenience were from time to time adopted. At one time it was proposed to make wheat a legal tender. Great numbers of Spanish dollars were punched as described by Mr. Ross. They are now very rare, and valued by the collectors of coins. It was found that the intrinsic value of the metal in the smaller piece was greater than its value in money, and it has been stated, although the writer cannot verify the statement, that an enterprising gentleman collected and shipped them to England to be sold as bullion, but the vessel in which they were sent was lost at sea and the silver with her. Later on, also, private individuals put in circulation their own copper coin, some specimens of which are now of very considerable market value and are sought for by collectors. Issues of small notes by others than Mr. Fitzpatrick were also made. They were redeemable in specie by their issuers, and, no doubt, were a convenience at the time. Advertisements of this kind of script may be seen in the newspapers as late as the "thirties." In January, 1825, a petition from several merchants and shop-keepers of Charlottetown, complaining of an importation of base copper coin, was presented to the Assembly and referred to a committee to prepare a bill to prevent the importation of such coin and for regulating the payment of copper coin throughout the Island.

### Prosperity, Settlers, Commerce, Etc.

Having thus disposed, for the present, of the troublesome question of currency, the Lieutenant-Governor found more satisfactory matter to put before the Assembly. He continued his Address in an optimistic tone, informing his hearers that:

"It is with the highest satisfaction that I can direct your views to brighter objects and am able to felicitate you on the vast acquisition of new settlers since the last session. The abundant increase of the last harvest of winter grain and all the plentiful crops of every kind, far exceeding any former year; to which may be added the cheering and animating prospects which the Island has from engagements already entered into, of erecting some saw and grist mills of very superior construction and public utility.

"The large supply of salt and other stores, lodged at different harbours for carrying on the herring and other fisheries the ensuing spring to a far greater extent than ever known here before,— the large contracts made by others for exporting square timber, besides the extended business of ship-building as it is now carried on, and the orders for preparing frames and materials for the erecting and completing of several mansion houses for the reception of some opulent and respectable proprietors among us, are all so many encouraging presages of the future wealth and prosperity of this hitherto too much neglected Island.

"It therefore seems only necessary for the present inhabitants and its Legislature, especially, to be united, faithful and true to their own interests and the country's good, in order to bring forward this valuable Island into that degree of estimation and notice to which, from its numerous and superior natural advantages it has so just and fair a claim. To accomplish which desirable ends, permit me, gentlemen, to recommend to you the high importance of candour and unanimity in all your consultations for the public welfare, and to assure you of my readiness cordially to concur with you in every salutary measure for the benefit of His Majesty's service, the prosperity of the Island and the general interest, harmony and happiness of all its inhabitants."

A peculiar and rather amusing incident occurred during this session. Mr. Cambridge, in an affirmation made in some proceedings before the House, was charged with using disrespectful language towards that Body, and was ordered to appear at the Bar of the House. He requested the House to allow him till 6 o'clock to make his apology. At 6 p. m. being called upon for his answer he presented a written paper to the Speaker. The House was then cleared, when the Assembly considered and rejected Mr. Cambridge's paper, and "being unanimous in opinion that some concessions should be made by him for the offence contained in his affirmation, deliberated on the particular words in which the same should be expressed. Having determined thereon, Mr. Cambridge was recalled and required to comply therewith, which he refused. Whereupon he was ordered to withdraw immediately. And it was 'Resolved, that the House, by taking any further notice of Mr. Cambridge by commitment or otherwise, would be gratifying him in doing what he seems to court, and therefore discharge him from any further attendance.'"

A motion was then made that the House do come to the following resolution, to wit:

"Resolved, that the said false and malicious words, contained in Mr. Cambridge's affirmation, be, on Saturday next, the 17th instant, burnt under the gallows by the sergeant-at-arms attending this House." Carried on a division nine to six. "And the sergeant-at-arms ordered accordingly."

In this session (1792) also the Act for the rescinding, annulling and making void the proceedings for the sale of lands in 1780 and 1781 was finally passed.

### BISHOP INGLIS VISITS CHARLOTTETOWN.

In May, 1789, Bishop John Inglis paid a visit to Charlottetown. He arrived from Halifax on the Dido, a frigate of twenty-eight guns, on Sunday, the 17th May, in the afternoon. Mr. Binney, senior, and Rev. Mr. Jones, a Roman Catholic priest, were also passengers. It was wet and the people were all employed in working up an intricate channel which leads to the harbour. This prevented the Bishop from officiating, as none could attend Divine service. The next day, he went on shore with Captain Sandys of the Dido and waited on Governor Fanning, "who received me very politely and called his Council and other principal gentlemen of the Island together on the occasion," . . . He dined with the Governor, twenty-two people sitting down to dinner.

The Bishop remained on the Island until the 26th, and rode out frequently with Governor Fanning to the adjacent parts. The inhabitants showed every attention in their power and were very hospitable. . . . "At different depths," he says, "from two feet to ten feet, there is a reddish freestone, which is the basis of the Island. . . . The timber is such as is found in northern climates, consisting of maple, beech, birch, pine, spruce, etc. The soil is excellent for grass and every kind of grain. Winter wheat does very well.

"There is no church or school house on the whole Island, although it has been in our possession upwards of twenty years, and the inhabitants are computed to be between five and six thousand, one-third of whom are supposed to be Roman Catholics, consisting of French and emigrants from the Highlands of Scotland.

"The Rev. Mr. DesBrisay, rector of Charlotte parish, a decent, sensible young man, is the only clergyman or minister on the Island. I desired him to call his churchwardens and vestry together. I expressed to them my astonishment at their neglect in building a church, and mentioned the pain I felt at not finding this mark of even their belief in the existence of a Supreme Being. I used other similar expressions to show my disapprobation of their neglect in this matter and to impress upon them a proper sense of it. . . . Wishing to avoid all crimination or retrospect to past transactions, I earnestly recommended the building of a church, and the taking of such steps as would tend to promote that necessary measure, and then left them to deliberate on and report to me, next day, the ways and means which they judged most elegible for the purpose.

"I consulted with Governor Fanning on the subject, who expressed the warmest desire to have the church built. . . . He drew up the form of a subscription for the purpose. The money subscribed was to be paid to Colonel Calbu and Major Gray for building a church on a plan I drew, and the Governor, himself, subscribed fifty pounds.

"On 21st May, the rector, churchwardens and vestry waited on me at the Governor's, where I lodged, with a decent and respectful address, in which they lamented their want of a church, and the causes which prevented them having one, hinting their wish to have my advice. I promised to return an answer before my departure. I then showed them the subscription paper, which I delivered to the churchwardens, requesting that they should carry it about and solicit subscriptions from the inhabitants. The measure was much approved. Besides a subscription the Governor intimated that he would apply to the Assembly at their next session for assistance. The overseers of roads offered to give up the pay allowed for that service to the same use. The Governor and Council, who had their choice of some lots near the town of Charlotte, offered to pay a certain sum for each lot towards building the church, in the hopes that it would encourage other owners of lots to do the same; and the officers of Government offered to give up their fees for the same laudable purpose. To these particulars should be added, that Captain Sandys very generously offered to assist with his men and boats, in transporting the timber for a church to the place where it was to be erected, and to employ his carpenter in preparing the frame, during his stay on the Island, after his return from Quebec."

It took a long time, near thirty years, to make the inhabitants realize that they should erect a place of worship for themselves, but once the idea was started they were very instant in the good work. Bishop Inglis must have been a strong man to start the seemingly inert mass.

"On Saturday, the 23rd May," says the Bishop, "I returned answer to the address of the rector, churchwardens, etc. The address and answer were printed the same day in the St. John's Gazette. I intimated my desire to preach, next day, on shore, but absolutely refused to preach in the coffee and ball room, where Mr. DesBrisay usually officiated, that I might in the most pointed manner show my disapprobation of the contempt thrown on Divine worship by having it celebrated in so very improper a place. If no suitable house could be found, I declared my resolution to officiate on board the Dido. The Governor offered his, but it was too small. Colonel Calbu and Mr. Patterson offered theirs also.* Mr. Patterson's was fixed on, as being the largest and most convenient. With the answer to the address, I drew up an official memorial to the Lieutenant-Governor-in-Council, setting forth the advantages of having churches built, glebe and school lands set apart, agreeably to the King's reservations and institutions. My astonishment and concern that nothing of this sort had been yet done in the Island; and making an earnest requisition that the King's instructions might be punctually complied with in the above particulars; particularly that without loss of time, a church might be built at Charlottetown. I consulted Governor Fanning on the subject of this memorial and he expressed a wish that it might be earnest and urgent on those points, which I complied with. The instructions to Governors, concerning a bishop, have not been sent to Governor Fanning."

Sunday, 24th, was fine. "About ninety people from the Dido, with the garrison, being part of the 42nd Regiment, attended Divine service at Mr. Patterson's, and these, with the inhabitants, made a congregation of about three hundred people and filled the house. The next day I went with a large party to see Governor Patterson's house. On this farm he is said to have laid out £5,000 sterling.

*Probably John Patterson, brother of the late Lieutenant-Governor.

"On Tuesday, 26th, we sailed from Charlottetown at ten o'clock with a light breeze in our favour."

CHARGES AGAINST FANNING, C. J. STEWART, ATTORNEY-GENERAL APLIN AND W. TOWNSHEND, COLLECTOR OF CUSTOMS.

Like his predecessor, Fanning had trouble with the proprietors. He seems to have acted with considerable tact, not lacking in firmness, and without making the personal enemies, who, in the end, proved too strong for Patterson.

As early as 1789 complaints were preferred against him. Mr. Dundas, Secretary for the Colonies, in that year wrote Fanning that "several of the proprietors of land in the Island of St. John, and merchants trading thereto and therein, having, by their memorials to the King, complained of your conduct and also of the conduct of several other officers of Government in the Island, the same has been under the consideration of a committee of His Majesty's Privy Council, I am to signify to you His Majesty's pleasure that you do, immediately on the receipt hereof, communicate the same to Peter Stewart, Joseph Aplin and William Townshend, Esquires, and that you do severally and respectively forthwith return full and particular answers to all the articles of the said complaint conformably to the said Order in Council.

"As the ship, by which this order is forwarded to you, will be detained about a month at the Island, it is expected that you do return your answer to the said complaints by that vessel, or by any other opportunity which may sooner offer."

The indictment of Fanning, Chief Justice Stewart, Attorney-General Aplin and William Townshend, Collector of Customs, consisted of general and loose charges of improper conduct in office, interfering with elections, failure of justice in the Supreme Court, etc., etc., and are pretty fully epitomized in the following memorial from Cherry Valley and Vernon River:

"We, inhabitants of Cherry Valley and Vernon River, beg to express our extreme regret at hearing certain complaints to have been exhibited against you and three other officers of His Majesty's Privy Council, injuriously representing your administration to have been factious and arbitrary, and those other gentlemen to have so grossly misbehaved in their respective offices as to bring His Majesty's government in this Island into popular hatred and contempt, and particularly stating that the administration of justice, since the restoration of the Chief Justice from his late suspension, has been partial and made subservient to the views and hopes of this pretended faction of Your Excellency's, with many other things of a criminal and unjustifiable import.

"On being made acquainted with so unexpected an occurence, we should do much injustice to our own feelings and conviction, as well as withhold from Your Excellency, that tribute of gratitude we owe you, if we omitted the opportunity we now have of assuring you of our entire disbelief of those injurious assertions, which so palpably contradict all our past experience of the conduct both of Your Excellency and of the other officers.

"We, therefore, desire to assure you that we have always found your administration to be mild and just and uniformly directed to the attainment of the great object of general prosperity of the Island, and that the conduct of the other gentlemen complained of, in the performance of the duties of their respective offices, we have always understood to be highly meritorious and altogether free from the malicious imputation of faction, oppression or injustice. The fair and impartial administration of the law since the restoration of the Chief Justice we particularly mark as a circumstance highly flattering to our future hopes and expectations."

From Prince County also, the inhabitants "particularly desire to thank Your Excellency for the method adopted since your arrival here, of choosing our representatives, whereby we have been relieved from this necessity, either of travelling from our homes to a great distance at inclement seasons, or be deprived of the privilege of giving our suffrages to those we would wish to represent us in General Assembly."

He tried to enforce the collection of the quit rents, and the proprietors complained of him and the other principal officials of the government to the Secretary of State. Their complaints were of the forced collection of rents, the escheating of their lands, and the uncertainty of tenure, to which, and not to their own neglect, they attributed the delay in settling the Island. Fanning successfully defended himself before the Privy Council, his agent in arranging his defence in London being Major Robert Gray, who seems to have gone to England for that purpose. He was private Secretary to the Governor, and his name was long a prominent one in the public life of this Island.

The following account of the proceedings is taken from the report of the committee of the Privy Council, "on certain complaints against Lieutenant-Governor Fanning, Chief Justice Stewart, Attorney-General Aplin and Wm. Townshend, Collector of Customs, officers of His Majesty's government in the Island of St. John."

"The memorial presented to Your Majesty carried the appearance of a complaint in the names of a considerable number of merchants, but before it came to be heard, out of eighteen that originally assembled to consider of this business, twelve of their meeting begged their names might be withdrawn, as the complaint had been preferred without their consent; so that six only remained as prosecutors, the rest disowning the whole proceeding. These were — Joseph Kirkman, Simon Yockney, John Harris, all late partners of John Cambridges; Alexander Fletcher, Chief of the Patterson faction in the Island; John Hill, a furious partizan of the Patterson faction, and John Cambridge.

"The general charge against the defendants is that they had formed a destructive combination to govern the Island at their pleasure; and, with this view, had jointly as well as separately, oppressed all those who opposed themselves to the arbitrary designs of the officers of this government, and the memorial states these persons, throughout, as associates and confederates. This charge, if proved, is a high misdemeanor.

"The committee expected to have seen express proof of the alleged combination or some circumstances from which a strong presumption of such combination must arise; but no evidence of this sort has been produced. On the contrary, it does not appear, from anything in this whole accusation, that any two of those gentlemen ever exchanged a word with each other, except when they met in Council; nor is there any proof of such a combination, from words or writing, spoken or written, by any of these defendants; so that the proof rests altogether upon the separate facts that are alleged.

"The committee, then, upon the strictest review of all the specific charges, are of opinion, not only that the aggregate of them is void of any proof of such a combination, as is alleged, but that the specific charges, taken separately, are fully answered. And that the whole accusation is groundless; and this will appear, by examining each charge by itself, which, together with their own opinion, the committee beg leave to humbly lay before Your Majesty."

First charge. "The Lieutenant-Governor is accused for dissolving the Assembly on his first arrival. The committee are of opinion he did right, because that was the very Assembly which, in conjunction with Lieutenant-Governor Patterson, had passed an Act to confirm the sales made under the illegal confiscations in disobedience to Your Majesty's Order."

Second charge. "That when, upon the election of members under this first dissolution, the sheriff returned that the poll had been disturbed by military interference, and that he could not venture to return them as duly elected, the Lieutenant-Governor is accused for issuing a new writ for a fresh election. At this time the whole Assembly were all chosen under one writ by all the voters on the Island; and the sheriff's objection went to the whole return, so that the election of all was equally impeached.

"The Lieutenant-Governor referred it to the Chief Justice and the Attorney-General. The Chief Justice thought the whole void, the Attorney-General differed. The committee are clearly of opinion that the opinion of the Chief Justice was right, but the accusers criminate the Lieutenant-Governor for not following the opinion of the Attorney-General, who was wrong, and bring this as a proof of an unlawful combination."

Third charge. "That he had altered the mode of election without authority. Instead of all being elected under one writ, he directed the election to be made under six writs and divided them for the three counties and three towns, a writ for each. Your committee hold that Fanning was right. All other charges were dismissed."

A number of charges were also preferred against the Chief Justice, the Attorney-General and the Collector of Customs. The judgment of the Privy Council concludes:

"Upon the whole, the committee are of opinion, which they humbly beg leave to submit Your Majesty, that the complaint ought to be dismissed.

"The committee cannot conclude without taking notice of a very unwarrantable attempt of complainants to introduce a vast mass of evidence against the defendants which they had no opportunity of answering. When the complaint first came to this Board, with the affidavits in support of it, the committee ordered it to be transmitted to the Island, and the defendants were, within a certain time, to deliver their answer, together with a copy of their evidence to the complainants, who had the liberty to reply, and they were to deliver their reply within a certain time, and then the whole was to be immediately sent over to England. Under this liberty of reply, the complainants thought fit to load their first accusations with new matter and new facts.

"His Majesty, taking the said report into consideration, was pleased to order that the several complaints be, and they are hereby, dismissed this Board."*

## MILITIA, — WAR WITH FRANCE.

In the beginning of May, 1793, the armed tender, Chatham, brought despatches directing the Lieutenant-Governor to transmit, without delay, an exact account of the "state of this Island," specifying its internal force in militia or otherwise, exclusive of His Majesty's troops (all of which were carried off in the tender), with the condition and number of their arms and accoutrements. He had at once required from Colonel DesBrisay, commanding the Island militia, an immediate return of the regiment under his command as required by the despatch. "Yesterday (6th May)

---

*Foot note to above, added by S. Cotterall, the Clerk of the Council,— "The greater part of this additional evidence has since been found to be fabricated by the malevolent and unprincipled agents of the Complainants; for, on a very general cross-examination, the witnesses examined by them have deposed, that they never swore, or meant to swear, to the facts contained in the additional affidavits brought forward by the Complainants. And it was very unfortunate that these cross-examinations did not arrive till the hearing was over; for they would have disclosed to their Lordships and the world the most malicious and wicked plot, on the part of the Complainants and their emissaries, to ruin the defendants, that was ever devised by the malignity of mankind."

he had received another despatch of 9th February last, from Right Hon. Henry Douglas, a principal Secretary of State, acquainting him that the persons exercising the supreme authority in France have declared war against His Majesty on 1st February, and signifying His Majesty's commands to instantly make the same to be made public in the Island under his charge. It was unanimously ordered by Council that a proclamation be immediately issued notifying the same.

"The Lieutenant-Governor submitted to the Council that repairs should be made to the battery at the Point and that the carriages to the cannon on the battery, which are entirely decayed and rotten, should be immediately repaired and put in a state of usefulness towards the security and defence of the town in case of attack. The Council, thinking it absolutely necessary, advised the Lieutenant-Governor to order the same to be done. Also, with Council's advice again, ordered Colonel DesBrisay to call out his regiment and, without loss of time, to inspect the several companies thereof and make a full return of the men with the condition and number of their arms and accoutrements, as required by the despatches, to be delivered to the Lieutenant-Governor for transmission to the Secretary of State without delay.

"The Lieutenant-Governor was further advised to write to all officers on half-pay resident on this Island asking if they desired to accept of commissions in the militia, as a preference would be given them, upon their signifying their willingness to render that public service in defence of this Island, as would be naturally expected, from a consideration of their services and zeal for the good of the service and the defence of His Majesty's subjects on this Island, and that the officers be requested to express, to the Lieutenant-Governor and Council, their readiness or otherwise to accept such commissions.

"The Lieutenant-Governor further acquainted the Board that His Majesty, taking into his most serious consideration the just and necessary war in which he is engaged with France, and putting his trust in Almighty God . . . had commanded a Public Fast and Humiliation to be observed. . . . The Lieutenant-Governor ordered the same to be observed here, appointing Friday, the 17th instant, as a day of public humiliation and fasting throughout this Island."

On 7th September, Fanning consulted the Council as to the expediency of making preparations for the better defence of the town and Island, as to whether it might not be prudent to make some works of defence and mount such of the cannon as should appear to be serviceable and necessary for such purpose. He, at the same time, communicated to the Board, despatches of 8th December and 7th January last from the Secretary of State, and stated that there did not appear to him, from his despatches, that there was likely to be an immediate cessation of hostilities. Whereupon it was unanimously advised that ". . . it was highly expedient and proper that some repairs should be made to the battery in this town and that such of the guns as are serviceable should be mounted." It was further advised that Colonel Lyons, Fort Major to the Island, should superintend and furnish an estimate of the expense which would attend the same, and that they be carried into effect immediately.

## War with Spain.

Despatches dated 27th August and 7th September, 1796, informed the Lieutenant-Governor that the most indubitable proofs of the hostile intentions of the Court of Spain against England had determined His Majesty to order his naval forces in every quarter of the world not to neglect any favourable opportunity that might offer of attacking the fleets of Spain either singly or united with those of France or Holland, or striking any other blow at the possessions of that Crown, and signifying to him the King's commands, that he should, in the most public manner possible, give such information to His Majesty's subjects in the Island, under his government, as might best enable them to prevent, on the one hand, any mischief they might otherwise suffer from the Spaniards, and on the other hand do their utmost in their several stations to distress and annoy them, by making capture of their ships and by destroying their commerce. And, therefore, the Lieutenant-Governor requested the opinion of the Board as to the most proper and effectual manner of publishing the purport of his Grace's despatches respecting the commencement of hostilities against the Crown and Court of Spain, their subjects and possessions, agreeable to His Majesty's commands. A proclamation publishing the same was ordered to be issued.

At a meeting of Council held 27th April, 1797, further despatches dated 27th October were submitted which informed the Lieutenant-Governor that "actual hostilities had taken place between Great Britain and Spain, and signified to him the King's commands that he should instantly cause the same to be made as public as possible in the Island under his government, that His Majesty's subjects, having this notice, take care on the one hand to prevent mischief which, otherwise, they might suffer from the Spaniards, and on the other might do their utmost in their several stations to distress and annoy them by making capture of their ships and, by destroying their commerce, for which purpose His Majesty has been pleased to order — LETTERS OF MARQUE AND REPRISAL OR COMMISSIONS OF PRIVATEERS, to be granted in the usual manner, but in the meantime, that the Lieutenant-Governor might give assurances to the owners of all ships and vessels that His Majesty will consider them as having a just claim to the King's share of all Spanish ships and property which they may make prize of." A proclamation was ordered to be issued accordingly.

In opening the session of the previous year Fanning again referred to the prosperity existing on the Island, "The flourishing state of which, it must be acknowledged, is most conspicuously evident from the greatly improved aspect and appearance of the face of the country in point of cultivation, but more unequivocally certain from the vast annual increase of our exports of various kinds of produce, and most distinguishably so in the valuable articles of wheat and black cattle."

He also calls attention to the church which had at last been built. "The erecting of a church in this town since the last session of the General Assembly, for the more decent and devout public worship of Almighty God, begun, and so far carried on, by private subscriptions, I persuade myself cannot be either unobserved by you, or regarded with indifference."

### IMMIGRATION.

For some reasons, there seems to have been considerable emigration from the Island during at least a part of Fanning's term of office. This was probably due to the unsatisfactory land conditions. In March, 1797, it had become so much a subject for anxiety that a memorial was adopted by the Assembly for a legislative enquiry into its cause, the report of which was forwarded, the following September, by the Lieutenant-Governor to the Secretary of State. Towards the close of Fanning's administration, however, there began to be an influx of settlers.

## NAME OF THE ISLAND.

In the seventh session of the Sixth General Assembly (the Long Parliament of the Island), the question of changing the name of the Island was again brought up. In his speech, opening the session, on 20th November, 1798, the Lieutenant-Governor said: "The name of this Island, having been found by long experience, frequently to occasion much prejudice and inconvenience to individuals, as well as to His Majesty's service, by the delay or miscarriage of government despatches and private letters, and even of merchandize and packages from England and other distant parts addressed to persons in this Island, being, through mistake, carried to St. John in Newfoundland, or St. John in New Brunswick, or St. John on the Coast of Labrador, or elsewhere; and these evils being likely, unceasingly, to occur and multiply, unless remedied by an Act of the Legislature as was attempted by a law passed in this Island, so long ago as the year 1780, and which Act was disallowed only on account of the prior appropriation of the name to which it was altered, as will appear by authentic documents, which I shall lay before you; I am induced to recommend to your consideration the great propriety and expediency of again passing an Act for that interesting and important purpose."

## 26TH NOVEMBER, 1798.

"A member of His Majesty's Council came down with a bill entitled 'An Act for Altering and Changing the name of this Island, from St. John to that of Prince Edward Island.'" The bill was put through its several readings, passed and was assented to (with a suspending clause, and received the Royal assent 1st February, A. D. 1799), on 26th November, since which time it has borne its present name of "Prince Edward Island."

## SELKIRK.

The Earl of Selkirk, who possessed estates to the extent of eighty-thousand acres, actively interested himself in peopling his lands. The year 1803 is a notable one in the history of Prince

Edward Island, for that was the year when the Dykes, the Polly and the Oughten cast anchor in these waters, having brought the "Selkirk settlers" from Scotland to make their homes on the Earl's estate. The three vessels brought, in all, about eight hundred people. They were a very fine class of immigrants. They settled in what is known by the general name of the Belfast district. Their descendants still occupy the lands and homes which their forefathers occupied and made. They were an enterprising and energetic people, who transmitted their vigorous dispositions, and their stalwart physique, to their children and their children's children. Descendants of these settlers have been distinguished in almost every walk of life. They are to be found in all parts of Canada and the United States, upholding the good name they inherited, and making their Island home known and respected wherever they may be. Their sons have distinguished themselves in every profession, trade and pursuit. In the days when Prince Edward Island boasted of her fleet of sailing ships, the men of Point Prim, and the other sections peopled by the descendants of these immigrants, were found commanding ships in every sea. There was scarcely a house which had not sent out its one or more master mariners; and they were of the best. Lord Selkirk did well for this Island when he brought these immigrants to its shores.

The Earl was of a restless and venturesome nature. Withal he was a great man. His name or titles are found in most widely separated regions of Canada, where they have been given to many localities. The Selkirk mountains, Fort Selkirk in the Yukon, Point Douglas (his family name), part of Winnipeg, settlements and roads in Prince Edward Island, were alike sponsored by him. Thomas Douglas, fifth Earl of Selkirk, Baron Doer and Shortcleugh, came of one of the oldest Scottish families, the Douglasses. He was the seventh son of Dunbar, the fourth Earl. He was born in 1771, at St. Mary's Isle, the Earl's seat in Scotland. He studied at the University of Edinburgh, where he became an intimate friend of Sir Walter Scott. His brothers all predeceased their father, on whose death, in 1799, he succeeded to the earldom at the age of twenty-eight. He had wealth, ability, enthusiasm, and lofty ideals; truly a remarkable man.*

---
*This sketch of Lord Selkirk is largely derived from Dr. Bryce's "Selkirk," in "The Makers of Canada" series, Vol. 8.

Before taking up colonization in Prince Edward Island, Selkirk had formed schemes for settlement in Western Canada. How early he formed plans is difficult to fix. He did so at least as early as the spring of 1802. Writing to Lord Hobart, Secretary for the Colonies, on 6th July of that year he says:

"Your Lordship hinted, also, that some lands might soon be open in the Island of Prince Edward, for a grant of which I should also apply, and would make similar exertions for their cultivation. By possessing these different grants in connection I could devote to them more of my time and attention than I could afford to either separately, and should, therefore, hope to render them more beneficial to myself and the public." He also asked for a grant of land in Upper Canada, adjoining the Falls of St. Mary, between Lake Superior and Lake Huron, and also of the mines and minerals he might discover along the north shore of these two lakes. The British Government, however, did not then encourage colonization there and, for the time at least, it encouraged the peopling of the Maritime in preference to the inland colonies of North America. Under these circumstances he made enquiries and learned that lots of land in Prince Edward Island might be purchased on terms which would indemnify him, were it not for the burden of quit rents and heavy arrears. However, this difficulty was arranged by the home authorities agreeing that the quit rents and arrears on lands purchased by him should be compounded on the most favoured terms.

In a representation by Lord Selkirk to Mr. Pitt in July, 1805, the Earl, referring to his transactions with Upper Canada and Prince Edward Island regarding land says he had obtained an order for a grant in Upper Canada, and that instructions were sent to the Governor of the province to set apart a township to be granted to him. This grant was accompanied by an offer of accommodation of a different nature if he would purchase lands in Prince Edward Island for his settlers. Though much against his own inclination, he complied with this recommendation, and conveyed to that Island the greater part of the emigrants with whom he was engaged.

Considering the terms of his Canadian grant as quite inadequate he did not think of availing himself of it, but previously to his determining on a settlement in Prince Edward Island, he had incurred expenses, which would have been lost if he had relinquished his grant, he was induced to visit that province to make a selection of a township and to send thither a few settlers, about twenty families, whom he could not employ to advantage in Prince Edward Island.

In 1803 he decided upon his settlement in Prince Edward Island. Some years later he inaugurated the settlement of Red River at or near Winnipeg. Becoming involved in legal troubles with the Hudson's Bay and Northwest Companies, his health gave way. He sought its recovery in the south of France, but without success. He died at Pau on 8th April, 1820.

The greater portion of his colonists were from the Isle of Skye. A number came from each of the shires of Ross, Argyle and Inverness, with a few from the Island of Uist. The three ships bearing his settlers arrived in Prince Edward Island in August, 1803; the Polly on 7th August, the Dykes, with the Earl himself on board, on 9th August, and the Oughten, with the men of Uist on board, on 27th August.

The beginning of the nineteenth century was a period of much distress for the British people. The Highlanders especially suffered. It was the period known as the "Highland Clearance," or "Clearances." These resulted from the policy, adopted by the great landowners, of reducing the number of small crofts or holdings to make sheep runs for large tenants, who, with ample capital, might develop the country's resources. It bore very heavily on the poor Highlanders. Selkirk laid plans for a systematic emigration policy, which would bring relief to his poor countrymen. The results are well known. He had beyond question the confidence of the people. His view was that settlement in the colonies would relieve the distress of crofter, farm labourer and operative alike.

### THE COMING OF THE POLLY, ETC.

Selkirk left Scotland in the midsummer of 1803, sailing in the Dykes, which left for the Gulf of St. Lawrence a few days before the departure of the other ships, his intention being to get to the proposed sites for settlement somewhat before the arrival of the Polly and the Oughten. They seem to have had a fair passage over, and on 3rd August found themselves, to their great surprise, north of Cape Ray and within the Gulf of St. Lawrence, not having reckoned on being so far advanced. Soon they made the "Bird" Islands, a little further Brion or Cross Island. The following day, August 4th, saw the Magdalen Islands at a distance, early in the morning, towards evening came near the North Cape of Cape Breton, high land with an even top reckoned about nine hundred feet in height. The land is bare of wood and appears quite barren.

Friday, 5th August, the ship was becalmed off Cape North, or rather a little to the southwest of Cape St. Lawrence, where they caught plenty of fish,— codfish when the vessel was stationary, and mackerel when she was moving.

Monday, the 8th August, they made Prince Edward Island at 5 a. m. at what they at first supposed was East Cape, but it proved to be the south side of the Island near "Bear Cape." "The land," notes the Earl in his diary, "on Lot 62, had a forbidding appearance, the wood small and nothing but spruce and birch, scarcely a tree the size of a man's thigh, and great part of it quite young. I learnt, on arriving at Charlottetown, that all this coast had been laid waste by a great fire, thirty or forty years before."

Thursday, the 9th August, "A favourable breeze brought us into Hillsborough Bay. On passing Point Prim, a vessel appeared lying in Orwell Bay, just at the situation pointed out for the Polly. They had sailed after us, yet it turned out they had got the start of us, as we shortly learned from a Charlottetown boat. Losing the tide we anchored off the mouth of the harbour. Major Holland, Fort Major, came on board and conducted me to the town, where we called on Governor Fanning, who asked us to remain, which we did. Dr. McAulay arrived in the evening. The Polly had had a remarkably quick passage and arrived on Sunday. It had been better had she arrived a little after rather than before me. Owing to this circumstance the people are to land, without any preparation for their reception, on an uninhabited spot. Had I been a week sooner, some kind of barracks might have been ready. The people, however, are setting about hutting themselves in wigwams.

"August 10th. We have another difficulty about provisions. The oatmeal promised has not arrived. The last harvest on the Island has been so poor that it is stated that no supply can be had here. The millers will only promise a trifle, and as all the trading people here are notorious for taking advantages, Mr. Charles

Stewart and others advised sending a schooner to Quebec or Halifax for a supply. After harvest it is expected there will be abundance, but the scarcity was so much apprehended this spring that the Council laid an embargo on exportation and opened the ports to American vessels, none of which came. This difficulty vanished on making a calculation of the quantity needed, which had been over-rated. A schooner from Pictou was in the harbour's mouth with ninety barrels of flour brought on speculation. This was purchased at ten dollars a barrel and would secure us till harvest or till the arrival of the Bess from New York.

"Mr. C. Stewart went down, with Dr. McAulay, to Orwell Bay to point out the situations. They had just arrived at the Polly when a message from me brought them back. Dr. McAulay had misunderstood my instructions and was proceeding to fix the people in two or three large villages instead of ten or twelve smaller ones. This my arrival rectified. Dr. McAulay was anxious to be back to the ship, as two or three country people had been on board circulating ill reports of the country. There are people who have set themselves down on the lands under the idea that they would revert to the Crown, and then they would have a claim of preference by their occupancy. These are now sour at finding themselves likely to be turned out and would gladly disgust the newcomers. Some people, also, on the neighbouring Lots, who have been in the habit of making hay on the marshes on Lot 57, are said to be ill-disposed.

"Dr. McAulay purchased a few tools and some iron for the people. We also got a small smith's bellows to supply the place of that we were obliged to leave at Tobermory, paying much more than its value in order to set C. McWilliams to work as soon as possible. Smith's work is exceedingly dear and difficult to procure here. A better bellows might be made in a few days if we had seasoned wood.

"I got comfortable lodgings in Mr. Cambridge's new house. On arriving, as the Dykes was long in getting up the harbour, I accepted the Governor's invitation to stay all night and he pressed me to remain next day, which I thoughtlessly did. This interfered considerably with business. The bonhomme's politeness is rather burdensome. He is a man of no superabundant head. The Chief Justice, Mr. Thorpe, dined with him, a native of the Kingdom

(Ireland) and not deficient in the natural qualifications of enhancing his own importance, 'and is hand and glove with all great people, and being here only on an occasional retirement for his health, etc.' He has, however, ideas and cleeks in his head to hang inferences upon, which does not seem the case with the Governor. Both of them speak highly of Charles Stewart.* In the course of yesterday the officers of the government and most of the principal people of Charlottetown called at the Governor's for me, of whom I saw Mr. DesBrisay, formerly Lieutenant-Governor, now Secretary, and Colonel Gray, who was Secretary to Governor Fanning when in Canada. . . .

"The oats of this Island, and barley also, are reckoned the best in America, the oats bringing a higher price at Halifax by 1s. a bushel than the oats of their own neighbourhood. . . .

"There is no regular mail from the Island. A scheme is now on foot for establishing one by subscription. (Strange that the Assembly does not do it from the revenues of the Island). Hitherto, they have depended on occasional opportunities from Halifax. Some gentlemen are now expected whose non-arrival has caused the departure of the mail to be delayed, day after day. . . . This must be one cause of the exorbitant charges of the merchants which everybody complains of. . . .

"The gross revenue runs between £400 and £500, of which fifteen per cent, £60 or £70, is allowed for collecting. The expenses of the Assembly amount to £80. The sheriff is allowed £20. Each road commissioner, nine in all, is allowed £9, or in the aggregate £81, besides expenses of police, gaol, prosecutions, etc., leaving barely £200 for roads and improvements. Thirty pounds a year is paid for rent of the Town House for holding Courts and Assembly. It is raised by a tax of 10d. per gallon on the importation of wines and spirits. The inhabitants are likewise liable for statute labour, four days of eight hours for each man, six days if he has a pair of oxen. The roads have lately been put under the management of three commissioners in each county named by the Lieutenant-Governor-in-Council, who fix upon lines and assign the statute labour to one or other road, appoint overseers to direct the application upon each. After the statute labour is completed a report of deficiencies is made and sums to a limited amount may

---

*For Thorpe, see Part VI *infra*. "Miscellaneous."

be laid out by the commissioners for making these up. The funds are insufficient, for there is but one road in the Island (Charlottetown to St. Peters) practicable for a wheel carriage. . . . There is a great need of an office for keeping the records, etc. At present they are tossed about the private house of the Registrar, in no sort of order, great part in loose sheets.

"The Assembly is elected by all resident heads of families (except Roman Catholics) in counties. Each of the three sends four members; each of the three towns sends two. Georgetown and Prince Town are no better than English rotten burghs, not having three houses each, though previous to an election new lots are sometimes applied for in order to make votes. The Assembly is elected for no determined period. The last was dissolved by the Governor after one year. The Assembly before that had continued for thirteen or fourteen years.

"On 13th August, having finished business with the Dykes, I set off for the settlement at the old French Village called Belfast,* . . . and went on board the Polly, from which everybody was landed, but there was still some baggage on board. . . . It was difficult to keep order along so great a number,— two hundred and eighty full passengers and nearly four hundred souls . . . The berths seemed pretty confined, though the abundance of hatches gave a good opportunity for air, yet it had proved very close in the hot weather. The berths were dirty enough.

"I found the people scattered along a mile of shore, a few in barns, etc., belonging to the unauthorized settlers — the rest in hovels and wigwams, built oblong like the roof of one of our European cottages and thatched in general with spruce boughs, some of them very close and fit to turn a good rain, . . . They have been so occupied with landing their baggage that nothing else has been done. Though the smith was sent down yesterday, he has not yet got to work. . . .

---

*Belfast in Prince Edward Island was not named for Belfast in Ireland. It is derived from the French words Belle Face — beautiful aspect or view — given to what is known as "Little Belfast" by the French who had a village there. Little Belfast is the section, below Eldon, facing for about two miles on the water and running back with a gentle rise for a mile or more. It is the only part of the shore there, which slopes down gradually to the water without high banks on the shore. Both above and below it are high banks overlooking the water. "Belfast" is a corruption and uniting of the two French words.

"The encampment had a very picturesque appearance under night; every hut, having a great fire near it, illuminated the woods, and each party sitting or moving around with their gypsy-like apparatus of pots and pans gave the light additional variety of play.

"Sunday, 14th August. From the lateness of the evening, I had seen few of the people last night. The most of them met us in the morning about breakfast time and we had a hearty shaking of hands. They came, in general, round me with a keenness and warmth, that, perhaps, had a little resemblance to the old feudal times. Being anxious to explore the country, in order for laying out the different lots, we proceeded, as expeditiously as possible, by the old French road or portage to Jenkyn's or Pinette River. The first half of the way is through old French cleared land, grown up with small timber of twenty or thirty years' growth. The further part is large timber with a considerable proportion of pines, etc. This is reckoned good land. On Pinette we embarked in a wooden canoe, leaving the people busy in bringing another across the portage, landed with Mr. Wright, the surveyor, and walked into the woods beyond the river.

"Dr. McAulay is to sound the people as to their inclination to purchase and the extent they aim at, which, as yet, he has little guess of, and for that purpose I stated to him that the proposed prices would be a half dollar per acre for back lands; one dollar for front; two dollars for old cleared; marsh or clear land, so far as can be given, five dollars. These I am given to understand are considerably below the current prices, when land is sold. John Stewart has sold a good deal at 10s., but, allowing instalments, some lots on Pownal Bay were sold at that price seven or eight years ago; but this Island has not partaken of the progress of the States. Indeed it is surprising that the land should sell at all, when gratuitous grants can be had in Nova Scotia and Cape Breton, and perhaps it is only owing to the imperfect knowledge and prejudices of the settlers that they do not go there. In New Brunswick, however, it is said to be difficult to get front lands and that the lands are of inferior quality. This may be a mere allegation of the proprietors here, who seem to have a sufficient portion of jealousy against Nova Scotia, and indeed any other colony. . . .

"The population of the Island is not well ascertained. It was reckoned about five thousand in 1795. In 1798, an imperfect census came out at 4,500. There was reason to suppose an omission of five hundred, making the total five thousand. To double in fourteen years, the increase in six would be about fifteen hundred. Immigrants in 1802 three hundred and fifty,— total six thousand eight hundred and fifty immigrants. Add immigrants in 1803, eight hundred and three, makes supposed population — seven thousand seven hundred and fifty.

"McEachern says fifteen hundred have come to it since, besides natural increase. Governor Fanning reckons now 10,000, but this is probably exaggerated. He reckons the Highlanders are above one-third. Robert Stewart reckons the freehold voters in Prince and Queen's at three hundred each. In King's County — the most populous but most Catholic,— only one hundred and fifty. This is only by guess.

### MILITIA.

"The militia has not been regularly enough mustered to be a standard of population and it is in a shameful state of neglect. The law of the Island only requires their being called out and exercised three days in the year, and it is much if this is complied with. A very small proportion have arms, and it is said that the people (absurdly enough) complain of doing anything as militia men.

### REGULAR ESTABLISHMENT.

"The military establishment, independent of militia, is very small indeed. When I arrived fourteen or fifteen artillery men was the whole garrison. A block-house of four guns, surrounded by a picket and ditch at the mouth of the harbour, was the only fortification. There are barracks for two or three hundred men. Latterly a subaltern's command of the 60th Regiment are arrived. During the war two companies of Provincial corps raised in Newfoundland were kept up.

### CIVIL ESTABLISHMENT.

"The civil establishment, paid by government from home, is £500 salary and £170 contingencies for the Governor; £400, (to which £100 is lately added) to the Chief Justice; Attorney-General £100; Collector of Customs £80. The Chief Justice's salary was further increased up to £500. The Assistant Judges receive no salary, the office is almost a name.' . . .

"It was only on 31st August that the last applications (McRae's) were finally agreed to. Before the 15th September, I understood that several log-houses in different Lots were set up."

On 27th August the Oughton arrived with the passengers from Uist. They are reported as not ill-behaved, only one individual having appeared turbulent, but lazy and always asking for medicines, though having no real sickness. These, Lord Selkirk decided to send to Township No. 10. They, however, after going part of the way returned and were disposed of elsewhere.*

SELKIRK'S GENERAL OBSERVATIONS.—THE FISHERIES.

"Much is said of the abundance of fish about the Island. Cod in the offing, rock-cod, mackerel, etc., in the bays. Herring come in about the breaking up of the ice. This circumstance will make it a popular place for the Highlanders. Shell-fish are in such abundance as to already be no inconsiderable aid to the newcomers. In the first settlement of the Island by the English (between the Canada and American wars), this is said actually to have saved the settlers from famine. They had begun by sowing on the old cleared land of the French, which, exhausted by frequent croppings, did not give the return expected, and while waiting for supplies from elsewhere, they had nothing but the fish to depend upon. Yet the present inhabitants derive little or no benefit from the fishery and follow it very little. The few fish that come to the Charlottetown market are brought in by the Indians. Some attempts have been made to establish a regular fishery (especially by Cambridge at Murray Harbour), but the people deserted the business and none of the English settlers follow it. The French on the north coast do, and own nine-tenths of the schooners, which are almost the only shipping belonging to the Island. They are not, however, regular fishermen, but follow it at the intervals of their agricultural business, a combination which never succeeds, and some of themselves are sensible of it. One of them observed — 'We be all farmer — all fisher — dat be de veri ting dat mak us all begars.''

"The French schooners are, in a general way, very ill found in

---

*The writer has been told that some of these people went over to Pictou County, in Nova Scotia, and settled there. He has not been able to verify this, and doubts its correctness.

rigging, yet accidents very seldom happen to them, they are so attentive to weather and acquire a wonderful sagacity about it. They even steer long distances without looking at their compasses.

"These French are the descendants of a few fugitives who concealed themselves in the woods, at the time the Acadian settlers were transported out of the country (during the Canada war). The villages at Pinette and Belfast, by them called Prime, were destroyed at that transportation."

### Shipping.

"It is computed that about seventy vessels belong to the Island, the greater part schooners of thirty to forty tons, some larger, but only one or two brigs or vessels of size. They are partly employed in fishing and partly in coasting-voyages, principally to Halifax and Newfoundland. The latter is the principal market for the products of the Island, and a very advantageous one for several articles, particularly well-fed beef, though a number of cattle are carried there to very little advantage when they are not in condition for immediate killing. The returns are said to come principally in rum. An ordinary schooner carries twenty to twenty-five head of cattle and perhaps a few sheep on the decks and with this number the owner sends a man to take care of them. In summer, cattle are sometimes taken on deck. A vessel of eighty tons has been freighted to Newfoundland for £90. There is scarcely any return freight except liquors, of which a good deal is smuggled, notwithstanding the lowness of the duty, as scarcely any obstruction is given.

"Many schooners built in the Island are sold in Newfoundland to good advantage. It is usual, in selling them, to reserve the sails, which are brought back to serve another turn. The Newfoundland market is sometimes extremely high —beef at 1s or 1/3 per pound in spring and in that season potatoes also come to a high market, sometimes to a dollar a bushel."

### Experts.

"The total exports of the Island, on an average of four years, to 1804, (higher considerably than the previous years) amount to: 387 head of cattle; 400 bushels of wheat; 480 sheep or hogs; 1,200 bushels of barley; 60 barrels of beef and pork; 3,000 bushels of oats; 15 cwt. of butter; 1,200 bushels of potatoes; Seal oil, sometimes 300 casks, and skins 600 to 1,200,— sometimes none of either. The lumber exported has been trifling and irregular."

### IMPORTS.

"The greater part of the imports are from Halifax. There is scarcely any direct communication with Britain, or the ultimate markets."

### TRADE AND SHIPPING.

A quarter of a century after Selkirk's account was penned, McGregor discussed the same subjects. He wrote:

"When the Island was possessed by the French, little trade was carried on. That government, lest it should draw off settlers from Louisbourg, discouraged its fisheries." Fishing was confined to two harbours — St. Peters and Tracadie.

"On being settled by the British a limited trade in fish, oil, sea-cow and seal skins was carried on with Quebec, Halifax and Boston. The fishermen were principally Acadian French, who used small shallops built on the Island.

"The facility with which the prime necessaries of life are obtained from the soil, is, at present, the greatest obstacle to the success of fishing establishments.

"A trade from which the Island has, and will likely derive considerable benefit, is carried on with Newfoundland, by building vessels for the seal and cod fisheries established there, and by supplying that market with black cattle, sheep, hogs, poultry, oats, potatoes, turnips, etc., the returns for which are made either in money, West Indies produce, or such articles as may best answer. Agricultural produce is also sent to Halifax, Miramichi and other places in Nova Scotia and New Brunswick. Beef, pork, sheep, hams, butter, cheese, oats, potatoes, flour and fish are occasionally exported to Bermuda.

"The branch of trade in which the largest capital has been invested, and that which has given employment to the greatest number of men, while it has, at the same time, been also of considerable benefit to the colony, is the building of vessels for the British market. Upwards of one hundred brigs and ships, measuring from one hundred and forty to fifty-five tons each, have been built in different parts of the Island within the last few years.

"When we view the position of Prince Edward Island, in regard to the countries bordering on the Gulf of St. Lawrence, the excellence of its harbours for fishing stations, and take into account that the whole of its surface may, with little exception, be considered a body of fertile soil, it does not certainly require the spirit of prophecy to perceive that, unless political arrangements may interfere with its prosperity, it will, at no very remote period, become a valuable agricultural as well as commercial country."*

### SELKIRK ON EMIGRATION.†

The people of Moydart, and some other districts in Inverness-shire, with a few from the Western Isles, were those who formed the Scottish settlements of Pictou in Nova Scotia, and of the Island of St. John. Of the settlers whom Lord Selkirk conveyed, in 1803, to Prince Edward Island, the greatest proportion were from the Isle of Skye; a district which had so decided a connection with North Carolina that no emigrants had ever gone from it to any other quarter. There were a few others from Ross-shire, from the north part of Argyleshire, and from some interior districts of Inverness-shire, all of whose connections lay in some part of the United States. Some, also, were from a part of the Island of Uist, where emigration had not taken a decided direction. The Earl had undertaken to settle his lands, which were British possessions, with emigrants who had contemplated going to the United States.

### DELAY IN ALLOTMENTS.

Those who receive gratuitous grants of land are often subjected to delay which more than counterbalance the advantages. The Loyalists, who were brought at the end of the American war to Nova Scotia, had to wait about a year, some of them nearly two, before the surveyors had completed their work and their allotments were pointed out to them. In Upper Canada, Lord Selkirk writes that he met with some emigrants who had left Scotland about two years before. They had been promised grants of Crown Lands, for which they had till then been waiting, and not till then had they received possession. In the interval most of their money was

---

*Account of Prince Edward Island, page 62 and *seq.*
†The next few pages are condensed from the Earl of Selkirk's "Emigration and the State of the Highlands," 2nd edition published in 1806.

expended, and in this exhausted condition they were beginning the cultivation of their property.

From the want of a general attention to keeping the settlements compact, and within reach of mutual assistance, most of the people, who begin on new and untouched land, are reduced to a situation of more than savage solitude. The practical difficulties that await them are sufficient to discourage the most hardy. The settler who begins on new lands has little access to the assistance of professed artificers. He must build his own house, construct his own cart, and make almost all his own implements.

When assistance has been granted with a liberal hand, particularly when gratuitous rations of provisions have been allowed, the effect has almost invariably been, by taking away the pressure of necessity, to render the settlers inactive, and to damp their exertions for overcoming the difficulties of their situation. A great portion of the Loyalists and disbanded Provincials, in Canada and Nova Scotia, performed scarcely any work, as long as they received rations from the governments; and when these were discontinued found themselves almost as destitute as if no aid had ever been given.

So lately as the year 1783, when the Loyalists were settled in Nova Scotia and Canada, it was not supposed that they could provide for themselves in less than three years. A great proportion did not accomplish it even in that time, and, when the bountiful support of government was discontinued, many of the settlements were abandoned.

Prince Edward Island, where Lord Selkirk established his own settlers, affords an instance in point. When it was first colonized by the English about 1770, many were brought from Europe, who, after being supported for two years by extraneous supplies, went away in disgust, spreading the idea that the country was incapable of cultivation.

He adds that few, perhaps, in their situation have suffered less, or seen their difficulties so soon at an end, as the people he took there. The population is estimated at about seven or eight thousand, thinly scattered along the shores. A great proportion of the lands, granted in 1767 in large lots, fell into the hands of absentees, who have paid no attention to their improvement and, in consequence, many very extensive tracts are totally uninhabited.

The settlement Selkirk himself had in view was to be on a part of the coast, where, for upwards of thirty miles, there was not a single habitation. His people, about eight hundred, reached the Island in three ships on 7th, 9th and 27th August, 1803. He had intended to come to the Island before any of the settlers, so as to make arrangements, but, on his arrival in Charlottetown, found that the most important ship, the Polly, had just arrived and the passengers were landing at a place previously appointed for that purpose. He, at once, went to the spot. The people had already found shelter in wigwams made after the Indian fashion.

The settlers had spread along the shore for about half a mile on the site of an old French village which had been destroyed and abandoned after the capture of the Island by the British in 1758. The land, formerly cleared of wood, was again overgrown with thickets of young trees.

The Earl arrived late in the evening, and it had a very striking appearance. Each family had kindled a large fire near their wigwams and around these were assembled groups of figures, whose peculiar national dress added to the singularity of the surrounding scene. Confused heaps of baggage were everywhere piled together beside their wild habitations; and by the numbers of the fires the whole woods were illuminated.

Owing to unforseen causes, it happened that three or four weeks elapsed before the settlers could have their allotments pointed out to them. The delay was pernicious. Attempts were made by interested parties to sow discontent and to entice them away to other places. They were not successful, but gave much trouble. The confidence of the settlers seemed to be shaken, and they became restless. It was not till they had dispersed to their separate lots, till by working upon them they had begun to form a local attachment, that the settlement could be reckoned as fairly started.

At this stage an alarming contagious fever broke out and caused anxiety. Selkirk had, however, as a companion a medical gentleman of skill (Dr. John Shaw, junior, afterwards of Annapolis in Maryland), through whose exertions the disease was soon alleviated and few fatal cases occurred. Very few settlers entirely escaped the contagion. This fever was an accidental importation. It was nearly eradicated when the settlers began to disperse to their separate lots upon which they had all begun to work before the middle of September. The settlers began the cultivation of their farms with their little capital unimpaired. Their principal expense was for provisions to support them during the winter and ensuing season; besides which all the most opulent purchased milch cows and some other cattle. Provisions adequate for the whole were purchased by an agent, and brought to the centre of the settlement.

A medical gentleman who came out with the emigrants settled in their midst. A blacksmith set up his forge, the only artificer deemed absolutely necessary. The settlers were concentrated within a moderate space. The lots were laid out so that four or five families, sometimes more, built in a little knot together, and the distance between these groups seldom exceeded a mile. This enabled them to render mutual assistance. They also gained experience.

The settlers were allowed to purchase in fee simple and, to some extent, on credit. Fifty to one hundred acres were allotted to each family, at a moderate price, but none was given gratuitously. Those who had not the capital were given three or four years to pay, during which time they could discharge the debt out of the produce of the land itself. The same principle was observed with regard to provisions. Nothing was given gratuitously. It was either paid for or sold on credit as a loan to be repaid with interest. There was no charity. They had to rely on their own industry.

Selkirk left the Island in September, 1803, and returned the end of the same month the following year. It was with the utmost satisfaction that he found his plans had been well carried out. The progress made was satisfactory to all concerned. He found the settlers securing the harvest. They had a small proportion of grain, but the principal crop was potatoes, of excellent quality, alone sufficient for the support of the settlement. There was universal satisfaction. He found, in general, the land in cultivation amounted to about two acres to each able working hand; in many cases considerably more. Several boats had been built and a supply of fish obtained. In little more than one year these people had made themselves independent. Most of them, at the time of his visit (September, 1804), were improving their habitations.

Mr. John McGregor, writing in 1828, gives interesting information with regard to Lord Selkirk and the Selkirk settlements a quarter of a century after he had planted them.* He writes:

"Numerous, indeed, are the examples I have known, of the prosperity of individuals, whole families and entire settlements in America. I would point out, in particular, the settlements formed by the late Earl of Selkirk in Prince Edward Island. Much has been said to the prejudice of that nobleman, and, well acquainted as I am with his views and measures, I am confident they were not only good and honourable in regard to himself, but honest and properly intended as respected every other person. . . .

"At the time the Island was taken from the French a few inhabitants were settled in this district (Belfast); but from that period the lands remained in a great measure unoccupied until the year 1803, when the late Earl of Selkirk arrived on the Island with eight hundred emigrants, . . . He brought his colony from the Highlands and Isles of Scotland, and by the convenience of the tenures under which he gave the lands, and by persevering industry on their part, these people have arrived at more comfort and happiness than they ever experienced before. . . . The inhabitants are all in easy circumstances, and their number has increased from eight hundred to nearly three thousand."

The Earl was himself of a restless and venturesome nature. He seems, after some years, to have wearied of his efforts here, and to have sought other fields. His name is well known in the history of Manitoba and Western Provinces and of the Hudson's Bay and Northwest rival companies. There he made his strong personality felt and thither he directed his efforts after leaving Prince Edward Island.

Although Fanning had many difficulties to contend with, had continual trouble with the proprietors over the quit rents, and encountered opposition and friction in numerous ways, he yet managed affairs with reasonable success. When his term of office closed in 1805, his successor found matters running with comparative smoothness. Fanning, himself, had gained the good will of the Island people and the approbation of the Home Govern-

---

*"Historical and Descriptive sketches of the Maritime Colonies of British America"— account of Prince Edward Island, etc., London, 1828.

ment. The latter granted him a life pension equal to his salary as a proof of their appreciation. The people, who had not been favourable to him when first he came among them, presented him with a most laudatory address, signed by a hundred and twenty-five of the leading men when he retired from office, to which he made a feeling reply, from which the following passage may be quoted:

"I came hither with the strongest prejudices against both the Island and its inhabitants; but, on my arrival, my former opinion has been done away with, and eighteen years continued residence has had the happy effect, not only to utterly remove these ill-founded prejudices, but, on the contrary, to excite, with each revolving year, an increasing partiality in favour of the Island, and a warm attachment to its inhabitants, and at present I have no other expectation or intention but of returning to pass the remainder of my days with you in this flourishing and delightful Island."

The address and reply were published on the 16th of February, 1805, in the fourth number of the "Royal Herald." The editorial business notice in this early Prince Edward Island journal is in itself interesting, as showing the conditions which prevailed at that date. The paper, which was printed by James Bagnall, printer to the King's most Excellent Majesty, it was announced, would be published regularly once a week, from the 1st of May to 1st of November, the remainder of the year once a fortnight. "The price to be sixteen shillings a year, to be paid one half in advance, at the time of subscribing, or on receipt of the first number in each half year. The paper to be punctually forwarded by every conveyance to those who may not have the benefit of living in the town. Country produce and furs will be taken as payment from those that cannot make it convenient to pay cash."

Until the coming of Lord Selkirk's settlers, little increase in population had taken place in Fanning's time. In fact, there was, as already intimated, an amount of emigration from the Island which caused the authorities concern. Still, the Island was becoming more prosperous, and was beginning to develop a trade, while agricultural operations were being successfully carried on. Mr. Stewart, who was thoroughly well informed on all matters relating to the Island, and an acute observer, informs us that: "Our fisheries, which had been gradually reviving since 1784, promised to become again considerable, and afforded the means of recommencing a trade with the West India Islands, by which we were abundantly supplied with their produce upon very moderate terms. Several cargoes of fish were also annually shipped for the European market, for which British manufactures salt and wine were brought in return. Besides the cod fishery, the herring fishery was begun, and promised well, and our merchants had found means to obtain a considerable share in the produce of the great salmon fisheries carried on in our neighbourhood on the continent. Upon the whole, there was every appearance of extensive and valuable fisheries being established to the great benefit of the Island, when the late war commenced, (*i. e.* the renewal of the war with France), since which the fisheries have been almost given up. Our articles of export now consist of wheat, barley, oats, salt pork, butter, furs, seal oil and oysters, to Nova Scotia, with live cattle and some timber to Newfoundland, and occasionally a few cargoes of squared timber to Great Britain. A few persons are also engaged in building ships, which are generally sold in Newfoundland. This is a business that will probably be carried on to a great extent, should the Newfoundland fisheries revive on the restoration of peace, as the great plenty of lumber in several districts, and the reasonable rates at which the necessaries of life are obtained, will enable us to build at a cheaper rate than they can do in Newfoundland, where the timber is now generally at such a distance from the harbours as to make it very expensive. Since 1792 the importation of any kind of provisions has totally ceased, and the export of these articles had gradually increased."

The provincial establishment was supported by grants from England, and the amount of revenue raised on the Island for public purposes was a mere trifle. The only taxes payable in 1806, when Stewart wrote, were a license duty on retailers of wines and spirituous liquors, a duty of ten pence a gallon on all wines and liquors imported, and two pence a gallon on all porter, ale or strong beer imported. The absurdly small revenue from these sources was the only fund for defraying the contingent expenses of government, and for providing roads and bridges and keeping them in repair. It is not surprising that the means of communication between parts of the province were bad. In the Assembly of 1785 the sum of £161 2s. 11d. comprised the total amount voted for the support of His Majesty's government. In 1786 the Assembly was in a more generous mood and voted £365 15s, 10d. In 1795 the vote was increased to £400.

## POSTAL ARRANGEMENTS.

Benjamin Chappell, the first postmaster, was appointed in 1802. He held office till his death at the age of eighty-seven, in 1825. He was succeeded by his son Richard, who held the position until his death in 1835. His daughter, Elizabeth Chappell, was then appointed postmistress of the Island in his place. She held office for a number of years when she retired, and Thomas Owen was appointed. For many years, during the Chappell regime, the one post office in Charlottetown served the whole Island.

## ROMAN CATHOLICS.

Well up to the close of the eighteenth century there appears to have been very little friction or ill-feeling in religious matters. Thirty years had yet to elapse before the Roman Catholic portion of the population should receive their civil rights and have the privilege of the franchise and of being represented in the Assembly by members of their own faith. Rev. Angus McEachern (later on Bishop of Charlottetown) was a man equally esteemed by Protestants and by members of his own flock. Harmony and goodwill seemed to prevail. It is, therefore, with a feeling of somewhat shocked surprise, that one finds in the journal of the House of Assembly for 23rd July, 1801, that the following address was unanimously agreed to:

"We, His Majesty's most dutiful and loyal subjects, the representatives of the Island, Prince Edward, in General Assembly convened, beg leave to express to your Excellency that, although we conceive that liberty of conscience ought to be fully allowed to all His Majesty's subjects of this Island, whatever their faith or religious tenets may be, yet that of late the encroachments made by the priests and their adherents, professing the religion of the Church of Rome, within this Island have become alarming, the attempts and endeavours to convert Protestants and their children to their faith, their public harangues, without regard to license or authority, their priests, in the habit of their Order, going in processions to funerals and festivals and other public occasions, the erecting crosses in different parts of the Island, particularly one near the side of a public road within the Royalty of Charlottetown, exhibited to the view of all passengers, and their zealous and unremitting labours to inculcate and propagate the Romish persuasion, in prejudice of the Protestant religion as established by law, we consider to be matter dangerous and offensive to His Majesty's loyal subjects, the Protestant inhabitants of this Island, and therefore beg leave to request that Your Excellency will be pleased to take the same into your consideration and adopt such measures on the occasion as in your wisdom you shall think fit."

### Church Missionaries.

On the same day (23rd July, 1801) that the above resolution was adopted it was ordered: "That a committee of this House be appointed to meet a committee of His Majesty's Council, during the recess, in order to make application to the societies in England and Scotland for the propagation of the gospel in foreign parts, to request they will be pleased to send one or more missionaries to this Island for that laudable and truly valuable purpose, and that in consideration of the present want of means for their sufficient support, the assistance of the societies may be requested."

The committee was appointed accordingly.

### Control of Public Funds.

On 2nd April, 1803, the Council, by Mr. Peter Stewart (the Chief Justice) sent down the public accounts. The Assembly forthwith took up the question which, for a considerable time, had been becoming more and more acute, of the control of expenditure. This question goes to the root of responsible government, the agitation for which in this Island, as well as in Canada, was beginning to take shape. Much time had yet to pass before the Assembly secured this control.

On the same day that the accounts were brought down, the following resolution was passed:

"*Resolved*, that it is the opinion of this House that the papers laid before the House containing public accounts, presenting little further than vague estimates, cannot be acted upon by this House and, therefore, order the same to be returned to the Treasurer."

"*Resolved*, It is the opinion of this House that it is necessary to the support of public credit, to the quieting the minds of the inhabitants of this Island, and to the rendering a more willing inclination in them to the paying of taxes, that the General Assembly should have the disposal of all public monies raised by them; and, therefore, consider it necessary, owing to the lateness of the session, that a committee be appointed to draft an address and have the same in readiness to lay before the House at the opening of the next session to be presented to His Majesty's Ministers, praying that instructions be sent to His Majesty's Governor, Lieutenant-Governor or Commander-in-Chief of this Island, to give his assent to such bills as may be passed for repealing former Acts of this Island on that subject complained of, and for placing the money of the public in the same channel as is customary throughout all His Majesty's other colonies."

LIEUTENANT-GOVERNOR DESBARRES

## PART V.

### CHAPTER III.

### LIEUTENANT-GOVERNOR DESBARRES.

COLONEL Joseph Frederick Wallet DesBarres, who was appointed to succeed Fanning in May, 1804, was an old man when he came to Prince Edward Island. He was a man of considerable ability and of literary and scientific attainments. The following account of him is taken from the Colonial Records:*

In 1755, after early training under eminent masters of military science, DesBarres received a cadet's warrant. Soon after he was given the choice of a commission in the Royal artillery or in the corps of engineers. Under the prospect of immediate active service, he preferred a lieutenancy in the 60th Regiment, and, in the spring of 1756, on the breaking out of the war with France, embarked for America. He raised some three hundred recruits and was ordered to form and discipline a force of field artillery, then much needed, which he commanded until the arrival from England of a battalion of the Royal forces.

In the spring of 1757, Schenectady being much harrassed by Indians, DesBarres proposed that he be sent to their principal settlements with a detachment of volunteers. He surprised them at night and made their chiefs prisoners. He gained their confidence so completely that they were restrained from further acts of hostility and became useful to the British army, in which a corps of them continued to be employed on scouting parties, until the close of the war.

He took an active part in the siege of Louisbourg in 1758, and was with Wolfe at Quebec, as an aide-de-camp, till the latter's death. When, in 1760, the British troops in Quebec were reduced to two thousand fit for duty, the preservation of the fortifications was committed to him as directing engineer.

---

*Archives, Col. Rec. Prince Edward Island. Vol. 21, p 67 and seq.

He carried on, or helped to carry on, surveys in Quebec, Nova Scotia, and Newfoundland, in the expedition to retake which, in 1762, he took part, serving as an engineer and quarter-master general. He received public thanks for his services. He was next ordered to New York on reconnoitering service. At the close of the war, in 1763, DesBarres was sent to make a survey of the coast and harbours of His Majesty's North American Dominions. In this work he was unremittingly employed for ten years, until the end of 1773, surveying the unexplored coasts of Nova Scotia. Sixty-three valuable harbours were found and surveyed, of which twenty-nine were fit for ships of the line, and nine capable of containing large fleets.

In 1784, on the establishment of Cape Breton as a separate province, he was appointed Lieutenant-Governor with the military command of that Island and of the neighboring province of Prince Edward Island. He left England for Cape Breton in October, 1784. In May, 1804, he was appointed Lieutenant-Governor and Commander-in-Chief of Prince Edward Island.

Like his successors in the government of Cape Breton, he had a stormy time while there. At the time of his appointment to Prince Edward Island he was over eighty years of age, but his age did not interfere with the discharge of the duties of his office, which he held for eight years. He seems to have developed a conciliatory spirit since leaving Cape Breton, near twenty years before. The machinery of government ran smoothly during his term in this Island, the province increased in population, and in other respects made good progress.

The new Lieutenant-Governor had a hard time in getting to the Island. On 25th September, 1804, he proceeded to Portsmouth to embark on the brigantine Polly, then lying off Spithead, engaged to sail under convoy, to carry him and his family to Newfoundland. On arrival at Portsmouth he was disappointed as to the condition of sailing with convoy. He then obtained from the commanding admiral the protection of an armed brigantine with letter to Admiral Young and Lord Gardner for the same purpose. After adverse and violent gales, the brigantine was at last compelled to seek shelter in Falmouth harbour, where she lay in a disabled state in want of fresh outfits, cables, etc. On 5th November, upon his arrival in Falmouth, he wrote Lord Camden setting out his plight, and pointing out that considering the lateness of the season and the great improbability of being able to reach Prince Edward Island or even Newfoundland, before the usual making of ice in the harbour on these coasts, he presumed His Lordship would see the necessity of his waiting where he was until spring, and taking passage in some of the earlier ships destined thither.*

## DesBarres Arrival.

DesBarres arrived in Charlottetown, 1st July, 1805. Writing to Lord Camden, he tells of being received and escorted through a numerous concourse of joyful people to the house of Lieutenant-General Fanning, where he met the Colonial Council assembled, and where, his Commission and appointment having been read and the usual oaths taken, the seals, command and administration of Prince Edward Island were delivered into his charge.

## Census.

On 6th August following, he submitted to Lord Camden the following state (extracted from a return taken in course of the last preceding month) of the population of the Island, viz.:

| | | |
|---|---:|---:|
| Number of males, above 60 years of age | 155 | |
| Number of males, from 16 to 60 years | 1,590 | |
| Under sixteen years | 1,937 | |
| Total males | | 3,682 |
| Number of females above 60 years of age | 121 | |
| Number of females from 16 to 60 years | 1,449 | |
| Number of females under 16 years | 1,705 | |
| Total of females | | 3,275 |
| Total population | | 6,957 |

He added that all classes in this Island appeared to him to vie with each other in their warm "attachment and loyalty to His Majesty and His Gracious Government."

He met the House of Assembly, for the first time, on the 12th November, 1805. In the early days, before responsible government, the Lieutenant-Governor was the author of his speeches to

---

*Letter DesBarres to Earl of Camden, Secretary of State, dated, Falmouth 6th November, 1804.

the House of Assembly, a fact to be borne in mind in reading the speeches to their "faithful Commons," of some of the gentlemen who held that distinguished position. In DesBarres' case, there was little in any session of the Legislature to call for comment. He was throughout mainly concerned with putting the Island in a state of defence. In his opening speech to the first House, he simply expressed his anxiety to provide for the welfare of the colony, and felt confident that, in his efforts, he would have the assistance of that body.

### THE LAND QUESTION.

The Assembly, in this session, again brought up the land question. On 20th November, they adopted a memorial to the King, in which after showing the neglect of the great number of proprietors to either settle their lands or pay their quit rents, they complained of the grievous discouragement under which they laboured, in finding that every measure adopted by them to accomplish that desirable end, though even under the auspices of His Majesty's gracious pleasure, have hitherto proved abortive, which leaves, in a great measure, in a wilderness state a colony in itself valuable and which only awaited the removal of the grievances complained of to make it of real and lasting importance to the mother state.

### DESBARRES' ACTIVITY.

DesBarres was eighty-three years of age when he took over the government of this province, but, despite his age, he seems to have, at once, visited different sections and to have made himself acquainted with Island conditions. On 4th December, 1805, only six months after his arrival, he wrote Mr. Edward Cooke, an official of the home government, that:

"In the course of my excursions to some of the remote settlements of this Island, I have been much delighted with the beautiful and picturesque appearance of the country, surrounded by seas swarming with fish, favoured with a soil peculiarly kind and easy of culture, and with numerous harbours and navigable rivers affording all desirable conveniences for carrying on the fishery and commerce to a great and profitable extent. With all these superior natural advantages and capabilities, it were but reasonable to suppose that Prince Edward Island ought to have arrived at a far more advanced stage of population, culture and commerce than that in which it is this day found to be. The enclosed abstract shows the actual state in respect to population and culture." . . .

"The resolution it (the General Assembly) passed relative to the quit rents and escheat Acts have greatly alarmed the proprietors of large tracts on the spot. Three of these have presented a memorial to me on that subject which I enclose."

POPULATION — CENSUS.

State of culture and estimated produce of the current year (1805) from a particular account dated 12th November, 1805,— Population, 7041. This includes eighty-four new settlers since last date.

| Acres Sown or Planted | | Estimated Produce | | Current Value | | Amounting to Currency |
|---|---|---|---|---|---|---|
| | | Bushels | Avg. per Acre | | | |
| 2,339 | wheat | 29,790 | 12¾ bush. | 5s | per bus. | £ 7,442.10.0 |
| 1,808 | barley | 13,389 | 13¼ " | 3s | "   " | 2,008. 7.0 |
| 1,349½ | oats | 25,317 | 18½ " | 1s 6d | "   " | 1,898.15.0 |
| 2 | rye | 25 | 12½ " | 4s | "   " | 5. 0.0 |
| 2½ | peas | 50 | 20 " | 5s | "   " | 12.10.0 |
| 1,358 | potatoes | 221,695 | 156 " | 1s 6d | "   " | 15,877. 2.6 |
| 127½ | turnips | 19,710 | 155 " | 1s | "   " | 985.10.0 |
| 118 | flax | 590 | 5 " | 7s 6d | "   " | 223. 5.0 |

| Acres Meadow Land | Hay Produced | Current Value in Island | Amounting to |
|---|---|---|---|
| 2,440 Upland | 2,195 Tons | 55s per ton | £6,036.5.0 |
| 4,347 Marsh | 6,012 Tons | 25s per ton | 7,526.5.0 |
| 6,787 acres | | | £13,562.10.0 |

Equal in sterling money to £12,206.5.0.

Stock of cattle, etc., on Prince Edward Island:

| | |
|---|---:|
| Breeding Mares | 392 |
| Horses | 444 |
| Colts under three years | 209 |
| Cows | 3,402 |
| Oxen | 1,701 |
| Young cattle under three years | 4,710 |
| Sheep | 11,756 |
| Swine | 8,111 |
| Value | £23,552.11.5 |
| | 12,206.05.0 |
| Total produce from culture and hay* | £35,758.16.5 |

A matter of present day interest, which for the first time was brought before this Assembly, was the proposal to establish a public market in Charlottetown. On 20th November, 1805, the Lieutenant-Governor sent a message on this subject to the House, in which he said:

"Convinced as I am of the obvious expediency of establishing, with apposite regulations, a public market in Charlottetown, I am induced to request your attention to the propositions contained in a memorial which Mr. Chalmers is to lay before you, for your consideration, improvement and legislative deliberation."

Two days later an "Act for Encouraging the Building of a Market in Charlottetown and establishing a public market thereat," was brought in and read a first and second time, when it was ordered that the House go into committee of the whole tomorrow morning on the Bill. On the morrow it was ordered to stand over till next session.

War was waging in Europe, and the struggle with the United States, though it did not break out until 1812, was already looming on the horizon. It threatened long before it came, and the governors of the British colonies were instructed to take measures to provide for the contingency of war. Throughout DesBarres' time he was ever anxious on this point and continually urged on the House of Assembly the necessity for the Island's defence.

---

*This census, taken two years after the coming of the Selkirk Settlers which were included in it, shows the population to have been disappointingly small and indicates that the emigration from the Island in the earlier years of Fanning's Administration, already referred to, was very considerable. It was largely due to the Loyalists and disbanded soldiers leaving the colony because they could not get titles to the lands promised them.

## DEFENCE.

Mr. Stewart, in 1806*, writing of the defence of Charlottetown, apart from the question of the militia, says: "The town is protected on the side of the harbour by two batteries; that of the west end of the town is mounted with eleven heavy guns, so disposed as to command every part of the harbour, the other is placed on the bank of the river in front of the town and mounts four guns, which also point to the harbour and the opposite side of the river; the entrance of the harbour is defended by a block-house mounting four guns, in front of which is a stone-battery mounting five guns, with a ditch, the whole well stockaded. . . . There is also a battery on the eastern side of the narrows, not at present in repair. . . . The barracks, at the west end of the town, consist of two separate ranges of buildings, each two hundred and sixty feet in length, which front each other, being divided by a spacious parade. They are calculated to accommodate upwards of three hundred men with their officers. . . . In point of accommodation they are not surpassed by any barracks in North America. Within the enclosure are an hospital, a store for provisions, and another for the ordnance, and a wharf in front of the town, two hundred and forty-eight feet in length, is a military erection." . . .

"On the west side of the harbour, Fort Amherst formerly stood on an elevated spot, three hundred yards from the water. It was erected immediately after the conquest of the Island — was a large square redoubt, with a broad deep ditch, mounted eighteen pieces of cannon and contained handsome barracks. Soon after its erection, it was twice attacked by the French and their Indian allies, but they failed in both attempts. The situation is commanded by higher ground at a small distance. On this account the fort was dismantled and destroyed by Governor Patterson soon after his appointment to the government.

In 1806, DesBarres summoned a new House of Assembly. In opening it, he referred to an increase of settlers which had taken place, but complained of the slow progress being made by the colony.

## MILITIA, ETC.

The Assembly, newly elected, met in its first session 1st December, 1806. It seems to have actively interested itself in

*Stewart's Prince Edward Island, p 12.

the question of defence. The House addressed the Lieutenant-Governor on the defenceless state of the Island which the members conceived demanded the most serious attention. They requested him to cause to be laid before them an account of the total number of effectives comprising the troops, in garrison and the militia, with the quantities of arms and ammunition now on hand. On the 12th the Lieutenant-Governor sent down a general return of the militia, etc.

Writing to Mr. Windham, Secretary for the Colonies, soliciting his attention to the state of the Island, DesBarres said: "I had, previous to leaving England, read the militia laws of Prince Edward Island and was led to expect a well-disciplined, armed and efficient militia. But no such thing had ever had any existence. All I could discover was a group of individuals, on whom commissions had been bestowed with various ranks, without any organization having taken place. I endeavoured to make the best arrangement circumstances allowed. I appointed officers in their respective districts, summoned all able men to join, and they were distributed and formed into companies and regiments. In result, and for the first time, after the lapse of nearly forty years since commencing the colonization of Prince Edward Island, there was a general muster of the militia. It amounts, officers included, to fourteen hundred and six, and there is no doubt of its progressive increase, and I fondly indulge the hope that from the good effects of your generous attention, you will see proper to recommend such aids and supplies as shall enable me to raise it into actual efficiency and permanent utility."

## PETITION FOR AID FOR SEVERAL MATTERS.

On the 13th December a joint petition of both Houses to the King praying for aid out of the quit rent funds, together with estimates therein set forth, was prepared. In it they submit for His Majesty's consideration the wants under which the colony labours, together with an estimate of the amount required for defraying the most pressing of its exigencies, in order duly to uphold the dignity of His Majesty's Government, accelerate the tardy population of the colony, stimulate a laudable spirit of industry and ingenuity among all classes, extend its culture and commerce and render it productive, not only of a pecuniary revenue; but also of, eventually, far more important benefits and advantages, being admirably well calculated by its situation, its fishing coasts, harbours, and numerous other natural qualities to become a nursery of valuable seamen and other useful subjects for the support, preservation and defence of the transatlantic Dominions.

Half a century had nearly elapsed since this Island was surrendered to the British, during which time it has been a constant source of expense, affording no adequate return. Progress has been slow compared with other colonies, yet its natural advantages have not been inferior — with a commodious situation, a healthy climate, and an active and laborious peasantry. The people are distributed in wilderness land, in small settlements and so poor as to be unable to spare, from their families, either that time or property which it would be necessary to devote to public purposes in order to facilitate the general concerns of the Island.

They hope that it may not be considered an imputation upon their public character, when they represent their deficiency in almost every necessary establishment of an infant colony. They represented that the revenue arising from an excise in this Island scarcely exceeds £400 per annum. The roads are entirely insufficient, though they have been, by laborious industry, cut through some hundreds of inhabited miles. And there were no public buildings, even a church having been erected almost entirely by private subscription. Thirteen hundred of the inhabitants have been lately embodied in the militia, yet there are but three hundred stand of arms on the Island. The people are anxious to render their colony a support, rather than a burden to the United Kingdom, but do not possess the means.

By a minute of the Lords Commissioners of the Treasury, the quit rents of this Island, for ten years, to 1st May, 1779 — at the then rate of £1,495 sterling, amounting to £14,950.0.0, as also a grant of Parliament of £3,000 sterling, were ordered (after the deduction of certain salaries due to the officers of government) "to be applied to the making of roads and other public works within the Island, by the Receiver-General," but no such application was ever made and the public are totally ignorant of the appropriation of such money or of the amount of quit rents since that period, no accounts thereof having been rendered to the Colonial Government of this Island.

By the account and estimate submitted herewith it will appear that a sum of £20,000, together with an annual allotment of £1,720, would place this Island upon a respectable footing, and enable it to proceed with vigour and activity in the prosecution of the before mentioned objects, which its people are jealously anxious to carry into immediate effect in case Your Majesty shall be pleased to order a part of the present quit rents to be appropriated to that purpose under the control of the Legislature of this colony.

ESTIMATE ANNEXED.

"An estimate of the expense for defraying the exigencies of His Majesty's Government in this Island:

| | |
|---|---:|
| Public roads, 500 miles and upwards, and bridges | £7,000.0.0 |
| Range of public buildings for Charlottetown, the metropolis of the Island | 3,000.0.0 |
| Government House and offices | 5,000.0.0 |
| Wharf at Charlottetown | 500.0.0 |
| School House and grounds at Charlottetown | 500.0.0 |
| A packet boat fitted for sea | 600.0.0 |
| A lighthouse on Point Prim | 300.0.0 |
| A Church, School House, Court House and Jail | 1,500.0.0 |
| Glebe and Grounds in Prince County } Ditto in King's County. | 1,500.0.0 |
| | £19,900.0.0 |

ESTIMATE OF ANNUAL ALLOWANCE

| | |
|---|---:|
| Additional allowance to three clergymen, one in each county, £100 each | £300.0.0 |
| Annual allowance for six school masters, two for each county, at £50 | 300.0.0 |
| Annual expenses of militia establishment | 350.0.0 |
| An auditor of Public Accounts, yearly | 50.0.0 |
| The Colonial Treasurer (in the event of an additional revenue) yearly | 100.0.0 |
| Two Assistant Judges at £50 each, yearly | 100.0.0 |
| Annual allowance to the Sheriff and for two deputies, one in King's County and one in Prince County and three gaolers | 100.0.0 |
| Annual allowance to master and crew of the packet and occasional outfits | 150.0.0 |
| Annual allowance to the colony agents | 120.0.0 |
| Annual allowance to the printer of government | 150.0.0 |
| Sterling | £1,720.0.0 |

In an address to the Lieutenant-Governor accompanying that to the King, the "Colonial Council and House of Assembly, in General Assembly convened, represented to His Excellency that they had taken into their consideration that part of His Excellency's speech which recommended the exertion of the Legislature towards the improvement of the Island, in consequence of which they had determined to represent their situation to His Most Gracious Majesty by the Petition which they therewith requested leave to lay before his Excellency, praying the Royal Bounty therein mentioned.

The Legislature's petition to His Majesty was not quite the reply to the recommendation in the opening speech which His Excellency had expected.

## MILITIA, ETC.

On 16th December, 1806, the Lieutenant-Governor sent lists of regulars, militia, ordnance, arms, ammunition, etc., to the Assembly, of which the following is a summary:

"Summary of Garrison at Charlottetown:

Royal Artillery.— One corporal, two privates.

Royal Newfoundland Regiment.— One subaltern, two sergeants, one corporal, one drumman, twenty-four privates.

(Sgd) JOHN FITZMAURICE,
12th December, 1806. *Town Major.*

## GENERAL RETURN OF THE MILITIA FORCES IN PRINCE EDWARD ISLAND.

### KING'S COUNTY REGIMENT.

| | |
|---|---|
| Commissioned Officers | 19 |
| N. C. O's. and Privates | 360 |
| Stand of Arms | 15 |
| Muskets | 7 |

### QUEEN'S COUNTY REGIMENT.

| | |
|---|---|
| Commissioned Officers | 23 |
| N. C. O.'s and Privates | 600 |
| Stand of Arms | 25 |

PRINCE COUNTY REGIMENT.

| | |
|---|---:|
| Commissioned Officers | 24 |
| N. C. O.'s and Privates | 380 |
| Stand of Arms | 65 |
| | |
| Total Commissioned Officers | 66 |
| N. C. O.'s and Privates | 1,340 |
| Stands of Arms | 105 |
| Muskets | 7 |

N. B.—The regimental returns (having been the first that were made to this office) may not be altogether correct.

A very few carbines and pistols have been returned, but in such a manner that they cannot at present be regularly entered.

(Sgd.) J. B. PALMER,
December 13th, 1806. *A. G. Mil.*

Also a detailed list of the guns, ammunition, etc.

In consequence of this return, the House of Assembly presented the following address to the Lieutenant-Governor:

"We, the representatives of His Majesty's Island, Prince Edward, in General Assembly convened, beg leave to express our thanks to Your Excellency for the several returns you were pleased to lay before us in compliance with our Address of 12th inst. These papers have been examined by us, with that requisite attention due so important a subject, and we are seriously impressed with a firm conviction that the defenceless situation of the Island loudly and imperiously calls upon us to make such representations to Your Excellency as may occasion the same being made known to His Majesty's Ministers and induce them to take those desirable steps, essentially necessary towards the ensuring the security and preservation of this valuable colony, which from the almost total want of disciplined troops, arms and ammunitions, in its present state, renders us not only open to insult from an enemy, but, in the event of an attack, actually incapable of making even a trifling defence.

"We have but one subaltern and twenty-eight men. A few great guns mounted and eight or ten rounds of ammunition, this with three hundred stand of small arms for our militia, and twelve round of ball cartridge for them comprise our whole means of defence. We, therefore, humbly pray Your Excellency may be pleased to take those desirable measures (by application) for a respectable force, with sufficient arms and ammunition, which the alarming necessity of the case so urgently requires."

At the close of the session of the Supreme Court, on 21st February, 1807, an address to the Lieutenant-Governor, referring to his activity in militia matters, pointed out that the internal defence of the colony occupied his early attention, with the result that a few ineffective companies of militia were soon increased and formed into three regularly arranged regiments, ready for discipline as soon as a fund can be found for that purpose.

They also express their indebtedness to the Lieutenant-Governor for an economical expenditure of the public labour on the highways, as well as for judicious directions as to the opening of roads, whenever the revenue should be sufficient to defray the expense of so necessary a measure. They went on to express gratitude for his vigilance and impartial investigation into the accounts of the colonial revenue now laid open to general inspection, a measure calculated to promote confidence among all classes of the people.

## POST OFFICE.

DesBarres, however, did not confine his attention to the militia alone. In 1806, he represented to the home authorities the expediency of establishing a post office at Charlottetown as, without such a measure, neither the public business of the Island, nor the operations of its trade can be carried on with requisite regularity and "desirable success."

## PUBLIC SCHOOL.

At the same time he pointed out that, there being no public school in Prince Edward Island, the necessity of endowing a school for the instruction of youth, with a moderate salary to the school master, is evident, and that such establishments are fixed in all the other colonies.

## POPULATION.

On October 1st, 1807, in a despatch to Lord Castlereagh, Secretary for the Colonies, DesBarres gave the actual state of the population in that year as amounting to a total of eight thousand seven hundred and thirty, a very large increase. In September of the following year the ship Clarendon, of Hull, James Hines, master, took 188 persons* from Oban for Charlottetown.

## LAND TAX.

In 1807 DesBarres endeavoured to supplement the very meagre revenue by a land tax, with the usual result of an outcry from those called upon to pay it. John Stewart, in a letter to Lord Castlereagh, is sorry to say that the colony is in a state of considerable ferment over an attempt made by Lieutenant-Governor DesBarres to lay a tax of a halfpenny an acre on all the lands in the Island, the forest and uncultivated part as well as the improved and productive. He declares it to be the first attempt of its kind that had ever been made in any British colony and measures, too, for the purpose of obtaining the consent of the Legislature will probably be found equally new. He suggested the appointment of a new governor.

## DEFENCE.

In March, 1808, the House of Assembly memorialized the Duke of Kent, who seems to have been looked upon as the special patron of the Island named after him, for his influence with the British Government to obtain a temporary allowance from the quit rents paid by the proprietors, to be laid out on the erection of public buildings, and in forming other establishments suitable and requisite for the convenience and respectability of the government, which, without help the inhabitants are unable to effect. They do not seem to have succeeded in their application, as the following year the Legislature itself passed an Act to raise money for these purposes.

On the very date of this memorial (28th March) the Lieutenant-Governor sent a message to the House of Assembly, in which he called attention to the necessity of providing measures for defence. He said:

"The uncertainty of the continuance of the peace and amity which has existed between His Majesty's Government and the

---

*Vol. 20 Col. Of. Records, Prince Edward Island p. 151.

United States of America, and the defenceless state in which the Island is at present left, without military protection, oblige me to call your particular attention to this circumstance, under a full persuasion that you will see the necessity of making provisions for a sufficient supply for the expenses, which must unavoidably attend the subsistence of the militia in the event of their being required to perform military duty; a small portion of which appears to me requisite until such time as an expected detachment arrives from Halifax."

The House of Assembly went into committee on this message and resolved, "That in the present state of the country, it was not in their power, after the fullest consideration, to devise any means for immediately defraying the expense of the subsistence of the militia, in case of their being called upon to do military duty, in the absence of the detachment of His Majesty's troops."

This was evidently a disappointment to the old soldier, who, in his speech proroguing the House, said, "That he had suggested raising such a sum of money as might enable him, in case of need, to resist and repel any hostile attempts, he had trusted that the justice and expediency of his recommendations would have appeared sufficiently obvious, important and forceful to prompt its successful result."

There can be little question that the Island was not in a position to do much at this time, but that they could have found some money is shown by the fact that the following year they provided means for raising sixteen hundred pounds for the erection of public buildings. But it should be borne in mind also that, while under our yearly governors, the House of Assembly could provide money for the public service, it had no control over its expenditure. This was always a sore question in British Colonies, before they obtained responsible government, or control of expenditure, and rendered them very chary of making grants. Much will be heard of this matter in the days of Lieutenant-Governor Smith, who succeeded DesBarres.

At this period, desertion from the navy and army was very common in North America. This was due to several causes. Many of the men were pressed into the service, and that mode of manning the ships was most unpopular.* The discipline on board, also, was very severe, and the treatment of the men often of a brutal character. Moreover, much better pay was offered in the United States mercantile marine. The right, claimed by Great Britain, to search United States vessels for such men, was one of the causes which led to the war of 1812. Statutes were enacted in various provinces with a view to lessening this evil. In Prince Edward Island an Act to prevent, under heavy penalties, the harbouring of deserters from the navy or the merchant service was passed, and rewards offered for apprehending deserters.

Doubtless impressed by the menace of war with the United States, the Council at the opening of the session for 1809, on 20th April, presented an address to the Lieutenant-Governor, expressive of their sense that the very singular political circumstances marking the executive government of the United States, called for the utmost vigilance and attention in preparing to repel any attempts which possibly may be meditated against this Island, and expressed the hope that under the blessing of a kind, protecting Providence, "the firmness and energetic valor of the inhabitants of Prince Edward Island will be found fully adequate to the purpose."

They added that "deeply impressed with the importance of improving our militia laws and establishing a love of good order, prompt discipline and due subordination among the inhabitants composing the militia, they would cheerfully concur in such measures as might be deemed expedient and in granting such

---

*"In July, 1807, the good ship Hope, of Bristol, Captain John Ford, was chartered by Andrew MacDonald and Sons, of Three Rivers (now named Georgetown), to bring out a cargo of merchandise, and there load a cargo of pine timber for Britain."

"While preparing to load, the sloop-of-war Halifax arrived at Three Rivers, and one morning the captain of the Hope was surprised by a visit from an officer and boat's crew, from the Halifax, boarding his vessel; and impressing, against their will and their own protest, the most able seamen he had, and taking them off on board the Halifax."

"The Hope was delayed for a long time, to the serious loss of all concerned. The master and the charterers sent a petition to Lieutenant-Governor DesBarres, setting forth the serious injury this practice would cause to the export trade of the province, and praying His Excellency to use his influence to have the men returned to them, if possible; and to put a stop to impressing seamen here; for it it was allowed to continue it would be impossible to charter vessels to ports in this province, where other men, equally qualified, could not be procured to navigate the vessels." It does not appear whether Captain Ford got his men back, nor do we know what the governor may have done to stop this practice in provincial ports, but we have met with no other record of later cases." The men in Her Majesty's navy now receive fair wages, good food and just treatment (which was not always the case at that time), and they are now quite willing to serve in the navy without being impressed. Under date of 30th June, 1805, Mr. Chappell has the following entry in his diary:

"The Vixen has two men pressed belonging to Malpeque."

supplies as might be necessary to render that force respectable and which the safety of the government might require."

In opening the session on 20th March, 1809, the Lieutenant-Governor expressed the hope "that they will view the political vicissitudes of their American neighbors, in the light of additional incitements, to being in constant preparation for repelling all attempts, which possibly may be meditated against this colony."

. . . .

He informed the Assembly that "since the close of the last session, His Excellency, Lieutenant-General Sir George Prevost, has, in consequence of his representations, ordered an additional supply of ordnance, arms, and ammunition as could be spared from Halifax for the service of this Island. A certain number of these arms would forthwith be distributed in the equipment of the militia."

PUBLIC BUILDINGS.

In the same session (25th March, 1809,) the Assembly again took up the question of public buildings and resolved:

1. "That it is essential to the dignity and honour of His Majesty's Government in this Island, the due and regular administration of justice and the security of property, that proper buildings be erected for holding the General Assembly, the courts of justice, the register office and a jail in Charlottetown."

2. "That it is indispensably necessary to make immediate provision for the erection of said buildings."

Five days later (30th March) a petition was presented from a number of inhabitants of Prince county against a 'Land Tax.' "

The same day, the House unanimously resolved, "That the most advisable and practicable mode of improvement of roads and erection of public buildings, is by an assessment at the rate of two shillings per each hundred acres of land in this colony which should be imposed for the above purpose."

In the session of 1810 the House reported that certain provisions should be made for defraying militia expenses as follows:

"The expense of drilling thirteen companies of militia at £5.0.0, £65,0.0. For purchasing forty drums and fifes, £50.0.0. Also for the purchase of one hundred and twenty picks, £45.0.0. for contingencies for the militia, £40.0.0.

### Loan to Build an Inn.

During this same session of 1810 it was, on motion, ordered that, "the sum of £100 be advanced, by way of loan, to Mr. Francis Garobbo, for the space of four years to assist him in the erection of a public inn, the same to be secured by mortgage on the premises, he paying lawful interest for the same."

On 21st August (1810) the Lieutenant-Governor, by letter, expressed his disappointment at the neglect of the Assembly to vote supplies for militia purposes, and on the same date, proroguing the House, he expressed his views at length strongly to the same effect.

In the session of 1812 (9th September) the Assembly passed a resolution to raise a sum of money by assessment upon land of two shillings for each hundred acres, to be paid into the hands of treasurers in the different counties, for the use of the militia and for highroads and bridges, provided that the sums to be applied to the use of the militia shall not exceed one thousand pounds.

During this session, the Assembly, in an address to the Lieutenant-Governor strongly censured Chief Justice Colclough relative to appointment of sheriffs, asserting that by some of his proceedings he would have the choice of juries and that, by others, he became solicitor, prosecutor and judge, and that they could no longer refrain from declaring his conduct to be dangerous to the lives, liberty and property of His Majesty's subjects, to such a degree as to render it inadvisable that the Chief Justice should be any longer continued in the discharge of the functions of his office which he hath proved himself unworthy of being entrusted with, and they pray that he be suspended from the exercise of his office until His Majesty's pleasure shall be known.*

### Expenditure.

The Finance Committee of this Assembly, which was evidently an active one, during the same session (on 28th September, 1812,) again took up the question of expenditure of public money, and reported: "That the mode of appropriating the monies raised by the Import Act has been the subject of creating much discontent and want of harmony in the colony, and an alteration in the Act

---

*For C. J. Colclough see "Miscellaneous" section VI, infra.

giving the House of Assembly its share in the appropriation of that money, would, in the opinion of the committee, conduce in a great degree to the prosperity of the Island and most certainly would produce in the House a spirit of liberality to meet the future exigencies of government." Evidently the germ of responsible government was developing.

Colonel DesBarres met the House for the last time this year (1812). The war with the United States had broken out. So far as it lay in his power he had acted with energy, and now sought to infuse some of his own enthusiasm into the Legislature. In his speech opening the session, he informed the House that, on receiving intelligence of war being declared by the United States against the United Kingdom, he had convened the Council and, with its advice, had sent an officer with confidential despatches to Nova Scotia. As a result of that mission he had the assurance from the Lieutenant-Governor and admiral commanding of affording "for the service and protection of the Island such means as the actual conjunction of affairs might occasionally require."

A very non-committal promise.

These hostile measures rendering it imperatively necessary to adopt vigorous means for efficient defence and security, he recommended as the primary and most pressing object of the Legislature's duty, a revision and improvement of the militia laws and regulations.

"The faithful prosecution and discharge of that important duty will, no doubt, afford you not only a gratifying opportunity of evincing your zeal and attachment to our most gracious Sovereign, and the best of constitutions on earth, but also of fostering the seeds of similar zeal and attachment amongst all ranks of individuals which compose our several militia corps, whose laudable disposition I contemplate with heartfelt satisfaction, and from whose genuine spirit and activity I am led to entertain the most sanguine hopes that in critical occurrences they will prove themselves amply deserving the encouragements and rewards apportioned to them by your justice and liberality."

The House promised immediate attention to the matter and a militia Act, or, more strictly speaking, an Act reviving former expired militia Acts, was placed on the statute book.

Before passing from the General Assembly of 1812, the last to be convened by Colonel DesBarres, it may be of interest to note the very high regard in which the earlier Houses of Assembly held their own dignity. They were determined that the most punctilious respect, not only from the public, but from its own members as well, should be insisted upon by the House, which did not hesitate to punish any disregard for its privileges, no matter by whom shown. Did a member see fit to be absent, without leave, or not to attend in proper time to his duties, Mr. Speaker very promptly despatched the sergeant-at-arms to bring the truant before the House. A curious incident in this connection is reported in the journal of 1812.

Mr. Worrell, one of the members for King's county, who resided at Morell, seems to have been of an eccentric character. He had absented himself from his duties, and the Speaker issued his warrant to bring him to the House. The warrant was entrusted to Mr. James Coles, who, after executing it, attended before the House, and stated that he had taken Mr. Worrell "and brought him to town, but that on the road from St. Peters, Mr. Worrell offered him his fees if he would let him go, which Coles refused to take; and Mr. Worrell said that, if Coles took the fees, he would have more fees to receive, by being ordered to go again after Mr. Worrell. And further that he (Mr. Worrell) said he would not have suffered himself to be taken had he known that Coles would not take his fees and discharge him."

During the same session, a rather amusing instance of the House's treatment of anything savoring of contempt on the part of outsiders occurred. The Solicitor-General informed the House that he had information that a professional gentleman, lately arrived in this Island, had said to one or more members, that the Speakers and members, then sitting, were not a House, but a convention, and moved that Benjamin Coffin, Esq., a member, be requested to state what he knew relative to the charge.

"Mr. Coffin stated that, on Monday last, he had seen Mr. Johnston, of this town, who had asserted to the effect that this House was not a House but a convention.

"Mr. Johnston being sent for, appeared at the bar and asserted that he was not bound to declare any professional opinion that he might have given.

"Mr. Coffin stated that Mr. Johnston had not been professionally employed, but had made the declaration beforementioned to several people in the street, at Mr. Sim's door.

"Mr. Johnston said that such was his opinion, and said he might have so expressed himself, and it still is his opinion.

"Mr. Solicitor-General moved, seconded by Mr. Nelson, that Mr. Johnston has been guilty of a high crime and misdemeanor in such his language, and that an humble address be presented to His Excellency, praying. that he would order His Majesty's attorney-general to prosecute Mr. Johnston for such offence," which was unanimously resolved. The address was accordingly prepared and presented to the Lieutenant-Governor.

Colonel DesBarres' term as Lieutenant-Governor came to an end in 1813, when representations which had been made to the home authorities with regard to the actual state of the Island, and the situation of Great Britain as to its relations with the United States of America, rendered it expedient, in the opinion of the British Government, that an active and efficient officer should be sent from England to relieve him in the charge of this Government. The Prince Regent, he was informed, had selected C. Douglas Smith, Esquire, to succeed him, who would leave England for the Colony with as little delay as possible. In consideration of DesBarres' length of service a suitable pension was ordered to be conferred upon him on his return to England.

DesBarres was a very old man. At the time of his recall from Prince Edward Island he was ninety-two years of age. He died in Halifax, 27th October, 1824. Mr. Murdock,* writes of him: "27th October, 1824, Colonel Joseph Frederick Wallet DesBarres, late Lieutenant-Governor of Prince Edward Island, and formerly of Cape Breton, died at Poplar Grove, in Halifax, aged 102 years. . . . I had the honor of attending the funeral of this eminent person. . . . His Honour, Mr. Wallace, the president,—most of the members of His Majesty's Council — the gentlemen of the bar, the officers of the army and navy, and many of the inhabitants, attended, by invitation, as mourners. . . . This amiable and valuable warrior was within one month of 103 years of age when he died. His scientific labours on our coasts,

---
*History of Nova Scotia, Vol. 111, p. 523.

and his reputation as one of the heroes of 1759, in the conquest of Quebec, under Wolfe, gave him a claim on the gratitude and reverence of all Nova Scotians."

The Acadian Recorder* added: "The chart, which he prepared from his own survey of this province, will give his memory claims of gratitude upon the nautical world, and could only have been produced by a man of surprising perseverance.

"We believe he was a native of Switzerland, and are informed he held a captain's commission under the Great Wolfe at the reduction of Quebec." One of his sons became a justice of the Supreme Court of Newfoundland; and a grandson held a similar position in the Supreme Court of Nova Scotia.

---

*November 6th, 1824, cited by Murdock.

## PART V.

### CHAPTER IV.

### CHARLES DOUGLAS SMITH, LIEUTENANT-GOVERNOR.

FOR a few months after Colonel DesBarres vacated the Lieutenant-Governorship, and before the arrival of his successor, Mr. Townshend administered the government. Mr. Smith succeeded Colonel DesBarres, in 1813. He was a brother of Sir Sydney Smith, the hero of Acre. He was very different in character from his predecessor, and, in fact, from all of the men who have administered the government of this Island. A man of most arbitrary and despotic temperament, it is difficult even to imagine how the British Government came to appoint such a man to the Lieutenant-Governorship of Prince Edward Island or to any other position of responsibility. Insolent and over-bearing he was quite unfitted for such a position. Unlike his predecessors he made no effort to make himself acquainted with the colony over which he was called upon to preside. He is charged with having, only once, during his ten years of office, gone into the country so far as eighteen miles from the town. During the ten years of his Lieutenant-Governorship, he convened the Legislature only four times, and each time there was almost open war between that body and the Lieutenant-Governor. In each case it was summarily prorogued or dismissed, with scant courtesy or gross insult. The House of Assembly was always ready to do battle with him, when it deemed its rights and privileges infringed upon, and yielded nothing. Smith was the worst type of public official— tyrannical, regardless of all popular rights, unconstitutional in his conduct, an autocrat. McGregor,* writing a few years after Smith had been recalled, says of him: "The period at which he entered upon the administration was as propitious as he could wish, the country being in a

---
*Account of Prince Edward Island. 92.

position to enable him to direct all its resources to the general advantage of the colony. Possessing, as he did, in an eminent degree, the friendship of Lord Bathurst, had he taken any interest in the welfare of the country which was committed to his care, he might have still governed it, with credit to himself, and satisfaction to the people, instead of making his administration obnoxious to almost every individual in the colony."

The Lieutenant-Governor called the Assembly together on 15th November, 1813. The late Rev. Dr. Sutherland, in his short History of Prince Edward Island, published an abstract of Smith's opening address, from which it is evident that there was nothing conciliatory about him, nor did his speech give any indications of weakness in that respect. In his speech, Dr. Sutherland tells us, "he told the members he had heard of dissentions and strife in the colony; that he would have called them together sooner, but he was not certain that the public good would be served by it; that since his arrival he had not witnessed any strife, and he hoped that the business of the country would be quietly prosecuted. However, as some of the messages from the House, which came before him, were not satisfactory, he concluded that the members were spending their time doing nothing, and on the 14th of January, 1814, he summarily dismissed them." His speech in proroguing the House exhibited bad temper and showed the arbitrary nature of the man. He said: "In remarking how little has resulted from the present meeting of the General Assembly, I am bound to declare my sense of your patient attention to business, and of your perfect readiness to co-operate in every salutary measure.

"I have had great satisfaction in affording you ample time and opportunity for examining and investigating whatever relates to the public expenditure. In this, and in all other respects, I have been actuated by the most sincere desire to pay very marked attention to your privileges. If this conduct on my part has not been altogether met on yours by a correspondent degree of liberality and confidence, it is a matter that, however it may form a ground for political regret, I, upon constitutional principles, shall forbear to comment upon.

"But, as, under present circumstances, the detaining you longer together does not seem likely to lead to any beneficial end, it becomes expedient to release you from further attendance, and to terminate the session."

The House, during the session, had taken up the public accounts, and devoted much of its time to reviewing and criticising the expenditure, much of it unauthorized. The demand for responsible government gained much in strength during this session.

The Assembly was not again convened until July, 1817. Its proceedings then were too independent to please the Lieutenant-Governor, and he dissolved the House. A new one was called together in 1818, which, not being more tractable than the former one, was suddenly dissolved and another elected in 1820. After the session of 1820, the House was not again convened until the early spring of 1825, when it was called together by Smith's successor, Lieutenant-Governor Ready, who was the antithesis of Smith and the best Governor the Island ever had. In the meantime Smith did as he pleased.

In October, 1816, he published a proclamation intimating that the King had extended to proprietors of land immunity from forfeitures, to which, under the original grants, they were liable, and also granting remission of quit rent arrears and fixing a scale for future payment. But before the amount had been fixed by the Home Government, he directed the Acting Receiver-General, in January, 1818, to enforce payment of arrears since 1816 on the old scale. This proceeding caused much distress, and the Home Government, when the matter was brought to its notice, ordered further action to be discontinued and the money exacted, over two shillings a hundred acres, to be refunded. It was intimated that the new rate would be enforced in future, but the following three years passed without any public demand being made, and the impression prevailed that no more quit rents would be demanded, particularly as payment was not exacted in the neighbouring provinces.

The period was an eventful one throughout the world. Napoleon now made his final desperate struggle, and was crushed. For nearly three years war with the United States continued. The Republic gained successes on the lakes, and her privateers did much injury to British commerce. But she did not have it all her own way on the water, where some brilliant work was done by the British; notably, the famous naval duel between the Shannon and the Chesapeake. On the other hand, the British kept her coasts in alarm, destroyed her trade, almost ruined the finances of the Republic, and of her Atlantic states; while, on land, the British and Colonial forces made a splendid record of victory for themselves. They carried on the contest under great disadvantages and usually against tremendous odds. In the beginning of the war they captured Detroit, though defended by immensely superior numbers. They won the victories of Queenstown Heights, Chateauguay, Lundy's Lane, Chrysler's Farm, Stoney Creek and others. In 1814, they captured Washington and seized a great part of the coast of Maine. At the close of the war, the British and Canadians were in possession of Michigan. Under an incompetent commander, and opposed by overwhelming numbers, they were defeated by General Harrison (afterwards President) at the battle of the Thames, where Tecumseh fell. The British were also repulsed in an attack on New Orleans, made really after the close of the war, but before the peace was known to the combatants. Notwithstanding this reverse and the fact that for a generation Great Britain had been engaged in a life and death struggle with Napoleon, and, at times, with all Europe, the British and Canadians had decidedly the best of the war with the United States in 1812-14. On the whole, the contest was most successfully waged by them. While its close found them in possession of a large area of United States territory, no hostile force had been able to maintain a footing on Canadian soil. During the war, Prince Edward Island suffered no molestation, and made steady progress.

On the 8th July, 1817, after three and a half years rule without its assistance, Smith convened the same House of Assembly, the second session of which he had so unceremoniously prorogued. The opening speech contained little of local importance, and gave no hint of the reason for not having convened the House during the long period since the last session. Matters went smoothly until the 6th August, when the House adjourned till the 14th. The members during the session, till this adjournment, had devoted their attention altogether to routine work, and to taking up such business affecting the province as they deemed expedient and necessary. They seemed to have determined to avoid any contest with the Lieutenant-Governor, until such time as they should have attended to the pressing business of the community. Consequently this part of the session was calm and uneventful.

But the House, while it held its complaints and grievances in abeyance, and preserved a most respectful attitude towards His Excellency, had not, by any means, forgotten its own dignity. Its members had carefully investigated the public expenditure, and voted a further supply. The speaker, on behalf of the House of Assembly of Prince Edward Island, presented the supply bill to His Excellency. The appropriations, they said, were not so large as they wished, but, knowing the limited means of the colony, they could not do more, and they reposed the highest confidence in His Excellency that the funds raised would be "strictly and honourably applied." To this bill the Lieutenant-Governor delayed his concurrence, in order to afford time for some requisite modifications which might render it unexceptionable. He then, after assenting to a few bills, prorogued the Assembly. In doing so, he assured the members that "in all that he had done or abstained from doing, on the present occasion, he had allowed himself to be actuated by constitutional principle alone." He intimated that when what he had reserved his assent to had undergone modification it might meet with his future concurrence.

During this session the question of education was taken up and a measure for promoting it and encouraging schools throughout the Island was adopted and passed by the Assembly, but was thrown out by the Council.

The Assembly was soon afterwards dissolved, and a general election held the same year. The new House met for the despatch of business on the 3rd November, 1818, In opening the session the Lieutenant-Governor referred, among other things, to the marriage of the Duke of Kent. Passing to local affairs, he expressed his satisfaction with the increase of industry, the great improvement in agriculture, evidenced by the abundant crops, yielding ample means of support for the Island's inhabitants and a considerable surplus for export. He assured the Legislature that whatever their collective wisdom might suggest would be met on his part with very calm consideration, "pure constitutional principles and an earnest desire to do good and to hinder evil." All this sounded very well, but, unfortunately, the views of the members of the Assembly upon constitutional principles differed materially from those of the autocratic governor.

On 5th November the House agreed to an address in reply to the speech. The address, while most dutifully expressed, severely criticised certain measures, "which were adopted here during the last winter to enforce payment of His Majesty's quit rents upon the original or old scale, and have produced the most distressing effects, particularly upon the lower classes of the community, arising chiefly from the ruinous costs and expenses thereby incurred, when it appeared to the inhabitants of this colony, by Your Excellency's proclamation, dated 1st October, 1816, that there was to be a fixed scale and a new rate of quit rents to commence."

The address further expressed the "hope that this branch of the Legislature will, at no distant period, in common with our neighbouring colonies, have a constitutional controlling power over at least part of the public monies of the Island."

The Assembly, the address proceeded, are so truly sensible of the want of good roads, that they would heartily do all in their power for their improvement, and also lamented "that the efforts of two branches of the Legislature, during the last session of the General Assembly, failed in meeting with His Excellency's concurrence, when they presented a bill, grounded, as they understood, on an Act now and for many years in force in the Province of Nova Scotia, which has rendered the roads excellent throughout that province, and which bill, besides affording us gaols in two of our counties would have highly improved the roads in the third."

They thanked His Excellency for his determination to meet their suggestions with very calm consideration, pure constitutional principles, and an earnest desire to do good and hinder evil, and, suggestively added that they were convinced that such disposition on his part would "best accord with the genuine principles of our incomparable constitution." His Excellency appointed two o'clock the following afternoon to receive the address in reply to the speech.

## DECLINING THE ADDRESS.

The following day (6th November) a message from the Lieutenant-Governor, by Mr. Carmichael, his private Secretary and son-in-law, was sent to the Speaker, in which His Excellency said that, "Desirous as the Lieutenant-Governor is, at all times, to put the best and most favourable construction upon every action of the House of Assembly, he, nevertheless, from a sense of propriety, feels compelled to decline receiving the address from them, intended to be presented this day, on the ground of its containing unconstitutional animadversions. He therefore regretted that the appointment for two o'clock of this day must stand annulled."

On 7th November the House of Representatives, in General Assembly convened, desirous of maintaining the utmost cordiality of sentiment and good understanding with His Excellency, and equally anxious that all their proceedings should be conducted with strict parliamentary correctness, and be couched in proper, respectful and constitutional language, had, with these views, taken His Excellency's message of yesterday into their most serious consideration, the result of which was that they could not find that their intended address to His Excellency, referred to in that message, contained any unconstitutional animadversion whatever, they, therefore, begged leave to request that His Excellency would be pleased to inform them when His Excellency would receive the address of this House, in answer to His Excellency's speech, delivered at the opening of this new Assembly.

The Lieutenant-Governor, in reply, lamented that they should have thought proper again to press the reception of the address which he had given so definite a reply upon. Did the objection to receiving it arise out of personal feeling alone, he would have a pleasure, and even a pride, in sacrificing it to maintain political union; but the question is far different, involving a constitutional principle of the first importance, and, therefore, a point that cannot possibly be conceded.

The Lieutenant-Governor expressed the trust that this matter would not interrupt the harmony he so much desired, and he repeated to the House the assurance of his unaltered and unalterable disposition to co-operate with them in measures for the public welfare.

The Assembly would not recede from its position, and the address was never received, the only instance, so far as the writer has been able to ascertain, of such an occurrence in the proceedings of the Island House of Assembly.

Undeterred by the fate of their address, the Assembly settled down to consider such matters as they thought to be in the interests of the province as calmly as if nothing out of the way had occurred.

However, the matter was, by no means, forgotten, and, on 20th November, it was unanimously "Resolved, that the address intended to have been presented to His Excellency the Lieutenant-Governor, in answer to his speech at the opening of this session, and the communications relating thereto, be inserted in the Prince Edward Island Gazette." Having passed this resolution the Assembly resumed their consideration of the ordinary business of the country.

A special committee to consider the public accounts submitted to the Legislature by His Excellency reported, very severely criticising some of the expenditures. They thought that the largest portion of the money spent on the militia might have been employed to more advantage on the impassable roads and bridges, for which it was intended.

A sum of £98 18s 4d had been expended in the department of the chief overseer and deputy chief overseers of roads, and the committee regretted that only the sum of £37 12s 0d had been laid out on the roads, bridges and implements for the same, when the revenue was intended to be chiefly laid out thereon.

£54 14d 5d had been paid Hon. W. Johnstone, and £7 to Hon. R. Gray, to be expended in a couple of law-suits. The committee could not, "consistent with their duty, refrain from observing that they conceived these charges to be of a most extraordinary nature, and a misapplication of the public money."

In foreign mails the committees were happy to observe that the receipts were nearly equal to the expenses, and they had great satisfaction in observing that the inland mails had been discontinued as the advantage arising therefrom was trifling in comparison to the expense.

£77 19s 1d had been laid out on the wharf in Charlottetown, and the committee conceived that this sum, together with the extravagant wharfage paid by the public, ought to have made more repairs and better improvements.

The committees were astonished to find that £316 3s 11d had been issued for which no warrants appeared, which issues, they were decidedly of opinion, were in direct violation of the Act respecting duties on wines, etc.

Finally the special committee begged "leave to remark that the monies raised by operation of the above recited Act have been the subject of much discontent and want of harmony in this colony; and an alteration in that Act, giving this House its share in the appropriation of that money, would, in the opinion of the committee, conduce in a great degree to the prosperity of the Island, and most certainly would produce in the House a spirit of liberality to meet the future contingencies of the government."

The report was agreed to. It was evident that hostilities of a pronounced character were pending between the Assembly and His Excellency.

On 8th December, 1818, the Assembly, in committee of the whole on the state of the colony, formulated a series of very grave charges against Chief Justice Tremlett,* which they presented to the Lieutenant-Governor, accompanied by an address, setting forth that the Assembly deemed it expedient that the said Chief Justice should be no longer continued in his office, and prayed that His Excellency be pleased to suspend him from the exercise of his office until His Majesty's pleasure should be known.

These resolutions are of such importance, as assertions of constitutional rights, and as showing the spirit of the people's representatives at that time, that they are worthy of being reproduced in full. Those against Tremlett were as follows:

1. Resolved, that the unnecessary extension of the sittings of His Majesty's Supreme Court of Judicature of this province, during the time Chief Justice Tremlett has presided in that Court, has been a severe grievance to His Majesty's subjects in this colony.

2. Resolved, that Trinity Term, 1814, continued for fifty-two days and only twelve jury cases were tried in that term; that Hilary Term, 1815, continued thirty-nine days and fifteen jury cases were tried in that term; that Michaelmas Term, 1815, continued seventeen days and only one jury case was tried in that term; that Hilary Term, 1816, continued forty-four days and only eleven jury cases were tried in that term; that Trinity Term, 1816, continued twenty-one days and only four jury cases were tried in that term; that Michaelmas Term continued eighteen days and only two jury cases were tried in that term; that Hilary Term, 1817, continued thirty-three days and thirteen jury cases were tried in that term; that Trinity Term, 1818, continued twenty-one days and nine jury cases were tried in that term.

*For Tremlett, see part VI. "Miscellaneous."

3. Resolved, that the duration of the terms of the said Court, in the times of the last and former Chief Justices, seldom exceeded six days, and that they were often less than six days.

4. Resolved, that the protracted sessions of the said Court have increased the expenses attending law suits, and induced the regular jurors to desert the Court in the midst of the business, rather than submit to the intolerable and ruinous attendances required of them, whereby talesmen of any description have been too frequently resorted to, and injustice to the parties has been the consequence, which has created great discontent throughout this colony and no small degree of contempt for the Court.

5. Resolved, that in consequence of Hilary Term, 1814, continuing through the whole month of July (in which month the statute labour has to be performed) many jurors and constables were fined for not performing their labour, while they were obliged to give their attendance to the Supreme Court, and in that Term the said Chief Justice kept the Court open and stayed proceedings from the 26th July until the 11th of August to accommodate two of the barristers who asked of him and obtained leave to quit the Court alternately.

6. Resolved, that in Hilary Term, 1818, the said Chief Justice did on the 18th day of that term, after all causes set down for trial had been heard, on a request made by the Attorney-General in behalf of the Acting Receiver-General of His Majesty's quit rents, agreed to keep the said Court open for the space of forty-one days longer, and did so keep it open for that period in order to enable the said Acting Receiver-General to accomplish certain proceedings in that Court under the Act of this Island for the recovery of quit rent against various lands on this Island, which proceedings were, in consequence, effected in that term, whilst the Legislature never contemplated the same as possible to be done within a shorter period than two terms.

7. Resolved, that by reason of the said last mentioned term being so extended, the said Acting Receiver-General, in the next term, being Trinity, obtained judgments against many valuable tracts of land for alleged arrears of quit rent on the old scale, and while a new scale was generally expected, that under these

judgments, so improperly and rapidly obtained, many extensive and valuable estates would, in all probability, have been sacrificed, and several of them, before the non-resident owners could be apprised of the proceedings taken and that impending ruin of their estates, by bringing them prematurely to sale, was only prevented by the most gracious Act of His Royal Highness, the Prince Regent, in lowering the rate of quit rent and ordering the proceedings for the old rate to cease.

8. Resolved, that the costs incurred for obtaining judgment, in respect of seven shillings sterling for one year's arrears of quit rent, against various town lots in Charlottetown, amounting, previous to the sale, to the sum of £7 12d 0d sterling each, reflects in the strongest manner on the Court which allowed the same.

9. Resolved, that the conduct of the said Chief Justice, in the aforementioned proceedings in respect of quit rents, was oppressive, illegal and a violent infringement upon the rights of property in this Island.

10. Resolved, that the judgments of the said Chief Justice Tremlett in the said Supreme Court have been tardy, fluctuating and indecisive, and his appointment to that high office has been, and is, a misfortune to this colony.

11. Resolved, that the said Chief Justice has brought contempt on his high judicial situation in this colony, by often sitting alone publicly to do the duty of an inferior magistrate or justice of the peace, in receiving from privates and others of the militia fines for alleged neglects of duty as such.

12. Resolved, that the said Chief Justice, in the important duty of annually nominating three fit and proper persons, one of whom to be chosen High Sheriff of this Island (which nomination is, by law, imposed on the Chief Justice) has often exercised the same illegally, by nominating persons who could not be required to serve, nor be fined for refusing; and in particular, the said Chief Justice has acted contrary to law and shown his total disregard to the welfare and internal peace of this colony by nominating the present High Sheriff of this Island, James Jackson, Esq., to fill that situation, well knowing him to be a person, who had, in last Hilary Term and before such nomination, been indicted and thereupon tried before him, the said Chief Justice, and found guilty of a most

heinous offence against the public peace, committed while the said James Jackson was in the commission of the peace.*

13. Resolved, that for the reasons aforementioned, it is unadvisable that the Chief Justice should be any longer continued in his office, which he hath proved himself at least incapable of filling with that dignity, learning, propriety and independence which are indispensably requisite in such office and that the British Constitution demands.

The report and resolutions were unanimously adopted.

The Assembly in an address of the same date declared they deemed it expedient that the said Chief Justice should be no longer continued in his office, and prayed that His Excellency might be pleased to suspend him from the exercise of his office until His Majesty's pleasure should be known.

Smith replied that the matter naturally called for his most serious consideration and speedy decision, but its importance made it necessary for him to deliberate well, before acting in any way or even giving any further answer.

The Lieutenant-Governor submitted the following notes on these resolutions.

He concurred as to first five resolutions. Then he says: "The sixth and seventh, though pointed apparently at the Chief Justice, are in reality an attack upon me. As to Court being kept open, as stated in the sixth, it was done by arrangement between the Acting Receiver-General of quit rents, the Attorney-General and the Chief Justice, who could have no motive but the furtherance of public business. The juries were dismissed so that there was no burthen of that kind upon the country and there was other business besides that related to quit rents carried on. The seventh I have desired the Acting Receiver-General to remark upon and I annex his observations.†

---

*James Jackson.— In the minutes of the Supreme Court for 23rd February, 1818, there is the following entry: The King on the prosecution of Stephen McEachern vs. James Jackson. Indictment for assault. The Grand Jury brought in a true bill, signed by Donald McKay, foreman, "for self and fellows."

The Traverser is arraigned and pleads not guilty. Ready for trial instanter. Jury sworn and impannelled. The Solicitor-General states the case for the Crown, calls witnesses who were cross-examined by Traverser. The Solicitor-General rests his case. The Traverser in person states his case and calls on the prosecutor as a witness. The Chief Justice charges the jury, who, without retiring, returned a verdict of guilty against the Traverser.

†No copy of his remarks can be found.

"I agree in the eighth resolution as to the high costs upon town lots; but it is rather remarkable they blamed the Court which taxed them, but say nothing of the Attorney-General who was to reap the benefit."

"The ninth is as unjust as it is intemperate. The Chief Justice conducted himself in strict conformity to the quit rent law. I am sorry to say I cannot controvert the tenth resolution; and I agree with the first part of the eleventh resolution for the reasons contained in the tenth and not for these assigned about the militia, on which subject I could never get him to do half what was necessary. I acquit him fully on the twelfth resolution. It is a subject on which I never had any reason to complain of him. As to the thirteenth resolution, I see as great a necessity for a new Chief Justice as they do, but I see a still greater one for a new Attorney-General, about whom they say nothing. The former may have been guilty of errors of the head, but it is the heart of the latter that is to blame."

The Assembly, on ninth December, preferred very serious charges against the High Sheriff, both in his office of sheriff and in his capacity of returning officer at the general election. The charges against the sheriff were embodied in the following resolutions:

"Resolutions on the State of the Colony re James Jackson, High Sheriff."

1. Resolved, that the evidence laid before the Committee of Privileges and referred to this committee, and also the further evidence now adduced, prove James Jackson, Esquire, the present High Sheriff of this Island, to be altogether unfit to be continued in that office.

2. Resolved, that the flagrant offence against the public peace in this Island, of which the said James Jackson, Esquire, was found guilty in Hilary Term last, has convinced the committee that he was not a proper person to have been afterwards nominated for sheriff

3. Resolved, that the present High Sheriff, having publicly, at the hustings in Prince Town, declared that he had a writ of execution against a voter and deterred him from voting, and named the plaintiff and defendant and the amount of the demand, and

having also declared that he had a writ against another voter at China Point, before either of said writs were served or executed, has been guilty of an offence which is odious in law, and therefore proved himself not worthy to hold his situation.

4. Resolved, that the said James Jackson, Esquire, High Sheriff, when acting as returning officer at the last general election has been guilty of several breaches of his duty in the following instance, to wit, at the election for Queen's county, by refusing to take the votes of Peter Robinson, Thomas Sims and Martin Heartz, previous to the poll being closed in Charlottetown.

Here follow a number of instances of improper behaviour at that election.

Ordered, that "An humble address be framed and presented to His Excellency, the Lieutenant-Governor, praying that he would be pleased forthwith to dismiss the said sheriff from his office, for highly improper conduct therein and cause a fit and proper person to be appointed in his place."

## Address.

The address to the Lieutenant-Governor founded on these resolutions, ran as follows:

"The House of Assembly, in General Assembly convened, having taken into their most serious consideration and heard evidence respecting the conduct of James Jackson, Esquire, the present High Sheriff of this Island in his official capacity, cannot refrain from declaring to Your Excellency that his conduct as High Sheriff and also before his appointment to that important office, has been dangerous to the rights, liberties, and properties of His Majesty's subjects within this Island to such a degree that this House conceive he should no longer be continued in said office.

"The House, therefore, humbly pray that Your Excellency may be pleased to remove the said High Sheriff from his official situation."

On motion to go into a committee of the whole house to take into consideration a message received from His Excellency, Mr. J. E. Carmichael, a son-in-law of the Lieutenant-Governor, came inside the Bar of the House and loudly said:

"Mr. Speaker, if you sit in that chair one minute longer as Speaker, this House will be immediately dissolved." The Speaker then asked Mr. Carmichael by whose authority. He answered, "By the Lieutenant-Governor's." The Speaker said, "Give it to me in writing." He said, "I will," and then said, "I will not. It is enough for you that you have received it." And he then retired in a most contemptuous manner.

While the House was considering the insult, the Lieutenant-Governor sent for the Speaker and, holding up his watch, said he would allow the House three minutes, before the expiration of which, if they did not adjourn, he would resort to immediate dissolution.

The House found the conduct of the said John E. Carmichael to be most unwarrantable and a high breach of the privileges of this House, and ordered that the Speaker should, forthwith, issue his warrant against him, the said John E. Carmichael, for said gross breach of privilege.

But the Assembly were not satisfied with preferring their charges against the Chief Justice and the High Sheriff. They considered that their most serious grounds of complaint were against the Lieutenant-Governor himself, and they were not disposed to overlook them, or to shirk the responsibility of formulating grievances and preferring them against His Excellency to the highest authority. Consequently, on 15th December, the House unanimously agreed upon a series of resolutions, asserting their rights and privileges, and impeaching the conduct of His Excellency. These resolutions are of much importance as showing the spirit of the people's representatives at that time as well as the very strained relations existing between them and the Lieutenant-Governor. They were as follows:

1. Resolved, that it is the undoubted privilege of this House to present addresses to the Lieutenant-Governor of the colony.

2. Resolved, that it is equally the right of this House to remonstrate or complain to His Excellency, the Lieutenant-Governor, of any public acts of his government, if it shall see it right so to complain or remonstrate.

3. Resolved, that the right of remonstrance, in its very nature, implies the right of this House to present its remonstrance to the Lieutenant-Governor and that it is his duty to receive it.

4. Resolved, that the address of this House, in answer to His Excellency the Lieutenant-Governor's speech, at the opening of the session, is loyal, respectful and constitutional.

5. Resolved, that the refusal of the Lieutenant-Governor to receive such address is without precedent, and tends to deprive His Majesty's loyal subjects in this Island of the most regular and constitutional channel through which their wants or grievances can reach the throne.

6. Resolved, that this House, notwithstanding the refusal of its address by the Lieutenant-Governor, has proceeded to the consideration of the public affairs of the Island and have passed various bills, yet it has never lost sight of its most undoubted right, which it is the duty of the House to assert and maintain unimpaired.

7. Resolved, that the refusal of the Lieutenant-Governor to receive the said address is a direct infringement of the rights of this House, and a breach of those ancient privileges which were asked for by the Speaker and acceded to by His Excellency in the usual form at the opening of the session.

8. Resolved, that a humble address be presented by this House to His Royal Highness, the Prince Regent, with a copy of His Excellency the Lieutenant-Governor's speech to it at the opening of the session, and the address of this House in answer thereto, which His Excellency has refused to receive, and also of these resolutions, and praying His Royal Highness will be graciously pleased to take such order in the matter as may insure to this House the future exercise of its rights and privileges now refused to it by Lieutenant-Governor Smith.

9. Resolved, that His Grace the Duke of Richmond, Governor-General and Commander-in-Chief of the Forces in British North America, be respectfully requested to transmit such address to His Royal Highness, the Prince Regent."

The House was then adjourned till 6th January, 1819. When it met, in that date, a message was received from the Lieutenant-Governor, stating that he had sent a copy of the address concerning the Chief Justice to the Secretary of State for the Colonial Department, requesting an early decision on the subject. With reference to the sheriff, the Assembly were certainly the proper judges of his conduct as returning officer, and he would not offer any opinion on that subject, but the Lieutenant-Governor was not aware of any impropriety committed by him as sheriff, and trusted the House would not expect him to make any change in that office until the regular annual period, now not distant.

The special committee appointed to prepare an address to the Prince Regent, in conformity with the Assembly's resolutions respecting the Lieutenant-Governor, having reported the same, the House adopted the report. The address was drawn in terms of the resolutions, a copy of which was to be forwarded with it, and closed with a prayer that His Royal Highness would be graciously pleased to adopt such measures as might secure to them the future exercise of their constitutional privileges.

It was ordered that the Speaker do, by letter, respectfully request His Grace, the Duke of Richmond, to transmit the said address to His Royal Highness, the Prince Regent.

This, however, was by no means the end of the Assembly's complaints and criticisms of Mr. Smith's conduct. They unanimously resolved "that it was a gross abuse and misapplication of the public money, on the part of Lieutenant-Governor Smith, to pay to John Edward Carmichael, Esquire, Acting Receiver-General of His Majesty's quit rents, sums of money for escheating townships numbers fifteen and fifty-five, as it appeared that the same sums had been issued without warrants, granted by and with the advice of His Majesty's Council, from the revenue of the Island, which arises by virtue of the several acts of the General Assembly passed in the twenty-fifth and twenty-sixth years of His present Majesty's reign, being directed to be laid out in making and repairing public roads and the further establishing ferries in this Island and such other uses to and for His Majesty's government as the Governor, Lieutenant-Governor or Commander-in-Chief for the time being, with the advice of His Majesty's Council, shall from time to time, order and direct."

The same day the Assembly adopted another address to the Prince Regent, requesting that he would "direct that this House may have the same control and power in appropriating the public monies of the colony as the Houses of Assembly in His Majesty's provinces of Nova Scotia and New Brunswick for many years had within those provinces, but in case Your Royal Highness in your wisdom shall not deem it proper to restore this privilege, the House humbly implores Your Royal Highness will have the goodness to meet the ardent wishes of their constituents by re-annexing this Island to the envied and flourishing province of Nova Scotia."

On the evening of 9th December, 1813, during the session of the House, the Assembly windows were smashed by Henry B. Smith, son of the Lieutenant-Governor. In the investigation ordered by the House it was clearly shown that the windows had been purposely broken. The House ordered that the Speaker issue a warrant against Mr. Henry B. Smith for wantonly, insolently and maliciously breaking the window of the Assembly Room on the evening of 9th December last, when the House was engaged in very serious business with closed doors, and the Attorney-General was directed to prosecute him for his outrageous conduct.

On 7th January, 1819, by operation of the Speaker's warrant, Henry B. Smith, acting provost marshal and naval officer,* was brought to the Bar of the House for breaking the windows of the Assembly Room in the Court House, and upon being questioned through the Speaker said, "I ups with my fist and slashed it through the window," and assigned no reason for his conduct. It was ordered that Henry B. Smith be committed to gaol during the pleasure of the House, and until he pay all expenses attending his commitment.

On 8th January, His Excellency prorogued the House without the customary address and so closed a very interesting and exciting session.

## IMMIGRATION.

During the year 1818, so stormy in a public sense, some new immigrants made homes for themselves here. Of these the fine settlement of New Glasgow was planted by W. E. Cormack, afterwards of St. John's, Newfoundland. The settlers were from the vicinity of Glasgow, Scotland. Mr. Cormack later performed a journey which, up to then, no other European had ever attempted, across Newfoundland,— a most arduous and perilous undertaking, when one considers the rugged and broken configuration of the country.†

---

*He was not of age, but a vacancy having occurred in these offices, his father, the Lieutenant-Governor, appointed Henry B. Smith to the position.

†McGregor — "Account of Prince Edward Island, p. 10 (note)."

Soon after his unceremonious prorogation of the Assembly, Smith dissolved the House, and a general election was held. Fourteen of the members of the late House were re-elected. The new House proved as independent and tenacious of its rights and privileges as was its predecessor. Dr. Angus McAulay, who was speaker in the old House, was appointed to the same position in the new. The House met on 25th July, and was summarily prorogued on 10th August.

On the 29th July, 1820, it was ordered by the Assembly that the Speaker lay before the House a communication to him, as Speaker of the late House, by His Excellency, the Lieutenant-Governor, enclosing an extract from a despatch from Earl Bathurst, dated 19th November, 1819, and the answer, if any, received from the late Duke of Richmond on the subject of the address to the Prince Regent. The Speaker, therefore, laid before the House his letter to the late Duke and His Grace's reply, and also a message from the Lieutenant-Governor to him, enclosing an extract from a despatch from Earl Bathurst, dated 13th November, 1819. An address to the Lieutenant-Governor was then prepared, requesting His Excellency to cause to be laid before the House a copy of the declaration of persons present in the House of Assembly on the 15th December, 1818, alluded to in the extract from Earl Bathurst's despatch.

On 31st July, Smith replied that: "The Lieutenant-Governor, on the most mature consideration, is of the opinion that he ought not to give any further information to the present House of Assembly than he felt it his duty to give to a former House, on a matter peculiarly relating to themselves. And feeling, also, the most anxious wish to transact all necessary public business with the General Assembly harmoniously, he is the more desirous not to enter into unnecessary retrospect, as that would certainly tend to lessen the good understanding, which he is so anxious should constantly subsist between all the branches of the Legislature."

The House, on 1st August, ordered that a committee be appointed to consider the several documents laid before this House on Saturday last, relative to Earl Bathurst's despatch to His Excellency, the Lieutenant-Governor, and also His Excellency's message of yesterday, in answer to the address of the House on the subject of the said despatch, and that the committee do report to this House thereon.

This committee reported that they found the resolutions made by the late House, on 15th December, 1818, alluded to in said despatch, were made and passed by that House, in a regular and constitutional manner, previous to an adjournment, with the consent of the House, and not by the members subsequently assembled in an irregular and unconstitutional manner, as alleged in a private declaration of persons, transmitted to Earl Bathurst; and the committee also found that the address of the late House, of the 5th January, 1819, to the Prince Regent, referring to the said resolution, was unanimously agreed to by the House, at which time Lieutenant-Governor Smith did not suggest that House to have been unconstitutionally convened. This report was agreed to by the House.

The Assembly next adopted and presented to His Excellency an address, requesting him to communicate to the House the answer, if any, received from the Secretary of State, to the address of 8th December, 1818, relative to Chief Justice Tremlett. In reply, the Lieutenant-Governor said that he had received a despatch from Earl Bathurst on the subject, bearing date 11th May, 1819, in substance as follows:

"His Lordship entirely approves of my having forborne to comply with the address of the House of Assembly, which prayed for the suspension of the Chief Justice; he remarks on the absence of the evidence against him, upon which the Assembly state themselves to have proceeded, and adds, that, unless some great and serious criminality be proved against the Chief Justice, he should consider himself bound to refuse his acquiescence to any proposal for his removal.

"Having thus made known the official reply I have received, you will feel yourselves authorized to communicate it in the most regular manner for the information of the House."

On 9th August, the House passed a resolution, on division by eleven to two, deeply lamenting "that His Excellency, Lieutenant-Governor Smith, in transmitting to His Majesty's Secretaries of State for the Colonial Department the address of the last House of Assembly, praying His Excellency to suspend the Chief Justice, did not transmit, along with the same, the resolutions upon which that address was founded, after the solemn and unequivocal manner in which that House declared their opinion concerning the

Chief Justice, upon the clearest and fullest evidence of facts adduced before them on that subject, so highly important to the administration of justice in this colony."

The Assembly, on 5th August, unanimously adopted a series of resolutions, embodying their grievances against the Lieutenant-Governor. They set out, in substance, that the House of Assembly are the sole judges of what are breaches of their privileges, and have at all times a right to complain to His Majesty of any such breach committed, or supposed to be committed, by the Lieutenant-Governor, or any other whom the House cannot bring to account by their immediate process. That the journals ought to be received by the Lieutenant-Governor as containing correct statements of the proceedings of the House.

"That the convening of the members of the last House of Assembly, and the laying at the same time before them the extract from Lord Bathurst's despatch, for their information, and then instantly dissolving them, without affording them any opportunity of making a reply, or of convincing Earl Bathurst of the facts, and also His Excellency's refusal to this House of complying with their address, requesting that he would be pleased to furnish them with a copy of the declaration of persons alluded to in Earl Bathurst's despatch, clearly evince to this House His Excellency's total disinclination fairly to enter into merits; and that he has attempted virtually to disfranchise the loyal inhabitants of this colony, by allowing the declarations of officious, unauthorized persons to be sent to His Majesty's ministers, in contradiction to the fair representations of the Legislative Assembly of this Island."

That the conduct of the Lieutenant-Governor has tended much to withdraw from him the confidence of the people. And they concluded with a resolution to present an address to the King, beseeching him to refer to the address of the last House, of 5th January, 1819, and the documents accompanying it, and also to these resolutions, and praying that His Majesty would make such order as would, in future, secure to this colony the constitutional rights of its inhabitants.

An address of the whole House, to the King, on the lines of the resolutions, was adopted, and the Speaker was instructed to request the Governor-General, the Earl of Dalhousie, to transmit it, with the documents, to His Majesty.

It was evident that the relations between the Lieutenant-Governor and the House of Assembly were becoming more strained.

The day following that on which they adopted the address to the King, the Assembly adopted the report of the committee on public accounts, which stated that, "in the application of the monies, there appear to your committee many payments which are of an unprecedented nature, but, as the House of Assembly have no control whatever over any part of the disposal thereof, your committee deem it unnecessary at present to make any further remarks thereon, more especially as the representations of former Houses on that subject have had no salutory effect."

The same day, the House adopted a resolution, deeply lamenting that the Lieutenant-Governor, in transmitting to the Colonial Department the address of the last House respecting the Chief Justice, did not also transmit the resolutions upon which it was founded, "after the solemn and unequivocal manner in which the Assembly declared their opinion concerning the Chief Justice, upon the clearest and fullest evidence of facts adduced before them on that subject, so highly important to the administration of Justice in this colony."

The House then asked to be relieved from further attendance at this time.

In his speech proroguing the General Assembly, His Excellency said: "It is impossible for me to pass unnoticed some of the proceedings of the Lower House, which have formally come to me through the copies of their Journals, which have been communicated. From them, it appears that certain resolutions, reflecting upon me, have been adopted, and an address to His Majesty framed and founded on them, which is to be transmitted through His Excellency, the Governor-in-Chief, a measure equally extraordinary and unnecessary, inasmuch as I should myself, if I had been applied to, have readily co-operated in any such measure that would have attracted His Majesty's attention to my conduct, whose faithful servant I am.

"The address in question would thus have reached the throne unquestionably much sooner, and, let me add, with more certainty, as it remains to be seen what conduct His Lordship may feel it consistent with his duty to adopt on so delicate a point as the interposing in the political concerns of a distant colony.

"Under any circumstances, my hearty and earnest desire to promote the public welfare will continue undiminished, feeling, as I trust I ever shall, superior to all party politics, and necessarily regarding with both regret and wonder those who allow themselves to be hurried away by them."

The next convention of the General Assembly was on 14th January, 1825, soon after Lieutenant-Governor Ready's assumption of the administration. In the intervening five years, Mr. Smith ruled without consulting the "faithful Commons." He appointed Mr. Ambrose Lane, his son-in-law, who had been a lieutenant in the army, to the position of Registrar and Master in Chancery, though he was not a lawyer. Another son-in-law, Mr. Carmichael, a gentleman against whom the Assembly had issued a warrant for contempt, was appointed Secretary of the province. His Excellency seemed as if he were determined to antagonize the people of the Island to the utmost. He caused the revenue to be collected and expended as seemed best to himself. He was accused of promoting litigation, with the object of making expenses for himself and his friends. He was charged with disturbing titles to lands which had been held for forty or fifty years in order to get fees for new grants, and of having by threats compelled parties who had obtained grants, while Mr. Townshend was administrator, to take out new ones, though Mr. Townshend's were perfectly good, and the forcing new ones to be taken out was only for the purpose of making costs. The feeling against the Lieutenant-Governor was rapidly nearing the boiling point. In June, 1822, a notice was posted up in Charlottetown, by J. E. Carmichael, Receiver-General (Smith's son-in-law) that that office would be kept open for payment of all arrears of quit rents due and payable within the Island. In December of the same year, he posted up another notice that payments must be made by 14th January; but due publicity was not given, nor warning as to the consequences of non-payment. In January a distress was levied on certain lands on Lots 36 and 37; then the officers proceeded to the eastern district of King's county and demanded instant payment, or promisory notes payable in ten days, on pain of their land and stock being sold. The people here were Gaelic-speaking Highlanders, with a profound respect for law, and dread of a bailiff, who, to meet the sudden and unlooked for demand, hauled their produce fifty or more miles to Charlottetown, in the winter, to redeem their notes. This influx of grain caused a glut in the market and a heavy decline in prices. These proceedings caused the utmost public indignation.

Petitions were presented to the Grand Jury, complaining of the conduct of the Acting Receiver-General and his deputies and true bills found against the latter; but no trial took place owing to the interference of the Lieutenant-Governor.

At length the leading men of the province determined to take measures to have the Lieutenant-Governor removed. Mr. John Stewart, already referred to several times, had long been the most prominent and influential man in the community, but had for some time been out of active public life. He now emerged from his retirement, and took the lead in the agitation against His Excellency. A memorial, signed by forty of the leading inhabitants, was presented to the High Sheriff of the Island, Mr. John McGregor, asking him to call a meeting of the inhabitants of Queen's county to consider the complaints and charges against the Lieutenant-Governor and to devise measures to remedy them, and also to call similar meetings, at intervals of a week, in each of the other two counties, for the same purpose.* McGregor called the meeting for Queen's county, in Charlottetown, on 6th March, 1823.

The notice or memorial, asking to have a meeting called, states that this step was taken because of a "number of respectable persons being determined to rouse the colony into a proper sense of the injuries which have been inflicted on its inhabitants from the same source." This source, of course, was the Lieutenant-Governor.

In the minutes of Council for 11th February, 1823, the Lieutenant-Governor caused to be read a letter from the High Sheriff, enclosing an application from certain landed proprietors requesting him to convene public meetings in the three counties. His Excellency asked the opinion and advice of His Majesty's Council how far under all the circumstances it would be prudent and proper to allow the proceedings in question to take place.

---

*John McGregor was then High Sheriff for the whole Island. He was a native of the Island. He later went to England and became Secretary of the Board of Trade in London and representative for Glasgow in the House of Commons. He was the author of a History of North America in three volumes, a copy of which is in the Prince Edward Island Legislative Library. He also published "Historical and Descriptive sketches of the Maritime Provinces of British America "including an account of Prince Edward Island," London, 1828. A copy of this is in the Archives at Ottawa. It is of value to the student of Prince Edward Island History.

The Councillors declared their opinion to be: "That it would not be proper for the proceedings to take place under the sanction of the High Sheriff," and therefore advised that the Colonial Secretary as such and as Clerk of the Council do make the following communication to the High Sheriff."

### LETTER TO THE HIGH SHERIFF.

COUNCIL CHAMBER, February 11, 1823.

SIR: "I am directed to acquaint and warn you that at a meeting of His Majesty's Council held this day, the subject of the public meetings lately called by you to take place at the different times and places stated in your public notice of the 6th instant, it was considered that it was not proper that the proceedings in question should take place under your sanction as High Sheriff of this Island."

J. E. CARMICHAEL,
*Col. Secty. and Clerk of H. M. C.*

His Excellency directed the High Sheriff's letter enclosing the requisition to convene meetings in the three counties to be entered on the minutes of the Board as follows:

SHERIFF'S OFFICE, February 8, 1823.

*To His Excellency the Lieutenant-Governor.*

SIR: "On the 6th instant, I received a requisition for public meetings of which the enclosed is a copy. After deliberating with much coolness upon the propriety of acceding to such a request, I found I could not (without acting contrary to the practice of the sheriffs in England and to the solemn oath I have taken) but agree to call such meetings as are asked for in the requisition."

J. McGREGOR,
*Sheriff.*

Requisition enclosed, in substance, "To John McGregor, Esq., High Sheriff:"

SIR: We, loyal subjects, free-holders and lease holders, in different parts of the Island, in the present alarming state thereof, threatened with proceedings by the Acting Receiver-General of quit rents, the effect whereof cannot fail to involve a great part of the community in absolute ruin, feel impelled (when the Island has been, nearly three years, deprived of that constitutional protection and support which might be expected from our Colonial Legislature) to call upon you, as High Sheriff, to appoint general meetings of the inhabitants to be held in the three counties, that they may have an opportunity, according to the practice of the parent country, of consulting together for the general benefit and joining in laying such a state of the colony at the foot of the Throne, for the information of our Most Gracious Sovereign, as the present circumstances thereof require. Trusting to your attachment to the general welfare, your spirit, patriotism and good sense, we do hereby call upon you, to appoint a general meeting of the inhabitants of each county, and we do also request that you will personally give your attendance at each of these meetings, whereby you will be able to vouch for the spirit of loyalty, decorum, perfect propriety, with which they will be conducted. . . .

(Sgd.) J. STEWART,
and thirty-eight others.

At a meeting of the Council on 15th February, 1823, the sheriff's reply to Mr. Carmichael's letter of the 11th was read:

SHERIFF'S OFFICE, 12th February, 1823.

SIR: I have the honour to acknowledge the receipt of your official letter of the 11th inst., stating "that at a meeting of His Majesty's Council held yesterday you were directed to acquaint and warn me that the meetings called by me at the different times and places stated in my public notice of the 6th inst., it was considered that it was not proper that the proceedings in question should take place under my sanction as High Sheriff of the Island.

"In answer to which I take leave to inform you, that in executing the duties of my office (conscious of unimpeached loyalty and integrity), I am resolved to do so according to rights with which I am invested by the laws of the Island and agreeable to the practice of England.

"I feel the utmost confidence in the objects and views of those by whom the requisition has been signed, being directed solely to an address to their Sovereign, stating the present difficulties of the colony and that the intended meetings will, on the part of all concerned in that object, be conducted with loyalty and propriety.

"I should, therefore, feel myself wanting in that regard, which every person holding my present situation owes to the interest of the colony, if I were to shrink from giving the sanction of my presence, as High Sheriff of the Island, to the intended meeting."

To J. E. CARMICHAEL, ESQ.,  
    *Col. Secty. and Clerk of the Council.*

J. McGREGOR,  
*High Sheriff.*

Which being taken into consideration it was ordered, in Council, that the High Sheriff should be superceded and that the Colonial Secretary be directed to communicate the same in the following words:

"(Dated as today)"

SIR: I am directed by His Excellency, the Lieutenant-Governor in Council, to acquaint you that you are superceded from the office of High Sheriff of this Island.

J. McGREGOR, ESQ.

J. E. CARMICHAEL,  
*Colonial Secretary.*

And that, in consequence of the foregoing supercedure, it be made known to the under sheriff, acquainting him that the whole duties of the office devolve upon him in pursuance of the Act 26; Geo. III., Cap. 15 Sec. 8.

At the meeting of 24th February the following letter from the High Sheriff was read:

CHARLOTTETOWN, 19th February, 1823.

SIR: I beg you will inform His Excellency that in consequence of a supercedias having this day been read in Court, by which His Excellency has been pleased to supercede me in the office of High Sheriff of this Island, I feel it necessary to ask that I may be made acquainted with the charge upon which I have been so superceded.

"I have also to beg that you will state to His Excellency that Cecil Wray Townshend, Esq., late Under Sheriff, never gave me any security in that office, and that I did, before the execution of the supercedias, revoke, annul and make void the Indenture by which I had appointed him Under Sheriff."

To G. S. SMITH, ESQ.,  
    *Provincial Secretary.*

JOHN McGREGOR,  
*Late Sheriff.*

The Council were of opinion that no answer to this letter was necessary, and that it did not appear necessary that the public notices for meetings should be annulled.

On 8th April, His Excellency informed the Council that, notwithstanding the admonition given the late Sheriff McGregor, certain public meetings, convened by him, had taken place and that various offensive resolutions had been alleged to have passed at such meetings which, it is understood, are to be sent home to His Majesty's Government. Upon which His Excellency was urgently advised to convene a Council for the express purpose of considering the present political state of the colony, which, necessarily, is considerably augmented by the circumstance of its being currently reported that certain law officers have been concerned in the drawing of the resolutions in question, which material fact is most highly requisite to be investigated in order that due notice may be taken of such conduct should it have actually taken place.

At a meeting of Council held 6th May, 1823, Mr. Hill was sworn in as High Sheriff. The Chief Justice informed him that it was proper that the circumstances should be made known to him, which had occasioned the removal of Mr. John McGregor, the late High Sheriff, from the office of sheriff, and which was in consequence of his conduct with respect to certain public meetings convened in this Island.

His Excellency then gave the High Sheriff the following admonition:

"Mr. Sheriff,— The circumstances under which you are called to your present office clearly point out the caution that is necessary in every public measure that you may have occasion to adopt.

"The attempts that have been made, and are making, to traduce and caluminate this Government cannot be unknown to you, but principles of public duty must now induce you carefully to avoid lending yourself in any measure or degree to persons capable of such conduct. Let me solemnly warn you to beware of such mis-guiders of the public mind and at the same time to express my confident reliance that you will not, on any point, allow yourself to be influenced by the public leaders or more secret advisers of faction; let them, in their individual capacities, carry their own accusations, wherever their presumption may lead them, but let not any officer belonging to the Government be an aider or abetter of those who endeavour to bring it into odium or contempt.

"Execute the duties of your office, sir, with steadiness, propriety and impartiality and confidently rely upon my support as long as you may deserve it."

At the Charlottetown meeting, the complaints and charges were formulated in a series of resolutions of great length, expressed with clearness and remarkable vigor. They repeated and elaborated all the charges and complaints that had been preferred by the House of Assembly in the last sessions, and the meeting expressed their high approval of the conduct of the Assembly. The charges against the Chief Justice and the former High Sheriff were set out fully. His Excellency's refusal to accept the address in reply to his opening speech, from the Assembly, in 1817, was scathingly denounced. The expenditure of public money in unwarrantable ways, in costs to the Governor, his son-in-law and others, as well as in ways other than those for which it was intended, were fully set forth. In short, all the charges previously made in the Assembly, and many additional ones, were included and amplified in the resolutions of the meeting which, it was resolved, should be embodied in a petition to the King, with a prayer for redress, and for the removal of the Lieutenant-Governor from his said office in this Island.

Messrs Stewart, McDonald, Mabey, Rollings, Dockendorf, Owen and McGregor were chosen a committee to act for the country. They were instructed, first, to embody the resolutions in an address to His Majesty, King George IV, concluding with a prayer for redress, and the removal of Lieutenant-Governor Smith; second, to send the same around the county for signatures; third, to transmit the same to His Majesty.

The meetings for the other counties were duly held and passed resolutions, differing somewhat, but to the same effect.

The committee had the address largely signed, and it was published in full in the Prince Edward Island Register, in September and October of the same year.

A charge against Smith was, that he, as Chancellor of his own Court, had sanctioned heavy and vexatious additions to the fees since the appointment of his son-in-law, Lane, as Registrar and Master. On the pretence that this was a gross libel and contempt of the Court of Chancery, he on 14th October, 1823, immediately on the publication, on the complaint of Lane, commenced action against the Queen's county committee to manage the Address to the King, all the members of which, except Mr. Stewart, were served with attachments issued by him as Chancellor out of the Court of Chancery and committed to custody. Mr. Stewart only got notice of his proposed arrest two hours before the officers arrived to arrest him. He escaped to Nova Scotia with the petitions and proceeded to England.* Smith then determined to impose heavy fines on the other members of the committee, but public feeling was so incensed that he decided discretion was the better part of valour and delayed proceedings. The publisher of the Register, Mr. J. D. Haszard, was brought before the Chancellor, but, upon giving a full explanation of the publication, he was discharged by the Chancellor with a severe reprimand.†

The report of the attachment appeared in the Register of 25th October, and in the same number appeared the following:

"We understand that Captain John Stewart has gone to England to lay the petitions of this Island before His Majesty."

The other six members of the committee had been arrested, but Mr. Stewart escaped and went to England, where he presented the Address before the proper authorities.

His six fellow members were brought before His Excellency, as Chancellor, on Mr. Lane's charges of contempt. The hearing lasted for several days in a crowded court house. The proceedings

---

*The writer has been told by descendants of Mr. Stewart that he escaped by being carried on board a schooner in an empty cask.

†In July, 1823, Mr. J. D. Haszard published in his paper, the Prince Edward Island Register, all the proceedings. He was forthwith haled before the Court of Chancery charged with contemptuous libel of the Court and its officers. He was asked if he would disclose the authors of publication, which he did. They were Messrs. Stewart, McGregor, Mabey, Dockendorf, Owen, Rolling and McDonald. Addressing Mr. Haszard, the Chancellor said: "I compassionate your youth and inexperience; did I not do so, I would lay you by the heels long enough for you to remember it. You have delivered your evidence fairly, plainly, clearly, and as becomes a man; but I caution you, when you publish anything again, keep clear, sir, of a Chancellor! Beware, sir, of a Chancellor!" and Mr. Haszard was discharged. This was one of the last of Smith's public exhibitions of tyranny. His reign was rapidly closing in. On 21st October, 1824, Colonel Ready arrived to succeed him, and was hailed with acclamations by the people. An address was also presented to Smith, on his departure for England, signed by the members of Council, principal officers of Government, and two justices of the peace. He left no regrets among the people over his departure.— Campbell, History of Prince Edward Island.

JOHN STEWART

and arguments of counsel were of great length, and were reported very fully in the Register newspaper. On the close of the hearing, the accused demanded that judgment should be given and the penalty inflicted at once, but the Chancellor decided to take time to consider, and they were allowed to go free until called upon, or, in a word, they were let go on suspended sentence. Nothing further, so far as the writer has seen, was done in the matter.

The Chancellor suspended the Attorney-General (Johnston) for speaking in Court, when members of the Committee, who had been brought to the Bar, had been ordered into custody, without being allowed the privilege of being heard, except by petition. After this Governor Smith remained within the barracks gates, apparently inactive as respected the local affairs of the colony, until he left the Island, after the arrival of his successor, Colonel Ready.

On the 24th of the following July (1824), the Register contained a copy of the following notice:

DOWNING STREET, May 22.

"The King has been pleased to appoint Lieutenant-Colonel John Ready to be Lieutenant-Governor of Prince Edward Island, in the Gulf of St. Lawrence, in the room of Charles Douglas Smith, Esq., resigned."

So ended a very interesting constitutional episode, or series of such episodes, in the history of Prince Edward Island.

The Register of 24th October announced the arrival of Colonel Ready to assume the government. He came in the brig John, Captain Chantier, twenty-eight days from Bristol. He at once proceeded to the barracks, the residence of the late Lieutenant-Governor, where he was received by Mr. Smith and the members of His Majesty's Council.

Mr. Stewart came out in the same ship. The Register is careful to express the "grateful feeling that prevails towards Mr. Stewart, our active and energetic envoy, to whose promptitude, exertion and ability we are in great measure indebted for the gratifying and auspicious event which has resulted from his mission to England and which we hail as a new and happy era to this hitherto much neglected, though naturally highly favoured Island."

Mr. Archibald arrived on Sunday, the 21st November, and was sworn in as successor to Chief Justice Tremlett.*

### RESPONSIBLE GOVERNMENT — CONTROL OF EXPENDITURE.

The Assembly vigorously insisted on their right to control supplies, and in this same session, on 24th March, 1825, Mr. Speaker, in presenting the revenue bills, delivered the following address to the Lieutenant-Governor. . . .

"It becomes my duty to state, in behalf of His Majesty's faithful subjects, the House of Representatives, that they have granted their supply, at present, chiefly from the high consideration in which they hold Your Excellency's character, and in the fullest belief that the produce of the revenue will be faithfully applied to the objects for which it has been granted, and when I state to Your Excellency that it appears to us, upon the fullest consideration of the subject, that the revenue, for a long series of years, antecedent to your happy arrival among us, has been grievously misapplied, I trust, under the circumstances, Your Excellency will not be surprised, when I state on this occasion that the colony looks forward, with much anxiety, to the period when Your Excellency may feel yourself at liberty to give your assent to an annual Act for appropriating the whole of the revenue, a boon which will give the highest satisfaction, and be long and gratefully remembered."

Mr. McGregor, writing of this period, gives very interesting information regarding agriculture and the social customs of the people, from which the following has been extracted.

### AGRICULTURE.†

Wheat is grown in abundance and has been frequently exported to Nova Scotia. . . . "With more attention, vast quantities might be raised and manufactured into flour for the

---

*Archibald was a leading lawyer in Nova Scotia. While Chief Justice of Prince Edward Island he never resided there. It was understood, on his appointment, that he should be permitted to reside in Nova Scotia. This is shown by the following reply, made 11th February, 1825, by Lieutenant-Governor Ready, to an address from the Assembly on the subject:

"Gentlemen,— I am not aware that it was communicated to me officially, but on Mr. Archibald's appointment to the Chief Justiceship, I was informed that it was with the understanding that he should have permission to reside in Nova Scotia."

For Archibald, C. J., see part VI, Miscellaneous.

†Account of Prince Edward Island, p. 51 and seq.

West India market. Winter wheat has been found to answer well, but the inhabitants seem careless about its cultivation. . . . Barley and oats thrive well and are, in weight and quality, equal to any met with in the English market and superior to what are produced in the United States.

"Both summer and winter rye produce weighty crops and are not liable to casual failures. Its cultivation, however, is not much attended to. Buckwheat will grow and ripen well, but there is scarcely any raised.

"Beans always produce a certain and plentiful return. . . Peas sometimes yield fair returns, but are not a regular and secure crop. . . . Potatoes of a kind and quality equal to the produce of any country are raised in great quantities and are exported to the neighbouring provinces and sometimes to the West Indies.

"Flax is raised of an excellent quality, and manufactured by the farmer into linen for domestic use. This article might be cultivated extensively for exportation. . . . All the culinary vegetables common in England arrive at great perfection.

"Cherries, plums, damsons, red and white currents, ripen well and are large and delicious."

The wheat and oat harvest commences generally after the first of September; "some use a cradle for cutting their grain and, afterwards, make it up in sheaves and stooks. The common way is to reap and lay it up in sheaves, and then stook and gather it in the same manner as in England." . . .

## Domestic Animals.

"Milch cows, and such horses and cattle as require more care than others, are housed in November, but December is the usual month for housing cattle regularly. . . .

"From want of due regard to rearing and breeding pigs, one-half the number on the Island are tall long-mouthed animals, resembling greyhounds nearly as much as they do the better kind of hogs."

With regard to domestic animals in the Island, the writer has extracted the following from a very interesting manuscript by Mr. Charles C. Gardiner of Charlottetown, now in the Dominion Archives at Ottawa. Mr. Gardiner has long been recognized as an authority on live stock in Prince Edward Island, so that anything in that line from his pen cannot be other than interesting. Mr. Gardiner writes:

"It does not appear by any records that I have had access to, that for many years after the Island was captured by the British, there were any domestic animals imported to the colony, but that the horses, cattle, sheep and swine, found here on the arrival of the Loyalists were the breed originally bred and owned by the French Acadians, and were the same description of animals that can be seen, at the present time, in some districts in the province of Quebec.

"It is evident, however, that considerable improvement must have been made in the cattle kind, for in 1818, at the Market House in Charlottetown, a veal was sold that was reared in the vicinity of Charlottetown, three weeks old, well lined and covered with fat, weighing one hundred and forty pounds. The notice appearing of it, at that time, says: 'This instance fully shows what attention and skill can produce, if applied by the industrious husbandman.'

"As early as 1811, improvement in matters pertaining to agriculture must have been engaging the minds of some, for in that year a Farmers' Society meeting was advertised to be held on the 23rd April, at Thomas Robinson's Long Room, Charlottetown, when officers would be chosen, and of which J. B. Palmer, father of the late Chief Justice Palmer, was the president.

### Forest Fires.*

"Great and serious injury to the country, and loss to individuals, have been caused by allowing fires to spread through the woods. Whole forests, on thousands of acres, have been, in this manner, destroyed; and the land by remaining uncultivated is impoverished by heavy crops of tall herbs, (called fireweeds), with white, yellow and lilac flowers, which spring up the first and second years after the woods are burnt, and exhaust the soil more than two crops of wheat would. Wild raspberries and bramble bushes spring up also and cover the ground, after the second and third years, as well as young birches and other trees.

*McGregor.

"These fires present, at times, the most sublime and grand, though terrific and destructive appearance. The flames are seen rushing up the tops of the trees and ascending an immense height among the tremendous clouds of black smoke, arising from a whole forest on fire; the falling trees come down every moment with a tremendous crash, while the sparks are flying and crackling, and the flames extending to every combustible substance, until it be quenched by rain, or until it has devoured everything between it and the cleared lands, the sea or some river.

### Careless Cultivation.

"The general system of cultivating the farms all over the Island is so careless and slovenly, that it appears astonishing that so many of the settlers raise a sufficiency to support their families. Composts are rarely known, and different manures that would fertilize the soil are also disregarded. In many of the bays, rivers and creeks, several banks of *mussel mud* abound. . . . These form an extremely rich manure, containing about forty-five parts of the carbonate of lime, and known by experience to impart fertility, for ten or twelve years, to the soil. Seaweed, which is thrown on the shores in great quantities, especially on the north side of the Island, is another excellent manure, particularly for barley; and even the common mud, which abounds in the creeks, may be applied to advantage. It is pleasing, however, to observe that a better mode of cultivating the soil, and a superior system of management have begun among the farmers. This arises from the force of example, set by an acquisition of industrious and careful settlers from Yorkshire in England and from Dumfrieshire in Scotland.

### Society.

"As there are scarcely three families in the town (Charlottetown) who come from the same part of the United Kingdom, and as the grades in which they moved, as well as their education and habits, must have been dissimilar, it follows that a considerable diversity of manners is observed among them.

"During the administrations of Governor Patterson, General Fanning and Governor DesBarres, the best circle of society in Charlottetown was allowed to be elegant and respectable and, however much the members who compose it might have differed in their views and opinion, as regarded the political affairs of the colony, they did not allow either to interfere with the public amusements or the private acts of hospitality. Indeed, the politeness and attention with which respectable strangers were received, became proverbial. During the course of Governor Smith's long administration, those social and kindly feelings which united society, became, unhappily, weakened in proportion as the number of its respectable members gradually diminished; some of whom left blanks, at that period particularly difficult to be filled up.

"The appointment of Colonel Ready will likely have on society, as well as on public affairs, an agreeable and useful influence, and an increasing population, together with liberal encouragement given education, will produce beneficial effects. . . .

### Amusements.*

"The amusements of Charlottetown, although not so extensive, are much the same as in Quebec and Halifax. During winter, assemblies are held once a month or oftener. There is an amateur theatre. Picnic parties are common in summer and winter. Dinner parties were at one time usual, but have not been so for some time past. The principal gentlemen in Charlottetown generally dine together at one of the hotels, on the anniversaries of the titular saints of the three kingdoms, as well as during the sittings of the Colonial legislature and of the Supreme Court. Skating, fishing and shooting are other sources of pleasure. A public subscription library, on a liberal and respectable footing, affords a variety of entertaining and standard works. Almost every householder keeps a horse, and driving during winter is a favourite amusement of all classes.

### Pursuits of the People.†

"When travelling through the settlements we discover the inhabitants to consist of Englishmen from about every county in the Kingdom; Scotchmen, who, it is true, predominate, from the

---
*McGregor, p. 66.
†McGregor, p. 68.

Highlands, Hebrides and the southern counties; Irishmen from different parts of the Emerald Isle; Acadian French; American Loyalists, and a few Dutch, Germans and Swedes.

"The English farmer does not reconcile himself so readily as the Scotch settler does to the privations necessarily connected, for the first few years, with being set down in a new country . . . and it is not till he is sensibly assured of succeeding and bettering his conditions that he becomes fully reconciled to the country.

. . . The American Loyalists, are, in general, industrious and independent in their circumstances, extremely ingenious, building their own houses, doing their own joiner work, mason work, glazing and painting. The men make their own shoes, their ploughs, harrows and carts, as well as their sledges; the women spin, knit, and weave linens and coarse woollen clothes for domestic use.

### Winter Employment.*

"The farmers are employed during winter in attending to their cattle, threshing out their corn, cutting and hauling home firewood for winter use and a stock of fuel for summer.

"The low price of rum and the vast numbers of houses, along all the roads, which retail it, form the most baneful evil connected with the country, and is the grand cause of any wretchedness that may be met with.

### Churches.

"The first place of worship built in the Island directly in connection with the Kirk of Scotland, stands at Pinette River in the centre of the Selkirk settlements. It has been built about two years. A large church, connected with the Kirk of Scotland, was commenced, about two years ago in Charlottetown, and will soon be finished.

"Besides that, in Charlottetown there is another English church at St. Eleanors, a handsome building lately erected.

"The Roman Catholics have a large chapel at St. Andrews, where Bishop McEachern resides. He has, with the Catholics of this Island, those of New Brunswick, Cape Breton and the Magdalens Islands under his care. There is a handsome Catholic

---
*McGregor, p. 75.

church at Charlottetown and about twelve others in different settlements. The free exercise of all religious opinions is tolerated and the Roman Catholics alone are precluded from being members of the Assembly or voting at elections. This disability, it is hoped, will soon be removed.*

## Lands for Settlers.†

"Not more than thirty thousand acres are at present held by the Crown. Woodlands in convenient situations may, however, be purchased for from five shillings to two pounds per acre, and leases in perpetuity, or at least what amounts to the same thing, for nine hundred and ninety-nine years, can be obtained at the annual rent of one to two shillings per acre and, in some situations, for less. So that, taking into consideration the advantages of residing in the vicinity of a well disposed society; of the opportunity that is afforded of having the younger branches of a family instructed in the rudiments of education; of roads communicating between all the settlements; corn-mills and saw mills being almost everywhere in the neighbourhood; and having the benefit and convenience, by living near shipping ports, of ready markets for the produce of the land or the sea, it may reasonably be concluded that the terms upon which lands can be had in this Island are more favourable than in any part of the States or Upper Canada."

## Walter Johnstone's Letters.‡

"Being all ready on 18th April, on board the Brig Diana of Dumfries, we sailed next morning at four o'clock, from the foot of the river Nith. All the passengers, forty-five in number, later became more or less seasick. On the 28th day we saw American land, supposedly the south side of Cape Breton, but the fog was so thick we could only discern the shore, and had to stand out to

---

*It was removed in 1830, two years after McGregor wrote.
†McGregor, p. 80.
‡Letters descriptive of Prince Edward Island by Walter Johnstone, a native of Dumfrieshire, written in 1820 and 1821, published at Dumfries in 1822.
On the title-page the author has a note, in which he states that he went out for the express purpose of surveying Prince Edward Island and collecting information on the subject of emigration. During two summers and one winter he was anxiously engaged in the prosecution of this object. He states that his small volume will be found to contain a particular account of the climate, soil, natural productions and mode of husbandry adopted in the Island; together with sketches of scenery, manners of the inhabitants, etc., etc., the whole being intended for the guidance of future

sea and steer backwards and forwards on the Banks of Newfoundland for eight days. When it cleared, passing Cape North, we entered the Gulf of St. Lawrence. On Friday morning we made Prince Edward Island about nine o'clock, rising like a dark cloud from the bosom of the ocean. Approaching the shore we discovered little clearances here and there, next the houses. About three o'clock we were so near as to require a pilot. Three young men came in a canoe cut from a solid tree. Their dress consisted of jacket and trousers, all of Island manufacture, like Scotch blanketing, home-dyed blue. They wore moccasins and, upon the whole, had rather a rough appearance, but discovered great agility, polished manners and spoke English as fine as Londoners. This was Three Rivers. Next morning we entered Murray Harbour and were comforted by the appearance of the settlement, not large but regularly settled and cleared a considerable way back from the water's edge. Their manner of fencing with wood has rather an uncouth appearance to the eye of a Briton. We saw some Indian females cross us in two canoes of birch bark, whose dress had a curious appearance at a distance."

He describes them fully and gives this description of the squaw's hoods: "The females wear a hood made of blue cloth; they take a piece of cloth in the form of a half sheet of large paper, overlapping two of the corners, in the way that grocers make up their papers to wrap small parcels in, and placing this upon their heads with the long tapering point uppermost, and the two loose corners hanging down at each ear, they have a very grotesque appearance."

Writing from Charlottetown, 20th October, 1820, he says that he finds nothing so much lacking as money and good ministers. He then goes on to describe the woods and the appearances of the country. He begins by observing that the country is one entire forest of wood, distinguished by the natives as soft wood and

---

emigrants, particularly as to what implements and necessaries it might be proper to provide themselves. It may be added that Johnstone was not an educated man. These letters are addressed to Rev. John Wightman, minister of Kirkmahoe, Dumfrieshire, by whom they were edited and published. Johnstone was clearly a very observant man well versed in agriculture. His pamphlet consists of nine letters covering about seventy pages. The writer has deemed it well to insert in the text a somewhat full epitome of this pamphlet as he knows of no means that would bring the condition of the Island, the state of its people, before his readers, more clearly than a description of this kind given by a shrewd observer. The letters were written about the middle of Lieutenant-Governor Smith's regime, but are inserted at the end, so as not to break the sequence of events in the struggle between Smith and the Assembly. The first letter was dated Murray Harbour, May 30th, 1820.

hard wood. Each of these embrace a great variety of kinds, such as oak, ash, elm, beech, maple, birch, alder and poplar, and many other kinds which rank among the second division, while white pine, hemlock, spruce, var, juniper (larch), rank among the former.

"The whole Island, when viewed at a distance at sea, looks as if there were not a tree on it. The trees grow so close together, and are so equal in height, that in spring their dark colour resembles heath; but upon a nearer approach to the shore, the wood assumes the appearance of strong growing hemp, for it is everywhere, in the southern parts of the Island, choked with spruce round the shore, as thick in proportion as hemp will grow. . . . Round the greater part of the Island the flowing tide washes the bottom of a steep bank of various heights, from four to more than twenty feet, and where the greater part of this bank is not solid rock the sea is wasting the bank in exposed situations considerably. . . . Of all the different kinds of wood upon the Island, the beech, when growing separate by itself, is the most beautiful. The ground it occupies is the freest from underwood, or anything to obstruct one's way, while in summer it furnishes the most delightfully refreshing shade over the head of any I have met with. The land where it abounds, is the easiest cleared, both as to the cutting, burning and rotting of the stumps, and the land, when cleared, is reckoned the second best in quality of any on the Island. A mixture of hard wood, with a small portion of soft in it, is next to beech in beauty, easiness to clear, and is also indicative of the best land on the Island. Hemlock, a kind of fir that is split into laths in Scotland, grows in clumps. Some of it is found of an amazing size, being from two to three and a half feet in diameter, and from fifty to seventy or eighty feet high, with a few puny, mutilated branches near its top. These trees are exceedingly heavy to cut and pile and very difficult to burn. The stumps will stand undecayed in the ground twenty or thirty years, before they can be easily eradicated. The soil congenial to the production of this kind of wood may be reckoned the third in quality on the Island; yet, in backward seasons, it will surpass any other description of soil in the quality of grain it produces. Pine, which we call Scotch fir at home, is not found but in detached trees, here and there in the woods, and is now all cut everywhere near to the shores. Spruce and var fall next to be noticed. The ground naturally productive of these may be ranked as the worst in quality of any in the Island. It is all of a swampy nature; that is, a soil with much of the white sand I spoke of upon the surface and a red clay below, of such an adhesive nature as not to allow the wet to get down to a proper depth. . . . Barrens: These have few or no trees upon them, but are covered with a kind of shrub they call myrtle, which over-runs the surface like heath, but resembles galls that grow in the mosses in Scotland. This land is very dry and sandy, and in its present state well deserves the name it obtains. It would be easily cleared, but would require much dung or good soil to make it productive. But except in the neighbourhood of St. Peters there is little of this upon the Island.

### Forest Fires.

"When fire gets hold of woods much mixed with soft wood, it runs sometimes several miles and forms in its progress, I am told (and I partly saw it), one of the most awful scenes in nature; flying when the wind is high with amazing rapidity, making a noise like thunder, and involving the neighbourhood in a dense cloud of smoke. . . . More than sixty years ago a great fire was kindled on the north side of the Island, it is said by a spark from the pipe of an Indian, which over-ran the greater part of the northern shore. The ground it over-ran is still discernable, being all sprung up of spruce, var, and white birch of, apparently, forty or fifty years growth. But burnt woods are to be seen in the neighbourhood of almost any settlement, some of them of considerable magnitude."

### Detailed Description of the Island.

On 30th July, 1821, Johnstone writes: " . . . I have now travelled over the greater part of the Island on both the southern and northern shores, from East Point as far west as Bedeque on the one side and Malpeque or Princetown on the other. I have also crossed over the Island from the one shore to the other at four different points and traversed much of it several times over. . . . The soil of the whole Island has been thrown up by water; it is, therefore, very fine and nearly all of one kind and quality and is laid upon a bottom of red soft freestone, which, in some parts of the shores, rises no higher than the level of the sea and in other parts not so high. But where it does rise to a considerable height on the shores it is so soft and loose in its contexture that the frost and tide are wasting it in exposed situations considerably. . . . The land is low and level, but there is little of it a dead level. . . . There are gentle rising grounds, but no high hills, at least none deserving the name of mountains.

"I shall proceed round the shores beginning at East Point. After leaving this Point a little on the south-east side of the Island, the sea has receded from the land a good way, where a large sand-ridge is found upon the back of it, when the tide comes and goes by an entrance a considerable way to the southwest. This is called East Lake. Another lake to the west of this is called West Lake. The land bordering on these lakes is good, and lately settled from Perthshire. The scenery is beautiful and romantic but it is far from market. . . . After we leave these lakes the land is thinly settled, and the woods, at present (1821), much infested with mice; but when the lands are more cleared, this evil will be less prevalent.

"The next place is called Colville Bay on the map, but 'Souris,' or 'Mice,' by the French. The next is Fortune Bay, a beautiful old settlement, with a good deal of clear land on it, and a number of schooners belonging to it, which trade to Newfoundland, Halifax, etc. . . . There is excellent herring fishing here in the month of May, and the people attend from a considerable distance with their nets to catch them. The next place we come to is Cardigan Bay or Three Rivers. This is the best harbour on the Island. It has the greatest depth of water, easiest of entrance, the best sheltered, earliest open in spring and latest in shutting in the fall or winter. One of the three principal towns projected by Government, called Georgetown, is intended to stand here. . . . A small house or two is all that it can yet boast of. To the west of this, about twelve miles, we come to Murray Harbour, which may be entered, it is said, by vessels of nearly three hundred tons burthen, at high water. This is a very pleasant, thriving and comfortable settlement. . . .

"From the shore a little west of Murray Harbour, at a place called 'White Sands,' across the Island to Savage Harbour, on the north shore, it is about thirty-five miles more. . . .

From White Sands to Wood Islands there are several miles of excellent front land, unsettled. Passing Woods Islands, we come to Belle Creek, Flat River, Jenyn's River, or Prinnet (Pinette). After passing this we come to Point Prim. On the north side of this, Orwell Bay runs into the land a long way. On the south of it the settlements of Belfast, the settlers are Highlanders and mostly Protestants, with this Bay, Pownal and Hillsborough Bays, all connected, the Island is much cut up. At the head of Hillsborough Bay we enter the river of the same name, and the harbour of Charlottetown. . . . On the northwest side of this river, about four miles above its junction with the Bay of the same name, stands the beautiful town of Charlottetown, with its streets all regularly laid out. . . . There is a large square in the middle of the town, where the Court House, the High Church and Market House stand with plenty of open ground for drilling the militia, executions, etc., etc.

"As we pass out of the harbour's mouth along shore towards the west, there are few settlers till we come to a place called Disabble (Desable); then to Crappo (Crapaud), where small vessels load with timber. . . . A little to the west is Tryon River, a very small river but the prettiest settlement in the Island. . . . The clearances are long and regular, the arable land rising gently behind the marshes and both dry and convenient for all the purposes of agriculture. Here the Island begins to narrow as we proceed on the Cumberland Cove, Augustine Cove, Cape Traverse and Seven Mile Bay, and a little further west a large Bay called Halifax Bay intersects the Island on the southern side, and Richmond Bay on the north, so that, I believe, the Island is not more than three or four miles in breadth between the head of one bay and the other."

"The head of this bay is divided into two branches, one of which is called Dunk River and the other Wilmot Cove. Around these is Bedeque, which is truly an excellent, well-cleared settlement. The settlers, however, are both ignorant and indolent farmers, and much of the land is running wild and barren under their management.* Bedeque has a good harbour for shipping.

"A little to the west, Cape Egmont juts cut and recedes to a cove beyond it of the same name. West Cape, half way down it,

---

*This description would not apply to the Bedeque of today.

and Cape Wolfe still farther. But it is all unsettled here, as it is all round the west end of the Island. But at the North Cape I have been told there is a farm under such good management that it is the most productive of any on the Island. From this the land is all unsettled till we come to Cascumpec or Holland Bay. . . . Here are great ranges of sand-hills along the shore. . . . We next come to Richmond Bay, which is very large and spacious, with good anchorage for ships of heavy burden. . . . On the west side of this bay there is a good settlement on Lots 13, 14 and 16. On the eastern side of this bay is Malpeque or Princetown, intended as the third county town on the Island, though not a single house of it has hitherto been built. The lands round it were long since settled, and the firewood is nearly all destroyed and far to haul. To the eastward we have a long track of shore, without any harbour, till we arrive at New London, where schooners can enter. The land here is good and there are large clearances. A little way from there, we come to Great Rustico or Harris Bay, which is said to admit only small fishing schooners. The next settlements are Brackley Point and Little Rustico or Cove-Head, which are old and good clearings, though the harbour will admit only small schooners. To the east of this a little way we come to Tracadie, or Bedford Bay. This is also an old settlement, mostly peopled with Roman Catholics. No large vessels can enter here. . . . The next place is Savage Harbour, which is of little importance in any respect whatever. . . . A little to the east we come to the bottom of St. Peters Bay, which runs in a slanting, easterly direction about ten miles into the country.

"This was the principal seaport at the time the French were masters in the Island; but the entrance has now become narrow and difficult, and will only admit small craft. From the entrance to this Bay to Surveyor's Inlet or North Lake, near East Point, a distance of thirty-five or forty miles, there is no place of shelter for vessels of any kind whatever. The shore is settled all the way and the land cleared a considerable way back. The settlers are Highlanders from Long Island and Roman Catholics. They raise large and good crops here, having plenty of kelp driven in upon the shore to manure the land with, but their knowledge of agriculture is very deficient. . . . I have now completed my route round the whole Island, for this inlet is very near East Point whence I set out.

## Roads.

"The road to St. Peters is the most public, best finished road in the Island. When it leaves Charlottetown it is broad and spacious. Subdivided farms, under decent management, are to be seen as we pass on to Mr. Wright's mills. Here is a flour, oat and barley mill, threshing machinery, brewery and distillery. When we reach St. Peters, the road turns to the right and along the south side of St. Peters Bay, passing over three separate rivers on wooden bridges, one of which is one hundred and forty-five yards long. At the head of the bay it separates; one branches to the right crosses over the Island, by five houses, to the Bay of Fortune, the other to the left to the northern shore, along which it winds its way to East Point.

"Another great road leaves Charlottetown for Malpeque, from which the roads lead off on the right to Great Rustico and New London, and on the left to Tryon and Bedeque. A few years ago this road was forty miles long through continued wood, without a house to shelter or refresh the weary traveller. It is now settling fast, and several houses are opened, furnishing accommodation for both man and horse. Another road from town leads across the North River in a westerly direction, passes on by the head of West River, Desable, Crapaud and Tryon. One branch then, on the right, penetrates through twelve miles of wood, to Bedeque, which is now rapidly settling; and the other branch on the left to Cape Traverse and Seven Mile Bay. A fourth road from town leads across the Hillsborough river on a regular ferry, and, proceeding in an easterly direction through Lot forty-eight and part of forty-nine, a branch takes off on the right, by Cherry Valley, across Orwell Bay to Belfast, Flat River and Wood Islands. The main road passing through the remainder of Lot forty-nine, to the head of Vernon River, divides, one branch to the right leads to Murray Harbour through seventeen miles of woods, without a house. Here are crystal brooks that never freeze, with the best land along their banks upon the Island. The other branch on the left leads through eleven miles of wood to Georgetown or Three Rivers. There is excellent land in the middle of this wood and settlers are beginning to pitch their tents upon it.

## The Inhabitants.

"The settlers generally live long and are exceedingly healthy. Allow me to make a few remarks about the inhabitants themselves. I must say they are a motley mixture of almost all nations; yet, various as the countries from which they have emigrated, and the customs prevalent in each of them, they are remarkably assimilated here into one form of living, dress, general conduct and manners. Some of them were driven from their native homes by misfortune, others by their vices, and a few were allured by the flattering hopes of obtaining great possessions, riches and splendor, but whatever was the cause of drawing or driving them hither, they are all placed on a level and taught one lesson namely, that *if they wish to eat they must work*.

## Hospitality.

"The people are hospitable in the extreme. Any man may travel from one end of the Island to the other if he keeps out of taverns, without being at one-half penny of expense. If his entertainers' portion be sometimes scant, still it may be said he gives it with a good will.

## Children.

"The children here thrive uncommonly in infancy and in general are as big and stout at twelve months old as those in Scotland at fifteen or sixteen. As their bodies grow faster in youth than there, so the vigour and strength of their minds appear to grow in proportion. I was told by a teacher from Scotland that the children here would learn as much in school in three months as they would do at home in twelve. At the age of ten years they have the freedom of speech, and the fortitude and boldness of a Scottish boy of twenty. As the women here are uncommonly fruitful, and few children die in youth, the families, of course, are many of them large, and as it often happens that the older branches marry at a very early period and shift for themselves, — that is they take a new farm and enter it,— the youngest son, in this case, falls to be possessor of his father's clear farm.

## Dress and Food.

"Their dress is mostly of homespun, duffles, stuffs and druggets, dyed blue. When they have a web to thicken, as they call it, they collect a dozen girls or more to perform the operation; and after it is over the young men assemble and a merry night is made of it in drinking, dancing, and making up of matches. Their food consists, commonly, of wheaten bread, potatoes, codfish, herrings and pork, with tea of some kind or other, or milk.

## Shell-Fish — Mussel-Mud.

"They have great numbers of lobsters, oysters, and various other kinds of shell-fish and some seals. There are great banks of mussels in several of the rivers. The stuff (mussel-mud) found in these banks, when laid upon the land, brings the best crops of any I saw on the Island, and to have some of these mussel-banks near one's farm is a great advantage.

## Live Stock.

"The black cattle are degenerating in size and weight. One of the old settlers told me the oxen, since he came to the Island, were decreased in weight over two hundred pounds. . . . The swine also have degenerated very much. . . . Their sheep, also, would be the better of being improved in the breed.

## Fish.

"Of the finny tribe, I begin with the herring. No sooner is the ice cleared out of the rivers and bays in the spring, than great shoals of herring rush in to many of them in various parts of the Island principally on the north and eastern sides. The settlers catch them with nets and barrel them up for family use, all the year round. But herring and potatoes are poor feeding at the best, and their herrings, caught in the spring, are poorer in themselves than those of Scotland.

"The next that make their appearance are a very small kind of fishes, about the size of one's finger, called smelts. These are driven in upon some of the shores with the tide in such amazing numbers that with a drag-net one might fill several barrels with them during one tide. The cod-fish follow these and next make their appearance, and the people continue fishing them the whole summer over, a little way from the shore, with hooks and lines. They make oil from their livers which they burn in lamps for light in the winter.

"Mackerel also occasionally visit the rivers and bays. There are a few salmon in some of the rivers (although I never saw any caught, except by the Indians), and a smaller kind of fish called salmon-trout are caught in several places, I thought them the finest eating of all the fish that they had. There are also bass, haddock, sturgeon, perch, flounders, eels, tommy-cods, alewives, etc. Many of the natives prize the eels above all the other fish, but I never ate them with a good relish, though they are certainly the fattest and strongest fish in Prince Edward Island.

### Exports and Markets.

"They export live stock of all kinds, grain and potatoes, to Newfoundland; and grain, pork and potatoes to Miramichi, and grain and potatoes to Halifax. . . . The Islanders enjoy a privilege which many of the labouring classes at home cannot at present obtain; they may all be employed in cultivating the ground; and the ground, I have heard it said, is so very grateful that no man ever yet bestowed prudent labour upon it but it repaid him for his toil. . . . If, instead of going a-fishing, fowling or making timber, they were to repair to the shores to collect kelp and sea-weed, to the mussel-beds for what they call *mussel-mud*, or to the woods to gather ferns to rot them down to manure, and to the sides of their marshes, to throw up compost hills, in all these ways they might provide good manure for their land.

### Compares Upper Canada, Nova Scotia and New Brunswick.

"Upper Canada has a richer, stronger soil, but it is far from markets, both for imports and exports; and in many parts of it they have no good water. Besides, almost every one that goes there takes the fever and ague; and other fevers, which they call the lake fever and common fever, are also prevalent. . . . New Brunswick, including St. John and Miramichi, has a soil, in general, more sandy and light, except a long way up St. John's River, than that of Prince Edward Island. Nova Scotia and Cape Breton have timber as heavy as it is upon the Island, and after that is cleared away, the stones found upon many parts require as much labour as the wood to clear the soil and make it fit for agriculture; and the grain and potatoes are seldom so good in their quality as upon the Island, and much oftener a failing crop is to be expected from the injurious nature of the fogs and blighting damps. And as the Island has the most pure and beautiful air, water of the very best quality in numerous springs, or at no great depth to sink for, a dry pleasant soil for cultivation when once cleared of the timber, almost the whole of it sufficiently fertile for all the purposes of agriculture, and seldom a failing crop but when the cultivator has himself to blame for it,— its local situation the most convenient for trading in all directions, and none of the inland parts far from the shore, protected on all sides from the rude incursions of a foreign foe, and requiring only more settlers, more mechanics of every kind more clearances, better roads and bridges, oat and barley mills, etc., to render it as pleasant a place to live in as the climate will admit of."

## PART V.

### CHAPTER V.

## LIEUTENANT - GOVERNORSHIP OF COLONEL JOHN READY.

#### 1824-1831.

IN Prince Edward Island the name of Colonel John Ready, Lieutenant-Governor of the province for 1824-1831, must ever be held in honour. He was not long in winning the confidence and respect of the people. During his first summer here he visited almost every section of the Island. He made the public interests his own; acquainted himself with the country and its needs. With energy and ability he devoted himself to the work of building up and improving the province. Not by precept alone, but by his own example and active exertions, and largely at his own expense, he led the way in promoting the Island's welfare. He was a grandfather of Lord Milner, famed in South Africa and Egypt as well as in the wider concerns of the empire. Colonel John Ready, after his return to England, became a major-general in the British army and Governor of the Isle of Man, which position he held at the time of his death.* He encouraged agriculture, which he saw must be

---

*He had two sons. The elder, Colonel Charles Ready, after commanding the 71st Highlanders (now the Highland Light Infantry) in the Crimean War, settled in Canada. He married Miss Ellen Hincks, daughter of Sir Francis Hincks, very prominent in the public life of Canada before and at the time of Confederation. A number of Colonel Charles Ready's descendants now live in Canada. Two of these, great-grandsons of the Lieutenant-Governor, joined the Berkshire regiment in the British army early in the late war. One of them was killed in Flanders. The other, also a John Ready, very young when he joined, served with distinction, gaining the M. C. and D. S. O. for personal gallantry. He attained the rank of captain, serving right through the war to the end, when he returned to Canada where he is now living.

The Lieutenant-Governor's younger son, Colonel John Ready, was also a soldier. He served in the Afghan War of 1878-1881 as major in the 66th (now the Berkshire regiment), which he afterwards commanded. His two sons, Colonel Basil Ready, and Major-General Felix Ready (C. M. G., D. S. O.), who was Adjutant-General of the army in Mesopotamia during the late war, reside in England.

Lieutenant-Governor Ready had three daughters, the eldest of whom died of consumption in Charlottetown and is buried in the Old Protestant cemetery in Elm avenue. The second was the mother of Lord Milner. The third married a Mr. Pollock Henry and died without issue.

LIEUT. GOVERNOR READY

the staple industry of the Island. To improve the stock, he imported from England, for breeding purposes, some of the finest animals that have been brought here. He gave an impetus to the profession of agriculture, which it has never lost. More than once he visited all parts of the Island, informing himself of its capabilities and wants, and at the same time making himself familiar with the condition of the people, and gaining a first-hand knowledge of their needs.

Shortly after his arrival he caused a general election to be held. The Legislature was convened on 14th January, 1825. In the opening speech His Excellency gave, as his reason for so soon calling the members together, the need of revising and continuing such beneficial acts as had expired, or were about to expire, and for considering such other measures as were necessary for the welfare and good government of the Island. He announced his intention, when the season permitted, to make himself personally acquainted with the state of the Province.

Much useful legislation was enacted at this session. Among other matters, the Legislature took up and enacted measures for the encouragement of education; for the preservation of oysters; for regulating juries; for regulating pilots; for regulating the fisheries of the Island; for preventing injuries from improper burning of woods (a very live question in Canada to-day); for providing revenue; for regulating the performance of statute labour. A large sum, from the small revenue, was devoted to roads and bridges. A bill to prevent the importation and circulation of base copper coin was introduced, but, on the motion for a third reading, got the six months hoist. This matter has been referred to elsewhere. It has an interest in itself, as indicating the difficulty experienced owing to the want of proper circulating currency.

A curious case of treatment of an obnoxious petition occurred on the 7th February, when, after reading a petition on behalf of the inhabitants of Lot Eighteen, it was ordered that it lie on the table. The Attorney-General moved an amendment, that it be thrown under the table; and the amendment carried.

The House went carefully into the expenditure since 1820, severely criticising many of the items. The various grievances and complaints against the late Lieutenant-Governor, against the registrar of the Court of Chancery, and the proceedings before referred to, were gone into fully and submitted to His Excellency. The Assembly took up the trade and commerce of the Island. They called attention to the Act of the British Parliament, regulating trade between His Majesty's possessions in America and the West Indies, and between other places in America and the West Indies, whereby the monoply of colonial trade had been relaxed, and a more extensive market opened to the commerce of the British possessions, greatly to the benefit of the neighbouring colonies, each of which has one or more ports from which the free trade may be carried on, but no port in this Island is named in the Act, whereby this colony is deprived of this commerce; and begged His Excellency to bring the matter to the notice of the Secretary of State with a view to having one or more Island ports thrown open to this trade. They suggested Charlottetown, Three Rivers and Richmond Bay as the ports which would most benefit the trade of the Island, by being made free ports.

The House was prorogued 24th March, 1825, and met, in its second session, on 12th October of the same year. In the meantime Colonel Ready had endeavoured to make himself fully acquainted with the state of the Island, and had visited almost every part of it. On opening the session, he congratulated the Legislature on the increasing industry and tranquility he had everywhere witnessed.

## Appropriation Bill.

The struggle between the Assembly and the Council with regard to the expenditure of public funds came up, in an intensified form, at this and subsequent sessions during Colonel Ready's term of office. On 25th October, 1825, the Council agreed to the Appropriation Bill, but, while doing so, ordered the following protesting resolution to be handed to the Assembly by the Clerk of the Council. It was read and ordered to be placed on the journals of the House.

Council Chamber, October 27th, 1825.

"On motion, it was ordered, that the following resolution be entered upon the Journals of this House, and that a copy thereof be sent down to the House of Assembly with the Appropriation Bill.

"His Majesty's Council have been induced to give their assent, at this time, to the Appropriation Bill for A. D. 1826, from the consideration that the session is now near a close and great inconvenience might be experienced by the colony were we to reject it, although there are several appropriations and clauses contained in it which are deemed very objectionable; but His Majesty's Council wish it to be understood, in future, that, while they will at all times earnestly endeavour to give effect to the measures of the House of Assembly, they will also be disposed to exercise their right of deliberating separately upon every measure for which provision is to be made in the Appropriation Bill, from any moneys raised, or to be raised, by virtue of any other Act or Acts of the General Assembly, and that His Majesty's Council will not, in future, be disposed to give their assent to any bill for appropriating such moneys unless the several sums and services therein contained shall have been previously submitted by the House of Assembly, in separate resolutions, for the concurrence of the Council, and shall have severally received their assent."

In the following session* the Assembly defined their position as follows:

"All supplies to be raised or charged on the subject in this Island, in the Legislature, and granted to His Majesty, are the sole gift and grant of the House of Assembly; and all Bills for granting such aids and supplies ought to begin with the Assembly; and that it is the sole right of the Assembly to direct, limit and appoint, in such Bills, the ends, purposes and limitations of such grants, and that the Council ought not to alter or change the same; and in like manner, that as it is the sole right of the Assembly to originate Bills of Aid and Supply to His Majesty, and to direct, limit and appoint, in such Bills, the ends, purposes and limitations of such grants, so it is the right of the Assembly to direct, limit and appoint, in separate bills, the uses, ends and limitations of such grants of aids and supplies to His Majesty which ought not to be changed or altered by the Council."

On 10th April, 1827, a committee of the Assembly appointed to confer with a committee of the Council touching the resolution of 27th October, 1825, reported that "they had asked a committee of the Council whether the Council had adhered to their said resolutions, inasmuch as a knowledge of their determination might

---
*Journal, 27 March, 1827.

materially influence the Assembly in passing Supply; . . . And that the sole purpose of the Conference was to learn whether the Council did, or did not, adhere to their resolutions of 27th October, 1825."

The committee of Council said a reply would be given without delay, and the same day the following answer was given to the committee of the Assembly:—"That the committee of His Majesty's Council, having reported the subject matter of their former conference, with the committee of the House of Assembly, His Majesty's Council had directed the committee to state that they see no reason to induce them to deviate from the principle expressed in their resolution of 27th October, 1825;" and the Council refused to pass three of the revenue Bills.

### Reject Appropriation Bill.

The next session, that of April 28th, 1828, a conference was held with a committee of the Council on Appropriation Bills. The speaker informed the committee of Conference that:—"The House orders the committee appointed to confer with the committee of His Majesty's Council on the Bill of Appropriation to enter into no discussion with them on any items of appropriation, and to inform the committee that any attempt to do so will be deemed an encroachment on the rights of this House, in matters of supply."

On 29th April, the Council again refused to pass the Appropriation Bill.

On 30th October, 1827, Right Honourable William Huskisson, His Majesty's principal Secretary of State for the Colonies, wrote the Lieutenant-Governor:—"You will do well to express to His Majesty's Council the regret with which I learn that they have thought fit, now, for the first time, to act upon a claim of at least doubtful right, which has been more prudently suffered, hitherto, to lie dormant, and which, in its nature, it is not very easy to reconcile to the principles of the British Constitution." This despatch was not laid before the Assembly until 1st May, 1828.

The Assembly, addressing the Lieutenant-Governor, say, that "as His Majesty's Council have been pleased to assign their reasons for the adoption of so unusual a course as intercepting His Majesty's supplies for the use of the Island, and thereby stopping all the public works so requisite in a new country, this House cannot but express its entire dissent from a measure so replete with impolicy and so entirely at variance with the best interests of the colony."

On the same day the Assembly, by message to the Council, expressed their regret that the misconstruction attributed to its Speaker, of the unauthorized communication between him and His Honour the President of His Majesty's Council touching the appropriation, should have taken place, and should have induced His Majesty's Council to tax the House of Assembly with making an unfounded statement, a charge which the House is of opinion might, with more justice, be applied to the statement of His Majesty's Council. This message was sent up by Mr. Owen. The Council in reply sent a message to the Assembly to acquaint them that the Council decline transacting any further business with that House until the message sent up by Mr. Owen be expunged from their Journals.

The following day the Assembly sent a message in reply, in which they say:

"The Assembly cannot but regret that His Majesty's Council should have so far forgotten what is due to the Assembly, and indeed to themselves, as to demand from this House that it should expunge from its Journals that or any other record of its proceedings; a demand equally intemperate and unparliamentary, and one with which the Council never could have hoped that this House should comply, still less ought His Majesty's Council to have expected a compliance with any demand accompanied with a threat to this House.

"The House of Assembly holds it a duty it owes to itself, and the country it represents, to tell His Majesty's Council that its demand is rejected, and that its threat has had no other effect on this House than to create a feeling of regret and mortification that His Majesty's Council should have hazarded a proposal to this House so derogatory to its rights and privileges."

At the same time they presented an Address to the Lieutenant-Governor setting forth the splendid progress made since he arrived here, which would be checked or stopped by the proceedings of the Council in stopping supplies.

In the following session (27th March, 1829,) a committee of Council to confer with the Assembly, expressed the regret of the

Council that a cause of difference, originating in a personal misunderstanding, should have given rise to feelings which have ultimately so seriously involved the harmony of both Houses as to have produced a cessation of business. . . . To renew a good understanding, without which no public good can be effected, the Council propose, in order to promote this desirable end, that the original cause of the existing difference, comprised in the application of the House of Assembly for an Appropriation Bill, together with the whole of the recriminatory resolutions, be expunged from the Journals of both Houses, a system of compromise, the adoption of which the Council conceived, could not be deemed inconsistent with the dignity of either body.

On 29th March the Assembly refused the Council's proposition, but declared themselves as "willing and desirous that the past should be forgotten, and that they were ready to proceed to the despatch of business in conjunction with His Majesty's Council as if the unhappy differences had never existed."

Henceforth during Colonel Ready's Lieutenant-Governorship, nothing occurred to mar the harmony existing between the two Houses. The Lieutenant-Governor, in his opening speech at this session, closed with a strong appeal to both Houses to adjust their differences in the interests of the colony. It may be assumed that it was to his influence that the renewal of good relations between the two Houses was due.

It seems curious that the "Act declaring that baptism of slaves shall not exempt them from bondage," passed in 1781, was not repealed until this session, having remained a blot on the statute book for forty-four years.

A petition from the Roman Catholic inhabitants for the right to vote at elections for the House of Assembly was brought up on the 20th October, but, owing to the advanced state of the session, was deferred until the next, "when the same ought to have, and is entitled to, the serious consideration of the House."

The Assembly, during both these sessions, gave much consideration to the improvement of means of communication. They urged the extension of the roads and their widening and improvement. In the Lieutenant-Governor they found a man able and willing to forward their views to the utmost.

During the recess, immediately preceding the session of the General Assembly which met on 20th March, 1827, Colonel Ready had spent much time in England, where he had interested himself intelligently and practically in the welfare of the province. While there he had purchased a number of valuable horses, cattle and sheep, which he imported to the Island, and which did much to gain for this province the high reputation it long held for good live stock. Though His Excellency himself, in his speech, did not refer to this matter, yet the Assembly, in their reply, recognized its value, and expressed their appreciation of its importance to this province.*

Into his speech the Lieutenant-Governor breathed an optimistic spirit. He mentioned his strong impression of the improving state of the Island. Referring to the improvement in internal communication since last session, he said:

"The western line of road has been completed up to Prince Town. Surveys have been made for the purpose of carrying on this line to Cascumpec and the North Cape, its final object.

"The roads to Georgetown, the Bay of Fortune, and other settlements, have undergone material improvement."

Reference was made to the benefit that would be afforded by an inland post. He strongly recommended the formation of an agricultural society. Encouragement to a commencement of Georgetown and Prince Town was recommended, especially the former, as being particularly eligible for a fishery. He also congratulated the Assembly upon an increased revenue.

The House of Assembly, by resolution, asserted its sole right to originate and grant supplies, and to limit and direct the ends and purposes of such grants, which ought not to be changed or altered by the Council.

The petition of the Roman Catholic inhabitants, which had been brought up in the last session, was brought up again, and the

---

*In these importations the thoroughbred stallion Roncevalles, and the mare Roulette, were brought to the Island. The former was famed in the early equine history of Prince Edward Island. It may interest horsemen of the present time to know the pedigrees of these two animals. The Register of 30th May, 1826, had the following: "In our last we noticed the landing of a horse and a mare imported from England by the Lieutenant-Governor for the purpose of improving the breed in this colony. The horse, Roncevalles, is thorough-bred, English; stands fifteen hands three inches high, colour dark bay with black legs. He was got by Skiddow out of Parisot, by Dragon out of Young Flora, sister to Spadilla by Highflier, Flora by Squirrel, Angelican by Snap. Skiddow was got by Gohanna out of Catherine (sister to Colibu), Gohanna by Mercury; Mercury by Eclipse.

"The mare, Roulette, is by King of Diamonds out of a Soothsayer mare; dam by Sir Peter out of Lucy, by Florizelle, out of Frenzy, the dam of Phenomenon."

following resolution was now moved:—"Resolved, that it is the opinion of this House that the right of voting at elections of members to serve in the General Assembly ought to be extended to His Majesty's subjects of the Roman Catholic religion within the Island, and that the election laws should be altered conformably to this resolution."

This resolution was lost on the casting vote of the speaker, John Stewart. Mr. Stewart was personally in favour of it but voted contra on the ground that it had not yet been settled in England, and on the further ground that a constitutional point of such importance ought not to be settled by a bare majority formed by the Speaker's casting vote.

### INLAND MAILS.

The Assembly took up the matter of inland mails, and recommended His Excellency to take such steps as he thought proper to have an inland mail to Prince Town at least once a week in summer, and once a fortnight in winter, returning by Traveller's Rest (Kensington), where a postmaster might be appointed, thence by Bedeque and Tryon River to Charlottetown, and also towards East Point and to Three Rivers; and that this House would make good, in a future session, any expenses attending the same. This seems to have been the beginning of the Island's internal mail service, with its numerous mail routes and offices. The postmaster of Charlottetown was directed to open a number of post offices and to establish the necessary courier routes. The system began operations on the 1st July following. The western route was ninety miles in length, the eastern over one hundred miles and the southeastern fifty-three miles.

### POST OFFICE IN PRINCE EDWARD ISLAND.*

"The earliest period in which we find a postal service in operation in Prince Edward Island, is 1801 (Quebec Almanac, 1802, p. 11). John Ross is mentioned as postmaster in that year. He was succeeded by Benjamin Chappell, in whose hands and those of his family the postmastership remained for over forty years."

---

*This account of the early Post Office in Prince Edward Island is taken from "The History of the Post Office in British North America, 1639-1870," by William Smith, Cambridge Press. Mr. Smith has very kindly allowed the writer to make such use as he saw fit of this very excellent History.

The system, or want of system, of bringing mail matter from England to the Island was the cause of much dissatisfaction. In November, 1802, the Assembly placed their grievances before the Lieutenant-Governor in the following address:

"We, having considered the various miscarriages, to which letters and parcels addressed to persons on this Island are subjected, owing to their being enclosed in the Halifax mail and left in the post office there, exposed, from whence they have been committed to the custody of any individual willing to take charge of them, by which means they have frequently been lost or intercepted, humbly request that Your Excellency will be pleased to represent to His Majesty's Secretary of State the above insecure and uncertain mode of conveyance of letters from England to this Island, and request that he will be pleased to direct that a separate mail or bag be made up and enclosed at the post office in London, directed for the postmaster in this Island and forwarded in the packet with the Halifax mail at the usual periods."

In this connection the following extract from a letter, dated 1st March, 1807, from Lieutenant-Governor DesBarres to Chief Justice Caesar Colclough, then in Halifax, throws much light on the inconvenience suffered by people on the Island owing to the irregularity of the mails.* "Nearly five months have elapsed since a line from England had reached this Island; judge then how comfortable any intelligence from these will be to us. In this view chiefly, the Indians, who, with my public despatches, carry this, are lured to proceed in an ice-boat to the Nova Scotia shore and thence to Halifax, where they are to deliver the bag of letters to Mr. Charles Hall, merchant, there, who will put the letters in a course of being forwarded to their address. Mr. Hall is requested by the postmaster of this place, at my instance, to collect all the letters and packets, directed for this Island, for which purpose the Indians will be kept in waiting during four or five days at Halifax, by whom such bag of letters, as may be made up, will be brought thither. Allow me, therefore, my dear sir, to entreat the friendly co-operation of your kind offices in the promotion of this object, and believe me to be, etc., etc., etc.

J. F. W. DesBarres."

---

*Col. Correspondence for Prince Edward Island 1807, Vol. 19.

"The connections with the mainland and the mother country were maintained for some years by such vessels as happened to visit the Island. The postal service of the Island was within the jurisdiction of Nova Scotia. It was not, however, until 1816 that the Deputy Postmaster-General made any mention of the Island service in his reports to the General Post Office in London."

He then informed the Postmaster-General that when Lord Selkirk was in Nova Scotia, some years before (1803), that nobleman urged upon him the necessity of a courier service to Pictou and thence to Prince Edward Island by packet. This service was established in 1816, and an arrangement was made with the Island Government by which the postage was to be applied, as far as it would go, to maintain the packet and pay the postmaster's salary, and the Government would make up the balance.

"There were no accounts between the Island post office and the General post office. The postmaster simply presented to the Deputy Postmaster-General periodical statements of postages collected and his expenses, together with a receipt for the deficiency, which was paid by the Government. This arrangement had the immense advantage that from the very first the Island service was in the hands of the Local Government, which carried on the post office with no more than a formal reference to the General post office. The postage from Charlottetown to Halifax was eightpence."*

"A post office was opened in Charlottetown in the beginning of the nineteenth century, and until 1827, it was the only institution of the kind on the Island."

"Letters remained in the post office till called for."

## Capes Mail Route.

In the winter of 1829-1830 an attempt, made to send mails by Cape Traverse, was found more expeditious and safer than by the old Wood Islands route. Hence this route was followed until the establishing of winter steam communication after the Confederation of the Canadian provinces.†

The sole right of the House of Assembly to initiate money bills and control supply again came up. A lengthy correspondence

*Smith, 185 and seq.
†Sutherland.

between the House of Assembly and the Council took place, the former steadily insisting upon its rights, and the latter claiming that, under the instructions to Governor Patterson, under which the House of Assembly was constituted, that House did not, exclusively of the Council, possess the right claimed.

Perhaps the most important Act of this session was one for taking the census, being the first of its kind in this province. All previous estimates of population were mere estimates and not to be relied on. On taking the census under this Act the population of the whole Island was found to be 23,473, considerably more than was supposed, while Charlottetown could boast of 1,649 inhabitants out of the total. The expense of taking this first census, as shown by the public accounts submitted to the House the next session, amounted to £163, surely a very moderate sum for such a work. At the same time the costs of the inland mails, which were established by His Excellency, by virtue of the resolution of the House already referred to, amounted to £75 12s 9½d.

## The Agricultural Society.

This society, formed on the earnest suggestion of Lieutenant-Governor Ready in his opening speech to the Assembly in 1827, did, for many years, a most useful work in the interests of agriculture. Importations of pure bred animals, from time to time, wrought a great improvement in the Island live stock. At the same time it imported seed, grain and roots for the renewal and improvement of the kinds already on the Island. Branch societies were formed at St. Eleanors and Prince Town, which were most beneficial in promoting agricultural operations along lines similar to those adopted by the parent society. Mr. McGregor, writing of this period says:—"Governor Ready has since (since the second session of 1825), been in England, but has again returned to the Island; the improvement and prosperity of which appear with him paramount to every other consideration. The roads all over the Island have been widened and made fit for carriages. New bridges have been erected and old ones repaired. The House of Assembly have appropriated money for supporting schools in the settlements. Agriculture and the breeding of cattle are encouraged, and what has been effected in so short a time proves how much might have formerly been done, without any expense, but the proper application of the colonial revenue."*

### APPROPRIATION BILL.

In his speech to the Legislature on 5th March, 1829, the Lieutenant-Governor expressed the great pleasure he had in stating, as well from his own personal observation as the information he had received, that every useful branch of industry is steadily advancing. The revenue has increased, affording a considerable surplus beyond the receipts of last year. . . . The fisheries, so long neglected, appear to be reviving; a branch of industry of the first importance as well to the agricultural as to the commercial interests, opening a market for the produce of the farmer and furnishing the means of a most valuable export.

Public schools are increasing in number under the operation of the present School Act and their beneficial effects are most sensibly felt. The Act, however, as it relates to the organization of classical schools, appears susceptible of improvement, with the view of opening to the youth of the colony the means of receiving a more extensive course of instruction.

"The rejection of the Appropriation Bill last session has caused much embarrassment in the administration of the Government and impeded the advancement of the colony. . . . I cannot but express my sincere hope and expectation . . . that the first moments of your sitting will be occupied in an earnest endeavour to bring the unfortunate misunderstanding of last session to an amicable adjustment. . . . To bring matters to this end a system of united compromise appears to me the best mode for both parties to pursue."

Writing to Sir George Murray a few weeks later he expresses his very great satisfaction that the misunderstanding of the last session had been adjusted and that both branches are going on with the public business in much harmony.

### EDUCATION.

As far back as the session of March, 1790, Fanning, in his opening speech, said:—"Sensitive as we all must be of the rapid

---
*McGregor,— Sketch of Prince Edward Island.

improvement of the agriculture, and the success of our fisheries, the extension of commerce and the increase of our inhabitants in this Island, it becomes my indispensible duty, in obedience to His Majesty's royal instructions, *to recommend to you the expediency of entering upon some methods for the erecting and maintenance of schools, in order to the training up of youth to necessary knowledge of the principles of religion and virtue.*" The House cordially endorsed his recommendation.

In 1796 Lieutenant-Governor Fanning again called the attention of the Assembly to the great duty they owed to the present rising and succeeding generations,"of making some provision and endowment for the permanent establishment of a public school or academy for the better education and instruction of the youth of this Island."

In November, 1798, "An Act for raising a revenue for erecting and maintaining Public Schools in this Island," passed the Assembly but was thrown out by the Council.

In July, 1801, Fanning again urged the making provisions for the erection and endowing of a public school or academy, . . . and that some provision be also made for the erection of a school house and apartments for the residence of a school master for the time being.

The same day Mr. Stewart introduced a bill for raising a revenue for erecting and maintaining public schools and for empowering the Lieutenant-Governor to appoint trustees and directors of said schools. This was rejected in committee. Mr. Stewart then moved to bring in a similar bill for Queen's county alone, which met with the like fate.

In March, 1803, Mr. Douglas brought in a bill for the encouragement of schoolmasters, which was ordered to stand over till the next session.

In July, 1817, a bill for promoting education and encouraging schools throughout the Island passed the House but was rejected by the Council.

And in July, 1820, Lieutenant-Governor Smith said that "A commencement is about to take place, without delay, of a system of necessary education, on the National plan, highly conducive to the interests of the rising generation, and which will be supported on my part in every feasable degree that the pecuniary means at my disposal may be considered equal to."

The Act for the establishment of an academy in Charlottetown became law in the session of 1829. The Act empowered the Lieutenant-Governor to incorporate certain Government officers, two members of Council, and three members of the House of Assembly as trustees of a classical academy to be established in Charlottetown, declare the salaries and number of masters to be employed, branches to be taught therein and the powers and authority of the trustees.

Owing to inability to raise a loan for building the academy, it did not come into actual use until 1836, when it was opened as the Central Academy. It fulfilled the purposes of its creation excellently well. In 1860, on the visit of His Royal Highness the then Prince of Wales (afterwards Edward VII) the name was changed to Prince of Wales College, which it still bears, where the good work of the old academy has been continued and widened out, with the result that it has a reputation second to none in Canada for institutions of its character and scope.

About the same time St. Andrew's College was founded, by the Right Reverend Angus Bernard McEachren, first Roman Catholic bishop of Charlottetown, a man equally honoured and respected by those of his own flock and by the Protestant inhabitants of this Island.

The new college was opened on St. Andrew's day, 30th November, A. D. 1831. It was under the patronage of the Bishop of Charlottetown and was presided over by Rev. Edward Walsh, a learned Irish priest, the college's first rector. It was, subsequently, moved to Charlottetown, and, with a changed name, developed into the splendid educational institution, known far and wide as St. Dunstan's College.

In the session of 1828, His Excellency called attention to the agricultural improvement, which exceeded that of any former period, both as regarded the proper cultivation of the soil as well as the improvement in horses, cattle and farm stock of every description. The public accounts submitted during this session show, to the great pleasure of the House, an expenditure of £277 8s 9d toward the support of schools in the Island. The committee expressed their trust that every encouragement might be afforded to so desirable an object.

## MILITIA.

In June, 1829, His Excellency transmitted to the Secretary of State in charge of colonial affairs, an address from the Assembly praying for a proportion of arms and accoutrements for the militia. "The militia," wrote the Lieutenant-Governor, "musters at present 5,400 men. We have, also, two very good companies of artillery of seventy men each, and a troop of cavalry of forty; which would be increased to fifty, provided they were furnished with swords and pistols. There is a very good spirit in the militia, at present, and, if provided with arms as is the case in Nova Scotia and New Brunswick, they would clothe themselves and become, in a very short period, a body equally respectable as those of the neighbouring colonies."

The session of 1830, which opened on 4th March, was the sixth and last of this House of Assembly. The increased cost of education, as evidencing the anxiety of the people to avail themselves of its advantages, was referred to with much satisfaction in the Lieutenant-Governor's speech. But the great subject mentioned in the speech was the conferring by the Imperial Parliament upon His Majesty's Roman Catholic subjects those rights and privileges which had been previously alone enjoyed by his Protestant subjects, and his calling upon the Legislature here to relieve the Roman Catholics of the disabilities they laboured under. This Act was passed, and inequalities which should never have been introduced into the New World were done away with.

This Assembly had been a most active and useful one, and had enacted a large amount of valuable legislation. It was composed of a superior class of men, several of whom possessed abilities much beyond the common, and were also possessed of a thorough knowledge of their constitutional rights. The great struggle for responsible government made immense headway during the terms of Lieutenant-Governors Smith and Ready. With the former, the struggle was against unconstitutional and arbitrary power, despotically wielded by the individual who administered the government. In the latter case, it was against the oligarchic council, which, quite irresponsible, arrogated to itself powers and privileges properly vested in and belonging to the representatives of the people. The Assembly, well aware of its rights, and well led, asserted and maintained its position with firmness and dignity.

Its work was difficult at best, but it was rendered much less onerous, than otherwise it would have been, by the assistance derived from the wisdom and conciliatory policy of His Excellency Lieutenant-Governor Ready.

Summary of the Island's position at end of Lieutenant-Governor Ready's Term (1831):*

### REVENUE.

The revenue of the Island amounted, in 1830, to £4,709 5s 8d, independently of the Parliamentary Grant (British) of £2,820. It is derived principally from an impost of ten pence currency, per gallon, on all wines and spirituous liquors, and two pence on ale, porter and strong beer imported into the Island.† . . . There was at this time an Act of the Legislature, before the Privy Council, for raising a revenue by an assessment on land for the purpose of building a Government House and other public buildings.
. . .

### MILITARY ESTABLISHMENT.

The garrison of this Island consists of a captain, subaltern, and forty-three rank and file from the garrison of Halifax, Nova Scotia, who are relieved every year and are no expense to the Island. A sergeant and five gunners of the Royal artillery are also stationed here. There is a town major and deputy ordnance store-keeper.

### JUDICIAL ESTABLISHMENT.

The judicial establishment consists of the Chief Justice, whose salary is voted by Parliament (British). He has no other emoluments, and an assistant judge, who has no salary or other emolument. This latter gentleman is not a professional man. The Supreme Court sits three times a year. There are no circuits. The Lieutenant-Governor presides in the Court of Chancery.

---

*Archives, Colonial correspondence.
†The drink bill of the Island at this time was enormous and was a heavy handicap to the progress of the colony. In the year 1825 there were imported into the province fifty-four thousand gallons of rum; two thousand five hundred gallons of brandy; three thousand gallons of Geneva and two thousand gallons of wine. The population was twenty-three thousand. Imports were valued at £85 337s 0d and exports at £95 426s 0d. It is, but fair to point out that some of this huge importation of rum was taken in part payment for small vessels, a considerable number of which were annually built for and sold in Newfoundland. Some of this was resold for export. Still, making every possible allowance, the drink bill was enormous.

## Ecclesiastical Establishment.

The ecclesiastical establishment consists of two clergymen, one stationed at Charlottetown and the other at St. Eleanors.

There is no parsonage house and the church is in a most ruinous state. A subscription has been entered into for building a new one — but it is feared there will not be enough funds raised to carry on the undertaking. The majority of the inhabitants are either Roman Catholics or dissenters. . . . There is a new church nearly finished at New London, but without a clergyman. The rector of St. Eleanors officiates there every second Sunday.

## Education.

There are three grammar schools in the Island,—at Charlottetown, Georgetown and Prince Town,— the masters of which are appointed by the Lieutenant-Governor. The master of the Charlottetown School received one hundred pounds a year; the masters of the other two schools fifty pounds each. The Governor and Council appoint five trustees to each school, who examine the school half yearly, look into the discipline of the school and give the master a certificate of their having done so, upon which he receives his salary.

There is also a school in Charlottetown which is conducted under the National or Lancastrian system, under the Superintendence of the committee of the Society for Promoting the Gospel, the master of which receives from Government twenty-two pounds ten shillings a year. Besides there are district schools throughout the Island, the masters of which undergo an examination before a Board of Education appointed by the Governor in Council and who receive twelve pounds annually from the colonial funds. In 1830 there was expended for this service three hundred and twelve pounds, nineteen shillings and four pence.

## Agriculture.

The Island is an agricultural country. The great article of export is agricultural produce.

## Public Works.

The only public work, undertaken in 1830, was a new jail in Charlottetown. There are no public buildings in the Island with the exception of a small court house and a market house, both in Charlottetown.

## Population.

The last census was taken in 1827, the population was then 23,473, but it is very much increased since that time. There is every reason to believe that the population is now at least 30,000. There has been a great influx of immigrants within the last few years.

## Price of Wheat and Other Grains.

The following table gives the average price per bushel of wheat and other grains from 1st July to 31st December, 1830. It is from a return made by Lieutenant-Governor Ready to Sir George Murray, Secretary of State, in a despatch of 14th January, 1831.

| Month | Wheat | Barley | Oats |
|---|---|---|---|
| July | 1/6 | | |
| August | 1/6 | | |
| September | 5/6 | 2/7½ | 1/6 |
| October | 5/6 | 2/11 | 1/3 |
| November | 5/6 | | |
| December | 5/6 | 2/9 | 1/6 |

Also similar return from 1st January, 1831, to 1st July, 1831, from Lieutenant-Governor Ready to Lord Goderich, Secretary of State.

| Month | Wheat | Barley | Oats |
|---|---|---|---|
| January | 6/6 | | 1/4 |
| February | 6/6 | 3/– | 1/4 |
| March | 6/6 | | 1/6 |
| April | 5/– | 3/– | |
| May | 5/– | | |
| June | 5/– | | |

## IMMIGRATION.

During 1829-1830 many immigrants arrived from the Old Country. Among these, in June, 1829, were eighty-four from the Island of Skye, who settled chiefly about Belfast. In the autumn of the same year thirty-five came from Newfoundland. In May, 1830, Rev. John MacDonald brought out two hundred and six persons from Greenock in the Corsair. These were all Roman Catholics, some from Ireland. They settled near Johnston's River. In June the Collina brought seventy-four from Devon and Cornwall, and sixty-three from Plymouth. The Hannah brought thirty from Ireland via Newfoundland, and soon after fifty arrived from Suffolk via Quebec. In August of the same year eighty came from Norfolk and Suffolk.

### THE FIRST STEAMER.

The first steamer, according to the Prince Edward Island "Register" of August, 1830, to enter Charlottetown harbour was named the Richard Smith. She was owned by the Pictou Mines Company. She came into the harbour on 10th August, 1830. She remained till next day. Before leaving she took Lieutenant-Governor Ready and a party of his friends for a sail up the river.*

### THE ROYAL WILLIAM.

The second, which arrived in September, 1831, was the Royal William, of 1370 tons. She was built in Quebec to trade between Quebec and the Maritime Provinces, and on her first voyage called at the Island capital. In 1833 she crossed the Atlantic propelled entirely by steam power, being the first ship to do so. That year she sailed from Pictou for Gravesend, where she arrived after a very stormy passage. She was subsequently sold to the Spanish Carlists and used as a war ship. She was wrecked in the Mediterranean. In March, 1830, the merchants and principal inhabitants of Charlottetown petitioned the Assembly for a grant in aid of the intended intercourse by steam between Quebec and Halifax, in order of induce the steamship proprietors to make Charlottetown a port of call. It is probable that it was in response to this movement of the townspeople, that the Royal William called at Charlottetown the following year.

*Prince Edward Island Magazine, Vol. II, p. 373-4.

This narrative has now been brought down through the early period of the Island's story, the Discovery, the French Ownership, the short period of annexation to Nova Scotia, the trials and struggles of the pioneer days, and has gone, somewhat, into the opening stages of the fight for responsible government. Lieutenant-Governor Ready met the new House in 1831, but the session of 1830 marks a great constitutional change, the greatest before responsible government, and is therefore a fitting place to close this volume.

In 1831, to the profound regret of all classes, Colonel Ready was recalled and Captain Sir Murray Maxwell appointed to succeed him, but died before leaving England. The people petitioned to have Colonel Ready retained, but too late. Sir Aretas W. Young, a worthy successor, had been appointed to the position, and arrived in Prince Edward Island in September. Colonel Ready was deeply regretted by all. His tenure of office was distinguished "by activity, energy and usefulness." Population largely increased and commerce and agriculture took on renewed life during his term on the Island.

## Presentation of Plate.

In the session of 1831, the Legislature, to mark their appreciation of Colonel Ready and of his services to the colony voted a sum of £400 currency, equal to £300 sterling for the purchase of plate for presentation to him on his departure from the Island. The following inscription, prepared by a joint committee of the Council and Assembly, was inscribed on the plate:—"Presented to Colonel John Ready, late Lieutenant-Governor of Prince Edward Island, in North America, by the inhabitants of the colony, as a mark of the high sense which they entertain of his eminent public services whilst in the administration of the Government, the important duties of which he ably, impartially and zealously fulfilled from the 21st day of October, 1824, to the 27th day of September, 1831, a period of nearly seven years, with no less honour to himself than advantage to the people."

History of Prince Edward Island

PART VI
**MISCELLANEOUS**

SECTION I
**The Churches**

## CHAPTER I.

## ST. PAUL'S CHURCH, AND THE PARISH OF CHARLOTTE.

DURING several decades of its earlier existence, the story of St. Paul's Church, Charlottetown, is the story of Protestantism in Prince Edward Island. More than one hundred and fifty years have passed since the appointment of its first rector. The church and its parish of Charlotte have had, at least in pioneer days, a varied career. For more than a quarter of a century the congregation had only a room fitted up in an inn in which to hold services. There were no roads, no public schools, no public conveniences of any kind in the Island. At the time of the first rector's appointment the total population did not exceed one hundred and fifty families.

When by an Imperial Order in Council of 28th June, 1769, the Island of St. John was equipped with a Government separate from that of Nova Scotia, His Majesty George the Third, "in his pious concern for the advancement of God's glory," ordered that one hundred pounds sterling should be allowed for the stipend of a minister. In August of the same year, the Rev. John Caulfield, clerk, was, by Royal warrant, appointed rector of the parish of Charlotte, so called after Her Majesty Queen Charlotte. He was required to repair to his charge at the same time as the Governor (Patterson). Also the Rev. R. Grant was appointed chaplain to the Governor on a salary of fifty pounds sterling.

Mr. Caulfield held the position for over four years and, it is to be assumed, drew his salary, but never saw fit to leave England. Mr. Grant, also, never visited the Island.

The need of a church was felt. As early as 4th December, 1769, the proprietors of the province petitioned the Lords Commissioners of the Treasury, setting out that in order to attract settlers, etc., "it is absolutely necessary that there be, as soon as possible, a church, etc., erected in Charlottetown," and as there were no funds belonging to the Island, the petitioners prayed their Lordships to take the premises into consideration, and grant such relief as to their Lordships should seem proper.

Walter Patterson, appointed Governor in 1769, arrived in Charlottetown 30th August, 1770. He was sworn into office on the 19th September of the same year. Almost at once he began applying to the Home Government for funds to build a church. On the 25th October, writing to Lord Hillsborough, he said:

"I take the liberty to report what I have often had the honour to mention to Your Lordship, before I left London, the great want of a church, a jail, and a courthouse, and the impossibility there is of our being able to build them for many years at the expense of this Island. The necessity I find from experience to be much greater than I could then imagine. We have not, at present, even a barn nor any other place to assemble the few people in, who are already here, to Divine Worship; the ill consequence the want of which will produce, Your Lordships and all His Majesty's Ministers are much better judges than me." He then goes on to say that he has "no draft" for such a building, but that, "there are proper people belonging to the public works at home from whom Your Lordships might have drafts made to your satisfaction." He estimates the cost of the church at one thousand pounds sterling.

Lord Hillsborough, replying on 2nd January, 1771, assured the Governor that he was "sensible of the propriety and necessity of your having a church, etc., and will endeavour, so far as depends upon me, to obtain some provisions for erecting these buildings."

On the 6th of March, 1771, Lord Hillsborough wrote again, enclosing the Nova Scotia estimates, giving the sum of one thousand pounds sterling granted by Parliament for building the church.

Before receiving the estimates, on the 23rd of May, Mr. Patterson, replying to Lord Hillsborough's despatch of 2nd January, says: "I am happy Your Lordship sees the necessity of our having a church, etc., and I wish, with all my heart, Your Lordship may succeed in your endeavour to procure us money to carry them on."

Writing again on 24th July, the Governor expressed his great pleasure in receiving the estimate giving the money for the church, and assures his Lordship that he will carry on this service with the strictest economy, and in such manner as he trusts will give satisfaction.

He also reported that he had changed the plan of the town. Among other things he had reserved the site of the present post office for a church. On 4th December, 1771, Lord Hillsborough wrote authorizing Patterson to set about building.

Unfortunately, the salaries of the Civil List were in arrears and Patterson, instead of building a church, applied the money towards their payment. Consequently, there was no church for nearly thirty years. In the meantime services were conducted in a room in Richardson's tavern on Queen street.*

The congregation also needed a clergyman. Mr. Caulfield, though holding the office of rector, had never come near his charge. In the autumn of 1773, Rev. John Eagleson, of Fort Cumberland, held services and preached three times in Charlottetown. There were probably others, but, if so, the writer has not found any record of their services.

Writing to Lord Dartmouth, 2nd September, 1773, the Governor said: "I can no longer forbear representing to your Lordship that the minister appointed for the town has not, as yet, made his appearance among us, nor has he ever once thought proper to assign any reason for his absence, nor do I believe he has ever made application anywhere for leave.

"The want of one is a cause of great complaint among the inhabitants and a reason given by some people for quitting the Island, after coming to it with a design to settle here. We have our children of all ages unchristened. I myself have two, one of them upwards of two years old. These are circumstances of such a nature that no consideration but the non-payment of our salaries would have prevented my taking notice of it before now. But lest we forget that there is such a thing as religion entirely, I must, with the greatest deference, beg Your Lordship's interposition in this matter; and if Mr. Caulfield does not immediately take possession of his living that we may have some other minister appointed to it who will."

Lord Dartmouth, on 26th November, 1773, wrote a very sharp letter to Mr. Caulfield, in which he said: "That notwithstanding your having been appointed by His Majesty's warrant, minister of Charlotte parish in that Island, as long ago as the month

---

*Richardson's tavern was on the present site of Carter & Co's., seed-store.

of August, 1769, you have not yet been inducted or officiated in your parish. I think it fit to acquaint you that such neglect of duty in a clergyman will not be, as it ought not to be, passed over, and, although I am aware that the cure of the said parish is granted to you during your life, I shall think it my duty to recommend to His Majesty to appoint an assistant minister, to whom the whole salary will be directed to be paid by the agent of the Colony."

On December 1st, 1773, Lord Dartmouth, replying to Patterson, wrote: "The conduct of Mr. Caulfield, in neglecting to repair to his benefice is highly indecent and improper and it gives me the greatest concern, as I find that by the terms of His Majesty's warrant for his admission he cannot be regularly superceded upon that ground. The allowance, however, of the stipend proposed for him is certainly within the power of Government, and, though Mr. Caulfield cannot be removed, yet I do not see any objection to the stipend being allowed to any other person appointed by the King to do the duty."

The Governor, on receipt of this, wrote Lord Dartmouth, requesting that Mr. Edward Patterson, a young clergyman then officiating in Ireland, might be named by His Lordship to the King for that purpose.

Replying on 7th January, 1775, Lord Dartmouth said: "It would have been very agreeable to me to have accepted your recommendation of Mr. Edward Patterson to be minister of St. John's in the room of Mr. Caulfield, but I had, before I received your letter, yielded to the solicitations of Mr. DesBrisay in behalf of his son, who has lately taken orders.

Mr. DesBrisay, who was Lieutenant-Governor of the Island and who had not yet left England, procured the resignation of Mr. Caulfield, enclosed it to Lord Dartmouth, whom he asked to have his son, Rev. Theophilus DesBrisay, appointed rector. His memorial, dated 15th May, 1774, was as follows:

"Your memorialist has received accounts from St. John of the inhabitants of that Island being in the greatest distress for want of a clergyman among them to preach the gospel; and that there are now children there, three or four years old, not yet baptized." He went on to pray his Lordship to recommend his son, Rev. Theophilus DesBrisay, to be appointed in the room of Rev. John Caulfield, resigned.

The Rev. Theophilus DesBrisay was appointed minister of the parish of Charlotte by Royal warrant dated 21st September, 1774. He was not quite twenty years of age, having been born in Thurles, county Tipperary, Ireland, 9th October, 1754. He did not set out for his charge until the autumn of 1775. He was rector of the parish of Charlotte until his death 14th March, 1823. He was the only Protestant clergyman until the closing years of the eighteenth century. The Rev. Dr. James McGregor, the eminent Presbyterian divine of Nova Scotia, between whom and Mr. DesBrisay a warm feeling of friendship existed, wrote of him: "I became acquainted with him, and was always welcome to preach in his church, which I uniformly did when I could make it convenient. His kindness ended not but with his life."

On 23rd November, 1775, while on his way out to Charlottetown, he was at Canso, wind-bound on a vessel conveying Mr. Spence, a member of the Island Council, to the same destination. There they were captured by two American privateers which had plundered Charlottetown, and were carrying off Mr. P. Callbeck, administrator of the Government in Mr. Patterson's absence in England, and Surveyor-General Wright, to General Washington's headquarters then in Cambridge Heights. They seized Mr. Spence's vessel and made the passengers prisoners. After a short detention they released Mr. Spence and family and Mr. DesBrisay, giving them only their clothes and bedding. The rest of their effects were carried off. They reached Charlottetown in a small schooner procured by Mr. Spence.

There Mr. DesBrisay found no church, no provision for food or housing, and no prospect of being paid his stipend. He, therefore, took duty as a chaplain on board one of His Majesty's ships of war, visiting his parish when he could. He remained in that position about two years.

In 1777, the British Government assumed the payment of official services, previously charged on the quit rents (but not paid), and thenceforth the rector received one hundred and fifty pounds sterling regularly paid. He then entered upon his duties, the first entry on the parish records being made in 1777. Since then the parish has never been without a rector residing in the province.

Mr. DesBrisay resided at Covehead, on the north side of the Island for about twenty years, coming into Charlottetown for the week's end to perform his ministerial duties. In addition to his clerical office, he was a Justice of the Peace, and an overseer of the roads.

On Sunday, 17th May, 1789, H. M. S. Dido arrived at Charlottetown, four days out from Halifax, having on board the Right Reverend Charles Inglis, D. D., Bishop of Nova Scotia.*

For nearly thirty years the Island continued to appeal to the Imperial authorities for a grant out of the quit rents or other funds for the purpose of providing a church, a jail and a courthouse. It never seemed to occur to the people that they should get to work and build a church for themselves, as they were very well able to do. Lumber suitable for the edifice was growing on some of their streets.

In 1795, after many years, the first real steps towards building a church were taken, when Lieutenant-Governor Fanning brought before the Council a petition for building a church by subscription of sundry persons and praying for a grant to them, their heirs and assigns, of an interest in the site and building to be erected thereon. It was advised that the grant be made. The church was to be "for the use of the Established churches of England and Scotland." Nothing further was done until May, 1797, when the list of subscriptions was so far completed and the plans so advanced as to warrant the drawing for pews.

It was not until 23rd April, 1800, that the actual work of construction began, on the site of the present post office. The frame was set up the following October, and the church seems to have been opened for services the next year. The new church (the first St. Paul's) could seat a congregation of three to four hundred.

In 1801 the rector moved into Charlottetown, where he resided till his death, which took place 14th March, 1823. He was sixty-nine years of age. A writer in the Prince Edward Island "Register" of 12th October, 1824, describes the rector's life and labours in simple and appreciative language as follows:

"Among his flock he lived as a father among his children, no unpleasing formality, no ridiculous pedantry, no affected importance disgraced his professional intercourse; grave without austerity, good-humoured without unbecoming familiarity, the welfare of his parishioners was his chief aim and the sanctity of his

*For particulars of the Bishop's visit see *ante*, Part V, Fanning.

heart was visible in all his acts, he truly sought the interest of the truth. The increased duties which he performed latterly were too much for his enfeebled frame, but his end was the end of peace."

During his incumbency, a Sunday school was established in connection with St. Paul's, a matter in which that church seems to have been in advance of the times.

In June, 1828, the Rev. L. C. Jenkins was inducted as rector and continued to hold that office for twenty-six years. On 30th July following a committee was appointed to select a site for a new church. The committee memorialized Lieutenant-Governor Ready, setting forth the necessity of a new Episcopal church, "set apart for the worship of Almighty God, in accordance with the rites of the Established Church of England, in consequence of the present edifice being in a ruinous state, and the original grant thereof conveying a right to the use thereof in favour of the ministry of the Scotch Establishment which prevents its consecration by the Bishop." At the request of the Committee the Governor in Council consented to grant the eastern portion of Queen square, which had been originally reserved for a jail and court house, as a site, and the required amount having been pledged by individual subscribers, the Society for the Propogation of the Gospel, and the Government, a contract was let on August 8th, 1831.*

On 10th August, 1833, when nearly finished it was blown down. Difficulties from various causes delayed further work, which was not resumed until 1835. The new church was finished and occupied the next year. The site was conveyed to the rector, churchwardens, etc., on 8th August of the same year, and on the 21st it was consecrated by Right Rev. John Inglis, Bishop of Nova Scotia, by the name of St. Paul's Church.

The pews were of the high-box style; special ones of double size were provided for the Lieutenant-Governor, the members of the Council, the House of Assembly and the officers of the garrison. Near the entrance two were reserved for strangers. The others were private property and the proprietary rights were jealously guarded.

In 1840, the Diocesan Church Society for the Island was formed. Soon afterwards, on the suggestion of Captain Orlebar

---

*P. Pope, "The Church of England in Prince Edward Island" in "Past and Present of Prince Edward Island," pp. 263-264.

of the Hydrographic Survey, an infant school was established. A school-house was also built, which was used for all parish purposes and for other church meetings until a few years ago when it was pulled down and replaced by the present handsome stone structure.

In 1858, Rev. David Fitzgerald, graduate of Trinity College, Dublin, and an honorary D. C. L. of King's College, Windsor, was inducted as rector and held the position for nearly twenty-eight years, when he resigned.

In 1887, the old rectory was sold and the present one of red Island sandstone faced with grey Nova Scotia stone was completed and occupied in 1889.

The contract for a new church was executed 23rd October, 1894, and the corner stone laid 30th May following. On Sunday, 3rd May, 1896, divine service, which had been held in old St. Paul's for nearly sixty years, was held there for the last time, and the next Sunday was held in the new church, which was consecrated on 29th July following. All seats were made free, thus ending forever the pew system which had prevailed in the two previous churches.

## CHAPTER II.

## THE ROMAN CATHOLIC CHURCH IN PRINCE EDWARD ISLAND,

SOMEWHAT extended reference has already been made to the position and organization of the Roman Catholic Church in the Island of St. John, during the continuance of French rule. That organization, in fact the whole ecclesiastical fabric, as it existed before the taking of Louisbourg and, with it, the Island of St. John, was broken up by that event. It is true that some few of the French inhabitants, mostly around Malpeque, escaped deportation. They were subsequently rejoined by some of their former compatriots who had fled from the Island in 1758, but even with this addition they were few in number. It is safe to say that there was no settled organization, and little, if any, missionary work, during the next fourteen years. It is not the writer's intention to make further reference to the religious establishment, during the French regime, than he has already done. Rev. M. Millard, a priest of that period, was allowed to remain in the Maritime provinces, owing to his great influence with the Indians, but he died in 1762. It is very doubtful if missionaries were ever sent to occupy the ground, and, if sent, it is most doubtful if any of them ever found their way to the Island. It may, therefore, be assumed that from 1758 to 1772, a period of fourteen years, no priest officiated in the Island, and there was no ecclesiastical organization there.*

### REV. JAMES McDONALD — 1772-1785.

When the ship Alexander sailed from Scotland bearing two hundred and ten emigrants, all Roman Catholics, sent out by Captain John McDonald to settle on his Tracadie estate, there came with them the Rev. James McDonald, to whom authority was given, by the Bishop of Quebec, to take religious charge of the

---
*See "The Early History of the Catholic Church in Prince Edward Island." Rev. John C. McMillan, Chapter VI.

Scotch settlers and also of the remnant of the French settlers who still remained on the Island. It is to be regretted that more is not known of the life work of this pioneer missionary priest than has been handed down. When he came out to the Island of St. John he was a young man in his thirty-sixth year, in the prime of his manhood. He was the first English-speaking priest to do missionary work in the Island. When he was nineteen years of age he went to the Scots College in Rome, where he was ordained priest in 1765. He at once returned to Scotland where he remained, carrying on his ministry, until he left the old land, in 1772, to accompany the emigrants going out to the Island of St. John. Like many other of those educated in the continental schools of Europe, he was an excellent linguist, being conversant with Italian, French and English, not to overlook what may be called his mother tongue of Gaelic.

He spent his first winter with the French settlers at Malpeque. At the same time he caused the Scotch settlers in Tracadie to erect a church, small indeed, but sufficiently large for their then purposes. It was a log building thirty by twenty, thatched with straw. It was situated at Scotch Fort. The year after his arrival (in 1773) he paid a visit to Quebec, where he was received with the utmost kindness by the Bishop and clergy. So far as the writer has seen that was his only visit to Quebec.

It is clear that he was most zealous in the discharge of his duties. Single-handed and alone he attended to the religious needs of his Scotch and French flocks for a period of thirteen years. The arduous nature of his work, in what was then a new and a wilderness country, wore out a constitution never very robust. He died in 1785 at the age of forty-nine years. He was buried in the French cemetery at Scotch Fort, where last year (1922) his name, with that of his successor, the Right Reverend Angus MacEachern, Bishop of Charlottetown, was inscribed on the splendid monument then erected to the memory of the settlers of 1772.*

For five years after Rev. James McDonald's death there was no priest in the Island of St. John. It is possible that there may have been an occasional visit by one, but, if so, the writer has not seen

---

*See "A brief account of the R. C. Church in Prince Edward Island up to 1860" by Rev. James Morrison (now Bishop of Antigonish) in "Prince Edward Island Past and Present," p. 280-281. Also "The Early History, etc., by Rev. John C. McMillan," p. 44-47.

RIGHT REV. ANGUS BERNARD MacEACHERN, FIRST BISHOP
OF CHARLOTTETOWN

any record of such visit. Soon after Rev. James McDonald's death, Bishop Desglis commissioned one John Doucet, an Acadian of Rustico, to perform marriages and administer baptism throughout the Island. Outside of this there does not appear to have been any religious organization.

### BISHOP MACEACHERN.

In August, 1790, there arrived in the Island of St. John, a very extraordinary young man, in the person of the Reverend Angus Bernard MacEachern, afterwards the first Bishop of Charlottetown. The story of his life, for nigh unto a half century, is the story of the Roman Catholic Church in the Island. He was the son of Hugh (Ban) MacEachern, who, with his wife and six children, had come to St. John's Island in the Alexander in 1772. Hugh (Ban) was in easy circumstances, and instead of settling on Captain MacDonald's estate purchased land at Savage Harbour. Angus Bernard was in his fourteenth year when his parents came to St. John's Island. He was left with Bishop Hugh MacDonald, Vicar Apostolic of the Highland district, to be educated. He was sent to the Roman Catholic College at Samlaman in the autumn of 1772, where he remained for five years studying the ordinary branches of commercial education. In August, 1777, he went to Spain and took up his classical studies at the Royal Scots College at Valladolid. He was ordained priest in 1787 and returned to Scotland where he carried on missionary work for a short time in the western Highlands. In August, 1790, he arrived in St. John's Island.

For some years he made his headquarters at Savage Harbour. Early in 1791 he began a large stone house on his father's farm. It was intended both for a residence and chapel. This chapel, the church at Scotchfort, and a delapidated log-building at Malpeque, were the only churches under his charge, when he commenced his ministrations in the Island. The work that devolved upon the young priest was almost beyond the powers of one man to perform. He had charge of the Roman Catholic population of the whole Island, French as well as Scotch, English and Irish. He had no one to assist him in his work. On the contrary he was compelled to extend the field of his labours to Cape Breton and the mainland. At first there were practically no roads or means of communication other than on foot. For twenty years he was alone. He travelled over his large territory with unwearying energy. Like St. Paul he was "in journeyings often."

Ten years after his coming to the Island he removed from Savage Harbour to St. Andrews, where his house was famed for hospitality. Here his parishioners purchased a two hundred acre farm, where Mr. MacEachern for the future resided. There he built his church which, as Dr. McMillan points out, was really the first cathedral in the Island. There also he built St. Andrews College to which reference has already been made.

In the closing year of the century two assistants, Rev. Messrs. deCollone and Pichard, joined the Rev. Mr. MacEachern in his work. Rev. M. Collone was stationed at Charlottetown, Rev. M. Pichard made his home in Rustico and had charge of the French mission, while Rev. Mr. MacEachern continued in charge of the Scotch mission, including Cape Breton and a considerable section of eastern Nova Scotia.

In 1803, the Right Rev. P. Denant, Bishop of Quebec, visited Prince Edward Island. It was the first visit of a Roman Catholic bishop to the Island. He left his home near Montreal in May, 1803, proceeded to Boston, thence he took passage by sea to Nova Scotia. He spent some time in Nova Scotia, which was within his own diocese of Quebec, and thence passed over to Prince Edward Island. From Charlottetown he proceeded to Tracadie and St. Andrews, where he spent several days. He then visited the French missions at Rustico and Malpeque. Thence he crossed over to New Brunswick and back to Quebec. He had made a very thorough pastoral visit, one involving enormous physical as well as mental exertion on his part. The Abbe de Collone was transferred from Charlottetown to Rustico whence, severing his connection with Canada, he soon returned to France. The Rev. M. Pichard was also removed from Rustico to a mission in Nova Scotia. Mr. MacEachern was thus again left, alone, in sole charge of the Island.

## Bishop Plessis.

In 1812 Bishop Plessis of Quebec paid a visit to this outstanding section of his immense diocese. He visited most parts of the Island and was enabled to realize the vastness of the work Rev. Mr. MacEachern had to do. A mere list of the names of some of the places he had in his charge gives but a faint idea of the labour he had to undergo. It included such centres as Rollo Bay, St. Margaret's, St. Andrew's, East Point, Three Rivers, Tracadie, Charlottetown, Rustico, Malpeque, Grand River, Egmont Bay, Indian River and Tignish, in all of which churches were now built or about to be built. There were, moreover, the missions of Nova Scotia and Cape Breton to be visited. It was clear that the work, from a physical standpoint alone, was too much for any one man. Shortly after the Bishop's visit Rev. M. Beaubin came over and made his home at Rustico, whence he took in the Acadian missions and so relieved Mr. MacEachern of that heavy part of his labours.

In the meantime building operations, under his directions, were going on in many parts. In 1815 a site was secured in Charlottetown for a church, and shortly afterwards the first St. Dunstan's Cathedral was erected there.

In 1821 Mr. MacEachern was consecrated as Bishop of Rosen. The Island, however, was not, at this time, made a separate diocese, and owing to the scarcity of priests, the bishopric added much to the labours he had to go through. However, this scarcity was now beginning to be remedied. The year 1822 witnessed the ordination of the first Prince Edward Islander to the priesthood. This was the Rev. Bernard Donald MacDonald, afterwards to succeed Bishop MacEachern as Bishop of Charlottetown. He at once returned to the Island and took charge of the Acadian missions.

Bishop MacEachern had long felt the need there was for an institution for secondary education in Prince Edward Island. To meet this need he founded the college at St. Andrews, to which reference has already been made.

In the year 1829, the Diocese of Charlottetown was formed separate from that of Quebec, and included also the Magdalen Islands and the Province of New Brunswick. Bishop MacEachern was appointed, by Papal Bull, to the new bishopric. Owing to the slowness of travel in those days the document did not reach Prince Edward Island until the following year (1830).

Bishop MacEachern had for some years taken up the question of Catholic emancipation. In 1825 a petition signed by nine hundred Roman Catholics, asking to be placed in the same position as their Protestant fellow subjects, was introduced in the Assembly but, on the plea that the session was too far advanced to take up so important a question, it was put over to the next session. It was brought up the following session (1827) when it was rejected. Eventually, after the passing, in 1829, by the Imperial Parliament, of an Act for relieving His Majesty's Roman Catholic subjects from civil and military disabilities, the question was disposed of in Prince Edward Island, in the session of 1830, when an Act for the relief of His Majesty's Roman Catholic subjects was placed upon the statute book. Reference has already been made to this question in an earlier part of this work.

In 1829 Bishop MacEachern was appointed a Justice of the Peace by Lieutenant-Governor Ready. He was, also, at a much earlier date, appointed a commissioner or overseer of roads in the St. Peters section of the colony, as in that year "the Legislature adopted the report furnished by him concerning the state of the roads" in his district.* The old Council minutes contain several orders as to work to be done under his inspection.†

This great missionary priest, after a long life of intense labour, was seized at St. Peter's Bay with a stroke of paralysis. By his own wish he was carried back to his own house at Savage Harbour, where, a few days later, on 22nd April, 1835, in the seventy-sixth year of his age, he passed to his reward. He was a man held in the highest esteem not only by members of his own church but also by Protestants as well.

---

*Rev. John C. MacMillan, "Early History, etc.," p. 270.

†Instances of orders: Minute of Council, 15th November, 1823,—"It was this day ordered that the Morell, Midgell and Halton River bridges should undergo a temporary repair, under the inspection of the Reverend Catholic Bishop MacEachern."

Meeting of Council, 4th May, 1824, Extract: "Had a certificate from Bishop MacEachern stating that the Morell bridge had been completed according to agreement amounting to £22 10s 0d." "Warrant issued" (for the amount).

Council Meeting, 19th July, 1826, Extracts, Minute. . . . Read Reports from Bishop MacEachern, Commissioner of the St. Peters District, viz.:—"On the bad state of the roads between Morell and the Gulf shore and stating Pine Creek bridge required to be re-planked. Ordered that the Bishop be authorized to advertise the said bridge at public vandue and to specify the manner in which it is to be built." Report upon Morell bridge, recommending four additional blocks and covering at the ends. Ordered that the Bishop be authorized to have the work done at the cheapest rate.

## CHAPTER III.

## THE PRESBYTERIAN CHURCH IN PRINCE EDWARD ISLAND.

IT has already been pointed out that for the first few decades of British rule in the Island of St. John and Prince Edward, to give it its two succeeding names, the story of St. Paul's church and the parish of Charlotte was the story of Protestantism in Prince Edward Island. This does not mean that other Protestant churches had not members or adherents in the colony. It means, rather, that none of the others, the Presbyterians, the Methodists, the Baptists, during this period, had any organization or clergymen representing these Christian churches. That there were considerable numbers of lay Presbyterians admits of no question. The first considerable influx of settlers came to the Island in A. D. 1770, when one hundred and twenty families, in two parties under the auspices of Sir James Montgomery and Mr. Stewart respectively, came to Richmond Bay intending to make their homes on the properties of these two proprietors. It will be remembered that the second of these parties was shipwrecked in October of that year, when attempting to make the harbour. These immigrants came from Argyleshire in Scotland and were mainly, if not entirely, Presbyterians. Later on others came out, who settled at Cove Head, St. Peters and Bay Fortune. Some came from Morayshire and settled at Cavendish, while others went to Georgetown and vicinity.*

These people did not bring a minister of their own church with them and, for over twenty years, saw none. The Presbyterians, however, were probably better equipped than other bodies to keep up and maintain the forms and teachings of their church. The Scotch Presbyterian, in religious matters, was essentially a reader and student of the Bible. It was taught by parent to child. Family worship, consisting of reading from "The Book," exposition

---

*Rev. T. F. Fullerton,—"Precis of the History of the Presterbyian Church in Prince Edward Island," published in "Past and Present of Prince Edward Island," p. 305a.

by the head of the household, followed by a prayer, often of great length, was conducted daily in the household. The Shorter Catechism was well thumbed by youth. No day was allowed to close without praise and thanksgiving being offered up to Almighty God and to His Son. This good custom continued among the immigrants, though without the guidance of a "minister." Consequently the "faith of their fathers" was maintained so that when a missionary did reach them he found a spiritual soil that, to some extent at least, had been kept tilled. To this cause may be assigned the quick springing into activity of Presbyterianism in this province when, at length, ministers of their own belief did come among the people.

These ministers found a people, among whom not only were the forms of their church worship maintained, but among whom, also, the same doctrines were taught, that they had learned in Scotland, the same religious customs that they knew in the old land they knew and cherished in Prince Edward Island. It is very probable that the clergymen, when they did come, found religious conditions that were quite similar to those which had prevailed in Scotland twenty years before. It was this religious Presbyterianism, become the very life of the people, in their lonely settlements, that sent Geddes to the South Seas, which sent George Gordon to his martyrdom in Eromanga and his brother James to take his place and share his fate. It is to be regretted that this good and grand old custom of family worship which did so much for these old pioneers is not today, the writer believes, observed as it formerly was.

The first Presbyterian missionary to the Isle St. John was the Rev. James McGregor, who paid it a visit in 1791. Dr. Fullerton, in the article already referred to, tells us that: "The ministrations of Dr. McGregor were thoroughly appreciated wherever he went, and not a few heard, for the first time, a service conducted by an ordained minister. The absence of any Church organization and the eagerness of the people for the Church of their forefathers, was pathetic in the extreme. Dr. McGregor's brief visit had won some to the side of truth and righteousness and had kindled the enthusiasm of the faithful, who for years had been longing for a "Church." The impression made upon him is best set forth in his own words: "I represented the destitute state of Prince Edward Island (to the Synod) in general, that I had not preached in Charlottetown nor in a number of other small settlements which never had the gospel preached to them; that Mr. DesBrisay seldom preached but in town; that the only other clergyman on the Island was a Catholic priest, and that the most gospel they got was from Methodists. But all the answer I got next summer was that the Synod sympathized with me, but could find no one willing to come to my assistance."

Dr. Fullerton, in the article already quoted, preserves a very interesting account, from Dr. McGregor's pen, of the first meeting which took place in 1791 between him and Rev. Mr. DesBrisay and of the life-long friendship that thenceforth existed between the two men: "The session (of Pictou), wrote Dr. McGregor, "appointed me two Sabbaths to St. Peters and two to Cove Head. Having taken a passage to Charlottetown, the metropolis, sixty miles from Pictou harbour, I landed next day after an agreeable passage. I was directed to a Mr. Rae, a Scotch merchant, a sober man, with whom I lodged agreeably. The next day I hired a horse and rode out to Cove Head, sixteen miles, on an agreeable road (then the only road on the Island). Near the end of my journey I missed my way, and calling at a house for information, met the landlord at the door and asked him to show me the way to Mr. Millar's. Pointing with his hand across a creek or small bay, he said, 'There is Mr. Millar's, you have missed your way a little, but I will send a boy round with the horse and put you across the creek in a canoe and your way will be shorter than if you had not missed it. Please to walk in and rest a little.' I thanked him for his kindness, accepted his invitation, and he gave my horse to a boy to take to Mr. Millar's. I was most agreeably entertained while I stayed. The gentleman easily found what I was and expressed his happiness that a Presbyterian minister had come to visit the Presbyterians there, but I had no courage to attempt ascertaining what he was. He accompanied me to Mr. Millar's and addressed me there: 'Mr. Millar, I have brought you what you have been long looking for, a Presbyterian minister, and I hope he will do you much good.' Mr. Millar thanked him affectionately and, after a little conversation, the gentleman returned home. After a cordial welcome from Mr. Millar, and mutual enquiries after each other's health, I asked him who the gentleman might be. He replied, 'It is Parson DesBrisay, the Church of England clergyman of the Island, a Calvinistic preacher, a man of liberal sentiments and of a benevolent disposition!' 'And where does he preach?' 'He rides every Sabbath to Charlottetown and preaches in the Church there.' 'And why does he not reside in town?' 'It is a wicked place, and he is more retired and happy in the country.' I afterwards became acquainted with him and was always welcome to preach in his church, which I uniformly did when I could make it convenient. His kindness ended not but with his life."

"Occasional visits from Doctor McGregor, who at one time or another, visited all the settlements, was the only supply received until 1800, at which time arrived the Rev. Mr. Urquhart, a minister of the Church of Scotland. He was the first to establish any organization." He made Prince Town his headquarters. He remained only two years, removing in 1802 to Miramichi, where he died.

The Rev. Peter Gordon, a preacher from the General Associate Synod, in Scotland, succeeded Mr. Urquhart, as minister of Cove Head, St. Peters, and Bay Fortune. He was really a missionary in charge of the Presbyterians of the whole Island. He died at the close of two years in his ministry.

In 1810, the Rev. Mr. Kier was ordained to the pastoral charge of the Presbyterian people of Prince Edward Island and established himself at Princetown, and the following year the Rev. Edward Pidgeon joined him, taking over the congregations of Cove Head, St. Peters and Bay Fortune. With the coming of these two devoted missionaries the Presbyterian Church in the Island may be considered as firmly established. Mr. Pidgeon, after a ministry of ten years in the Island, was succeeded in 1821 by the Rev. Robert Douglas.

The growth of the Presbyterian body was a rapid one, necessitating, in 1821, the formation of the Presbytery of Prince Edward Island, with the Rev. John Kier as its first Moderator.

In 1823, the Rev. John McLennan was sent out by the Church of Scotland to minister to the spiritual needs of the emigrants from the Highlands and Islands of Scotland. He ministered, not only to the people of Belfast, but also to the people of Wood Islands, Georgetown and Murray Harbour. He also preached, occasionally, in Charlottetown, Cherry Valley and New London.

Up to this period there had been no Presbyterian organization in Charlottetown. In 1825, however, a public meeting was called to take this matter into consideration with the eventual result of the erection of St. James Church, the first Presbyterian place of worship in the town.

The year 1825 saw the coming of two men whose names became household words in the Presbyterian body. These were the Rev. Mr. Patterson and the Rev. Mr. Dunbar. The former accepted a call to the congregation of Bedeque, which had recently separated from Richmond Bay, and continued his labours there until his death in 1882, a continuous pastorate of fifty years. Mr. Dunbar took charge of the congregation of Cavendish and New London. Afterwards he retired from the active ministry and became prominent in educational matters.

Perhaps the most remarkable man in the Presbyterian Church of the earlier days was the Rev. Donald McDonald, who came to the Island in 1827, and for forty years preached to the people of all sections of the colony. He was a very extraordinary man, possessed of great personal magnetism. He built up the largest congregation or following that has been formed by any one man in the Island. His commanding influence was felt by all with whom he came in contact. The effect of his teaching was marked during his lifetime and, to this day, it continues potent in many parts of the province.

The pioneer ministers have been followed by worthy successors. The organization of the Church has been established on a solid basis. With the increase of population the old territories were subdivided and the congregations became more compact and more readily worked. The Presbyterian Church is now in a strong position and is the largest Protestant denomination on the Island.

### Foreign Missions.

Even a mere sketch, such as this is intended to be, would be imperfect without a reference to the missionary work of the Presbyterian Church in the earlier days. In 1838, the Rev. Dr. Geddie settled and became pastor of the congregation of Cavendish and New London. But the charge of a congregation in Prince Edward Island was not the work for which he was intended or, possibly, for which he was best qualified. He was possessed with a consuming zeal for foreign missions. He established missionary organizations in his own and in other congregations, and in 1845 he himself went forth, the first missionary to the heathen from the Presbyterian

Church in Canada. His field was the Island of Aneiteum in the South Seas, where he laboured for over twenty years, or nearly until his death in 1872. So successful were his efforts that he could truly say, when leaving his mission, that "when I landed on Aneiteum there was not a Christian, and before I left there was not a heathen on the island." This was the beginning of Presbyterian foreign mission work in Canada which has now grown to goodly dimensions.

## The Martyrs.

Following the example of Dr. Geddie, the Rev. George N. Gordon, of Alberton, P. E. Island, took up mission work in the island of Eromanga in the South Pacific. Unlike Geddie he was murdered by the natives among whom he laboured, the first Canadian martyr in the foreign mission field. His brother, Rev. James D. Gordon, took up his brother's work and met the same fate at the hands of the natives among whom they laboured. The work has never been halted, and today Presbyterian foreign missions are a great Christian force in the out-lying places of the earth.*

---

*In 1904, the late Rev. John M. McLeod, for eighteen years pastor of Zion Church in Charlottetown, published a comprehensive "History of Presbyterianism in Prince Edward Island." The writer recommends this volume to Presbyterians, who desire to inform themselves with regard to their Church's history in this province.

Covering a smaller field is a "Historical Sketch of Zion Presbyterian Church, Charlottetown, Prince Edward Island, from its erection to February, 1908," by the late Samuel C. Nash, for many years head of His Majesty's excise in this Island. Though limited as to the area of which it treats, this is a valuable pamphlet, well worthy of reading by the members of Zion Church and by others interested in the religious history of Charlottetown.

## CHAPTER IV.

## THE METHODIST CHURCH IN PRINCE EDWARD ISLAND.

THE great religious movement in Great Britain, associated with the names of John and Charles Wesley, could not but have its effect also in the new and outlying parts of the empire. Men of the loftiest character, of a high order of eloquence, and filled with zeal in the Master's service, they exerted a marvellous power over the spiritual life of the English-speaking people. Without separating from the Church of their fathers, they broke through the formalism which, in their day, characterized the Church and brought the teachings of Christianity home to the common life of men.

The Wesleys were great men, and they soon built up a body of followers which has continued to grow, though its founders have long since gone to their reward. A new light was casting its beams over the religious world and its rays were beginning to illumine the minds of men. The Wesleys did not teach or preach a new religion. They brought home to their hearers the religious truths which they already held. But they brought home those truths in a way that was new, to which people were unused. They clothed the dry bones with flesh and blood. They made of the Saviour a great living personal force. They sought out the men and women of town and country, they got hold of the miner, the mechanic, the worker, and inspired them with their own zeal. In meetings in the open air, in sheds, anywhere, they gathered together all who would come, and preached the simple gospel so that all could understand. They produced the beautiful hymns that go by Wesley's name and which reach home to the very hearts of hearers. Formality was not considered. The one great object was to reach the heart, to bring the message to all, to enthuse. They reached the great middle classes, they appealed to the labourer and to the needy, inspiring their hearers with some of their own earnestness.

The movement soon became a mighty one. It was impossible that it would not reach the outlying stations of the empire. Some few of Wesley's disciples found their way to the Island of St. John in the early days of British rule. There is no very early record of the Methodist Church in the Island, although there were adherents. Their story, like that of the other Protestant denominations, was for the first few decades the story of St. Paul's Church and the parish of Charlotte. It was not till the opening years of the eighteenth century that they became an active body.

The first to become prominent in religious matters was Benjamin Chappell, who came to the Island from London in 1775. He was a convert and friend of John Wesley and was thoroughly imbued with the views of that great teacher. Mr. Chappell was a man of fair education and of much ability. He first settled in New London where he remained for a few years, working at his trade of a carpenter and joiner, to which he seems to have added that of millwright. That he had plenty of employment is shown by the entries in his day book, where he kept a minute record of his daily work. In this book he also made brief entries of all sorts of happenings. This book is known as "Chappell's Diary" and is of much value to any who wish to search out the story of the Island during the many years over which the entries extend.

After a few years living in New London, Mr. Chappell, with his family, moved into Charlottetown and made his home on Water street, where his residence still stands. Here he was evidently kept very busy. The writer has not found any record of his taking an active part in religious matters previous to 1801. In that year, Thomas Dawson, a local preacher of ability, came to the Island and settled up the East or Hillsborough River. He was an Irishman and had been an officer in the Royal Irish Artillery.*

During 1801 and following years prayer meetings seem to have been pretty regularly held. At Christmas of that year Mr. Dawson preached at the Coffee House. This is the first report of his preaching that the writer has found. It occurs in Chappell's diary. The entry for 15th August, 1802, states that Mr. Dawson preached, and adds that "This is three times we have used the rooms for Mr. Dawson in preaching." For years the custom was kept up, and

---

*H. Smith —"Methodism in Prince Edward Island," in "Past and Present of Prince Edward Island," 314a.

then were preachings and prayer-meetings week days as well as Sundays. For a time Mr. Dawson was the principal preacher. Several times mention is made of the number of times he preached in the room, such as the seventh and eighth time. Meetings were also held at Mrs. Smith's, by Mr. Dawson. Some of the entries state that he preached at the room by leave of the pastor. He also extended his ministrations beyond Charlottetown, going to Murray Harbour and other parts of the Island. A Mr. Murchiston is mentioned as taking part in the work. Mr. Dawson died of blood-poisoning on March 4th, 1804. Other men took up the work. The names of Messrs. Black, Avard, McGregor, Bulpit and others are familiar during this period.

Among the earliest of the lay preachers was Joshua Newton, collector of customs, who frequently held services and preached in Charlottetown. Joseph Avards, one of Wesley's men, came to the Island from England in 1806. For a number of years he preached and held services in Charlottetown or in the outlying districts. It was in response to his appeal that, in 1807, the London Missionary Society sent out the Rev. James Bulpit, the first ordained Methodist minister to come to the Island. He resided in Charlottetown until his death in December, 1849, but had retired from active work in 1815. His wife also conducted a school for many years. He was succeeded by the Rev. John Hick, who, in 1816, preached his first sermon in an unfinished chapel on the north side of Richmond street between Queen and Pownal. Mr. Hick remained for a year on the Island and was succeeded by Rev. John B. Strong, who arrived in the autumn of 1816. Small chapels had now been built at Murray Harbour and in Bedeque. Henceforth a continuous series of ordained ministers filled the various circuits, and the Methodist body continued to grow.

The premises on Richmond street were soon found too small to accommodate the congregation, and in 1833 a site for a new chapel was purchased on the corner of Richmond and Prince streets. In 1863-1864 the continual growth of its membership made it incumbent on the Church to provide increased space for the congregation, and accordingly the large brick edifice on Prince street was erected. The Methodist Church, throughout the Island, has grown and prospered until it is, today, next to Presbyterianism, the strongest Protestant denomination on Prince Edward Island. It is not the design of the present volume to enter into the early struggles of the several Christian denominations, beyond giving a bare outline of their beginnings, so further reference will not be made to the Methodist Church in Prince Edward Island. Those who desire to delve deeper into the subject will find much valuable information in the article on "Methodism on Prince Edward Island," in "Past and Present of Prince Edward Island," by Mr. Henry Smith, already referred to, and also in several articles in the local press by the same gentleman.

## CHAPTER V.

## THE BAPTIST CHURCH IN PRINCE EDWARD ISLAND.

SO far as the writer has been able to ascertain the Baptist Church had no representatives in Prince Edward Island until some years after the close of the eighteenth century. The first mention of a Baptist preacher being in the Island that the writer has found is in Chappel's diary for Wednesday, 13th May, A. D. 1812. It simply states, "A Baptist preacher at Bulpit's house, a good man."

Except on this one occasion, recorded by Mr. Chappel, the preacher does not seem to have preached in the colony, and nothing further is heard of him. There was no settled or regular organization of the Church as a religious body until a considerable time after his visit. Since their actively coming into the field the Baptists have progressed steadily though somewhat slowly, until now they form an important and compact body, with churches spread over many sections of the province. Their churches here are now united with those of Nova Scotia and New Brunswick in the Baptist Convention of the Maritime Provinces.

In the period proposed to be covered by this volume, there can hardly be said to have been any general Baptist organization bringing the scattered parts together into a compact body. The individual has to be considered rather than the Church of which he was a member. As was the case with the Presbyterians, the earliest Baptist workers came from Scotland. The earliest of these was John Scott, who lived and farmed at the North River, where many of his descendants still reside. He was a gifted local preacher. He not only preached at his home at North River, but also extended his ministrations further afield to St. Peters Road, West River and other sections, where he preached especially to the Scotch residents whom he addressed in their native Gaelic. He exercised considerable influence over the people to whom he preached.

Alexander Crawford was the next man to take up the work in Prince Edward Island. In 1809 he emigrated from Scotland to Nova Scotia where for a time he taught school and preached. He then settled permanently in Prince Edward Island. Some of his doctrinal views were not those of the Church, and in consequence he never united with the Baptists of Nova Scotia. He was a man of good education and of much energy. He organized the Baptist churches at East Point, Three Rivers, Lot Forty-eight, Tryon and in other sections of the country. Missionaries from Nova Scotia visited the Island and did much to smooth out the religious differences just referred to. Among others, in the summer of 1825, Rev. C. Tupper, father of the distinguished Canadian statesman, spent some time, with considerable success, in missionary work on the Island.

The following year (1826) the Rev. Joseph Crandall and Rev. Theodore Seth Harding took up the work begun by Mr. Tupper. They exercised a powerful influence over their congregations and the Baptist body was considerably built up and strengthened by their efforts. During their ministrations the first Associated Baptist Church was organized at Bedeque in 1826.

The Rev. Samuel McCully came to the Island and visited various parts of the colony. He was considered a powerful preacher. At North River he held meetings in the house of William Dockendorff, who represented Queen's county in the provincial House of Assembly. In October, 1830, he organized the North River Baptist Church, which is still one of the most important in the Island. Mr. Benjamin Scott, a licentiate from Nova Scotia, was wrecked at Lot 49 in 1830, and began to preach where he so strangely found himself. Rev. Hezekiah Hull came to the scene in 1831 and organized a church there of which Mr. Scott afterwards became the minister.

Up to this period the Baptist community depended upon missionaries for their religious ministrations, but it was now decided to have ministers of their own. Accordingly, in 1832, Messrs. Benjamin Scott, John Scott and John Shaw were inducted by Rev. Edward Manning and Rev. Theodore Harding, then doing missionary work on the Island, into their respective pastorates of Alexandra, North River, and Three Rivers. They were the three earliest pastors as distinguished from missionaries. To the Messrs. Scott reference has already been made.

John Scott had been a school teacher and Independent local preacher. In 1832, the year of his induction, he organized a church at Three Rivers (Georgetown), where he resided, and the next year (1833) he organized another at East Point. In both these were a number of persons who were known as "Scotch" Baptists, from the fact that the early preachers in these sections had come from Scotland.

In 1863 a church consisting of nine members was organized in Charlottetown by Rev. George McDonald, at that time doing missionary work in the colony. From small beginnings it has grown into a strong body, with excellent church and minister's residence. This church has been fortunate in having, from time to time, several strong men holding its pastorate. Churches continued to be organized until they have been fairly well planted throughout the province.

For many years the Baptist churches of Prince Edward Island were connected with the Eastern Baptist Association of Nova Scotia. With the growth of the denomination on the Island came the necessity of an Association of their own. This need was satisfied in July, 1868, when the Prince Edward Island Baptist Association was organized at North River by representatives of all the churches gathered there for this specific purpose. The earnest and eloquent words with which the writer of the account of the Prince Edward Island Baptists, from which the foregoing is derived, closes his account, might well be adopted for guidance by other Christian denominations and by secular bodies as well. He writes:

"The veteran leaders, who in past years nobly laboured for the best interests of their fellow men, have entered into their rest. A new generation has risen up to carry forward the enterprises entrusted to their care, and the diligent review of the history of those, who have laid with patient hands the strong foundations of our colonial prosperity, should inspire present workers with a zeal and energy worthy of the splendid example set before us by our forefathers."*

---

*"Prince Edward Island Baptists" by Rev. William H. Warren, M. A., in "Past and Present of Prince Edward Island," pp. 295-304.

History of Prince Edward Island
PART VI
**MISCELLANEOUS**
SECTION II
**The Early Chief Justices**

## CHAPTER VI.

## JOHN DUPORT, FIRST CHIEF JUSTICE OF THE ISLAND OF ST JOHN.

JOHN Duport was an attorney. He came out to Halifax with Governor Cornwallis, in June, 1749. At a Council held by Cornwallis, then Governor of Nova Scotia, on board the Beaufort, ship of war, on 18th July of the same year, Duport was appointed a Justice of the Peace for the township of Halifax. In February, 1752, he was appointed a Judge of the Inferior Court of Common Pleas for the county of Halifax. In 1773 he was made secretary of Governor Hopson's Council. He performed the duties of secretary of the Council of Nova Scotia for many years. In 1766, "on considering the want of a sufficient number of copies of the laws of the province," and the great necessity of a correct and complete edition, it was ordered by the Council, that Mr. John Duport prepare such edition, which shall be printed in folio by Mr. Robert Fletcher, he furnishing 200 copies, for which he shall be paid £180. On 31st October, 1766, the House of Assembly voted Mr. Duport the £60 to be paid him for preparing the edition of the laws for the press. On 31st July he was voted £30 for past services.

Jonathan Binney, a native of Hull, a small village near Boston, elected a member of the Nova Scotian House of Assembly for the town of Halifax in 1761, in the year 1768 was made Second Judge of the Island of St. John and was afterwards sent to Canso as Collector of Duties and Superintendent of that place, and the same year was appointed Collector of Import and Excise at St. John's Island. Mr. Duport was appointed Second Assistant Judge of the Supreme Court of the Island of St. John's, and in 1770 was appointed Chief Justice of that Island.*

At the time there were no other judges at all on the Island, and no lawyers except Mr. Phillips Callbeck, the Attorney-General,

---
*Akins N. S. Archives, page 694, note. Murdock's History of Nova Scotia, Vol. II, p. 493.

whose title to and qualifications for the position were never questioned, but who could not be spared from the positions he already held.

There was then much difficulty in procuring provisions on the Island of St. John. The officials procured their winter supplies from Halifax. Mr. Duport, when leaving Nova Scotia, evidently was not aware of this fact, as the first notice there is of him, after his arrival, is a short statement in the first despatch to Lord Hillsborough, by Governor Patterson, after the latter's arrival here, dated 21st October, 1770, in which the Governor says:

"I have been obliged to give Mr. Duport, our Chief Justice, leave to return to Halifax for this winter, as he had neglected to lay in provisions for himself and family, during the summer. They must otherwise have been starved."

In a despatch of the 25th of the same month the Governor says that he himself was sworn in on the 19th of September, and that he then gave "the Chief Justice a commission for holding the Supreme Court of Judicature, and on the 24th of September, the Court was opened for the despatch of business. This was evidently the first Court held here after the organization of the Island as a separate Government.

## SALARY £200.

The Chief Justice's salary was only £200 a year, and that was to be paid out of the quit rents supposed to be paid by the proprietors of the Island, and, as they did not pay, he was always in arrears. Indeed, his story is a very pathetic one. It is best gathered from the correspondence and does not need much comment.

On 23rd April, 1771, he wrote Lord Hillsborough from Halifax, the first of a series of apparently well founded complaints. He says, after alluding to his leave of absence, "The Governor also gave me leave to draw for my first year's salary, due in May last, on Mr. Smith, his agent in London, which I have accordingly done; but my bills have not been paid, as Mr. Smith informs me that he had not money in his hands occasioned by the backwardness of the proprietors in paying their quit rents. . . . I would humbly submit to Your Lordship's judgment and consideration the present salary of £200, annexed to my office and the manner of its being paid . . . and hope Your Lordship will be of the opinion that it may admit of some addition and that the payment of it may be made certain quarterly, in order to enable me to support the expenses naturally attending the settlement of a new country. . . . My whole dependence for subsisting myself and family is on my salary, and the failure of the regular payment of that must reduce us to the utmost distress in a place where ready money is expected for every necessary of life. I would further beg leave to remark to Your Lordship that I am grown old in the public service, having been an assiduous and faithful servant of the Crown for upwards of twenty-two years, and have always had the approbation of His Majesty's Government in every employment with which I have been entrusted." Incidently this throws a strong side light on the hardships and difficulties that settlers and officials had to encounter here in the early days.

Lord Hillsborough's reply, dated at Whitehall on 3rd July, 1771, afforded little comfort to the distressed Chief Justice. He says: "I hope Mr. Smith will so far succeed in his application to the proprietors of lands in the Island of St. John, as to procure such a payment of the quit rents as shall enable him to discharge what is due on account of the salaries of the officers on the civil establishment; I cannot, however, on any account, at present, recommend any payments beyond what the quit rents will answer, but when the Island shall be in a situation to make some further provisions for the support of its establishment, I shall most readily acquiesce in any proposition for the increase of your salary, out of such funds as shall be provided for that purpose by Act of Assembly."

In a despatch of 3rd September, 1771, the Chief Justice refers to the establishment of terms of Court, and convictions at the last one held. He also reverts to his own troubles, and incidentally points out that Cape Breton was suffering depression in its fishery business, which, he says, is chiefly owing to the heavy duty on spirits to which it is liable, owing to being annexed to Nova Scotia, and suggests as a remedy for Cape Breton's troubles that that Island and the Magdalens should be annexed to the Island of St. John. He also asks to be appointed Chief Justice of South Carolina, which position he understood to be vacant.

The request was not granted, and he had to continue in great distress and embarrassment a couple of years longer, when he died.

The office of Chief Justice was then put in commission by the Governor. The commission to act as Chief Justice was dated 14th February, 1774, and was issued to Robert Stewart, John Russell Spence and Thomas Wright.

Governor Patterson, in his despatch, dated 21st May, 1774, to the Home Government, announcing Mr. Duport's death and his provision for filling the office says: "Mr. Duport, our Chief Justice, died of the gout in his stomach on the 29th of last January. He was a remarkable instance that temperance and sobriety alone is not sufficient to eradicate nor prevent the fatal effects of that disorder. He lived for five years on a milk diet, and even after he left it, he drank nothing but water. His food must likewise have been the plainest kind, at least during the last four years of his life, yet he was subject to very long and severe fits.

"If ever death was a welcome guest to any man, he must have been so to Mr. Duport, for his life was a constant scene of difficulties and distresses since he came to reside in this Island, and at a period, too, when age renders most people unfit to struggle with hardships. They were chiefly for want of his salary being punctually paid, but as I wait in daily expectation of that matter being settled on a proper footing, I shall not, at present, give your Lordship any further trouble on the subject.

"As there is not a lawyer upon the Island capable of executing the office of Chief Justice as it ought to be, except the Attorney-General (Mr. Callbeck), who cannot be spared from the places he already holds, I judged it the most prudent method of proceeding to have it executed by three persons, in the manner directed by their commission, a copy of which shall accompany this to your Lordship. But as this was done only through necessity, not by any means to my satisfaction, nor perhaps not altogether to the inhabitants, it caused me to wish most earnestly the place was filled by an able lawyer, and to intreat Your Lordship will recommend such a one for it to His Majesty as speedily as it can be done with convenience."

## CHAPTER VII.

## PETER STEWART, SECOND CHIEF JUSTICE OF THE ISLAND OF ST. JOHN.

AS has been seen in the account of Chief Justice Duport, upon his death the chief justiceship was placed in Commission. Not one of the three commissioners was a lawyer. The only lawyer in the province was the Attorney-General. The office was in commission for nearly two years. Apparently on the recommendation of the Earl of Warwick,* who wrote of him on 12th December, 1774, that he "was bred to the law and had upwards of twenty years practice in it," Mr. Peter Stewart was appointed to the vacant position. The Earl added that, "He is a large proprietor on the Island and has nearly two hundred people thither, who have been settled upwards of two years.† He had a large family of ten children, several of whom, particularly John Stewart, became very prominent figures in the early period of Prince Edward Island's history. On his way to the Island, with his wife and children, he was shipwrecked and lost nearly all his personal property. He did not get his commission until A. D. 1776. He had a chequered experience for the twenty-five years during which he held office.

During the early years of his Chief-Justiceship, relations between him and the Governor seem to have been of a most amicable kind. He was a man of fair parts well qualified to discharge the duties of his office. His eldest son, John, the author of a description of Prince Edward Island published in 1806, was a man of great energy and ability, who was for long the foremost man in the community to which he rendered very important services. The Chief Justice was also popular with the House of Assembly, which in the session of March, 1784, unanimously adopted a resolution "requesting the Home Government to increase the Chief

---
*Letter from Earl of Warwick, *ante*, p. 173.
†This reference must be to the settlers brought out in 1770, four years before.

Justice's salary." It recites his high standing, ability and integrity; the grant of an additional £200 a year to the Chief Justice of Nova Scotia; that he had a large family of eleven children; that he only receives £400 a year now, and that "On his arrival in November, 1775, he had the misfortune to be ship-wrecked, by which he had suffered the loss of the greatest part of his property." This resolution was ordered to be forwarded by the Speaker in the name of the House.

Up to this time matters had gone smoothly, but now, owing to domestic differences, the friendship formerly existing between the two men and their families was replaced by a feeling of bitter enmity. This came to a climax in the course of a general election held that year (1784).

### Reasons for Dissolving the House.*

Patterson, in giving Lord North his reasons for dissolving the House, says: "I dissolved the Assembly on 14th last January and issued writs for a new one to meet on 6th March following.

"The establishment of peace and the revival of trade induced me to bring forward a plan to lay the foundation of a revenue for the future maintenance of the civil establishment, agreeably to His Majesty's Royal Proclamation.

"The Council unanimously concurred in this measure and several merchants were consulted as to what articles would bear taxing with least prejudice to our infant commerce.

". . . A very violent opposition did take place, but not from the merchants. Mr. John Stewart, son of the Chief Justice, a very intemperate young man, travelled through the Island, unknown to me, and infused into the peoples' minds the dread of a general tax. He represented me as hostile to the colony, that I intended making slaves of them by laying an impost on every article of their produce, to even seize their cattle by force, in short that they would be a ruined people if they did not resist me and chose such representatives as he should recommend.

"This conduct of Mr. Stewart . . . was rendered more successful by the conduct of Chief Justice Stewart, who

---

*Patterson to Lord North, 15th April, 1784, Dom. Archives, Col. Cor. Prince Edward Island, Vol. V, p. 161,— 1784.

. . . appeared at the elections as counsel for the candidates brought forward by his son and corroborated what he had advanced, declaring publicly that such taxes were in contemplation. . . This left no doubt in the minds of the people, and consequently the election was carried in favour of his son's list. . . ."

Becoming apprehensive of what Patterson might do, Stewart, on 2nd June, 1784, wrote to Lord Sydney, "I have every reason to believe an attempt is now to be made of depriving me of my place of Chief Justice, which I have held since 1775, and of turning me and my numerous family of eleven children out of our only subsistance."

A commission was issued by Patterson suspending the Chief Justice and appointing Thomas Wright, Alexander Fletcher and Robert Gray to be justices or judges of the Supreme Court.

### Charges Against the Chief Justice.

Patterson's charges against the Chief Justice were as follows:

"First, For having abetted his son, Lieutenant John Stewart, and others, in opposition to the known wishes of the Governor, in choosing an Assembly, who were a discredit and unequal to the business of the country.

"Second, For divulging a secret of Council at the hustings during the time of polling, by saying the Governor intended laying a heavy tax upon the country, thereby inflaming the minds of the people against the Governor, in order to influence them in their choice of candidates, by which the Governor was prevented from carrying into effect His Majesty's Royal instructions, in which he is commanded, as soon as may be, to lay the foundations of a revenue for the support of the civil establishment.

"Third, For advising disobedience to the Governor's authority and to the laws of the country, whereby the business of the public cannot be carried on to any good effect and the whole Island is thrown into confusion."

On 25th February, 1788, more than a year after Fanning's taking over the Lieutenant-Governorship, in a new House of Assembly, Mr. Charles Stewart moved "that the House, considering the situation of the Chief Justice of the Province, do request that His Excellency, the Governor, will be pleased to cite the late

Lieutenant Governor (Patterson) and the present Chief Justice before him and his Majesty's Council to enquire into the suspension of the Chief Justice and to take such measures thereupon as may be proper and necessary." This motion was defeated by an almost unanimous vote, two members voting for it and thirteen against. The reason for this vote, in all probability, was that the matter was being taken up elsewhere.

On 30th May, 1789,* Chief Justice Stewart, in a memorial, of this date to His Majesty's Privy Council, prays among other things, "that Your Lordships will restore him to the execution of his office, from which he has been near four years suspended to his great loss and injury."†

On 25th May, 1790, the Lieutenant-Governor (Fanning) acquainted the Council that he had received a public despatch dated 2nd September, 1788, from Mr. Grenville, one of His Majesty's Secretaries of State, informing him that His Majesty, by His Order of 15th June, 1787, had referred to the Lords of the Committee of Council for hearing complaints, the despatch from Walter Patterson, Esquire, then Lieutenant-Governor of the Island of St. John, to Lord Sydney, containing his reasons for having suspended Peter Stewart, Esquire, from the office of Chief Justice of the said Island.

"Their Lordships have reported to the King their opinion that Mr. Stewart ought to be restored to his said office, which report His Majesty, by his Order in Council of 8th August last, copy of which I enclose, approved; and I am commanded by the King to signify to you his pleasure, that you do, immediately, restore the said Peter Stewart, Esquire, to his office of Chief Justice of the Island of St. John.

"The Lieutenant-Governor informed the Board that he had, immediately on receipt thereof, restored Peter Stewart, Esquire, to his office of Chief Justice of the Island of St. John."

Mr. Grenville's letter to Lieutenant-Governor Fanning of second September, 1789, dated at Whitehall, regarding Chief Justice Stewart was a follows:

"His Majesty, having referred to the Lords of the Committee of Council for hearing complaints, a letter from Walter Patterson,

---

*Archives, M. S. bound, Prince Edward Island M. 177.
†This Memorial is signed,—"On behalf of my father, J. Stewart."

Esquire, at that time Lieutenant-Governor of the Island of St. John, to Lord Sydney, one of His Majesty's principal Secretaries of State, containing his reasons for having suspended Peter Stewart, Esquire, from the office of Chief Justice of the said Island, their Lordships have reported to the King their opinion that Mr. Stewart ought to be restored to his said office, which report His Majesty has, by his order in Council of the 28th August last, copy of which I enclose, been pleased to approve, and I am commanded by the King to signify to you his pleasure, that you do immediately restore the said Peter Stewart to his office of Chief Justice of the Island of St. John."

On 24th November, 1789, the Lieutenant-Governor replying to Mr. Grenville said:

"I was induced in June last, by and with the advice of His Majesty's Council, to restore Mr. Chief Justice Stewart, until His Majesty's pleasure should become known, to the execution of the duties of his office, from which he had long been suspended by my predecessor. I am to this day ignorant of the specific charges of the suspension and therefore cannot form any opinion of the nature and weight of them."

Chief Justice Stewart had been suspended from the duties of his office for four years. The writer has been unable to find any valid reason for his suspension, which seems to have been an outrageous abuse of authority on the part of Lieutenant-Governor Patterson. Stewart seems to have been a painstaking and upright judge. He does not appear to have had any serious difficulties to contend with during the remaining years of his judicial career. Towards the close of the year 1800 he retired from active work, and resigned his office after a service of a quarter of a century. He died five years later, on 10th November, A. D. 1805.

## CHAPTER VIII.

## THOMAS COCHRAN, THIRD CHIEF JUSTICE OF PRINCE EDWARD ISLAND.

THOMAS Cochran, sometime Chief Justice of Prince Edward Island, was a son of Hon. Thomas Cochran, who in 1784 was Speaker of the House of Assembly of Nova Scotia, and, in 1788, was a member of the Council of that province. The Cochran family was a distinguished one. It consisted of five, three sons and two daughters. Of these one son, William, became a general in the British army, another became Attorney-General and afterwards Chief Justice of Gibraltar. One daughter married Commodore, afterwards Sir Rupert George, and another became the wife of Dr. John Inglis, the second Bishop of Nova Scotia.

Thomas Cochran, the eldest son and the subject of this sketch, was born in Halifax. He entered King's College, in Windsor, Nova Scotia, in 1789, one of the first batch of matriculants in that institution. Shortly after graduation, he studied law at Lincoln's Inn and was called to the Bar in 1801. The same year, he was appointed Chief Justice of Prince Edward Island. He was supposed to be the youngest man, in the history of the Empire, to attain to so dignified a position. Cochran held the office of Chief Justice a very short time, a little over one year. Nothing of importance transpired during his tenure of the position. Interest in his career centres in its tragic ending. His commission, as Chief Justice, was dated 24th October, 1801. That of his successor, Robert Thorpe, bore the date of 10th November, 1802.

On 25th June, he was appointed Judge of the King's Bench of Upper Canada. He was not thirty years of age, yet Lord Hobart, in writing to Lieutenant-Governor Hunter, expressed his satisfaction as to Cochran's ability to fill the position. In his letter, dated 31st May, 1802, Lord Hobart says:

"Mr. Cochran, at present Chief Justice of the Island of Prince Edward, will proceed to your government as *puisne*, in the room of

Mr. Alcock. These arrangements will, I trust, ensure a continuance of the regularity and ability with which the business of the Courts in the two provinces have so long been conducted."

In the opening years of the nineteenth century, two brothers named Farewell, from the United States, established a trading post for furs at what is now Port Whitby. In 1804 they made a trip into the Indian country, taking with them a hired man named John Sharp, pitching their camp at Ball Point on Walpole Island in Lake Scugog. One day on their return from a trading expedition, they found Sharp murdered, his head having been smashed with a heavy club.

The crime plainly had been committed by an Indian. The Farewells trailed the murderer, a well-known Indian, Ogetonicut, and traced him to the Peninsula of East York, now Hiawatha Island, in the Harbour of Toronto.

A brother of Ogetonicut, named Whistling Dick, had been killed the previous year by a white man and Ogetonicut had openly threatened revenge. Lieutenant-Governor Hunter had promised that the slayer of Whistling Dick should be punished, but he could not be arrested; Ogetonicut, becoming impatient of delay and in vengeance for his brother's murder, determined to kill some other white man, and murdered Sharp.

After some demur, the Indians delivered Ogetonicut to the officers of the law and he was lodged in the gaol of the Home District for trial. There was doubt as to whether the crime had been committed within the Home District, and a survey disclosed it as being within the Newcastle District, within which it had to be tried. The land travelling was bad, and most of the traffic was by the lake in canoe, whale-boat or schooner.

The Provincial Government had a schooner, named the Speedy (Captain Thomas Paxton), which was ordered to convey the prisoners to Newcastle. Captain Paxton objected to making the voyage, about 100 miles, as the schooner was not sea-worthy, but his objections were over-ruled and he was ordered to sail. In the schooner went the Assize judge, Mr. Justice Thomas Cochran. With him went Solicitor-General Gray as Crown prosecutor. With him also sailed Angus McEachern, of the Upper Canada Bar, who had been Clerk of the Legislative Assembly of the province during the first two Parliaments and was now a member of the third, who was to defend the Indian. There were also Mr. Fisk (the High Bailiff of York), two Indian interpreters, Mr. Herchimes, a York merchant, and several witnesses — in all with captain and crew, thirty-nine persons. The Speedy set sail on 7th October, 1804; "the weather being even then stormy; she was sighted the following day opposite what is now Lakeport, about ninety miles east of Toronto, but was never seen again. Judge, counsel, constable, prisoner, witnesses, interpreters, merchant, captain and crew were all engulfed in the angry waters and not even a spar of the schooner ever again came to mortal ken. A single hencoop came ashore, which was supposed by some to have belonged to the unfortunate vessel, but even that is doubtful."*

---

*Authorities for above: King's College (Nova Scotia) Records:—"Church Work," Halifax, N. S., 1921; "Lives of the Judges of Upper Canada," by David R. Read; Toronto, Russell and Hutchison 1888. "Robert Isaac Day Gray, First Solicitor General of Upper Canada," by Hon. Mr. Justice Riddell of the Supreme Court of Ontario:—Canadian Law Times, Vol. XLI, No. 7, July, 1921.

## CHAPTER IX.

## ROBERT THORPE, FOURTH CHIEF JUSTICE OF PRINCE EDWARD ISLAND.

UPON the resignation of Thomas Cochran as Chief Justice of Prince Edward Island, Robert Thorpe, a member of the Irish Bar, was appointed to the vacant position. The writer has been unable to learn much about him before his coming to Prince Edward Island. He, for some unknown reason, had become a protege of Lord Castlereagh's. One would not go far wrong, as suggested by Mr. Justice Riddell,* in conjecturing that the reason had something to do with the union of Great Britain and Ireland. It was through Castlereagh's influence that Thorpe was appointed Chief Justice of Prince Edward Island. His commission bore date the 10th day of November, A. D. 1802. Mr. John A. Mathieson (now Chief Justice Mathieson)† writes of Thorpe that: "He failed to make history, from which fact it is fair to assume that he succeeded in his office." This is perfectly correct, so far as Thorpe's career in Prince Edward Island is concerned, but it is by no means the case with regard to his subsequent career.

While Thorpe held the Chief Justiceship, the Earl of Selkirk came to the Island, in 1803, bringing with him over eight hundred settlers from Scotland. While on the Island he met Thorpe at Lieutenant-Governor Fanning's. Selkirk, who was a shrewd observer, gives the following sketch of the Chief Justice: "The Chief Justice dined with him (Fanning). Mr. Thorpe, a native of the Kingdom (of Ireland) and not deficient in the natural qualifications of enhancing his own importance, and is hand and glove with all great people, being here only on an occasional retirement for

---

*Mr. Justice Thorpe, "The leader of the First Opposition in Upper Canada," by William Penwick Riddell, LL. D., F. R. S. (Can.), Justice of Supreme Court of Ontario, Canadian Law Times, Vol. XL, No. 11, p. 915.

†"Bench and Bar," in "Past and Present of Prince Edward Island," p. 129.

health, etc. He has, however, ideas and cleeks in his head to hang inferences upon, which does not seem to be the case with the Governor.*

Owing to irregularity in the receipt of his salary, Thorpe, in 1804, visited England to get matters straightened out. On the voyage he was captured by the French. He gives an account of this adventure in a letter to the Earl of Camden, dated Duke street, Westminster, 7th November, 1804, as follows: "Owing to a misconception relative to my salary as Chief Justice of St. John's (Prince Edward Island), almost the entire of my first year's income was withheld. . . . With the approbation of the Governor, I determined, by my personal appearance, to rectify the mistake and prevent, in future, any derangement of my affairs. Off the coast of Ireland I was captured by the French and carried into Passage in Spain, from whence escaping to Bilbao, I, with difficulty, procured a passage to England; the season will not permit my immediate return as I had intended, and have, therefore, to request Your Lordship's permission to remain here until spring."

Fanning and Thorpe could not agree, and it was determined to send the latter to another position. He was appointed Puisne Justice of the Court of King's Bench in Upper Canada, succeeding Mr. Cochran, his predecessor also in the Supreme Court of Prince Edward Island, who was drowned in the Speedy. "He arrived in York (now Toronto) in September, 1805. He seems to have considered himself an emissary of the Imperial Government and a spy on the colonial administration; he certainly tried in every way to "enhance his own importance."† When leaving Prince Edward Island, as a parting salutation, he characterized the people there as, "the worst people in the world are at Prince Edward Island. . . . I blessed you for sending me away."‡

Thorpe had been but a short time in Upper Canada before he began a bitter campaign against the Governor and the government. A vacancy in the representation of Durham, Simcoe and the East Riding of York having occurred, Thorpe contested the constituency and was elected by a large majority. He seems to have consolidated

---

*Selkirk's Diary, No. 1, Archives, 11th August, 1803.

*Mr. Justice Riddell, 40 Can. Law Times 916-917.

†Letter, Thorpe to Under Secretary Cooke, October 1, 1805. Canadian Archives, Q. 303, p. 177
— Riddell, p. 917.

all the elements in the House which were hostile to the Government, and proceeded to build up an opposition party, of which he was the leader. He continued his activities outside the House. Francis Gore, the Governor, complained of his conduct to Wyndham, Secretary of State, and he was rebuked.

Mr. Justice Riddell, in the article already referred to, gives an account of what followed: Mr. Justice Powell had heard in England that it was intended to suspend Thorpe. "With Gore's (the Governor's) perfect approbation, Powell, before the arrival of Castlereagh's despatch, called on Thorpe and told him what was coming. He also told him that if he would ask Gore for leave of absence, before the matter became public, he would receive it and money to convey him to Europe. That he at once refused, said he could not be removed without a hearing before the Privy Council, and claimed that everything he had done was by direction of the Secretary of State. He left the province without leave of absence and without the knowledge of the Governor. . . . His suspension was made final . . .; he never again appeared in Canada; and no other judge has ever offered himself for election to the Lower House of Upper Canada."*

Returning to England, Thorpe was appointed Chief Justice of Sierra Leone, where he remained many years. From there he brought home a budget of complaints. To again quote Mr. Justice Riddell, he was cashiered for this. . . . It was not the mere bringing of complaints to London which proved fatal to Thorpe. He made a most vigorous, if not virulent, attack in print against the African institution and its predecessor, the Sierra Leone Company, organized for the benefit of free blacks on the West Coast of Africa. Neither director nor manager escaped the lash of his pen. Wilberforce was, by implication, charged with hypocrisy; Zachary Macaulay (father of Lord Macaulay) with making money out of the pretended charity, and all were implored to let the unfortunate blacks alone. Perhaps his worst offence was making public that while a poor black settler, Kisil, could not get his pay for work and labour done long before for the Company, Macaulay (then lately Secretary and always director) received fifty guineas for importing ten tons of rice into England from the West Coast of

---

*Riddell, pp. 921, 922.

Africa; and while £14 5s 4d was spent "for clothing African boys at school," £107 12s 0d went "for a piece of plate to Mr. Macaulay." Thorpe was unwise enough to expose the seamy side of charitable institutions; and "when we consider that H. R. H. the Duke of Gloucester was president; Lords Lansdowne, Selkirk, Grenville, Calthorpe, Gambies and Teignmouth were vice-presidents, members of Parliament like Wilberforce, Babington, Homer, Stephen, Wilbraham, etc., were members of the institution, and that Wilberforce was a bosom friend of Pitt's, we need not wonder at Thorpe's dismissal.*

*Mr. Justice Riddell, Can. Law Times, Vol. XL, pp. 922, 923. See also Read's "Lives of the Judges of Upper Canada," p. 77 and seq, Rowsell and Hutchison, Toronto, 1888.

## CHAPTER X.

## CAESAR COLCLOUGH, FIFTH CHIEF JUSTICE OF PRINCE EDWARD ISLAND.

CHIEF Justice Colclough is best known to fame by Bushe's impromptu on his crossing a ferry, near Ballina, in a violent storm. With several other barristers, going on circuit, Colclough had arrived at the ferry while a very bad storm was raging. The ferryman feared to attempt a crossing. Mr. Colclough, who had business of importance awaiting his arrival, threw his saddle-bags into the boat and ordered the man to put him across. Bushe, instantly composed the following:

> "While meaner souls the tempest keeps in awe,
> Intrepid Caesar crossing Ballina
> Shouts to the boatman, shivering in his rags,
> You carry Caesar and his saddle bags."\*

He was appointed Chief Justice on the recommendation of Lord Camden in consequence of services performed during the rebellion of 1708, in Ireland, with which his Lordship, as Lord Lieutenant of that country, was acquainted. He was appointed on the first of January, 1806, with a yearly salary of £500, payable in London.

Colclough reached Halifax, on his way to the Island, on 24th November, 1806, too late to get over except by ice boats, in which he did not choose to trust himself and family. He had, therefore, to remain in Halifax all winter. In the meantime he had heard from the Island, from the Governor and the Attorney-General, and was sorry to find the utmost ill-will between them and each wished to engage him. Chief Justice Blowers of Nova Scotia advised him not to arrive on the Island, if possible, until the day previous to the

---

\*The writer, writing from memory, believes that this appeared in Shiell's Memoirs, and in Barrington's (Sir Jonah) Sketches of the Irish Bar, two racy works, very popular, half a century ago, copies of which he has been unable to procure for verification.

sitting of the Supreme Court, as he would thus get on the Bench without being supposed to be biased by any one, and his decisions would have the credit of impartiality. He intended, as far as was consistent with his duty, to support the Governor, "as his principal ever has been to so do by the existing government."*

Lieutenant-Governor DesBarres, writing from Charlottetown to Edward Cook, on 2nd July, 1807, says: "I am happy in informing you that our Chief Justice arrived here two days ago, and that he is this moment sitting on the Bench, where he is much wanted. He appears to me to be a man of whom nothing but good is to be expected."

Colclough, for a time, held the confidence of the House of Assembly as well as that of the Lieutenant-Governor. On 7th April, 1809, the House unanimously resolved that, "contemplating with great satisfaction the beneficial effects resulting to this Island from able, upright and dignified administration of justice, since the arrival of Chief Justice Colclough thereon — Ordered, that the thanks of this House be presented to him for the same, and also ordered that the Speaker do enclose the foregoing resolution to Chief Justice Colclough."

The good feeling between the Lieutenant-Governor and the Chief Justice did not long continue. On 14th August, 1809, he writes: "With infinite regret I feel it a duty I owe to myself to request that you will obtain permission for me to resign my situation as President of the Council or that Governor DesBarres may be directed to treat me and other gentlemen, who may differ in opinion from him therein, at least with decency and good manners, and not take the liberty of desiring one of our most respectable members to act honestly."

The good opinion gradually veered to the opposite point,† "In 1812 some of his friends in the Assembly introduced a resolution that the thanks of the Assembly should be presented to the Chief Justice for the firm and dignified conduct he had evidenced in his judicial capacity since arrival in this Island.

"The object evidently was to strengthen his hands in a contest then going on between him and Governor DesBarres, but the resolution was voted down, twelve to four, and thus became a weapon in the hands of his opponents.

---
*Colclough to Edward Cook, dated at Halifax, 19th May, 1807.
†Mathieson, "Past and Present of Prince Edward Island," pp. 130, 132.

"The majority in the Assembly followed up their triumph by passing a direct vote of censure upon the Chief Justice, setting forth that in certain proceedings taken in his Court against members of the 'Loyal Electors,' a society formed by the settlers in opposition to the proprietors, he had acted as solicitor, prosecutor and judge, and that, by seeking to appoint the sheriff he also aimed at having the choice of juries. His conduct was characterized as so dangerous to the lives, liberties and properties of His Majesty's subjects as to render it inadvisable that he should be longer continued in the discharge of the functions of his office. In accordance with the resolution an address was presented by the Speaker, Honourable Ralph Brecken, to the Lieutenant-Governor, praying for the suspension of the Chief Justice until His Majesty's pleasure should be known. The governor lost no time in granting the prayer of the Assembly, and the suspension took place in October, 1912. Shortly afterwards Governor DesBarres was recalled and the Chief Justice reinstated, but his usefulness in this field was gone."*

At this time Chief Justice Tremlett of Newfoundland had got himself into trouble with the people and Legislature of the "Ancient Colony," not dissimilar to Colclough's experience in Prince Edward Island. Each had become very unpopular. They exchanged positions in 1813. Tremlett was sent to Prince Edward Island on board one of His Majesty's ships, and Colclough was taken to Newfoundland in the same dignified manner. He arrived in St. John's in September, 1813. Judge Prowse† writes that "Chief Justice Colclough lived in the house near Mr. Eden's shop, Rawlin's Cross. He had a royal coat of arms over his door, and compelled every one to take off his hat when passing the house." Colclough remained in St. John's for three years; he was "not much of a lawyer, and a very sorry administrator." In note to page 391, Judge Prowse describes the two men: "Both these legal luminaries were at the time under a cloud, and it was considered a good arrangement to give each a new sphere, so a man-of-war carried Chief Justice Tremlett to the Island, and on her return voyage in October (September) brought back the illustrious Caesar." From notes furnished by the late Lieutenant-Governor Howlan and Judge

---

*Mathieson, p. 130.
†History of Newfoundland, pp. 390-1, Notes 1 and 2.

Alley of Prince Edward Island, Prowse adds the following: "Colclough, an Irish barrister belonging to an old family in Wexford, was appointed Chief Justice of the Island on the 1st May, 1807. For the first few years he gave great satisfaction; afterwards he got into trouble with Governor DesBarres and was suspended in September, 1812. Colclough claimed the right to appoint the sheriffs; he showed himself a partisan on the side of the proprietors against the settlers society known as the 'Loyal Electors.' DesBarres was recalled through the influence of the proprietors, and Colclough was reinstated, but as he was greatly disliked in Prince Edward Island, and Tremlett was unpopular in Newfoundland, they exchanged offices."

## CHAPTER XI.

## THOMAS TREMLETT, SIXTH CHIEF JUSTICE OF PRINCE EDWARD ISLAND.

THOMAS Tremlett, the sixth Chief Justice of Prince Edward Island, had, previously to his appointment to that office, held a similar position in Newfoundland for a period of ten years. He was not a lawyer himself and he succeeded two doctors and a Collector of Customs in the position of Chief Justice of Newfoundland. Tremlett, or Trimlett, was a merchant. "His firm had been very large Newfoundland merchants; they came to grief through some outside speculation, and, in accordance with the custom of the country, he received a Government office. There never was a more independent, upright judge than Tremlett; his decisions gave great offence to his quondam friends in the trade. They made constant complaints against him; finally they embodied their grievances in a long elaborate petition containing three specific charges of injustice. The Governor, Admiral Duckworth, furnished the old chief with the complaints against him. His reply was unique. Here it is in full:

"To the first charge, Your Excellency, I answer that it is a lie, to the second charge, I say, that it is a damned lie, and to the third charge it is a damned infernal lie, and, Your Excellency, I have no more to say. Your Excellency's obedient servant.

THOMAS TREMLETT."*

---

*Prowse, History of Newfoundland, pp. 360, 361. In a foot note,Judge Prowse says that besides this letter there was a formal official one from Tremlett. In a second note (p. 361) he gives the despatch of Governor, Admiral Duckworth, on the charges against Chief Justice Tremlett. In substance the Admiral writes:

"The Chief Justice of Newfoundland, as far as my intercourse with him has enabled me to judge, is a person who will not be influenced in the discharge of his duty by the approbation or disapprobation of any man. . . . Of his abilities I am far from thinking poorly. . . . He is certainly a man of great diligence and application, but he has by an irritability of temper, and a certain rudeness of manner which are natural to him, and by separating himself entirely from the society of the people of the town, rendered himself in the last degree unpopular; and however circumspect his future conduct may be in the discharge of his public duties, he will never be approved by them. . . . The complainants are urgent for a public examination of evidence upon the spot, alleging that they are not equal to a discussion with the Chief Justice on paper;

Tremlett was sustained in his position both by the Governor and the authorities in England. It was, however, considered desirable that a man of more legal knowledge, of more popular manners, and unconnected with local interests, should be appointed. His Lordship was, therefore, transferred to Prince Edward Island. The choice next fell upon an eccentric Irish gentlemen of good family, Caesar Colclough, who was Chief Justice of that Island. Tremlett was the last of the unlearned; subsequently the head of the Supreme Court had to be a barrister of not less than seven years standing.

Arrangements were arrived at for the exchange of positions between Tremlett and Colclough, which were carried out as set forth, in the sketch of Colclough preceding this article.

Tremlett was certainly unfit to fill the office of a judge in either Newfoundland or Prince Edward Island. His ignorance of law and of the practice of the Courts were insuperable obstacles to his satisfactory discharge of the duties of the chief justiceship. His personality was also against him. He was a crusty old bachelor,

---

that his representations are filled with falsehood, and that there is no other method of proceeding effectually than that of a public enquiry at which they may be able to bring forward their witnesses upon oath. . . .

"It is my duty to state distinctly, in this report, that in whatever instances his judgments may have erred, I have not found in any part of the Chief Justice's conduct the most remote appearance of corruption, nor when I had called upon the complainants, have they ventured to charge him with it in any instance."

In a report by the Lords of the Committee of Council for Trade and Foreign Plantations, dated 13th June, 1812, their Lordships, referring to complaints preferred by the merchants of St. John's against the Chief Justice, say; That, . . . "after a full enquiry and deliberation it does not appear that any act of wilful injustice has been sanctioned by Chief Justice Tremlett, nor is there any well attested proof of partiality or opinion or of any unaccountable delay or unwarrantable decision.

Under these circumstances, their Lordships have not recommended His Royal Highness to dismiss the Chief Justice from the high and important position which he fills and H. R. H. is therefore pleased to continue to confide to him the charge of administrating justice in the Island of Newfoundland."

In a separate paper, "their Lordships attribute the unpopularity of the Chief Justice not to any actual misconduct in his judicial capacity, but in some degree to the invidious nature of the duties which he is called upon to execute as well as to the ungracious manner in which they may be occassionally performed. Although there may have existed no ground for serious complaint and still less for any charge of partiality or corruption there can, however, be little doubt that whilst the Chief Justice is continued in his present position there will not be that general satisfaction and confidence that ought in all cases to accompany the administration of justice; and although H. R. H. will on no account consent to the dismissal of the Chief Justice or to any act which might imply the least suspicion of his integrity or even any disapprobation of his past conduct, H. R. H. would nevertheless be desirous that some arrangement should be made by which Mr. Tremlett might be employed with less embarrassment and inconvenience to himself and with greater prospect of advantage to the public service. . . . .

(Sgd.) BATHURST.

and was most profane in his language. He had a fair amount of ability and common sense. In this respect he had an advantage over Colclough, who had only a superficial knowledge of law, and no common sense. Tremlett's difficulties were largely due to his ignorance of law and practice, and to make matters worse the assistant judges were not lawyers and had never made a study of law.

An order for a commission under the seal of Prince Edward Island, appointing Thomas Tremlett Chief Justice of that colony was issued by command of His Royal Highness the Prince Regent at Carleton House. It bore date the 8th April, 1813. The commission itself was dated 22nd November of the same year. He held the position for over ten years, supported by Lieutenant-Governor Smith. He was finally removed at the same time and by the same means as Smith.

Between the two the Island was kept in a continual turmoil.*

---

*A fairly complete account of Tremlett and Chief Justice of Prince Edward Island has already been given in Part V, *ante*, to which the reader is referred for further particulars.

## CHAPTER XII.

## S. G. W. ARCHIBALD, SEVENTH CHIEF JUSTICE OF PRINCE EDWARD ISLAND.

MR. ARCHIBALD, the seventh Chief Justice of Prince Edward Island, arrived on Sunday, the 21st November, 1824, and was sworn in next day as successor to Chief Justice Tremlett. He was also appointed President of the Council. He was a member of the Nova Scotia bar, Solicitor-General and Speaker of the House of Assembly of that province.* He was a good lawyer, a man of ability, and well qualified for the position. Yet it was a very extraordinary appointment. He was a resident of Nova Scotia and could only attend to his duties in Prince Edward Island during the summer months. During the winter he was shut out by the ice.

Less than three months after his arrival, on 9th February, 1825, an Address of the Assembly to Lieutenant-Governor Ready prayed him to inform the House whether it was intended that Chief Justice Archibald should be permitted in future to reside in Nova Scotia and this colony be deprived entirely of his eminent talents in the Legislature, as well as his essential services for the greatest part of the year as Chief Justice. The Lieutenant-Governor answered that he was informed that on Mr. Archibald's appointment it was with the understanding that he should have permission to reside in Nova Scotia.

"It does not appear that he ever contemplated moving to this Island. He merely came here to attend the sessions of the Supreme Court and then returned to his practice in Nova Scotia.

"Complaints were soon heard from the Legislative Assembly that the distinguished abilities of the Chief Justice were not available to the government of the colony. Legal business could

---

*Mathieson, "Past and Present of Prince Edward Island," p. 136.

not be satisfactorily carried on even during vacation in the absence of the one judge who knew the law, but to make matters much worse, he was prevented by storms and ice from reaching the Island to attend the winter terms.

"It was suggested that the terms of the Court should be changed to suit the judge, but it was decided in the end to change the judge and let the terms stand. He resigned the chief justiceship in 1828, and was succeeded by the Hon. E. Jarvis, who discharged the duties of his office for twenty-five years with satisfaction to the colony."

# APPENDICES.

### APPENDIX A.
PATTERSON'S COMMISSION AS GOVERNOR OF THE ISLAND OF ST. JOHN.

### APPENDIX B.
PATTERSON'S INSTRUCTIONS.

### APPENDIX C.
FURTHER INSTRUCTIONS.

### APPENDIX D.
FURTHER INSTRUCTIONS.

### APPENDIX E.
PATTERSON'S COMMISSION AS LIEUTENANT-GOVERNOR.

# APPENDIX A.

## Walter Patterson's Commission as Governor.

Walter Patterson, Esq.,
  Governor of the Island of Saint John.*

George the Third, by the Grace of God of Great Britain, France and Ireland, King, Defender of the Faith, etc. To our trusty and well beloved Walter Patterson, Esquire, Greeting; Whereas, We did, by our letters patent bearing date the eleventh day of August, one thousand seven hundred and sixty-six, in the sixth year of our reign, constitute and appoint our trusty and well beloved William Campbell, Esquire, commonly called Lord William Campbell, to be our Captain-General and Governor-in-Chief in and over our Province of Nova Scotia, bounded on the westward by a line drawn from Cape Sable across the entrance of the Bay of Fundy to the mouth of the River Saint Croix by the said river to its source, and by a line drawn due north from thence to the southern boundary of our colony of Quebec to the northward, by the said boundary as far as the western extremity of the Bay des Chaleurs to the eastward, by the said Bay and the Gulph of St. Lawrence to the Cape or promontory called Cape Breton in the island of that name, including that island, the island Saint John and all other islands within six leagues of the coast, and to the southward by the Atlantic Ocean from the said Cape to Cape Sable aforesaid, including the island of that name and all other islands within forty leagues of the coast, with all the rights, members and appurtenances whatsoever thereunto belonging, for and during our will and pleasure as by the said recited Letters Patent, relation being thereunto had may more fully and at large appear; Now Know You that We have revoked and determined, and by these presents do revoke and determine, such part and so much of the said recited Letters Patent and every clause, article and thing therein contained as relates to or mentions the Island of Saint John. And further know you that We, reposing especial trust and confidence in the prudence, courage and loyalty of you, the said Walter Patterson, of our especial grace certain knowledge and mere motion have thought fit to constitute and appoint, and by these presents do constitute and appoint you, the said Walter Patterson, to be Captain-General and Governor-in-Chief, in and over our Island of Saint John and territories adjacent

*Public Archives of Canada, Series M, vol. 593, pp. 1-12.

thereto in America, and which now are or heretofore have been dependant thereupon; and We do hereby require and command you to do and execute all things in due manner which shall belong to your said command and the trusts We have reposed in you according to the several papers and directions granted or appointed you by this present Commission, and the instructions and authorities herewith given to you or by such further powers, instruction and authorities as shall at any time hereafter be granted or appointed you under our signet and sign manual or by our order in our Privy Council and according to such reasonable laws and statutes as shall hereafter be made and agreed upon by you with the advice and consent of the Council and Assembly of the Island under your government in such manner and form as is hereafter expressed. And our will and pleasure is that you, the said Walter Patterson, do after the publication of these our Letters Patent, and after the appointment of our council of our said Island in such manner and form as is prescribed in the instructions which you will herewith receive in the first place, take the oaths appointed to be taken by an Act passed in the first year of the reign of King George the first intituled (An Act for the further security of His Majesty's person and government and the succession of the Crown in the heirs of the late Princess Sophia, being Protestants, and for extinguishing the hopes of the pretended Prince of Wales and his open and secret abettors). As also that you make and subscribe the declaration mentioned in an Act of Parliament in the twenty-fifth year of the reign of King Charles the Second, intituled (An Act for preventing dangers which may happen from Popish recusants), and likewise that you take the oath usually taken by Governors in other colonies for the due execution of the office and trust of our Captain-General and Governor-in-Chief in and over our said Island and for the due and impartial administration of justice. And further that you take the oath required to be taken by Governors in the Plantations to do their utmost, the several laws relating to trade and the plantations be duly observed, which said oaths and declaration our Council of our said Island, or any three of the members thereof, have hereby full power and authority and are required to tender and administer to you and in your absence to our Lieutenant-Governor of our said Island. All which being duly performed you shall yourself administer unto each of the members of our said Council and also to our Lieutenant-Governor of our said Island the said oaths mentioned in the said Act intituled (An Act for the further security of His Majesty's person and government and the succession of the Crown in the heirs of the late Princess Sophia, being Protestants, and for extinguishing the hopes of the pretended Prince of Wales and his open and secret abettors). As also to cause them to make and subscribe the aforementioned declaration and to administer unto them the usual oaths for the due execution of their places and trusts; and We do further give and grant unto you, the said Walter Patterson, full power and authority from time to time, and at any time hereafter, by yourself or by any other to be authorized by you in this behalf, to administer and give the oaths mentioned in the said Act for the further security of His Majesty's person and government and the succession of the Crown in the heirs of the late Princess Sophia, being Protestants, and for extinguishing the hopes of the pretended Prince of Wales and his open and secret abettors, to all and every such person and persons as you shall think fit who shall at any time or times pass into our said Island or shall be resident or abiding there; and We do hereby authorize and empower you to keep and use the Public Seal, which will be herewith delivered to you, or shall be hereafter sent to you, for sealing all things whatsoever that shall pass the Great Seal of our said Island. And We do hereby give and grant unto you, the said Walter Patterson, full power and authority, with the advice and consent of our said Council, to be appointed as aforesaid so soon as the situation and circumstances or our Island under your government will admit thereof and when and as often as need shall require, to summon and call general assemblies of the freeholders and planters within the Island under your government in such manner as you in your discretion shall judge most proper or according to such further powers, instructions and authorities as shall be at any time hereafter granted and appointed you under our signet and sign manual, or by our order in our Privy Council, and our will and pleasure is that the persons thereupon duly elected by the major part of the freeholders of the respective counties, parishes or townships, and so returned, shall before their sitting take the oaths mentioned in the said Act intituled (An Act for the further security of His Majesty's person and government and the succession of the Crown in the heirs of the late Princess Sophia, being Protestants, and for extinguishing the hopes of the pretended Prince of Wales and his open and secret abettors) as also make and subscribe the aforementioned declaration, which oaths and declaration you shall commissionate fit persons under the Public Seal of that our Island to tender and administer unto them, and until the same shall be so taken and subscribed no person shall be capable of sitting, though elected. And We do hereby declare that the persons so elected and qualified shall be called and deemed the Assembly of our said Island of Saint John, and that you, the said Walter Patterson, by and with the advice and consent of our said Council and Assembly, or the major part of them, shall have full power and authority to make, constitute and ordain laws, statutes, and ordinances for the public peace, welfare and good government of our said Island and of the people and inhabitants thereof, and such others as shall resort thereto, and for the benefit of us, our heirs and successors, which said laws, statutes and ordinances are not to be repugnant but as near as may be agreeable to the laws and statutes of our Kingdom of Great Britain, provided that all such laws, statutes and ordinances of what nature or duration soever be within three months or sooner after the making thereof transmitted to us under our Seal of our said Island for our approbation or disallowance of the same, as also duplicates thereof by the next conveyance. And in case any or all of the said laws, statutes and ordinances not before confirmed by us shall at any time be disallowed and not approved and so signified by us, our heirs or successors, under our or their signet or sign manual, or by order of our or their Privy Council, unto you, the said Walter Patterson, or to the Commander-in-Chief of the said Island for the time being, then such and so many of the said laws, statutes and ordinances as shall be so disallowed and not approved shall from thenceforth cease, determine and become utterly void and of none effect, any thing to the contrary thereof notwithstanding. And to the end that nothing may be passed or done by our said Council or Assembly to the prejudice of us, our heirs and successors, we will and ordain that you, the said Walter Patterson, shall have and enjoy a negative voice, in the making and passing of all laws, statutes and ordinances as aforesaid, and that you shall and may likewise, from time to time as you shall judge necessary, adjourn, prorogue and dissolve all General Assemblies as aforesaid. And we do by these presents give and grant unto you, the said Walter Patterson, full power and authority, with the advice and consent of our said Council, to erect, constitute and establish such and so many Courts of Judicature and Public Justice within our said Island under your government as you and they shall think fit and necessary for the hearing and determining of all causes, as well criminal as civil, according to law and equity and for awarding execution thereupon, with all reasonable and necessary powers, authorities, fees and privileges belonging thereunto, as also to appoint and commissionate fit persons in the several parts of your government to administer the oaths mentioned in the aforesaid Act, as also to tender and administer the aforesaid declaration to such persons belonging to the said Courts as shall be obliged to take the same; and we do hereby grant unto you full power and authority to constitute and appoint judges and in cases requisite Commissioners of Oyer and Terminer Justices of the Peace, sheriffs and other necessary officers and ministers in our said Island for the better administration of justice and putting the laws in execution, and to administer or cause to be administered unto them such oath or oaths as are usually given for the due execution and performance of offices and places and for the clearing of truth in judicial causes; and we do hereby give and grant unto you full power and authority when you shall see cause, or shall judge any offender or offenders in criminal matters or for any fines or forfeitures due unto us fit objects of our mercy, to pardon all such offenders and to remit all such offences, fines and forfeitures, treason and wilful murders only excepted, in which cases you shall likewise have power upon extraordinary occasions to grant reprieves to the offenders until and to the intent our royal pleasure may be known therein. We do by these presents authorize and impower you to collate any person or persons to any churches, chapels or other ecclesiastical benefices within our said Island as often as any of them shall happen to be void. And we do hereby give and grant unto you, the said Walter Patterson, by yourself or by your captains and commanders by you to be authorized, full power and authority to levy, arm, muster and employ all persons whatsoever residing within our said Island, and as occasions shall serve to march from one place to another or to embark them for the resisting and withstanding of all enemies, pirates and rebels, both at land and sea, and to transport such forces to any of our plantations in America if necessity shall require for defence of the same against the invasion or attempts of any of our enemies, and to execute martial law in time of invasion or other times when by law it may be executed. And to do and execute all and every other thing or things which to our Captain-General or Governor-in-Chief doth or ought of right to belong. And we do hereby give and grant unto you full power and authority, by and with the advice and consent of our said Council, to erect, raise and build in our said Island such and so many forts and platforms, castles, cities, boroughs, towns and fortifications as you, by the advice aforesaid, shall judge necessary, and the same or any of them to fortify and furnish with ordinance, ammunition, and all sorts of arms fit and necessary for the security and defence of our said Island, and by the advice aforesaid the same again, or any part thereof, to demolish or dismantle as may be most convenient. And forasmuch as divers mutinies and disorders may happen by persons shipped and employed at sea during the time of war, and to the end that such as shall be shipped and employed at sea during the time of war may be better governed and ordered, we do hereby give and grant unto you, the said Walter Patterson, full power and authority to constitute captains, lieutenants, masters of ships and other commanders and officers, and to grant to such captains, lieutenants, masters of ships and other commanders and officers to execute the law martial during the time of war according to the directions of an Act passed in the twenty-second year of the reign of our late Royal grandfather, intituled An Act for amending, explaining and reducing into one Act of Parliament the laws relating to the government of His Majesty's ships, vessels and forces by sea, and to use such proceedings, authorities, punishments and executions upon any offender or offenders who shall be mutinous, seditious, disorderly or any way unruly, either at sea or during the time of their abode or residence in any of the ports, harbours or bays of our said Island as the cause shall be found to require according to martial law and the said directions during the time of war as aforesaid; provided that nothing herein contained shall be construed to the enabling you or any by your authority to hold plea or have any jurisdiction of any offence, cause, matter or thing committed or done upon the high sea or within any of the havens, rivers or creeks of our said Island under your government by any captain, commander, lieutenant, master, officer, seaman, soldier whatsoever, who shall be in our actual service and pay in or on board any of our ships of war or other vessels acting by immediate commission or warrant from our Commissioners for executing the office of our High Admiral, or from our High Admiral of Great Britain for the time being under the Seal of our Admiralty, but that such captain, commander, lieutenant, master, officer, seaman, soldier or other person so offending shall be left to be proceeded against and tried as their offences shall require either by commission under our Great Seal of Great Britain as the statute of the twenty-eighth of Henry VIII directs, or by commission from our said Commisioners for executing the office of our High Admiral of Great Britain for the time being according to the aforementioned Act intituled An Act for amending, explaining and reducing into one Act of Parliament the laws relating to the government of His Majesty's ships, vessels, and forces by sea, and not otherwise; provided, nevertheless, that all disorders and misdemeanors committed on shore by any captain, commander, lieutenant, master, officer, seaman, soldier or other person whatsoever belonging to any of our ships of war or other vessels acting by immediate commission or warrant from our said Commissioners for executing the office of our High Admiral, or from our High Admiral of Great Britain for the time being under the Seal of our Admiralty, may be tried and punished according to the laws of the place where any such disorders, offences and misdemeanors shall be committed on shore, notwithstanding such offender, being in our actual service, and born in our pay on board any such our ships of war or other vessels acting by immediate commission or warrant from our said Commissioners for executing the office of High Admiral or our High Admiral of Great Britain for the time being as aforesaid, so as He shall not receive any protection for the avoiding of justice for such offences committed on shore from any pretence of his being employed in our service at sea; and our further will and pleasure is that all public money raised or which shall be raised by any Act hereafter to be made within our said Island be issued out from warrant from you by and with the advice and consent of the Council and disposed of by you for the support of the government and not otherwise. And we likewise give and grant unto you full power and authority, by and with the advice and consent of our said Council, to settle and agree with the inhabitants of our said Island for such lands, tenements and hereditaments as now are or hereafter shall be in our power to dispose of, and them to grant to any person or persons upon such terms and under such moderate quit rents, services and acknowledgements to be thereupon reserved unto us as you, with the advice aforesaid, shall think fit; which said grants are to pass and be sealed by our Public Seal of our said Island, and being entered upon record by such officer or officers as shall be appointed thereunto shall be good and effectual in law against us, our heirs and successors. And we do hereby give you, the said Walter Patterson, full power and authority to order and appoint fairs, marts and markets, as also such and so many ports, harbours, bays, havens and other places for the convenience and security of shipping and for the better loading and unloading of goods and merchandise in such and so many places as by and with the adivce and consent of our said Council shall be thought fit and necessary. And we do hereby require and command all officers and ministers, civil and military, and all other inhabitants of our said Island to be obedient, aiding and assisting unto you, the said Walter Patterson, in the execution of this our commission and of the powers and authorities herein contained, and in case of your death or absence out of our said Island to be obedient, aiding and assisting unto such person as shall be appointed by us to be our Lieutenant-Governor or Commander-in-Chief of our said Island, to whom we do therefor by these presents give and grant all and singular the powers and authorities herein granted to be by him executed and enjoyed during our pleasure or until your arrival within our said Island; and if upon death or absence out of our said Island there be no person upon the place commissionated or appointed by us to be our Lieutenant-Governor or Commander-in-Chief of the said Island, our will and pleasure is that the eldest councillor who shall be at the time of your death or absence residing within our said Island shall take upon him the said administration of the government and execute our said commission and instructions, and the several powers and authorities therein contained, in the same manner and to all intents and purposes as other our Governor or Commander-in-Chief should or ought to do in case of your absence until your return, or in all cases until our further pleasure be known therein. And we do hereby declare, ordain and appoint that you, the said Walter Patterson, shall and may hold, exercise and enjoy the office and place of our Captain-General and Governor-in-Chief in and over our said Island of Saint John, with all its rights, members and appurtenances whatsoever, together with all and singular the powers and authorities hereby granted unto you for and during our will and pleasure. In witness, etc., witness ourself at Westminster the fourth day of August, 1769.

BY WRIT OF PRIVY SEAL.

## APPENDIX B.

### Patterson's Instructions.*

*Instructions to our trusty and well-beloved Walter Patterson, Esquire, our Captain-General and Governor-in-Chief in and over our Island of Saint John, and the territories adjacent thereto in America, and which now are or heretofore have been dependent thereupon. Given at Our Court at St. James' the fourth day of August, 1769, in the ninth year of our reign.*

First. With these our instructions you will receive our Commission under our Great Seal of Great Britain, constituting you our Captain-General and Governor-in-Chief in and over our Island of St. John and the territories dependent thereon in America; you are therefore to fit yourself with all convenient speed, and to repair to our said Island of St. John, and being arrived at Charlottetown within our said Island, which we do hereby appoint to be the capital of our said Government, and the chief place of your residence, you are forthwith to cause our said Commission to be read and published, in such manner and form and with such solemnity and ceremonial as is usually practised on like occasion in our other colonies in America. And you are to take upon you the execution of the place and trust we have reposed in you, and the administration of the Government, and to do and execute all things in due manner that shall belong unto your command according to the several powers and authorities of our said Commission under our Great Seal of Great Britain, and these our instructions to you or such further powers and instructions as shall at any time hereafter be granted or appointed you under our signet and sign manual, or by our order in our Privy Council.

Second. The powers and directions contained in our said Commission to you under our Great Seal of Great Britain will fully point out to you our royal intention with regard to the form and constitution of Government which is to be established within our Island of Saint John; the first object of your duty will therefore be to constitute a Council to advise and assist you in the administration of the affairs of our said Government, which said Council is for the present to be composed of the following persons, viz.,

---

*Public Archives of Canada. Commissions and Instructions — Prince Edward Island, 1769-1839. Series M, vol. 593.

Thomas DesBrisay, Esquire, our Lieutenant-Governor of our said Island, or our Lieutenant-Governor of our said Island for the time being; our Chief Justice of our said Island for the time being, William Allanbey and David Higgins, Esquires; and of such and so many other persons, chosen by you from amongst the principal inhabitants and proprietors of land in our said Island, as shall make up the number of twelve; which said persons so chosen by you shall be to all intents and purposes members of our said Council until our royal will and pleasure be further known or until we shall think fit to appoint other persons in their stead. It is nevertheless our will and pleasure that the said Chief Justice shall not be capable of taking the administration of the Government upon the death or absence of you, our Governor or Commander-in-Chief for the time being.

Third. It is the further will and pleasure that our said Council, so to be constituted as aforesaid, shall have and enjoy all the powers, privileges and authority usually exercised and enjoyed by the members of our Councils in our other American colonies, subject nevertheless to the like rules, restrictions and limitations as to their attendance, suspension, and removal as are prescribed with respect to the Councils of our other colonies by our instructions to our Governor thereof; that is to say, that, if it shall at any time hereafter happen that there are less than seven members of our Council resident within our said Island of Saint John you shall in that case choose as many persons out of the principal inhabitants of our said Island as will make up the full number of the Council to be seven and no more; which persons so chosen and appointed by you shall be to all intents and purposes councillors in our said Island till either they shall be confirmed by us or by the nomination of others by us, under our sign manual and signet, our said Council shall have seven or more persons in it.

That you do suspend and remove any of the members of our said Council from sitting, voting and assisting therein, if you shall find just cause for so doing, and appoint others in their stead until our pleasure shall be known; but that you do not suspend or remove any of the members of our Council, when they shall have been confirmed by us as aforesaid, without good and sufficient cause, nor without the consent of the majority of the said Council, signified in Council after due examination of the charge against such Councillor, and his answer thereunto; and in case of suspension of any of them you are to cause your reasons for so doing, together with the charges and proofs against such person, and his answer thereunto, to be duly entered upon the Council books, and forthwith to transmit copies thereof to us by one of our principal Secretaries of State; nevertheless if it should happen that you should have reasons for suspending any of the said persons not fit to be communicated to the Council, you may in that case suspend such persons without the consent of the said Council; but you are thereupon immediately to send unto us by one of our principal Secretaries of State an account of your proceedings therein, together with your reasons at large for such suspension, as also your reasons at large for not communicating the same to the Council, and duplicates thereof by the next opportunity.

That if any of the members of our said Council shall hereafter absent themselves from the said Island, and continue absent above the space of six months together, without leave from you or from our Commander-in-Chief for the time being first obtained under your or his hand and seal, or shall remain absent for the space of one year without our leave given them under our royal signet and sign manual, their place or places in the said Council shall immediately thereupon become void; and that if any of the members of our said Council then residing in the Island under your command shall hereafter wilfully absent themselves when duly summoned, without a just and lawful cause, and shall persist therein after admonition, you suspend the said councillors so absenting themselves till our further pleasure be known, giving us timely notice thereof; and we do hereby will and require you that this our royal pleasure be signified to the several members of our Council aforesaid and entered in the Council books of the Island under your Government as a standing rule.

Fourth. That establishing such and so many Courts of Judicature as shall be found necessary for the due and impartial administration of justice, and the directing the rule of their proceedings will necessarily become an immediate and important object of considerable consideration; it will therefore be your duty to give the fullest attention to it, to consult and advise with the person whom we have appointed to be our Chief Justice of our said Island as to the measures proper to be pursued for this purpose, governing yourself therein as far as difference of situation and circumstances will admit by what had been approved and found most advantageous in respect to such establishments in our neighbouring colony of Nova Scotia; and taking especial care that, at the same time, nothing is omitted from which our good subjects there may derive that privilege and protection which the British Constitution allows them in all parts of our dominions, they be not harrassed and vexed with unnecessary attendances and proceedings, or oppressed by exorbitant fees or demands; but that on the contrary justice be administered in the most speedy and effectual way, and all fees of offices and officers of every kind settled by you with the advice of the Council upon a plan of the greatest moderation. And to the end that nothing may be done or finally established in our said Island of St. John under your Government without our consent or approbation, you are by the first opportunity and with all convenient speed to transmit unto us by one of our principal Secretaries of State, authentic copies of all acts, grants, orders, commissions, or other powers by virtue of which any courts, offices, jurisdictions, pleas, authorities, fees and privileges have been settled or established for our confirmation or disallowance; and in case any or all of them shall at any time or times be disallowed or not approved then such and so many as shall be so disallowed or not approved, and so signified by us, shall cease, determine and be not longer continued or put in practise.

You are to take care that no man's life, member, freehold or goods be taken away or harmed in our said Island, otherwise than by established and known laws not repugnant to be as much as may be but agreeable to the laws of this Kingdom.

Sixth. Whereas, we are above all things desirous that all our subjects may enjoy their legal rights and properties, you are to take especial care that if any person be committed for any criminal matters (unless for treason or felony plainly and especially expressed in the warrant of commitment) he have free liberty to petition by himself or otherwise the Chief Judge or any of the Judges of the Common Pleas for a writ of habeas corpus, which upon such application shall be granted and served on the provost marshal, gaoler or other officer having the custody of such prisoner, or shall be left at the goal or place where the prisoner is confined; and the said provost marshal or other officer shall, within three days after such service (on the petitioners paying the fees and charges and giving security that he will not escape by the way) make return of the writ and prisoner before the judge who granted out the said writ, and there certify the true cause of the imprisonment, and the said judge shall discharge such prisoner, taking his recognizance and security for his appearance at the Court where the offence is cognizable, and certify the said writ and recognizance into the Court, unless such offences appear to the said judge not bailable by the laws of England.

Seventh. And in case the said chief judge or any of the judges of the Common Pleas shall refuse to grant a writ of habeas corpus, on view of the copy of commitment, or upon oath made of such copy having been denied the prisoner, or any person requiring the same in his behalf, or shall delay to discharge the prisoner after the granting such writ, the said chief judge or other judge shall incur the forfeiture of his place.

Eighth. You are likewise to declare our pleasure, that in case the provost marshal or other officer shall imprison any person above twelve hours, except by a mittimus setting forth the cause thereof, he be removed from his said office.

Ninth. And upon the application of any person wrongfully committed, the said chief judges or any of the said judges shall issue his warrant to the provost marshal or other officer to bring the prisoner before him, who shall be discharged without bail or paying fees. And the provost marshal or other officer refusing obedience to such warrant shall be thereupon removed; and if any of the said judges denies his warrant he shall likewise incur the forfeiture of his place.

Tenth. You shall give directions that no prisoner being set at large by an habeas corpus be recommitted for the same offence but by the Court where he is bound to appear; and if any of the said judges, provost marshal, or other officer, contrary hereunto, shall recommit such person so bailed or delivered, you are to remove him from his place, and if the provost marshal, or other officer having the custody of the prisoner, neglects to return the habeas corpus, or refuses a copy of the commitment within six hours after the demand made by the prisoner or any other in his behalf, he shall likewise incur the forfeiture of his place.

Eleventh. And for the better prevention of long imprisonments, you are to appoint two Courts of Oyer and Terminer to be held yearly, viz., on the second Tuesday in December and the second Tuesday in June; and you are to recommend to the Assembly, when met, forthwith to make provision for defraying the charge of holding such courts.

Twelfth. You are to take care that all prisoners in cases of treason and felony have free liberty to petition in open Court for their trials, that they be indicted at the first Court of Oyer and Terminer, unless it appear upon oath that the witnesses against them could not be produced; and that they be tried at the second Court or discharged; and the said chief judge or other judge, upon motion made the last day of the sessions in open Court, shall discharge the prisoner accordingly; and upon refusal of the said judge and provost marshal or other officer to do their respective duties herein, they shall be removed from their places.

Thirteenth. Provided always, that no person be discharged out of prison who stands committed for debt by any decree of chancery, or any legal proceedings of any court of record.

Fourteenth. And for the preventing of any exactions that may be made upon prisoners you are to declare our pleasure that no chief judge or oth er judge of our said Court of Common Pleas shall receive for himself, or clerks, for granting a writ of habeas corpus, more than two shillings and sixpence, and the like sum for taking a recognizance, and that the provost marshal or other officer shall not receive more than five shillings for every commitment, one shilling and three pence for the bond the prisoner is to sign, one shilling and three pence for every copy of a mittimus, and one shilling and three pence for every mile he bringeth back the prisoner.

Fifteenth. And further, you are to cause this our royal pleasure, signified to you by the nine articles of instructions immediately preceding this, to be made public and registered in the Council books of our said Island.

Sixteenth. You are to take care that all writs be issued in our name within our said Island.

Seventeenth. The forming a lower House of Assembly or House of Representatives for our said Island of Saint John is a consideration that cannot be too early taken up, and ought to be maturely weighed; for until this object is attainable the most important interests of the inhabitants will necessarily remain without that advantage and protection which can only arise out of the vigour and activity of a complete constitution. The division already made of the Island of Saint John into counties, parishes and townships will naturally suggest to you what ought to be established in respect to the places that should elect representatives: and by a due attention to what has been found practicable and convenient in forming the like constitutions in the late established colonies of Nova Scotia and Georgia, you cannot materially err in such other regulations incident to this institution as may be necessary, until the form of it and the rules and method of proceeding can be more precisely defined by a permanent law. It will be necessary, however, in forming this essential establishment, that the greatest care should be taken that no colour or pretence is given for the assumption of any powers or privileges by the said lower House of Assembly or House of Representatives which have not been allowed to Assemblies in our other colonies; and that their mode of passing laws, and the exercise of that negative upon those laws which we have thought fit to reserve to you by our commission under our Great Seal, do conform to, and correspond with those regulations and restrictions which have been established in this respect in our other American colonies. That is to say,

That the style of enacting laws, statutes and ordinances to be passed in the Island be by the Governor, Council and Assembly, and no other.

That each different matter be provided for by a different law, without including in one and the same Act such things as have no proper relation to each other.

That no clause be inserted in any Act or ordinance which shall be foreign to what the title of it imports; and that no perpetual clause be part of any temporary law.

That no law or ordinance whatever be suspended, altered, continued, revived, or repealed, by general words; but that the title and date of such law or ordinance be particularly mentioned in the enacting part.

That no law or ordinance respecting private property be passed without a clause suspending its execution until our royal will and pleasure is known, nor without a saving of the rights of us, our heirs and successors, and of all bodies politic and corporate, and of all other persons except such as are mentioned in the said law or ordinance and of those claiming by, from and under them; and before such law or ordinance is passed proof must be made before you in Council, and entered in the Council books, that public notification was made of the party's intention to apply for such Act in the several parish churches where the lands in question lie, for three Sundays at least successively, before any such law or ordinance shall be proposed. You are to transmit, and annex to the said law or ordinance, a certificate under your hand that the same passed through all the forms above mentioned.

That in all laws or ordinances for levying money or imposing fines, forfeitures or penalties, express mention be made that the same is granted or reserved to us, our heirs and successors, for the public uses of our said Island and the support of the government thereof, as by the said law or ordinance shall be directed. And you are not to permit any clause whatsoever to be inserted in any law for levying any money, or the value of money, whereby the same shall not be made liable to be accounted for unto us here in this Kingdom and to our Commissioners of our Treasury, or our High Treasurer for the time being, and audited by our Auditor General of our Plantations or his deputy.

That all such laws, statutes and ordinances be transmitted by you within three months after their passing, or sooner if opportunity offers, to us by one of our principal Secretaries of State, that they be fairly abstracted in the margents and accompanied with very full and particular observations upon each of them; that is to say, whether the same is introductive of a new law, declaratory of a former law, or does repeal a law then before in being. And you are also to transmit in the fullest manner the reasons and occasion for enacting such laws or ordinances, together with fair copies of the Journals of the Proceedings of the Council and Assembly, which you are to require from the clerks of the said Council and Assembly.

That you do not pass or give your assent to any bill or bills in the Assembly of our said Island of an unusual or extraordinary nature and importance, wherein our prerogative or the property of our subjects may be prejudiced, or the trade and shipping of this Kingdom any ways affected, until you shall have first transmitted unto us by one of our principal Secretaries of State the draught of such a bill or bills, and shall have received our royal pleasure thereupon, unless you take care that there be a clause inserted therein, suspending and deferring the execution until our pleasure shall be known concerning the same.

That you do not give assent to any law that shall be enacted for a less time than two years, except in cases of imminent necessity, or immediate temporary expediency; and that you do not re-enact any law, to which the assent of us or our royal predecessors has once been refused, without express leave for that purpose first

APPENDIX B.   457

obtained from us, upon a full representation by you to be made to us by one of our principal Secretaries of State, of the reasons and necessity for passing such law; nor give your assent to any law for repealing any other law passed in your government; whether the same has or has not received our royal approbation, unless you take care that there be a clause inserted therein suspending and deferring the execution thereof until our royal pleasure shall be known concerning the same.

That no law for raising any imposition on wines or other strong liquors be made to continue for less than one whole year; as also that all other laws made for the support of government shall be without limitation of time except the same be for a temporary service and which shall expire and have their full effect within the time therein prefixed.

That you do not assent to pass any Act in our Island of St. John under your government whereby bills of credit may be struck or issued in lieu of money, either to you the Governor or to any Lieutenant-Governor or Commander-in-Chief, or to any of the members of our Council or Assembly, or to any other person whatsoever except to us, our heirs and successors, unless there be a clause inserted in such Act declaring that the same shall not take effect until the said Act shall have been approved and confirmed by us, our heirs and successors.

That you do not upon any pretence whatsoever, on pain of our highest displeasures, give your assent to any law wherein the natives or inhabitants of the Island of Saint John under your government are put on a more advantageous footing than those of this Kingdom, or whereby duties shall be laid upon British shipping or upon the product or manufactures of Great Britain upon any pretence whatsoever.

Eighteenth. It is equally unnecessary and impracticable to point out to you in these our instructions all the various and important objects to which the several constitutions, both legislative and judicial, herein before established and defined will apply; such objects will be very many in the first establishment of government and will require an exertion of the greatest activity and discretion as to the rules and principles by which the proceedings either of the Council, Assembly or Courts of Judicature are to be governed in all cases not herein before provided for or explained. Many useful precedents may be found in the instructions to our Governor of Nova Scotia, a copy whereof is hereunto annexed, and by which you are to regulate your conduct as far as different circumstances will admit in all cases wherein they refer to establishments of a similar nature.

Nineteenth. The having a revenue competent to all the necessary services of government, both fixed and incidental established, upon a solid and permanent foundation, is essential to every civil institution of this nature, and ought to be one of the first objects of legislation, the establishment already formed will point out what the extent of that revenue should be and the nature of the duties and taxes to be granted to us for this purpose must depend upon circumstances that can neither be known nor judged of here, and upon a full consideration of what has been found most beneficial in other infant colonies in the like case. It will, however, be your duty, so soon as a General Assembly is formed, to recommend this matter to the consideration of the House of Representatives and require them in our name to grant to us such revenue as may amount to all the expenses of government upon some certain estimate.

Twentieth. In the meantime, and until such revenue can be established, we have taken into our royal consideration a proposal made by the principal proprietors of lots or townships within our said Island of Saint John by which they respectively engage to take out fresh grants for their lots under the seal of our Island of Saint John, in exchange for those they have already taken out under the seal of our province of Nova Scotia upon the following terms and conditions. That is to say,

That one moiety of the quit rent originally reserved on such lots and to commence at the expiration of five years from the date thereof shall, by the terms of these new grants, commence and become payable to us, our heirs and successors, from and after the first day of May last past.

That the other moiety, the payment of which was to take place at the expiration of ten years, shall, by the terms of the said new grants, not commence and become payable until the expiration of twenty years from the date thereof.

Twenty-first. As this proposal has in view to enable us to make provision for the support of government within our said Island until the inhabitants thereof shall be in a condition to provide for that purpose by a proper revenue arising out of the duties and taxes granted to us by Act of Legislature, we have thought fit graciously to accept the same; and therefore our will and pleasure is, that you do forthwith, upon your arrival in your Government, cause the said proposals, the original whereof in writing and subscribed by the proponents will be herewith delivered to you, to be registered and entered upon record upon the Council books; and that you do forthwith proceed to pass fresh patents under the seal of our said Island for the respective lots upon the terms and conditions above mentioned, for which patents no fee or reward whatever shall be taken either by yourself or by any other person acting under your authority.

Twenty-second. The annual amount of the quit rents which will thus become due and payable to us is estimated as follows, That is to say:

## Appendix B.

Twenty-six Lots at six shillings per one hundred acres, a moiety of which is..................................................................................780
Twenty-nine Lots at four shillings per one hundred acres.............580
Eleven Lots at two shillings per one hundred acres........................110
Rent of Town and Pasture Lots uncertain............................................

It is therefore our will and pleasure that out of the produce of our said revenue of quit rents so to be paid, as aforesaid, you do take to yourself as Governor of our said Island the sum of five hundred pounds sterling per annum, and that you also do cause the following annual salaries to be paid out of the said revenue to the several officers hereinafter mentioned, that is to say,

To the Secretary and Register of our said Island, one hundred and fifty pounds.

To the Chief Justice of our said Island, two hundred pounds.

To the Attorney General of our said Island, one hundred pounds.

To the Clerk of the Crown and Coroner, eighty pounds.

To the Provost Marshal, fifty pounds.

To a minister of the Church of England, one hundred pounds.

And it is our further will and pleasure that the said salaries, as well to yourself as to the rest of the officers above-mentioned, do commence and become payable from and after the first day of May last past, and that the same be paid quarterly by our Receiver General of our quit rents for our said Island, or his deputy, pursuant to warrants signed by you, our Governor, with the consent of our Council for our said Island, as directed by our commission under our Great Seal of Great Britain; provided, nevertheless, that it be understood, and we do hereby declare it to be our royal will and pleasure, that if the foregoing appropriation of our said quit rents shall fall short of the appointments above mentioned, either by a failure of consent in any number of the proprietors to the alterations proposed in the terms of their grants, or hereafter by any accident or casualty whatever, the salaries and allowances to the several officers above mentioned shall be diminished in proportion. And it is our will and pleasure that neither yourself, nor any other of our officers for our Island as aforesaid, shall be entitled to any part of the said salaries and allowances, nor shall any warrant be granted for the same, unless you or they be resident upon our said Island, excepting only when yourself or any of our said officers respectively shall be absent by leave from us under our signet and sign manual or by order in our Privy Council, in which case one full moiety of the salary and of all perquisites and emoluments whatsoever, which would otherwise become due unto you or to our said officers respectively, shall, during the time of such absence, be paid and satisfied to the person on whom the administration and execution of government, or of such offices, as aforesaid, shall devolve or be conferred; provided, nevertheless, and it is our royal intent and meaning, that whenever we shall think fit to require you by our especial order to repair to any other of our Governments in America for our particular service, that then and in such case you shall receive your full salary, perquisites and emoluments, as if you were then actually resident within our said Island of Saint John, anything in these instructions to the contrary in any wise notwithstanding.

Twenty-third. And in order the more effectually to secure and enforce the payments and collection of the quit rents due to us upon all grants of land, as aforesaid, and upon which the support of our Government is to depend, it will be an essential and immediate object of your attention to consider, with the advice of our Council, of some proper law to be passed within our said Island for that purpose, in which you will conform as near as may be to what has been approved and established for that purpose in our other colonies under like circumstances.

Twenty-fourth. The annexed copy of our order in our Privy Council on the 26th day of August, 1767, will fully inform you of the plan we have thought fit to adopt for the settlement of our said Island of Saint John, and for the distribution of lands there under all descriptions; you will therefore be particularly careful to carry the said plan into full execution, and more especially in laying out the lands we have thought fit to reserve for the towns within our said Island, taking care that all reservations whatever for public uses be made justly and exactly so as fully to answer our royal intentions therein.

Twenty-fifth. And whereas, it hath been represented unto us that there are now sundry stores, materials and provisions belonging to us within our said Island which we have thought fit to entrust to the care and custody of a storekeeper appointed for that purpose, with instructions to obey such directions as he shall receive from you touching the disposal and application thereof to the public service, it is therefore our will and pleasure that you do, upon your arrival in our said Island, take an account of such stores, materials and provisions as are under the care of our storekeeper, as aforesaid; and you are to cause the said stores and materials to be applied and disposed of for the public use and benefit in such manner as shall appear to you to be most advantageous for our service; and in case our said storekeeper shall have sold, or otherwise disposed of the provisions, or any part thereof (which being perishable would not continue long fit for public use) in that case you are to require of our said storekeeper an account of the produce of such sale, making him such an allowance out of the sum that shall be produced therefrom as you shall think a proper reward for his trouble in this business.

Twenty-sixth. You are to permit a liberty of conscience to all persons (except Papists) so they be contented with a quiet and peaceable enjoyment of the same, not giving offence or scandal to the Government.

Twenty-seventh. And whereas, nothing can more effectually promote the peace and happiness of our subjects there, and impress upon their minds a just sense of religion and morality than an uniform and regular observance of those rites and duties which our holy religion require, you will therefore have a very particular attention to this important object, and to that end you shall take especial care that God Almighty be devoutly and duly served throughout your Government; the Book of Common Prayer as by law established read each Sunday and holiday; and the Blessed Sacrament administered according to the rites of the Church of England.

Twenty-eighth. You shall be careful that the churches, hereafter to be built within our said Island, be well and orderly kept, and that, besides a competent maintenance to be assigned to the minister of each orthodox Church, a convenient house be built at the public charge for each minister; and you are in an especial manner to take care that one hundred acres of land for the site of a church and as a glebe for a minister of the gospel, and thirty for a schoolmaster, be duly reserved in a proper part of every township, conformable to the directions and conditions annexed to our Order in Council of the 26th of August, 1767, hereinbefore referred to.

Twenty-ninth. You are not to prefer any minister to any ecclesiastical benefice in that our Island without a certificate from the Right Reverend Father in God the Lord Bishop of London, of his being conformable to the doctrine and discipline of the Church of England, and of a good life and conversation, and if any person preferred already to a benefice shall appear to you to give scandal, either by his doctrine or manners, you are to use the proper means for the removal of him.

Thirtieth. You are to give orders forthwith that every orthodox minister within your Government be one of the vestry in his respective parish; and that no vestry be held without him, except in case of sickness, or that after notice of a vestry summoned he omit to come.

Thirty-first. You are to enquire whether there be any minister within your Government who preaches and administers the Sacrament in any orthodox church or chapel without being in due orders, and to give an account thereof to the said Lord Bishop of London.

Thirty-second. And to the end the ecclesiastical jurisdiction of the said Lord Bishop of London may take place in that Island so far as conveniently may be, we do think fit that you do give all countenance and encouragement to the exercise of the same, excepting only the collating to benefices, granting licenses for marriages and probate of wills, which we have reserved to you our Governor and to the Commander-in-Chief of our said Island for the time being.

Thirty-third. We do further direct that no schoolmaster be

henceforth permitted to come from England and to keep school in the said Island without the license of the said Bishop of London, that no other person now there or that shall come from other parts shall be admitted to keep school in that our said Island of Saint John without our license first obtained.

Thirty-fourth. And you are to take especial care that a table of marriages established by the canons of the Church of England be hung up in every orthodox church and duly observed, and you are to endeavour to get a law passed in the Assembly of that Island for the strict observance of the said table.

Thirty-fifth. The Right Reverend Father in God Edmund, late Lord Bishop of London, having presented a petition to His late Majesty King George I, humbly beseeching him to send instructions to the Governors of all the several plantations in America that they cause all laws already made against blasphemy, profaneness, adultery, fornication, polygamy, incest, profanation of the Lord's Day, swearing and drunkenness in their respective Governments to be rigorously executed, and we, thinking it highly just that all persons who shall offend in any of the particulars aforesaid should be prosecuted and punished for their said offences, it is therefore our will and pleasure that you take due care for the punishment of the aforementioned vices, and that you earnestly recommend it to the Assembly of our said Island to provide effectual laws for the restraint and punishment of all such of the aforementioned vices, against which no laws are as yet provided; and also to use your endeavours to render the laws in being more efficacious by providing for the punishment of the aforementioned vices by presentment on oath to be made to the temporal Courts by the church wardens of the several parishes at proper times of the year to be appointed for that purpose; and for the further discouragement of vices and encouragement of virtue and good living, (that by such example the infidels may be invited and desire to embrace the Christian religion,) you are not to admit any person to public trusts or employments in the Island under your Government whose ill fame and conversation may occasion scandal. And it is our further will and pleasure that you recommend to the Assembly to enter upon proper methods for the erecting of schools in order to the training up of youth to reading and to a necessary knowledge of the principles of religion.

Thirty-sixth. And whereas, you will receive from our Commissioners for executing the office of High Admiral of Great Britain and of our Plantations a commission of Vice Admiralty of our said Island, you are hereby required and directed carefully to put in execution the several powers thereby granted you.

Thirty-seventh. And there having been great irregularities in the manner of granting commissions in the Plantations to private ships of war, you are to govern yourself, whenever there shall be occasion according to the commissions and instructions granted in this Kingdom, copies whereof will be herewith delivered you. But you are not to grant commissions of marque or reprizal against any Prince or State, or their subjects in amity with us to any person whatsoever without our especial command. And you are to oblige the commanders of all ships having private commissions to wear no other colours than such as are described in an Order in Council of the 7th of January, 1730, in relation to colours to be worn by all ships and vessels except our own ships of war.

Thirty-eighth. Whereas, divers Acts have from time to time been passed in several of our colonies in America, imposing a duty of powder on every vessel that enters and clears in the said colonies, which has been of great service in furnishing the magazines with powder for the defence of the said colonies in time of danger, it is our express will and pleasure, and you are hereby required and directed to recommend to the Assembly of our said Island to pass a Law for collecting a Powder Duty, and that the law for that purpose be made perpetual, that a certain time in the said Act not exceeding twelve months be allowed for giving notice thereof to the several masters of vessels trading to our said Island; and that for the more ample notification thereof a proclamation be also published in your said Government declaring that from and after the expiration of the time limited by the said Act for such notice, no commutation shall be allowed of but upon evident necessity which may some time happen, whereof you or the Commander-in-Chief for the time being are to be the judge, in which case the said master shall pay the full price gunpowder sells for there, and the monies so collected shall be laid out as soon as may be in the purchase of gunpowder. And you are also to transmit every six months to us by one of our principal Secretaries of State an account of the particular quantities of powder collected under the said Act in your Government, and likewise a duplicate thereof to the Master General or principal officers of our ordnance.

Thirty-ninth And in case of distress of any other of our Plantations, you shall, upon application of the respective Governors thereof to you, assist them with what aid the condition and safety of our Island under your Government can spare.

Fortieth. You are likewise, from time to time, to send unto us by one of our principal Secretaries of State as aforesaid, an account of the wants and defects of the said Island, and what are the chief products thereof; what new improvements are made therein by the industry of the inhabitants and planters; and what further improvements you conceive may be made or advantages gained by trade, and which way we may contribute thereunto.

Forty-first. If any thing shall happen that may be of advantage and security to our said Island which is not herein or by our commission provided for, we do hereby allow unto you, with the advice and consent of our Council, to take order for the present therein, giving unto us by one of our principal Secretaries of State speedy notice thereof that so you may receive our ratification, if we shall approve of the same. Provided always, that you do not by colour of any power given you commence or declare war without our knowledge and particular commands therein, except it be against the Indians upon emergencies, wherein the consent of our Council shall be had and speedy notice thereof given unto us by one of our principal Secretaries of State as aforesaid.

Forty-second. And you are upon all occasions to send to us, by one of our principal Secretaries of State, particular account of all your proceedings and of the condition of affairs with your Government.

Forty-third. And whereas, great prejudice may happen to our service and the security of the said Island by your absence from those parts, you are not upon any pretence whatsoever to come to Europe from your Government without having first obtained leave for so doing from us under our sign manual and signet or by our order in our Privy Council.

Forty-fourth. And whereas, we have been pleased by our commission to direct that in case of your death or absence from our said Island, and in case there be at that time no person upon the place commissionated or appointed by us to be our Lieutenant-Governor or Commander-in-Chief, the eldest councillor whose name is first placed in these instructions to you, and who shall be at the time of your death or absence residing within our said Island, shall take upon him the administration of the Government, and execute our said commission and instructions, and the several powers and authorities therein contained in the manner therein directed. It is nevertheless our express will and pleasure that, in such case, the said eldest councillor or President shall forbear to pass any Act or Acts, but such as shall be immediately necessary for the peace and welfare of our said Island, without our particular order for that purpose, and that he shall not take upon him to dissolve the Assembly, if it should happen that there should be an Assembly then in being, nor to remove or suspend any of the members of our said Council, nor any judges, justices of the peace or other officers, civil or military, without the advice and consent of at least seven of the Council. And our said President is to transmit to us by one of our principal Secretaries of State, by the first opportunity, the reasons for such alterations, signed by himself and our Council.

## APPENDIX C.

### Further Instructions to Patterson.*

George R. (L. S.)

*Additional Instruction to our Trusty and Well-beloved Walter Patterson, Esq., our Captain-General and Governor-in-Chief in, and over, our Island of St. John, and the Territories adjacent thereto in America, and which now are, or hereafter shall be, dependent thereupon. Given at Our Court at St. James, the 31st day of August, 1782. In the twenty-second year of our reign.*

Whereas, laws have been passed in some of our colonies and plantations in America, by which the lands, tenements, goods, chattels, rights and credits of persons, who have never resided within the colonies where such laws have been passed, have been made liable to be attached for the recovery of debts in a manner different from that allowed by the laws of England in the like cases; and whereas, it hath been represented unto us that such laws may have the consequence to prejudice and obstruct the commerce between this Kingdom and our said colonies, and to affect public credit; it is therefore our will and pleasure that you do not on any pretence whatever give your assent to, or pass any Bill or Bills in our Province under your Government, by which the lands, tenements, goods, chattels, rights and credits of persons who have never resided within our said Island shall be liable to be attached for the recovery of debts due from such persons, otherwise than is allowed by law in cases of the like nature within this our Kingdom of Great Britain, until you shall have first transmitted unto us, by one of our principal Secretaries of State, the draught of such Bill or Bills, and shall have received our royal pleasure thereupon, unless you take care in the passing of such Bill or Bills that a clause or clauses be inserted therein suspending and deferring the execution thereof until our royal will and pleasure shall be known thereupon.

*Public Archives of Canada. Series M, vol. 593.

## APPENDIX D.

### ADDITIONAL INSTRUCTIONS TO PATTERSON.*

GEORGE R. (L. S.)

*Additional Instruction to our Trusty and Well-beloved Walter Patterson, Esq., our Captain-General and Governor-in-Chief of our Island of St. John, in America, or to the Commander-in-Chief of our said Island for the time being. Given at our Court at St. James, the 24th day of July, 1783. In the twenty-third year of our reign.*

Whereas, it hath been represented to us that certain of our loving subjects, proprietors of lands in our Island of St. John, in commiseration of the distress to which many of our faithful subjects, heretofore inhabitants of the provinces and colonies, now the United States of America, are reduced in consequence of their loyalty and adherence to their allegiance to us, have agreed to transfer and convey certain proportions of the lands by them respectively held by grant from us to such of our said faithful subjects who may be inclined to settle thereupon, and their heirs and assigns forever in fee. In order, therefore, to promote such the laudable intentions of our said loving subjects, and to encourage the settlement of our subjects under the description aforesaid, who may be inclined to avail themselves of those intentions, it is our will and pleasure that you do give directions that all conveyances and other deeds necessary for transferring such parts of the lands as shall be agreed to be conveyed to our faithful subjects aforesaid be prepared by our Attorney-General of the said Island of St. John and when executed be duly recorded in the Secretary's office of the same and that the Secretary of the said Island shall make out a docquet of all deeds so recorded, specifying the name of the proprietor conveying, of the persons to whom the land is conveyed, the quantity of land conveyed, and the number of the Lot of which the same was a part; which docquet shall from time to time be delivered by him to the Receiver-General of our quit rents who shall discharge in the rent roll such proprietors from any future quit rent upon the land so conveyed, for which the person to whom the same is conveyed, his heirs or assigns, shall thereafter stand

---

*Public Archives of Canada. Series M, vol. 593.

chargeable in the said rent roll. It is nevertheless our will and pleasure that no land conveyed as aforesaid shall be liable to the payment of any quit rent to us, our heirs and successors, till ten years after the date of the respective conveyances.

And in order to relieve our subjects who have agreed to convey a part of the lands held by them as aforesaid, it is our will and pleasure that any arrears of quit rent that may have been due and unpaid upon the quantities of land which they may convey shall be remitted, and they discharged therefrom; or in case such arrears shall have been paid, our Receiver-General of the quit rents shall repay to the person or persons so conveying so much of the last payment made as shall have been paid for the part of the lands so conveyed. You are, however, to take especial care that under colour of complying with this our instruction, no collusive conveyances are made in order to obtain a remission of arrears of quit rent, but that in every instance the indulgence and encouragement hereby granted be confined to actual and bona fide conveyances for the purposes hereinbefore mentioned and no other. And in order to prevent any persons disaffected to us and our Government from becoming settlers in our said Island, it is our will and pleasure that all persons who shall be desirous of availing themselves of the good intentions of our said living subjects and to become settlers upon the lands to be conveyed to them as aforesaid shall, before the execution of the conveyance by them to be made, besides taking the usual oaths directed by law, also make and subscribe the following declaration in the presence of you or our Commander-in-Chief for the time being, or of such person or persons as by you or him shall be appointed for that purpose, viz., "I, A. B. do promise and declare that I will maintain and defend to the utmost of my power the authority of the King in his Parliament as the supreme Legislature of this Island." And it is our further will and pleasure that the following condition and exception be inserted in and made a part of every conveyance which shall be made of lands within the meaning of this our instruction, that is to say, "It is hereby further covenanted and agreed by and between the parties above mentioned, that if the lands hereby granted and conveyed by the said A. B. to the said C. D. and his heirs as aforesaid, shall at any time or times hereafter come into the tenure or possession of any person or persons whatever, inhabitants of our said province, either by virtue of any deed of sale, conveyance, enfeoffment or exchange, or by gift, inheritance, descent, devise or marriage, such person or persons, being inhabitants as aforesaid, shall, within twelve months after his, her or their entry and possession of the same, take the oaths appointed by law and make and subscribe the following declaration, viz., 'I, A. B., do promise and declare that I will maintain and defend to the utmost of my power, the authority of the King in his Parliament as the supreme Legislature of this Island,' before some one of the magistrates of the said Island, and such declaration and certificate of the magistrate that such oaths have been taken shall be recorded in the Secretary's office of the said Island within two months after taking and making and subscribing the same. In default of which this present conveyance every part and condition thereof shall be void to all intents and purposes, and it shall and may be lawful to and for the said A. B., his heirs or assigns, again to enter upon and repossess the lands and premises hereby granted and conveyed, and every part and parcel thereof, anything herein contained to the contrary notwithstanding." And it is our further will and pleasure that our Surveyor-General of lands for the said Island, or his lawful deputy for the time being, shall lay out and survey the several parts and portions of lands which shall be conveyed to our faithful subjects aforesaid, and shall enter the several surveys or plats thereof of record in his office. And you, or our Commander-in-Chief for the time being, with the consent of our Council, shall grant a certificate to the said Surveyor-General for the actual expense attending such survey, to be ascertained upon oath, together with one-half the usual and accustomed fees of office upon the same, directed to the Receiver-General of our quit rents for our said Island, who shall pay and discharge the same out of any monies belonging to us which shall be in his hands; and you shall also grant certificates from time to time to our Attorney-General for his pains in preparing the deeds of conveyance hereinbefore mentioned, provided the same shall not exceed ten shillings for each deed, and also to our Secretary for one-half the usual and accustomed fees of office, for recording such deeds of conveyance, directed to our Receiver-General of quit rents, who shall pay and discharge the same in like manner. And you shall transmit to us through one of our principal Secretaries of State a distinct account of what conveyances shall be made and certificates given as herein directed, and also transmit a duplicate thereof to our High Treasurer or the Commissioners of our Treasury for the time being.

## APPENDIX E.

### Patterson's Commission as Lieutenant-Governor.*

GEORGE THE THIRD, by the Grace of God, King of Great Britain, France and Ireland, Defender of the Faith, etc. To our Trusty and well-beloved Walter Patterson, Esq. GREETING: Whereas, we did, by our letters patent bearing date at Westminster the fourth day of August, in the ninth year of our reign, constitute and appoint you, the said Walter Patterson, to be our Captain-General and Governor-in-Chief in and over our Island of Saint John and territories adjacent thereunto, in America, and which then were, or theretofore had been dependent thereupon, during our pleasure, as in and by the said recited letters patent, relation being thereunto had more at large appear; and whereas, by our warrant under our sign manual bearing date the thirty-first day of July, in the said ninth year of our reign, we did constitute and appoint Thomas DesBrisay, Esq., to be Lieutenant-Governor of our said Island of Saint John for and during our pleasure, as in and by our said recited warrant relation being thereunto had may more at large appear; and whereas, we thought fit to annex our said Island of Saint John to our Government of Nova Scotia, and by our letters patent, bearing date at Westminster the day of this instant September, to appoint John Parr, Esq., to be our Captain-General and Governor-in-Chief of our Province of Nova Scotia and our Islands of Saint John and Cape Breton, and to revoke our letters patent herein before recited, whereby we did appoint you, the said Walter Patterson, to be our Captain-General and Governor-in-Chief of our said Island of Saint John, as in and by the said recited letters patent relation being thereunto had may also more at large appear. Now know ye that we, hereby revoking our said recited warrant constituting and appointing the said Thomas DesBrisay to be our Lieutenant-Governor of our said Island of Saint John, and reposing especial trust and confidence in your loyalty, courage and prudence, do, by these presents, constitute and appoint you, the said Walter Patterson, to be Lieutenant-Governor of our said Island of Saint John and the territories adjacent thereunto during our pleasure, with such powers and

---

*Public Archives of Canada. Series M, vol. 593.

authorities according to such directions as are or shall be expressed in our commission and instructions to our Captain-General and Governor-in-Chief of our Province of Nova Scotia, and our Islands of Saint John and Cape Breton, now and for the time being, whose orders you are from time to time to observe, and we hereby command all our officers and subjects of our said Island of Saint John and the territories adjacent thereunto, to take due notice hereof, and obey you as our Lieutenant-Governor accordingly. Given at our Court at St. James the..................................................day of ................................1784, in the twenty-fourth year of our reign.

By His Majesty's Command,

SYDNEY.

# Bibliography.

In preparing this volume, the author has consulted the following:

1. John Stewart — "Account of Prince Edward Island."
2. Rt. Rev. M. F. Howley — papers read before the Royal Society of Canada.
3. Dr. S. E. Dawson — "The St. Lawrence."
4. Bagster — "Jacques Cartier."
5. Dr. Stewart — Encyclopaedia Brittanica, 9th Edition.
6. Archbishop O'Brien — paper read before the Royal Society of Canada.
7. Ganong.
8. Sir Joseph Pope — "Cartier."
9. John Calder Gordon.
10. "Americana."
11. "Micmac Place Names," recorded by Dr. Rand and collected by Col. W. P. Anderson.
12. Doublet's Letter Patent.
13. Rev. A. E. Burke, in P. E. Island Magazine.
14. Abbe Casgrain — "La Seconde Acadie."
15. Champlain's maps, 1612 and 1634.
16. Treaty of Utrecht.
17. Nova Scotia Archives — Akin.
18. Villejoin — Commandant of Isle St. Jean.
19. St. Pierre's Concession.
20. P. E. Island Magazine.
21. Late Professor Caven, articles in P. E. Island Magazine.
22. Rev. John C. McMillan — "Early History of the Catholic Church in P. E. Island."
23. Dominion Archives.
24. Colonial Correspondence (Archives).
25. French Archives, copies in Ottawa.
26. De La Ronde.
27. Sir Andrew McPhail — "Canada and her Provinces."
28. DeRoma's Grant
29. Colonel Franquet — Plans for Fortifications.
30. Thomas Pichon.
31. Rev. George Sutherland — "History of P. E. Island."
32. Sir John Bourinot — "Canada," Story of the Nations Series.
33. Hannay — History of Acadia.
34. O'Hagen — "Canadian Essays."
35. Edward Richard — "Acadia."

36. Rev. W. H. Warren — "P. E. Island Baptists."
37. Articles of Capitulation of Louisbourg.
38. R. Montgomery Martin — "The British Colonies, their History, Extent, Condition and Resources."
39. "Canada and its Provinces."
40. Longfellow's Evangeline.
41. General Amherst's Instructions to Colonel, Lord Rollo.
42. Anonymous Account of the loss of the Duke William.
43. Rev. M. Gerard, Cure of Point Prim, to M. the Rev. L'Isle Dieu.
44. Captain Pile — Ship "Achilles," — Nova Scotia Historical Society.
45. Smethurst's Account.
46. Surveyor-General Holland's Report.
47. John McGregor — History of North America.
48. John McGregor — "Historical and Descriptive Sketch of the Maritime Provinces of British North America"— London, 1828.
49. Lieutenant-Governor Francklin's Despatches, etc.
50. Patterson's Correspondence and Despatches.
51. Phillips Callbeck's Correspondence.
52. Mr. Wright's Correspondence.
53. Mr. Benjamin Chappell's Diary.
54. Campbell's History of P. E. Island.
55. C. C. Gardiner's M.S. History (Archives).
56. Fanning's Addresses to the House of Assembly.
57. Royal Instructions.
58. Report of Land Commission of 1861.
59. Lord Durham on Escheat in P. E. Island.
60. Newspapers.
61. "Sketches of Highlanders," etc., by Colonel R. C. McDonald.
62. "A Knight of the Eighteenth Century," by Miss Anna McDonald.
63. "A Chapter in Our Island History, 1772," a Lecture by the late Rev. Dr. McDonald in Charlottetown, 1882, published in the Herald Newspaper.
64. Lutterlot's Proposals.
65. Statutes of the Island.
66. P. E. Island "Register."
67. Halifax Herald, 13 November, 1920.
68. The Annual Register.
69. Selkirk's Diary.
70. Fanning's Description of the Island.
71. Victor Ross — "History of the Canadian Bank of Commerce."
72. Bishop John Inglis Diary of visit to the Island in 1789.
73. "The Makers of Canada."
74. Selkirk's "Emigration and the State of the Highlands," 2nd Edition, 1806.
75. Acadian Recorder, 6th November, 1824.
76. Minutes of the Supreme Court of P. E. Island.
77. "P. E. Island, Past and Present."
78. P. E. Island Register Newspaper.
79. Walter Johnston's Letters.

80. History of the P. O. in B. N. A. by Wm. Smith.
81. Rev. T. F. Fullerton — in Past and Present of P. E. Island.
82. Lamont's Biography of Rev. Donald McDonald.
83. History of Presbyterianism in P. E. Island, by Rev. John M. McLeod.
84. Historical Sketch of Zion Church by Samuel C. Nash.
85. Henry Smith — Methodism in P. E. Island.
86. King's College Records.
87. "Church Work," Halifax, 1821.
88. David R. Reid — "Lives of the Judges of Upper Canada."
89. Hon. Mr. Justice Riddell, Ontario Supreme Court.
90. Hon. J. A. Mathieson, Chief Justice of P. E. Island, in "Past and Present P. E. Island."
91. Prowse's "History of Newfoundland."
92. G. W. Barrington's Remarkable Voyages and Shipwrecks," London, not dated, *re* loss of the "Duke William."

# Index.

## A.

| | | Page |
|---|---|---|
| ABAGWIT / ABEGWET / APAGWIT — Variations of Indian name, (See also "Epagwit" and Minegoo.) ......(note) | | 15 |
| ABEL'S CAPE tragedy | | 233, 234 |
| ACADIA, Refugees from | | 70, 71 |
| Their terrible destitution | | 70, 71 |
| ACADIANS, employed in 1763 cutting pine at Three Rivers | | 122, 123 |
| ACCOUNTS PUBLIC, Report of Special Committee on | | 320 |
| ADMIRALTY, a Court of, for Island of St. John (4th August, 1769) | | 149 |
| AGRICULTURE and FISHERY | | 247 |
| AGRICULTURAL SOCIETY formed | | 373 |
| Improvement (1828) | | 376 |
| AMHERST, GENERAL — Instructions to Lord Rollo | | 87 |
| General Whitmore | | 89, 90 |
| AMHERST, FORT erected | | 94, 95, 297 |
| destroyed by Patterson | | 297 |
| "ANNABELLA", 1770, with immigrants, wrecked | | 153 |
| APPROPRIATION BILL (1825) Council passes under protest | | 364 |
| (1828) rejected by Council | | 366 |
| Colonial Secretary's despatch re same | | 366 |
| Correspondence re | | 366, 367, 368 |
| ARTICLES OF CAPITULATION OF LOUISBOURG | | 78, 79 |
| ARCHIBALD, CHIEF JUSTICE | | 344, 438, 439 |
| ASSEMBLY, House of, Established 1773, disrespectful language concerning, punishable | | 256, 257 |
| Act voiding land sales passed by | | 257 |
| how elected (Selkirk) | | 275 |
| defence, address from on | | 302, 303 |
| expenditure, claims sole control of supply | | 308, 309, 318, 329, 344, 365, 372 |
| jealous of its dignity, curious instance | | 310, 311 |
| Lieutenant-Governor Smith dissolves (1817) | | 315 |
| new one elected (1819) | | 315 |
| dissolved and new elected (1820) | | 315 |
| session held in 1820 and not again till 1825 | | 315 |
| convened by Lieutenant-Governor Ready, 1825 | | 315 |

|  | Page |
|---|---|
| ASSEMBLY, of 1817, investigates expenditure | 317 |
| voted supply | 317 |
| voted, Smith delays concurrence | 317 |
| prorogued | 317 |
| dissolved | 317 |
| Smith's speech to new (1818) | 317, 318 |
| address in reply critical | 317, 318 |
| censures Quit Rent collection proceedings | 318 |
| Smith refuses to receive address of | 318, 319 |
| considers refusal | 319 |
| find nothing unconstitutional in address | 319 |
| ask when it will be received | 319 |
| Lieutenant-Governor persists in refusal to receive | 319 |
| address ordered to be printed in Gazette | 320 |
| windows, while in session, smashed by son of Lieutenant-Governor | 330 |
| Smith's son arrested on Speaker's Warrant | 330 |
| prorogued without usual address | 330 |
| dissolved and general election | 331 |
| request for papers refused by Smith | 331 |
| committee to consider documents | 331 |
| report agreed to | 332 |
| censures the Lieutenant-Governor | 332, 333 |
| address to King *re* Smith forwarded per Governor-General | 333 |
| adopt report on public accounts (1820) | 334 |
| resolution *re* Smith and Tremlett | 334 |
| Smith's speech proroguing | 334, 335 |
| correspondence with Council *re* Appropriation Bill | 366, 367, 368 |
| protest Council's refusal to do business *re* supply | 367 |
| address to Lieutenant-Governor *re* same | 367 |

B.

| | |
|---|---|
| BAPTIST CHURCH, Sketch, early History in P. E. Island | 409, 411 |
| BALLOT, whole Island given to proprietors by | 130, 131, 132 |
| BARLEY, and other grains, price of, in 1730 | 380 |
| BONAVENTURE, Governor in 1749 | 50 |
| had garrison of 100 | 50, 51 |
| BRITISH AND FRENCH struggle for supremacy, ends | 82, 83 |
| BUGEAU, AMAND | (note) 49, 50 |
| BURSLAY, ABBE, brought by St. Pierre | 23 |

C.

| | |
|---|---|
| CABOT, JOHN, landfall | 2, 3 |
| first voyage in the Matthew | 3 |
| objective | 3 |

# INDEX.

|  | Page |
|---|---|
| CABOT, JOHN, landfall made 24th June, 1497 | 3 |
| Cape Breton | 4 |
| landed twice, same day | 5 |
| landfall, Archbishop O'Brien on (note) | 5 |
| CANADA, Island affiliated to | 208 |
| CALLBECK, P., Attorney-General, Administrator of Government, and Thomas Wright carried off by privateers to Washington's Camp | 180 |
| see privateers | 188 |
| raised company, armed from Halifax | 191 |
| fortifications started by | 191 |
| proposes to raise 100 men | 191, 194 |
| defence, takes measures for land | 193 |
| measures approved by General Howe | 193 |
| convenes Assembly (1776) | 194 |
| in 1779, suggests adding to forces | 245, 246 |
| died 1790 | 246 |
| public monument voted | 246 |
| inscription to be placed on | 78, 79 |
| CAPITULATION OF LOUISBOURG, Articles of | 80, 81 |
| population at time of | 335 |
| CARMICHAEL'S incapacity and tyrannical conduct | 335 |
| son-in-law of Smith appointed to office | 326, 327 |
| outrageous conduct of | 327 |
| warrant issued against | 1 |
| CARTIER, JACQUES, discovers Island | 8 |
| life and character of | 0 |
| sails from St. Malo | 9 |
| Bonavista, Newfoundland, reaches | 9, 10 |
| Labrador and Newfoundland, explores | 10 |
| Magdalens, discovers | 10 |
| Sea Cows abounded there | 11 |
| landfall on P. E. Island, where? | 11, 12 |
| sails along north shore westwardly | 11, 12 |
| rounds North Cape | 13 |
| lands at four places | 13 |
| finds no harbours | 13 |
| did not know it to be an Island | 288 |
| CHAPPEL, BENJ. first postmaster | 376 |
| CENTRAL ACADEMY | 136 |
| CHARLOTTETOWN, the capital | 133 |
| Georgetown and Princetown laid out by Morris | 144, 145 |
| buildings and stores in 1768 | 144 |
| earliest described | 164, 165 |
| town plan and description of | 51 |
| Harbour, first chart of | |

|  | Page |
|---|---|
| CENSUS, A. D. 1728–1735–1753 | 23 |
| of 1728, increase of population | 23 |
| where settled | 27 |
| of 1735 total settlements | 27 |
| of 1805, population | 29 |
| of 1829, Act to take | 293 |
| population | 373 |
| expense of | 373 |
| CHIGNECTO, strengthening of, urged | 373 |
| CHIEF JUSTICES, early — brief sketches of | 37, 38 |
| CHURCH, Court House and jail urged by Patterson | 415, 439 |
| Grant to build | 155 |
| how expended | 157 |
| account of expenditure asked for in 1784 | 157, 158 |
| brought up in New House | 158 |
| built | 158, 159 |
| CHURCHES, brief sketches of | 267 |
| CIVIL ESTABLISHMENT (1803) | 385, 411 |
| "CLEARANCE, HIGHLAND" | 277 |
| CLIMATE, Holland's description of | 271 |
| COCHRAN, Chief Justice — Tragic fate of | 129 |
| COLCLOUGH, Chief Justice | 424, 426 |
| suspension of, asked by Assembly | 431, 434 |
| COUNCIL appointed, 1770 | 308 |
| constitution of | 153 |
| members of, dismissed | 176 |
| threw out Appropriation Bill (1827) | 205 |
| (1828) | 366 |
| refuses to do business with Assembly | 366 |
| COURTS of C. P. and General Sessions opened | 367 |
| Supreme, established | 145 |
| CUMBERLAND rebels lay siege to Fort Cumberland | 153 |
| plan raid on Charlottetown | 190 |
| seize ship at Pictou | 190 |
| CURRENCY, lack of | 190 |
| debentures to provide, suggested | 251, 253 |
| leather notes | 251, 252, 253 |
| "Holy Dollar." | 253 |
| treasury notes | 253 |
| copper coinage, private | 254 |
| bill prohibiting base coin, defeated | 255 |
|  | 363 |

D.

|  |  |
|---|---|
| DEFENCE, Callbeck takes measures for land | 191, 194 |
| Lieutenant-Governor Fanning urges provision for | 249 |
| Stewart describes means of | 297 |

# INDEX.

|   | Page |
|---|---|
| DEFENCE, Lieutenant-Governor DesBarres reports on state of | 298 |
| address of Assembly on | 302, 303 |
| Lieutenant-Governor DesBarres urges measures for | 304, 305 |
| DENYS, NICHOLAS, comes to Acadia in 1632 | 17 |
| gets concession in 1656 | 17 |
| describes Island | 18 |
| made no permanent establishment | 18 |
| first to exploit Cape Breton coal | 19 |
| DEPORTATION of French from Island | 84 |
| not justifiable | 84, 85 |
| to France | 98 |
| houses on Island not destroyed | 99 |
| more tragic than the expulsion from Acadia | 87 |
| see "Duke William." | |
| DESBARRES, Lieutenant-Governor | 291, 312 |
| career of | 291 |
| concerned for defence | 294 |
| recommends establishing a post office | 303 |
| tries to enthuse Legislature for defence | 309 |
| recommends revision of Militia Law | 309 |
| retired on pension | 311 |
| his great age | 311 |
| surveyed coasts of Nova Scotia | 312 |
| served with Wolfe at Quebec | 312 |
| died at Halifax, aged 103 | 311 |
| DESBRISAY, Lieutenant-Governor applies for Lieutenant-Governorship of N. S. | 196 |
| DESERTIONS from army and navy | 305 |
| causes of | 305, 306 |
| DILIGENT AND HUNTER, H. M. S., stationed at Charlottetown | 188 |
| DESCHAMP, ISAAC, first Magistrate and Justice of the C. P. | 135 |
| arrives | 145 |
| DOUBLET, CAPTAIN | 16 |
| gets grant of St. John and Magdalen Islands | 16, 17 |
| DRINK BILL of Island (1825) (note) | 378 |
| DURHAM'S, LORD, land question referred to | 227 |
| strong report to Lord Glenelg by | 222, 223, 224 |
| DUKE WILLIAM, transport, account of the | 95 |
| marriages on board | 98 |
| voyage and loss with prisoners | 96 |
| sails for France under cartel | 100 |
| in good order | 100, 101 |
| sights "Violet," another transport in distress | 101 |
| "Violet" with 400 founders | 102 |
| starts plank-butt | 102 |
| abandoned | 102, 110 |

480 HISTORY OF PRINCE EDWARD ISLAND.

|  | Page |
|---|---|
| DUKE WILLIAM, prisoners lost on | 110 |
| sight three ships, which leave them to their fate | 105, 106 |
| captain and crew take to boats | 107 |
| land near Penzance | 110 |
| M. Gerard, cure of Point Prim, on board, and saved | 112 |
| M. Gerard letter from | 112 |
| Captain Piles states ship unseaworthy | 114 |
| statement doubtful | 114, 115 |
| DYKES | 77, 78 |
| DYKES, name of one of Selkirk's ships | 271 |

E.

|  |  |
|---|---|
| ECCLESIASTICAL ESTABLISHMENT (1830) | 379 |
| EDUCATION, measures promoting, thrown out by Council (1830) | 317 |
| grammar schools | 377 |
| teachers' pay | 379 |
| EGMONT, EARL, applies for great of whole Island | 379 |
| Feudal System, proposes to introduce | 118 |
| application refused | 118, 119 |
| second memorial for same, unanswered | 119 |
| third memorial for same, refused | 119 |
| EMIGRATION from Island early in Fanning's time | 119, 120 |
| influx later | 267 |
| EPAGWIT, an Indian name for Island (note) | 267 |
| ESCHEAT, for non-payment of quit rents proposed | 15 |
| of lands, proceedings | 198 |
| Court of, agitation for | 200 |
| memorial to Crown for | 216 |
| land commission 1861, report on | 216, 217 |
| EXPORTS, great increase of (1796) | 225 |
|  | 267 |

F.

|  |  |
|---|---|
| FANNING, Lieutenant-Governor (1786–1805) arrives | 206, 235 |
| Patterson refuses to retire | 206 |
| Patterson's letter of refusal | 240 |
| career, sketch of | 235, 239 |
| American view of | 237, 238 |
| Selkirk's opinion of | 238, 239 |
| John McGregor on | 239 |
| journey to Charlottetown | 240 |
| visits eastern sections in summer, 1787 | 240, 241, 242 |
| account of journey | 240, 242 |
| population, estimate of | 242 |
| reports on Island (1789) | 247, 248 |
| defence, urges provision for | 249 |

# INDEX. 481

|  | Page |
|---|---|
| FANNING, Spain, volunteers to serve in war against | 249 |
| complaint against Fanning and others | 260, 264 |
| committee of P. C., heard by | 262, 264 |
| complaints dismissed | 262, 264 |
| the charges | 263 |
| trouble with proprietors | 285 |
| gains popular good-will | 285 |
| granted pension equal to salary | 286 |
| address to and reply | 286 |
| FERGUS, member of Council, lost | 166 |
| FIRE, The "Great Fire," 1738 | 54, 55 |
| FOREST FIRES | 353 |
| FISHERIES, etc., prosperity of Island (1790) | 249 |
| FISHERY, prohibited by French | 69 |
| to be encouraged by British | 120, 121 |
| land on coast reserved for | 122 |
| reserves when original grants made | 228 |
| FITZROY, SIR CHARLES, Lieutenant-Governor in 1837 | 221 |
| circularized proprietors *re* tenant grievances | 221 |
| FOOD-STUFFS, prices of in 1778 | 196 |
| FORT AMHERST, erected | 94, 95–297 |
| FRANCE, war with (1793) | 264, 266 |
| militia called out | 265 |
| public fast and humiliation | 265 |
| Letters of Marque | 267 |
| FRANQUET, tours Island | 43, 44, 45, 46 |
| tours, object military | 43 |
| visits settlements (North Shore) | 43, 44 |
| prepares plans of Forts (see plans 42, 44, 46) | 43 |
| found Three Rivers deserted | 45 |
| DeRoma's title outstanding | 45 |
| Gauthier, N. visits | 45 |
| eulogizes soil, etc. | 45 |
| church, settles site for | 46 |
| road, LaGrande source to St. Peters planned by | 46 |
| makes first chart of harbour | 51 |
| children, impressed by number or | 70 |
| FRENCH AND BRITISH struggle for supremacy ends | 82, 83 |
| FRANCKLIN, Lieutenant-Governor of N. S. starts settlement | 135 |
| details of his measures | 136 |
| issues commission for Court of C. P., etc. | 136 |
| clergyman, urges appointment of | 138 |
| suggests stationing ship and troops | 138 |
| submits four estimates cost of establishment (note) | 138, 139, 140 |
| expense deemed excessive | 147 |
| expenditure, explains | 147 |
| FUNDS, public assembly claims right to control (1803) | 289 |

## G.

| | Page |
|---|---|
| GARDINER, C. C., on domestic animals | 345, 346 |
| GAUTHIER, NICHOLAS, life and character of | 46–50 |
| GEORGETOWN, laid out by Morris in 1768 | 133, 146 |
| GOMEZ, STEPHEN, claim as discoverer of Island | 6, 7 |
|     skilful navigator | 6 |
|     deserted Magellan | 6 |
|     discovers Strait of Canso | 7 |
|     explored coast from Florida to Cape Breton | 7 |
| GOVERNMENT, officers of, arrive | 145 |
|     composition of | 179 |
|     Parliament votes £3000 for Civil | 195 |
| GOVERNORSHIP abolished, 1784 | 207 |
|     Lieutenant substituted | 208 |
|     Lieutenant, Patterson appointed | 208 |
| GRAY, CAPTAIN ROBERT | 243 |

## H.

| | |
|---|---|
| HALDIMAND applies for remaining French settlers | 116 |
| HARBOURS, best for trade, etc. | 125 |
| HARVEY, Sir John, appointed Lieutenant-Governor, 1831 | 221 |
| HIERLEHY, arrives with four companies from New York | 189 |
| "HIGHLAND CLEARANCE" | 271 |
| HOLLAND, SAMUEL, appointed Commissioner to make general survey of B. N. A. | 123, 124–136 |
|     nearly lost off Cape Breton | 123 |
|     travels over land to Quebec | 123 |
|     description by, of Island and its products | 124, 125 |
|     of fish and game | 127, 128 |
|     McGregor's account of | 128 |
| HOLMES, Admiral and Associates apply for grant of Island | 122 |
| HOWE, CAPTAIN EDWARD, murder of | 67 |

## I

| | |
|---|---|
| IMMIGRANTS, SCOTCH (1770) wrecked entering harbour (note) | 153 |
|     in 1770, 1771 and 1772 | 167, 168 |
|     Letterlott's proposal to bring German | 174, 175 |
|     from Scotch Highlands | 250 |
|     (1829 and 1830) | 381 |
| IMMIGRATION (1818) | 330 |
| IMPORTS AND EXPORTS in 1803 | 279, 280 |
| INGLIS, BISHOP JOHN, visit (1789) | 257–260 |
|     diary of | 257–260 |
|     urges building church | 258, 259 |
|     refuses to preach in tavern ballroom | 259 |
|     memorializes Council *re* building church | 259 |

# INDEX.

| | Page |
|---|---|
| INDIANS, (Micmac) warlike | 41 |
| peace made with | 42 |
| Colonne Abbe, presents claims of, in 1806 | 232 |
| INHABITANTS, return of, in 1768 (with names) | 146 |
| INN, Government advance money to build | 308 |
| ISLAND, discovery of | 1-15 |
| abandoned for a century | 14 |
| Champlain's maps, appears on | 14 |
| Breton's and Basques resorted to | 14 |
| importance recognized | 20, 21, 37, 38 |
| captured by British in 1745 | 35, 36 |
| restored by Treaty of Aix-la-Chappelle | 36 |
| prosperity of, during the war | 36, 37 |
| golden age of | 37 |
| settlers, Acadian and French | 39 |
| settlements in 1728 | 38 |
| Acadians desire French rule | 39 |
| Pichon's description of | 56, 60 |
| French efforts to settle | 63 |
| store-house for Louisbourg | 63 |
| destitution of inhabitants | 73, 82 |
| settlements ordered destroyed | 75 |
| capitulation of Louisbourg, included in | 75 |
| Rollo, Colonel Lord, sent with 500 men | 75 |
| inhabitants ask to remain | 75 |
| crops raised by French on | 76 |
| likely exaggerated | 76 |
| supplied meat, grain, etc | 99 |
| survey ordered (by British) | 120, 121 |
| full report to be made | 120 |
| divided into counties | 121 |
| counties into parishes | 121 |
| parishes into townships | 121 |
| Walter Johnston's letters on exports and markets (1821) | 360 |
| other provinces comparison by | 360, 361 |
| townships to share natural advantages | 121 |
| town-site in each county | 121 |
| church site and glebe in parish | 121 |
| divisions regular grants of, to be made | 121 |
| grants not to exceed 20,000 acres | 121 |
| affiliated with Canada | 208 |
| name, changed to Prince Edward | 248 |
| Act changing name, allowed | 268 |

## J.

| | |
|---|---|
| JOHN, ISLE ST., first mention of | 13 |
| JACKSON, SHERIFF, resolution of Assembly censuring | 325, 326 |
| his criminal record | 325 |

|  | Page |
|---|---|
| JAIL, new, erected | 380 |
| JOHN THE BAPTIST, places named for | 268 |
| JOHNSTON, WALTER, letters of (1821)..........(note) | 350 |
|     account of voyage out | 350, 351 |
|     account of Murray Harbour | 351 |
|     describes Squaws Cap | 351 |
|     country a forest | 351, 352 |
|     wood, varieties of | 352 |
|     description of | 352 |
|     forest fires, description of | 353 |
|     mice | 354 |
|     description of Charlottetown | 355 |
|     roads | 357 |
|     inhabitants of mixed nationalities | 358 |
|     hospitality of people | 358 |
|     large families | 358 |
|     precocity of children | 358 |
|     dress of settlers | 359 |
|     food of settlers | 359 |
|     shell-fish | 359 |
|     mussel-mud | 359, 360 |
|     live stock degenerating | 359 |
|     fish, varieties | 359, 360 |
| JUDICIAL ESTABLISHMENT (1830) | 378 |

### L.

|  | Page |
|---|---|
| LANDS OF ISLAND, lotteried | 130, 131, 132 |
|     method of lottery | 130, 131 |
|     report Trade and Plantation Commissioner approving same | 131 |
| LANDS, proprietors offer one-quarter of lands for Loyalists | 202 |
|     sales of 1881, House Committee considers sale of | 203 |
|     Committee report on sales | 203, 204 |
|     Act confirming 1780, 1781 sales disallowed | 204 |
|     Act confirming leads to Patterson's dismissal | 204 |
|     held for speculation | 225 |
| LANDLORDS, mostly absentees | 232 |
|     or represented by agents | 232, 233 |
| LAND PURCHASE ACT 1858 | 225, 226 |
|     estates purchased thereunder | 226 |
| LAND COMMISSION, 1861, report by | 226, 227, 228, 229, 230, 231 |
|     report on Church and Glebe lands | 229, 230 |
|     on French claims | 230, 231 |
|     on Indian claims | 231, 232 |
|     report on escheat | 225 |
|     non-payment of quit rents cause trouble from first | 225, 294 |
| LAND TAX proposed | 304, 307, 308 |
| LEGAL TENDER — Fish, grain, etc., suggested to be made | 205, 206, 251 |

|  | Page |
|---|---|
| LIVE STOCK, ETC., at time of capture (1758) | 77 |
| LOCATION of towns, reasons for | 125, 126, 127 |
| LOCUSTS destroy crops, 1749 | 53 |
| LOUISBOURG, derived supplies from Island | 72, 73 |
|     captured in 1745 | 34 |
|     restored by Treaty of Aix-la-Chappelle (1749) | 43 |
|     re-captured in (1758) | 72 |
|     siege and capture of (1758) | 74 |
|     articles of capitulation of | 78, 79 |
| LOUTRE, LE | 41, 42 |
|     Indians, influence over | 41, 66 |
|     bitter enemy of British | 64 |
|     a sinister figure | 65 |
|     Beausejour, present at capture of (1755) | 64, 65 |
|     escaped to Quebec | 65 |
|     reproached by his Bishop | 65 |
|     captured at sea (1756) | 65 |
|     prisoners in Jersey | 65 |
|     Howe, murder of Captain Edward | 67 |
|     analysis of character | 67 |
|     Casgrain, Abbe, on | 68 |
| LOYALISTS, located on lands escheated in 1781 | 202 |
|     difficulty of getting their grants | 212 |
|     additional instructions *re* | 214 |
|     minutes of Council *re* grants to, mutilated and suppressed | 214, 215 |
|     Royal Commissions (1861) report on | 215, 216 |
|     Fanning, presses claims of | 215 |

## M.

|  | Page |
|---|---|
| MAILS, Island | 370 |
|     routes | 370 |
|     irregularity of | 371, 372 |
|     system of carrying | 371, 372 |
|     winter | 373 |
|     Cape Traverse — Tormentine, winter route | 372 |
| MALPEQUE, principal Indian centre | 41 |
|     white settlers (1728) | 41 |
| MARKET for Charlottetown proposed | 296 |
| MARRIAGE, first Christian on Island | 24 |
|     of French on transport | 98 |
| MARQUE, letters of (1793) | 267 |
| MAXWELL, SIR MURRAY, appointed Lieutenant-Governor | 382 |
|     died in England | 382 |
| MEMORIAL of Council and Assembly state wants of the province | 298 |
|     estimate of funds required | 299, 310 |
| METHODIST CHURCH, sketch of early history in P. E. Island | 405, 408 |
| METIVIER, ABBE, missionary priest with M. Breslay | 23 |

# 486    HISTORY OF PRINCE EDWARD ISLAND.

| | Page |
|---|---|
| MISSIONARY work (French) | 24 |
| MISSIONARIES, French | 51, 52 |
| MISSIONARIES (English) sought from S. P. G. (1801) | 389 |
| MICE, plague of | 60, 152 |
|     awful devastation by | 60 |
|     description of, by Pichon | 60 |
|     Souris named for | 354 |
| MILITARY ESTABLISHMENT (1830) | 378 |
| MILITIA, settlers join McLean and Goreham's regiments | 189 |
|     Independant Companies from New York | 189 |
|     two Companies raised in 1794 | 189 |
|     removal of troops to Halifax | 198 |
|     general muster made by DesBarres | 298 |
|     returns (December, 1806) | 301, 302 |
|     1829 mustered 5,400 men | 377 |
| MINEGOO, Indian name of Island (note) | 15 |
| MINES AND MINERALS, reserved out of grants | 122 |
| MIRAMICHI, people starving | 75 |
| MORRIS, chief surveyor of N. S. | 145 |
|     lays out Charlottetown, etc. | 145 |

## Mc.

| | |
|---|---|
| MCDONALD, CAPTAIN, brings over 300 immigrants (1772) | 168, 169 |
|     joins British forces on outbreak of American revolution | 169 |
|     property of, sold for quit rents in his absence | 169 |
|     petitions for remission of quit rents | 169, 170 |
|     opposite opinions of | 171, 172, 173 |
| MCEACHERN, Bishop arrives on Island (1790) | 250 |
|     Bishop of Posen (1821) | 250 |
|     Bishop of Charlottetown (1831) | 250 |
|     St. Andrews' College founded by | 250 |
|     character of | 250 |
|     see Miscellaneous "The R. C. Church in P. E. Island | 395 |
| MCGREGOR, JOHN, Sheriff for whole Island (note) | 336 |
|     called meetings on memorial of leading men to consider charges against Smith | |
|     meeting for Queen's county, 6th March, 1823, for McGregor (note) | 336 |
|     notified improper to preside over meetings | 337 |
|     correspondence with Council | 337, 338, 339 |
|     dismissed by Lieutenant-Governor Smith | 339 |
|     public meetings held by him | 340 |
|     Hill appointed to succeed as sheriff | 340 |
|     Hill admonished by Smith | 340, 341 |

# INDEX. 487

|  | Page |
|---|---|
| McGREGOR, JOHN, account of P. E. Island (1829) | 344–350 |
| on agriculture | 344 |
| on domestic animals | 345 |
| forest fires | 346, 347 |
| careless cultivation | 347 |
| mussel-mud | 347 |
| society | 347 |
| amusements | 348 |
| pursuits of people | 348, 349 |
| nationalities of settlers | 348, 349 |
| winter employments | 349 |
| churches | 349, 350 |

## N.

| | |
|---|---|
| NAME OF ISLAND Act to change to New Ireland disallowed | 196, 197 |
| inconveniences from name "St. John" | 196 |
| reasons for disallowance | 197 |
| Prince Edward Island, changed to | 268 |
| NEW GLASGOW, settled (1818) | 330 |
| NOVA SCOTIA, annexed to | 118–149 |

## O.

| | |
|---|---|
| O'BRIEN, Archbishop on Cabot's landfall (note) | 5 |
| "OUGHTEN"— One of Selkirk's ships | 271 |
| OATS and other grains, price of, in 1830 | 380 |

## P.

| | |
|---|---|
| PATTERSON, appointed Governor of Island of St. John | 148, 149 |
| sworn in | 149 |
| arrives in Charlottetown | 150 |
| Acadians, settlers on township No. 13 | 151 |
| description of Island | 151 |
| mice, plague of | 152 |
| instructions as Governor | Appendix B |
| commission as Governor | " A |
| further instructions | " C |
| further instructions | " D |
| commission as Lieutenant-Governor | " E |
| further descibes Island | 166 |
| goes to England (1775) | 178 |
| returns in 1780 | 195 |
| reports great improvement | 196 |
| delays submitting draft Act to repeal statutes of 1773, 1781 | 200–204 |
| dismissal, leads to his | 204 |
| speech submitting draft repealing Bill | 204, 205 |

|  | Page |
|---|---|
| PATTERSON, draft bill thrown out | 205 |
| "criminating complaint" against, by proprietors | 205 |
| councillors dismissed | 207 |
| obstructs new government | 207 |
| returns to England | 207 |
| PENSENS, M. DE, — Governor (1730) | 28 |
| PETITION, curious treatment of a, by Assembly | 363 |
| PICHON, visits settlements (1752) | 55, 60 |
| character and life of | 55–60 |
| a traitor | 55, 56 |
| describes Island | 55, 60 |
| PINE, Acadians employed cutting | 122, 123 |
| POLLY, one of Selkirk's ships | 271 |
| POPULATION at capitulation | 80, 81 |
| return of in 1768, English by name | 146 |
| in 1805 | 293 |
| arrivals from New York, Jersey and Pennsylvania | 146 |
| increase of | 151 |
| in 1770 | 167 |
| in 1803 | 277 |
| and produce, tables | 295, 296 |
| in 1807 | 303, 304 |
| in 1827 | 380 |
| in 1830 | 380 |
| PORT LA JOIE, not a fishing centre | 28 |
| descent by British on, in 1745 | 34 |
| destruction at | 34 |
| twenty-eight British killed or captured at | 34 |
| inhabitants of, offer submission | 35 |
| hostages given by settlers of | 36 |
| British attacked by De Montesson at | 36 |
| settlers of, became neutral | 35, 36 |
| an agricultural settlement | 39 |
| POST OFFICE arrangements (Fanning) | 289 |
| DesBarres recommends establishment of | 303 |
| in P. E. Island | 370, 371, 372, 373 |
| earliest service in P. E. Island | 370 |
| POSTMASTER, Benjamin Chappell the first (1802) | 288 |
| died (1825) | 288 |
| daughter Elizabeth succeeded him | 288 |
| PRESSING SEAMEN (note) | 306 |
| PRESBYTERIAN CHURCH, sketch of early history of, in P. E. Island | 399, 404 |
| PRINCE EDWARD ISLAND, name St. John changed to | 248 |
| PRINCETOWN laid out in 1768 | 133 |
| PRINTING PRESS (1788), first in Island | 246 |
| statutes printed in this | 246 |

INDEX. 489

|  | Page |
|---|---|
| PRIVATEERS, fitted out by French | 94 |
| Americans raid Charlottetown | 180 |
| Americans carry off Messrs. Callbeck and Wright, the former being Administrator of Government | 180 |
| "Americana," account of said, in | 180 |
| Washington's instructions to | 180, 181 |
| Callbeck and Wright's account of raid | 181, 185 |
| capture Rev. T. DesBrisay | 184 |
| Councillor Spence and family | 184 |
| commanded by Broughton and Selman | 180 |
| prisoners released by Washington | 185 |
| Spence's account of raid to Lord Dartmouth | 185, 186 |
| plunder settlers' supplies | 196 |
| reports of Callbeck and Wright | 187, 188 |
| Malpeque plundered by | 189 |
| St. Peters raided by (1778) | 189 |
| two reported in 1781 | 198 |
| PRODUCE AND POPULATION, 1805 | 295, 296 |
| PROPRIETORS, petition for separate Government | 139 |
| separate Government granted | 140 |
| ask Lord Commissioner of Treasury for a church, court house and jail | 149 |
| break their agreement | 150 |
| quit rents default in paying brought before Home Government | 176 |
| efforts to compel discharge of their obligations thwarted by proprietors | 225, 226 |
| PUBLIC BUILDINGS urged | 307 |
| PUBLIC SCHOOL, need of shown | 303 |

## Q.

| | |
|---|---|
| QUIT RENTS to be levied | 121 |
| higher than in other provinces | 121 |
| to defray costs of Government | 179 |
| proprietors make default of payment | 188 |
| escheat to recover proposed | 198, 199 |
| arrears of, accumulate | 199 |
| Act for their recovery (1773) | 199 |
| British Government make order to collect (1776) | 199 |
| proceedings to recover (1781) | 199 |
| Act to legalize sale of lands in arrears (1781) disallowed | 200 |
| Home Government draft bill to repeal Act of 1773 and to disallow Act of 1781 | 200 |
| require it submitted to and passed by Assembly | 200 |
| lots sold in 1781 for | 200, 201 |
| arrears of compounded | 220 |
| Smith's tyrannical conduct in collecting arrears from small owners | 315 |

## R.

| | Page |
|---|---|
| READY, Colonel John Ready, Lieutenant-Governor, arrives | 343 |
| Lieutenant-Governor, 1824-31 | 362 |
| sketch of family (note) | 362 |
| agriculture encouraged by | 362, 363 |
| live stock, improvement of | 363, 364 |
| convened Legislature (1825) | 363 |
| much legislation | 363 |
| live stock imported by | 369 |
| recalled in 1831 | 382 |
| plate presentation of, to | 382 |
| RECOLLECTS — replace Sulpicians at Port la Joie | 27 |
| remain until 1752 | 27 |
| REVENUE AND EXPENDITURE, 1803 | 274, 275 |
| 1830 | 378 |
| REFUGEES FROM ACADIA | 70, 71 |
| See Acadia | |
| ROADS, badness of communication | 163 |
| good, urged by Patterson | 163 |
| to Princetown built by him | 163 |
| statute labor proposed | 177 |
| ROLLO, COLONEL LORD, sent to take possession of Island on fall of Louisbourg | 87 |
| Amherst's instructions to | 87 |
| distinguished career of | 89 |
| advises erection of Fort at Head of Hillsborough | 93, 95 |
| notes Island's fertility | 94, 99 |
| ROMA, DE — Concession to | 31 |
| forms new Company at Three Rivers (1831) | 31 |
| extensive establishment at | 32, 33 |
| ships built by | 33 |
| destroyed by New England warship | 33, 34 |
| ROMAN CATHOLICS | 288 |
| petition for franchise | 368, 369, 370 |
| rejected by Speaker's vote | 369, 370 |
| reasons for his vote | 370 |
| granted (1830) | 377 |
| ROMAN CATHOLIC CHURCH, sketch of early history in P. E. Island | 393-398 |
| RONDE, DE LA, organized Fort La Joie | 29 |
| describes Island | 29, 30 |
| RONCEVALLES, imported by Ready (1826) | 369 |
| ROQUE, DE, visits settlements | 53, 54 |
| census taken by | 53 |
| population in 1752 | 54 |
| RUSTICO, named from Rassicot, a settler | 40 |

## S.

| | Page |
|---|---|
| SAW AND GRIST MILLS at Savage Harbor (French period) | 40 |
| SAWYER'S, REAR-ADMIRAL, visit (1788) | 244 |
| first Flag Ship to visit Charlottetown | 244 |
| SCALPS, charges against French | 79 |
| Boscawan, Stewart & McGregor, charges by | 79 |
| McPhail | 79 |
| discredited by, doubtful | 80 |
| SCHOOLS | 373, 374 |
| SEA COWS, Cartier reports as abounding in Magdalens | 10 |
| fishery | 153, 154, 155 |
| accommodation for to be reserved | 122 |
| destruction of | 153 |
| SELKIRK, settlers | 268 |
| sketch of the Earl | 269 |
| granted lands in Canada | 270 |
| purchased lots in P. E. Island | 270, 271 |
| colonists from Skye, Ross, Argyle and Inverness | 271 |
| come in three ships (Dykes, Polly and Oughten) | 271 |
| "Highland Clearance" | 271 |
| arrival of ships | 271, 272 |
| diary | 272 |
| tells how Assembly elected | 275 |
| landing of settlers | 272 |
| his opinion of Fanning | 273, 274 |
| sets out for Belfast | 275 |
| settlers scattered along shore | 275, 283 |
| general observations of | 278 |
| fisheries | 278 |
| shipping | 279 |
| exports and imports | 279, 280 |
| delays in allotments | 281 |
| allowed to purchase in fee | 284 |
| McGregor's account of | 285 |
| SEPARATE PROVINCES, estimated expense of | 144 |
| SETTLERS in new country | 282 |
| sent by St. Pierre | 25 |
| from France and Acadia (1720-21) | 25, 26 |
| St. Pierre's retire to Cape Breton | 28 |
| French settlers of Malpeque escape deportation | 99, 100 |
| (Scotch) arrive A. D. 1770, 1771-1772 | 157 |
| relief measures thwarted in London | 219 |
| influx of | 255 |
| SETTLEMENTS connected by water or ice | 40 |
| saw and grist mills in (French) | 40 |
| farms well stocked (French) | 40 |
| farming | 77 |

|  | Page |
|---|---|
| SETTLEMENT from other parts of Empire opposed by British Government | 167 |
| DesBrisay censured for advertising for settlers from Ireland | 167, 168 |
| SHIPBUILDING, by St. Pierre | 30 |
| SHIPS, hostile captured and brought to Charlottetown | 189 |
| SHIRLEY, Governor, urged fortifying neck of land between Bay of Fundy and Bay Verte | 42 |
| SLAVES, negro, St. Pierre permitted to hold | 23 |
| baptism not to, exempt from bondage | 197 |
| Act *re* baptism repealed | 368 |
| SMITH succeeds DesBarres as Lieutenant-Governor | 313 |
| character of | 313, 314 |
| speech opening session | 314 |
| refuses to receive address | 318, 319 |
| ungracious speech in proroguing | 314 |
| Assembly brings charges against | 327, 328 |
| Address of Assembly ordered sent to Prince Regent | 328 |
| Duke of Richmond requested to transmit | 329 |
| Assembly charged with misapplication of public funds | 329 |
| appoint his sons-in-law, Lane and Carmichael, to offices | 335 |
| complaints against | 335 |
| outrageous conduct of Carmichael | 326, 327 |
| warrant issued against him | 327 |
| Sheriff McGregor calls meetings to consider Smith's conduct | 336 |
| John Stewart takes lead against | 336 |
| meeting prefers charges against | 341 |
| committee appointed to prepare Address to King against | 341 |
| Address against, published in Register | 341 |
| as Chancellor issues warrant against committee | 342 |
| Stewart escapes and goes to London | 342 |
| other members tried for contempt by | 342, 343 |
| Attorney-General suspended | 343 |
| recalled | 343 |
| SMETHURST, first Briton to attempt fishery | 122 |
| St. Peters (1763) | 122 |
| Pine at Three Rivers, employed to preserve | 122 |
| SMUGGLING (1788) | 244, 245 |
| Patterson implicated in | 244, 245 |
| SOUTH LAKE, settlement at | 41 |
| SPAIN, rumours of war with | 249, 266, 267 |
| STEAMSHIP, first "Richard Smith" | 381 |
| Royal William | 381 |
| STEWART, JOHN, charged with mutilating journals of House of Assembly | 158 |
| took lead against Lieutenant-Governor Smith | 336 |
| PETER, recommended as Chief Justice | 173 |
| with settlers shipwrecked in 1775 | 190 |

|  | Page |
|---|---|
| ST. ANDREWS College founded | 376 |
| ST. JOHN'S ISLAND. See Island. | |
| ST. PAUL'S CHURCH and Parish of Charlotte, sketch of early history | 385, 392 |
| ST. PIERRE, obtains grants | 20, 21 |
| terms of his grants | 22 |
| permitted to hold negro slaves | 23 |
| settlers sent by | 25 |
| shipbuilding by | 30 |
| concession revoked | 28 |
| established fishing station | 29 |
| commercial capital, settled by | 25 |
| SQUARES IN CHARLOTTETOWN | 165 |
| SUPPLY, See Assembly | |
| SUPREME COURT, established | 153 |
| terms of established | 165 |
| SURVEY, HOLLAND'S | 123–130 |
| of B. N. A. ordered by | 123 |
| of Island to be first | 123 |

### T.

|  |  |
|---|---|
| TAXES, in Fanning's time | 387 |
| on land proposed | 304, 307, 308 |
| TECUMSEH, death of | 316 |
| TOWNS, location of and why | 125, 126, 127 |
| laid out by Morris | 133, 134 |
| reservations in | 134 |
| TOWNSHIPS, lottery of | 130, 131, 132 |
| terms in grants of | 133 |
| TRADE AND SHIPPING (McGregor) | 280 |
| in Fanning's time | 287 |
| TRADE AND COMMERCE (Lieutenant-Governor Ready) | 364 |
| free trade with British possessions asked for | 364 |
| ports proposed to be free | 364 |
| TRAVERSE, TORMENTINE CAPES, winter mail route | 372 |
| TREMLETT, C. J., sketch of his career | 435, 437 |
| grave charges, by Assembly, against | 321, 324 |
| suspension asked for | 321, 324 |
| resolution censuring | 321, 322, 323, 324 |
| resolution, Lieutenant-Governor Smith's comments on | 324, 325 |
| succeeded by Archibald | 344 |

### U.

|  |  |
|---|---|
| UTRECHT, Treaty of | 19 |
| influx of Acadians after | 19 |
| UNITED STATES, war of 1812 with | 309, 315, 316 |
| British Canadian victories | 316 |
| Washington captured | 316 |
| British-Canadians have best of war | 316 |

## V.

| | Page |
|---|---|
| VERAZANNO | 6 |
| French claims based on his discoveries | 6 |
| coasted along U. S., N. S., C. B. and Newfoundland | 6 |
| VILLEJOIN, last French Governor of Island | 72 |
| prepares for defence | 72, 74 |
| letter from, to French Minister | 91 |
| supplies, his lack of | 72 |
| VIOLET, transport with prisoners from Island for France lost with all on board | 101, 102 |

## W.

| | |
|---|---|
| WAR of 1812, with the United States | 309 |
| with Spain | 249, 266, 267 |
| with France | 264 |
| WASHINGTON, capital of the U. S. captured | 316 |
| WHEAT, barley and oats (1830) price of | 380 |
| WINTER MAIL SERVICE, crossed at Wood Islands, 1775 | 178 |
| crossing | 194 |
| WRIGHT AND CALLBECK — See "Privateers". | |

## Y.

| | |
|---|---|
| YOUNG, SIR ARETAS W., Lieutenant-Governor | 382 |
| arrives 30th September, 1831 | 382 |

THE END.

www.ingramcontent.com/pod-product-compliance
Lightning Source LLC
Chambersburg PA
CBHW060908300426
44112CB00011B/1389